Approaches to Teaching the Works of Oscar Wilde

Edited by

Philip E. Smith II

D1548046

The Modern Language Association of America
New York 2008

For information about obtaining permission to reprint material from
MLA book publications, send your request by mail (see address below),
e-mail (permissions@mla.org), or fax (646 458-0030).

Library of Congress Cataloging-in-Publication Data

Approaches to teaching the works of Oscar Wilde /
edited by Philip E. Smith II.
p. cm. — (Approaches to teaching world literature ; 103)
Includes bibliographical references (p.   ) and index.
ISBN 978-1-60329-009-8 (alk. paper)
ISBN 978-1-60329-010-4 (pbk. : alk. paper)
1. Wilde, Oscar, 1854–1900—Study and teaching.   2. Wilde, Oscar,
1854–1900—Criticism and interpretation.   I. Smith, Philip E.
PR5824.A58 2008
828′.809—dc22   2008021366

Approaches to Teaching World Literature 103
ISSN 1059-1133

Cover illustration of the paperback edition: Photograph of Oscar Wilde,
by Alfred Ellis and Walery. London, March 1892(?)
Courtesy of the William Andrews Clark Memorial Library,
University of California, Los Angeles

Printed on recycled paper

Published by The Modern Language Association of America
26 Broadway, New York, New York 10004-1789
www.mla.org

CONTENTS

PREFACE TO THE SERIES

In *The Art of Teaching* Gilbert Highet wrote, "Bad teaching wastes a great deal of effort, and spoils many lives which might have been full of energy and happiness." All too many teachers have failed in their work, Highet argued, simply "because they have not thought about it." We hope that the Approaches to Teaching World Literature series, sponsored by the Modern Language Association's Publications Committee, will not only improve the craft–as well as the art–of teaching but also encourage serious and continuing discussion of the aims and methods of teaching literature.

The principal objective of the series is to collect within each volume different points of view on teaching a specific literary work, a literary tradition, or a writer widely taught at the undergraduate level. The preparation of each volume begins with a wide-ranging survey of instructors, thus enabling us to include in the volume the philosophies and approaches, thoughts and methods of scores of experienced teachers. The result is a sourcebook of material, information, and ideas on teaching the subject of the volume to undergraduates.

The series is intended to serve nonspecialists as well as specialists, inexperienced as well as experienced teachers, graduate students who wish to learn effective ways of teaching as well as senior professors who wish to compare their own approaches with the approaches of colleagues in other schools. Of course, no volume in the series can ever substitute for erudition, intelligence, creativity, and sensitivity in teaching. We hope merely that each book will point readers in useful directions; at most each will offer only a first step in the long journey to successful teaching.

Joseph Gibaldi
Series Editor

PREFACE TO THE VOLUME

After the revaluation of the traditional literary canon in the late twentieth century, teachers and students now explore most of Oscar Wilde's works in courses ranging from topics that fit traditional curricular classifications, such as nineteenth-century survey, single-figure study, and history of the novel or drama, to courses using newer approaches, such as cultural studies, Irish studies, or queer theory. Therefore I have planned this book to be an inclusive resource for teachers who might wish to consider an approach to a single work or to most of Wilde's writings.

The classroom and curriculum are laboratories for proving and improving teachers' assumptions and methods. Just as literary research with no connection to teaching can produce ingenious interpretation or pointless scholarship, teaching without reference to research and scholarship can produce uninformed and pointless pedagogy. All the essays in this collection reflect the experience of teachers who have proved their approaches repeatedly and successfully with their students. Furthermore, their essays have been refereed and critiqued by anonymous reviewers and by the MLA Publications Committee. The result is a volume of substantial contributions to the study and teaching of Oscar Wilde.

I am grateful to the MLA series editor, Joseph Gibaldi, for encouraging a volume devoted to Wilde's works, and to the MLA acquisitions editor Sonia Kane, for her advice and consideration over the several years required for the preparation of the book. The dean of arts and sciences at the University of Pittsburgh approved my sabbatical leave, which helped me in the preparation of this volume.

Thanks for technical wizardry to Richard Moore and Richard Parent, who assisted in the formatting of the text from many separate and variously prepared digital files.

I have enjoyed learning from the contributors to this volume as I have read and edited their essays. My undergraduate and graduate students in Wilde seminars have taught me much about the praxis of teaching and about what new eyes and minds can bring to study and interpretation of Wilde.

Finally, for support and encouragement in this project as in all things, I give heartfelt thanks to Susan Harris Smith.

—PES

Part One

MATERIALS

Classroom Texts

The Oxford edition of *The Complete Works of Oscar Wilde* will be, when it is complete, the standard authoritative text for reference. However, at this moment only four volumes—*Poems and Poems in Prose, De Profundis [and] Epistola: In Carcere et Vinculis, The Picture of Dorian Gray,* and *Criticism: Historical Criticism, Intentions, The Soul of Man*—have been printed, and their high purchase prices make them most unlikely to be chosen for classroom adoption. Nevertheless, anyone teaching the poems, the novel, the critical essays, or Wilde's letter from prison will find in them the best reference texts. The edition of poems includes over twenty poems unpublished in Wilde's lifetime; *Dorian Gray* appears in both the 1890 and 1891 texts; Wilde's letter from prison appears in the original truncated and full versions; the critical essays are newly edited with notable changes, especially in *The Rise of Historical Criticism;* and all four volumes feature extensive sections of commentary with textual notes, publishing information, biographical references, and glosses for allusions. In addition, teachers and students interested in *De Profundis* should look at the handsome color facsimile of the manuscript, published by the British Library in 2000 with a useful introduction by Merlin Holland.

The best choice for a one-volume, comprehensive classroom collection and the edition referred to by contributors to *Approaches to Teaching the Works of Oscar Wilde* is the *Collins Complete Works of Oscar Wilde: Centenary Edition,* updated from an older Collins edition in 1999. This volume is well suited for any course that has a substantial number of assigned readings in Wilde, because it includes the stories and novel, the plays (but with the four-act version of *Earnest*), the poems and poems in prose (in the chronological order established by the Oxford edition), and the critical essays together with selected journalism and letters. Another useful but more limited volume is the Oxford World's Classics selection, *Oscar Wilde: The Major Works,* edited by Isobel Murray, which includes *The Picture of Dorian Gray* and three stories, two critical dialogues, four plays, three poems, three poems in prose, and some aphorisms. Murray edited other volumes in the same series, including Wilde's *Complete Shorter Fiction.* A comparable collection, Ian Small's *Oscar Wilde: Complete Short Fiction,* contains the stories, the prose poems, and "The Portrait of Mr. W. H."

Works published during Wilde's life are in the public domain, so there are many collections and single-text editions of the fiction, drama, and criticism from which instructors may choose according to the needs of their syllabi. Some of these volumes are worthy of note—for example, the New Mermaid editions of the plays edited by Russell Jackson (*Earnest*) and Small (*Lady Windermere's Fan*) are precursors of the Oxford edition of the complete works now in preparation; they contain useful introductions, textual notes, and glosses. Other noteworthy editions of *Earnest* are Joseph Bristow's The Importance of Being Earnest *and Related Writings*, which includes an introduction, notes, and two of Wilde's essays and his aphorisms; and, as a reference, Joseph Donohue and Ruth Berggren's *Oscar Wilde's* The Importance of Being Earnest, which contains extensive introductory essays about theater history, illustrations, and copious glosses for allusions in the play. Instructors seeking a collected edition of the five major plays are well served by Peter Raby's The Importance of Being Earnest *and Other Plays*, which has a useful introduction and notes as well as texts of the four society comedies and *Salomé* that have been reviewed against the New Mermaid editions. Richard Cave's edition of the plays for Penguin (2000) is a comparable collection but contains an additional play, *A Florentine Tragedy*. The Norton Critical Edition of *The Picture of Dorian Gray* prints both the *Lippincott's* (1890) and revised book (1891) versions together with a selection of critical essays that is useful for intensive study of the novel.

Online Texts

Because most of Wilde's writing is out of copyright, it can be published online in computer-searchable form. The copy-texts for online publication must also be in the public domain, and therefore they will not reflect recent textual scholarship. However, the use of Web sites for additional text assignments or for the ability to search online texts can be a useful supplement to up-to-date editions. Students and teachers who wish to track down the citation of particular ideas or images, for example, can search quickly through some or all of the online texts. Since Web sites come and go, only a few recommendations are made here, with the expectation that teachers will search for current sites. The Corpus of Electronic Texts (CELT) is an Irish site of relatively long standing; since 1997, it has maintained a large and growing selection of Irish literary texts. Most of Wilde's fiction, poetry, drama, and criticism is online at the CELT Wilde home page: www.ucc.ie/celt/wilde.html. The source-text information for the various selections is given under "Background Details and Bibliographic Information." Other Web sites that offer texts by Wilde are *Bibliomania* (www.bibliomania.com/) and *Project Gutenberg* (www.gutenberg .org/wiki/Main_Page).

Critical articles from refereed journals are increasingly available for downloading through online database searches by search engines like *Google* or through proprietary sites (e.g., the MLA annual bibliographies) which are provided by subscription services like EBSCO, usually through institutional library connections that require users to have a computer account that is authorized by a college or university.

The Instructor's Library

This section lists scholarly and critical resources that teachers may find useful. It is intended to help teachers in need of guidance for preparation and further study or to recommend directions for students. Since the explosion of critical attention attending the theoretical questioning of dominant paradigms of literary approaches in the 1970s and 1980s, there have been many books and essays that focused on Wilde from a number of new approaches. In the first three-quarters of the twentieth century, critical opinion placed him in the realm of minor figures of the late Victorian period. Since then, however, Wilde and his work have undergone a major revaluation by people using the entire apparatus of scholarly and critical exposition and interpretation, from the editing and publication of a new collected edition on modern principles to the use of a variety of critical perspectives that have led to new interpretations of his writing.

Reference Works

A few volumes—an encyclopedia, guides, and bibliographies of Wildean scholarship and criticism—can be crucially helpful for teaching, research, and criticism. Karl Beckson's *The Oscar Wilde Encyclopedia* (1998) features entries for all Wilde's works, which contain summary accounts with publication and manuscript information; for many of his friends, family, and contemporaries; and for critical terms, locations, and general topics. The book is indexed, and many entries contain scholarly references; thus it serves as an excellent starting point for fuller study or for a review of crucial information.

A valuable and extensive guide to publications by and about Wilde, Thomas A. Mikolyzk's *Oscar Wilde: An Annotated Bibliography* (1993) gathers listings for about a century of work into one volume. Small's two guides, *Oscar Wilde Revalued: An Essay on New Materials and Methods of Research* (1993) and *Oscar Wilde: Recent Research* (2000), contain material of great value to instructors, including evaluative essay-lists of critical books, articles, and research materials. Small's volumes not only give guidance on the location and status of manuscript materials, they also offer his critical lens as a way to winnow scholarly and critical work produced in the second half of the twentieth century. Similarly, Melissa Knox's *Oscar Wilde in the 1990s: The Critic as Creator* (2001) surveys, by chapters devoted to critical categories, a large selection of important books and essays written on Wilde during the decade. *Palgrave Advances in Oscar Wilde Studies* (2004), edited by Frederick Roden, contains ten chapters in which scholars survey the state of Wilde criticism by critical category (e.g., I am the author of an essay on philosophical approaches). For particularized searches and, of course, for the most up-to-date bibliography, one should consult the annual lists produced by the MLA and also by *Victorian*

Studies. The MLA database is particularly useful because it is available to subscriber libraries in computer-searchable form.

Biographical Resources

The conflicting ideas and images of Wilde arising from interpretations of his self-fashioned celebrity, his public notoriety, and the "real" or private man and his family have always interested students and teachers of Wilde. Wilde publicized himself. Though he expressed disdain for journalism, he carefully and consciously created personae that he offered to reporters and writers for newspapers and magazines. His public appearances, bisexual life, trials and imprisonment, and the censorious contemporary reaction as well as the later adoption and reappropriation of Wilde as a gay martyr helped generate a transatlantic notoriety, which, for over a century, has overshadowed his literary achievements and produced a set of biographical questions of continuing and powerful interest. Students are likely to have culturally loaded preconceptions about Wilde before beginning to study his work. Teachers will therefore find assignments requiring biographical interpretation and understanding to be perennially interesting. Teachers interested in exploring the many biographies and biographical critical approaches should consult the relevant chapters in both of Small's guides to research materials, *Oscar Wilde Revalued* and *Oscar Wilde: Recent Research.*

A place to begin for an overview of Wilde's life in relation to his writing is John Sloan's *Oscar Wilde* (2003), one of the Oxford World's Classics Authors in Context series. This volume introduces Wilde's relations to social, literary, and intellectual issues and would be a good choice for a single-author course on Wilde. There are several recent popular biographies that portray a sensationalized Wilde, but the best biography for breadth and depth of material is Richard Ellmann's *Oscar Wilde*, published in England in 1987 in an edition with different pagination than the American edition of 1988, which also silently corrected a few errors. All references in our volume are to the American edition. Ellmann became seriously ill and died as the book was in the last stages of production; regrettably, it was printed with many errors uncorrected, including the theory, since discredited, that Wilde died of syphilis and the famous miscaptioning of a photograph of Alice Guszalewicz, the Hungarian opera singer, as "Wilde in costume as Salomé" (illus. facing 429). Even so, Ellmann's biography remains the standard account. Fortunately, Horst Schroeder, a German scholar dedicated to improvement of Ellmann's book, has published an invaluable companion to the biography, *Additions and Corrections to Richard Ellmann's Oscar Wilde*; the revised and enlarged second edition corrects over a thousand errors, with page citations to both the English and American printings of the biography. Teachers or students interested in learning more about the details of particular moments of Wilde's life would do well to search out Schroeder's revisions and amplifications of Ellmann.

Anyone interested in the biographical approach should also browse E. H. Mikhail's two-volume collection *Oscar Wilde: Interviews and Recollections* for reprinted accounts of Wilde from journalists, friends, and acquaintances during and after his lifetime. A compact set of introductions and illustrations of some of Wilde's associates appears in Simon Callow's *Oscar Wilde and His Circle* (2000), a volume in the British National Portrait Gallery series Character Sketches. Two biographers from the 1990s take up the neglected issue of Wilde's Irish heritage: Davis Coakley's *Oscar Wilde: The Importance of Being Irish* (1994) gives the Irish context of Wilde's youth and young manhood, and Coakley supplies many details of Wilde's education; Richard Pine's *The Thief of Reason: Oscar Wilde and Modern Ireland* (1995) attempts to define essential Irishness of national identity in relation to Wilde and to modernist writers. Jeff Nunokawa's *Oscar Wilde* (1993) provides a brief introductory narrative of Wilde's life, a "portrait of the artist as a gay man" (61). Jonathan Fryer, in *André and Oscar: The Literary Friendship of André Gide and Oscar Wilde* (1998), focuses on the last decade of Wilde's life and his relationship as literary and homoerotic mentor to Gide. Douglas Murray's *Bosie: A Biography of Lord Alfred Douglas* (2000) provides a useful account of this contentious personality, which is of interest for its perspective on Wilde and for its account of Douglas's forty-five years of life after the death of Wilde.

The current state of biographical materials concerning Wilde has been significantly improved by the intervention of his grandson, Merlin Holland, who with Rupert Hart-Davis has edited and reissued with many additions and improvements the essential and fascinating volume *The Complete Letters of Oscar Wilde* (2000), which merits reading and consultation for any serious study of Wilde. Holland's collection of Wilde family photographs, *The Wilde Album* (1998), gathers together many of the relevant images of Wilde and his circle. Holland has also published a crucial transcript of Oscar Wilde's first trial, *The Real Trial of Oscar Wilde* (2003; in England published as *Irish Peacock and Scarlet Marquess: The Real Trial of Oscar Wilde*). Teachers and students interested in the questions raised by Wilde's trials should also consult H. Montgomery Hyde's *The Trials of Oscar Wilde*, which is more than fifty years old and was compiled from newspaper accounts but remains the best source for the two latter trials. Hyde can be usefully supplemented by Jonathan Goodman's *The Oscar Wilde File*, which tells the story of the trials and reproduces many illustrated newspaper accounts and photographs. Ed Cohen's *Talk on the Wilde Side* (1993) investigates the newspaper accounts of Wilde's trial in the context of the construction of middle-class norms of heterosexuality in nineteenth-century social and sexual discourses in Britain. Finally, Michael S. Foldy's *The Trials of Oscar Wilde: Deviance, Morality, and Late-Victorian Society* (1997) contains a critical account of the trials in their social and biographical contexts.

Teachers and students who wish to look at reproductions of original editions and primary documents can do no better (unless they live and work in Los Angeles) than browse *The Oscar Wilde Collection*, forty reels of microfilm that reproduce most of the special collection of Wilde materials at the William Andrews Clark Memorial Library (UCLA).

Critical Collections

An efficient way to begin preparation of teaching materials for classes on Wilde would be to inspect several recently published collections of critical essays that offer different viewpoints for interpretation and that also contain useful bibliographies of criticism. Peter Raby's *Cambridge Companion to Oscar Wilde* (1997), for example, contains useful introductory essays on contexts, on Wilde's several identities as writer (poet, journalist, dramatist, fiction writer, critic), and on particular works and themes. Several more collections offer wide-ranging selections of recent essays: Regenia Gagnier's choices in *Critical Essays on Oscar Wilde* (1991) represent the burgeoning of Wilde criticism in the 1980s and reflect the work of critics primarily in the United States. *Rediscovering Oscar Wilde*, George Sandulescu's collection of papers from the 1993 conference on Wilde at the Princess Grace Irish Library in Monaco, has thirty-seven essays from European and American critics on a variety of topics. Jonathan Freedman's *Oscar Wilde: A Collection of Critical Essays* (1996) contains a miscellany of interpretive essays on Wilde as critic, on *Salomé* and *The Importance of Being Earnest*, and on *The Picture of Dorian Gray*. Jerusha McCormack's *Wilde the Irishman* (1998) presents essays arguing for the influence of an Irish heritage on Wilde. Eiléan Ní Chuilleanáin's *The Wilde Legacy* (2003) contains eight essays and a panel discussion from a Dublin conference; four essays concern the Wilde family in Ireland. Giovanna Franci and Giovanna Silvani's *The Importance of Being Misunderstood: Homage to Oscar Wilde* (2003), another collection of conference papers, has essays on a variety of topics, including biographical approaches to Wilde and some of his family, interpretations of major and minor works, a section on the fairy tales, and articles on Wilde and film. A third collection of conference papers, *Oscar Wilde: The Man, His Writings, and His World* (2003), edited by Robert Keane, contains twenty-two essays on an interesting variety of biographical and critical topics, including three on *Dorian Gray*. Joseph Bristow's collection *Wilde Writings: Contextual Conditions* (2003) features essays about Wilde's work in social, political, journalistic, theatrical, and other contexts. Finally, a classic in the field and a basic work for any instructor interested in contextualization is Karl Beckson's *Oscar Wilde: The Critical Heritage* (1970), indispensable critical essays and reviews of Wilde's works that appeared during and after his life.

Critical Studies

Single-volume studies of Wilde range from thematic accounts attempting to encompass all his writing to approaches and interpretations limited to particular works or kinds of works. Some useful biographical approaches that include critical considerations of his work have been mentioned above. An introductory author-and-works book, often in a publisher's series aimed at undergraduate libraries, can be a valuable way for students and teachers to begin their studies. Volumes such as Neil Sammells's *Wilde Style: The Plays and Prose of Oscar Wilde* (2000), Anne Varty's *A Preface to Oscar Wilde* (1998), and Raby's *Oscar Wilde* (1988) include reasonably recent critical readings and up-to-date bibliographies. Older introductory volumes, such as John Stokes's British Council pamphlet *Oscar Wilde* (1978) and Donald Ericksen's *Oscar Wilde* (1977) in the Twayne series, may still have value because of their approaches to thematic issues, but their bibliographies have been superseded. Josephine Guy and Ian Small offer a new approach to the author-and-works book in *Studying Oscar Wilde: History, Criticism, and Myth* (2006), a title in the ELT Press's 1880–1920 British Author Series. Promising jargon-free prose, they provide "snapshots of how specific *kinds* of academic research" can be important to the general reader. Their chapters take up the biographies of Wilde and criticism of *De Profundis*, *Intentions*, the plays, and the fiction. Their commonsensical explanations challenge "the Oscar of popular mythology" (vii) created by biographical readings of the works and question the scholarly interpretations that have argued for Wilde as a serious writer.

Single-volume studies reflecting an author's thesis rather than the requirements of a series are helpful though often limited by their critical focus and selection of texts. Some studies attend to all or most of Wilde's work, while others limit their approach by genre, theme, or critical theory. Recent serious criticism of Wilde begins effectively in the 1970s, with scholarly criticism such as Rodney Shewan's *Oscar Wilde: Art and Egotism* (1977) and J. E. Chamberlin's *Ripe Was the Drowsy Hour: The Age of Oscar Wilde* (1977), both of which revalued Wilde's writing after archival research into his intellectual formation. Shewan's book remains a valuable account of Wilde's works as expressions of individualistic identity, and Chamberlin's makes a compelling case for the breadth of Wilde's knowledge of late-nineteenth-century philosophical, scientific, and social-scientific thought. Christopher Nassaar's *Into the Demon Universe* (1974) constructs a psychoanalytic and biographical approach for understanding the connection between shame or guilt and Wilde's writing; it can be instructively contrasted with recent queer-theory approaches. Norbert Kohl's *Oscar Wilde: The Works of a Conformist Rebel* (1980; trans. 1989) takes a traditional man-and-works approach but thoroughly evaluates texts and criticism.

In the wake of late-twentieth-century cultural and critical theory, thesis-driven studies of Wilde have broadened from literary-historical scholarship and appreciation to other modes of approach. One of the first critics to deploy Continental critical theory in the appraisal of Wilde was Gagnier, whose influential and useful *Idylls of the Marketplace: Oscar Wilde and the Victorian Public* (1986) considers Wilde's writing and performance as a celebrity as an unresolved duality of cynical and idealistic responses to art and to his public audiences. In her view,

Wilde's stylistic doubleness positions Wilde to resist being appropriated by consumerism. She analyzes three of the critical essays, the comedies and *Salomé*, *The Picture of Dorian Gray*, and *De Profundis*. Her interpretation of Wilde's duality of cynicism and idealism in his self-presentation to the marketplace has engendered other studies. Xiaoyi Zhou's *Beyond Aestheticism: Oscar Wilde and Consumer Society* (1996) analyzes Wilde's contradictory textual and personal performances as a self-created subject and his ideas of the self as revealed in the characterizations of his major works. Zhou sees Wilde as interpretable through the critical dialectic of modernism and postmodernism. He concludes with a Jamesonian estimate of Wilde as a writer who positions himself in relation to consumer culture and in so doing anticipates the postmodern abandonment of the "depth model" of traditional thought (216). Paul Fortunato's *Modernist Aesthetics and Consumer Culture in the Writings of Oscar Wilde* (2007) revises Gagnier's interpretation by claiming that Wilde's conception of art is completely commodified. Fortunato sees no complications or contradictions in Wilde's early modernist aesthetics of surface: he reads *Lady Windermere's Fan* as a comedy of self-indulgent superficiality that embodies a triumphant aesthetics of consumerism in the characterization of Mrs. Erlynne.

Some theoretically inflected, thesis-driven critical studies from the 1990s that teachers may find worth consulting are Patricia Behrendt's *Oscar Wilde: Eros and Aesthetics* (1991), a biographically and psychoanalytically oriented approach through an understanding of sexuality and textuality; Guy Willoughby's *Art and Christhood: The Aesthetics of Oscar Wilde* (1993), which finds in Wilde's characterizations of Jesus as a secular Christ in the fairy tales, "The Soul of Man under Socialism," and other works a unifying concept of aesthetics; Jody Price's political reading of Wilde as individualist and socialist in *"A Map with Utopia": Oscar Wilde's Theory for Social Transformation* (1996); and Michael Patrick Gillespie's pluralistically inclusive reader-response approach, *Oscar Wilde and the Poetics of Ambiguity* (1996). Each of these four studies has a focus arising from strong dependence on an argumentative thesis, but they are all open to criticism, either because they are limited to their own view (Behrendt, Willoughby, and Price) or because they accommodate all views (Gillespie).

Teachers interested in Wilde's plays may learn much from the collections of essays and the relevant chapters of the general studies listed above; but there are also several books that critique Wilde's drama. Two studies are useful but dated. Alan Bird's *The Plays of Oscar Wilde* (1977) addresses Wilde's plays chronologically, with attention to their contemporary reception. In *Oscar Wilde* (1984), a title in the Grove Press Modern Dramatists series, Katharine Worth provides a reliable introduction to the literary and theatrical history of Wilde's plays, remarking on important productions as she performs summary readings and critiques.

Two more recent books have focused new attention on Wilde's dramatic sources and texts for the plays, leading to revaluation. Kerry Powell's *Oscar Wilde and the Theatre of the 1890s* (1990) performs an essential service for teachers and students, because it analyzes Wilde's four society comedies and *Salomé* intertextually, tracing the influence on his work of Ibsen's plays; of contemporary British and Continental, especially French, well-made plays and farces; and of many obscure and sometimes unpublished plays. Powell sees Wilde as a professional playwright seeking a distinctive voice and mode while being motivated by the large financial rewards available from theatrical success. Powell's readings of the plays and their performance histories make substantial contributions to the study of Wilde the playwright and man of the theater, but they are not strongly connected to Wilde's other writing, especially to its importance in critical and social theories.

Sos Eltis's *Revising Wilde: Society and Subversion in the Plays of Oscar Wilde* (1996) capably argues that there are connections between Wilde the playwright and "the revolutionary Oscar Wilde . . . who challenged social, sexual, and moral conventions, satirizing and subverting the orthodox values on which Victorian society was based" (5). Eltis considers *Vera* and the four society comedies but, significantly, not *Salomé*. Her approach, building on Powell's, uses Wilde's contemporary theatrical contexts and also works from the textual histories of the plays to show that Wilde added socially subversive meanings in his revisions of the plays. Eltis's argument for Wilde as a subversive playwright runs counter to scholars like Powell and Small, who contend that Wilde was concerned more with professional success and profits than with ideas and social subversion. This critical disagreement makes an interesting focus for teaching Wilde's plays.

Wilde's criticism is often taught in association with other works, like the plays (e.g., *Dorian Gray*), or in its own right, in a course on the history of criticism and theory or on Victorian literature. Wilde's criticism draws attention in several ways. It is enjoyable to read, but Wilde's rhetorical mode is often paradoxical and his range of references daunting. Readers have argued for decades about his seriousness and about the coherence of his critical ideas across essays. Did Wilde have a consistent or even evolving set of cultural and literary theories? Do his critical views revise themselves while also reflecting a systematic and coherent position, or do they contradict themselves without aiming at coherence? The texts are usually understood to be the four periodical essays ("The Truth of Masks," "Pen, Pencil and Poison," "The Decay of Lying," and "The Critic as Artist"), which he republished in *Intentions*, as well as "The Soul of Man under Socialism," "The Portrait of Mr. W. H.," "The Rise of Historical Criticism," and the several lectures and many pieces of critical journalism. Two anthologies of Wilde's criticism likely to be in university libraries could be useful for teachers: Richard Ellmann's *The Artist as Critic* (1970) has a useful introduction and a selection of texts that includes journalism and reviews; Stanley Weintraub's *The Literary Criticism of Oscar Wilde* (1968) has an introduction, notes, and glosses. Teachers should also consult the general critical studies of Wilde for chapters or analyses of the critical works. They may also wish to consult the critical commentary accompanying *Oscar Wilde's Oxford Notebooks: A Portrait of Mind in the Making* (1989), which I edited with Michael S. Helfand, because it contains an extensive analysis of Wilde's critical essays understood in relation to the extensive notebook entries recording his readings in classical and modern philosophy, history, literary criticism, sociology, anthropology, political economy, science, and other subjects.

Among the three recent notable books on Wilde's criticism, Laurence Danson's *Wilde's* Intentions: *The Artist in His Criticism* (1997) presents a discursively allusive reading of the volume's four essays as well as of "The Soul of Man under Socialism" and "The Portrait of Mr. W. H." Danson argues that Wilde's criticism can best be understood in the contexts of its revisionary relations to preceding criticism and its reception when published. Danson also usefully locates Wilde's critical ideas in relation to his poetry, fiction, and plays and to other contemporary literature. But he fails to take into account much recent scholarship on Wilde's intellectual formation, especially in regard to the philosophical, scientific, and social-scientific subjects Wilde studied at Oxford, recording significant passages and his own thoughts in his notebooks. These notebook entries undergird his criticism onward from the time of his long treatise "The Rise of Historical Criticism" (1879), an essay Danson also does not consider. Danson's argument that there are everywhere unresolved paradoxes and contradictions underlying Wilde's major critical views should be read as part of the conversation about the philosophical coherence (or lack of it) in his critical theory.

Julia Prewitt Brown's *Cosmopolitan Criticism: Oscar Wilde's Philosophy of Art* (1997) argues that Wilde's critical theory reflects his education in idealist philosophy. Brown asserts that, in its attempt to identify and attain an "ethical aesthetic" (51), Wilde's critical theory parallels the ideas of other nineteenth-century writers like Kant, Schiller, Kierkegaard, and Nietzsche. Finally, in its cosmopolitanism, she claims, it anticipates the work of twentieth-century critics like Walter Benjamin. Her analysis includes major sections on "The Decay of Lying," "The Critic as Artist," "The Soul of Man under Socialism," "The Picture of Mr. W. H.," *The Picture of Dorian Gray*, and *The Importance of Being Earnest*, as well as briefer mentions of other works.

Finally, Bruce Bashford, in *Oscar Wilde: The Critic as Humanist* (1999), argues that Wilde is a subjectivist and formalist critic who assumes that "meanings are always *someone's*, are always attached to or embodied in a person" (11). Bashford attends to the hermeneutics of reading; to creativity in art and criticism in the work of the critic; to the relations between ideas of romantic selfhood and criticism; and to the analysis of rhetoric in Wilde's writing, in chapters that analyze "The Decay of Lying," "The Critic as Artist," "The Portrait of Mr. W. H.," "The Rise of Historical Criticism," and *De Profundis*.

Three recent critical approaches to Wilde can be useful to instructors. One, the focus on an Irish Wilde, has already been mentioned in regard to biographical approaches and to anthologies. The biographies by Coakley and Pine and the two collections of essays, the first edited by McCormack and the second by Ní Chuilleanáin, give an overview as well as some specific applications of the approach and its attempts to find connections among Wilde's familial and national heritage, his interest in Celtic literature, and his major works. They can be usefully supplemented by Vicki Mahaffey's *States of Desire: Wilde, Yeats, Joyce, and the Irish Experiment* (1998), which places Wilde in the midst of Irish modernism, seeing the power of language used by writers as emblematic of Irish identity and resistance to British culture. Jarlath Killeen's *The Faiths of Oscar Wilde: Catholicism, Folklore, and Ireland* (2005) argues that several of Wilde's major works reveal the shaping influence of his belief in Irish folk Catholicism. Killeen's *The Fairy Tales of Oscar Wilde* (2007), the first book devoted to Wilde's two collections of fairy tales, interprets both collections as subversive of Victorian English pieties but conservative in their Irish folk–Catholic morality. For Killeen, Wilde is "both a didactic children's writer and a social radical" (14).

An extremely productive critical approach to Wilde has emerged from the explosion of gender, gay, and queer-studies criticism in the last two decades of the twentieth century. Some founding books in this movement, notably Eve Kosofsky Sedgwick's *Between Men: English Literature and Male Homosocial Desire* (1985) and *Epistemology of the Closet* (1990), the latter of which contains a chapter on Oscar Wilde, helped generate a revaluation of texts and contexts that has shaped both popular culture and our reception of literary and cultural history. Important books following in the wake of Sedgwick with significant mentions, chapters, or sections on Wilde are Richard Dellamora's *Masculine Desire: The Sexual Politics of Victorian Aestheticism* (1990), Jonathan Dollimore's *Sexual Dissidence: Augustine to Wilde, Freud to Foucault* (1991), Alan Sinfield's *The Wilde Century: Effeminacy, Oscar Wilde, and the Queer Moment* (1994), Linda Dowling's *Hellenism and Homosexuality in Victorian Oxford* (1994), Christopher Craft's *Another Kind of Love: Male Homosexual Desire in English Discourse, 1850–1920* (1994), Joseph Bristow's *Effeminate England: Homoerotic Writing after 1885* (1995), Graham Robb's *Strangers: Homosexual Love in the Nineteenth Century* (2004), and Morris B. Kaplan's *Sodom on the Thames: Sex, Love, and Scandal in Wilde Times* (2005). Fryer's *André and Oscar*, mentioned earlier in the section on biographical resources, brings a nonspecialist's approach to the story of the relationship between Wilde and Gide. Gary Schmidgall's *The Stranger Wilde* (1994) explores Wilde's gay identity in a lengthy, popular rather than scholarly, and only casually organized reading of the life and works. It repeats, among other errors, Ellmann's mistake of identifying the Hungarian opera singer Alice Guszalewicz as Wilde in drag in the role of Salomé. Cohen's *Talk on the Wilde Side*, mentioned earlier in connection with Wilde's trials, brings a serious approach to social history and to the analysis of sexual discourse to bear in consideration of how Victorian British normative definitions of homosexuality operated in constructing Wilde's reputation during and after the trials. Nunokawa's *Tame Passions of Wilde: The Styles of Manageable Desire* (2003) thoughtfully reads a number of Wilde's key texts, notably "The Critic as Artist," *The Importance of Being Earnest, The Picture of Dorian Gray, Salomé*, and

"The Soul of Man under Socialism," in search of a theory of Wildean desire. Shelton Waldrep's *The Aesthetics of Self-Invention: Oscar Wilde to David Bowie* (2004) considers Wilde not only as a student of German idealist philosophy but also as the creator of a self-consciously performative and commercial public personality in ways that have influenced such twentieth-century cultural figures as David Bowie, Truman Capote, and Andy Warhol.

In contrast to most recent critics, who have read Wilde from the perspectives of Irish nationalism, gay studies, postmodern theories of spectacle, or identity politics in the consumer culture of capitalism, Josephine Guy and Ian Small offer a corrective view in their empiricist and materialist study *Oscar Wilde's Profession: Writing and the Culture Industry in the Late Nineteenth Century* (2000). Basing their interpretation on the inspection of Wilde's manuscripts, his business correspondence, his earnings for his dramatic productions, and his transactions and contracts with publishers, Guy and Small argue that Wilde was "much more complicit with than critical of the commercial interests of late nineteenth-century British literary and theatrical culture" (12). Their accounts of his practices as writer, including his habits of revision and of plagiarism, suggest to them that "Wilde was a writer who did not have an abundance of either intellectual resources or material" and that his "creative imagination worked best in what was a fairly narrow area, that of the aphorism or polished one-liner" (281). His success, they argue, arises from his quotability and his entertaining indulgence in genre-driven writing that pleased audiences. This approach, which reduces Wilde's motivation to pecuniary interest alone and limits the scope of intellectual and creative authorial intention, is reminiscent of demystifying approaches to popular or hack writers. But it does not take into account approaches that depend on readers' reception (e.g., psychological, gender), and it discounts approaches that find homologies between Wilde's work and fin de siècle or contemporary ideas and texts.

Intellectual and Critical Contexts: Fin de Siècle Europe and America

There are vast amounts of associated materials that teachers of Wilde may find useful, ranging from general information about late Victorian literary history and culture to philosophical, scientific, and social-scientific documents. Many other specific sources are suggested in the books and articles listed above and in the articles in this volume.

Despite the plenitude of contextual material, some recommendations may help teachers and students who seek information about Wilde's literary, historical, and social environment. A classic survey of the period, with eyewitness traces of the literary tastes of the time, is Holbrook Jackson's *The Eighteen Nineties: A Review of Art and Ideas at the End of the Nineteenth Century* (1913). Other useful perspectives from those who lived in the period may be found in Mike Jay and

Michael Neve's *1900: A Fin-de-Siècle Reader* (1999), a collection of short but provocative excerpts from writers concerned about the meanings and consequences of late-nineteenth-century developments in areas such as evolutionary science, psychology, religion, spiritualism, sexology, racism and colonialism, and feminism. Several recent books and collections of essays focus on the culture of fin de siècle England. Three may be of particular interest to students and teachers of Wilde: first, Small's *Conditions for Criticism: Authority, Knowledge and Literature in the Late Nineteenth Century* (1991), an essay on the intellectual backgrounds of literary critical work and the change from the Arnoldian (or Wildean) man of letters to the professional critic; second, Elaine Showalter's *Sexual Anarchy: Gender and Culture at the Fin de Siècle* (1990), a comparative study of literary and social representations of sexuality at the turn of the century, with some provocative opinions (and occasionally erroneous, since she repeats the Ellmann biography's mistake of captioning the photograph of an opera singer as Salomé as Wilde in drag), especially about Wilde's relation to feminism; and, third, Bram Dijkstra's *Idols of Perversity: Fantasies of Feminine Evil in Fin-de-Siècle Culture* (1986), a cultural inventory of decadent-movement literary and artistic visions of women in Europe with strong resonance for Wilde's *Salomé*.

Finally, two guides to the period centered on London can be useful to students and teachers who may be unfamiliar with the city's role in a variety of literary, social, political, and cultural movements, many of them connected to Wilde. Wolf Von Eckardt, Sander Gilman, and J. Edward Chamberlin's *Oscar Wilde's London: A Scrapbook of Vices and Virtues, 1880–1900* (1987) contains many illustrations and introductory but sometimes superficial accounts of urban entertainments and depravities, in the East End and the West End. Karl Beckson's more substantial *London in the 1890s: A Cultural History* (1992) insists on the variety and complexity of a decade that saw the decline of Victorianism and the rise of modernism in the city at the heart of the British Empire. This useful book is sewn through with references to Wilde and other literary figures like Yeats, Symons, Shaw, Moore, Kipling, and Ibsen. Beckson provides chapters on cultural movements such as the rise of socialism and anarchism, the artistic adoption and enactment of decadence, the rise of Celticism, the campaign against prostitution, the new women and the beginnings of feminist redefinitions of suffrage and sexuality, the new drama, the culture of homoeroticism and its opponents, the new journalism, Zolaism, and the lures and consequences of empire.

Selected Web Sites

Several Web sites that contain searchable texts of Wilde's works are mentioned above. Other sites devoted to Wilde are of varying quality; some may be associated with university courses, but many are maintained by amateurs, fans, or students, and they can appear and disappear or be abandoned, so I recommend only a few and suggest that instructors search for current links themselves. A long-standing resource with reliable information in short articles with cross-references is *The Victorian Web* (www.victorianweb.org/); it has useful navigation buttons and can help with basic information on many subjects and writers, including Wilde and his context; the links to Wilde will yield several sites, including *Oscar Wilde* (www.cmgww.com/historic/wilde/), posted by his grandson, Merlin Holland, on which there are several pictures of Wilde as a child and a young man. An extensive collection of photographs as well as information about the best collection of Oscar Wilde materials in North America can be found at the William Andrews Clark Memorial Library site (www.humnet.ucla.edu/humnet/clarklib/). Finally, a helpful Web-based publication is the *Oscholars*, an online illustrated international journal of news, reviews (theater, books, music, exhibitions, Web sites) and republished and translated work concerning Wilde, his family, and circles, to be found at www.oscholars.com and www.irishdiaspora.net. In the archives are twenty-nine monthly issues June 2001 to October 2003; a new series has begun as of summer 2006. There are appendices, special supplements, and bibliographies. Subscription details may be obtained from the editor (oscholars@gmail.com).

NOTE

All quotations from Wilde in this volume, unless otherwise indicated, are from the *Collins Complete Works of Oscar Wilde: Centenary Edition*.

Part Two

APPROACHES

Introduction:
Wilde's Challenge to Teachers

"Education is an admirable thing. But it is well to remember from time to time that nothing that is worth knowing can be taught" (1242 ["A Few Maxims"]). Wilde's maxim challenges any teacher: how, indeed, might we teach anything worth knowing about the master of paradox? One constant of Wilde's writing is witty subversion of social conventions and linguistic structures, and therein one finds a compelling reason why teaching Wilde is not only worthwhile but also a critical pleasure. Though readers may interpret and learn independently of teachers, literature does not teach itself to students: good teaching requires instructors who can explain their rationales for choosing an approach from the plenitude of interpretations and who can clarify the effects of contexts, forms, and theories. The teachers who wrote essays or responded to the survey for this collection provide a cross-section of helpful approaches to the commonly assigned texts from Wilde's oeuvre.

Beginning in the 1980s there was a major scholarly and critical revaluation upward of Wilde's importance as a representative late Victorian writer. Though his writing has always enjoyed popularity, Wilde had been routinely dismissed as a witty poseur and minor figure until well after the middle of the twentieth century. The publication of his letters, biography, and notebooks as well as new critical attention to his ideas produced a reestimation of his work. Now, wherever literature written in English is studied, teachers assign selections from Wilde in a variety of university English and Irish literature courses, from graduate seminars and upper-level specialized courses to period surveys for majors; his writings also appear in composition, theater, and criticism courses as well as cultural studies, gender studies, and gay studies courses. Outside the anglophone first world, Wilde's works have been widely adopted for university curricula in English and in translation.

University teachers of Wilde have developed approaches that reflect queer theory, poststructuralism, and discourse theory. More traditional approaches depend on the contextual relation of Wilde's texts to form and genre, to theater history, art history, and literary history. Teachers and scholars see his writings as inhabiting a pivotal moment at the conclusion of the Victorian period and the beginning of modernism; some instructors teach them as prescient anticipations of postmodern literature and culture.

Simply to list the kinds of courses in which Wilde's texts are assigned only begins to suggest the range of contemporary approaches to teaching Wilde. Instructors have developed interesting and different plans for teaching his work, from single texts to as much of the oeuvre as one can assign in a semester. Survey respondents report teaching graduate seminars devoted to Wilde alone or to topics featuring his work, such as decadence or fin de siècle literature. Respondents also list undergraduate senior seminars, major-authors courses, and special courses on Wilde alone or paired with another figure—for example, Shaw.

This collection begins with three approaches to teaching Wilde in an intensive course: the first is Bruce Bashford's explanation of building students' critical understanding and acuity through what he calls an inferential approach to interpretation of Wilde's poetry and fiction. The second is Neil Sammells's nuanced exploration of teaching Wilde as an Irish writer whose life and art are characterized by performance and play, as exemplified in two seemingly quite different texts, "The Soul of Man under Socialism" and *The Importance of Being Earnest*. The third is my account of a course organized around teaching Wilde's writing and intellectual development in association with other formative and characteristic works from the 1890s.

Survey respondents report that the insights of queer theory have been particularly useful for interpretations of Wilde's fiction, with much attention paid to *The Picture of Dorian Gray*. The essays on Wilde's fiction begin with Shelton Waldrep's approach to teaching *Dorian Gray* in a course on the Victorian novel. Noting that Wilde's novel successfully supports interpretations emerging from the major theoretical configurations, Waldrep describes how he adds a postcolonial reading of gothic romance. Nikolai Endres considers Wilde's novel in an upper-level undergraduate course on gay and lesbian literature. He teaches students to read the erotic codes in the novel through study of contextual discourses involved in the late Victorian image of homosexuality. Jonathan Alexander approaches *Dorian Gray* by asking students to compare the novel with three twentieth-century film versions in order to consider changing representations of homosexuality and their relation to prevailing ideologies of sexual morality and individual identity. Two more essays in the collection address Wilde's short fiction and fairy tales. D. C. Rose suggests what he calls a quizzical approach to teaching the short stories and gives examples of its application to several of them, especially "Lord Arthur Savile's Crime." Nicholas Ruddick uses two fairy tales, "The Happy Prince" and "The Nightingale and the Rose," to teach students how Wilde's aesthetic ideas can be interpreted as a critique of Victorian-era utilitarian social policies.

Since their first productions, Wilde's comedies, led by *The Importance of Being Earnest*, have been revived constantly in the theater and film repertory; they have been studied in English and theater departments almost as long. Two essays treat the comedies generally, and another four address each play individually. Sos Eltis describes how she introduces aspects common to all four plays using film versions of *An Ideal Husband* in company with the play text. She focuses on Wilde's critique of ideals, his use of dandies and criminals as protagonists, and his interrogation of the roles of women in middle-class and upper-class society. Then she compares Wilde's use of dramatic language and theatrical conventions with that of other 1890s plays as a transition to students' consideration of his other three comedies. Melissa Knox argues for a biographical approach to understanding the plays, noting that Wilde's critical theory connects creativity and confession and therefore sanctions the interpretive investigation of the characters' lives and confessions as analogues to events from Wilde's life. She suggests a set of readings from Wilde's criticism and letters that enables her approach.

Francesca Coppa takes the position that Wilde's first comedy, *Lady Windermere's Fan*, not only incorporates many of the melodramatic conventions of nineteenth-century plays but also, in its use of those conventions, anticipates modern and postmodern plays. Kirsten Shepherd-Barr teaches *A Woman of No Importance* in ways that call for students to be acquainted with the play's dramatic and theatrical contexts, especially its connections to Ibsen and to the well-made play. Robert Preissle situates *An Ideal Husband* in a comparative arts course, challenging students to analyze the play as literary text, performance text, and film text (using Oliver Parker's 1999 film adaptation).

The Importance of Being Earnest is the most accessible and most often assigned of Wilde's plays at every level of the curriculum, from introductory first-year writing and literature courses to graduate seminars taught in English and theater departments. Alan Ackerman describes teaching the play as a textual location for ideas of literary form and freedom. His exploration of formal resonances includes both the mechanical, from Aristotelian plot requirements to Bergsonian theory of comedy, and the organic, especially Plato's theory of forms and Hegel's philosophy of development. Ackerman shows students how the play fulfills and questions forms; his approach leads to an understanding of the play's claims for freedom.

Like *Earnest*, *Salomé* has had great success since the beginning of the twentieth century, especially outside Britain; it flourished as an avant-garde poetic drama, as an opera, and in film versions. Several essayists and survey respondents reported *Salomé* to be the most engaging and most difficult of Wilde's texts for students, because it raises many issues, from literary symbols and the religious and sexual implications of biblical source material to questions of necrophilia and transgendered identity to the interpretation of Wilde's language and Beardsley's illustrations.

The variety of approaches justified my making *Salomé* a special topic for this collection. There are inevitably a few commonalities among these essays, but significant and instructive differences make the five collected here worthy of attention. First, Eszter Szalczer's interdisciplinary historicist approach to theater and drama situates the play as a *Gesamtkunstwerk* with artistic roots in French symbolist drama. Szalczer suggests how upper-level undergraduates and graduate students can be divided into small groups to prepare research projects on the play for presentation to the class. Joan Navarre focuses on the differences between the biblical sources and Wilde's play in order to prepare students for interpretation based on the motif of looking. She introduces students to Laura Mulvey's theory of the gendered gaze at the same time that she asks them to analyze the play for the language and presentation of looking and desire. Beth Tashery Shannon takes visualization in a different direction. Her students also approach the play by comparing it with biblical sources, but they read and view the play as it relates to Beardsley's images, to censorship, to French symbolist fiction (Huysmanns) and poetry (Mallarmé), and to the subject of Salomé in European painting, especially the images of Gustave Moreau. Petra Dierkes-Thrun approaches *Salomé* using twentieth-century film and popular cultural appropriations of the playwright and play. She begins with consideration of the text and its nineteenth-century contexts but screens a biography of Wilde and three other films based on the play. She shows how the popular reception of Wilde as homosexual illustrates the difficulty of deciding issues of transgendering, sexual identity, and acculturation. Samuel Lyndon Gladden asks students to explore the thematic dualities of erotic/pornographic and sacred/profane as well as the play's representations of religion and sex. He contextualizes his approach by having students listen to operas; look at paintings, a graphic novelization of the play, and films; and read Wilde's "The Sphinx" and *La Sainte Courtesaine; or, The Woman Covered with Jewels* (c. 1894) before they focus on the text of *Salomé* with the Beardsley illustrations.

Teachers who responded to the survey reported that they assign Wilde's critical essays in *Intentions* as well as "The Soul of Man under Socialism" and "The Portrait of Mr. W. H." as major texts in their graduate and undergraduate seminars or single-author courses devoted to Wilde. This collection includes two essays on Wilde's criticism. Joe Law teaches *Intentions* in literary criticism surveys and single-author courses on Wilde. When he assigns the essays at the beginning of a single-author course, some of the issues they raise—for example, self-realization and the corollary denial of the unified self or the relation of language to thought—can usefully be traced through Wilde's fiction, drama, and poetry. In turn, acquaintance with Wilde's major works helps students return to the critical essays with greater interest. Law also connects Wilde's criticism to its roots in the works of Plato, Sidney, Arnold, Ruskin, Pater, and other writers, suggesting relations that might be drawn in courses on Victorian prose writing or literary criticism.

Jarlath Killeen suggests having students work with the two textual variants of "The Portrait of Mr. W. H." First he builds on students' responses to their reading of both texts by introducing historical issues of textual authority and theoretical knowledge sufficient to produce a laboratory for deconstruction. Then he argues for an opposing historicist interpretation of "Mr. W. H." based on religious controversies of the nineteenth century. Students have the responsibility for choosing interpretations and arguments to justify them. The approach brings Wilde's texts, which themselves tell a story of literary criticism, into a classroom enactment by students.

The final group of essays deals with Wilde's trials and later work. The trials themselves have become an important subject for study, with an especially contemporary resonance for gay consciousness and queer theory. Survey respondents indicate that Wilde's prison letter, *De Profundis*, is usually assigned in single-figure courses and is an important text in gay studies and gender studies.

S. I. Salamensky describes an approach to teaching the trials she has used in a cluster of literature, drama, and performance courses at upper and lower levels. Study of the trials and their investigation of sexual conduct and truth make an effective opening for students to pursue and critique issues of ethics and difference, the role of the artist in society, and the judicial system, as they are represented in language.

Frederick Roden considers "The Soul of Man under Socialism" and *De Profundis* as religious literature. He teaches them in graduate and undergraduate Victorian literature surveys as a culminating assignment to the semester's readings. Teaching both texts under the rubric of tolerance, he asks students to contrast the Christian socialism of "The Soul of Man" and the Christlike individualism of the prison letter.

Heath A. Diehl assigns *De Profundis* in an introductory literature course titled Coming Out Narratives. Using a comparative approach, he couples Wilde's letter with Moisés Kaufman's play *Gross Indecency*. He supplements the readings in Wilde and Kaufman with essays on queer theory and the history of sexuality, producing assignments designed to lead students toward greater acuity in critical reading and writing as well as a greater sense of the interplay of divergent or contradictory interpretations of history.

Joseph Bristow asks students to combine a careful look at the background of *The Ballad of Reading Gaol* with a close reading of the poem's hybrid discourses: realistic, Romantic, poetic, and propagandistic. He investigates the literary provenance of Wilde's ballad, noting its distinctive differences from poems by Kipling and Henley and its debts to other works, notably by Shakespeare, Coleridge, Hood, and Housman. The publication history and reception of the poem lead Bristow to a reconsideration of the controversies aroused by study and analysis of *The Ballad of Reading Gaol*.

As this volume came together, I read and reread the approaches to the benefit of my own teaching. All the essayists share a common concern not only to advance the study of Oscar Wilde but also to represent teaching as a professional commitment informed by scholarship and critical inquiry. Pedagogy in the best sense implies sharing between teacher and students as well as among teachers. These essays should have a practical effect on what happens in classrooms as well as in studies. There is no last word or single best approach; rather, teachers should find thoughtful and different contexts that will spur them to imagine their courses or to rethink and perhaps revise their goals, assignments, and classroom methods.

The Critic as Student:
An Argumentative Approach

Bruce Bashford

Teaching Oscar Wilde to undergraduates is easy; teaching Oscar Wilde to undergraduates is hard. This isn't a Wildean paradox, since paradoxes arise when two truths genuinely conflict, while each of these two statements is true in a different sense. In the junior- and senior-level courses I've taught devoted entirely to Wilde (what we call a major-author course), my students not only have found Wilde delightful but also have been immediately engaged by his answers to what Matthew Arnold considered the basic moral question of "how to live." Both responses make the teaching easy. But I've also found it hard to teach Wilde as completely as I'd like in a "student-centered" mode. After defining my sense of *student-centered*, I explain how Wilde may be approached in this mode and indicate the difficulties encountered in this approach.

My notion of *student-centered* comes from a course our department developed as an introduction to the English major: Literary Analysis and Argumentation. While at first glance the course looks like one in New Critical close reading, what gives it a distinct character is the assumption that interpretations can be stated as arguments. The basic task the course poses for instructors is finding the right questions to initiate and guide class discussion as well as to serve as paper topics. These are questions that locate points in a work where a reader is asked to make important interpretive decisions; where there is textual evidence available to support a reader's decision; and where that evidence, at least initially, seems to point in more than one direction.

Teaching on the basis of these questions produces a class that's student-centered in a sense that goes beyond simply having students do most of the talking. Whatever the specific question we set for a paper assignment, we follow it with a second: How do you know? This second question requires students to make explicit how they have drawn their interpretive inferences. Since such reflection isn't something they're used to doing, they have to develop the habit of stepping back, as it were, to make clear to themselves why they read a text as they do. It's what they see when they step back that gives them their argument for their claims. We also routinely require students to state the opposing case— the case for an initially plausible reading that they aren't endorsing—and explain why their reading is preferable. This exercise requires even more perspective on their own thinking, but by about mid-semester we can ask our students if a possible question for a paper will work: if the material can sustain different lines of argument about a significant interpretive problem. In class sessions, the instructor, having posed a question, guides students' collective effort to answer it. This guidance can involve keeping a shorthand record on the board of what's been settled and what hasn't, being sure students who disagree speak to one another, asking students who haven't contributed where they stand, and drawing students back into the talk when the insightful remark they made earlier will be easier to appreciate. Classes can resemble debates, but the overall feel is cooperative, and students whose readings have been rebuffed may later help strengthen the opposing view. The goal is to have the class determine which reading or readings can be best supported from the evidence at hand. If no consensus emerges, the fail-safe position is to reflect on why the inquiry got as far as it did and no further. These are student-centered classes in the strong sense that they run on what students can do, on their success in reasoning together about the interpretive problems a text presents.

Since we've designed the course to emphasize one critical skill, it cannot serve as a complete pedagogical model for our other courses. In this course, for instance, we aren't concerned with coverage, while instructors in other courses do feel an obligation to survey a body of material. Except for some remarks about coverage later, I leave it to other contributors to this volume to discuss this matter; I concentrate on the possibility of teaching Wilde through argument in response to inferential questions. "The Ballad of Reading Gaol" and *The Picture of Dorian Gray* furnish my principal examples. Along the way I make brief remarks about "Lord Arthur Savile's Crime." I begin by using Wilde's best-known poem to illustrate the kind of question I have in mind.

In our introductory course, we choose works because they present prominent inferential problems; works that properly belong in other courses may not. Wilde's works present such problems more than one might think. At the end of "Lord Arthur Savile's Crime," for instance, when Lord Arthur declares that he owes to chiromancy "all the happiness of my life," Lady Windermere dismisses this claim as "nonsense!" (183), inviting readers to consider who is right. Students' efforts to support either side provide a focus for interpreting the story. It may be more useful, however, for me to discuss the harder case, where the text doesn't so readily provide the question.

Three stanzas from "The Ballad of Reading Gaol" are usually marked off as a unit by asterisks (as in the recently published *Complete Works* [*Poems* 196]):

> Yet each man kills the thing he loves,
>   By each let this be heard,
> Some do it with a bitter look,
>   Some with a flattering word.
> The coward does it with a kiss,
>   The brave man with a sword!
>
> Some kill their love when they are young,
>   And some when they are old;
> Some strangle with the hands of Lust,
>   Some with the hands of Gold:
> The kindest use a knife, because
>   The dead so soon grow cold.
>
> Some love too little, some too long,
>   Some sell, and others buy;
> Some do the deed with many tears,
>   And some without a sigh:
> For each man kills the thing he loves,
>   Yet each man does not die.   (884; lines 37–54)

These stanzas follow a unit of six that opens the poem. That unit ends after the speaker has told us that the trooper is in prison for murdering his wife and will be hanged, with the lines, "The man had killed the thing he loved, / And so he had to die" (883). A possible argumentative question, one I've actually used, is, "By the end of these three stanzas, has the speaker changed his mind? How do you know?" While this question isn't posed for readers as explicitly as the disagreement at the end of "Lord Arthur Savile's Crime," the verbal resemblance between the two lines concluding the three stanzas above and the two lines concluding the earlier section suggests that, having finished the unit above, we're to return to the earlier lines to some point.

Teaching through the use of this kind of question enables an instructor to prepare for class sessions by becoming acquainted with the interpretive territory before the students do—a quite different procedure from preparing a lecture by considering what sequence of topics will make it easiest for students to follow. It's a matter of identifying the large- and small-scale interpretive problems students will encounter and the various lines of possible argument about each. In the classroom, the instructor consults this prior acquaintance to help students make what progress they can.

In a class discussion prompted by my question, I'd listen for the following: that students would early on read "kill" in these stanzas as figurative rather than literal. If they didn't immediately explain how they know a figurative meaning is present, I'd ask them to, which they could do by citing the means of the killing: "a bitter look" and "a flattering word" are not lethal weapons. I'd expect this observation to raise the question, In what sense, then, is the thing loved killed? Or perhaps, What's killed? These questions prompt the interpretive work common to answering the larger question either way, how to translate lines 39 to 52, all describing instances of killing. Students can again work with the means of killing. They have said, for instance, that it's the beloved's spirit that's killed—as opposed to the whole living person—reasoning from the kind of damage done by Lust and Gold. I'd also listen for signs of diminishing returns: are we to think that "with many tears" and "without a sigh" also describe means of killing, or do they describe manners of killing? If I had to, I'd suggest that we recognize that this question occurs to a reader and move on. I'd expect, certainly hope, that someone see that the last two lines of the first two stanzas are distinctive, since in both places the speaker states a definite preference for one means of killing over others. We'd need the basis of the preferences explicated.

I'd listen for students' mention of the "Yet" that begins a stanza and begins a line at the end of a stanza and of the "For" in line 54: words that help us follow the logic of the speaker's thought. When someone uses the "For," I'd ask for a synonym and then see if other students agree with that choice. Someone might offer "Since": each earlier "some" kills, must do so, since each man kills the thing he loves. Or someone might say "Therefore," taking line 54 as a conclusion reached through induction. Both possibilities bring us to the issue that the original question tries to make specific: What does the speaker see in his general principle or conclusion? Both positions on the question can cite the two uses of "Yet" as evidence that the speaker sees a disparity between the treatment of the trooper and people at large. The "no change of mind" position can argue that the speaker sees this disparity as unjust—and that's as far as the evidence will let us go. The "change of mind" position will claim we should take another inferential step: in the speaker's view, if everyone's not punished, then the trooper shouldn't be either. It might cite as evidence of the speaker's attitude the resemblance between the two kinds of killing he prefers, by sword and knife, and the trooper's murder of his wife (that the trooper used a knife is itself an inference to be argued). If by the period's end students have clearly formulated these two lines of argument, I'll feel we have had a thoughtful encounter with the poem even without reaching unanimity.

Since this is a student-centered approach, it seems fitting that students help me present it. The responses of two students to an assignment on *The Picture of Dorian Gray* help me consider three difficulties encountered by an inferential approach to Wilde as well as make more concrete the character of the approach. The first of these difficulties, and the most pervasive, is that the rhetoric is spare in Wilde's fiction. I'm using *rhetoric* in the sense it has in Wayne

Booth's *The Rhetoric of Fiction*: all the directions, all the clues that an author embeds in a text to communicate a determinate view of a fictional world to readers (xiii). (That view can be, of course, that the world is ambiguous.) In some of Wilde's works, we do get ample help in judging the fictional world and its inhabitants. In *The Devoted Friend*, for instance, we know from the disparity between the Miller's professions of friendship and his treatment of Little Hans that the Miller is definitely not a friend.

But Wilde's fundamental habit of mind, his constant reversal or inversion of our common attitudes and expectations, means that he doesn't usually give us guidance in such an explicit form. Rather, he states the reversal and leaves it to us to work it out. Our work is easiest to do for his paradoxical aphorisms, where the reversal is visible enough to point us toward a resolution. "The tragedy of old age," observes Lord Henry, "is not that one is old, but that one is young" (154), which, however we finally render it, surely directs us to distinguish between a person's chronological age and his sense of himself. In the longer works, the reversals become structural principles rather than almost apparent propositions. As Norbert Kohl has noted, "Lord Arthur Savile's Crime" parodies—in my terms, reverses—the conventions of the detective story: "instead of a search for the criminal, we have the character's search for the crime; [Lord Arthur's] problem is to *become* a criminal, not to catch one" (63). *Dorian Gray* is structured by having Dorian's portrait age and reflect his moral decline, while Dorian's person does neither: a reversal of the view that art is immortal and that—for the Wilde of the preface to the novel, anyway—art is separate from the moral sphere. In each of these cases, Wilde presumably intends the work as a whole to present the resolution of the reversal, but the work's greater length and density of detail make this resolution much harder for readers to grasp than with an epigram. And so we do the best we can.

The following paper assignment on *Dorian Gray* asks students to confront this first difficulty. While it's an assignment that has produced satisfying results, students have shown me, by their responses, how to make it better.

> *The Picture of Dorian Gray* appeared first in a magazine published in Philadelphia. Wilde later revised the magazine version for publication as a novel, adding material in a number of places. In chapter 19, for example, he added the section beginning with Dorian's asking, "What would you say, Harry, if I told you that I had murdered Basil?," and running through Harry's saying, "No: we have given up our belief in the soul. Play me something" (152, 154).
>
> (a) What should a reader notice in this passage, that is, what are the main inferences and judgments it asks us to make? How do you know?
>
> (b) This chapter is Harry's last appearance in the novel. Does the additional material identified above make any difference in our view of him, that is, do we make any inferences or judgments that we could not make from the rest of the chapter? Why do you say yes or no?

At some point in your answer to (b), briefly indicate what someone who opposed your view might say and explain why your view is more convincing.

Students receive the assignment when we begin discussing the novel over several class periods. The intention behind part *a* is to connect our class sessions and the paper assignment. It says, We're going to be drawing inferences about the novel together in class: let's see you do that in a passage we won't discuss.

It is part *a* of the assignment that turns out to need revision most, but the student in this excerpt from her paper is able to do well with it. For her, Wilde added the material to portray Dorian's being forced to confront "his guilty conscience." Here's her initial support for this claim:

Student 1

Dorian's dependence on Harry partly contributes to this increased sense of self-reproach. From the outset, when he suggests responsibility for Basil's murder, Dorian gazes at Wotton "intently" for a response (152). He is needy, curious, and dependent on Harry's opinion. Harry's reaction thus spurs in Dorian a sense of doom, which is renewed throughout the passage. For example, Harry insists that it is not in Dorian to commit a murder, affirming that "all crime is vulgar" and that it "belongs exclusively to the lower orders," who see it simply as "a method of procuring extraordinary sensations" (152). Albeit Harry does not believe Dorian could be capable of murder, this spurs in Dorian a renewed sense of his own vulgarity. In assigning murder to the lower orders, Harry is implying that it is vile and bestial, something attainable by atavistic beings who have no grasp on "civilization" or art to procure their "extraordinary sensations." Dorian, fully aware of his responsibility for Hallward's death, is frightened by this remark, evident when he retorts, "A method of procuring sensations? Do you think, then, that a man who has once committed a murder could possibly do the same crime again? Don't tell me that" (152). Dorian does not want to believe he could again be capable of such a heinous act.

I might ask this writer to mark off her inferences from her evidence more distinctly: to do more of what she's doing when she uses "evident when." It's already clear, however, that she's inferring Dorian feels fear and self-reproach when Harry explains why Dorian couldn't have murdered Basil; that is, as readers, we should see something that Harry doesn't. Knowing that Dorian did kill Basil, we obviously assume that the crime is present to Dorian's consciousness, that his "Don't tell me that" reveals his discomfort at applying Harry's explanation to himself. The student goes on to support her claim that Dorian's "sense of doom . . . is *renewed* throughout the passage," but this excerpt should initially suggest the feel of writing from a student-centered class: she is patiently working out for herself how she reads the passage and why.

An excerpt from another student's paper brings out the weakness in my question. For this writer, the additional material "asks the reader to ponder a very likely question. Does Lord Henry know that Dorian Gray killed Basil? It is evident in their conversation that Lord Henry is aware of the murder." Here's part of her support for this claim:

Student 2

Perhaps the most obvious statement of [this] knowledge is given by Lord Henry when he comes out of nowhere with his "half-closed eyes" and says, "By the way, Dorian . . . 'what does it profit a man if he gain the whole world and lose'—how does the quotation run?—'his own soul?' " (153). Harry knows that Dorian will react to such a statement if he is guilty, because it is a direct insult against everything Dorian stands for. It is Dorian who had gained all of the worldly, societal achievements and yet forfeited his soul by killing his only link to his soul, Basil. Such a carefully planned question like this is typical of Lord Henry's indirect assault against Dorian. When Dorian reacts, Lord Henry, "elevating his eyebrows in surprise" (153), having already received a definite answer to the murder of Basil, simply plays off the question with a story about a preacher using the phrase. It is observable by Lord Henry's careful question and his physical reaction that he is aware already that Dorian killed Basil. When Lord Henry ends the conversation with, "No: we have given up our belief in the soul" (154), he is again solidifying the fact that he knows Basil is dead as a result of Dorian.

The problem isn't that this student isn't arguing: she too is a reader making her own way. She's reasoning from the aptness of Harry's biblical quotation—"a direct insult against everything Dorian stands for"—to an intent on Harry's part: we're to see him confirming his belief by this "careful question." She also uses the physical descriptions of the two men to support her claims, remarking before this excerpt, "if this [scene] were a play, it would be obvious that Lord Henry knew more than he was letting on."

The problem—mine, not hers—is that she isn't able to take into account as she formulates her argument the possibility raised later in the first student's paper when the first student pauses to reflect on her "assumption" that Henry never suspects Dorian murdered Basil:

Student 1

Of course, one could argue against this assumption and debate that Wilde put an additional passage in chapter 19 in order to exemplify Wotton's suspicion and mistrust of Dorian Gray. But such an argument would prove fallacious for a couple of reasons. Wotton, as already seen, constantly refers to Dorian's perfection, to a good soul who has a life which is not marred by experience. Even though Wotton seems suspicious of Dorian, asking questions and making suggestions which bear a striking resemblance to Dorian's guilt, these are innocent conjectures. It is from Dorian's point of view that these comments seem suspicious, because he is daunted by an overbearing sense of fear, fostered from the degradation of his own soul. When Harry asks about the profit of gaining the whole world and losing one's soul, it's only because he was affected by the "drama" of the man who spewed the question. The "wet Sunday, an uncouth Christian in a mackintosh, a ring of sickly white faces under a broken roof" was, as he says, "good in its way, quite a suggestion" (154). He has amiable feelings for romance, and music, which is not an "imitative" art (154); he wishes that Basil could have come to "such a really romantic end" (152), as Dorian suggests. Henry enjoys finding romance in life, finding drama in waking reality. He's enchanted by Dorian because life has been his art. Dorian has set himself "to music"; his days are his "sonnets" (155).

This excerpt has the closely reasoned character that virtually defines my sense of student-centered. I particularly like the way it packs evidence into its rebuttal. It points to the significance of Harry's many favorable remarks about Dorian in the passage; it uses point of view—since we know Dorian's guilt, we share his point of view—to assign the air of suspicion in the scene to Dorian; and it collects several signs of Harry's aesthetic sensibility, which make plausible his account of why the quotation has stuck in his mind—the argumentative point being that no further motive for his repeating it is necessary.

In the future, then, I might replace my part *a* with the question these students addressed: Should we think that Harry knows Dorian murdered Basil? The intention behind part *a* was to have students draw inferences before answering a question about the significance of the added material; that Wilde made the addition seemed a sufficient basis for a question. The results taken as a whole, however, showed me that I'd stopped short of doing something basic to my approach: helping students confront a specific interpretive decision. The first student above defines such a decision when she reflects on her "assumption" and so improves the assignment. When the second student answers part *b* later in her paper, which explicitly asks that an opposing view be addressed, she does so well. In responding to my part *a*, however, she gives us the evidence only for her reading and would benefit from being aware that she's asking us to make a decision that could be made otherwise.

To restate what I learned from the assignment in the more general terms I used earlier: in the middle of the additional material, Harry and Dorian have a sustained exchange about the portrait. Harry expresses his admiration for it, asking, "[W]hat has become of that wonderful portrait [Basil] did of you?" Dorian is uncomfortable throughout, declaring, "The memory of the thing is hateful to me" (153). Since we understand the difference between Harry's and Dorian's attitudes toward the portrait because we understand the portrait's special power, the exchange brings the novel's basic reversal explicitly into the scene. And since Dorian's murder of Basil is a direct consequence of the reversal, both my students have the reversal in mind in the excerpts above, and they address the exchange over the painting elsewhere in their arguments. But even when the novel's basic reversal is so prominent, it doesn't direct a reader through the scene in a particular way. It doesn't function like a paradoxical aphorism, where the underlying act of mind is visible enough to nudge us toward a resolution. To make our way, we have to rely on Wilde's local rhetoric, and since that's spare, students must reason about evidence carefully. My students reminded me that they are in the best position to do so when they approach the material from an argumentative perspective.

A revised part *a* could, I think, stand as a complete question for a short paper or for an examination question. Some reflection on part *b*, however, will let me consider a second difficulty my inferential approach encounters, what I'll call a tactical difficulty, since it involves course management. A late colleague once observed that our Analysis and Argumentation course shows that the simplest things are hardest to do: he meant that explaining how one knows what seems obvious—easily known—can be surprisingly hard. It can also, as my excerpts from students show, take a surprising amount of time to support even a few inferences. Since I always follow up writing assignments with the consideration of selections from papers—usually from papers that take opposite positions—these assignments consume class time as well as students' work at home time. Therefore it is difficult to balance a commitment to students' working things out for themselves with covering a body of material. One way to meet this difficulty in part is to be sure that assignments have thematic scope—that is, I ask students to argue their views on large-scale interpretive issues posed by the work.

While my part *b* is a good question as it stands, my students again have shown me how it might be improved. It's a genuine question: it's not obvious that we couldn't gain whatever insight we get into Harry in the added material from the shorter, magazine version of the chapter. In the added material, for example, Harry says, "I have sorrows, Dorian, of my own, that even you know nothing of," and then remarks, "I am amazed sometimes at my own sincerity" (154), which indicates that Harry sees himself as speaking in a manner he usually doesn't. But one might hear this note of "sincerity" in the shorter version too, since Harry acknowledges being terrified by death and admits missing Victoria, his wife who has run off with a musician, since while "married life is merely a habit, a bad habit. . . . [O]ne regrets the loss even of one's worst habits. . . . They are such an essential part of one's personality" (152). The question also has thematic scope. As students reflect on pieces of evidence like these to answer it, they're considering a possibility important for the novel as a whole: that Harry, who as a younger man is described as "brilliant, fantastic, irresponsible" in talk (43), is losing energy, running down, and that this decline is somehow a comment on his entire philosophy of life.

Still, the first student above, in the course of arguing no for part *b*, suggests how the question could be given even more scope. She cites instances in both the new and original material where Harry expresses "to Dorian the reality that people cannot change" and observes, "This idea, that individuals cannot change, dominates Dorian. It's evident in the beginning of chapter 20, when he questions the irretrievability of his horrific acts, and in a fatal plight tries to destroy the visual representation of his soul." She is correct. That Dorian does explicitly recall a portion of chapter 19 in chapter 20 suggests the question, "Does the material Wilde added to chapter 19 change our understanding of the final chapter?" The issue can be argued either way, and the argument still allows, even requires, discussion of Harry. It has more thematic scope, however, because it shifts attention to Dorian, whose story the novel is, and to what surely occupies our attention as readers, the resolution of the main plot line.

This problem of coverage is made more complex by a third difficulty encountered by an inferential approach to Wilde's works. It is specific to Wilde and so not solely a matter of course management. While his spare rhetoric presents a problem as we construe his works, moving through them sequentially, this third problem concerns his larger purposes. I've pointed to "Lord Arthur Savile's Crime" as an example of Wilde's explicitly posing an inferential question for readers: Does Lord Arthur's happiness depend on chiromancy, or is this belief, as Lady Windermere says, nonsense? The evidence points both ways: Lord Arthur is thinking not only of Podgers's prophecy but of Podgers himself providing the victim it requires—something we know that Lady Windermere doesn't. On the other hand, we have her direct report that Podgers "was a dreadful impostor" (182), which Lord Arthur doesn't hear. There's more evidence for both sides distributed throughout the story, which confirms the relevance of the question. When Wilde republished the original serial version of the story, however, he changed its subtitle from "A Study in Chiromancy" to "A Study in Duty," and we hear a lot about Lord Arthur's sense of duty as he tries to fulfill the prophecy. What's not clear is how pursuing the question that so prominently ends the story is to be connected with attending to the equally prominent theme of duty. Lord Arthur's notion of duty can sound so much like self-indulgence that Kohl concludes, "it is not his duty that Lord Arthur is fulfilling, but a flagrant violation of it" (63).

Perhaps, then, there's a compound reversal in the story that inverts the concept of duty, the conventions of the detective story, and the usual relation of chiromancy to truth. Or—the possibility has to be faced—Wilde is pursuing more than one formal purpose in the story. For my approach, it's desirable at some point in discussing a work to pose a question that's comprehensive in the sense of being about the work's governing purpose, but it's sometimes hard to be confident one has found such a question about a Wilde text. (That the evidence for answering the question of who is right in the disagreement between Lord Arthur and Lady Windermere is scattered throughout the work doesn't ensure that the question is comprehensive.) The fail-safe position here is to make this difficulty the object of class attention: to have students consider whether there are competing purposes in a work that prevent formulating such a question. This method keeps students from feeling that the class's encounter with a work has left it in a jumble; instead they're clear about what they could decide and what they couldn't.

While the difficulties I've described emerge clearly in a student-centered class, they aren't peculiar to it. Speaking as much of professional readers as of students, Peter Raby has observed that Wilde's "works and personality mock the commentator from behind a shifting display of masks" (*Oscar Wilde* 144). Because Wilde is hard to interpret, because his fictional rhetoric is terse and his purposes sometimes hard to discern, he's particularly vulnerable to thesis-driven approaches that look to his works for certain preferred ideas. In my undergraduate classes, I introduce secondary commentary on Wilde as other voices doing what we are doing: presenting and supporting interpretations. I'd like my undergraduates to be acquainted with various critical perspectives on Wilde, but it's more important to me that my students learn to hold the proponents of these perspectives to the same standards of interpretive argument to which they hold themselves.

The Irish Wilde

Neil Sammells

As recently as 1981, students were told by a "guide to Anglo-Irish literature" that "[Wilde's] plays have no Irish dimension" and that we cannot think of Wilde as being molded by influences that were molding Ireland during his lifetime (Warner 5). With the rise of postcolonial criticism in Irish studies over the past two decades—so that it is now in some respects the dominant discourse in Irish literary and cultural studies—such an assertion now looks unsustainable as well as unfashionable. Wilde, like many another aspiring writer, left Ireland for the larger stage of London as soon as he decently could, but he has been recently reclaimed as Irish by academics with as much entrepreneurial energy as he has been rebranded by the Dublin heritage and tourist industries. (Twenty years ago, when I first started taking students to Dublin on field trips, Joyce was everywhere, Wilde nowhere—certainly not lounging in Merrion Square.) *Wilde the Irishman* is the title of a 1998 collection of essays (McCormack), and the phrase has become a critical commonplace.

Such a reclamation poses some serious pedagogical issues. Noting the importance of Irishness to Wilde (both in terms of historical, political, and cultural contexts and in how he saw his nationality) is not the same as encouraging students to scrape away a supposedly English surface to his work in order to expose an Irish or Celtic core. Such an approach is potentially both reductionist with respect to the texts and essentialist with respect to race and nationality: a distinctly un-Wildean approach to Wilde. Students need to be made aware not just of the degree to which his Irishness was written out of his work in most critical assessments before 1980 but also of the problematic assumptions inherent in recent attempts to relocate him in the Irish literary canon.

The hugely influential 1991 *Field Day Anthology of Irish Writing* provides a good test case. Christopher Murray, for instance, identifies a subversive potential in the characteristic Irish wit of dramatists from Farquhar to Shaw and Wilde, who were determined enemies of English falsity. But Murray also feels that the subversion was typically compromised: "from William Congreve to Oscar Wilde the profile of the expatriate Irish playwright is of the polished man of letters, as eager for social status in England as for literary fame. He wrote primarily to please the English arbiters of taste." Political questions hardly entered Irish drama, he claims, until the arrival on the scene of W. B. Yeats (Deane 1: 502, 507). Murray's views seem a sophisticated elaboration of Daniel Corkery's mechanistically nationalist *Synge and Anglo-Irish Literature* (1931), which is to be found elsewhere in the anthology and which condemns expatriate writers like Wilde, "who did not labour for their own people," preferring to write "for their kinsfolk in England" (2: 1008). Murray is not alone among the editors in finding Wilde's work compromised by its English context. Seamus Deane says

of Wilde's poetry that it is vulgar in its facility of feeling and rhythmic automa-
tism. As in all of Wilde's work, "the subversive, even radical critique of society
that is implicit in what he has to say, finds no release within the linguistic conventions which he mocked but by which he remained imprisoned" (2: 721). For
Murray and Deane, then, Wilde's is a story of compromise, of metaphoric imprisonment in English convention anticipating literal incarceration in Reading
Gaol. Declan Kiberd, however, offers a different analysis. Claiming that Wilde
was to the end of his days a militant republican, Kiberd sees his expatriate status as a confrontation rather than a compromise: "he and Shaw challenged, by
personal behaviour, as well as artistic skill, the prevailing stereotypes of the
Irish in Britain" (2: 372). This, I think, is the key. Students who encounter
Wilde as part of the newly, and self-confidently, compiled Irish literary canon
need alerting to the dangers of an implicit narrative of contamination, which invokes an Irish essence that cannot survive its English environment. The Irish
Wilde is best understood not in essentialist terms and best explained not in
terms of personal and artistic defeat.

Jerusha McCormack says that her volume *Wilde the Irishman* seeks to "rein-
state [Wilde's] spirit back in its own haunting grounds: to relocate its origins and
its effect in its native Ireland and in the spiritual territory that Wilde himself understood as home to the collective unconsciousness of his race" (5). Such recu-
peration can be undertaken not just in the name of cultural authenticity but also
for an authentic culture, or one imagined as authentic; and its tone veers constantly toward the elegiac. Deirdre Toomey's discussion of the fairy tales in Mc-
Cormack's collection, for instance, describes Wilde as tied to a dying Irish oral
culture by what Yeats called his half-civilized blood (35), thus relocating him in
an organic community that has yet to succumb fully to modernist fragmentation
of its social structures, sense of identity, and modes of representation. The temptation to see Wilde as defined by these origins is strong. Owen Dudley Edwards
decides, for instance, that Oscar Fingal O'Flahertie Wills Wilde was "a hostage
to Irish cultural identity" (McCormack 58). I labor this point not simply because
I wish to contest direct and simplistic nationalist readings of Wilde but also because I work hard to ensure that students are aware of the dangers and ironies of
applying notions of authenticity to Wilde's life and work—particularly notions of
cultural, national, and sexual authenticity. Indeed, one of the principal characteristics of his writing is its determined deconstruction of essentialisms of all
kinds: one of the elements of a consistent political and aesthetic strategy.

Despite the occasional dramatic declaration of his Celtic blood, Irishness was
for Wilde a form of discursive play and performance. He took a starring role as
an Irishman in late Victorian society. As such, his Irishness is not compromised
by his English contexts but is deliberately and willfully compromising: a dramatic posture he adopts in order to confront and transform the very Englishness he needs for his theatrical effects. That nationality was histrionic for
Wilde is evidenced by his reaction to the banning of *Salomé*. "I am not English.
I am Irish, which is quite another thing," he claimed—while simultaneously an-

nouncing his intention to take up French citizenship (qtd. in Mikhail, *Oscar Wilde: An Annotated Bibliography* 188). What I am not suggesting, however, is that seeing Wilde's Irishness as in some ways performed diminishes the significance of his nationalist politics, as voiced, for instance, in his damning review of J. P. Mahaffey's *Greek Life and Thought: From the Age of Alexander to the Roman Conquest* and what he regards as his old tutor's antidemocratic and antinationalist reading of ancient and contemporary history (Ellmann, *Artist* 80–84). As is clear from his praise of Wilfred Scawen Blunt—who was an Irish nationalist, though English by birth, and imprisoned in Galway Gaol for his attachment to the cause—Wilde recognized that nationalism could be a self-conscious and deliberate choice rather than determined exclusively by nationality and notions of "blood ties." We should see Wilde's nationalism as part of a nexus of radical political sympathies helping to characterize his work and not as atavistic in any sense. In effect, it is the style of being Irish, and for Wilde, as we know, in matters of great importance, style, not sincerity, is the vital thing.

Wilde's nationalism is "A Study in Green." This is the subtitle of his essay on the artist, forger, and serial killer Thomas Griffiths Wainewright, "Pen, Pencil and Poison," in which he claims that a fondness for green—the national color—denotes an artistic temperament in individuals and is said in nations to denote a laxity of morals (1095). Green, in other words, is the color of the artist, the decadent, the subversive, the Irish. This series of sliding identifications is crucial to our understanding of the importance to Wilde of both his nationality and his nationalism. His penchant for the green carnation buttonhole is symptomatic: it is the badge of a homosexual coterie, a demonstration of the self-consciously modern and refined taste that prefers the artificial to the natural, and a declaration of national allegiance that refracts and politicizes both. The green carnation is, in effect, a languidly insistent and coded declaration of difference: a multiform signifier.

Writing in 1933, G. J. Renier claimed that although Wilde's homosexual temperament was present to a fairly marked degree, it was not enough to prevent marriage and procreation, but "upon this temperament was imposed a lack of self-control due to his nationality" (4). He goes on to suggest that "it is not through persecution but through science that the mass production of homosexuals will be averted" (96). More recent attempts to articulate Wilde's nationality with his sexuality have been, thankfully, less sinister, and they have frequently taken as their subject the complex interrelation of the two in the ways Wilde was seen and described. Michael Foldy, for instance, suggests that the threat Wilde was regarded as posing at the time of his trials was not simply a matter of his "sexual deviancy": he came to symbolize the "very antithesis of Englishness" as his sexuality and nationality coalesced in the discourses of "healthy" late Victorian society (xv). Owen Dudley Edwards claims that Wilde's Irishness was in the dock at the Old Bailey as much as his sexual deviancy and that his compatriot Edward Carson cracked Wilde's English facade when, during cross-examination, he invited "very Irish responses to his heavy-handed questions about alleged immorality in Wilde's writings." The press made the connection, alluding to "the Irish QC." As Edwards puts it, "Come down to the Old Bailey and watch the Paddies whack" (12). Indeed, Frank Harris, Wilde's contemporary, made the same point, claiming a confusion in English minds between Wilde and an Irish terrorist group that had assassinated a British cabinet minister: "I have seen enough of English justice and English judges and English journals to convince me that Oscar Wilde had no more chance of a fair trial than if he had been an Irish 'Invincible' " (167). Terry Eagleton's version of Wilde announces, in *Saint Oscar*, that he objects to the trial on the grounds that "no Irishman can receive a fair hearing in an English court because the Irish are figments of the English imagination. I am not really here; I am just one of your racial fantasies" (23). Interestingly, Eagleton's fictional Wilde conceives of his "doubleness" in terms that link him with real Irish "traitors" such as Roger Casement and William "Lord Haw-Haw" Joyce: he is, he says, a fifth columnist, "a spy, a changeling, an alien smuggled into the upper class to corrupt their offspring" (23). Similarly, the Irish novelist John Banville explores, in *The Untouchable*, this concatenation of Irishness, homosexuality, and treachery in explicit terms: he transmogrifies the "real" Sir Anthony Blunt—Keeper of the Queen's Pictures and spy for the Russians—into the Irish Victor Maskell. Wilde is clearly one of the models for this "Queer Irish Spy": aesthete, classical scholar, married gay predator, outsider/insider, man of many masks (47).

"The Soul of Man under Socialism" is Wilde's most dangerous, most subversive essay and should be the focus for any discussion with students about Wilde's politics. Originally published in the *Fortnightly Review* in February 1891, the essay argues that the abolition of private property, marriage, the family, and poverty will result in a utopian society in which—on socialist lines—the state withers away, allowing everyone to become a full-fledged individualist, an artist, relieved of the "sordid necessity of living for others" (1174). The role of art in bringing about this revolution is vital: an artist is a type of political agitator. Wilde recognizes the importance of ideology and of the false consciousness that allows the poor to accept their lot: "no class is ever really conscious of its own suffering. They have to be told of it by other people, and they often entirely disbelieve them" (1176). He is characteristically acute on the complicity of Christianity in the maintenance of capitalist ideology, offering consolation as it does to the "virtuous poor" (1176). The essay provocatively restyles Christ (along lines suggested by Ernest Renan in his *The Life of Jesus*) as a revolutionary, a protosocialist with the message, "You should give up private property. It hinders you from realising your perfection" (1180).

Wilde was undoubtedly influenced by his compatriot George Bernard Shaw in targeting Christianity in this way: Lawrence Danson suggests that Wilde's decision to write on socialism was somewhat pragmatically influenced by the success of *Fabian Essays*, to which Shaw contributed in 1890 (*Wilde's* Intentions 93). Furthermore, "The Soul of Man" may have fed back into the preface to Shaw's *Major Barbara* (1907), with its savage attack on "Crosstianity" and the seven deadly virtues; Shaw certainly attempts a series of Wildean paradoxes in his championing of socialism, based on the "universal regard for money," which he claims is the "one hopeful fact in our civilization, the one sound spot in our social conscience" (21). But the Irish connection does not end there. Edwards argues that the essay's general political message is complemented by an immediate and specific polemical purpose. "The Soul of Man" is implicit evidence of Wilde's nationalism as well as an explicit proclamation of his socialism. Wilde's attack on journalism is a "furious denunciation of the British press and its destruction of Parnell." The Irish home ruler is the central absent presence in the argument, according to Edwards, and Wilde's failure to mention him by name was not a matter of deliberate concealment: "he simply seems to have been in so white a heat that he failed to allow for a life for his essay beyond the date of its magazine" (11). It is obviously the topical example of the Irish political hero's being destroyed by a divorce case that lies behind Wilde's condemnation of the way "serious, earnest, thoughtful" journalists nail their ears to the keyhole and

> drag before the eyes of the public some incident in the private life of a great statesman, of a man who is a leader of political thought as he is a creator of political force, and invite the public to discuss the incident, to exercise authority in the matter.   (1189)

Edwards is right to point out this specific and urgent context because it means we cannot simply dismiss "The Soul of Man" as abstract and willfully impracticable; its socialism is intimately connected with a larger radical political agenda that embraces Wilde's Irish nationalism and his feminism. In addition to the influences of Baudelaire, Shaw, and Renan, Wilde draws heavily on William Morris, the Taoist philosophy of self-culture, and European anarchist thinkers such as Kropotkin; but we should not let the characteristic eclecticism of the essay detract from the secure and sophisticated theoretical underpinnings of its radicalism.

In my experience, students who have come to Wilde because they know and enjoy his plays or *Dorian Gray* have a lot of trouble taking his politics seriously. They will read "The Soul of Man," if at all, as an exercise merely in posturing. Of course, it is another performance among many, but no less important for that. The truth is that Wilde's political sympathies have always met with a skeptical response. Harris, one of Wilde's few supporters to offer practical help and advice as the storm gathered to break over Wilde during his trials, claimed that his republicanism, for instance, was not even skin-deep and that his political prejudices were really those of the English governing classes "and were all in favour of individual freedom, or anarchy under the protection of the policeman" (66).

Recent scholarship should help students challenge this judgment. Sos Eltis, for instance, has usefully documented Wilde's personal contact with the world of émigré radicals and anarchists in the London of the 1880s and 1890s: the world satirized as radical chic in "Lord Arthur Savile's Crime." Wilde tried to organize a

petition in support of the Chicago anarchists in 1886; was a friend of S. M. Step-
nyak, who had assassinated the chief of the Russian secret police; and stood bail
for the young John Barlas, who showed his anarchism by firing a pistol outside the
Houses of Parliament in 1891 (17–18). He was also personally acquainted with a
number of well-known members of the French artistic avant-garde, such as Félix
Fénéon and Adolphe Rette, who were prominent in revolutionary and anarchist
politics. Eltis also emphasizes the seriousness of Wilde's feminism, claiming that
Wilde was a consistent champion of women's rights and supported all the primary
demands of late-nineteenth-century feminism—in particular the campaigns for
women's suffrage and greater access to higher education (7). Central to this claim
is Wilde's editorship of *Woman's World*. Wilde transformed the magazine when
he took it over in 1887, signaling his womanly rather than feminine agenda by
changing the name from *Lady's World*. As editor, Wilde introduced "a high intellectual content" and "radical tone," dropping articles on "pastimes for ladies" and
giving space instead to those arguing for women's right to equality of treatment
with men and to a greater role in public and political life (6–13). Although some
critics, such as Sally Ledger, have described Wilde's contribution to feminism as
at best equivocal, Eltis insists that the brevity of Wilde's tenure as editor—he
quickly tired of the day-to-day routine of running the magazine—should not detract from his commitment to the cause.

"The Soul of Man" was published in the same issue of Harris's *Fortnightly
Review* as "The Celt in English Art," by the influential anthropologist, Darwin-
ist, essayist, and novelist Grant Allen. Allen argued that the conquered Celts
would eventually overturn English dominance and emerge as political as well as
cultural leaders. He regarded the "great and victorious aesthetic movement" as
part of "the general racial, political, and social return-wave," a Celtic reflux that
would result in the triumph of Celtic ideals: "imagination, fancy, decorative
skill, artistic handicraft; free land, free speech, human equality, human brotherhood." Allen stressed what he saw as the connection between "the decorative
revival and the Celtic upheaval of radicalism and socialism" and pointed to
William Morris and Wilde as leading exemplars of this common aesthetico-
political project (272). We need not accept that, because he shared the pages of
the *Fortnightly Review* with Allen, Wilde also shared Allen's belief in the racial
origins of aestheticism or Allen's faith in eugenics. The crucial point is that both
authors make a provocative intertwining of aestheticism, radicalism, and socialism in the name of Celticism. For Wilde, Irishness and Celticism are not essentialist notions legitimating forms of authenticity but floating signifiers he
appropriates for his own tactical and strategic purposes: principally to define his
own otherness, his oppositional stance, his rejection of authority.

So when approaching Wilde's Irishness, we need to find ways of helping students read his work that do not involve the cracking of a code. Wilde is not an
Irish writer underneath. It is, appropriately, Shaw who puts his finger on it, when
reviewing *An Ideal Husband*. Wilde, he declared, "is England's only thorough
playwright. He plays with everything; with wit, with philosophy, with drama, with

actors and audience, with the whole theatre" ("Two New Plays" 44). This playfulness Shaw identifies, rightly, as an offensive tactic: he counts Wilde as an ally in subversion, emphasizing their shared status as aliens. "Ireland," he claims, "is of all countries the most foreign to England." England's colonial relation to John Bull's Other Island is thus redefined. The arrogant assumption of assimilation is replaced with an insistence on foreignness, on otherness, and its principal target is earnestness and sincerity. To the Irishman, says Shaw, "there is nothing in the world quite so exquisitely comic as an Englishman's seriousness" (45).

What Shaw describes as pervading levity, I would characterize as stylization: the playfulness with which Wilde fashions the clash of genres, for instance, and the way he stylizes English. From a postcolonial perspective, Wilde is a colonial subject operating within the discourses of his imperial masters. As a member of the Anglo-Irish ascendancy and a nationalist he is contemptuous of English dominion (witness his scathing expose of insider dealing at the heart of the imperial metropolis in *An Ideal Husband*) yet implicated in it. This paradox is enacted in his precise deployment, and disarming, of the discourse of the colonial masters: he and his characters speak with an almost extraterritorial precision that exploits English to its own destruction. Nowhere, of course, is this strategy more evident than in *The Importance of Being Earnest*, which is Wilde's most stylized, most playful, and hence most political play. To ask students to read it, for instance, as a gay play underneath is to use the surface/depth model of analysis, which Wilde's work explodes: it is an attempt to stabilize the text's meaning, to authenticate and fix it. The play's radicalism is to be found not by excavating it and returning it to an authentic and specific gay politics but in recognizing how it counters a pernicious authoritarianism, personified by Lady Bracknell, with a deliberate and self-conscious emphasis on the liberatory potential of style, as exemplified in the lying antics of the young lovers. Nor is *Earnest* a socialist play underneath: it is socialist in its fascination with surface and in its manner. "The Soul of Man" shows that Wilde associates socialism with a future that is aesthetically as well as materially satisfying and one in which authority in all its forms has been deconstructed. The self-conscious playfulness of *The Importance of Being Earnest* is an act of faith in that utopian future, in which the exquisites, and not Lady Bracknell, will rule.

As teachers we need to alert students to the fact that Wilde's sense of his Irishness and its associated politics are much more interesting and subtle than a reductive anti-Englishness approach would imply. His opposition to essentialisms and authority of all kinds would have made him less at home in Eamon de Valera's free, fantasy island of athletic youths and comely maidens than he was in the English Victorian culture that destroyed him. To teach Wilde's Irishness is to confront the shifting complexities that define his work and to get students to examine not just the ways they read but the ways in which they conceive of nationality and nation: pedagogy through paradox, constructing Wildean ways of reading Wilde. But then, as Wilde reminds us, nothing that is worth knowing can be taught (1242).

Oscar Wilde and the 1890s:
A Single-Figure Course

Philip E. Smith II

> We, in our educational system, have burdened the
> memory with a load of unconnected facts, and laboriously
> striven to impart our laboriously-acquired knowledge. We
> teach people how to remember, we never teach them how
> to grow.
>
> —Wilde, "The Critic as Artist"

I designed my seminar on Oscar Wilde and the 1890s for graduate students
and, in an alternate version, for senior English majors. My ambition has been to
provide a structure that enables students to pursue their own interests in Wilde
in the context of the seminar's shared enterprise: their explorations and discoveries should enable mutual intellectual growth. In both graduate and undergraduate seminars, a focus on the works of Oscar Wilde centers the reading and
research done by students, but readings from several other late-nineteenth-
century writers introduce critical and contextual ideas that can frame the students' work on Wilde or provide students with points of entry to related
projects. My fall 2005 course description directs the intention this way:

> This graduate course presents the major works of Oscar Wilde (poetry,
> fiction, drama, and criticism) in the context of other texts from Europe-
> an (Ibsen, Nietzsche, Nordau) and anglophone (Arnold, Ruskin, Pater,
> Shaw, Wells, Morris, the new women) writers at the end of the nine-
> teenth century. Wilde's writing is considered in relation to aestheticism
> and the art-for-art's sake movements as well as in relation to nineteenth-
> century philosophical and scientific discourses. Contemporary critical
> approaches to Wilde inform student reports and projects. The students'
> major work is to produce a paper suitable for presentation at a confer-
> ence and (in the best cases) for publication. The last two meetings are
> devoted to oral presentations of the semester's research by every mem-
> ber of the seminar.

As I have developed the course over the last decade, the selected contextual
readings have slowly changed. In past versions of the course, I included texts
like G. B. Shaw's *Plays Unpleasant* (1898), H. G. Wells's *The Time Machine*
(1895) and *The Island of Dr. Moreau* (1896), and Arthur Morison's *A Child of
the Jago* (1896), all of which had significant merits. But a fifteen-week semester,
two weeks of which are devoted to students' presentations of their research,

does not offer a leisurely opportunity to read extensively, so I dropped these three authors and added Henrik Ibsen's *Ghosts* (1881), *Hedda Gabler* (1890), and Mike Jay and Michael Neve's *1900*, an anthology of short selections excerpted from documents characteristic of issues and trends in the fin de siècle. I also include Friedrich Nietzsche's *On the Genealogy of Morals* and selections from Max Nordau's *Degeneration*.

I ask students to read using some major thematic foci of my choosing but also to bring to the course their own cultural and literary-theoretical interests, which will help them shape their critical research projects. I want them to become acquainted with Wilde's writing, roughly in chronological order, under the rubric of literary and social theories of the 1890s concerning writers' proposals about the art of life (and the life of art) connected with socialism, science, and aestheticism (and their ideological dark sides, decadence and degeneration) as well as with issues of power and gender definition accompanying the emergence of homosexuality, feminism, and such associated cultural categories as dandyism and the new woman. But I expect students to find and pursue research projects that connect to their own interests in Wilde and with their developing commitments to literary and cultural theories.

The classroom process I use combines assigned presentations with discussion of assigned readings. Since I want students to begin thinking about their research projects early in the term, I ask each one to prepare and present a five-minute report, with accompanying handout, on a major critical or scholarly text. At the same time, I ask for proposals that at least identify the range of interest and associated texts for a project. These projects are circulated to the seminar so that each reporter on a research book will be able to advise about its possible use by seminar colleagues. I want two or three reports presented at each class meeting, sometime between the third and the tenth week of the seminar (first drafts are the eleventh week) so they can be of use to everyone's process of preparing a project draft. I also ask students to choose one of the major assigned texts and to prepare a report connecting it both to its nineteenth-century contexts and to their own interests. I encourage open-ended reports, which produce questions for discussion, rather than conclusive opinions about the assigned reading.

I ask students to begin the semester by reading some of the dominant Victorian critical and aesthetic ideas, which are expressed by Matthew Arnold in "The Function of Criticism at the Present Time," Walter Pater in the preface and conclusion to *The Renaissance*, and John Ruskin in *Modern Painters*. All three men helped Wilde define his own critical and creative theories. I want students to understand that at the heart of late-Victorian aestheticism there existed a debate about the nature of knowledge and perception. Arnold's well-known Platonic idea of seeing "the object as in itself it really is" (317) and Ruskin's notion of seeing, both of them idealist formulations implying an essential truth or knowledge to be intuited through art, are contrasted by Pater's subjectivist, impressionist, and materialist formulation, "to know the object as in itself it is perceived" (*Renaissance* xix). For introductory critical background on this topic, I refer students to Wendell Harris, Richard Ellmann (*Artist* xi–xii) and to *Oscar Wilde's Oxford Notebooks* (42–43). This critical debate helps them contextualize issues in Wilde's criticism, especially in "The Decay of Lying" and "The Critic as Artist," but it also suggests paths for teaching his creative writing.

I assign a selection of Wilde's poems beginning with two contrasting sonnets, "Hèlas!" and "Theoretikos," which introduce some of the critical issues connected with Wilde's position as a poet who speaks for Romance and the "soul's inheritance" but also for the "heritage of centuries" in art and culture in the respective poems (864, 776). The remaining poems I assign are "The Garden of Eros," "Impression du Matin," "Charmides," "Panthea," "The Harlot's House," "Humanitad," and "The Sphinx"; the prose poems I assign are "The Artist," "The Doer of Good," "The Disciple," "The Master," "The House of Judgment," and "The Teacher of Wisdom." I expect these choices to suggest issues and topics that students will choose to follow up in the poetry as well as in later texts. For example, "The Garden of Eros" pays conventional homage to some of Wilde's poetic and aesthetic fathers, Shelley, Keats, Byron, Swinburne, Morris, Ruskin, and Rossetti, the group he would later write about in his American lecture "The English Renaissance of Art." "Charmides," "Panthea," and "Humanitad," though quite different in their subjects, are alike in alluding to Pater's conclusion to *The Renaissance* and his advice for cultivating passionate awareness of the pulse of life. "Charmides" and "Panthea" suggest the thematic appeal of sexuality, both as narrative of transformation (looking ahead to *Dorian Gray*) and as a principle of life indebted to William Wordsworth's nature and Walt Whitman's all-encompassing Kosmos. "Humanitad," in its praise of Giuseppe Mazzini and republicanism as well as in its invocation of a humane Christ, looks forward to "The Soul of Man under Socialism." "Impression du Matin" and "The Harlot's House" sample Wilde's ability to turn Blakean and Poe-esque urban descriptions to his own effects; both poems anticipate his depiction of London in "Lord Arthur Savile's Crime" and *Dorian Gray*. The prose poems suggest Wilde's oracular tone with scriptural narratives and his life-long interest in reconciling human desires with the model of a human Christ, and they look forward to, among other works, "The Soul of Man under Socialism," the prison letter known as *De Profundis*, and the fairy tales.

After the poems, over a period of two weeks, I assign Wilde's four short stories and a selection of the fairy tales together with "The Rise of Historical Criticism," "The Truth of Masks," and "Pen, Pencil, and Poison." Like the poems, the short fictions help students focus on some of the critical issues raised by Arnold, Pater, Ruskin, and Wilde; they consolidate impressions of readers who have begun to correlate or contrast thematic ideas, such as transgression, which students might locate in "The Devoted Friend," "Lord Arthur Savile's Crime," "Pen, Pencil, and Poison," "Hèlas," and "Charmides." I follow the short fiction with a week devoted to Wilde's criticism and literary theory—that is, the two remaining essays from *Intentions,* "The Decay of Lying" and "The Critic as Artist." I also assign "The Soul of Man under Socialism," "The Portrait of Mr. W. H.," Nordau's chapter on Wilde from *Degeneration,* and the first essay from Nietzsche's *On the Genealogy of Morals.* This week's assigned work is more than can be discussed in depth in a single three-hour session, especially with two or three research reports on the agenda. However, depending on students' interests in introducing works for discussion, it is possible to look at two or three of the essays and to begin thinking about the Nietzsche selection.

These critical essays reappear in discussions over the remainder of the semester as students begin to realize their implications for Wilde's ideas about culture and aesthetics; for his individualism and utopian social thinking; for his notions of the roles of artist and critic; for his incorporation of science and philosophy into criticism and creation; for his pronouncements on personality, self-perfection, soul, and the importance of the figures of the sinner and of Jesus Christ in regard to the formation of subject position. By juxtaposing these readings and ideas with Nietzsche's genealogy of "good and bad" and "good and evil," I invite students to compare and contrast the ways in which both Nietzsche and Wilde challenge the dominant paradigms of middle-class culture through the transvaluation of terms, through aphorisms, and even through the technique of dialogue.

For the next two weeks, my reading assignments juxtapose *The Picture of Dorian Gray* (divided in half: chapters 1–8 and 9–20) and the two final essays from Nietzsche's *The Genealogy of Morals.* Students can compare, for example, Nietzsche's idea of the "will to power" with Wilde's ideas on the differences between art and life as characterizing the power of creation (throughout "The Decay of Lying") or on sin as an element of progress (in "The Critic as Artist" [1121]) and of course in Dorian Gray's development of the "new Hedonism that was to recreate life, and to save it from that harsh, uncomely puritanism" (99). I also want them to note that Nietzsche's reminders to call ideas into question should be deployed to interrogate the homologies as well as the contrasts between his views and Wilde's. For example, Nietzsche's pronouncement that "art, in which precisely the *lie* is sanctified and the *will to deception* has a good conscience, is much more fundamentally opposed to the ascetic ideal than is science" (153–54) recalls Wilde's position in "The Decay of Lying," that "[t]he only form of lying that is absolutely beyond reproach is lying for its own sake, and the highest development of this is, as we have already pointed out, Lying in Art" (1090). Such examples do not begin to exhaust the possibilities for comparative analysis of Wilde and Nietzsche, but they do suggest how such analysis might be incorporated into students' projects.

I ask students to consult with me about possible topics as soon as they think of them; the earlier the start, often the better the project. By week 6 of the semester, when students are reading the first half of *Dorian Gray* and the second essay in *On the Genealogy of Morals,* I expect them to turn in a written project proposal based on the direction they have taken since my consulting with them. The proposal is not meant to be a promissory note; rather, it is a way to stake out territory that students may explore further, modify, or abandon as they work through the course assignments and compare notes on research with their colleagues. I hand back the proposal with comments and suggestions for development; the first draft of the project is due in week 11 and is returned by week 13. In the fall semester, which is usually when I teach the course, there is an intervening week for Thanksgiving. Finally, in weeks 14 and 15 students present their projects in a conference setting for the class. But at the time the proposal is due, half the seminar sessions remain. I scale back the length of reading assignments somewhat for the second half of the course, because I expect students to be working on their project as well as doing the work of the course.

The week after we finish *Dorian Gray* and Nietzsche, the project proposal is returned, and the assignments turn to drama, the area of Wilde's greatest success and last development. The first plays discussed are Ibsen's *Ghosts* and *Hedda Gabler*, contextualized by the section on Ibsen from Nordau's *Degeneration*.

Ibsen, like Nietzsche and Wilde, is one of the artists, writers, and thinkers condemned by conservatives as a symptomatic figure of European cultural degeneration, but his phenomenal influence on European drama, and on English drama in the 1890s, makes him a crucial figure to study in relation to Wilde. The plays are remarkable as documents of nineteenth-century European theater history and as works in the history of culture and particularly, with the problem plays, of issues connected with late-nineteenth-century feminism. *Ghosts* introduces many of Ibsen's dramaturgical devices connecting themes with moments of text and atmosphere, his innovations in the structure of the *pièce bien faite* that move from farcical and melodramatic plot turns to revelations of idea and character at key structural places. The thematics of liberation and tension between bourgeois culture and the avant-garde are replayed in the tension of awakened ghostly relations between Mrs. Alving and Pastor Manders and in the return of Oswald from Paris to confront the consequences of his family history and his own generation. Just as *Ghosts* famously offers a kind of alternative to *A Doll's House* (what would have happened if Nora had not walked out and slammed the door on her marriage) and was therefore of significant interest to feminists throughout Europe, so *Hedda Gabler* presents a compelling character study of an haute bourgeoise attracted to the freedoms promised by freethinkers and feminists but frustrated by her lack of courage and her social conditioning. Mrs. Alving, Nora Tesman, and Hedda Gabler can all be read comparatively with the characters Wilde imagines in his society plays.

Kerry Powell observes that "Wilde himself was not counted among the Ibsenites or their detractors, yet to a significant degree measured his work as a playwright against the example that Ibsen set" (*Oscar Wilde* 75). Wilde's society plays gain considerable resonance when they are read next to Ibsen's problem plays. Instead of the tragic ironies that permeate Ibsen's plays, Wilde creates ironies and dilemmas with comic or melodramatic consequences. The plays are suitably ambiguous in meaning that they have generated interesting critical controversies—for example, over whether the plots and speeches involving Wilde's female characters might be read as furthering the agenda of feminism or confirming the patriarchal paradigm. We read the four society comedies in the ninth and tenth weeks of the semester. They are usually welcome texts for students who wish to prepare presentations to introduce discussions. They also offer the opportunity to raise the question of the plays' relation to Wilde's fiction, criticism, and poetry as well as to the question of popular culture versus art.

Another entrance to the question of drama as art might be found in the discussion of *Salomé*, which occurs in the eleventh week of the semester, when the first drafts of student projects are submitted. We read *Salomé* with the first half of Elaine Showalter's anthology *Daughters of Decadence*. In contrast to the society plays, this verse drama raises again issues of aestheticism and decadence in art, of romance versus realism—as did *Intentions* and *Dorian Gray*. Discussion of the play also invites student reports on the cultural background, analogues in art history, musical and film versions, and the issues raised by feminist and gender theories. *Salomé* offers a fulcrum for students to stage their thinking about the representation of women in Wilde and, beginning with the illustrations by Aubrey Beardsley, in the late nineteenth century. Bram Dijkstra's *Idols of Perversity: Fantasies of Feminine Evil in Fin-de-Siècle Culture* is a particularly useful critical book to have a student introduce to the seminar at this point in the semester.

Salomé also resonates well with the short fiction in Showalter's anthology, since the stories by the new women both challenge and accommodate male fantasies of women at the same time that they show signs of participating in the awakening of feminism and in the beginnings of modernism. Showalter's *Sexual Anarchy* pairs well with *Daughters of Decadence* and is another useful book for a student report, especially in the light of her critical reading of Wilde's homosexuality as decadent and aesthetic and therefore antipathetic to feminism (174–76). In all sorts of ways, from a detail like the prevalence of cigarette smoking as a sign of liberation from Victorian values to the utopian and prophetic fables of Olive Schreiner, the stories in *Daughters of Decadence* represent transatlantic responses to the avant-garde social and artistic climate of the 1890s for upper- and middle-class women. For example, the fictions focused on women writers (Mabel Wotton's "The Fifth Edition," Constance Woolson's "Miss Grief," and Vernon Lee's "Lady Tal") make a set of interesting and contrasting analogues to the lives and careers of the dominant (and very Henry Jamesian) male writers. The story with the greatest resonance for Wilde is "Suggestion," by his friend Ada Leverson, who shows her appreciation for the aristocratic amorality Wilde portrayed in *Dorian Gray* and his society comedies in her characterization of Cecil "Cissy" Carington. Showalter claims that the story offers "a pointed critique of Wilde's narratives" (xii), but it can as easily be read as Leverson's homage to Wilde by allowing the manipulative Cecil the opportunity to expose heterosexual hypocrisy.

During week 12, the second on *Daughters of Decadence*, I ask students to begin reading Wilde's prison letter, *De Profundis*, and we discuss it in week 13 together with his letters to the *Daily Chronicle* on prison reform and with *The Ballad of Reading Gaol*. Many students interested in queer theory or gender issues already know something about Wilde's trial and the aftermath, and they find the documentary history of the trials as well as the publication history of *De Profundis* interesting topics for a seminar presentation as well as for a research paper. Merlin Holland's edition of the transcript of the first trial, *The Real Trial of Oscar Wilde* (entitled, in Ireland and Britain, *Irish Peacock and Scarlet Marquess: The Real Trial of Oscar Wilde*) and his facsimile edition of *De Profundis* (Wilde, De Profundis) make useful subjects for in-class reports, as does Jonathan Goodman's illustrated collection of documents and newspaper reports and transcripts, *The Oscar Wilde File*. Theater students are often interested in reporting on plays such as Moisés Kaufman's *Gross Indecency* and David Hare's *The Judas Kiss*, which imagine the relationships among Wilde, Robert Ross, Alfred Douglas, and others in the dramatic events of April 1895 and after.

Discussion of *De Profundis* in week 13 ranges through the issues raised in the text, refracted by students' reading of most of Wilde's writing over the preceding weeks. The power of Wilde's account of his fracturing relationship with Douglas brings a new focus to his writing in relation to accounts of his life. The refiguring of the concept of soul and the figure of Christ continues a thread present in the writings since his poems. Wilde's references to events in his life extending back to Oxford and to moments in his written works as premonitory or ironic in the light of experience have immediate force and poignancy. Questions can be raised about what Wilde calls "the evolution of my life and character" (1059). Questions about his commitment to his cultural and aesthetic agendas arise from the letter's claims for literary art and from these two repeated sentences: "The supreme vice is shallowness. Everything that is realised is right" (981). Discussion about students' responses to *De Profundis* also needs to take into account Wilde's affecting representations of prison life in his two letters to the *Daily Chronicle* and in *The Ballad of Reading Gaol*. The combination of these texts in the last week unfailingly produces interesting observations and cross-references to the research papers that students by this point in the semester have expended much work in preparing.

The last two meetings of the seminar allow students to present a conference on Wilde. As I read and comment on the drafts of their papers, I also begin to group them thematically into panels of three or four presentations each, sometimes with the possibility that students' interests have enabled two or more interpretations of the same text. Although the written length for papers is set at twenty pages or more, I ask that the presentations be kept to fifteen to twenty minutes, or no more than ten pages of double-spaced text to be read. I suggest to students that just as they have made suggestions for one another's research over the course of the semester, this set of presentations raises the bar by simulating the conferences to which they are encouraged to submit work. Therefore, as an informed audience, they should aim to reinforce what works well and to provide a critique of any aspects that could be strengthened, with the understanding that everyone's work will receive the same kind of attention.

The students' selection and performance of research and writing engage their interests and critical abilities in their encounter with the course syllabus I have designed. If there is synergy between my design and their interests, challenging work can result. Since I aim not only to acquaint students with a substantial number of Wilde's writings in context but also, and more important, to provide an occasion for students' research and critical interpretation, the proof of success lies mainly in the work they do. A list of titles is no assurance of the quality of work, but I can at the very least suggest the range of inquiry undertaken by recent students by showing a selection of their papers, organized by subject (see the appendix to this essay). One paper, written by a senior, won the university's annual Ossip Award for the best research paper by an undergraduate; others, by graduate students, have been accepted for publication and for presentation at conferences.

APPENDIX:
SELECTED SEMINAR PAPERS

Poetry

"Oscar Wilde's Poetic Aesthetic" examines Wilde's reviews of other poets for his judgments, then applies them to a sample of his poetry.

"The Influence of Dante's Poetry on Wilde," written by a senior, is now the basis for a PhD dissertation in Italian literature.

Fiction and Fairy Tales

"Building the Book Beautiful: Artists at Work in *A House of Pomegranates*": the author's curiosity was piqued when she discovered that Frankel's *Oscar Wilde's Illustrated Books* pays scant attention to *A House of Pomegranates*. Finding microfilm reproductions unacceptable, the author visited a library that had a copy of the text and its dim illustrations. Her essay effectively read the illustrations and suggested interpretations that illuminated the stories as well as the illustrations and the book as a collaborative design.

"Toward Rereading Wilde's Fairy Tales: Another Look at 'The Devoted Friend' ": the author's insight about rereading the tale to children enabled her to formulate and revise a penetrating interpretation of the story, which was accepted for publication in *Children's Literature* 36.

"The Paradox of Christian/Cultural Fragmentation within Oscar Wilde's 'The Fisherman and His Soul' "

"The Wilde Changeling: The Beauty of the 'Other' in Oscar Wilde's Fairy Tales"

"A Hylo-Idealistic Romance of Duty: Courtship in Oscar Wilde's Short Fiction"

Drama

" 'Please Don't Put Us Down as Ibsenites!': The Publicity, Performance, and Reception of the 1891 London Debut of *Hedda Gabler*": the Robins-Lea production drew Wilde twice to the theater; he was a friend and sponsor of Elizabeth Robins, who played Hedda.

"Influences and Ideals: An Expanded Analysis of the Parallels between Ibsen's *Pillars of Society* and Wilde's *An Ideal Husband*"

"The 'Passion of Maternity' in Oscar Wilde's *Lady Windermere's Fan*"

"Worlds of Will within Wilde's *Salomé* and Ibsen's *Brand*: A Paradigm of the Influence of the 'Other' "

Criticism

"The Function of Paradox at the Present Time: Irony, Eros, and Ethics in Oscar Wilde's 'Critic as Artist' "

"Oscar Wilde and the Art of Self-Care" examines Foucault's idea as parallel to Wilde's idea of soul in "The Soul of Man," *Dorian Gray*, "The Critic as Artist," and *De Profundis*.

"Consumer as Critic?" This paper concedes Wilde's alliance with socialism but, drawing on Veblen, Said, and others, sees Wilde focusing on the consumer rather than on the wretched laborer. The paper explores several key texts to show Wilde producing the Platonic critic (Jesus) while rejecting the connoisseurship of Dorian Gray.

"Synaesthesia and Transgression in 'The Critic as Artist' and *Salomé*"

"The Critic as Modern: Oscar Wilde's Philosophy of Immanence." Beginning with Benjamin's idea of truth as an ideal still possible in an immanent world, the essayist recapitulates Wilde's intellectual background, then reads "The Critic as Artist" and *The Picture of Dorian Gray* as an inverse pair.

Journalism

"Oscar Wilde and *The Woman's World*: Gender Negotiation and Aesthetic Engenderment"

The Trials

> "Subversion in the Courtroom: Legal Strategies and Sexual Typing in the Case of Regina vs. John Douglas"

De Profundis

> "The True History of *De Profundis*"
> "The Artist in Prison: Creative Suffering in *De Profundis*"
> "The Mythology of the Self in *De Profundis*"

Gray Zones:
Teaching *The Picture of Dorian Gray* as a Victorian Novel

Shelton Waldrep

The Picture of Dorian Gray is a fascinating text for students for much the same reason it continues to interest—and perhaps confound—scholars: it is difficult to define. Indeed, the book presents a series of paradoxes, ever-shifting definitional paradigms, that keep you guessing as to what the novel is really about, at the same time allowing readers to enjoy the hunt for a foundational moment. Given the popularity of the novel among scholars working in queer theory, a common approach to anchoring the book is to see it as a coming-out narrative. Yet, as Jeff Nunokawa and others have noted, as soon as homosexuality is seen as the key to Dorian's identity, the novel's logic goes off track ("Homosexual Desire" 313). Likewise, if you approach *Dorian Gray* as an aestheticist text that resists the hard world of fact, you also have to explain the Jim Vane plot and the naturalist impulse that it seems to represent—one praised by Walter Pater, no less.

The best way to approach the book is to allow for a variety of perspectives while still maintaining connections among them. The novel, after all, gets to have everything at least two ways—to present meaning as a series of Russian nesting dolls in which anything that we think we know is really the kernel of something else entirely. The novel's structure seems to suggest that everyone's favorite theoretical approach is always apropos: queer, Freudian, Marxian, New

Critical, biographical, whatever. Each can fit equally well into the book's meta-morphic confines, much as the book itself can function as an appropriate text for a wide array of classes, from an introduction to fiction to a course on the most subtle points of hermeneutics. Yet the book's protean ability is based on a particular version of the gothic, one that Judith Halberstam has defined as "a discursive strategy which produces monsters as a kind of temporary but influential response to social, political, and sexual problems" (75). Under the guise of avoiding the questions of the Victorian era altogether, Wilde is actually summing up his century and providing a solution, however tentative, to its growing problem of representation, of verisimilitude, gone dangerously out of control as realism loses its ability to stabilize meaning at the century's end.

While I have taught *Dorian Gray* in a number of different pedagogical situations, one structure I have found that does justice to the novel's multiple meanings has been to place it in historical context near the end of an undergraduate or graduate survey of the Victorian novel that traces the nineteenth-century gothic. Specifically, I look at *Dorian Gray* as incorporating a shift from what Susan Meyer calls "reverse colonization" (112) toward the concept of degeneracy. According to Meyer's theory, while empire expanded outward, it also opened itself up to the possibility of reverse influence: the racial other might in fact come home to the heart of the empire to disrupt the social fabric.[1] In order to familiarize the class with Meyer's ideas, I spend the first meeting lecturing on the historical background of the Victorian period and emphasize that our course will focus not only on close readings of the texts but also on the ways in which the novels reflect their cultural and historical milieu.

With each novel in the course we adopt a variety of critical stances that have been popular with critics in the past for examining that particular novel, but we use the postcolonial approach as a common thread for connecting all of them. I usually begin the discussion of Wilde's novel by providing students with background information on the book—its publishing history, author's biography, critical response, and then move on to a general discussion of important themes, characters, systems of symbolism, and so on. Finally, we spend time on individual passages, attempting especially to look for patterns of meaning. The various strains that we follow in class, such as the intertwining of the postcolonial with questions of the other via the gothic, are substantiated by specific passages. I also use editions with supplementary critical essays and assign essays to be read before the work is discussed in class. Both the Bedford and Norton editions contain essays that emphasize the representative criticism made of the novels, though the Bedford editions also provide background information on various critical schools (psychoanalytic, Marxist, poststructuralist, postcolonialist, etc.). Because my current institution requires classes in critical theory for English majors and graduate students and because most of my colleagues teach from this perspective, I can assume that my students have some familiarity with the general concepts. We might read *Jane Eyre* but also the selection from Sandra Gilbert and Susan Gubar's landmark feminist study of the novel, *The Madwoman in the Attic*, or *Wuthering Heights* and J. Hillis Miller's deconstructive take on a few of its key scenes. In either case, students are exposed simultaneously to the novel as well as to the many different ways that are available for reading it.

While novels are frequently changed or added to the class, I try to keep a set of core texts that can be used to track the movement of the gothic from race and nationality to blood and (pseudo) science: currently *Emma, Jane Eyre, Wuthering Heights*, Elizabeth Gaskell's "The Old Nurse's Story," *The Lifted Veil*, and *Dracula*, though doubtlessly many others would fit this list.[2] I like to begin with Jane Austen because, while pre-Victorian, her novels illustrate the fact that postcolonial themes and interests are present in the English novel even before the emergence of such properly Victorian figures as the Brontës or George Eliot, and in *Emma* we can see signs of Austen's familiarity with the world beyond the village. The discussion of "the slave-trade" that occurs in volume 3 shows that Austen was not only aware of outside politics but even used it in this novel as a metaphor for the story she wrote (196).[3]

The reference to colonialism in *Emma* will emerge as a major theme in the Victorian era proper. In *Jane Eyre* we look at the attempt to confine the racial other, literally, to the attic.[4] Meyer does an excellent job of teasing out the orientalizing aspects of the text, from the liminal Creole identity of Bertha Mason to the way in which that identity is carried over to other characters in the book as the novel represents race as anxiety. Thornhill, like Jane Eyre, is haunted by the need to distance the racial other. In *Wuthering Heights*, Heathcliff is the racialized other (Irish? American?) who comes back from a mysterious three-year absence with money and a plan to avenge himself on all who had formerly enslaved him.[5] Emily Brontë takes much further the conceits of *Jane Eyre*, but she also asks more difficult questions about the marginalization of race during the early years of Victorian empire.

That during the middle point of the Victorian period the reverse imperialism of the first half of the century slowly becomes more scientist and neogothic can be seen in both Gaskell's "The Old Nurse's Story" and Eliot's *The Lifted Veil*. The mesmerism, clairvoyance, and reanimation in Eliot's novella point the way, in other words, toward the plot of Wilde's novel. By the time we get to the late Victorian period, this gothic anxiety has broken through the realist text that contained it as the lingering aspects of a ghost story to become the main story itself. In looking at Gaskell's extremely popular "The Old Nurse's Story," we see the gothic in the form that it is best known today—that is, the haunted house story. We also examine how the gothic allows the representation of things normally out of bounds to realist fiction: patriarchal violence, for example. The gothic becomes a mode in which women can speak directly to one another about the margins of safety. In her novella, Eliot posits a more individualistic take on the gothic as an exploration of the limits of consciousness. While both Eliot and Gaskell see the gothic as being partly about the limits of communication, Eliot's version emphasizes not the need for women to communicate with one another but rather the gothic as a device for switching between the literal and the mystical, the world of fact and the realm of sensation.[6]

Wilde seemed to know that the shift from high Victorianism to the steady-state decline of the last two decades meant a shift from the racial other to one based on blood. The result is *Dorian Gray*. *Dracula* and any number of other novels that move the anxiety about a racial other from visible skin to invisible blood show the same shift. England becomes infected with otherness. The other has bred into the English genome a decline that parallels the waning of empire, of the Victorian moment, and represents the cultural logic of race mixing. The fear now borne out so strikingly in Cesare Lombroso and Nordau was that this otherness had become impossible to detect. Like Dracula a few years later, Dorian could walk among the living, and no one would be the wiser. Even the aristocracy was no longer safe. Blood now meant biology, and with that came the unpacking of everything that race had stood in for. Dorian Gray is as mutable as the text he haunts and a perfect symbol of late Victorian anxieties. A protagonist who goes to opium dens and frequents the docks of London, the border zone between England and its watery contact with the rest of the world, he is also an aristocratic personage, a social being whose downfall presages the end of an era. In this sense, the use of the gothic is ultimately parallel to the oriental as Edward Said has defined it: an imaginary Western construct that functions as a zone for containing uncouth appetites for sex and violence that are supposedly avoided or contained in the typical high Victorian text.

With the appearance of Bram Stoker's Dracula, the gothic has its biggest star, an example of the unnatural East that comes to the heart of empire, late Victorian London, with the specific goal of preying on the unsuspecting population, of doing Heathcliff on a grand scale by turning victims into willing slaves who nightly infect others with their blood in order to spread their cause, secretly, throughout the country.[7] The secondary essays in the Bedford and Norton editions of *Dracula* are especially helpful for teasing out how the book conflates sexual and racial identity. Essays in the Norton edition by Phyllis A. Roth, Franco Moretti, Christopher Craft, Stephen D. Arata, and Talia Shaffer, for example, delineate the argument that Jonathan Harker, as he moves from the West toward the East (Transylvania), is entering a part of the globe that has no stable identity. It has been, as Dracula explains, conquered and reconquered so many times that it now exists only on a slippery geographic and metaphoric border between West and East (i.e., the Orient). The sexual encounters that Harker has while in Castle Dracula are equally ambiguous: homoerotic with Dracula or orgiastic with the three mysterious female vampires who almost overtake him. In addition to raising concerns about the function of the popular novel in the nineteenth century, *Dracula* also raises questions about the relation between a novel and its extraliterary manifestations—in this case, the long shadow cast by the film versions in the next century.[8]

The concept of degeneracy mirrors the fin de siècle fear of entropy, failing empire, guilt, and the general death knell of the Victorian era.[9] The Irish and Gypsies have now become homosexuals, Jews, and to some extent even women, who literally sap the lifeblood from the culture. A new kind of gothic results that posits a monster at its center, a figure of foreignness who is made up of different identities and characterized by an excess of meaning or signification. This new type of gothic itself has a somewhat vampiric relation to the realist writing of the day and functions much like the hidden secret of late Victorian fiction. One might argue that Victorian writing was in essence gothic and that by the 1890s these traits simply emerged to destabilize realism once and for all. Certainly, as Halberstam argues, Wilde's novel is a sort of literary drag performance that is excessive, having too much meaning (60).[10] It is gothic in its very ability to express what was everywhere repressed in more realist writing but still breaks out in gothic moments.

The question of homosexuality that arises out of the cultural anxieties embodied in the gothic can be linked to Wilde's careful development of a public persona. The book registers both as his personal attempt to reconcile his transition from family man to dabbler in the homosexual demimonde and his concomitant desire to resist being defined as what we now call gay but more accurately might call queer. That is, I return to the question with which one often begins: Is Dorian gay? If not, then what is he? And just how is it that over one hundred years after publication, we still have to ask that question? This approach to the novel is informed by the scholarly work that sees Wilde's trials as, among other things, the moment when homosexuality moved from being defined as an activity to an identity and when previous codes of masculinity were shut down as effeminacy became not only synonymous with homosexuality but also with emasculation.

In order to make these points, I assign selected readings from Jonathan Freedman's *Oscar Wilde: A Collection of Critical Essays*. For an advanced undergraduate or graduate version of this course, students read the pieces by Ed Cohen, Rachel Bowlby, Eve Kosofsky Sedgwick, and Wayne Koestenbaum, which provide an overview of the work on Wilde in general and *Dorian Gray* in particular as it relates to queer theory and commodification. Essays by other scholars can be used to supplement those in Freedman's collection, especially for a graduate seminar. Extremely useful for the theme of this course overall is Curtis Marez's "The Other Addict: Reflections on Colonialism and Oscar Wilde's Opium Smoke Screen," which provides a theory for the orientalizing traits in the novel— namely, that Dorian is an exploration of Wilde's own plight as a racialized Irishman. Caricatured in both Britain and America as "Black, Native American, and Chinese," Wilde was himself seen as "non-Western" and hence associated with "degenerate, feminine traits" (272) autonomous from his sexuality. To further strengthen the idea of Wilde's prescience, we watch Hugh Thomson's 1997 documentary of Wilde, which was presented as part of the BBC's Omnibus series and later rebroadcast on the Bravo cable network. We discuss the strengths and the weaknesses of this portrait of Wilde as

> "the first pop star" . . . crediting Wilde explicitly with being the inventor not only of gay male style and culture in the twentieth century, but of all the attitudes and spectacles of rebellion that came to prominence in the 1960s through masculine rock-star figures, and that reached their apex with the punk bands and the glam rock singers of the 1970s and 1980s.   (Stetz 92)

By approaching the novel from more than one perspective, I reproduce my experience of how students themselves attempt to make sense of the text. That is, they seem to respond to the novel as a challenge in which they readily apply various theoretical methodologies to the plots, characters, and themes. The novel's infinite interpretability, however, resides not only in the gothic's ability to create a matrix in which to reflect sexuality, race, nationalism, and so on but also in the novel's own self-conscious approach to interpretation. *Dorian Gray* is all about interpretation, whether it is the challenge laid down in the infamous preface to see only what you dare to see in the text or in the endless debates on aesthetics and the practice of everyday life that we receive either from Lord Henry or the unnamed narrator. We never know quite what to make of Wilde's desire that his text be infinitely interpretable. As with his masterpiece, *The Importance of Being Earnest*, the novel plays with the instability of meaning, which can be seen most especially in Wilde's use of language. Frequently overloaded and encrusted with detail, connotation, and resonance, the language almost ceases to function as anything other than a sculptural form calling attention to itself in proportion to how much space (or time) it inhabits. Wilde's novel, in other words, lends itself to the method of deconstruction generally and to structuralist or poststructuralist approaches to language in particular.

Nowhere can this attention to language be better seen than in the novel's opening paragraph, with its emphasis on synesthesia, the prose poem, Japan, and stylization. We know we are being asked to read in a different way. I ask a student to read the paragraph aloud and note the ways that Wilde calls attention to the sounds of the words—almost separately from the sense. If we have discussed Pater's prose or Algernon Swinburne's poetry, we are in an even better position to compare and contrast Wilde's attempt to create the static effects of the Orient. The book as a sort of antinovel, something that reads against the grain of Victorian realism, establishes our theme of the mingling of sexuality, orientalism, and antimimeticism. But I also emphasize that Wilde is exploring technique here—asking readers to open themselves up to the possibilities of form. The idea is to teach a way of reading the novel that is appropriate for and in concert with the author's goals.

In order to set up levels of interpretation, I offer my own take on the essential characters and plot strains. I begin with Harry, a dandy figure that most people would associate with Wilde or with previous dandies; Harry is married but divorces later on. Unlike Basil, perhaps, Harry appears to be immoral, though his epigrams contain wisdom. Basil, by contrast, is the true artist, has a homoerotic attachment to Dorian, and puts his actual soul into his portrait. Dorian inadvertently sells his soul for immortal beauty; his momentary vanity in Basil's studio dooms him, though he perhaps finally learns the extreme importance of the soul. He is ultimately responsible for several murders, two suicides, and so on, while the paradox of the novel is that his beauty conceals his horrors beneath a comely surface.

Through lecture and discussion I try to get students to realize that the apparent homosexual triangle is more complicated than one might at first think. The book does not allow for easy answers: the parts can be constantly combined and recombined, like a literary Rubik's Cube. Basil's feelings for Dorian, expressed on canvas, are yet denied by Basil as art; they may simply be the surface of something else, such as erotic attraction. Of course, Basil's feelings are associated with exposure, and it is fear of exposure that causes Dorian to kill him. The two are intimately linked. Harry awakens a new consciousness in Dorian, one connected to a "Hedonism" (99) that includes drugs, blackmail, and ruining the lives of other men. Though Harry is enacting a form of seduction through pedagogy that is obviously homoerotic (à la Plato's Socrates), he slowly disappears from the book, and the homoerotic, dandified seduction through the ear via words that he represents for Dorian is taken over by the mysterious book. We can read Harry's wonderful witticisms but do not know exactly what the book does to Dorian—though we do see some of what it might mean in chapter 11, where Dorian re-creates the obsessions of Joris-Karl Huysmans's Des Esseintes.

Though Wilde's book seems to be all about the closet—to universalize homosexual desire or dissipate it throughout the text—homosexuality does not actually act as the key it seems to be for unlocking either Dorian's secret or the secret of the text. Indeed, it is never clear that Dorian is not heterosexual. At the end, he may even be homophobic in his murder of Basil and blackmailing of Alan Campbell. The novel moves from the romantic toward the naturalistic, and the world of the Vanes slowly takes over the novel as Dorian leaves the epicene world of the wealthy to slum his way into an orientalized world that almost catches him in a net of class revenge. He eludes both worlds, only to die at his own hand in an ending that can only be explained as a supernatural and inevitably moral conclusion to a book that tries to teach a lesson even as it seems to subvert that very message.

I do not allow the moralistic ending of *Dorian Gray* to slide by the students or, again, to be explained as just another strange convention that we have to put up with when reading Victorian writing (Jane Eyre's telepathic message from Rochester notwithstanding). We look in particular at the change in point of view in the novel's last paragraphs, in the sentences that read, "He seized the thing, and stabbed the picture with it," and, "There was a cry heard, and a crash" (159). I ask students to explain what has suddenly changed about the text that we are reading. Though students are probably unaware of it at the time of their first reading, the text undergoes a massive shift in point of view. "He seized the thing," but, "There was a cry heard." Agency—or the active mood—momentarily disappears. Before we are told that Dorian has died, we know that something has happened by the fact that the text is suddenly in search of someone or something to inhabit. Dorian vanishes from the story, and the text registers this implosion. When he is finally identified by his rings in the last sentence of the novel, we already know that his soul has escaped.

This exercise in close reading shows students that Wilde's novel, while Victorian in time frame, continues to be experimental, even protopostmodern, to the very end. We discuss just how this ending changes everything that has come before it—most especially our sense that the novel has at its core any stable sense of realist narrative or even reality. We also discuss other work that the ending might be doing, such as functioning as a critique of the dandy as, perhaps, an attempt by Wilde to comment on an earlier notion of his own performative self that he has now rejected. For some students, the ending is out of sync with the rest of the novel and seems a sort of way out for Wilde. That is, the novel can be witty and subversive all it wants as long as the protagonist comes to some sort of just end. Problems that may result from a gay reading of the novel—that yet another gay character ends up dead—are something we also have to discuss.

Despite the importance of the novel's ending, the various strains uniting the course come together in an earlier scene: Dorian's nightmarish trip to the wharves of London, where the text comes closest to naming or hinting at his sins. We begin the section with Wilde's description of opium mentioned just before Dorian's departure: "It was a small Chinese box of black and gold-dust lacquer. . . . Inside was a green paste, waxy in lustre, the odour curiously heavy and persistent" (133). As we move closer to the docks of east London, Wilde makes it clear that we are entering an area of the unknown, a space marked out by the orientalizing effect of drug use. Once Dorian arrives, he engages in shadowy conversations hinting at either drugs or sex. Just as Jane Eyre hides her name from the Rivers family and Heathcliff lacks a surname, Dorian succeeds in withholding his identity from the denizens of the docks much as he withheld it from the Vane family. It is only at the end of the chapter that he is identified by the linking of Sibyl's pet name for him, "Prince Charming," to his actual name (137). The text is concerned with how to name itself, or its sin, and the naming is resisted as long as possible. Though the Duchess of Monmouth notes a few pages later, "I am quite satisfied with my own name, and I am sure Mr. Gray would be satisfied with his" (140), Dorian quips, "To define is to limit" (141).

Despite Wilde's rage against aspects of Victorian society—its sense of moral superiority and trumpeting of mimeticism—his novel can be seen as truly Victorian, connected to its century as much as anything by Dickens or Eliot. Ultimately we need to reexamine the idea of Wilde as a Victorian. Students like to see him as a foreshadowing of what was to come, but I think it is sometimes the instructor's job to reposition Wilde in reference to other forms of Victorian cultural production. One can certainly see him as the center of the late Victorian period, but I am interested in reexamining the beginning and end of his career, periods of time when he was in transformation. At the beginning, he was absorbing influences; at the end, he was, arguably, trying to decide what sort of legacy he represented—or could represent—after the trials reduced his ability to signify in as many registers as before. Whether *Dorian Gray* is a cul-de-sac of Wilde's own making—an evolutionary branch that failed—or an attempt at a transformative artistic statement about the ugliness of reality, it remains his most complex and sustained work of prose fiction and a provocative text for teaching the end of a major historic period.

NOTES

I would like to thank Phil Smith for his help in putting this essay together and for pushing it more toward the teacherly realm. I have tried throughout to locate and call attention to scholars who have influenced what I say in the classroom, but, like other instructors, I tend to put everything into my lectures that I can—including, but not only, extensive reading, my own notes as a student, posted messages to discussion boards, and so on. In other words, I am probably not always able to give credit where it is due, as teaching seems to me in many ways a much more cooperative enterprise than publishing is, and one of the greatest compliments is to have one's ideas used in the classroom.

[1] Of particular importance in Meyer are chapters 2 and 3, where she discusses *Jane Eyre* and *Wuthering Heights*, respectively.

[2] I frequently focus on women writers in an effort to show that finding a female authorial voice is central to understanding how the Victorian novel became the dominant literary genre for the century and mutated into something different from the realist novel altogether—the novels of the decadent male writers of the late Victorian era.

[3] The seemingly radical interpretation that the novel receives in the movie *Clueless* (1995) is better at making viewers aware of Austen's subtle use of language, character development, and plot than most period versions of Austen's novels.

[4] Bertha's imprisonment is symbolic not just of Rochester's guilty conscience but also of the attempt to locate the racial other in a different body, a different geography. Bertha is Jane's opposite and as such is the important double—the shadow—of everything that Jane must deal with in overcoming obstacles to married life: a potentially violent man, cultural difference, an acknowledgment of passion and sexuality. As Elsie Michie suggests, Rochester—if not other characters, too—is racialized in the novel. Bertha cannot ultimately be contained and may well be, like the people from warm climates that England has subdued, not just a burden or a responsibility but also a part of the culture now as well.

[5] For more on Heathcliff and his possible racial permutations, see Eagleton, *Heathcliff*.

[6] For more on the inner/outer, private/public, self/other dichotomies in Eliot and her characters, see Kucich 114–200.

[7] Note not only that Heathcliff is called a vampire (among other things supernatural) but also that vampires are mentioned in *Dorian Gray* and that Dorian kills Basil with

a knife to the throat (117), echoing the attack by Bertha Mason, with her teeth, on Mr. Mason in *Jane Eyre* (214).

[8] For instructors wishing to explore the relation between Dracula as a character in the novel and Dracula as a character in film and other popular media, there now exist three excellent essays on the vampire figure and the rise of cinema by Kittler; Stewart; and Thomas. Francis Ford Coppola's film version of the novel, misleadingly entitled *Bram Stoker's* Dracula (1992), takes a lot of liberties by inventing a romantic subplot that puts Dracula into a sympathetic light. But it is still brilliant at interpreting the novel and updating some of its metaphors, such as the fear of blood as deadly contagion.

[9] For more on the concept of degeneracy, one can assign a portion of Nordau's *Degeneration* for students to read. The chapter entitled "Decadents and Aesthetes" from the section "Ego-mania" is the obvious place to start, though this reading might be more suitable for graduate students, given its numerous references to the literature and culture of the time.

[10] Halberstam provides a nuanced description of the late gothic monster in her discussion of *The Strange Case of Dr. Jekyll and Mr. Hyde* and *The Picture of Dorian Gray* (53–85).

Teaching *The Picture of Dorian Gray* as a "Gay" Text

Nikolai Endres

In Gay and Lesbian Literature, an upper-level elective for English majors cross-listed with Women's Studies, I assign *The Picture of Dorian Gray* and some of Oscar Wilde's other queer works, together with primary literature from ancient Greece to modernity and secondary works on critical theory. The course is best taught as a discussion class, with occasional short lectures and many student presentations, group work, creative papers, reserve reading, and other collaborative projects, all of which are particularly useful for Wilde, the great literary absorber and plagiarist of himself. Also, since Basil Hallward, at the very outset of *Dorian Gray*, voices concern, even guilt ("Your rank and wealth, Harry; my brains, such as they are—my art, whatever it may be worth; Dorian Gray's good looks—we shall all suffer for what the gods have given us, suffer terribly" [19]), we address homophobia, homosexual scandals, Wilde's trials, Victorian hypocrisy, and medicolegal research.

Students often react to *Dorian Gray* with perplexity. Where does Wilde say that Dorian Gray is gay? Homosexuality is officially withheld: *"The Picture of Dorian Gray invokes the queer image, to some readers at least, despite at no point representing it"* (Sinfield, *Wilde Century* 103). True, but a specific examination of Wilde's life (see Sato and Lambourne; McKenna), of other works that deal with love and sex, and of literary models reveals an abundance of clues. Having a PhD in comparative literature, I am versed in comparative approaches; as a classicist I am able to trace Wilde's allusions to the past; as a student of gay and lesbian studies I am familiar with the several frameworks in this emerging field. My pedagogical approach is a close and detailed reading, occasionally speculative rather than definitive. My students thus enrich their understanding of Wilde's erotic code by both facilitating and appreciating the educational strategies that the class as a whole provides.

A helpful prereading activity is to screen Wilde's stirring defense in court (for instance, as performed in the movie *Wilde* with Stephen Fry):

> "The Love that dare not speak its name" in this century is such a great affection of an elder for a younger man as there was between David and Jonathan, such as Plato made the very basis of his philosophy, and such as you find in the sonnets of Michelangelo and Shakespeare. It is that deep, spiritual affection that is as pure as it is perfect.
>
> (qtd. in Hyde, *Trials* 236; see *Dorian Gray* [92])

I then ask my students a simple question: If you wanted to convey homoerotic activity but were prohibited from speaking it out, how would you do it? Most of their (usually resourceful) answers map out our procedure. Since Dorian engages in so many crimes and since they are all mentioned, what does it mean that one crime remains unspoken? Does not its very omission draw attention to it? Or, would not the explicit naming of sex have been aesthetically vulgar? In *Dorian Gray*, Wilde loves to create an aura of mystery: years ago, for example, Basil suddenly disappeared and caused "such public excitement, and gave rise to so many strange conjectures" (18; see 98). It is almost uncanny how Wilde is foreshadowing his own life.

Despite Wilde's stipulation concerning the impersonality of art, we may not neglect certain biographical details. On a handout, I collect miscellaneous phrases. Wilde famously revealed to André Gide, "I have put my genius into my life; I only put my talent into my work" (Gide, *Si le grain* 348). In *De Profundis*, he contends, "I was a man who stood in symbolic relations to the art and culture of my age" (1017). Is he telling us to be on the lookout for symbol and allegory? Another testimony also invites us to relate Wilde to Dorian: "Basil Hallward is what I think I am: Lord Henry what the world thinks me: Dorian what I would like to be—in other ages, perhaps" (*Letters* 352). Thus Dorian is "perhaps" Wilde, the "posing somdomite [*sic*]"—the unspellable love? Why is Wilde evoking "other ages"? Last, students are intrigued by Karl Beckson's observation that Wilde uses the adjectives "wild" and "wilder" and the adverb "wildly" thirty-four times in *Dorian Gray* ("Wilde's Autobiographical Signature"). We look forward to Wild(e) times to come.

Next, we tackle the question of cultural constructs and fluid gender roles. At the end of the nineteenth century,

> no longer is sexuality generally judged as male/strong/regrettable against an asexuality that is female/weak/laudable . . . the usual pattern is natural/heterosexual/good versus unnatural/homosexual/despicable.
> (C. Nelson 545–46)

Drawing on Michel Foucault (43), I explain that homosexuality as a gay lifestyle is not necessarily applicable to the Victorian age, although there are many similarities. Eve Sedgwick suggests that the Victorian frame of mind staunchly adhered to an image of the homosexual, which comprises "effeminacy, transvestitism, promiscuity, prostitution, continental European culture, and the arts" (*Between Men* 173; see Sinfield, *Wilde Century* 12). We put her theoretical groundwork to the test, seeking examples for each quality, in order to enhance our grasp of Dorian's sexual activity and preference.

For effeminacy—and one might invoke here Karl Heinrich Ulrichs's famous self-description as *anima muliebris virili corpore inclusa* (esp. 364; "a woman's soul trapped in a man's body")—we note sundry analogies. In physical appearance Dorian takes after his mother, Lord Henry exhorts him to avoid the sun, Dorian easily and quickly breaks into tears, he faints like a Victorian woman in distress, the color of his lips is scarlet, and he dyes his hair gold. He displays exotic flowers, sweet fragrances, precious jewels, all feminine objects in a commodity culture. We also discuss the fact that there are far more indoor settings, the exclusive sphere of the Victorian "angel in the house," than outdoor. (Of course, indoors, or the fear of the public, is also the setting of the closet. After Dorian has his painting carried upstairs, he locks the door to the attic, closes all the windows, and draws the curtains.) Wilde, too, was (controversially) seen by some of his contemporaries as effeminate.[1] Dorian further discovers the charm of drag (102). We come up with valuable insights on the (gay) ramifications of his effeminacy: like a woman (in terms of ideology), he is beautified, closeted, objectified, gazed at, kept immaculate, protected from the sun, and dolled up.

Then, in a report on previously assigned articles (e.g., Endres; Martin, "Parody"; Losey), two or three students analyze Walter Pater's new hedonism, its indebtedness to Epicureanism, and Dorian's gross sexualization of it. Henry proposes:

> [I]f one man were to live out his life fully and completely, were to give form to every feeling, expression to every thought, reality to every dream . . . the world would gain such a fresh impulse of joy that we would forget all the maladies of mediaevalism, and return to the Hellenic ideal.   (28)

But it is Dorian's tragic flaw not to realize that Henry is blatantly contradicting himself, for how can Dorian lead a life "fully and completely" if his self-development is inhibited by an overpowering master, who, Pygmalion-like, has decided to fashion him? (A smart student termed it "verbal S/M.") Dorian's attempt at Hellenism and its spontaneity of consciousness logically fails, and he eventually falls back to strict Hebraism: "Yet it was his duty to confess, to suffer public shame, and make public atonement. There was a God who called upon men to tell their sins to earth as well as to heaven" (158). By casting his desire in the form of language, Henry circumvents possible accusations of homosexual seduction, whereas Dorian finds satisfaction only in real excess. Basil presents ample evidence (of course, he cannot speak out the unspeakable) that Dorian directs his licentiousness toward men:

> Why is your friendship so fatal to young men? There was that wretched boy in the Guards who committed suicide. You were his great friend. There was Sir Henry Ashton, who had to leave England, with a tarnished name. You and he were inseparable.   (112)

In the same vein, Pater's conclusion, from which new hedonism's carpe diem derives, was not reprinted in the second edition, for it might mislead "young men" (*Renaissance* 186). What kind of life is Dorian (mis)leading?

I conclude with Pater's famous review, which elicits a heated discussion:

> A true Epicureanism aims at a complete though harmonious development
> of man's entire organism. To lose the moral sense therefore, for instance,
> the sense of sin and righteousness, as Mr. Wilde's heroes are bent on doing
> so speedily, as completely as they can, is to lose, or lower, organisation, to
> become less complex, to pass from a higher to a lower degree of self-
> development.   (qtd. in Beckson, *Oscar Wilde: The Critical Heritage* 84)

Many students may argue that Dorian has to die because he violated the Christian doctrine of the indissoluble coherence of body and soul. But he would have seemed guilty even to a classical and medieval audience: like Prometheus, he is driven by the hubris to create a human being, his other self; like Faust, he signs a diabolical pact. It seems what Dorian really wanted to achieve was a Romantic ideal: a soul and body at ease in nature, in an idyllic *locus amoenus* (see 99). Furthermore, sometimes an advanced student versed in classical philosophy points out Henry's (deliberate) misunderstanding of Epicurus: pleasure (*hedone*) is indeed the goal in life, but as a means for achieving tranquillity of mind; Epicureanism is no swinish sensuality. For Dorian, though, hedonism is a convenient justification for a life of homosexual profligacy: "Eternal youth, infinite passion, pleasures subtle and secret, wild joys and wilder sins" (84); "He had mad hungers that grew more ravenous as he fed them" (98); "brawling with foreign sailors in a low den" (106). Do these elusive yet hard-core terms not camouflage (gay) pornographic scenarios? That is indeed the conclusion the class normally draws.

Next, we look at Dorian's own prostitution. He is, of course, not selling his body for money; rather, he keenly prostitutes himself to drugs and the devil. Even so, one student elaborated that the James Vane scene outside the opium den simulates a pickup and that Dorian is indeed prostituting himself by offering his body to secure power. That is not a bad guess. Wilde picked up prostitutes, but he was wise enough to conceal his "feasting with panthers" (1042 [*De Profundis*]). Liberal-minded students often voice quibbles here. Is Dorian the person to reproach? Is it not first of all a society that refuses to acknowledge domestic partnerships or civil unions? The number of sexual acts with various partners rapidly decreases in a marriage. Ideally, there is no extramarital sex. In the absence of legal protection, what else remains for Dorian than frequenting brothels?

From mercenary sex we move to Dorian's travels and Wilde's Francophilia: "to read Greek and speak French are two of the greatest pleasures in the cultivation of Life" (*Letters* 814). Several reviews of *Dorian Gray* (in the Norton Critical Edition) dismissed the novel as dangerously French. Why? The Continent had an irresistible attraction for homosexuals, because the *Code Napoléon* had decriminalized sex between consenting adults. When Basil is assassinated by Dorian, he is on his way to Paris; Dorian and Henry travel to Trouville (Hole Town? True Town?) in Normandy and to a city in a French colony, Algiers (where they own a "walled-in house" [106]), the mecca of homosexual artists. Dorian spent an autumn in Venice, another El Dorado, where a "wonderful love . . . stirred him to mad, delightful follies" (121). When he goes to Nottinghamshire, entertaining "fashionable young men" and astounding with his "wanton luxury" (106), he is visiting the home of the celebrated Lord Byron. After successfully pursuing many components of Sedgwick's list, I introduce another of her tenets.

One ideological approach to homosexual discourse is that of "a narrative that makes explicit, in idealizing and apparently contemporaneous terms, the outdated or obsolescent values of an earlier system, in the service of a newer system that in practice undermines the basis of those values" (Sedgwick, *Between Men* 70). In their discussion of *Endzeitstimmung*, for example, " '*Fin de siècle*,' murmured Lord Henry. '*Fin du globe*,' answered his hostess. 'I wish it were *fin du globe*,' said Dorian with a sigh" (130), Dorian and Henry are deliberating and questioning values that are on the verge of breakdown (*fin de siècle* as *fin de sexe*?). I photocopy seminal secondary materials that establish these values and that show how they were being interrogated in the 1890s.[2] By promoting a new form of friendship, both Henry and Basil are shifting the Victorian emphasis on male intimacy and bonding from the social and political to the (homo)sexual. This is how we best understand Henry's bold exclamation, "I give the truths of to-morrow" (140), and Cyril's conviction, "Literature always anticipates life" in "The Decay of Lying" (1083–84), and Lord Illingworth's creed in *A Woman of No Importance*, "The future belongs to the dandy" (493). With the aid of photographs and readings, I direct my students to the tenuous figure of the dandy. The dandy dedicates his leisure time to the cultivation of his mind and body; he neither produces (Victorian man) nor reproduces (Victorian woman); he makes aesthetics his religion, and he straddles the past and the present with his nostalgia for aristocratic values and contempt for egalitarian democracy.[3] Wilde maintains, "Dandyism is the assertion of the absolute modernity of Beauty" (1242 ["Maxims"]). What is so modern and prophetic about the dandy? Does it include (homo)sexual liberation and emancipation?

Next, Roman Catholicism offers a wealth of information. At first, students are puzzled because they equate the Church with biblical injunctions against Sodom and Gomorrah, but when I throw out questions such as "Does the pope wear a dress?" or "Did Jesus marry?" or "Is mass campy?" or "Why are angels naked?," their imaginations flare (see also Sedgwick, *Epistemology* 140). Dorian shows a great interest in the statue of Saint Sebastian (105), golden monstrances, ecclesiastical vestments, candles, and transubstantiation—significant for its duplicity of the wafer as both bread and Christ's body, which mirrors his own double life. In his imaginative ritual, he kneels—but not just to pray. He watches the priest in his "stiff" vestment, who "slowly" moves aside a "veil." What is the priest really showing (baring) to Dorian? This scene of oral temptation is homoerotically heightened by "boys" in "lace and scarlet," tossing fuming censers in the air, making invisible a sexual spectacle that Dorian and the priest are performing on the steps of cold marble (100–01). I also show a copy of Guido Reni's *San Sebastian* (in Kaye 285), one of Wilde's favorite paintings. In an age of stigmatization and ostracism, Sebastian was a "gay saint." During the reign of Diocletian, he came to the rescue of Christian soldiers (for which the emperor had him executed in 287), thereby confessing his Christianity; this coming-out story probably inspired Shakespeare in *Twelfth Night* and Wilde in "The Grave of Keats." Tantalizingly, we find, Sebastian is usually depicted as shot full of arrows, but his portraits show a figure who seems to be experiencing "unalloyed bliss, despite, or because of, all the 'arrows' sticking into him" (Knox, *Oscar Wilde: A Long and Lovely Suicide* 80).

We turn to Dorian's romantic involvement with a woman, indeed an obstacle to our gay reading. We first scrutinize Sibyl's femininity. Strangely, almost all women fall for Dorian, so there would have been ample choice—had he been interested. With the help of Wilde's poems (e.g., "The Sphinx" or "The Burden of Itys") or his short story "The Fisherman and His Soul," we suggest that the blurring of gender lines is frequent in Wilde. Dorian rarely sees Sibyl as a woman but quite often as a boy. As Stephen Greenblatt establishes, in Shakespearean theater it is neither sex nor names that yield gender markers but clothing, a finding comparable to Wilde's "The Truth of Masks." Several students investigate the roles Sibyl plays (never forgetting that all Shakespearean women were played by men). The first night Sibyl acted Juliet, the second night Imogen, the third night Rosalind as a boy, in "man's apparel" pretending to be Ganymede in *As You Like It* (2.4)—"as Dorian likes it," a student once exclaimed in class (to great approval). It is only after Sibyl's performance as a cross-dressed Rosalind that Dorian introduces himself to her, not after she plays a woman, Juliet or Imogen. Also, in Shakespeare's comedy, Rosalind *en travestie* asks Orlando to accept her as the person she is, as a man, persuading Orlando to love "him" as a man (3.2). Dorian's Miss-appropriation of Sibyl indeed complicates and stimulates my students' impression, and sometimes we even speculate: is Dorian subversively asking a boy to marry him?

Another question arises: Is Dorian honest in his proposal? He tells Henry, "I did not treat it as a business transaction" (65). If we consider the notion of marriage as a financial affair (as, for example, the social constraints in Jane Austen's novels or Wilde's comedies dictate), Dorian never really wanted to marry her, because marriage during the Victorian period *was* a business venture. Sibyl's mother is referring to such a deal: "Of course, if this gentleman is wealthy, there is no reason why she should not contract an alliance with him" (57). Basil objects to Dorian's engagement in familiar terms: "But think of Dorian's birth, and position, and wealth. It would be absurd for him to marry so much beneath him" (63). Lord Henry thinks of Sibyl as Dorian's mistress (50), and for him, "the one charm of marriage is that it makes a life of deception absolutely necessary for both parties" (20). He does not seem to be affected when his wife, who bears the same name as the queen, runs off with someone else (152). Sibyl simply does not signify for Dorian, as her family name underscores.

Another vivid discussion ensues over the yellow book. Several candidates for the book have been proposed, but for our purposes, J. K. Huysmans's *À Rebours* (*Against Nature*) stands out, because it complements the Sibyl Vane episode. One night Huysmans's protagonist, Des Esseintes, goes to a circus, where he watches the performance of a female acrobat: the conspicuously named Miss Urania (a tribute to Pausanias's Aphrodite in Plato's *Symposium*), who has muscles of steel and arms of iron. Initially he sees her as a woman and feels no desire to approach her. But then he observes a heightening masculinization. Later he finds out that his man still has distinctively feminine features and is repelled (ch. 9). For both Dorian and Des Esseintes, Sibyl and Miss Urania express a fearful femininity. Both Des Esseintes and Dorian indulge in vaguely homosexual activities and unconventional settings. Dorian removes his affair with Sibyl to an Arcadian idyll: "I forgot that I was in London, and in the nineteenth century. I was away with my love in a forest that no man had ever seen" (65). Des Esseintes escapes to the Renaissance in order "to realise in the nineteenth century all the passions and modes of thought that belonged to every century except his own" (96). To advance class discussion, I remind students that Wilde himself evoked "other ages." The influence of *À Rebours* is monumental: "Dorian Gray had been poisoned by a book" (109). Is homosexuality a poison or contagious (like AIDS nowadays)? Paradoxically, how does such a profound concordance undercut the individual that *Dorian Gray* purports to celebrate?

Other allusions in *Dorian Gray* are to Petronius's *Satyricon*, whose protagonists are all bisexual, and to Edward II's love for Piers Gaveston as related by Christopher Marlowe. Furthermore, Dorian reads about Roman emperors: Tiberius, Caligula, Domitian, Nero and his catamite Sporus, Elagabalus (all in ch. 11), whose infamous (homo)sexual escapades Suetonius's *Lives of the Caesars* graphically relates and whom Wilde often used as code names in his letters, such as his reckless "Neronian hours, rich, profligate, cynical, materialistic" (*Letters* 577; see 604–05). When Basil compares Dorian to Antinous, he has exactly the emperor Hadrian's love for his beautiful boy in mind (23; see *Letters* 705). At this point, I send my students to the library and Internet to research more obscure but nonetheless pregnant figures: Adonis, Silenus, Hermes, Cupid-Eros, Ganymede, Hylas, Marsyas, satyrs, Montaigne, Michelangelo, and Winckelmann. . . . With all these venerated allusions, we bear out one critic's claim:

> Any historical, literary, or mythical association with the classical world or with the contexts of classical literature became a signifier for homoerotic content, which was conflated with highly eroticized homoerotic plots and special verbal coding.   (Fone 90)

Speaking of classical antiquity, according to sexology in the 1890s the Dorian tribe was credited with "inventing" or introducing the practice of pederasty in classical Greece (see Dellamora, *Apocalyptic Overtures* 43–64), and that Dorian has no father is relevant, too, for his situation is akin to Greek *paiderastia*: the older man acts as a surrogate father for the boy. In a telling typographic error (Freudian slip?), the *Star* reports Wilde as having testified in court that "[e]very man would see his own son in Dorian Gray," while in reality Wilde said "sin" (in E. Cohen 163; see Wilde, *Letters* 266). Crucially, Henry has no son, and Basil Hall*ward* thinks of himself as Dorian's guardian. Naturally, then, Dorian, in his "candour" and "purity" (27), is susceptible to the influences of a more experienced man, hence the novel's classification as a (negative) bildungsroman. In addition, Basil's love for Dorian is highly idealistic: "You became to me the *visible incarnation* of that *unseen ideal* whose *memory* haunts us *artists* like an exquisite dream" (89; my emphasis; see *Letters* 363, 397). The expressions in italics reflect pure Platonism: the artist's attempt to represent an ideal form of which the soul initially had knowledge but that it lost in its descent to earth.

Platonism of course evokes homoeroticism, which Wilde extolled in "The Portrait of Mr. W. H.":

> In 1492 appeared Marsilio Ficino's translation of the "Symposium" of Plato, and his wonderful dialogue, of all the Platonic dialogues perhaps the most perfect, as it is the most poetical, began to exercise such a strange influence over men, and to colour their words and thoughts, and manner of living . . . subtle suggestions of sex in soul, in the curious analogies it draws between intellectual enthusiasm and the physical passion of love, in its dream of the incarnation of the Idea in a beautiful and living form, and of a real spiritual conception with travail and a bringing to birth.   (324; see also Ellmann, *Oscar Wilde* 298)

We explore the sexual references (encoded in platonic love) to "wonderful," "enthusiasm," "strange," "influence," "sex in soul," "in*carn*ation," "conception," or "travail." What is Wilde trying to say here, especially to an audience educated in the classics?

To bring my students back to the present, I look at Basil's first meeting with Dorian. The excerpt inevitably hits close to home for teenagers:

> I suddenly became conscious that some one was looking at me. I turned half-way round, and saw Dorian Gray for the first time. When our eyes met, I felt that I was growing pale. A curious sensation of terror came over me. I knew that I had come face to face with some one whose mere personality was so fascinating that, if I allowed it to do so, it would absorb my whole nature, my whole soul, my very art itself. . . . I was on the verge of a terrible crisis. . . .   (21)

Is this love? The love of Basil's life? Does it ring true? Is he levitating? What is love at first sight like? How can pen put a taboo to paper? Is it still platonic? Last but not least, an oral report on Basil's love for Dorian in the more explicit serialized version (in the Norton Critical Edition [*Picture*]) plus Wilde's date changes (see Ellmann, *Oscar Wilde* 277) help clarify Basil's profound infatuation and its homoerotic tinge.

To deepen our understanding of Wilde's code, we investigate fauna and flora as well. Flowers were Wilde's life: "for me . . . flowers are part of desire" (1057 [*De Profundis*]; see *Letters* 576). In our initial encounter, Dorian buries "his face in the great cool lilac-blossoms, feverishly drinking in their perfume as if it had been wine" (30); our last image is his "withered" body (159). He drops a spray of lilac and watches a bee "creeping into the stained trumpet of a Tyrian convolvulus." Just as the bee stings the flower, so Henry penetrates Dorian, and both are stained in the wake of their orgasms. "The flower seemed to quiver," just as Dorian was "stirred by some new emotion." With postorgasmic bliss, the flower "swayed gently to and fro" (31–32). This famous bee incident—which compares interestingly with the bee in *The Importance of Being Earnest* (377) and of course with Marcel Proust's bumblebee in *Sodom and Gomorrah* (3–33)—offers my students an abundance of ideas: penetration, insemination, honey-flattery, camouflage, and so on. Flowers also figure prominently in gay circles. Why? Is it a flower's somewhat phallic image, or the petals' shedding quality, or the flower's rainbow colors, or the leaves' poison, or the blossom's androgynous reproduction, or its eternal youth and beauty, or the proverbial pansy? Since it is usually women who receive flowers, is Dorian effeminized?

Once again, we consider Wilde's keen interest in the classics. In Greek lyric poetry, *anthos* ("flower") is often a homoerotic symbol. In this context, I go back to Dorian's hymn to Sibyl (a Greek name)—"with a little flower-like face, a small Greek head with plaited coils of dark-brown hair, eyes that were violet wells of passion, lips that were like the petals of a rose" (49)—which could have been lifted out of the *Greek Anthology*, a collection of verse addressed to boys. In mythology, Apollo loved Hyacinth but accidentally killed him and transformed him into a flower; Narcissus, a flower of epicene gender in Greek, loved himself. Hyacinths and narcissi are all over Dorian Gray's flower bed. In an incriminating letter to Bosie (the Prince Fleur-de-Lys), Wilde wrote, "I know Hyacinthus, whom Apollo loved so madly, was you in Greek days" (*Letters* 326; see 746, 774; see also 1245 ["Phrases"]). In another letter, Wilde envisions "an unknown land full of strange flowers and subtle perfumes, a land of which it is joy of all joys to dream, a land where all things are perfect and poisonous" (*Letters* 185). Walt Whitman in *Leaves of Grass* dreams of the country in which the calamus blossoms (96–116). The green carnation (see Robert Hichens's novel) was a symbol of recognition among Parisian homosexuals. *Punch* chose sunflowers and lilies to hint at Wilde's decadent aestheticism: for example, in one of the magazine's fancy portraits (no. 37), "O. W." muses, "O, I feel just as happy as a bright Sunflower!" (Schmidgall 59). Dorian, in his "rose-red youth" and "rose-white boyhood" (29), may suggest two (female) fairy-tale characters, Snow White and Rose Red.

Although flowers are beautiful, they are quite useless; probably only a botanist knows their biological function. Is Dorian's (homo)sexuality valueless? According to Basil (note the name), Dorian is so shallow that after Basil gave away his "whole soul" to him, Dorian treated it "as if it were a flower to put in his coat, a bit of decoration to charm his vanity" (24). Are flowers metaphors for forbidden, homosexual desire? Henry ambivalently compares Dorian's nature to a flower that "had borne blossoms of scarlet flame" (52), and his notorious yellow book contains "metaphors as monstrous as orchids" (96). Dorian intends to sow poppies after Sibyl's death (81), draws flowers after Basil's murder (120), and orders his servant to procure orchids ("testicles" in Greek) after the interview with Alan Campbell (126). Reading between the lines and leaves, my students eventually associate flowers in *Dorian Gray* with homosexuality. An insider outrageously suggests:

> Homosexuality, like an interest in flowers, is a sign of effeminacy. Homosexuals, like flowers, have no reason to exist; they delight only themselves. Homosexuals are sterile. . . . They blossom in the form of works of art.
> (Bartlett 46)

Wilde himself mused, "A work of art is useless as a flower is useless. A flower blossoms for its own joy" (*Letters* 292). Everything seems temporary, hectic, evanescent.

We conclude with the ending, which is the moral of *Dorian Gray*. Wilde writes:

> All excess, as well as all renunciation, brings its own punishment. The painter, Basil Hallward, worshipping physical beauty far too much, as most painters do, dies by the hand of one in whose soul he has created a monstrous and absurd vanity. Dorian Gray, having led a life of mere sensation and pleasure, tries to kill conscience, and at that moment kills himself. Lord Henry Wotton seeks to be merely the spectator of life. He finds that those who reject the battle are more deeply wounded than those who take part in it.
> (*Letters* 259)

In the end, vice is punished, but is virtue really rewarded? Up until the final pages, Dorian prospers, since, as Wilde seems to be saying, beauty and glamour get one everywhere: "The soul is a terrible reality. It can be bought, and sold, and bartered away" (154). After the deaths of Basil, Alan Campbell, and James Vane, it is only Dorian's conscience that effects his ruin. The picture and Dorian have totally merged; the one must perish with the other. Dorian's homosexual double life prevails until the very end. My students differ widely on the ending. Is there a need for closure (of the closet)? Does coming out mean death? Could it be that with Dorian's demise, Wilde may have wished to exorcise this aspect of his being—namely, the tragedy (as imposed by society) of homosexuality? In Victorian literature, it seems, more women than men commit suicide, but Sedgwick sees the novel's climax as a defeminization of suicide that destroys the "feminocentric Victorian version" of typical sentimentality (*Epistemology* 150). Some of my students then stand Sedgwick on her head, for when stabbing himself, Dorian really penetrates himself.

The depiction of homosexuality is unsympathetic. Although Basil's homo-eroticism creates his finest art and Henry's love for Dorian Henry's most powerful philosophy, Dorian's friendships are one-sided. Dorian aestheticizes Sibyl, which is his approximation of the painting—that is, of himself. When someone falls out of love, he can always direct his desire at someone else; but being in love with oneself inaugurates the fall into self-hatred in the form of suicide. At the end, Dorian painfully grasps his narcissistic trap: "I wish I could love. . . . But I seem to have lost the passion, and forgotten the desire. I am too much concentrated on myself. My own personality has become a burden to me. I want to escape" (147). *Dorian Gray* ends on a high note of modernism: dysfunctionality, failure, sycophancy, frustration.

NOTES

[1] He was considered effeminate by Julian Hawthorne, Edmond de Goncourt, Arthur Symons, Toulouse Lautrec, Henry Labouchère, W. S. Gilbert and Arthur Sullivan in *Patience*, and the editors of *Punch*. See Ellmann, *Oscar Wilde*; Hamilton; Paglia.

[2] For example, Beckson, *London*; Bredbeck; Bristow, "Wilde" and *Effeminate England*; E. Cohen; W. Cohen, *Sex Scandal*; Craft; Danson, *Wilde's* Intentions; Dellamora, *Masculine Desire*; Dollimore; Dowling; Felski; Foldy; Kopelson, *Love's Litany*; Showalter, *Sexual Anarchy*; Sinfield, *Wilde Century*; Vicinus.

[3] See Charles Baudelaire's "Le peintre de la vie moderne" and his fascinating prototypes of *le dandy*: Caesar, Catiline, Alcibiades, Byron (1177–80). For secondary sources, see Adams; Gagnier, *Idylls*; Nunokawa, "Importance"; Moers.

APPENDIX:
RESERVED READING

One approach is to consider Wilde's classical background. We explore literary manifestations of homoerotic desire in ancient Greece and Rome (and in biblical times) and investigate how Wilde often uses these instances as an erotic code. We further look at the dissemination of platonic love or "Greek love" in the British university system:

> Bible, 1 and 2 Samuel (David and Jonathan)
> Homer, *Iliad* 9, 16, 18, 19, 23 (Achilles and Patroclus)
> Plato, *Symposium* and *Phaedrus*
> Plutarch, *Dialogue on Love*
> Pseudo-Lucian, *Affairs of the Heart*
> Vergil, *Aeneid* 5 and 9 (Nisus and Euryalus)
> Petronius, *Satyricon*
> Juvenal, satires 2 and 9
> Suetonius, *The Twelve Caesars*
> Greek and Roman homoerotic poetry

Marsilio Ficino's commentary and Benjamin Jowett's translation of the *Symposium*
Michelangelo, *Poems*
Kenneth Dover, *Greek Homosexuality*
Craig Williams, *Roman Homosexuality*

Many of these primary materials have become available in T. K. Hubbard's *Homosexuality in Greece and Rome.*

Some of the English classics Wilde read at Oxford and other contemporary works also feature prominently in *Dorian Gray*:

William Shakespeare, *As You Like It* and the sonnets
Christopher Marlowe, *Edward II*
John Keats, "camelion poet"
Lord Tennyson, *In Memoriam*
Walter Pater, conclusion to *Studies in the Renaissance* and *Marius the Epicurean*
J. A. Symonds, "A Problem in Greek Ethics" and *Poems*
Medical, social, and political writings by Edward Carpenter and Havelock Ellis
W. S. Gilbert and Arthur Sullivan, *Patience*

Contemporaneous homoerotic poetry (Walt Whitman included) can be found in Brian Reade's *Sexual Heretics*; other sources can be found in Chris White's *Nineteenth-Century Writings on Homosexuality.*

The French influence on Wilde is pervasive:

Marquis de Sade
Théophile Gautier, *Émaux et camées* and *Mademoiselle de Maupin*
Charles Baudelaire on the dandy
J. K. Huysmans, *À Rebours*
decadent literature

Finally, among comparatively modern gay novels are:

E. M. Forster, *Maurice*
André Gide, *Corydon*, *If It Die*, and *The Immoralist*
Marcel Proust, *Sodom and Gomorrah*
Thomas Mann, *Death in Venice*
Mary Renault, *The Charioteer* and *The Persian Boy*
Christopher Isherwood, *The Berlin Stories* and *Christopher and His Kind*
Gore Vidal, *The City and the Pillar*
James Baldwin, *Giovanni's Room* and *Another Country*

Evelyn Waugh, *Brideshead Revisited*
Marguerite Yourcenar, *Memoirs of Hadrian*
Andrew Holleran, *Dancer from the Dance* and *Nights in Aruba*
Yukio Mishima, *Forbidden Colors*
Patricia Nell Warren, *The Front Runner*, *Harlan's Race*, and *Billy's Boy*

Dorian Gray in the Twentieth Century: The Politics and Pedagogy of Filming Oscar Wilde's Novel

Jonathan Alexander

In *The Celluloid Closet: Homosexuality in the Movies*, Vito Russo suggests that the interest in filming Wilde's *Picture of Dorian Gray* is nearly as old as the film industry itself. The novel has inspired many different artists to adapt the story to various media, to various ends. *Oscar Wilde on Stage and Screen* (1999), by Robert Tanitch, describes a multitude of performances—in film, television, theater, musical theater, and opera—of Wilde's works. Film versions range from an early Danish silent of 1910 to the 1983 American television film *The Sins of Dorian Gray*, which presents Dorian as a woman.

Interpretations of the novel invariably highlight its examination of aesthetics and its connection to an ethics of self-development. For instance, Michael Patrick Gillespie argues strenuously that the novel promotes an aesthetic engagement with ethics, known as the new hedonism, that Lord Henry asserts early in the novel. In Gillespie's words, the new hedonism "makes a direct claim for the shaping effect of art upon one's character, and it asserts the primacy of a doctrine of pleasure that absolves individuals from the ordinary responsibilities for their actions" ("Ethics" 145). At the same time, Gillespie recognizes that "any number of readers" have offered, "in a definitive fashion, very different interpretations based upon a variety of ethical positions ranging from harsh condemnations to unqualified reproach of Dorian's behavior" (152–53).

It is interesting that most of the filmed interpretations are preoccupied with the novel's perceived sexual content. But this preoccupation should not surprise, given both the reception of the novel since its publication and Wilde's subsequent trials and the increased connection throughout the twentieth century between sexuality and identity. Shelton Waldrep argues that "[p]lays and films may not be able to treat Wilde's homosexuality with less delicate gloves than in the past, but it is still the mere fact of this activity that the versions can never escape" ("Uses" 50). While some critics debate whether the novel drops hints, as it were, that some of Dorian's vices may include homoerotic encounters, Waldrep is correct in suggesting that Wilde's queerness has influenced our reception not only of Wilde himself but of his works as well. In fact, Alan Sinfield has read Wilde's trials and retroactively the publication of the novel as the grounds on which Western culture established its understanding of the modern homosexual (*Wilde Century* 104).

Preoccupation with the queerness of the novel goes hand in hand with Michel Foucault's assertion that, particularly in the last hundred years, "[i]t is through sex . . . that each individual has to pass in order to have access to his own intelligibility, . . . to the whole of his body, . . . to his identity" (155–56).

Indeed, in the film versions of the novel, the largely ethical and aesthetic considerations of the novel are subsumed into, some might even say eclipsed by, a consideration of the role of the (queerly) sexual in the making, and undoing, of identity. But no representation of sexuality is without its ideological assumptions and implications. Pedagogically, examining these transformations of the novel into film can be quite revealing about shifting ideologies with regard to the depiction of sexuality and its relation to identity and morality. For instance, in being attentive to how sexual vice, in particular homoeroticism, is depicted or actively suppressed in each film, students have the opportunity to think critically about shifts in sexual politics and in the politics of representation from one end of the century to the other.

Reviewing *Dorian Gray* through the lens of various film representations gives students a specific sense of changing attitudes about homoeroticism and its representation; methods of suppressing, foreclosing on, or closeting the homoerotic in the service of bolstering dominant paradigms of meaning making and morality; and the use of the homoerotic to forward a particular film's (usually moralistic) agenda. Students can be attuned to such shifts in the treatment of queerness when given a few simple comparative exercises. For instance, they could be asked to

> compare a film version with the novel, noting what scenes, characters, and allusions have been added or deleted and to what effect;
> compare two or more film versions, either with the novel or with one another, noting changes in presentation. Such comparison works particularly well with versions in which the novel's plot has been updated to reflect a more contemporary setting.

Each exercise allows students to explore how changes in the representation of the novel also affect changes in the representation of sexuality; they can then reflect on the ideological implications or meanings of each change.

In this essay I offer a discussion of three major, readily available film versions of *The Picture of Dorian Gray* and describe how each either figures the homoerotic or elides discussion of it. Through comparative analysis of these films with the original source material, instructors and students can explore changing views about sexuality, queerness, and their relation to identity throughout the twentieth century.

The Picture of Dorian Gray (1945)

The Picture of Dorian Gray, directed by Albert Lewin for MGM, is considered a film classic. Lewin seems to have had a moral goal in making this film; he "decided everything was going to be in black and white because of the good and evil symbolism. [He] packed it full of symbols" (qtd. in Tanitch 378). Indeed, the film is intent on recuperating the novel as a moral tale, and its dual use of sexuality and suppression of queerness shows students how mainstream art, such as the popular cinema, revises the more radical elements of an artwork for its own purposes. One way to unpack this revision for students is to have them work through both the film and the book, noting significant changes, particularly in the deletion or addition of characters and in the alteration of key bits of dialogue.

For instance, students may note that in the film portrayal of Dorian some careful editing was done. Tanitch notes that "Dorian's perversion was suggested by the fact that he admired the drawings of Aubrey Beardsley and read Oscar Wilde!" (378). That, however, is about as far as the filmmakers take Dorian's perversion. Tanitch suggests that "Lewin avoided censorship by leaving Dorian's unspeakable crimes to the cinemagoer's imagination. The most explicit scene was the one in which Dorian blackmailed Allen Campbell by threatening to tell his wife" (379). What Dorian threatened is left tantalizingly open for consideration—or projection. Indeed, it is the careful skirting around such allusions that merits attention, and students can be assigned the task of detailing the many ways in which even the smallest reference to the homoerotic is made obscure.

The temptation scene with Hallward and Wotton parallels the novel well, and many lines of dialogue are lifted directly from Wilde's text. When queried about why he has painted the portrait, though, Basil mystifies his inspiration, suggesting that a power outside him guided his hand, effectively suppressing the homoeroticism present in the novel. Rather, we hear that the painting has a "mysterious quality," and Basil's "attraction" to Dorian is never discussed. Lord Henry is much more faithful to Wilde's novel, and he emphasizes in his monologues and epigrams the themes of youth, self-development, influence, and the necessity of yielding to temptation—all described as he captures and imprisons a butterfly in a plate of water. All the key Wildean concepts and concerns are trotted out here, but the film's narrator overlays his own interpretation, describing Wotton's little speeches as full of the "praise of folly" and the "creed of pleasure."

In depicting Dorian's debauchery, the film is more suggestive than explicit, and I have had students keep note of all the extratextual effects that signal how we are supposed to respond to Dorian as a character. Students observe, for instance, the use of muted lighting to depict the shadowiness of his pursuits. We also see one of Dorian's bizarre parties, featuring a mystical dancer, which can be read in a number of ways. On the one hand, the scene continues to emphasize the spiritual (through what we are supposed to read as Dorian's fascination with the demonic, perhaps); on the other hand, by associating Dorian with the oriental, it suggests that he may be under an alien, evil influence. The scene begs for a postcolonial reading, in which Eastern influences are coded as evil.

Changes to characters and the addition of extra characters assist this film in its ideological enterprise. Notably, Sibyl Vane is not an actress but a singer in a bar or salon, The Two Turtles. This change helps reveal how the film's director sought to make the story a cautionary one, not one concerned with the connection between aesthetics and ethics, as Gillespie suggests. Most notably, Sibyl's artistic talent is downplayed, and Dorian falls out of love with Sibyl not because she loses her acting abilities but because Lord Henry suggests that he tempt her innocence. Not as pure as Dorian thought, she fails Henry's test. The narration thus moves from the question of Sibyl's artistic talent to the question of her sexual purity. The sexuality, repressed earlier in the scene with Basil, returns— though heterosexualized this time and used as a gauge of innocence. Tracing this change, in this and later film versions, is a useful exercise for at least two reasons: first, the move from aesthetic to sexual considerations underscores the importance of the sexual to identity throughout the twentieth century; second, the use of sexuality to enforce moral codes provides an opportunity to understand how sexuality, as a form of knowledge, is also an exercise of social power.

The opening temptation scene in this film is also noteworthy for its introduction of an additional character: a young girl, Gladys, who is Basil's niece and ward.[1] She becomes important in providing a dramatic love interest, and, interestingly enough, we see her appear in later film versions as well. In fact, Gladys reenters, all grown up, to suggest the passage of time—and to create a spiritual foil for Dorian's ever-growing wickedness. Dorian finds it hard to be insincere with her, and Gladys wants to marry him against the advice of yet another new character, David Stone, who would like to marry Gladys himself. Her function in the film is clearly to prick Dorian's conscience. She is a figure from his youth, his innocence—a reminder of what he once was. In an interesting online article on this film, Karin Wikoff argues that the introduction of Gladys "makes the idea of her ruin more horrible, since she is the niece of the friend Dorian murders." To tease out the heterosexualizing importance of Gladys and David to the film, I prompt students to think about what the film would be like without their presence.

To engage students in close readings of the novel, I ask them to keep track of changes in dialogue, which can be both quite specific and quite ideologically loaded. In the famous conversation between Dorian and Basil, the painter alludes to the various things that are being said about Dorian, and changes in this dialogue, from novel to film, are significant. For instance, Basil wonders why Dorian's friendship is so fatal to people—not to the young men mentioned in the novel. We see a small but telling deemphasis on the homoerotic, and it is played simultaneously alongside a reemphasis of the spiritual drama. As Dorian shows Basil the portrait, we see a cross in the background, masterfully created by a play of light and shadow. You cannot help but see it as Basil asks, "Do you know how to pray, Dorian?" And, perhaps in an effort to reassert heterosexual feeling in the scene, the film gives Dorian an additional motive to kill Basil: "Gladys must never know."

The end of the film stresses its moral interpretation of the novel, and comparison is revealing. Dorian seems increasingly interested in pursuing what Lord Henry calls his "strange impulse to be good," but scene after scene reveals Dorian as a hunted and haunted man. The lesson is clear: once the path of wickedness is chosen, it leads to inevitable destruction. According to the narrator, Dorian vows to "find peace in a life of humility and self-denial," but he knows that the painting would always "tempt his weakness," so it must be destroyed. He looks for one last sign of goodness in the portrait, perhaps changed for the good by his decision not to marry Gladys. There is nothing, so he stabs the portrait, with the expected result. Lord Henry and others come rushing in and discover the body lying underneath the swinging lamp, an image reminiscent of the gallows. In a final emphasis of the spiritual lesson we are to glean from this film, Henry mutters, "Heaven forgive me." Even the evil tempter in this moral drama finally sees the light.

The Secret of Dorian Gray *(1970)*

In later film versions, the homoeroticism largely elided in 1945 begins to creep in, suggesting greater openness in discussing and representing queerness. One film from the 1970s risks much more representation of sexuality in general and queerness in particular—with very different results from that of the earlier MGM film. Massimo Dallamano's *The Secret of Dorian Gray* is willing to explore the philosophy of new hedonism and not condemn it outright or as heavy-handedly. Subtitled "A Modern Allegory Based on the Work of Oscar Wilde," this film is a fascinating, updated version of the story set in modern London. According to *Images in the Dark, The Secret of Dorian Gray* offers "a wonderful compendium of outlandish 1960s mod clothes and the slightly right-of-hip denizens who assist Dorian in his descent to Hell" (R. Murray 293).

The film emphasizes beauty, even self-pleasure—perhaps a comment on the new hedonism of the 1970s—and it is worth having students compare the aesthetic philosophies set forth in the first chapter of the novel with the rendering of pleasure in the film. They might notice that *The Secret of Dorian Gray* is willing to show us what self-development looks like in the twentieth century; that is, it has a distinctly sexual dimension.

In its exploration of a new hedonism, the film is delicious. The sex scenes, even when the music is a trifle spooky or eerie, are often playful. Unlike any of the other films, this film titillates with images of Dorian's corruption. In one scene, as Dorian is concluding his deal with the aged Patricia, the two walk through a horse stable and Dorian takes her from behind. We see scene after scene of similar exploits, one woman after another, and then scenes with two women. Finally, Henry approaches Dorian while the young man is showering; in a frightfully clichéd moment, Dorian drops his bar of soap and Henry comes to the rescue, as it were. This encounter leads to a wonderful montage of Dorian cruising men for sex, which, we are led to believe, he finds with a black man in a public toilet. In the confrontation with Dorian, Basil notes that Dorian has corrupted many, in many different ways, including "that young boy," and says that there is "no degradation you haven't lived through."

The film also establishes more of an aesthetic-ethical tension. Henry maintains that "we're all responsible for our own lives—and nothing else" and that "beauty is more important than genius." Dorian pursues beauty, claiming a responsibility only to and for himself. While the portrait deteriorates, we can't help but relate to or at least sympathize with the handsome, pleasure-seeking Dorian. Using this film, I have had students debate in class where our sympathies should lie, with pleasure or ethics. The beauty of this film is that it presents the pursuit of pleasure as so enticing that we have a hard time condemning Dorian. While the conclusion invites moralizing, with Henry's asking Dorian shortly before the end of the film, "What does it profit a man?" (after Mark 8.36), this film is much more willing than the 1945 version to play with, in Gillespie's words, "the primacy of a doctrine of pleasure." Having students trace this theme, again through comparisons, might help them question what changes made it possible, between 1891, 1945, and 1970, to film a version of the novel that could explore a new hedonism without recourse to heavy-handed moralizing.

The Sins of Dorian Gray *(1983)*

Given the increased willingness to film sexually explicit material, to tease out sexuality and queerness in the film versions, and given an increased awareness of women's issues and gender inequalities, it seemed inevitable that someone would want to portray Dorian Gray as a woman. The 1983 American television film *The Sins of Dorian Gray* presents us with just such an updated *Dorian Gray*, with its own twists aided and abetted by the gender switching of some of the main characters.

In plot, *Sins* is a relatively faithful if melodramatic adaptation. But the changes in gender provide students with an opportunity to explore the ideological bents of this film. Dorian is an aspiring actress from very humble origins; Henry Lord is a fashion mogul who tempts her away from her acting ambitions to pursue a corrupting career in a shallow and corrupt fashion industry; and Stuart Vane is a married, would-be musician whose simplicity and naïveté eventually lead the increasingly worldly and career-minded Dorian to dump him—with tragic results. It is clear that our sympathies are supposed to lie with Stuart, who is creating art, while Henry is simply promulgating shallow, possibly damaging stereotypical ideals in his advertisements. A different kind of sexual politics from that of the earlier films is at play here, and it can lead to interesting class discussion. In the earlier films, Sibyl was limited by class and gender; in *Sins*, a man is trapped by his class and marital obligations: he's neither rich nor savvy enough to manage a complicated affair with a powerful woman. At the same time, Dorian's

potential power as a woman is critiqued by the film's heavy-handed treatment of
the aesthetic theme. Stuart is a free artist, not a professional: he plays what he
wants and how he wants and is clearly intended to be a contrasting figure to Dorian, who has just sold her soul to the fashion industry.

The love plot unravels to reveal Dorian as a selfish monster and Stuart as a
selfless victim. Dorian wants Henry to help Stuart professionally; Henry,
though skeptical, agrees, though he calls him Dorian's "plaything of an idle
hour." Henry manages to get Stuart a spot on the *Dick Clark Show*, but Stuart
is on "booze and pills" and can't perform. He tells Dorian, "I just can't do this
for you." She coldly responds, "He's not who I thought he was—or could be."
Dorian and Henry go to dinner, and Henry tells Dorian, "I never approve or
disapprove of anything. . . . I represent all the misadventures you never had the
courage to commit." Dorian, taken with Henry's temptation, asks him to make
love to her. We see, nearly simultaneously, a distraught Stuart Vane on his mo-
torbike, driving frantically. As Henry is leaving Dorian's apartment, *post coitus*,
Stuart shows up and forces his way in. They talk, and Dorian castigates him:
"You let me down. . . . You're not the person I was in love with. . . . You blew
your big chance. . . . I thought you were strong." Dorian is cold and calculating,
hardly the sweet waitress from earlier in the film. Tragedy, of course, ensues.

Dorian has chosen pleasure and selfish career ambitions over aesthetic purity, and it becomes difficult to identify with her—or so the film would have it.
The film thus uses the novel's aesthetic themes to privilege the pursuit of art
over a shallow concern with pleasure and career. She pays a heavy price for her
choice. If we think of the film as being essentially queered by the gender
switching—a transgendering of the plot, if you will—then we might expect the
film to provide a feminist reading of the story. It doesn't. The sexual politics at
play is one in which the man, Stuart Vane, is the victim of a cold, calculating,
and heartless sexuality—the sexuality of a woman in control. This queering of
the plot serves the purposes of a fairly moralistic lesson on two fronts: beware
both the shallow pursuit of beauty and pleasure, and beware the powerful
woman. A wonderful assignment I have tried asks students to envision, before
seeing the film, what a female Dorian might be like and how the story might
consequently unfold. Some portray Dorian as a feminist, overcome eventually
and tragically by sexism. Comparing such versions with *The Sins of Dorian
Gray* is both amusing and intriguing: students see clearly how a feminist reading of the story is denied in the moralizing of this film.

Comparing representations of pleasure and debauchery is also enlightening,
and students could create charts that contrast pleasure in the novel, in this film,
and in an earlier film. Unlike *Secrets*, *Sins* does not show us much of how Dorian
is debauched. Instead, after twenty years have passed, we see that she has become difficult to work with. She is now a first-class bitch—spoiled, smoking,
drinking, and rampaging. She's a caricature of the spoiled model. Her makeup
artist, Tracey, calls her "an empty, beautiful, vicious nothing"—"just an image."
Compared with earlier versions, this film is the most preoccupied with aesthetic

issues, but the simplistic dualism—true art good, fashion industry bad—replaces Wilde's more complex arguments for the connection between the aesthetic and ethics.

Each of the film versions discussed here offers students an opportunity, through a series of carefully constructed comparisons, to see the ways in which any radicality implicit in the original novel—whether it be of an aesthetic, ethical, or sexual dimension—is quickly and effectively co-opted by the film industry to promote a particular moral reading. The films invariably figure the new hedonism as the pursuit of sexual pleasure, and it is largely condemned outright. Queer sexualities are often repressed or used as a marker of moral degeneration. Indeed, as the century wore on, the gradual introduction of specifically homoerotic or queer images was used not to advance a new hedonism or a reevaluation of the connection between pleasure and ethics but to buttress a fairly puritanical moral code. In fact, one could argue—and students should be encouraged to pursue this line of questioning—that the use of sexuality in the films, often added to the plot of the novel, is calculated to perform just such sociocultural work. Examining these films with students shows them how representations of sexuality have changed over the course of the twentieth century.

NOTE

[1] Her character is developed perhaps out of a few sentences toward the end of the novel, in which Wilde's narrator suggests that Dorian fell in love with someone late in life.

The Shorter Fiction
Approached and Questioned

D. C. Rose

The place of Wilde's shorter and shortest works in his canon of writing offers a point of access to the complexity of Wilde as an author. It is not simply that he was a multifaceted writer, able to turn to poetry, short story, play, essay; it is more that in each genre he left a body of self-standing work independent of the rest. Yet no individual work of Wilde stands quite alone, for all feed into the veins that he worked: class, aestheticism, gender (even though coded), the magic of imagination, Christianity, the power of money. Because he can appear light-weight, he can be trivialized, and the search for meaning must be intensified accordingly. No other author in history, unless it be Shakespeare, has had so many operas, symphonic suites, films, puppet versions, and one-person shows derived from his life and work, and this hinterland beckons to the student.

Critical attention has been able to admire one genre and dismiss the others without the critic's diminishing Wilde's status: *The Picture of Dorian Gray* plus *Salomé* versus the comedies; "The Ballad of Reading Gaol" plus *The Harlot's House* versus the *Poems* of 1881; *De Profundis* plus *Intentions* versus *The Duchess of Padua* plus *A Florentine Tragedy*. Such partitioning presents a problem instead of offering a solution. What actually are Wilde's stories? And where do we allocate their place in teaching either Wilde or the genre? This challenge for students applies to all the texts discussed. One cannot read Wilde as one can read Conrad or Hardy, Yeats or Joyce (or E. Nesbit). There is little in the way of plot or even characterization to examine. What one scrutinizes is Wilde's ability as a teller of tales, more at home (let it be argued) in these works than in *The Picture of Dorian Gray*, which, as a novel, is very oddly constructed. It is a basic point, but students need to come to a view of why they find the stories appealing or unappealing, riveting or boring.

Whereas there was considerably more to Wilde's project than being merely a teller of tales, his method of rehearsing epigrams and anecdotes in conversation before incorporating them into texts licenses this approach. Notably, as I suggest below, the stories connect with Wilde's other writings as well as with other contemporary modes of fiction, touching and exploring genres such as the gothic and supernatural, to the cult for London that appears in writers as diverse as W. E. Henley and John Davidson, Conan Doyle and Saki. To these stories Wilde brought his quizzical Irish eye, mocking and yet often affectionate; his indignation was ironic, not savage, poised between his desire for social success and his frequent weariness with that success. His epigrams, so often quoted, serve all these purposes, and to rediscover their placing in his work is to understand their import.

There has been a curious reluctance among Wilde's critics to grapple with the shorter fiction, the convenient term for "Lord Arthur Savile's Crime," "The

Canterville Ghost," "The Sphinx without a Secret," "The Model Millionaire," and "The Portrait of Mr. W. H." (hereinafter "Crime," "Ghost," "Sphinx," "Model," and "W. H."), the works that are not classified as stories or tales. In his introduction to the 1930 Everyman's Library edition of Wilde, Hesketh Pearson glided past the shorter fiction in order to get on to *The Picture of Dorian Gray*, indicating unease with these fugitive works (*Oscar Wilde's Plays*). Fortunately, one need no longer defer to Pearson as a critic (he thought *An Ideal Husband*, *Lady Windermere's Fan*, and *A Woman of No Importance* "dated beyond repair" [x–xi]); the distance we have traveled is indicated in the 1991 Everyman's Library edition, where Pearson's introduction has been replaced by one by Terry Eagleton (Wilde, *Plays*). Eagleton, however, while writing forcefully about much of Wilde, omits reference to the shorter fiction altogether.

Turning to more specialist publication, one finds that even so popular a work as "Crime" is explored only by Alfons Klein, and there is no essay material on "Sphinx" or "Model." "Ghost" has attracted more attention, but it is slight enough and barely accessible (Green; Guy; Klein; Schroeder, "Oscar Wilde"; Søderman; Wilburn). Only with "W. H.," perhaps because it is itself a critical as much as an imaginative work, has attention been substantially engaged, even though *substantially* is still a relative term. A bibliography is given in the appendix to this essay. (Naturally, the wider biographic and critical material on Wilde should also be consulted, and differences of emphasis and methodology between general and specific studies are themselves worth attention [see Small, *Oscar Wilde Revalued* and *Oscar Wilde: Recent Research*].) Much thesis material may be found by consulting *Dissertation Abstracts International*, accessible through various portals online. Moreover, Wilde's popularity inspires frequent new editions, now usually with introductions and notes.

Many of the elements for informing critical debate were for a long time therefore largely absent. The position changed only as the work of Wilde as a whole attracted contemporary academic scrutiny, which I have summarized as the change from Pearson to Eagleton. Most new approaches contain textual analysis and invite response. Such criticism is complicated by the difficulty of grouping the shorter fiction under any rubric other than length. "Crime," for example, is better grouped with the four comedies, exhibiting much of the Mayfair ambience that characterizes them. "Sphinx," a trifle, is also a society tale. "Ghost," with its comedic aspects, is midway between these but may be closer to the group of tales "The Young King," "The Birthday of the Infanta," "The Fisherman and His Soul," and "The Star Child," given its supernatural and Christian elements and the lightness of touch in its prose. Evaluations of these figure prominently in studies by Bruce Bashford, Philip Cohen, Lawrence Danson (*Wilde's Intentions*), and Christopher Nassaar. These studies reveal a diversity of approach that mirrors the ambiguities and ambivalences of Wilde himself.

Wilde's own view, not necessarily to be taken *au pied de la lettre*, hardly helps: that the stories were "studies in prose, put for Romance's sake into a fanciful form. Meant partly for children, and partly for those who have kept the child-like faculties of wonder and joy" (*Complete Letters* 354 [letter to G. H. Kersley, 15 June 1888]). This statement is well-meant but tendentious, for it underplays the complexities. What if they had not been "put . . . into a fanciful form"? To invert a familiar trope, these stories are for adults of all ages. Of course, all fairy tales can be subjected to this analysis, and the distance is considerable between the anthropologist's study and the nursery. Why has Wilde's shorter fiction not attracted the analysis of a Bruno Bettelheim, a Clande Lévi-Strauss, or even an Angela Carter?

"Ghost" is a link between the shorter fiction and the shortest fiction, *"The Happy Prince" and Other Tales* (published by David Nutt, May 1888, and reprinted during Wilde's lifetime only once, in 1889) and *The House of Pomegranates* (Nov. 1891), in which Wilde published a collection of nine tales in all. But what sort of tales? In 1960, in the first edition devoted to bringing all nine together, the Bodley Head published them as *Fairy Tales*: "The Happy Prince," "The Nightingale and the Rose," "The Selfish Giant," "The Devoted Friend," "The Remarkable Rocket" (from Wilde's first collection), "The Young King," "The Birthday of the Infanta," "The Fisherman and His Soul," and "The Star Child" (from the second). This grouping proclaimed a view of the nature of these tales that separates them from the shorter fiction in a way that can hardly be justified, particularly in the case of "The Star Child" and "The Young King." Nevertheless, this convention maintained itself through subsequent editions, much reinforced when contemporary publishers began issuing illustrated editions, which placed the stories in different readership age groups. These publishing choices form the basis for a comparative study of intended readers as well as provide different interpretative foci. Thus the stories also formed the Gollancz 1976 edition as *The Fairy Stories of Oscar Wilde*, the ninth reprint being issued as a Gollancz Children's Paperback. In 1986, Walker Books issued *The Selfish Giant*, publicized as "one of the best loved of all children's stories." In format, price, and tenor of the illustrations, this edition was specifically aimed at younger children. In contrast, the 1996 edition of *Giant* published by Macdonald Young Books is aimed by the same criteria at older children. The illustrations by Valentine Sirel to the Sator edition of *The Happy Prince* of 1983 seem to place the book midway between these two groups.

This ambiguity can be pursued through other editions, for even the short fiction has frequently attracted the same sort of illustration as the shorter fiction (see the appendix to this essay). The critical treatment of these editions varies from whimsical marginal notes to serious interpretation of the text. A new slant was added in 1992, when P. Craig Russell, who had illustrated a number of operas, embarked on a five-volume edition of Wilde's tales in comic strip format. To English or Irish minds, this development doubtless consolidates the identification of the tales as children's literature; to the American and French, the format bridges the gap between adults and young people. Russell also produced a version of *Salomé*. "For adults," said the publishers, "here are tales exquisitely spun and remarkably insightful. For children, what better way than beautiful comic art to bring them back to reading and the love of books?" This statement overlooks the grim (pun intended) side of many of the tales. Vyvyan Holland is clear that his father "told us all his own written stories, *suitably adapted for our young minds*" (53; emphasis added). The point is that there is no easy dividing line between young minds and older ones, in a spectrum from "The Devoted Friend" to *The Picture of Dorian Gray*. Assessing the position of both the short and the shorter fiction along this spectrum is a task for teachers and students.

The orality of these tales, like so many of the prose poems and even passages in *Dorian Gray*, was rehearsed in Wilde's conversation, and reading them as texts to be spoken (or, rather, reading much of Wilde aloud) gives them a dramatic interest. Fortunately, many are available on audiocassette or CD (and LP and even 78s), which a university library should be able to provide. A short list is given in the appendix to this essay, and students can be encouraged to listen outside the classroom to prepare for discussion within.

To move between the shorter fiction group of stories and those not part of the canon formed in 1888 and 1891 is to travel by easy stages. A thematic connection is imposed if one considers that "Ghost" and "The Selfish Giant" are the two tales by Wilde illustrated by Lisbeth Zwerger (resp., *Canterville Ghost* and *Selfish Giant* [1991]), yoking them in the convention of children's fiction. With "Ghost," certainly a narrative that evokes in Wilde's phrase "faculties of wonder and joy" (*Complete Letters* 352 [letter to G. H. Kersley, 15 June 1888]), one enters territory explored at greater length elsewhere by Wilde: his ambivalent attitude toward Americans, his engagement with aristocracy, his exploration of the gothic (even if to subvert it), and his gift for fine writing.

Sometimes the parts war against the whole, as if Wilde had not entirely made up his mind for whom he was writing. In "Ghost," Virginia Otis, echoing Wilde's dead sister, Isola, sits uncomfortably in the same narrative with her awful twin brothers. The story also exemplifies the eclectic nature of Wilde's culling of sources. While Otis may indeed be, in Mariano Baselga's exposition, an epenthesis of the Greek *hostis*, that is, "anybody" (15), it was also a name readily at hand. Otis lifts were crossing the Atlantic, being notably installed in the Eiffel Tower in 1889. The name indicates Wilde's view of American social climbing, and it opens the way into a discussion of Wilde's own snobbery and his views on society, foreigners, and the other. Arguably it reveals his uncertainty when balanced between the company of the rich and famous by day and the working class renters by night. He also mocks the conventions of gothic, of which the best example perhaps is how the indelible bloodstain has to be supplemented from Virginia Otis's paint box. This joke well illustrates how exhausted the gothic tale had become, ready to be replaced by the psychological tale. The Otis family, dealing practically with the specter in "Ghost" (published in 1891), and Sherlock Holmes and Dr. Watson, dealing with the spectral hound in *The Hound of the Baskervilles* (published in 1901–02 but set in 1889), display a rationalist rejection of the supernatural. In atmosphere too there is no great distance to be traveled from Canterville Chase to Baskerville Hall. It is a much longer way from Canterville Chase to Bly, the haunted house in Henry James's *The Turn of the Screw* (1898), where the children, unlike the young Otises, become the victims. Here parallel readings extend and develop our grasp of Wilde's achievement and his place in the literary conventions of the day. One can also look at the representations of the housekeepers Mrs. Umney, Mrs. Barrymore, and Mrs. Grose and how they function in the texts.

Mockery of the paranormal also characterizes "Crime," where Wilde again shows both his fascination with the aristocracy and his perception of the vapid nature of their pursuits. Like "Ghost," "Crime" can be seen as part of the project of Wilde's engagement with tales of the inanity of upper-class society, explored in more extended fashion in *A Woman of No Importance*, *Lady Windermere's Fan*, *An Ideal Husband*, and *The Importance of Being Earnest*, with which plays it forms a unity. (There are stage versions of "Crime" by Constance Cox, Ronald Llewellyn Phillips, Robert Carrickford, and Antoinette Duffy; there was even a version of it broadcast on Russian television in 1991). "Crime" opens at a reception given by Lady Windermere, although this is not the Margaret of *Lady Windermere's Fan*. First published in three parts in May 1887, it is clearly a proving ground for the plays, and any discussion of them that leaves out this story is vitiated. The stage versions of "Crime" open up a useful field of inquiry about such transmutations.

One can also see in Wilde's gibes at anarchism the stirrings of a critique of its practitioners developed by Joseph Conrad in *The Secret Agent* and G. K. Chesterton in *The Man Who Was Thursday*. How far does this approach undermine Wilde's own leanings to a philosophical anarchism? Does it support or negate his position set out in "The Soul of Man under Socialism"? In that essay, he espouses a sort of anarcho-bohemianism, wanting control to be removed as the requisite of a free society and seeing such absence of control as specifically necessary for the artist (and perhaps the student). In his rejection of "physical force" anarchism (1188), how far was he also distancing himself from the Irish nationalists who advocated it? Is Wilde setting forth, in his own way, some of the terrorism debates of today?

Savile's flight through nighttime London is a novel depiction of the flâneur; it aligns Savile with other London prowlers, crisscrossing the city in search of, or fleeing from, adventure or experience. Robert Louis Stevenson's Mr. Hyde and Prince Florizel; Holmes and Watson; Wilde's Dorian Gray, Ernest and Gilbert, and John Worthing; E. W. Hornung's "gentleman cracksman" A. J. Raffles; Saki's dandy Clovis Sangrail; the music hall character Burlington Bertie (played *en travesti* by Vesta Tilley)—all in their several ways are Baudelairean flâneurs. Raffles is just such an artist-criminal as attracted Wilde; Sangrail is the character Wilde might have invented had he lived. The detailed routes through London in the Holmes stories ("The Sign of Four" is a useful example) provide an idea of the nighttime London of Dorian Gray and Arthur Savile. Wilde's contribution to this cast of wealthy idlers adds considerably to the depiction of London in late Victorian literature, giving both a social reading to his work and placing it in our conventions of urban interpretations. How do Wilde's characters compare with the others?

Given the second wave of the gothic in late Victorian England, of which *Dr. Jekyll and Mr. Hyde* and *Dracula* are the key texts, Wilde's ironic take on the genre comes as both welcome light relief and the suggestion that the gothic was not always taken with the high seriousness with which we have come to invest it. It also serves as a useful reminder that the author of *The Picture of Dorian Gray* was a satirist. He could form, but he could also mock. "Ghost" especially becomes as much a distancing from secret lusts and scarlet sins as Max Beerbohm's *The Happy Hypocrite*, a specific riposte to Wilde's project.

"Crime" does, however, afford another entry into the study of Wilde— namely, the evocation of his milieu through use of names. Wilde uses names that for his contemporaries carried a freight of association that we need to recover in order to come to a view of his reception. His names have a very different purpose from that used by, say, Charles Dickens or Maurice Maeterlinck (for whose works Wilde asked while in prison), and one can discuss the difference between labels as emblems and labels as symbols. Setting aside that between the first appearance of "Crime" in serial form in May 1887 and its publication as *"Lord Arthur Savile's Crime" and Other Stories* in October 1891, Wilde had been proposed for membership of, and rejected by, the Savile Club, one can notice that Lady Chiltern's first name, Gertrude, was also the name of Lady Savile, wife of the third baron, of Rufford Abbey, Rufford being a name Wilde uses in "Crime," "Ghost," *A Woman of No Importance*, and *Lady Windermere's Fan*. Also note that, while Algernon Moncrieff lives in Half Moon Street, Septimus Podgers (the chiromantist in "Crime") lives at 103a West Moon Street. Half Moon Street is off Piccadilly, in which street the Savile Club was at 107. (Arthur's Club was at 69 St. James's Street.) Here is a complexity that repays a close reading. The confines of Wilde's fashionable London were narrow enough.

East of Half Moon Street runs Clarges Street; next again is Bolton Street, and one may relate Lady Bracknell's "dear Duchess of Bolton" to it (368). Henry James had lived in Half Moon Street in 1869 and at 3 Bolton Street after December 1876, but the most interesting of Half Moon Street's residents was Percy Bysshe Shelley. These streets all run into the north side of Piccadilly, as does Albemarle Street, home of the Albemarle Club, to which both Oscar and Constance Wilde belonged and where the Marquess of Queensberry left with the hall porter the famous calling card inscribed "To Oscar Wilde posing Somdomite [*sic*]" (Ellmann, *Oscar Wilde* 438). At number 41, the fashionable dining club Amphitryon had flourished for a while in the 1880s. Carter's Hotel in Albemarle Street was where Queensberry was staying at the time of his exchange with Bosie Douglas that ended in the latter's telegram, "WHAT A FUNNY LITTLE MAN YOU ARE" (418). Albemarle Street was, and is, also the address of John Murray,

Byron's publisher (and Conan Doyle's). The market in which Lane says that he cannot find cucumbers, even for ready money, is Shepherd's Market, behind Half Moon Street. It is still possible to buy cucumbers there. Stratton Street, another couple of minutes away, gave its name to the Honorable Victoria Stratton, Mrs. Allonby's mother-in-law (*Woman of No Importance*). Hertford Street, where Alan Campbell lived (*Dorian Gray*), is about a three minutes' walk from Half Moon Street and connects with Curzon Street, where Lord Henry Wotton, Lord Goring, Lady Clementina Beauchamp, and Mrs. Erlynne all lived (and where, at number 19, Disraeli died in April 1881). Lord Windermere need not have been profligate in paying Mrs. Erlynne's rent—the *poule de luxe* Cecil Hamilton lived in a Curzon Street house rented at twelve guineas a week. Savile Row, the center of fashionable tailors' establishments, is off Vigo Street (where the Bodley Head was situated), behind the Albany, where "Ernest" Worthing lived at B4 and where A. J. Raffles also lived. Grosvenor Square, the home of Dorian Gray and Sir Robert Chiltern, and Grosvenor Street, the home of the Bracknells, are within another six minutes' walk. Charles Street, where Wilde briefly lived at number 9, runs from the southwest corner of Berkeley Square to where Chesterfield Street connects it to Curzon Street.

Of this part of London, Ian Malcolm (who married Lillie Langtry's daughter) recalled:

> Scores of leisured young men, elegant and accomplished, were to be seen everywhere and at all times of the day and night; they played a more ubiquitous rôle in London Society than they do to-day. Immaculately dressed, they rode or walked in Rotten Row from eleven-thirty for an hour or so, when it was time to put on frock-coat and tall hat for a lunch-eon engagement at the club or elsewhere. (35)

This is clearly the world of Algernon Moncrieff and Arthur Savile. Wilde's May-fair, layered with references and correspondences, is contained within a quadrilateral of hardly more than half a mile each side. A small world, it is as agreeable a starting place for urban mapping as a literary conceit as it is for an afternoon stroll. Though the flâneur is an essentially Parisian concept, these texts show the success of its relocation to London and offer clues to how it may be relocated yet again to other cities at other times, from the New York of the "upper ten thousand" to the San Francisco of the flower children.

The mapping is easily done. Any teacher with *PowerPoint* can access online maps and use them in class. The Web site www.multimap.com can be a starting point for London, and the city's Victorian time is also readily accessible through a number of photographic archives. Further exploration of the resources pro-vided both online and in print by the Education Department of the Museum of London (www.museumoflondon.org.uk/) will help place Wilde's London in the context of the methodology of urban studies. The Westminster City Archives maintain an elaborate Web site that should be visited (www.westminster.gov

.uk/libraries/archives/index.cfm). Students should be encouraged to seek out such resources, which of course can be brought into service of the rest of London fiction, from Dickens to Kureishi. The annual Literary London Conference, supported by both a journal and a Web site (www.literarylondon.org), is also a developing resource here. For those interested in comparative literature, how London emerges through Wilde can be read in conjunction with how Paris (the starting point of "Sphinx") emerges through Zola or Maupassant (see http://expositions.bnf.fr/Zola).

More serious territory is entered on with "W. H.," more novella than long short story. The alignment is closer to "The Decay of Lying" and "The Critic as Artist" than to the rest of Wilde's work. This is not so much Wilde the story teller, still less Wilde the social observer, as Wilde the intellectual speculator, whose questioning could trench rather alarmingly on the forbidden field of homosexuality, though in a manner sufficiently coded for him to silence Edward Carson in *Regina v. Queensberry:*

> CARSON. I believe you have written an article to show that Shakespeare's sonnets were suggestive of unnatural vice?
> WILDE. On the contrary, I have written an article to show that they are not. I objected to such a perversion being put upon Shakespeare.
> (Hyde, *Famous Trials* 113)

How far "W. H." illuminates our view of Shakespeare and is of use in Shakespeare studies is debatable. The critical work on it tends to be by Wilde scholars rather than Shakespeareans. It is well worth subjecting to scrutiny by a sixteenth-century specialist. It can be seen more pertinently as part of the late-nineteenth-century interest in Shakespeare, as exemplified in the actor-managers Henry Irving, Herbert Beerbohm Tree, William Poel, and Frank Benson, on whom much has been written, and in the writings on Shakespeare by Edward Dowden and Shaw and Frank Harris. "W. H." is therefore a text for any discussion on the representation and reception of Shakespeare. The narrative structure is a complex one, and how it functions is not obvious on first reading; but in serving to distance the ultimate author (Wilde) from the narrators and commentators of the text, the story can be seen in a context of authorial masks, a vital concept in the understanding of Wilde and much of the coded literature (especially the homosexual literature) of the day. This idea can be developed with reference to "Model," which otherwise is a nugatory piece in which the last line appears to have been written first and the narrative composed to lead up to it. But "Model," a tale of a millionaire who through a whim wishes to be painted as a pauper and is taken for one by a caller to the artist's studio, can run deeper than that, and reading it both with *The Picture of Dorian Gray* and with Henry James's "The Real Thing" will show that depth. As with the "Sphinx," where a woman with a mystery turns out not to have one, we are being led into Wilde's views on the truth of masks and into coded reference to his own multiform personality, not sexual merely but also social and national. Although "Model" serves very well as an introduction to the queer reading of texts, "Sphinx" implies that a mask can hide the absence of face, which suggests that Wilde also saw the limitations of always assuming that what is hidden is more interesting than what is on the surface, a quizzical rather than a critical approach.

This approach, mutatis mutandis, also suggests a closer look at *The Duchess of Padua* and *A Florentine Tragedy* as late Victorian reconstructions of Renaissance themes, cutting from study of text to study of representation. Here reference to the iconography (to Morris, Burne-Jones) is essential. How does this idea sit with the Victorian representation of social themes, flight into the past, or conjuring up an idealized future?

Wilde's shorter fiction is flexible enough to appeal to students at almost any level. I have suggested that, close reading aside, a quizzical approach, testing the texts for contributions to the overarching ideas, may be more useful to students in encouraging independent thought than a more formalistic engagement with the texts. Perhaps something of Wilde's own mastery of language might even rub off!

APPENDIX:
SUPPLEMENTAL BIBLIOGRAPHIC
LISTS FOR THE SHORT FICTION

ILLUSTRATIONS

By Dorothea Braby. Wood engravings in *Lord Arthur Savile's Crime*. London: Rodale, 1954. Afterword by Edward J. Fluck. Limited to 1,000 numbered copies.

By John Gaastra. For *The Young King*. London: Folio Soc., n.d.

By Robert Geary. Of "Lord Arthur Savile's Crime" and "The Sphinx without a Secret." In *"The Canterville Ghost" and Other Stories*. Retold by John Davage. Penguin Readers Level 4. Harlow: Pearson Educ., 2003.

By Maurice Henry. Of "The Canterville Ghost," "Lord Arthur Savile's Crime," "A Model Millionaire," and "The Sphinx without a Secret." In *Le fantôme de Canterville et autres contes*. Ed. Jean-Luc Steinmetz. Paris: Livre de Poche, 1988.

By Jean Kerleroux. Of "Lord Arthur Savile's Crime," "The Canterville Ghost," "The Sphinx without a Secret," "The Selfish Giant," "The Remarkable Rocket," "The Fisherman and His Soul," "The Devoted Friend," "The Happy Prince," "The Birthday of the Infanta," "The Nightingale and the Rose," and "The Star Child." In *Le crime de Lord Arthur Savile et autres contes*. Paris: Érable (François Beauval for subscribers only), 1974.

———. For *Le crime de Lord Arthur Savile et autres contes*. Les chefs d'œuvres de mystère et du fantastique. Paris: Érable, 1969.

By David Roberts. Of "The Model Millionaire" and "The Sphinx without a Secret." In *"Lord Arthur Savile's Crime" and Other Stories*. Adapt. Bill Bowler. Oxford: Oxford UP, 2003.

By Günter Schöllkopf. Of "The Canterville Ghost" and "Lord Arthur Savile's Crime." In *Zwei Novellen: Das Gespenst von Canterville und Lord Arthur Saviles Verbrechen*. Fwd. Annemarie Hofmann. Stuttgart: Riederer, 1967?

By Lisbeth Zwerger. For *The Canterville Ghost*. Salzburg: Neugebauer, 1986.

Recordings

"The Canterville Ghost" and Other Stories [*Model, Crime*]. Retold by Stephen Colbourn. Audiocassette. Oxford: Heinemann English Language Teaching, n.d.

Collected Short Stories. Read by Frank Muller. Oxford: Isis, n.d.

Lord Arthur Savile's Crime. Read by John Moffatt. London: Penguin, 1997.

Lord Arthur Savile's Crime. Read by John Standing. Talking Tape Company, n.d.

The Nightingale and the Rose; The Remarkable Rocket; The Selfish Giant. Audiocassette. Monte Carlo: Monaco-Ireland Arts Soc., 1995.

Oscar Wilde's Fairy Tales. Read by Simon Callow. London: Hodder Headline Audiobooks, 1995.

Oscar Wilde's Fairy Tales. Read by Seamus Moran. New York: Ion Rhapsodes ser., 1995.

The Short Fiction of Oscar Wilde. Read by Jude Law and Joan Allen. Pleasantville: Face/Off, 2000.

Teaching Wilde's Fairy Tales: Aestheticism as Social and Cultural Critique in "The Happy Prince" and "The Nightingale and the Rose"

Nicholas Ruddick

It is not difficult to get students to read and enjoy Oscar Wilde's works, and it is all too easy to get them to debate the significance of his life. But how does an instructor convey to a class Wilde's importance as the late nineteenth century's foremost theorist and advocate of aestheticism? Wildean aestheticism was far more than a rehearsal of the slogan "art for art's sake." It offered both a radical critique of the crudely utilitarian materialism of the late Victorian era and a decadent (or precociously protomodernist) insight into the superannuated state of nineteenth-century Romanticism. Students can certainly come to evaluate Wilde's role in intellectual history through an examination of his major essays in tandem with his novel *The Picture of Dorian Gray* (1891). However, I have found that the study of a pair of shorter and more accessible works can quickly lead classes to a clear and by no means superficial understanding of the significance of Wildean aestheticism. Students of late-nineteenth-century literary and cultural history will greatly benefit from instructors who can lead them through a careful analysis of "The Happy Prince." Instructors who can reveal something of the complex engagement of "The Nightingale and the Rose" with the Romanticism of Hans Christian Andersen will illuminate for fairy-tale classes a key moment in the development of the literary fairy tale in English.

Oscar Wilde's first important book was a slim volume, *"The Happy Prince" and Other Tales* (1888), containing five short fairy tales. The proposition that short fantastic fictions apparently intended for children can be used to introduce undergraduates to weighty matters of intellectual history might seem excessively paradoxical to instructors unfamiliar with the fairy tale as a genre. Yet although the fairy tale, through the famous collections of the Grimms and Andersen, had by the mid–nineteenth century come to be associated with young readers, there is no essential connection between the genre and children (see, e.g., Zipes, Introd. xi). There is evidence that adults were the primary intended readership of Wilde's fairy tales. Wilde sent copies of *The Happy Prince* collection to such childless luminaries as John Ruskin and Walter Pater, and in a letter of 1888 he noted that the tales "are studies in prose, put for Romance's sake into a fanciful form: meant partly for children, and partly for those who have kept the childlike faculties of wonder and joy, and who find in simplicity a subtle strangeness" (*Complete Letters* 352). In 1891, in response to criticism that his later volume of tales might not please children, he wrote, "Now in building this *House of Pomegranates* I had about as much intention of pleasing the British child as I had of pleasing the British public" (302).

"The Happy Prince" is unlikely to be much enjoyed by children today. Its plot is too static, its vocabulary too complex, and its style, influenced by the fin de siècle prose poem, too stilted. Undergraduates, by contrast, may dismiss the tale at first reading as too slight or childish to merit much attention. Instructors might begin by asking the class for their thoughts on the Councillor's description of the statue of the late Happy Prince: "He is as beautiful as a weather-cock . . . only not quite so useful" (271). Depending on the level of the course, it may be necessary to provide a little Victorian intellectual context to get the discussion rolling. The Councillor, who articulates the values of the dominant class in the city, is a utilitarian of the crudest kind. That is to say, he believes that if something is useful to oneself, then it is likely to make one happy, therefore it must be morally good, and therefore it may be called beautiful. As money can be very useful, and someone who has a lot of it is likely to be happier than someone who has none, then—so the utilitarian argument went—wealth must be morally good, and the more expensive an object is, the more beautiful it must be. (Such logic could also be used to explain why the poor lived in ugly squalor and were predisposed to crime.)

To Wilde, this utilitarian philosophy was nothing more than a specious justification of selfish acquisitiveness, and it may be necessary to remind students at this point that utilitarianism, the ethical theory formulated by Jeremy Bentham (1748–1832), was supposed to conduce to the greater good of the majority, not of the already privileged individual. The Happy Prince's statue is "useful" and "beautiful" to the city's ruling class because it demonstrates the equation between happiness and high monetary value. Put another way, in life the Prince was happy because he was rich; now that he is dead, his gilded and bejeweled statue usefully advertises the city's dominant ideology—namely, that wealth equals happiness. More sophisticated students, when asked why the Councillor adjudges the statue to be not as useful as a weathercock, will be able to deduce that his failure to understand how an ideological tool might be as valuable as a literal one marks him as a truly crude utilitarian.

In *De Profundis* (1949), Wilde called himself "a born antinomian" (1019), by which he meant that it was in his nature to reject socially established morality. Even more than the essay "The Soul of Man under Socialism" (1891), "The Happy Prince" reveals the antinomian Wilde, a Wilde particularly appealing to bright undergraduates, through its exposé of the social and moral consequences of extreme laissez-faire capitalism, the economic system justified by crude utilitarianism.

The tale describes a city in which the laboring masses are exploited by a wealthy idle minority, artists without independent means starve, and among the poor there is neither assistance for the sick nor protection for the abused. Only posthumously does the Prince come to understand that his former happiness was the result of ignorance insulated by unearned wealth, for now that he is raised high on a pedestal, he can see "all the ugliness and all the misery of [his] city" (272). Some students may here be struck by the tale's contemporary relevance: its suggestion that the city's utilitarian materialism, an ideology (masked by various euphemisms) still powerful today, is little better than a doctrine of greedy selfishness that encourages haves to oppress have-nots with impunity.

To test whether students are following Wilde's critique of utilitarianism, one might ask them why the Prince's statue, having been stripped of its gold and jewels by the Swallow for redistribution to the needy, is no longer useful or beautiful to the city's rulers. Most should be able to reply that the statue now fails to demonstrate the equation between happiness and wealth. The instructor might at this point ask the class to think about issues of value raised by the tale. To the city's rulers the statue has no artistic value—that is, no beauty of the kind valued most highly by Wildean aestheticism—for they acknowledge only material value. To them the unadorned statue's worth is equal to not a penny more than the cash value of the metal out of which it is made. Moreover, the city values highly only what is literally superficial—here, the statue's gilding and gems. According to Wildean aestheticism, however, the superficial cannot have true value.

Students might be reminded that in *De Profundis* Wilde reiterates the axiom, "The supreme vice is shallowness. Whatever is realised is right" (1002, 1020). With the words, "As he is no longer beautiful he is no longer useful" (276), the Art Professor at the University pronounces doom on the statue: thereby Wilde evidently wished to show that the late Victorian academy shared and promoted the utterly distorted aesthetics of the age. For true value in the city, as the end of the tale makes clear, lies outcast in the dead Swallow and the broken lead heart of the Prince. Both may be monetarily worthless, but in spiritual terms they are priceless symbols of charity and self-sacrifice for the common good. In Wildean aesthetic terms, both the Prince and the Swallow have transcended the superficiality of their nature and achieved self-realization.

Though Wilde produced only a small body of fairy tales, the best are significant enough to form part of the essential canon of nineteenth-century tales, a fact recognized by two excellent recent fairy-tale anthologies intended for undergraduates (see Hallett and Karasek; Tatar). Instructors in fairy-tale classes who approach the genre chronologically might summarize its nineteenth-century history as follows. From 1812 on, the Grimm Brothers as part of a nationalistic cultural project published what they (often mistakenly) believed to be quintessentially German folk tales that they had transcribed from oral sources. Soon realizing that middle-class parents were adapting their tales to tell to their children, the Grimms in subsequent editions of their collection altered and polished the tales with the developing children's literature market increasingly in mind. Profiting from the Grimms' example, Andersen, who grew up in humble circumstances in the twilight of the Danish oral folk tradition, became world famous after 1835 for fairy tales, specifically intended for children, that he had adapted from traditional sources (e.g., "The Tinderbox" [1835]) or that he had composed himself (e.g., "The Emperor's New Clothes" [1837]). Andersen, strongly influenced by the Romantic movement, frequently included elaborate natural descriptions and autobiographical themes in his tales (e.g., "The Ugly Duckling" [1844]), many of which, unlike typical folk tales, ended unhappily for the protagonist (e.g., "The Little Mermaid" [1836]). Wilde wrote in a nineteenth-century fairy-tale tradition transformed by Andersen. Indeed, Andersen was by far the most important influence on him as a fairy-tale writer (for the secondary influence of Wilde's mother, Speranza, see P. Cohen 73–75; Horan 76–78), and Wilde often paid overt homage to his Danish master. Whenever "The Happy Prince" is taught, some students will notice that one of Andersen's most famous protagonists, the Little Match Girl, makes a guest appearance in Wilde's tale as an embodiment of the plight of the urban poor.

When discussing Andersen's influence on Wilde, fairy-tale critics have tended to emphasize the differences between the writers, often at Andersen's expense. It can be a useful heuristic strategy to ask students who have read first Andersen's, then Wilde's tales to evaluate some critical extracts comparing the two writers. For example, Isobel Murray feels that Wilde "avoids Andersen's cloying moments, and generally transcends him" (10). Responding to Murray, Jack Zipes claims that "Wilde's underlying purpose in writing his tales would be 'subversion' rather than 'transcension.' He clearly wanted to subvert the messages conveyed by Andersen's tales" (*Fairy Tales* 114). Maria Tatar, who believes that Andersen's female protagonists tend to promote the virtues of subservience and "cheerful self-effacement," notes that "despite the superficial resemblance to Andersen's tales, Wilde's stories sound very different ideological chords" (216, 249), for Wilde was a shrewder and more radical social critic than Andersen.

Students are likely to find some truth in such observations, but many will probably also come to feel that the critics insufficiently acknowledge Wilde's considerable positive debt to Andersen. They will have noted that Wilde took from Andersen not only characters and motifs (e.g., the Little Match Girl's cameo in "The Happy Prince" and the many borrowings from "The Little Mermaid" in "The Fisherman and His Soul" [1891]) but also the technique of using the fairy tale as an allegorical vehicle "to express his own inner development in a form free from social scrutiny" (Martin, "Oscar Wilde" 74). Student essays comparing Andersen and Wilde often begin by noting, for example, that without the precedent set by Andersen, Wilde's most powerful fairy tale, "The Nightingale and the Rose," could not have been written.

In courses on the fairy tale, I find that "The Nightingale and the Rose" is best approached after students have familiarized themselves with two tales by Andersen, "The Swineherd" (1842) and "The Nightingale" (1844). In "The Swineherd," an impoverished young prince disguised as a swineherd seeks the hand of an emperor's daughter, to which end he gives her a nightingale that sings "as though all the melodies ever composed lived in its throat" (Hallett and Karasek 238) and a rose from a tree on his father's grave that blooms only once every five years. But she, unable to see the value in a real nightingale and rose (as opposed to costly artificial ones), rejects him. By making her a musical rattle, he eventually purchases from her the kisses she did not give him before, but when her father catches her in the act of embracing a swineherd, he has them both thrown out of his castle. The reader expects the lovers now to rejoice in their union as a compensation for their reduced circumstances, but the quasi-Romantic plot takes a harshly realistic turn. The swineherd-prince rounds on the princess: "I have come to despise you. . . . You did not appreciate the rose or the nightingale, but you could kiss a swineherd for the sake of a toy. Farewell!" (242). Students need not be familiar with "The Happy Prince" to see that there can be no happy ending for the swineherd-prince and the former object of his affection, because the couple's value systems are incompatible. She, a materialist, shares the dominant values of her society; he, a true Romantic, recognizes that the emotional, aesthetic, and spiritual values represented by the nightingale and the rose are far more precious than the kind of gifts that she covets.

From Andersen's tale, Wilde borrowed not only the motifs of the nightingale and rose but also the theme of irreconcilable value systems. Careful readers may conclude that Wilde in "The Nightingale and the Rose" neither transcends nor subverts "The Swineherd." Rather, he intensifies the social critique already strongly evident in Andersen's tale, as if to track, by maintaining a close intertextual relation between his tale and Andersen's, the development of a sociohistorical process. During Andersen's time, Wilde implies, true love was still possible—the swineherd might have found a simple girl of the people who shared his uncorrupted values. By Wilde's time, however, the rampant and pervasive materialism of society has made romantic love impossible.

For Andersen, the emperor's court represents the corrupt values of the wealthy, the swineherd the unspoiled values of the poor. To ask a class why Wilde sets the tale not in the feudal class structure of the traditional fairy tale, as Andersen did, but among the bourgeoisie, the dominant class of the nineteenth century (and today), often provokes an interesting discussion. Many students will have discovered the direct relevance of Wilde's sociological critique to their own lives. The girl is the daughter of a professor, not an emperor; the Student is poor only temporarily. Having given up the impractical nonsense of romantic love and returned to his dusty books, the Student will undoubtedly earn his degree (his study of philosophy was only a utilitarian means to an end), join the professional middle class, and eagerly subscribe to their philistine values. As one of my class once observed with an uneasy smile, once the Student is earning a handsome salary, he will be sure to attract plenty of eligible young philistine women.

In "The Nightingale and the Rose," Wilde made a further significant change from "The Swineherd" by using a bird as protagonist rather than a human lover. But even here he was beholden to Andersen, who often made effective use of a nonhuman protagonist—for example, in such tales as "The Ugly Duckling," "The Daisy" (1838), and "The Butterfly" (1861). But the tale that most clearly influenced Wilde's elevation of the bird to protagonist is Andersen's "The Nightingale." Set in a fairy-tale China, this story concerns an emperor's court of fabulous wealth and beauty that is nevertheless culturally moribund, totally constrained by its own absurd rituals.

The emperor has learned that visitors to China always praise the song of a nightingale who haunts the margins of his palatial gardens. Never having heard of this creature, he orders that it be brought before him. Despite its drab appearance the bird sings so beautifully that the emperor, weeping for joy, has it caged and allowed out only for walks with its legs bound with silk ribbons. But then the emperor is presented with an artificial nightingale, which sings as well as the real one and is studded with costly jewels. This he prefers to the real bird, which, now ignored, leaves the palace. Soon the artificial nightingale breaks down, and the emperor himself falls mortally ill. But just as Death is about to claim the emperor, the real nightingale returns from the gardens and charms Death away by its song. The grateful emperor offers the bird any reward it might choose, but the nightingale refuses a material recompense, wanting only its freedom to roam China so that it can sing to the emperor of both the good and evil it finds there. To the emperor, it confides that it has already been amply rewarded by "the tears from your eyes; and to a poet's heart, those are jewels" (Hallett and Karasek 216).

Instructors will find that a comparison between Andersen's "The Nightingale" and Wilde's "The Nightingale and the Rose" will help classes understand the extent to which Wilde broke with the belated Romanticism dominating his own age. It has been noted that Andersen's tale is "a virtual primer in Romantic imagery and values, with the nightingale itself representing the artist in defiance of the complacent narrow-mindedness of society" (Hallett and Karasek 184). For Andersen, the nightingale as Romantic poet is able to rejuvenate society on certain conditions: that the powers that be are responsive to his song (this is the redemptive significance of the emperor's tears), that they are able to understand that there can be no replacement for an authentic poet, that they learn to value the poet's art more highly than material things, and that they allow the poet complete freedom of expression.

Students will find that there is little here with which Wilde would have disagreed. But though his nightingale is also a Romantic poet, he implies that Romanticism itself is no longer what it was in Andersen's time. Part of that change has been caused by the consolidation of that soul-destroying ideology, utilitarian materialism, so that while Andersen's nightingale had the power to restore life to a dying emperor, the song of Wilde's nightingale only precedes her own futile death. In senior classes, instructors may want to use the nightingale motif to help sketch crucial differences between the mentalities of the earlier and later nineteenth century. If Andersen's singer is a close relative of the "immortal Bird" of Keats's "Ode to a Nightingale" (Abrams et al. 851), then Wilde's fin de siècle nightingale is more akin to "Le rossignol" ("the nightingale") of Paul Verlaine's poem (1866), tearfully going through the motions of "célébrant l'Absente" (48; "praising the Absent One" [49]). For Wilde, indeed, the now permanent Absentee is not the lover but romantic love itself.

There are many other threads to pursue in teaching these two fine fairy tales, which, like Wilde's other short fictions, have still not received sufficient close critical attention. As far as autobiographical themes are concerned, both tales suggest Wilde's conscious identification with the figure of the martyred Christ. (This identification is even more evident in other fairy tales by Wilde, such as "The Selfish Giant" [1888] and "The Young King" [1891].) A specifically homosexual theme is hinted at in the emotional movement of the Swallow away from the (female) Reed toward the Happy Prince (see Martin, "Oscar Wilde" 75–76; Snider 5). A study of the role of the Young Syrian in Wilde's *Salomé* (1894) may well offer an insight into the nature of the Nightingale's feelings for the Student and the meaning of her self-sacrifice. There will never be enough class time available to exhaust the meaning of Wilde's two best tales. If for a term-paper topic students are asked to discuss Hesketh Pearson's pronouncement in 1946—"Like all who have expressed themselves in stories or plays for children, from Hans Andersen to James Barrie, [Wilde] was emotionally undeveloped" (*Life* 141)—they are likely to produce lively essays that will greatly differ in approach but have in common a mixture of amusement and outrage at the impercipience of the biographer.

An Introductory Approach to Teaching Wilde's Comedies

Sos Eltis

Wilde's social comedies—*Lady Windermere's Fan*, *A Woman of No Importance*, *An Ideal Husband*, and *The Importance of Being Earnest*—often prove to be frustratingly recalcitrant texts for students. The carefully crafted witticisms and epigrams, the melodramatic plot lines, and the overriding impression that "style, not sincerity, is the vital thing" (406) can lead students to dismiss the plays either as out-of-date commercial vehicles or as simply trivial (with little awareness of Wilde's complex and ironic use of the term). The following approach is designed to crack the plays open, making students aware of the literary, social, and moral issues that run through them. The aim is to enable students to engage with both their substance and style and the intrinsic links between them and to locate the plays in the wider context of Wilde's writing and the late nineteenth century.

I have found *An Ideal Husband* to be the best starting point for revealing the complexity, subtlety, and depth of Wilde's theater. It centers most overtly on topics of clear relevance both to the late nineteenth century and the modern political world, contains the greatest profusion of contradictory lines of argument, and has a morally unresolved ending. There are also, very usefully, two different film adaptations of the play, directed by Alexander Korda (1948) and Oliver Parker (1999). *An Ideal Husband* is also a good starting point because it has been most persistently underestimated by critics, both at its first performance and in modern academic debate. With its political intrigue, luxurious settings, and convenient but unconvincing plot contrivances, the play is all too easily dismissed as high-class melodrama. Wilde himself complained in 1895 that the critics had misjudged his play. They had, he said, missed "its entire psychology . . . they really thought it was a play about a bracelet. We must educate our critics—we really must educate them" (495 [*The Sketch*]).

My first step is, therefore, to present students with a range of critical responses to the play's first production in January 1895. A number of Victorian critics voiced their confusion at its moral scheme, unsure whether they were meant to rejoice over "the escape of a sinner from the penalty of his sin" or sympathize with a criminal politician because he had "an abnormally good wife" (Rev. of *An Ideal Husband*; Walkley). George Bernard Shaw's response to the play is particularly suggestive, with his emphasis on Wilde's provocative playfulness and Sir Robert's "assertion of the individuality and courage of his wrongdoing as against the mechanical stupidity of his stupidly good wife" ("Two New Plays"). My experience has always been that students also feel a strong urge to resolve their reading of the play toward a coherent and unambiguous conclusion, erasing many of the contradictions and tensions in the text. The variety of responses from Victorian and modern critics, therefore, helps introduce the idea of the play's moral ambiguity.[1] I then use classroom discussion, drawing on students' multiple readings, to draw out some of the inherent problems and highlight conflicting lines of argument. The four most compelling areas of debate can be outlined as follows:

The role of ideals.   Wilde's ubiquitous attacks on puritanism and the danger of a narrowly absolute morality are echoed in the numerous criticisms of moral idealism. Sir Robert Chiltern accuses women of idealizing men rather than loving them as complete, flawed human beings (552–53); Mrs. Cheveley discourses on how the "modern mania for morality" leaves politicians open to blackmail, as the slightest whiff of scandal can ruin a career (528); Lord Goring's final speech to Lady Chiltern urges her to abandon ideals and judgment for love and tolerance (579).

Conversely, idealism is simultaneously positioned as the alternative to cynical careerism and fraud. Sir Robert first rejects Lady Chiltern's political idealism when he is intent on backing the Argentine canal scheme in order to safeguard his reputation (533–34). Mrs. Cheveley is the chief critic of ideals, but her amoral and cynical approach reduces politics to a "clever game" (520) and offers a poor alternative to Lady Chiltern's absolutes. Nor does the play's conclusion resolve the issue. While resolving the action, the endings to Wilde's plays deny a satisfying moral conclusion. *A Woman of No Importance* ends with the triumph of the puritans, Hester and Mrs. Allonby carrying Gerald off to the New World. At the finale of *Lady Windermere's Fan*, husband and wife still do not know the full truth about their morally complex world. *An Ideal Husband* leaves the promulgation of political ideals to continue unchecked. The *Times* lauds Sir Robert's "Unblemished career. . . . Well-known integrity of character" (570) and so helps secure his seat in the cabinet. Similarly, Sir Robert may inveigh against the damaging tendency of women to idealize men, but he finally assures his wife that she is "the white image of all good things, and sin can never touch you" (581).

The criminal as hero.   Sir Robert Chiltern established his fortune by sell-ing a cabinet secret for money and is ready to give his political backing to a fraudulent scheme in order to safeguard his reputation. The play ends with his promotion to the heart of government. Far from being the repentant sinner, Sir Robert castigates his wife for her horror at his crime and rejects Lord Goring's pity, offering instead a defense of his own actions (535–40). "I had fought the century with its own weapons, and won," he declares (538), defending his pur-suit of power and criticizing his society's worship of money over merit. In this respect, *An Ideal Husband* can be linked to "The Canterville Ghost," "Pen, Pencil and Poison," "Lord Arthur Savile's Crime," *The Ballad of Reading Gaol*, and *De Profundis* as a work celebrating the criminal as hero, an oppositional figure to the hypocrisy, puritanism, and vested interests of the establishment.

The figure of Mrs. Cheveley, however, complicates any interpretation of the play as a subversive celebration of criminality. Her fraudulent dealings are closely linked to Sir Robert's, both through linguistic echoes—"it is a swindle. Let us call things by their proper names" (526, 528)—and through her claim to brotherhood: "The same sin binds us" (551). Sir Robert can be aligned with Wilde's praise for disobedience and rebellion in "The Soul of Man under So-cialism" (1176), but only when we ignore the politician's pursuit of wealth and power over others, in direct contradiction of the essay's philosophy. By fighting his century with its own weapons in order to enter the heart of the establish-ment, he is both a critic of society's values and an exponent of them. Whether the play's ending is supposed to be cynical satire on political corruption or a cel-ebration of moral tolerance and charity is a matter for debate.

The dandy as hero.   A number of modern critics have taken Lord Goring to be Wilde's mouthpiece, directly voicing his philosophy (see, e.g., Shewan 177–86; Mikhail, "Self-Revelation"). Goring masterminds the play's resolution, defeating the machinations of Mrs. Cheveley and persuading Lady Chiltern to support her husband's promotion. His speech on the superiority of a man's life to a woman's is placed in the traditional position for a play's moral message and is further validated by the stage direction, *"showing the philosopher that under-lies the dandy"* (578). Yet it is difficult to reconcile this speech with a number of other elements in the play. In advising Lady Chiltern to support her husband's ambition rather than risk losing his love, Lord Goring is directly contradicting Sir Robert's previous speech (552–53), claiming that men's love is unshakable, whereas women's love is conditional. Moreover, by valuing man's intellect and ambition above women's emotion, Goring validates the desire for power, which he had previously rejected, and sets himself in opposition to the values set forth in, for example, "The Soul of Man under Socialism." As a dandy, Goring is ini-tially a figure of ironic detachment and humorous tolerance, but these qualities are forfeited through his involvement in the play's action. As Sir Robert ob-serves to his friend, "You have never been poor" (537), and it is Goring's wealth that enables him to adopt the detached pose of the dandy but also implicates him in society's corruption, in a play where money is tainted.

Women's role and the separate spheres.   Goring's final speech to Lady Chiltern echoes the Victorian doctrine of the separate spheres, whereby the woman was confined to the private, domestic sphere, while the man's intellect and vigor suited him to the coarser influences of the public sphere. Mrs. Cheveley, energetically and unscrupulously involved in political maneuvering, could be viewed as a confirmation of the debasing influence of public life on female virtue.

Yet several elements complicate any reading of the play as advocating separate spheres. Sir Robert first introduces the notion of the discrete worlds of public and private when trying to fend off his wife's concern over his sudden support for the fraudulent canal scheme; he tells her that "public and private life are different things. They have different laws and move on different lines" (533). The concept is, thus, a convenient rhetoric for deflecting his wife's interest away from his criminal dealings. At the beginning of the play, Lady Chiltern is closely involved not only in her husband's career but also in her own political causes. At a meeting of the Women's Liberal Association she discusses "Factory Acts, Female Inspectors, the Eight Hours' Bill" (541), all humane measures designed to protect the rights and welfare of workers, criminals, and children and similar in spirit to the penal reforms for which Wilde campaigned after his imprisonment. The play's demonstration of the dangers of idealism offers a further challenge to the philosophy of separate spheres, a doctrine designed specifically to protect women's absolute purity from the cynical pragmatism of public life. Once again, the play's conclusion leaves it unclear whether Lady Chiltern is retiring to the domestic sphere, leaving her husband to pursue his political ambitions untroubled by moral qualms, or whether she will remain actively involved in his career now that she is more fully educated in the ways of the world.

These and any other issues brought out in discussion are then formulated into questions. For example, Does Sir Robert's entry into the cabinet constitute a happy ending?, or, Does the play finally confirm the wisdom of the doctrine of separate spheres for men and women? The students are divided into groups to debate the issues between themselves and are then invited to summarize the main points of their argument to the rest of the class. Wilde's use of the dialogue form, not only in his plays but also in his essays, makes his work particularly suited to this form of debate and discussion, enabling the students themselves to discover the complex structure of the plays without being pressured to resolve them into neat and final answers.

The two film versions of the play can usefully be introduced at this stage. Both of them powerfully demonstrate the urge to offer definite answers to the uncertainties raised in the play. The interpolated scenes in both films in which Sir Robert delivers his speech to the Commons, condemning the Argentine canal scheme, serve to confirm his true character. His moral probity and newfound determination to serve his country faithfully will render his future political success an unquestioned good. The moral ambiguity of the play is then displaced into other scenes. In the Korda film, the final credits roll on Mrs. Cheveley, clearly unscathed by her disappointment and still networking in the park. Parker's film, though far less faithful to the plot of the original, offers an interesting response to its moral complexities. In the penultimate scene (the last scene shows Lord Goring's marriage to Mabel), Lady Chiltern finally admits she has lied and is warmly congratulated, apparently for her new skill in deception rather than for her belated honesty, so that the film concludes as a comic celebration of moral imperfection.

Looking at details of the play in performance, whether on stage or on film, also emphasizes the role of luxury and wealth in Wilde's representation of late Victorian society. The opening stage direction and subsequent allusions to specific artistic schools indicate Wilde's deployment of visual signifiers in his conception of the play. The rich clothes, expensive tapestry, and luxurious furniture that fill the set are all tainted by the intrinsic connections Wilde reveals between wealth, power, and corruption. A consideration of different interpretations of individual roles can also demonstrate the difficulty of determining inner character from outward appearance or dialogue. The general absence of soliloquy; the constant emphasis on style, attitude, and reputation; the nonnaturalistic patterns of speech; and Wilde's constant questioning of the concept of naturalness all combine to offer an essentially performative interpretation of character. A consideration of appearance and inner psychology, the relation between seeming and being, in the socially rooted world of *An Ideal Husband* also serves as an excellent preparation for considering the even more elusive relation between surface and depth in *The Importance of Being Earnest.*

When we have thus examined the sophisticated crosscurrents running through the play, background reading can then usefully be introduced. The complex mixture of dramatic genres in *An Ideal Husband* and the range of issues and debates contained in it mean that it intersects with a wide range of contemporary texts, from Ibsenite and Shavian problem plays to fashionable comedies of manners, political lectures on gender roles and the female franchise, and accounts of the careers of prominent Victorian politicians. John Ruskin's description of the two separate spheres in his essay "Of Queens' Gardens" is of central relevance, but a variety of other contemporary writing on the role of the sexes and the issue of female suffrage can also prove valuable, a particularly useful anthology being Jane Lewis's *Before the Vote Was Won* (1987). Henrik Ibsen's *Pillars of Society* (1877), George Bernard Shaw's *Widowers' Houses* (1892) and Harley Granville Barker's *The Voysey Inheritance* (1905) can all be compared with *An Ideal Husband,* as plays that launch radical attacks on social corruption, questioning the role of ideals and the difference between morality and legality, while eschewing any neat resolution or closure. Arthur Wing Pinero's *The Cabinet Minister* (1890) offers a more conservative take on similar themes; it is particularly relevant, as Wilde appears to have borrowed a number of Pinero's plot devices and reworked them. Pinero's *The Weaker Sex* (1888) and *The Times*

(1891) also offer firmly conservative views on gender roles and social mobility and provide examples of the more resolved structure of the traditional well-made play. Henry Arthur Jones's *The Case of Rebellious Susan* (1894) is another play on gender roles and the position of women, and its hero, Sir Richard Cato, can be compared with Lord Goring as the play's apparent voice of wisdom. The career of the Irish Nationalist Party leader Charles Stuart Parnell is an informative contemporary example of the realities of reputation and the hypocrisy of the establishment, as, indeed, is Wilde's own career.

Having gained an understanding of the complexities of *An Ideal Husband*, students then have a strong basis from which to approach the other plays. Further class discussion of Wilde's stylistic techniques and of the central issues that run through the plays and how they connect to his other works is then all that is needed for students to undertake independent research.

The relation to Victorian dramatic genres must be considered in any approach to the plays. Just as Wilde's shorter fiction plays with the conventions of fairy tale, children's story, and oral folk tale and *The Picture of Dorian Gray* relates to both gothic horror and the detective story, so each play contains elements of more than one genre, whether in the form of linguistic styles, characterization, or plot devices. Characters even refer self-consciously to the conventions with which the play is negotiating, as when Mrs. Erlynne mockingly reproves her son-in-law for believing that she will behave like other literary fallen women: "I suppose, Windermere, you would like me to retire into a convent, or become a hospital nurse, or something of that kind, as people do in silly modern novels" (460 [*Lady Windermere's Fan*])

Lady Windermere's Fan and *A Woman of No Importance* both revolve around the issue of sexual mores and society's judgment of the fallen woman and so can be located alongside a number of other contemporary plays belonging to this genre: Pinero's *The Profligate* (1884), *The Second Mrs. Tanqueray* (1893), and *The Notorious Mrs. Ebbsmith* (1895); Jones's *Saints and Sinners* (1884), *The Case of Rebellious Susan* (1894), and *Mrs. Dane's Defence* (1900); and Shaw's *Mrs. Warren's Profession* (1893). *The Importance of Being Earnest* was identified as Gilbertian farce by a number of Victorian reviewers, and a reading of the play is informed by comparison with W. S. Gilbert's *Engaged* (1877) and *The Palace of Truth* (1870) and with Pinero's popular farces *The Magistrate* (1885) and *Dandy Dick* (1887). More unsettlingly, Joe Orton's sexually anarchic farces of the 1960s, *Entertaining Mr. Sloane* (1964), *Loot* (1965), and *What the Butler Saw* (1969), can be viewed as a modern development of Wilde's techniques and contain numerous linguistic echoes of the sexually punning subtext of *Earnest*.

The high-flown rhetoric and emotional intensity of the plays flirt with Victorian melodrama, and a reading of at least one or two of these Victorian plays is essential to enable students to locate Wilde's morally ambiguous texts against the overt struggle between virtue and vice that marks this genre. Several useful anthologies of Victorian melodramas are currently in print, including ones edited by George Rowell, by George Taylor, and by Michael Booth (Lights). Much critical debate has hinged on whether Wilde transcends or remains mired in popular dramatic conventions, whether he resolves his plays with a sentimental message of Christian charity or offers stringent criticism of the conflict between individual liberty and the constrictions and limitations of conventional society. The early social problem plays of Shaw and Ibsen, therefore, provide a vital context for locating Wilde in the socially engaged drama of the period. Norbert Kohl's *Oscar Wilde: The Works of a Conformist Rebel*, Kerry Powell's *Oscar Wilde and the Theatre of the 1890s*, and my *Revising Wilde: Society and Subversion in the Plays of Oscar Wilde* are all centrally concerned with the relation between Wilde's plays and those of his contemporaries.

Wilde's style is closely linked to questions of genre and moral interpretation. The highly ornate passages describing jewels, tapestries, and books disturb a moral reading of *Dorian Gray* by inviting aesthetic rather than ethical responses, and the mixture of inverted values, ironic detachment, sentiment, and humor in the narration of "Lord Arthur Savile's Crime" makes it difficult to identify a fixed moral stance or a final moral message. Similarly, the pattern of different styles and registers in the plays serves to complicate audience response, bringing into collision different genre expectations and standards of judgment. So, for example, in act 2 of *A Woman of No Importance*, Mrs. Arbuthnot addresses the father of her illegitimate son in the highly emotional and morally charged language of melodrama, while he responds in the coolly rational language of Ibsenite new drama. The audience is left unsure whether to judge their encounter as that of wronged innocent and aristocratic seducer or as two individuals vying for power in a sexually unequal society. Humor provides a further destabilizing influence, often working against any straightforward moral reading. In *A Woman of No Importance*, all the best jokes go to the decadent characters, while morally upright characters remain uncharismatically humorless. The plays can therefore be linked with Wilde's critical essays and the preface to *Dorian Gray* as part of a wider debate about authorial intentionality and the relation between ethics and aesthetics, morality and art.

The wealth of epigrams, which can easily mislead students (as it did Victorian reviewers) into dismissing the plays as a combination of clever wordplay and clichéd melodrama, also provides a route into the plays' underlying themes. Starting with Wilde's claim to have "summed up all systems in a phrase, and all existence in an epigram" (1017), students can be challenged to unpack the issues contained in any of the plays' paradoxes and witticisms. The question is then raised as to how these witticisms relate to the larger action of the play as a whole—often a highly revealing exercise. *Lady Windermere's Fan*, for example, contains numerous exchanges about the attractiveness of sin, the marketability of female virtue, and social convenience of amorality. *A Woman of No Importance* contains numerous comparisons between the sexes. *The Importance of*

Being Earnest is full of comments on marriage, gender, religion, class, wealth, education, and literature. A number of the paradoxes also destabilize the meaning of individual words and terms, thereby challenging the systems of value that lie behind them, reproducing in miniature his disruption of such orthodox terms of judgment such as "lying," "morbid," "selfish," and "immoral" in his essays. The linguistic gymnastics of *The Importance of Being Earnest* and its punning sexual subtext thus mirror the play's shifting gender roles, and they combine to subvert any stable notion of normality. Linguistic style thus becomes a means of signaling genre, disturbing judgment, concealing and revealing ideas, a weapon deployed quite consciously by both the playwright and his characters.

Armed with an awareness of these issues and left free to explore the complexity and linguistic wealth of Wilde's society plays, students quickly validate his boast that he "took the drama, the most objective form known to art, and made it as personal a mode of expression as the lyric or the sonnet" (1017 [*De Profundis*]). Through the years I have received thoroughly researched papers on a wide range of topics, where students have either worked exclusively on Wilde's plays or analyzed them in the wider context of his writing as a whole. Some of the most fascinating papers have considered paradox and epigram as a means of expressing moral ambiguity, the figure of the dandy as a site of political and artistic protest, the plays as a response to late Victorian social mobility and the politics of class and manners, and the question of identity and selfhood in relation to performance.

Having been shown the interplay between Wilde's dramas and other contemporary theater, students were also confronted with complex issues of originality, authorship, intertextual reference, and the inherent instabilities of audience response and reception. It is the recognition of this ambiguity and uncertainty that seems to be the key to opening up students' responses to Wilde and that makes teaching his work such an unpredictable and challenging pleasure. I rarely set essay titles, preferring to suggest areas for investigation, offering guidance on further reading as the students' interests develop. In fifteen years of teaching Wilde, I have witnessed an extraordinary range of critical responses to his work, in which the one consistent feature was the discovery of new depth, resonance, and possibility.

NOTE

[1] For a convenient anthology of critical responses, see Beckson, *Oscar Wilde: The Critical Heritage.*

A Method for Using Biography in the Teaching of Oscar Wilde's Comedies

Melissa Knox

Oscar Wilde's wonderful comedies can be taught in many ways, but I would argue for the broad use of his biography as a particularly fruitful method. Although biography is sometimes regarded as a stepchild of literary criticism, it pays to consider the two as Siamese twins joined at the heart. Few would challenge the notion that a brief biographic time line gives students ways of identifying with and understanding an author whose times, nationality, interests, efforts, dreams, and life problems might otherwise seem remote. A less accepted use of biography—particularly valuable in teaching Oscar Wilde—involves discovering how stylistic characteristics of an author's literary work as well as the stories the author tells and the characters he creates arise out of personal, private, and sometimes unconscious wishes. A new sense of the literary integration of Wilde's plays—especially of his four comedies—comes from knowledge of the emotional turmoil that plagued Wilde as he was writing them. It can be shown that the emotional integration he strove for as he was writing them supported their literary integration.

Wilde's work is an important entry point to his life, while for many other writers it is the other way around. His interest in self-analysis is well known and often expressed through his characters. "I am the only person in the world I should like to know thoroughly," confesses Mr. Dumby in *Lady Windermere's Fan*, adding, "but I don't see any chance of it just at present" (438). We can take this statement as Wilde's wistful confession. Like any writer, Wilde expressed his desire for self-understanding in his creation of comedy and tragedy. His declaration that he had put his genius into his life but only his talent into his work (Gide, *Oscar Wilde* 16) and his lifelong interest in the relation between his art and his life and in crafting his life as a work of art point to the importance of biographical investigation. Indeed, until the 1960s, almost everything written about him was grounded in biography and biographical speculation.

Ahead of his biographers, Wilde knew to connect literary analysis with biographical and autobiographical discoveries. His critical theory therefore underlies and inspires the approach I recommend. In his criticism, particularly in "The Critic as Artist," he observes that "Shakespeare might have met Rosencrantz and Guildenstern in the white streets of London . . . but Hamlet came out of his soul, and Romeo out of his passion. They were elements of his nature to which he gave visible form" (1142). Connecting literary creativity to confession, he remarks, "Man is least himself when he talks in his own person. Give him a mask, and he will tell you the truth" (1142). Fiction and other nonautobiographical forms brim over with self-revelation. Inventing characters and plots seduces the writer into self-exposure.

Thank you for visiting the Contemporary Jewish Museum.
Your opinions are important to us.

Please take a moment to answer a few questions about
your visit at **thecjm.org/survey**.

You will be entered to win an iPod Nano,
Supporter level membership, or a $150 gas card.*

*You can choose one of the three prizes

Wilde recognizes this phenomenon, asserting that "the more objective a creation appears to be, the more subjective it really is." That is, the less obviously autobiograpical it is, the more biographical knowledge helps unmask features of the author's personality. "The very landscape that Corot looked at was, as he said himself, but a mood of his own mind," Wilde writes, adding, "For out of ourselves we can never pass, nor can there be in creation what in the creator was not" (1142). Naturally the same truth applies to the reader and the literary critic. In the preface to *The Picture of Dorian Gray*, Wilde remarks, "It is the spectator, and not life, that art really mirrors" (17).

In the winter semester of 2002, I had the opportunity of teaching the seminar Oscar Wilde and His World to graduate students at the University of Bielefeld in Westphalia, Germany. All the students were fluent in English and most were German. Their nationality interested me, considering the history of Wilde's reception by German critics. Wilde's biography came in handy as a way to put Wilde in a particular German context and also encourage students who had never read a word of him to discover life patterns in his novel, his letters, his American lecture tour, his short stories, essays, surreal play *Salomé*, comedies, and tragicomic *De Profundis*.

Because most of my students were German and because many had little idea of the legal and emotional aspects of sexual practices in the nineteenth century, I read aloud to them an anecdote about the German reception of Wilde that was told by Wilde's first biographer, Robert Sherard. Sherard related that shortly after Wilde's release from prison, a young German was moved to defy English prudery and censorship of Wilde and to initiate "a Wilde 'boom' in Germany." In about 1899, Dr. Max Meyerfeld, "anxious to study England and the English," came to London. In his lodgings he came across a small volume of Wilde's *Poems in Prose*, read it, felt "absolutely fascinated." The next evening, he relates,

> I was dining out, and being seated at table next to a lady who seemed more than usually intelligent, and who obviously was well informed on English literature, I said to her: "Can you tell me anything about a writer called Oscar Wilde?"

He added that he'd never heard of Wilde before (*Real Oscar Wilde* 309–10). The lady refused to speak to him again, and the next day the host complained to Meyerfeld, asking him what he meant by "insulting a lady at my table." When Meyerfeld expressed his surprise, the host explained that Wilde was in prison and that "it was a great social offence to mention his name." This incident inspired Meyerfeld to buy everything Wilde had written and to introduce him to "[his] countrymen." He was apparently so successful that Wilde was later thought by some young Germans to be a German writer: "Herr Vilde, of course, he's a German. We have always been taught so" (310).

My students' surprise at the degree of ostracism faced by Wilde led to a discussion of reasons for the Victorian rejection of Wilde. I explained Freud's concept of repression as the mind's attempt to banish disturbing thoughts by relegating them to the unconscious. In this context, I suggested, a member of a society was expelled because he forced his contemporaries to perceive aspects of their own sexuality that frightened and enraged them. A teacher can point out that the rejection of Wilde, to the point of making the very utterance of his name a social indiscretion if not a crime, served the psychological purpose of reinstating the repressions that had been so disturbed by Wilde's exhibition of sexual freedom. The teacher might explore other literary analogues—for instance, the story of Phaedra.

The belief of the young German that Wilde was "of course" a German pleased my students, but I pointed out to them that it typifies the reactions of literary critics to the personality of Oscar Wilde, especially in the 1990s. Ever since he entered the ranks of canonized writers—that is, since the 1960s—every critic wants a piece of the action. Depending on whom one reads, Wilde is a gay man championing gay rights, an Irishman struggling against British dominance, an aesthete, a literary critic, and so on. He was all these things, and he was none of them. Something about Wilde, possibly what the Argentinean writer Jorge Luis Borges called his ability to be "nearly always right" (79), inspires us to identify ourselves with him and in that way to begin to understand him.

In my course we focused almost exclusively on the Wilde canon, because I believe that a thorough dose of Wilde—or rather the many different Wildes—offers more possibilities for connecting the man to the artist than can any biography or critical interpretation. Students often remarked on how different *Salomé* sounded from the comedies, how surprising it was to discover the depressed and distraught tone of *De Profundis* after the hilarity of *The Importance of Being Earnest*. I had suggested earlier that one reason Wilde's best-known work is funny is that he was often depressed and made jokes to cheer himself up. Only by reading as much of the canon as could be force-fed in fourteen weeks could students perceive the degree of his despair.

My students knew from guided forays into Steven Marcus and Peter Gay that sexuality in Victorian England was a vibrantly present but seldom openly discussed topic. Even so, they were shocked to see how deeply Wilde's sexuality was resented, and they immediately identified with Wilde as an isolated, rejected revolutionary, a version of him that spoke to them compellingly. Never mind the other Wildes introduced in photographs and in memoirs read aloud in class from various biographers: the foppish dandy, the Wilde with the Neronian curls, the Wilde with the decaying teeth, the Wilde who remarked that women "are a decorative sex. They never have anything to say, but they say it charmingly" (47), who asserted that "women appreciate cruelty, downright cruelty, more than anything else" (82), and who told his wife that he was going golfing when he was going out to find sex in the streets. For my students, as I suspect for many young students, he appeals most strongly as the hero martyr for the good cause of providing freedom to an oppressed sexual minority. For my German students it was the icing on the cake that a German helped popularize Wilde.

Wilde, who in "The Critic as Artist" referred to truth as "one's last mood," would have appreciated this approach (1143). I therefore ask students to relate this definition of truth to other truths emerging when critics project their worldviews on an artist's truths. In class, we read aloud selections illustrating Wilde's idea that in its deep irrationality literary criticism matches the greatest artworks. "The one characteristic of a beautiful form is that one can put into it whatever one wishes, and see in it whatever one chooses to see," Wilde wrote, adding that the "highest Criticism" is "the purest form of personal impression," which is moreover "the record of one's own soul" (1128, 1125). I tell students that I believe that art and literary criticism are confessions as much as they are perceptions, perceptions filtered through the experiences of one's soul. No wonder Wilde remarked that he lived "in terror of not being misunderstood" (1114).

This terror of having himself, his identity, understood, is, I suggest to students, an important element in his work. Each of his comedies deals with characters driven toward a decision about identity. Will Lady Windermere tolerate what looks like her husband's infidelity and remain a good, submissive wife? Or will she boldly rush into an affair with Lord Darlington? Will her mother, Mrs. Erlynne, reveal her true identity or masquerade as a heartless opportunist? In *An Ideal Husband*, will Robert Chiltern sacrifice his identity as a powerful politician preaching morality because he cheated his way to the top? In every comedy except for *The Importance of Being Earnest*, Wilde treats such problems with his customary mix of levity and serious argumentation. We are allowed to see the inner struggles of the characters and to hear a fair amount of moralizing, especially in *A Woman of No Importance*. *The Importance of Being Earnest* remains a different story, in which all conflict becomes an occasion for hilarity. I ask students what the difference in *Earnest* may say about a shift in Wilde's view of his identity.

To enable students to explore the problems of identity, I provide them with a selection of Wilde's confessions (drawn mostly from his letters) and pose the question of how his private agonies shaped his literary expressions. Even with graduate students, I stress the importance of knowing the dates of his letters and other literary works as well as of his birth, death, and important life events, like his marriage, his first meeting with Lord Alfred Douglas, and his prison years. Otherwise, it is not unusual for students to assert that Dorian Gray is based on the character of Alfred Douglas, although Wilde had yet to meet Douglas when he wrote *The Picture of Dorian Gray*.

Wilde's letters are rife with revelation: many a letter confesses a mood, a source of great joy or sorrow, or philosophically reflects on deception and self-deception. Since one cannot expect students to read all 1,562 letters, I select those that concern important stages of his life and especially conflicts and crises he experienced, and I point out that without the letters we would have little idea of the content of these conflicts. Relevant passages include those that expose the extent of turmoil that he routinely experienced. An example is this sad letter postmarked 4 August 1897, written during his first months after being released from prison:

> Nemesis has caught me in her net: to struggle is foolish. Why is it that one runs to one's ruin? Why has destruction such a fascination? Why, when one stands on a pinnacle, *must* one throw oneself down? No one knows, but things are so.   (*Complete Letters* 921)

I remark that the letter reveals an intense battle with himself, a struggle between a desire for self-preservation and a compulsion to throw himself down. Why, I ask students, did Wilde "run," as he writes, to his "ruin," and in what ways do we see him planning it in his comedies? What battle was he fighting and why? Here is an opportunity for the teacher to inform students about Wilde's affinity for battles, starting with a letter of his violently anti-British mother, written in 1850, four years before Oscar was born, which can be compared with his expressed wish to join a battle: "[A]h, this wild rebellious ambitious nature of mine. I wish I could satiate it with Empires, though a St. Helena were the end. . . . Is it my fault if I was born first cousin to Aetna and half-sister to Vesuvius?" (qtd. in Knox, *Oscar Wilde . . . Suicide* 5; his mother's letter, to an unidentified person, is in the University of Reading Library, originally from the archives of Elkin Matthews [TS 557, p. 27]).

Wilde's very name is compiled of heroes of ancient Ireland and warlike family relatives; Oscar Fingal O'Flahertie Wills Wilde is his full appellation. The first two names arose from the mists of Irish legend, and the O'Flaherties are known as "ferocious" in Galway (Knox, *Oscar Wilde . . . Suicide* 4). When as a grown man and highly successful playwright he got into the legal tangle that he knew would send him to prison, his mother told him that if he stayed in London, he would always be her son, but if he left, she would never speak to him again. He bowed to her wishes but remained ever unable to live up to her great expectations for him. One remembers his quip in *The Importance of Being Earnest*: "All women become like their mothers. That is their tragedy. No man does. That's his" (371).

But like son, like mother. She was never sure of the role she wanted for herself. Her comment in the volcanic letter quoted above, that she wishes she could satiate her ambition with empires, "though a St. Helena were the end," shows her ambivalence. To be hero and victor or martyr and victim for the Irish revolutionary cause remained a lifelong dilemma for her and one that she foisted on her son. "No man dies for what he knows to be true," Oscar sighed in "The Portrait of Mr. W. H.," an essay that was all about never being able to decide on identity—specifically, about the identity of Shakespeare's Mr. W. H. He added, "Men die for what they want to be true, for what some terror in their hearts tells them is not true" (349). Like most sons, he would have preferred to be like his father. A distinguished eye-and-ear surgeon, Dr. William Wilde strove for a reclusive life. Although he had many love affairs, he was happiest alone in a room doing research—he wrote copiously about Irish history and folklore, about anthropological findings in the west of Ireland, about medicine. Like his father, Oscar excelled as a student, winning the Berkeley Gold Medal at Trinity College, Dublin, and a Double First in Classics at Oxford. In a letter dated about 30 June 1889, he jests, "What is to become of an indolent hedonist like myself if Socialism and the Church join forces against me? I want to stand apart, and look on, being neither for God nor for his enemies. This, I hope, will be allowed" (*Complete Letters* 403). His own conscience did not allow it.

It is now possible to suggest to students that Wilde's battleground lay between these versions of his identity hinted at in this letter, even though all roads led to martyrdom. By the time he wrote *The Importance of Being Earnest*, he had come to the "pinnacle" that he mentions in his Nemesis letter. He had, in a sense, conquered the English as an Irishman, since he possessed the body as well as the soul of the eminent Marquess of Queensberry's son, Lord Alfred Douglas. Now was the time to gird his loins for a battle that must end in Pyrrhic victory, since its purpose shifted endlessly in his mind. Was it the goal of Irish patriotism or the civil rights of the homosexual? They merged in his mind. In a letter written after prison, he confessed, "A patriot put in prison for loving his country loves his country, and a poet put in prison for loving boys loves boys" (1019).

At this point, having provided much biographical background, one can ask students how they might read between the lines of Wilde's comedies preceding *The Importance of Being Earnest*. I ask them to look for signs of inner turmoil, of questioning his identity. Such a sign is this warning uttered near the end of *Lady Windermere's Fan*: "To shut one's eyes to half of life that one may live securely is as though one blinded oneself that one might walk with more safety in a land of pit and precipice" (463). In the same play, the first of his four comedies, Wilde has Lady Windermere reprove the seductive dandy Lord Darlington with, "I am talking very seriously. You mustn't laugh, I am quite serious" (421). When, shortly thereafter, she again reproves him, saying, "Lord Darlington is trivial," he asks her not to say that, and she asks, "Why do you talk so trivially about life, then?" His reply reveals Wilde's own need to joke about the conflicts that tormented Wilde, since he could not solve them: "Because I think that life is far too important a thing ever to talk seriously about it" (425).

But in *The Importance of Being Earnest*, Wilde does something completely different. His characters show no hint of moral or personal struggle. Could it be because the question of identity no longer troubled him? I ask students to consider the possibility that the comedies are blueprints for his life. The so-called Gribsby episode in *Earnest*, in which a young man is almost carted off to prison for debt, or the scene in *An Ideal Husband* in which a character is threatened with blackmail and treated to a grisly depiction of the newspaper coverage of his trial, sounds like a draft of Wilde's final identity. Wilde might be in earnest about something—martyring himself, for example—but he would no longer agonize about the rightness or wrongness of his decision. He would instead laugh, determinedly laugh, and the more desperate the situation, the louder the laugh.

In an interview published in the *St. James Gazette*, 18 January 1895, Wilde remarked that *An Ideal Husband* had "its philosophy" and defined that philosophy as "[t]hat we should treat all the trivial things of life very seriously, and all the serious things of life with sincere and studied triviality" (*More Letters* 189). In *Earnest*, he strikes the balance he longed for in the other comedies between seriousness and triviality. Identity, his most serious life question, becomes the play's greatest joke: the names of the men are the cause of the women's falling in love with them. The hero is a foundling, has therefore no true identity, having lost both his parents, but this is no tragedy—it is merely an occasion for keeping up appearances, for his future mother-in-law advises him that if he wants to marry her daughter, he must "acquire some relations" (370)—that is, enlist the services of people to parade as his mother and father in order to make him look respectable.

I ask students to consider Wilde's identification with his parents, the battle-ax mother and retiring father. If he felt driven all his life to fill, in an endless round, two opposing roles, then his tragic end makes sense. To be hero and victor—or to be martyr and victim—for the Irish revolution: these were the imperatives he felt had been thrust upon him by his mother. Only while writing *The Importance of Being Earnest* did he give up the idea that he might find some compromise that would allow him to go on living without provoking a disaster. Like the protagonist of an ancient Greek drama, he embraces the inevitability of a tragic end. Only his masterpiece, *Earnest*, boasts uninterrupted laughter, avoiding descents into shrill morality that had marred his earlier plays (e.g., when Hester, the puritan of *A Woman of No Importance* and named after Hawthorne's Hester Prynne in *The Scarlet Letter*, complains about the "shallow, selfish, foolish . . . wrong" English society [483]).

The Importance of Being Earnest gains much of its artistic integrity from the emotional message that it conveys—namely, that one should laugh about, not try to escape from, torturing uncertainty. Wilde was in earnest about enjoying every moment on the way to his execution, like the man in the bad joke who glances at the gallows as he is being led to them on a Monday morning and quips, "It looks like the beginning of a bad week." The courage and confidence with which Wilde delivers this message enter the veins of his audience, and it is this gift of his that raises his final comedy to the rank of masterpiece.

Wilde criticism of the 1990s is all about Wilde's identity, as I mentioned earlier. More specifically, it reflects a need to pin down the identity of this notoriously mercurial figure. What has not been discussed much in literary criticism is how Wilde's moods and concerns about his identity influenced the questions that biographers and literary critics have always been moved to ask about Wilde. His uncertainties plague us all. In a sense there seems little change between the endless Victorian and early-twentieth-century debates about whether Wilde was sincere and the tendency of critics of the last few decades to question what his true identity was. Both these approaches are the same that Wilde took to the serious study of himself, a study made bearable by his trivialities. He endlessly questioned whether he was sincere, and he endlessly revised his identity. He managed to hide his suffering in public but exhibited it in the tragic figures of his first three comedies—Mrs. Erlynne, Mrs. Arbuthnot, Robert Chiltern—while nudging his audience to fall into uncertainty about whether these figures are serious and sincere or only clowns and opportunists. Afraid that the audience might recognize a laugh as a momentary release from the abyss of despair, he laughed harder, laughing, in fact, to the bitter end. He fought his last battle on his deathbed. Flat on his back, knowing he was about to expire, he announced, "My wallpaper and I are fighting a duel to the death. One or the other of us has got to go" (Ellmann, *Oscar Wilde* 546).

APPENDIX:
THREE QUESTIONS TO ASK STUDENTS

Students might be asked the following questions based on confessional remarks made by Wilde in letters.

1. Letter written in the week ending 3 March 1877 to William Ward (*Complete Letters* 38–40)

What does this attitude of self-doubt reveal about Wilde's ways of thinking in general? Ask students what religion means to Wilde. Invite them to investigate the relation between his remarks about religion and his self-doubt. Call attention to his "dreams" of visiting Cardinal Newman, converting to Catholicism, enjoying "quiet and peace . . . in my soul" and to his confession in the next breath: "I need not say . . . that I shift with every breath of thought and am weaker and more self-deceiving than ever." Speculate—and seek evidence for—what made him experience doubt the most. Examine characters in his plays who express doubt. The teacher can provide examples. To give one example: Mr. Dumby, in *Lady Windermere's Fan*, has the following conversation with Lady Plymdale:

DUMBY.	What a mystery you are!
LADY PLYMDALE (*looking at him*).	I wish *you* were!
DUMBY.	I am—to myself. I am the only person in the world I should like to know thoroughly; but I don't see any chance of it just at present. (438)

2. Letter to H. C. Marriller, postmarked 12 December 1885 (*Complete Letters* 272)

Our most fiery moments of ecstasy are merely shadows of what somewhere else we have felt, or of what we long someday to feel. And, strangely enough, what comes of all this is a curious mixture of ardour and of indifference. I myself would sacrifice everything for a new experience, and I know there is no such thing as a new experience at all. I think I would more readily die for what I do not believe in than for what I hold to be true. I would go to the stake for a sensation and be a sceptic to the last! Only one thing remains infinitely fascinating to me, the mystery of moods. To be master of these moods is exquisite, to be mastered by them more exquisite still. Sometimes I think that the artistic life is a long and lovely suicide, and am not sorry that this is so.

What do Wilde's remarks on ecstasy suggest about his knowledge of his own mind and experiences, about the ways in which the unconscious mind works generally, and about the influence of childhood and childhood sexuality on adult experiences and sexual desires? (Here the teacher may also connect Wordsworth's assertion that the "Child is father of the Man" and Thomas Jefferson's confession in a letter that "I find as I grow older, that I love those most whom I loved first" with Freud's idea that childhood experience is the blueprint for adult romantic and sexual expectations). How would you interpret Wilde's description of the artistic life as "a long and lovely suicide"?

3. Letter to Philip Houghton, probably in February, 1894: "Your letter has deeply moved me. To the world I seem, by intention on my part, a dilettante and a dandy merely—it is not wise to show one's heart to the world—and as seriousness of manner is the disguise of the fool, folly in its exquisite modes of triviality and indifference and lack of care is the robe of the wise man. In so vulgar an age as this we all need masks" (*Complete Letters* 586).

What has "deeply moved" Wilde? How does he mask himself? Use this letter as a springboard to a discussion of how he had to mask and at the same time reveal his identities (as a gay man, as an Irishman, as a would-be lord, as a hero, as a martyr) to the world.

Teaching Melodrama, Modernity, and Postmodernity in *Lady Windermere's Fan*

Francesca Coppa

I usually teach the plays of Oscar Wilde in courses with the word *modern* in the title; most often, the class is Modern Drama. Certainly, *modern* is a word that Wilde himself was fond of using; many of his best epigrams are written on the subject of "modern life" or "modern culture" or some other "modern mania." And yet, situating his plays in dramatic modernity can be pedagogically difficult. By the time Wilde appears on my syllabus, I've already described the nineteenth-century theater against which the modern theater defines itself. I've explained the characteristics of the well-made play and the melodrama: the clear typology of characters (hero, villain, and ingenue), the use of contrivances to keep the plot moving (letters, mislaid papers, the sudden appearance and disappearance of key props and people), the presence of characters in disguise, the reliance on dramatic irony, the certainty of poetic justice. We've probably already studied plays by Henrik Ibsen and August Strindberg and perhaps George Bernard Shaw, and discussed the emerging dramatic theories of realism and naturalism. Then we turn our attention to an Oscar Wilde play—and lo and behold, his plays look more like their nineteenth-century counterparts than like the other modern plays in the course. Students pick up on his nineteenth-century construction immediately, though they tend to use words like "gimmicky" and "flat" to describe what they're seeing. And nowhere are Wilde's nineteenth-century roots more evident than in his first major stage play, *Lady Windermere's Fan*. Consequently, I've found it necessary to teach Wilde as melodramatist, modernist, and postmodernist all at once. His work defies simple categorizations; or, rather, it embodies multiple theoretical orientations simultaneously.

Without question, Wilde considered himself a modern playwright, and like most other playwrights of his era, he was deeply influenced by the works of Ibsen. Ibsen's impact in Britain dates from about 1889, the year when both *A Doll House* and *Pillars of Society* premiered in London. The English stage had long been abandoned as a venue for serious work, but in Ibsen's wake, writing for the theater became not only profitable (mainly as a result of new copyright laws) but also intellectually respectable, a heady combination that drew many former novelists, essayists, and poets into writing for the stage.

The drama these writers produced was therefore strongly influenced by the Ibsenite model, which managed to be simultaneously realist and poetic. On the one hand, Ibsen holds the proverbial mirror up to life, depicting recognizable people struggling with familiar personal, psychological, and social problems; on the other hand, he elevates these people and problems to the extent to which they become archetypal, mythical, emblematic, and highly dramatic. Nora

Helmer is both a specific middle-class lady of her day with highly individuated habits and an everywoman whose articulation of dissatisfaction rocked an entire class. Hedda Gabler is both an illustrative human psyche incapable of coping with the restrictions of the female role and a tragic character as unique and complex as Hamlet. It was, in fact, as a maker of tragedy that Ibsen impressed Wilde, who told a friend that he admired *Hedda Gabler* because he "felt pity and terror, as though the play had been Greek" (Powell, *Oscar Wilde* 79). The nineteenth century had failed to produce credible tragedy; remove tragedy's cruel indifference to fate, its complexity of situation and motive, its sense of pathos and catharsis, and melodrama was what you had left. But modern drama's complex characterizations, socially taboo issues, and unpleasant or unfair endings provided fertile ground for tragedy. As a classicist, Wilde was attracted to the epic-poetic side of the modern drama movement (as opposed to Shaw, who was impressed by the realist-political strain and replicated Ibsen's issue-oriented discussions in his own work). Wilde therefore believed that to be modern was to be both poetic and highly tragic, and from this vantage point, his most obviously modern play is *Salomé.*

Despite not being realist, *Salomé* fits easily enough in the modern drama tradition, although it is rarely taught in modern drama courses. William Archer described the character of Salomé as "an oriental Hedda Gabler" (Powell, *Oscar Wilde* 79), and students can be made to see, as Wilde's contemporaries did, the clear continuities between Wilde's *Salomé* and works of modern drama such as *Hedda Gabler* and Strindberg's *Miss Julie*. For one thing, these plays all focus on strong, psychologically complex women who, as Kerry Powell notes, "represented a total contradiction of the serene purity with which the Victorian male endowed his feminine ideal" (79). While the lush biblical setting of Wilde's play is very far indeed from the middle-class drawing room associated with modern drama and the highly poetic language a far cry from modern drama's sensible discussions, Wilde's portrait of a woman crazed by sexual desire managed to evoke both ancient Greek tragedy and the emergent science of psychology. In modern drama, psychology replaces fate as the force determining a character's dramatic arc. As if to seal *Salome's* place as Wilde's most modern and intellectually daring work, the play was banned in England by the Lord Chamberlain's office, giving it a nearly unbeatable avant-garde cachet.

This is not to say that Wilde didn't experiment with the more conventional side of dramatic modernism. *An Ideal Husband* is written in modernism's more typical realist-political vein and contains the familiar issue-based conversation. I frequently teach *An Ideal Husband* in a unit that includes Ibsen's *A Doll House*, Strindberg's *The Father*, and Shaw's *Candida*, and students have no problem recognizing that Strindberg, Shaw, and Wilde each rewrite Ibsen in ways that illuminate their own preoccupations. All three playwrights can be seen to be arguing, for very different reasons, that the male is the doll in the doll house. For Strindberg, that argument expresses a fear of female control; for Shaw, it illuminates a labor relationship in which the master of the household lives in ignorance of the extent to which his mastery depends on his wife's service. In *An Ideal Husband*, Wilde responds to Ibsen by having Sir Robert Chiltern demand of his feminist wife, "Why can't you women love us, faults and all?" (552). This question responds to Nora in *A Doll House*, whose abandonment of her home follows hard on the realization that her husband is not the man she thought he was. More generally, in *An Ideal Husband* Wilde can be seen to be arguing against equalizing standards of morality and behavior between the genders. As Lord Goring notes in the speech most likely to infuriate students, "A man's life is of more value than a woman's. It has larger issues, wider scope, greater ambitions" (579). Wilde also implies that if the double standard must be eradicated, then both men and women should be held to the (lower) male standard rather than the (higher) female standard, a reversal of the then-current feminist position.

An Ideal Husband is Wilde's most obviously realist play, but it too fails to conceal its melodramatic underpinnings. Despite its modern conversation about moral standards, the plot ultimately turns on a stolen letter and the device of a mysterious brooch turned bracelet. Similarly, the titular fan in *Lady Windermere's Fan* is introduced to the audience with all the subtlety of a sledgehammer:

> LORD DARLINGTON.   And what a wonderful fan! May I look at it?
> LADY WINDERMERE.   Do. Pretty, isn't it? It's got my name on it, and everything.   (421)

Students are likely to find such exchanges laughably crude. They can hear the thud of a plot point's being dropped: the fan, and the mark of the owner's name on it, will surely be significant to the play's action. And this is just the first of *Lady Windermere's* contrivances. The farewell letter Lady Windermere writes to her husband, Lady Erlynne's secret identity as Lady Windermere's mother, the scene in Lord Darlington's rooms where both women hide behind conveniently placed draperies—all are staples of nineteenth-century (melo)dramatic construction. Students who have been trained to look for signs of modernity in drama—realist or naturalist details, an emphasis on setting and set design as indicators of characterization, depictions of a variety of social classes, complicated characterological psychologies, a focus on social issues—may well be disappointed with Wilde's trivial aristocrats, overt exposition, and blatant manipulation of props.

Yet it is precisely Wilde's use of these conventions in *Lady Windermere's Fan* that marks it as a modern, even a postmodern, play. Wilde uses the nineteenth-century devices to draw a sharp contrast between the melodramatic and modern sections of his play, and in doing so he is following a direct Ibsenite precedent. Ibsen employs a number of melodramatic conventions in *A Doll House*, seeming to present the audience with a clear-cut hero, villain, and ingenue and building suspense by means of that old Victorian standard, the blackmailer's letter. But these melodramatic devices ultimately demonstrate Nora's highly naive vision of the world, and they abruptly disappear from the play when her perception changes. Ibsen shows us that Nora's own narrative values are highly melodramatic; in many ways, her problems stem from the fact that her expectations seem to have been derived from the popular stage. The story Nora plots for herself is the sheerest melodrama: she fantasizes that when her husband discovers she has committed fraud to save him, he will spontaneously confess to the crime, whereupon she will drown herself. (Compare this story with the one Nora's friend Christine tells, that of a marriage based on necessity, an early widowhood, and having to support an invalid mother and two brothers.) Over the course of *A Doll House*, the melodramatic conventions break down: the play's ostensible villain, Krogstad, is persuaded to be merciful, whereas the play's ostensible hero, Torvald, looks out for himself. Nora therefore learns that the real world does not run according to the rules of poetic justice. At that point, the play sheds its melodramatic skin and becomes modern—becomes, in fact, a play that criticizes the melodramatic theater for miseducating its audience.

Like Ibsen's Nora, Wilde's Lady Windermere develops a more complex, modern understanding of the world over the course of the play. A self-described puritan, Lady Windermere believes in hard-and-fast moral rules that permit neither compromise nor forgiveness; in other words, her morality is as flat and Victorian as the dialogue introducing her famous fan. Wilde expertly orchestrates a melodramatic plot in which she threatens to strike Mrs. Erlynne, who she believes to be her husband's mistress, with her fan, ignorant of the fact that this woman is actually her mother. The blow is ultimately avoided, but a distraught Lady Windermere flees to another man's apartment as a way of rejecting her husband and his presumed infidelity, thus precisely replicating the circumstances that brought about her mother's fall from grace. Perhaps unsurprisingly, Mrs. Erlynne is the first to appreciate the gravity of Lady Windermere's mistake and determines that her daughter should not share her fate. Mrs. Erlynne saves her daughter by publicly sacrificing what little reputation she has left, which also means giving up all hope of future social redemption. So far, Wilde is playing straightforwardly from the melodramatist's handbook: the fallen mother in disguise has sacrificed herself to save her innocent daughter from the clutches of a libertine. In fact, Mrs. Erlynne's sacrifice provides the highly theatrical third-act curtain. Students can easily compare this scene with similar ones in nineteenth-century plays like Arthur Wing Pinero's *The Second Mrs. Tanqueray*.

But at this point, Wilde diverges from the familiar script just as sharply as Ibsen does at the end of *A Doll House*. When Torvald refuses to play the role that Nora has scripted for him, she abruptly calls her own marital performance to a halt, stopping the Victorian play in progress and questioning its theory and direction, its underlining assumptions. Eventually she abandons the stage for the real world, slamming the door on an entire theatrical genre. Mrs. Erlynne has a similar show-stopping moment as she, too, abruptly refuses her role in the drama. "Oh, don't imagine I am going to have a pathetic scene with her, weep on her neck and tell her who I am, and all that kind of thing," she scoffs. "I have no ambition to play the part of a mother" (459). "That kind of thing," followed shortly by a scene of breast-beating repentance, is precisely what the audience would have been anticipating. But, as Mrs. Erlynne tells us, "Repentance is quite out of date. And besides, if a woman really repents, she has to go to a bad dressmaker, otherwise no one believes in her. And nothing in the world would induce me to do that" (460).

Lady Windermere's Fan is notably lacking in poetic justice: not only does Lady Windermere escape the consequences of her mistake but so does Mrs. Erlynne. Wilde was obviously interested in the notion of poetic justice and wrote one of his best epigrams on the subject: "The good ended happily, and the bad unhappily. That is what Fiction means" (376). Certainly, he believed that poetic justice was a fiction, and in *Lady Windermere's Fan* he makes this view explicit by having Mrs. Erlynne reject the idea of redeeming herself through martyrdom:

> I suppose . . . you would like me to retire into a convent, or become a hospital nurse, or something of that kind, as people do in silly modern novels. That is stupid of you . . . in real life we don't do such things—not as long as we have any good looks left, at any rate.   (460)

Refusing the convent, Mrs. Erlynne manages to snag herself a rich husband literally on her way out the door, thus avoiding her typical theatrical destiny. As Powell notes:

> Shooting herself or contracting a disease is sometimes the only expiation a repentant mother can make, although in some cases she is permitted to work out her shame as a nurse or in a convent or even to rejoin her family after a scene of self-abasement before the wronged husband and child.
>   (*Oscar Wilde* 18)

Wilde further teases his audience by denying his play an obligatory scene—one of the key components of the well-made play—in which Lady Windermere learns the secret of Mrs. Erlynne's identity. The satisfactions of a melodramatic reunion scene are sacrificed to Mrs. Erlynne's more realistic desire to escape the situation rich and unencumbered by her daughter and grandchild—hardly the typical melodramatic ending for a woman with a past!

The only hint we get that Wilde might be preparing to diverge from the melodramatic script is the characters' ongoing preoccupation with their social roles, which foreshadows Mrs. Erlynne's rejection of "the part of a mother." I generally assign homework or in-class writing asking students to identify moments in which Wilde's characters show themselves to be performers; these writings then become the basis for discussion. "[O]n several occasions after I was first married," the Duchess of Berwick earnestly explains, "I had to pretend to be very ill, and was obliged to drink the most unpleasant mineral waters, merely to get Berwick out of town" (427). Mrs. Erlynne dismisses a photograph of her younger self by noting, "Dark hair and an innocent expression were the fashion then" (459). In this context, students see that the performative nature of human identity is one of the reasons that one should not make facile judgments about people's natures. "I don't think now that people can be divided into the good and the bad as though they were two separate races or creations," Lady Windermere realizes (456). The lesson is partly, as in Ibsen, a metatheatrical one: honesty, integrity, reputation, and honor can literally be staged. Part of what Wilde realized is that melodrama falls apart when the underlying certainties—that one can distinguish good from bad, reality from pretense, truth from fiction—stop being certain.

This emphasis on performance is one of the reasons that Wilde's plays are marked not only as modern but also as postmodern. Modernity, like repentance, is quite out-of-date, and Wilde's modern message, that one should refuse to conform to the rules of morality and society because the worst that can happen is social exile to the Continent, reads very differently in the wake of his arrest, trial, prison sentence, exile, and early death. If his plays tend to begin in melodrama and end in modernity, Wilde's very modern life was forced to conform to the rules of melodrama, including the literary breast-beating of *De Profundis* and his death in Paris in the fall of 1900.

In the postmodern age, it is the conjunction of melodramatic and modern styles that makes Wilde's work seem contemporary. Most good introductory essays on postmodernism will introduce students to terms like *pastiche, fragmentation,* and *collage,* and Wilde's work exemplifies these techniques. Wilde was a magpie, a mimic, some would even say a plagiarist; after all, the Oxford Union in 1881 rejected his first collection of poems, claiming that they were "for the most part not by their putative father at all, but by a number of better-known and more deservedly reputed authors" (Ellmann, *Oscar Wilde* 146). But while Wilde's poems are rarely taught, originality is no longer one of the primary criteria of greatness in the postmodern world of *Rosencrantz and Guildenstern Are Dead* or *Moulin Rouge.* Rather than label Wilde a plagiarist, we might see him as Michel de Certeau's poacher or Henry Jenkins's fan.[1]

For Certeau, a poacher is one who (in Jenkins's words) makes "an impertinent raid on the literary preserve that takes away only those things that are useful or pleasurable to the reader" (*Textual Poachers* 24). Wilde's work fits this definition in several ways. First, the very idea of poaching (which Jenkins preserves in the idea of the interpretive raid) emphasizes the degree to which both theorists see reading as a battle over cultural geography or what we might more evocatively call intellectual property.[2] The battle that Certeau describes dovetails nicely with recent postcolonial work on Wilde, which argues that as an Irishman he attempted to raid the intellectual, literary, and theatrical preserves of the dominant colonial power and to establish a position of cultural authority in it. Moreover, Wilde frequently uses (note that a nonpostmodernist would say "misuses") culture in hedonistic ways, to provide pleasure for his audience. For instance, he preserves many of the pleasures of melodrama while losing the strict morality on which it was built.

Jenkins, building on Certeau, defines a fan as one whose "response [to an art-work] typically involves not simply fascination or adoration but also frustration and antagonism, and it is the combination of the two responses which motivates their active engagement with the media" (*Textual Poachers* 23). In other words, despite the idea of a fan as a slavering devotee of a particular work, a fan may also be a highly analytic critic of that work.[3] While the fusion of adoration and analysis may seem a paradox, it is precisely the sort of paradox that is character-istic of postmodernism: the ability to sustain at the same time differing and pos-sibly even contradictory attitudes in a work.

All Wilde's plays embody this conflicting attitude, because Wilde is simulta-neously a lover and a critic of the melodrama (or, in Jenkins's terms, he is a fan). He clearly adores the cheap devices and grand speeches while distancing him-self from them both as a serious artist and a modern man. This bifurcated atti-tude toward melodrama—a genre that still dominates film and television—is familiar to many of our students (as expressed in statements like, "It's just tele-vision, but I love it," "It's cheesy, but I can't miss an episode"). A student in one of my drama courses at Muhlenberg College articulated Wilde's contradictory postmodern attitude toward melodrama in *The Importance of Being Earnest* by means of a contemporary parallel. "It's like *Scream*," he said excitedly, referring to the 1996 Wes Craven horror film. "It actually *is* the thing it's parodying."[4] This comparison, I thought, was particularly apt: *Scream* is a fully functioning horror movie that uses all the conventions of the genre even as it makes the spectator aware of these conventions and even often appears to be sending them up. But *Scream* is not a parody of horror films in the sense that *Airplane!* is a parody of airplane disaster movies. Rather, *Scream* is invested in frighten-ing its audience, and has itself inspired two parodies: *Scary Movie* and *Shriek If You Know What I Did Last Friday the Thirteenth*, both of which exhibit much less complex attitudes toward the source material.

Like *Scream*, *Lady Windermere's Fan* is aware of itself as belonging to a pop-ular genre defined by rules with which its (fannish) audience is familiar. In this way, Wilde's plays are structured precisely like his famous epigrams, and both are good precisely to the extent to which they demonstrate cleverness within that preexisting and recognizable structure. An epigram generally rewrites a proverb, that popular formulation of common wisdom that represents the voice of the people, the unknown and unknowable "they" of "As they say. . . ." They say, "Marriages are made in heaven," but Wilde instructs us, "Divorces are made in heaven" (359). The phrase is funny because it reverses a formulation already familiar to us. A more contemporary epigrammist, the comedian Roseanne Barr, tells us, "The fastest way to a man's heart is through his chest," and our pleasure is dependent on our already having absorbed the underlying cliché. A person who isn't familiar with that cliché, or thinks it so outmoded as to be irrelevant, is not the ideal audience for the epigram. Barr's epigram requires a certain level of investment in the original phrase, so that the reader experiences it as a weapon to be used against common, sexist wisdom about gender roles.

Similarly, an appreciation of Wilde's epigrams requires an investment in the form if not the content of the proverb. I used to be surprised that students sometimes reacted to Wilde's epigrams not with laughter but with resentment, as if he were lecturing them—and then I realized that, yes, of course he was lecturing them, because the forms of epigram and proverb are essentially indistinguishable. His epigrams may reverse the proverb's content, but he remains invested in the proverb's authoritative stance. As Regina Gagnier has so perceptively noted:

> [T]he astonishing thing about [Wilde's] wit is not that he could always find the right word to substitute for the key term of the platitude, but rather that he knew the platitudes so well to begin with. His mind was stocked with commonplaces, and these seem to have been there for the sole purpose of their subversion. The situation is one in which an outsider has to a stunning degree taken upon himself the reflective apparatus to mock the group on, and with, its own terms. The use of such tactics endears the speaker to the group the moment he mocks it. This is the technique of ironic reference: the use of popular symbiology by its critics in order to be both commercially competitive and critical.   (*Idylls* 7–8)

The technique of ironic reference Gagnier here ascribes to Wilde is familiar to our students—in fact, this kind of apolitical irony is the primary attitude of the culture they know best. They have been raised on a series of cultural products carefully designed to have things every which way[5] or, in Gagnier's phrase, "to be both commercially competitive and critical." Effectively teaching Wilde's plays, therefore, is often a matter of helping them map Wilde's literary moves onto their own postmodern experience, to train them to see the ways in which Wilde embraces both the proverb and the epigram, the oral and the written, the popular and highbrow, genre fiction and tragedy, and the melodramatic and the modern—all the ways in which he is a postmodern poacher of texts and, in more ways than one, Lady Windermere's fan.

NOTES

[1] An excellent excerpting of the key chapter of Jenkins's *Textual Poachers* can be found in his "Television Fans."

[2] Arguably, this battle between owners and poachers, at the very center of cultural production in today's postmodern world, has never been more heated. Consider the fact that the Disney Corporation, which has made much of its fortune by remaking fairy tales that were in the public domain, is the chief architect of a series of laws aimed to prevent these derivative works from ever passing back to the public. Wilde's works bear, in this sense, the mark of their moment in copyright history. As a commercial playwright, he would never have been as attracted to the stage if there hadn't been new copyright laws that made writing plays profitable, and yet his work certainly bears the stamp of an older literary culture in which rampant theatrical theft—particularly across national borders,

as theft between England and France or England and America was a routine matter—was the norm. Ten years earlier, he wouldn't have been interested in the stage; ten years later, he wouldn't have been able to write the same kind of blatantly derivative work.

[3] In this way, fans are members of a kind of grass-roots academy, critics who have developed a high degree of expertise in areas not currently considered worthy of the effort: *Star Trek*, baseball statistics, punk rock, and so on.

[4] The student was Steve Soroka, and the course was Modern Drama (fall semester, 2000).

[5] An example is a popular film like the Sandra Bullock vehicle *Miss Congeniality* (2000), which manages to appeal simultaneously to women and men, feminists and beauty queen contestants. The titular character's irony (as she mocks and yet becomes part of the pageant culture) may be harder for students to detect than the more blatant ironies of, say, *Moulin Rouge* (2001), which so unproblematically resuscitates all the melodramatic conventions of the nineteenth century, including the tubercular woman with a past who must tragically die for her sexual crimes. Or, as the film's Web site blandly put it: "GENERAL SURGEON'S WARNING: Never fall in love with a woman who sells herself, it always ends bad."

Wilde about Ibsen:
The Fusion of Dramatic Modes
in *A Woman of No Importance*

Kirsten Shepherd-Barr

A Woman of No Importance presents an exceptionally fine opportunity to teach students about a range of topics, from modes of drama and important developments in theater history to the specifics of Wilde's playwriting techniques. The Wilde play most students encounter is *The Importance of Being Earnest*, so *A Woman of No Importance* is new to them and shows Wilde in more experimental mode, before the superrefined achievement of the later play.

It may surprise students familiar only with *Earnest* that Wilde's plays are "essentially heavy social dramas disguised as comedies by a great deal of elegance and more wit" (M. Booth, *Theatre* 177). We still tend to think of his plays as light and effervescent, not heavy and serious, and of him as decadent aesthete more than social reformer. *A Woman of No Importance* is the ideal Wilde play to teach precisely because of the "schizophrenic" mixing of these two very disparate roles (Kaplan and Stowell 21). It offers the trademark epigrammatic wit of *Earnest* while also exposing the ways in which Wilde was juggling a range of dramaturgical influences as he developed his own style.

One of the joys of teaching Wilde these days is the wealth of scholarship on this once-neglected author. Not only is *A Woman of No Importance* a delight for the witty banter of most of its dialogue, but also it offers teachers superb resources to draw on for secondary readings. Katharine Worth's *Oscar Wilde* offered one of the first positive reassessments of this play, and the relevant chapter of her book should be required reading. Peter Raby's introduction to the Oxford World's Classics edition of Wilde's comedies should also be required, as should the relevant sections of his *Cambridge Companion to Oscar Wilde*. Some teachers may indeed prefer to use Raby's edition of the play because of his superb notes to the text. Kerry Powell's *Oscar Wilde and the Theatre of the 1890s* is invaluable, especially the chapters on the society plays and "Wilde and Ibsen." Sos Eltis's *Revising Wilde* is indispensable for teaching any of Wilde's plays, and it reflects the new scholarship on Wilde as a socially engaged, often radically progressive playwright. For graduate courses, one can assign these books in their entirety if there is time; at the very least, for both graduates and undergraduates, Eltis's chapter on *A Woman of No Importance* is essential for an understanding of the play's themes and theatricality, especially its radical treatment of women, and for crystal-clear textual analysis of the dialogue as well as insight into Wilde's dramaturgical strategies.

In my department (English), I teach modern drama and theater history at all levels: from a basic survey of Western drama (the Greeks to the present) for nonmajors to upper-level undergraduate courses in modern drama (Ibsen to

Pinter, Women Playwrights, British Drama) to graduate courses like Modern British Drama and Modern American Drama. *A Woman of No Importance* works well at all these levels, especially in courses that include Ibsen, who precedes Wilde on the syllabus (if one is following a generally chronological plan) and thus lays the groundwork for the kind of contextual analysis offered here. In Modern British Drama, where we read three of Wilde's plays (usually *A Woman of No Importance, The Importance of Being Earnest,* and *An Ideal Husband*), the play is central to understanding the techniques and influences Wilde was adapting as he developed a style that would fuse wit and elegance with deep social commentary. It is useful to provide a bibliography showing the explosion of Wilde criticism since about 1970.

The following suggestions are aimed at all kinds of levels and schedules, whether you can devote two class sessions to the play or more and regardless of whether this is the only Wilde play you have time for. Using your own selections from the play, you can condense or expand the suggestions. Many of the readings suggested here are of a suitable length to be put on electronic reserve, which makes them readily accessible for students and allows instructors to use them in a more versatile way than handouts—for example, by having students write discussion topics based on readings that can then be distributed and discussed by electronic discussion list or individual e-mail messages. Whatever the method used, I suggest having students apply their understanding of the readings to close analysis of the text of the play. Their discussion questions should reflect a testing of the ideas in the readings against the text itself, using specific examples.

Placing the Play in the Context of Theater History

Wilde liked to boast that act 1 of *A Woman of No Importance* was perfect because it had "absolutely no action at all" (Raby, Introduction xvi). This delightfully paradoxical claim helps direct students to think about staging and performance instead of reading the play purely as a literary text. Teaching the play as a part of theater history, and as a script for performance, brings its theatricality directly into focus as students read and discuss it from a practical standpoint. Theater reviews are especially helpful for reading the play as a script. A selection of reviews of the original production can be found in Karl Beckson's *Oscar Wilde: The Critical Heritage* (144–63), while John Stokes's *Oscar Wilde: Myths, Miracles, and Imitations* provides a fascinating analysis of reviews of revivals of *A Woman of No Importance* (157–61).

It can also be fun and illuminating to show students excerpts from contemporary accounts of the nineteenth-century stage, such as Jerome K. Jerome's *On the Stage—and Off,* which offers marvelous illustrations as well as an intimate account of the struggling actor's experiences, and the volume of firsthand theatrical documents compiled by Russell Jackson in *Victorian Theatre.* Such resources provide a vivid sense of the conditions in which Wilde was writing.

Finally, of special note in this regard is *Theatre and Fashion: Oscar Wilde to the Suffragettes*, by Joel Kaplan and Sheila Stowell. Their brilliant analysis of the costumes for *A Woman of No Importance* (20–27) includes illustrations from original publications and shows how fashion was used consciously to undermine the rigid categories of woman with a past and pure woman represented, respectively, by Mrs. Arbuthnot and Hester Worsley.

The theatrical approach focuses on the three dramatic modes that directly influenced Wilde's playwriting and that he tried to unite in this play: nineteenth-century melodrama, the *pièce bien faîte* or well-made play, and the radical new problem play pioneered by Henrik Ibsen and shown in London at precisely the time Wilde was working on his own society dramas. Before introducing these categories, it is also useful to point to an earlier tradition that was equally influential to Wilde: the English comedy of manners, represented by such plays as Richard Sheridan's *The School for Scandal* and Oliver Goldsmith's *She Stoops to Conquer*.

"Stop, Gerald, Stop!": Wilde's Appropriation of Melodrama

I start by giving students a thorough understanding of melodrama. Much good secondary material exists on this topic—for example, by James Redmond, James L. Smith, and Elaine Hadley—but a brief definition will do. They should understand the basic features of melodrama, such as heightened emotion, spectacle, and stock character types (hero, ingenue, villain, comic man, and comic woman) painted in broad strokes as either wholly good or bad. In addition, acting techniques reflected the content of melodramas: "larger than life; highly externalized; extravagant in gesture, movement, and facial expression; rhetorical in speech; and intensely emotional" (Booth, Lights xvii).

The melodramatic moments in *A Woman of No Importance* are highly problematic and have often been used by critics to show how weak the play is. A useful way into discussing them is to ask students to apply their definition of melodrama to the play and identify the play's melodramatic aspects. They usually point first to the end of act 3, when Gerald is about to slap Lord Illingworth in outrage at his pursuit of Hester but is stayed by Mrs. Arbuthnot's "Stop, Gerald, stop! He is your own father!" (503).

We discuss how this moment exemplifies both verbal and physical melodrama, focusing on the stage directions as indicators of the action. This focus points up the dramatic difference between the melodrama of this scene and the kind of restraint we are used to in the farcical *Earnest*, where characters languidly dispense epigrams and rarely lose their poise. Here, wild actions and heightened emotions rule. We suddenly hear Hester offstage saying, "Let me go!," and then see her running on "in terror." She "rushes over to Gerald and flings herself in his arms," exclaiming, "Oh! Save me—save me from him!"(502–03). Lord Illingworth appears, Gerald in "rage and indignation" denounces him and declares, "I will kill you!," and Mrs. Arbuthnot, "rushing across and catching hold of him," tries to restrain him. Gerald, "thrusting her back," swears, "Don't hold me—I'll kill him!," forcing his mother to blurt the immortal line that ends the act and reveals to Gerald his true patrimony. In the final stage directions, we get a melodramatic nonverbal tableau: "Gerald clutches his mother's hands and looks into her face. She sinks slowly on the ground in shame. . . . Lord Illingworth frowns and bites his lip" (503). All this excitement is packed into the last few minutes of the act.

A great exercise is to ask students to perform this scene in class rather than just read it aloud. Having them try to enact the stage directions while also speaking the lines exemplifies brilliantly the workings of melodrama and the demands of the stage in general. We then discuss how the scene represents melodrama and how Wilde is adapting the form to his own purposes. Is he importing it wholesale into his drama, or is there an implicit criticism of the form in his use of it? Does it seem contrived to students now? If so, why? It is also illuminating to discuss Richard Allen Cave's assertion that

> melodrama is crucial to Wilde's strategy: it underpins all his plays to intimate how slender a hold the society he depicts has on its professed stability and decorum; a fear of public exposure prevails and gives an edge of desperation to the characters' actions and speech.   (225)

Playing with the Well-Made Play

Having found our footing with melodrama, we move on to the well-made play, its origins in France, its successful adaptation to the English stage, and its immense popularity as well as its relation to other modes such as melodrama and the "cup and saucer" domestic drama. I lay out the main features of the well-made play: its tight, intricate plotting; reliance on objects either mislaid or falling into the wrong hands (jewelry, letters, handkerchiefs accidentally dropped and discovered by the wrong person); mistaken identities; surprise revelations—features all encompassed by the standard trajectory of exposition, situation, climax, and denouement. We discuss the obvious overlap with melodrama, which also includes many of these features, and note where the main differences lie. For example, well-made plays have a more nuanced development of emotion, though nowhere near the psychological sophistication Ibsen would introduce. Also, the presence of a *raisonneur* in many well-made plays offers a kind of detached commentary on the action not found in melodrama. Another key feature of well-made plays is their setting in upper-class society among people the middle-class audience aspires to emulate.

I ask students to find such elements in *A Woman of No Importance*, an assignment that works well in groups or as homework. I want them to understand this kind of drama from the inside out, not through some abstract definition that they will memorize and repeat verbatim on an exam but from working directly with the text. As creaky and predictable as it may seem to us now, this formula dominated the theater of its time, and unless students grasp its essentials, they will never fully appreciate the brilliant strategy Wilde employed by manipulating the well-made play for his own subversive purposes.

Ibsen's Modernization of the Drama

The final ingredient in our contextual mix is Ibsen. I provide a brief overview of the influence of Ibsen during the early 1890s in England and how he radically changed drama through formal innovation (adapting the well-made play, as Wilde and Shaw also did after his groundbreaking example), characterization, dialogue, and controversial themes. Ibsen is credited with being the father of modern drama for both formal and thematic boldness, but too often the latter is emphasized at the expense of the former. If there is time, we read short excerpts from various Ibsen plays, like *A Doll's House*, *Ghosts*, and *Hedda Gabler* (a play Wilde particularly admired), to illustrate his depth of psychological development; his daring treatment of social problems; and his naturalistic dialogue, which dispensed almost entirely with monologues and asides and increasingly came to reflect the cadences, interruptions, and evasions of everyday speech. Above all, he radically challenged existing roles for women, and he pushed women downstage to be the center of the drama rather than to inhabit shallow or predictable supporting roles.

As Powell beautifully illustrates in his chapter on Wilde and Ibsen, Wilde's development as a playwright occurred "in an atmosphere suffused with Ibsen" (*Oscar Wilde* 74). Indeed, "to a significant degree [Wilde] measured his work as a playwright against the example that Ibsen set" (75). Ibsen gave Wilde the impetus and means to challenge conventional notions of acceptable female behavior on stage. Ibsen's and Wilde's modifications of the well-made play focused particularly on dismantling the stark contrast between the good and bad women and the double standard by which men's sexual freedom was condoned while women were expected to remain pure. *A Woman of No Importance* boasts an astonishing variety of women, each distinct from the other; collectively they provide a glittering backdrop of female-dominated society against which the action of the play unfolds. At one end of the spectrum is the female dandy, Mrs. Allonby, not simply a great sparring partner for Lord Illingworth but also a radical commentator who repeatedly trumps him at his own epigrammatic games. At the other end is Hester Worsley, the American puritan whose name is reminiscent of Hawthorne's Hester Prynne and whose severe prudishness makes her dislike the dandyish Mrs. Allonby and initially shun the sinner Mrs. Arbuthnot.

Hester's name directs the audience to wonder from the outset whether this Hester will also be a victim of puritanism—in this case, her own. Such puritanism seems incongruous in one so young, beautiful, and rich, as the other characters around her often note. One of the most illuminating analyses of Hester comes in Powell's book (58–60) and should be assigned reading if possible. Powell shows how *A Woman of No Importance* deliberately uses Hester's name to invoke *The Scarlet Letter* and thus "engages in debate with Hawthorne's version of the story" (59). In particular, two stage adaptations of *The Scarlet Letter* in London in 1888 possibly prompted Wilde "to reassess prevailing ideas of woman's duty," for he "awards his heroine the happy exile that Hawthorne withholds . . . and lets off the seducer with a slap in the face" (60). Who wears the "A" in Wilde's version? And what happens to her? It is also useful to discuss what happens at the end of the play (the departure of Mrs. Arbuthnot, Gerald, and Hester to the "less unjust" New World [509]) in relation to Wilde's own experience of America, which is described by Richard Ellmann (*Oscar Wilde*) and other critics and biographers of Wilde.

Even the minor female characters are fleshed out and distinct from one another. A very effective assignment that combines learning about dramaturgical strategies as well as Wilde's attitudes toward women is to have students pick female characters in the play and analyze what Wilde does to give each one her particular stamp of identity. This assignment is a great way to teach such aspects of Wilde's dramaturgy as epigram and verbal patterning. For example, Lady Hunstanton's character is given its distinctiveness partly through her repeated and hilarious verbal tic of getting two incongruous things mixed up: "But I believe he said her family was too large. Or was it her feet? I forget which" (467). Some of her funniest lines are variations on this formula, and the laughter is in a sense cued by the expectation and recognition of this verbal pattern. Yet students should be equally alert to the politics of such linguistic choices. In this apparent bumbling lies a power that should not be underestimated; Lady Hunstanton's linguistic lapses are markers of her status in society, not merely silly and vapid remarks. Showing students how Wilde in effect trains his audience to laugh and at the same time to recognize the social codes such laughter contains can be one of the most rewarding exercises in teaching this play.

Finally, there is the title character. One of the most difficult elements of *A Woman of No Importance* for students today must surely be the character of Mrs. Arbuthnot. It can be hugely rewarding to start with the severity of her manner and dress, using excerpts from Kaplan and Stowell to show how in reality the actress playing Mrs. Arbuthnot was known for seductive female roles and wore a revealing, tight-fitting gown that was quite fashionable even while seeming to conform to the character's situation. The actress thus gave Mrs. Arbuthnot a mix of elegance and moral stature formerly denied to fallen women on stage (Kaplan and Stowell 26). Next we look at her interminably long speeches and their (to modern ears) rather leaden tone. Her impassioned speech to Gerald in act 3 ("Gerald, there was a girl once, she was very young . . ." [502]) just before the moments discussed above is one example of a melodramatic language that modern students find awkward, contrived, and totally at odds with the witty banter of the rest of the play. It is therefore essential to read these passages very closely: they are, perhaps unexpectedly, an indicator of Wilde's subversiveness.

Here we really discover the feminist side of Wilde, the former editor of *Woman's World*. Using Eltis's chapter on the play, we can begin to see what lies beneath Mrs. Arbuthnot's stilted tone in all such speeches: a searing indictment of philandering men who ruin women, which goes against the conventional double standard by which women had to be pure and men could sow their wild oats with abandon, and later (act 4) a triumphant rejection of the mantle of fallen woman as Mrs. Arbuthnot defiantly embraces the product of her downfall with another long speech that explicitly states, "[T]hough day after day, at morn or evensong, I have knelt in God's house, I have never repented of my sin. How could I repent of my sin when you, my love, were its fruit," and culminates with the words, "Child of my shame, be still the child of my shame!" (508–09).

This is a powerful and stunning plea for society to stop judging women on their sexual past and start allowing them to pursue more varied and liberated lives, and it is an idea pioneered by Ibsen in the plays that were most famous in England at the time: *A Doll's House, Ghosts, Hedda Gabler, The Master Builder*. These plays successively challenged what was seen as acceptable female behavior onstage (see Shepherd-Barr). Hedda longs to break out of the mold of that behavior, finding the prescribed roles for women too limited and stifling, but sees no acceptable alternatives yet. She is tragically ahead of her time. *Hedda Gabler*, made famous in London by the actress and ardent feminist Elizabeth Robins, captivated Wilde; he called it "new and fascinating" and saw it several times in 1891 (Shepherd-Barr 96). Mrs. Arbuthnot suggests a kind of Wildean turn on an Ibsenesque character, a transmutation that would occur again in his next play, *An Ideal Husband* (Powell, *Oscar Wilde* 81–88).

Wilde found a way of challenging conventional notions of femininity while seeming to endorse them. Mrs. Arbuthnot seems to accept her lot as a fallen woman yet proclaims that she is glad she sinned because it produced her beloved Gerald. Far from hiding her "shame," she announces it, and in the end it is Lord Illingworth who loses, being dismissed as "a man of no importance" (514). This is a pointed reversal of the usual formula of well-made plays featuring fallen women, from *La dame aux camellias* to *The Second Mrs. Tanqueray* or the melodramatic mainstay *East Lynne*, in which the woman with a past must be killed off by the playwright in order to capitulate to audience expectations and reassert the status quo.

Hester serves as a stand-in for the audience as she is taught to rid herself of prejudice against fallen women. She grows while most of the other characters remain static and trapped in their class-based prejudices. In addition to her representation of gender and class, it can be informative to see her in the context of sexuality, of Wilde's lifelong struggle as a homosexual and his concomitant hatred of the puritanical, self-serving morality of his time that branded certain groups outcasts. Students might not be aware of how consistently this antipuritan idea appears in his work and how he railed against puritanism in his letter to Lord Alfred Douglas written from prison, *De Profundis*, which is worth excerpting in relation to the play for its eloquent elaboration of such ideas as puritanism and duty.

At this point I alert students to the concepts of realism and naturalism in the theater (many will have encountered their quite different meanings in other genres) and the major differences between them. I also give students a sampling of the virulent criticisms of Ibsen expressed by theater reviewers in London, of which Wilde must have been aware. The idea is to give students a grasp of how Ibsen was new as well as a sense of his tremendous cross-cultural impact.

Unifying the Theatrical Influences

Having discussed how Wilde's three major influences, the Victorian melodrama, the well-made play formula, and Ibsen's new dramaturgy, come together in *A Woman of No Importance,* I then ask students how well they feel these are integrated and if there are elements in the play that do not readily fall into these categories. Students usually find that the play has a bipolar quality to it, lurching from comic to serious mode and never fully integrating the two. It is as if Wilde is still feeling his way toward his own true mode of playwriting. I briefly discuss how this experiment in challenging the conventions of the Victorian theater would be continued, and considerably improved, in the next society comedy, *An Ideal Husband,* culminating in farcical mode in *The Importance of Being Earnest*. While we see some of the same elements in this last play, the influence of Ibsen is now much subtler, the use of the well-made play is more skillful, and the quintessentially Wildean characteristics—epigram, verbal patterns, inversion of gender roles, dandyism—are essentially reified into a new form of theatrical art. But the social criticism, while brilliantly disguised, is no less prevalent.

It helps to contextualize Wilde's social commentary by mentioning the dramatic censorship that affected all British playwrights during this period (and until 1968) and that caused Ibsen's *Ghosts* to be refused a license for performance and many of his other plays to be performed by small, independent theater groups (Shepherd-Barr 10–11). Wilde was most directly affected by censorship in his efforts to get his play *Salomé* produced, an experience that is worth having students read about in any of the available biographies of Wilde. I want students to think about the extent to which his distinctive dramaturgy evolved out of the need to find ways of couching his criticisms of society so that his plays could pass the censor. This awareness helps counter the mistaken assumption many students have about Wilde as the apolitical, decadent aesthete interested only in "l'art pour l'art."

The pedagogical approach outlined here emphasizes context, theatricality, and dramaturgy. It assumes that you cannot fully understand and appreciate *A*

Woman of No Importance unless you know something about what came before it (and how the play is a reaction against that) and what was going on at the time Wilde wrote it (and how he assimilated it into the play). *A Woman of No Importance* is his direct response to a number of currents dominating the theater of his time, foremost among these being Ibsen. *A Woman of No Importance* marks one stage in Wilde's revision of Ibsen for the English stage. It is a dramatic experiment in mixing very different styles of playwriting. One needs the fullest theatrical context for the play to appreciate what Wilde is trying, with only partial success, to do. The play becomes, in many ways, a hallmark of early modernist theater. Thinking about the play in this context, students will also be asked to think about the concept of modernism and the role of theater in it. This approach avoids the traditional tendency to isolate theater from the other arts and brings our understanding of Wilde directly in line with the currents of contemporary scholarship on theater and modernism. The play may be an experiment that has yet to convince critics and audiences of its success, but it is a delightful experiment nonetheless.

Wilde in the Comparative Arts Course: Teaching *An Ideal Husband*

Robert Preissle

The Wildean critical renaissance since about 1980 has been fueled, as Philip Smith's introduction to this collection notes, by recently emergent critical approaches such as gay-lesbian study and poststructuralist theory. For the generalist or traditionalist as well, however, Wilde's works remain particularly interesting on a number of levels. One such level is in the context of comparative arts study, itself an emergent approach but one far more accessible to the nonspecialist educator and student alike. Both play text and performance text of Wilde's *An Ideal Husband*, coupled with Oliver Parker's 1999 film adaptation, are an especially rich combination for comparative arts study in both the transgeneric and transhistorical reception issues they raise.

In a contemporary narrative world that might well be termed the Age (Rage?) of Adaptation, the crucial light that transgeneric reception study can throw on the nature of differently received narrative art forms is often extinguished by the question of mere fidelity. Central to understanding any narrative art—in this case, a play as written, as performed, and as a film—is that each form has both similar and different capacities because of its reception mode. Plays as texts are far more suitable for transgeneric study than prose fiction, because of course they are ultimately meant for both reception modes, reading and watching-listening. Wilde's plays, as I discuss below, are especially interesting because of the particular moment in time at which they were created.

Transhistorical reception is also a critical issue in comparative arts study. Students of our own, or any, time bring a different cultural capital to their experience of a text, whether it be written, performed live, or seen and heard on film. In this respect, Parker's film version is in an intertextual dialogue with the play's reading text, a dialogue aimed at the more informed viewer; it is also actively engaged with the modern viewer who is not knowledgeable about either Wilde or his era.

Transgeneric Reception Issues

A key component of comparative arts study is how reception modes influence received meanings, and the differences among *An Ideal Husband's* play text, performance text (most likely to be imagined), and film text are extremely instructive about these different modes. As Ian Small notes, Wilde was in the first generation of playwrights who experienced "the phenomenon of published reading-texts of plays" (*Oscar Wilde: Recent Research* 90), so he expected his plays to find an audience of both readers and theatrical viewers and revised them for publication accordingly. Although students probably will not be able to see the play performed, an excellent technique to begin discussion is to ask them to highlight, as they read the play, its extradiegetic elements.

At the least, this exercise will reveal how far stage directions can be taken to convey meaning to readers versus watchers-hearers. The play text's opening describes "a large eighteenth-century French tapestry—representing the Triumph of Love, from a design by Boucher" (515). How will a performance text convey such written specifics, including the interplay of the tapestry's title with the narrative's action, or the association of Boucher's work with French aristocracy's "ornamental decadence" (de la Croix and Tansey 781)? Similarly, Mrs. Marchmont and Lady Basildon are seated on a "Louis Seize sofa" (515), continuing the (ironic?) connection being made to a decadent aristocracy.

The play text's extradiegetic elements also delineate specific characters. As Stephan Kohl has rightly argued, much of the play text's meanings are

> concentrated in the non-performable parts of the text . . . and it is the marked difference between the two acts of reception [reading and attending a performance] which allows some insight into the playwright's view of his audience.   (116)

Indeed, each of the major characters is introduced with a crucial stage direction, such as Goring's: "He is clever, but would not like to be thought so. A flawless dandy, he would be annoyed if he were considered romantic" (521). Typically for Wilde, most of these introductions introduce character dichotomies: for Mabel, tyranny/innocence; for Robert, passion/intellect; for Goring, dandy/philosopher.

The stage directions introducing the characters also create a metaphoric spine that continues the earlier noted reference to art. Gertrude is associated with Greek beauty, Mrs. Marchmont and Lady Basildon with Watteau, Lord Caversham with Lawrence, Mabel with a Tanagra figurine, Mrs. Cheveley with "A work of art . . . showing the influence of too many schools" (517), and Robert with Vandyck. For readers of Wilde's day, these references to specific artists may have served to specify character types in very particular ways, such as that "Watteau immediately encodes a sense of 'delicate eroticism'" (Bristow, "Dowdies" 54). Significantly, only Goring is introduced with no stage direction directly referencing art, a clear indicator to the play text's reader that for him alone no visual comparison can come close to being the measure of the man.

These examples of the different insights easily accessible to the reader as opposed to the viewer-listener are, of course, merely suggestive of the starting points for discussion. In Roland Barthes's terms, these elements are indices, and students can and should be encouraged to think about possible theatrical stagings that might convey similar meanings. For example, in the original stage production, Mrs. Cheveley's gown suggested her status as a villain because it depicted dead swallows. Mabel could be costumed in a more girlish way, and perhaps in white, to suggest her innocence. The major characters could even enter through separate wings and pause next to actual copies of works by the artists mentioned, while the conversation of the other actors ceases and lighting directs the viewer's attention to the entrance. Still, information such as that given about Robert's "complete separation of passion and intellect" (518) would be extremely difficult to convey in performance.

Discussing the play text versus performance text and then the film text should be a twofold move: the film text has similarities to and differences from both the other reception modes. My experience has been that students are far more capable of distinguishing the reading mode from the live performance mode than they are the live performance mode from the filmed performance. They often see film as recorded theater, and theater, like film, is a visual and aural more than a verbal medium. *An Ideal Husband* is one of the most effective works to use to show them that film is both different from and similar to a play text and a performance text.

The easiest place to start this discussion is with the similarities between performance text and film text that are also differences between both and play text. Performance and film texts seem to operate on the basis of mimesis rather than diegesis. Thus, in both theater and film, actors will portray roles and speak lines in certain ways; settings and costumes will actually (virtually, in film) be represented instead of described; character's movements will be through actual (or, again, virtual in film) space and time.

Although many critical differences between theatrical and film performance, such as film's ability to reshoot a scene and theater's always unique performance, will result from this opening discussion, my analysis focuses on two: differences in space and perspective. Wilde's play retains the Aristotelian unity of space, its action occurring in only three locales. Parker's film, by contrast, makes maximum use of film's ability to move seamlessly into many different places. In its first five minutes, viewers see Goring's bedroom, a public appearance of the Chilterns, Goring's bedroom again, the large public space of the park where several of the principals are riding, and then a montage sequence of preparations for the Chilterns' party, before settling into the play's first act, at the party. Later scenes are set at a gymnasium; a sauna; a play; another party; Boodle's Club; outdoors in a lower-class district; Gertrude's women's club meeting; and penultimately at the House of Commons, where Robert gives his speech denouncing the Argentine Canal scheme, among other things.

Picturing these spaces, necessarily only spoken of or assumed in the play and performance texts, does far more than simply open up the more limited perspective of a performance text. For modern viewers, seeing these characters in a large variety of spaces adds dimension to them. When Mabel remarks that Goring "rides in the Row at ten-o'clock in the morning" or when Robert remarks that "Lord Goring is the result of Boodle's Club" or when Mabel says, "You remember, we are having tableaux, don't you?" (516, 521, 545), viewers-readers of the play's era can conjure up those images, but modern viewers probably cannot. The addition of these spaces, then, is a crucial part of establishing the milieu in which the characters exist, a milieu that readers-viewers of the time would have been well aware of but that is now lost to many spectators.

The film also frequently juxtaposes these spaces to comment on the events taking place in them. Thus, the brief opening in Goring's bedroom shows a naked woman leaving his bed and his butler providing a bromide to soothe what the viewer assumes is a hangover. The next scene of Robert and Gertrude in a public space, being questioned by the media, quickly establishes that Robert is a responsible social servant, long out of bed and on the job while Goring lolls about. Later, while Gertrude and Mabel are shown at the tableaux, shots of Robert and Goring at a sauna are intercut; both pairs are talking about Goring's and Mabel's romantic lives, and the evident friendships in the couplings underscores that Goring and Mabel are an ideal pair, unlike Goring and Mrs. Cheveley or Mabel and Tommy. Finally, while Goring tries to entice Mrs. Cheveley, by romancing her, to give him the letter, Mabel is intercut: she is waiting at an art exhibit, in vain, for Goring to keep his engagement with her. The audience knows that Goring is acting to save Robert (although his attentions to the lovely Julianne Moore hardly seem forced), while Mabel plays the part of the uninformed innocent. These meanings are all available because of film's flexibility in juxtaposing spaces.

In addition to multiplying and juxtaposing spaces, the film takes advantage of its ability to slice up common spaces to focus the viewer's perspective in ways that would be difficult for a theatrical performance to achieve. This slicing is most evident in three scenes. First, at the Chilterns' party, as Robert and Mrs. Cheveley come to the end of their conversation about the letter, the newspaper editor appears, in high focus, in the background, reinforcing the threat of public exposure Robert faces. Later, while the principals are at a play, the camera cuts restlessly from one to another, reinforcing the fact that they are all engaged as much in looking at one another as in looking at the play. Finally, during Robert's speech, the camera cuts among him, Goring, Gertrude, and Mrs. Cheveley in a perfect example of the classical use of this device to increase dramatic intensity.

Students can be encouraged to compare how prose fiction uses space and perspective with how a play text, a performance text, and a film text do. They'll be surprised to find that prose fiction and film texts share the ability to use many spaces, to juxtapose spaces, and to slice up larger spaces into smaller ones, creating perspectives difficult to render on the stage. Although the mediums seem much more distant than performance text and film text do, their techniques bring them into a closer congruence.

Transhistorical Reception Issues

The cultural capital question occupies a central role in the larger context of transhistorical reception; the passing of time makes the question inevitable. Parker's film attempts to create a much fuller milieu for the play's narrative, fleshing out the characters and their lifestyles. I focus on three transhistorical aspects of the play text, performance text, and film text: their central scandals, attitudes toward women, and gay-homoerotic qualities.

As Peter Raby correctly notes, the play's central scandal is one that current audiences can "simply transpose [to] the general area of reference [of] some more recent comparable issue" ("Wilde's Comedies" 156). Indeed, *An Ideal Husband*'s focus on financial impropriety, blackmail, the boundary between private and public, and the power of the media makes the play the most accessible and relevant of all Wilde's society comedies, sad proof that the world of modern Western politics has changed little in a century.

But an important difference between the play or performance text and the film text is the film's decision to portray Robert's speech denouncing the Argentine Canal, and students should discuss this decision. Two points should be made. First, films meant to appeal to a comparatively large audience almost always engage in upping the stakes of the material from which they are adapted; the film clearly ups the stakes here. In both play and performance texts, only Robert's integrity and his and Gertrude's relationship are at stake. In Parker's version, Goring does not have Robert's letter before the speech, thus the threat to Robert's public life still exists. In addition, Goring's matrimonial future hinges on the speech. As Linda Williams, among others, argues, melodrama is "the foundation of the classical Hollywood movie" (42), and in melodrama, no matter what the specific genre, stakes are characteristically both heightened and multiplied.

Equally interesting is the content of Robert's speech. In rejecting the canal scheme, Robert references the need, as the century turns, to discard a national policy determined exclusively by commercial interests and embrace one informed by moral values. For a modern audience, itself located at the turn of a century, the commercial-moral contrast in the context of national policy, and Robert's clearly liberal stance, could not be more manifest.

To the extent that attitudes about women also fall in the political realm, students will surely want to discuss how the three texts approach women. Wilde's, and this play's, relation to women has been a matter of considerable commentary, with views ranging from misogynistic to protofeminist. The play text presents three quite different women: the evil dandy Mrs. Cheveley ("She is, for the moment, dreadful to look at" [567]); the puritanical Gertrude; and the modern and entirely suitable Mabel, a dandy in training without either Mrs. Cheveley's evil or Gertrude's stiff morality. Although a theatrical performance is not likely to be available, students can still be encouraged to discuss the effects that casting, costume, and alterations to the play's dialogue might have.

In all events, Parker's film considerably lessens the bite of Wilde's presentation of both sexes. The film's Mrs. Cheveley has not stolen the bracelet-brooch, nor is she at any point the near harridan in appearance that Wilde's stage direction, quoted above, calls for. Perhaps as a compensatory gesture, gone almost entirely is the play's biting satire about men or husbands from the mouths of Lady Markby, Mrs. Marchmont, and Lady Basildon; the combined effect is far more romantic comedy and far less satire. Predictably, Goring's "A man's life is of more value than a woman's" speech (579) is almost entirely elided; as Joel Kaplan argues, "The passage was already awkward in 1895, when Ada Leverson wrote a good-natured parody of it for *Punch*" ("Wilde" 258). Educators with students who have a specialty in theatrical studies will want them to research how recent productions have handled the women issues. Patrick Sandford's 1989 London revival, for example, like the film, cuts Goring's speech. In a transfer of Peter Hall's 1992 London production to Broadway in 1996, Clive Barnes wondered whether "the wicked Mrs. Cheveley overdoes the hissing melodrama a little bit, . . ." (qtd. in Tanitch 245). These productions can be discussed, of course, both on their own and considered in the light of how they might have influenced Parker's screenplay.

By far the most difficult transhistorical reception issues are posed by these texts' approaches to gay-homoerotic questions. One way to frame these questions is to introduce information about Wilde's biography—specifically, that during the run of the play, Wilde was convicted of indecency for what we would today call homosexual activities.

Students can be encouraged to consider how knowledge of Wilde's situation affects their interpretation of the play text as well as how that information might have affected audiences at the time. Students may find themselves making connections between the play's central conflict of public/private on the political level and public/private on the individual level. Scenes in the play may remind students of any number of current-day scandals involving the intersections of politics and sex, homosexual or otherwise. Students might be presented with the opposing views of commentators such as Robert Tanitch, who sees in the playtext a "homosexual subtext" (248), and Alan Sinfield, who argues, conversely, that "[s]exuality will not come properly into focus in *An Ideal Husband* because the play is not interested in it" ("Effeminacy" 40). Students' views can be expected to be quite as varied, but a key discussion point is how already received knowledge about the playwright might color interpretations of the play text.

Another aspect of Parker's film that lends itself to consideration of this issue is the casting. Students might be asked whether the casting of Rupert Everett, an openly gay actor, in the role of Goring, affects their reaction to or perception of the character's sexual orientation. Again, the oppposing opinions of commentators may prove useful in postscreening discussion. Tanitch, for example, argues that Goring is presented immediately as irrevocably heterosexual, since the film's opening scene depicts a naked woman leaving his bed. For viewers who are unaware of Everett's real-life status, the film demonstrates that sexual orientation is a matter of performance, not essence; for those aware of his status, the film's diegesis that supposedly celebrates heterosexuality is ironically and thoroughly undercut.

A significant intervention that the film engages in, unlike both play text and any performance text so far presented, is its introduction of a scene in which the principals are attending a performance of Wilde's *The Importance of Being*

Earnest. Although this scene has meanings on several levels, one of them surely is to make the transhistorical point that sexual orientation is no longer a bar to public success, much less a guarantee of criminal prosecution and public disgrace, as it was in Wilde's time. In keeping with the liberal leanings of the film, if modern politics has not progressed, at least the nominal treatment of women and gays has.

An Ideal Husband *and the Next World*

Perhaps the most difficult aspect of preparing a comparative arts course is choosing works that will be rewarding across the spectrum of possibilities. Those interested in transgeneric and transhistorical connections will find that *An Ideal Husband* is extremely well-suited. It allows for important explorations of three different reception modes (four, if one counts imagining a prose fiction version); encourages the examination of historically connected but different and removed audiences; and focuses on both continuing relevant social issues, in particular politics and the boundary between private and public life, and issues at the roots of the modern era and now more fully engaged, such as the women's movement and gay-homoerotic questions.

Like all Wilde's plays, *An Ideal Husband* is located at that unique moment in time when playwrights were first considering their works in the light of their possible widespread publication while at the same time unaware of their potential as film texts. As Mabel says to Lord Caversham about Goring's potential as a husband, "It sounds like something in the next world" (582). Mabel's comment, typically Wildean, might be interpreted as referencing either heaven as the next world or the next real world, the modern one that Wilde, among others, helped begin through his literature and his life. *An Ideal Husband* relates crucially to that latter next world in transgeneric and transhistorical ways that are significant, complex, and instructive both for comparative arts study and for our time on many larger levels.

Form and Freedom
in *The Importance of Being Earnest*
Alan Ackerman

A crucial feature of Oscar Wilde's work and life is the tension between freedom and form. I use this structural and thematic problem as an approach to teaching Wilde's dramas, though I also draw extensively on nondramatic texts. *The Importance of Being Earnest*, in particular, is a work that I teach in courses ranging from a large lecture course in Western drama for first-year undergraduates (hereafter DRM100) to a fourth-year seminar devoted entirely to Wilde (hereafter ENG420). This essay draws from various materials and teaching experiences but is intended as an aid for teaching *Earnest* to students with little or no prior exposure to Oscar Wilde.

Defining Form

First, what do we mean by *form*? When we speak of literary form, we refer to the structure or shape of a work, the construction of plot. In DRM100, I talk about models of dramatic form from Aristotle's *Poetics* to the well-made plays of the nineteenth century. Aristotle teaches that plot is more important than character. He describes different kinds of plots, favoring those that progress logically and that involve a moment of recognition and reversal. *Oedipus, the King* is his model for the finest type of tragic plot. Even in a course devoted to Wilde alone, it is worth noting the importance of Aristotle and Sophocles for establishing these paradigms, because Wilde was a classical philologist whose thinking was deeply informed by those models. *Oedipus* in particular represents the deterministic forces of plot, also of destiny, in a form that Wilde playfully employs, for instance, in his short story "Lord Arthur Savile's Crime: A Study of Duty," when the protagonist, whose palm has been read, worries, "Was there no escape possible? Were we no better than chessmen, moved by an unseen power . . . ? [H]e felt that some tragedy was hanging over him" (165). In this passage, there is an explicit analogy between literary form (tragedy) and social form (the real-life parts that men and women must play). Form obtains a level of such dominance that character, far from struggling against it, accepts it so completely as to be reduced to absurdity.

In discussions of form, Wilde frequently elides distinctions between art and life. In *The Picture of Dorian Gray* we are told that

> the canons of good society are, or should be, the same as the canons of art. Form is absolutely essential to it. It should have the dignity of a ceremony, as well as its unreality, and should combine the insincere character of a romantic play with the wit and beauty that make such plays delightful to us.
>
> (107)

Yet it is Dorian's opinion that "man was . . . a complex multiform creature that bore within itself strange legacies of thought and passion" (107). Social systems—the organization of interpersonal action from ceremonial forms of courtship to habitual, polite behavior, from the casual demands of family and friends to those of the law—are dangerous, for they can turn individual people into objects. "[A]ll sentences are sentences of death," Wilde writes in *De Profundis* (1057). Social form is inseparable from linguistic form, as Cecily's instruction in German grammar implies in *Earnest*. When her guardian, Jack, particularly wants her to behave, he lays special stress on studying German, which gives her a headache and, she thinks, makes her look plain. I ask students to consider how rules of grammar, like those of conventional behavior, may be deadly.

Texts as Idealizations and Slavery to Form

In *Earnest*, characters are compelled by a wide range of texts to perform parts for which their only apparent qualification is, by an absurd tautology, that they appear in those texts. Lady Bracknell tells Jack, "I feel bound to tell you that you are not down on my list of eligible young men, although I have the same list as the dear Duchess of Bolton" (368). Each character is bound not only by social but also by literary conventions. Ultimately, Jack/Ernest will appear qualified to marry Gwendolen because his name is found in the Army List. Rigid models determine the course of lives. Gwendolen explains her love to Jack:

> We live, as I hope you know, Mr. Worthing, in an age of ideals. The fact is constantly mentioned in the more expensive monthly magazines . . . and my ideal has always been to love some one of the name of Ernest. . . . The moment Algernon first mentioned to me that he had a friend called Ernest, I knew I was destined to love you.   (365–66)

Destiny is not cosmic, as it was for the Greeks, but determined by social conventions. The "false ideal[s] of our time" (1073 ["Decay of Lying"]) are shown to be disastrous in nearly every one of Wilde's plays. "Ideals are dangerous things," says Mrs. Erlynne in *Lady Windermere's Fan* (461). Yet those ideals have attained the status of truths, and they have become rigid because published in magazines and sermons. Even in trivial social situations, individuals are trapped by words, as Herod is, more seriously, in *Salomé*. "I am the slave of my word," he laments (599).

Form triumphs over freedom in the figures of servants, who appear to possess no thoughts or passions of their own. Good servants, in Wilde, represent ideal instances of form. In *An Ideal Husband*, Lord Goring's servant Phipps "has been termed by enthusiasts the Ideal Butler. . . . He is a mask with a manner. Of his intellectual or emotional life, history knows nothing. He represents the dominance of form" (553). Phipps, like Lane in *Earnest*, is merely functional, utterly lacking an interior life. Algernon says, "I don't know that I am much interested in your family life, Lane." And Lane replies, "No sir; it is not a very interesting subject. I never think of it myself" (358).

But in the service of the marriage plot, the young lovers are servants too. They do not become impassive, but their emotional life is generic. Wooing Cecily and simultaneously dictating as she writes, Algernon declares:

> Miss Cardew, ever since half-past twelve this afternoon, when I first looked upon your wonderful and incomparable beauty, I have not merely been your abject slave and servant, but, soaring upon the pinions of a possibly monstrous ambition, I have dared to love you wildly, passionately, devotedly, hopelessly. (393)

Of course, Algernon's rhetoric runs away with him (he serves the rhetoric, not the other way around), as form conquers content, since the hyperbole does not match the situation. He does not in fact love "hopelessly," and Cecily is hardly "incomparable," as we see when the *two* couples enact a double courtship. He is an abject slave and servant not only to Cecily but also to the literary and social demands of courtship. To be a servant in a bachelor's apartments or in a marriage plot is to be dominated by form. Behind the comedy of these lines is the transformation of a man into a thing.

Historicizing Form

> The form is mechanic when on any given material we impress a predetermined form, not necessarily arising out of the properties of the material, as when to a mass of wet clay we give whatever shape we wish it to retain when hardened. The organic form, on the other hand, is innate; it shapes as it develops itself from within, and the fullness of its development is one and the same with the perfection of its outward form. Such is the life, such the form.
>
> (Coleridge, *Coleridge's Shakespearean Criticism* 1: 224)

Mechanical Form

Dramatic theory in the nineteenth century largely focused on the relation between the rigid form of the well-made play (*pièce bien faite*) and the play's social or thematic content, including characterization. Eugène Scribe perfected the form that nearly every dramatist of the century wrote in or against. Before reading *Earnest* in DRM100, we study an example of the well-made play (such as Scribe's *Glass of Water*), discuss its paradigmatic structure and its influence. Scribe's *système du théâtre* generally involves an expository first act, at the end of which a conflict is initiated; roughly three acts of mounting tension; a climactic confrontation in the fourth act, with the hero temporarily at a loss; and a gathering of the entire cast onstage, when secrets are revealed and all is set right. The formula is employed to this day, with variations only in character, situation, and the machinery of complication. Often I ask students if they can name contemporary examples from television and movies of well-made dramas or formulaic works that privilege plot over character. Students in DRM100 should be able to describe not only ways in which *Earnest* conforms to aspects of Scribe's *système* but also aspects of the system that the play may be said to parody.

In *De Profundis*, Wilde writes that "life was changeful, fluid, active, and that to allow it to be stereotyped into any form was death" (1035). In *Earnest*, two people perish precisely because of form: Jack's younger brother, Ernest, dies of a severe chill, and Algernon's poor friend Bunbury is quite exploded. Both must be eliminated in the interests of the marriage plot, and since we are concerned entirely with their relation to the plot and not at all with their existence as characters, we laugh at their demise. It is the ease with which such characters are killed off that may have led George Bernard Shaw to describe this work as "mechanical" and "almost inhuman" ("Old Play" 42). I ask students if Shaw's disparaging terms can help us understand the play in a positive sense.

The relation between the rigidity and hypocrisy of French drama and that of English society is explicit in *Earnest*. Algernon explains to Jack that, in married life, "three is company and two is none."

JACK (*sententiously*).   That, my dear young friend, is the theory that the corrupt French Drama has been propounding for the last fifty years.

ALGERNON.   Yes; and that the happy English home has proved in half the time.   (363)

In comparing French drama to the English home and drawing a parallel between the corrupt and the happy, the play does not allow the former to disappear into the latter; on the contrary, it highlights the formal constructedness of each. Dramatic clichés are defamiliarized. "The suspense is terrible," says Gwendolen. "I hope it will last" (414). Wilde playfully depicts staples of Scribean drama: the lost-and-found parents and children, the fortuitous peripeteias. Characters are rushed breathlessly by the well-made plot. "Hesitation of any kind," Lady Bracknell says, "is a sign of mental decay in the young, of physical weakness in the old," and she proceeds to narrate and unconsciously parody a melodramatic plot: "Apprised, sir, of my daughter's sudden flight by her trusty maid, whose confidence I purchased by means of a small coin, I followed her at once by a luggage train" (407).

There are several nontheatrical texts with which *Earnest* should be read in order to develop an understanding of the relation of form and freedom. In ENG420,

I supply students with a handout of quotations from Henri Bergson's famous 1900 essay "Le rire" ("Laughter"). Here are a few excerpts from that handout:

> The vice capable of making us comic is . . . that which is brought from without, like a ready-made frame into which we are to step. It lends us its own rigidity instead of borrowing from us our flexibility.   (70)
>
> It is really a kind of automatism that makes us laugh—an automatism . . . closely akin to mere absentmindedness. . . . It is in this sense only that laughter "corrects men's manners."   (71)
>
> The ceremonial side of social life must . . . always include a latent comic element, which is only waiting for an opportunity to burst into view. . . . For any ceremony, then, to become comic, it is enough that our attention be fixed on the ceremonial element in it, and that we . . . think only of its form.   .   (89)

Bergson's notion of the comic as "something mechanical encrusted upon the living" (84) employs an idiom that must be understood in its historical context, an age of mechanical reproduction. Wilde, like Bergson, self-reflexively represents an industrial age that pervades even the English country garden. Cecily is supposed to be reading "Political Economy" and learning about the "relations between Capital and Labour," though she professes to know only the "relations between Capital and Idleness" (377). In this world, science and rationality (or logic) are privileged over humanistic thought. (Cecily believes in "Rational Dress" [377].) Fact is favored over fancy. Upper-class social relations, too, have become highly formalized.

The latent comic element in the ceremonial side of social life is exemplified in *Earnest* when Gwendolen, recognizing that Jack wants to marry her and acknowledging that she wants to marry him, insists nonetheless on a formal proposal.

> GWENDOLEN.   . . . I think it only fair to tell you quite frankly beforehand that I am fully determined to accept you.
> JACK.   Gwendolen!
> GWENDOLEN.   Yes, Mr. Worthing, what have you got to say to me?
> JACK.   You know what I have got to say to you.
> GWENDOLEN.   Yes, but you don't say it.
> JACK.   Gwendolen, will you marry me? (*Going on his knees.*)
> GWENDOLEN.   Of course I will, darling. How long you have been about it!   (366–67)

Ceremony is emptied of content, since the performance of the proposal is only a mechanical routine, but, then again, the insistence on loving an Ernest also empties the name of content. To love a man for being named Ernest betokens a fundamental absentmindedness.

Gwendolen, however, is not merely absentminded. Each of the four lovers indicates a life not totally dominated by form. But that life, like Bunbury, exists outside the confines of the play. Gwendolen offers an alternative conception of form in a metatheatrical comment. When Jack praises her by saying, "You're quite perfect, Miss Fairfax," Gwendolen responds, "Oh! I hope I am not that. It would leave no room for developments, and I intend to develop in many directions" (363–64). Character development would be a conventional expectation, but Wilde mocks that expectation here. Gwendolen does not develop in many directions. Her ultimate, predictable pairing with Jack is inscribed in the opening act. The conclusion, in fact, refers to the opening, and she appears neither more nor less wise when she says in the end, "Ernest! My own Ernest! I felt from the first that you could have no other name!" (418). Laughter is the result of such predictable, absentminded felicity.

Organic Form

The idea of development is deeply informed by the dominant ideology of progress that characterizes the nineteenth century. Darwin's evolutionary thought had an enormous influence on nineteenth-century drama, as it did on all aspects of social thought, and so did Hegel's *Phenomenology of Spirit* and later Marx's materialist conception of history. Communism, Marx wrote, "is the true resolution of the strife between existence and essence, between objectification and self-confirmation, between freedom and necessity, between the individual and the species" (84). It is not possible to do justice to these thinkers in a course for first-year undergraduates. But one must note Wilde's engagement with the thinkers of his century, when, for instance, in *Earnest*, German metaphysics is explicitly banished from the world of the play. Gwendolen dismisses the possibility that Jack is not Ernest by saying, "Ah! that is clearly a metaphysical speculation, and like most metaphysical speculations has very little reference at all to the actual facts of real life, as we know them" (366). Cecily is being instructed not only in the relations between capital and labor but also in German; though, as Lord Goring remarks in *An Ideal Husband*, "It is love, and not German philosophy, that is the true explanation of this world" (543).

For Wilde, two thinkers epitomize two theories of form: Plato and Hegel (1173 ["The Truth of Masks"]). In simple terms, Hegel's theory of form is itself evolutionary and temporal, unlike Plato's conception of ideal and static forms, which is epitomized in the parable of the cave. An aspect of the difference between Plato's theory of forms and Hegel's is indicated when Hans-Georg Gadamer writes of the latter in *Hegel's Dialectic*, "In the phenomenon of motion, spirit becomes aware of its selfhood for the first time. . . . Motion is 'the concept of the true soul in the world'" (13). This philosophy of the spirit is evident in Bergson as well, who posits a theory of drama against the comic: "What the dramatist unfolds before us is the life-history of a soul, a living tissue of feelings and events" (164). This philosophy is crucial in Wilde. Gilbert tells Ernest in "The Critic as Artist":

> Form is everything. It is the secret of life. . . . [I]t is Form that creates not merely the critical temperament, but also the aesthetic instinct. . . . Start with the worship of form, and there is no secret in art that will not be revealed to you.   (1149)

At this point, it is clear that we are talking about two notions of form: the mechanical and the organic, as I show in ENG420 by drawing on a Romantic vocabulary employed by critics from Samuel Coleridge to Walter Pater. Wilde's work frequently presents a notion of form that is not rigid, inherited, limiting, or mechanical but fluid or organic. "[F]orm and substance cannot be separated in a work of art," Wilde writes in "The Soul of Man under Socialism"; "they are always one" (1187). In *De Profundis*, he also writes, "What the artist is always looking for is that mode of existence in which soul and body are one and indivisible: in which the outward is expressive of the inward: in which Form reveals" (1024). This idea of expressive form is also represented in *Earnest*, not only in Gwendolen's sense of the possibility of developing but also around the edges of the drama. At the opening curtain we hear Algernon playing the piano, significantly offstage. "I don't play accurately," he says. "[A]ny one can play accurately—but I play with wonderful expression. . . . I keep science for Life" (356). An appreciation of the difference between mechanical and organic form (between form as limitation and form as revelation) offers a key to teaching ways in which Wilde imagines both aesthetic and ethical freedom. In "The Critic as Artist," Gilbert says:

> [T]he real artist . . . does not first conceive an idea, and then say to himself, "I will put my idea into a complex metre of fourteen lines." . . . He gains his inspiration from form, and from form purely, as an artist should.   (1148)

Here form is posited paradoxically as a source of art.

So, what happens to this sense of form in *Earnest*? It is excluded from a society that is sealed hermetically like a bubble. Wilde shows that to *progress predictably* is an oxymoron. This play dramatizes the fact that any work (or life) whose end is pre-scribed cannot be said to develop. Jack discovers his origin to have been an end, and Lady Bracknell declares indignantly, "I had no idea that there were any families or persons whose origin was a Terminus" (408). Of course, it is just such a circularity that allows for a reassuring inscription of the very forms Lady Bracknell previously thought threatened by such an unconventional entrée to high society. She says:

> To be born, or at any rate bred, in a hand-bag, whether it had handles or not, seems to me to display a contempt for the ordinary decencies of family life that reminds one of the worst excesses of the French Revolution. (369)

Social revolution is averted by identification with form so strict that Jack becomes not only a text but *the* text. He "realis[es] for the first time in [his] life the vital Importance of Being Earnest" (419). The circularity of plot, theme, and character precludes development. Form trumps freedom.

In ENG420 we read Wilde in the dramatic, social, and philosophical contexts of the late nineteenth century and see that Wilde's theoretical and dramatic works inform each other. *The Importance of Being Earnest* represents a world dominated by positivism, sentimentalism, a burgeoning popular press, and a tradition of bourgeois theater that privileges form over content and offers predictable plots and conventional characters. One may ask how the society became mechanical. In "The Critic as Artist," Wilde writes, "The security of society lies in custom and unconscious instinct. . . . The great majority . . . rank themselves naturally on the side of that splendid system that elevates them to the dignity of machines" (1141). In *Earnest*, engagements are determined by "the proper average that statistics have laid down for our guidance." Marriage is impossible without certificates of "birth, baptism, whooping cough, registration, vaccination, confirmation, and the measles; both the German and the English variety" (409).

Jack, who was in infancy mistaken for the manuscript of a novel, now finds his identity in another text, the word *Ernest* published in a list of names. The list itself does not develop; it is asyntactic in form. The neat logic of the play's conclusion suggests an identity between form and content and the liberating potential of organic form, but the importance of being Earnest that Jack discovers is too neat for life (just as to be Ernest is not necessarily to be Earnest). It is comically rigid. Algernon noted earlier that any sane person would seek, through Bunbury, to escape the box of Victorian marriage. And Gwendolen's final line serves as a corrective to the pre-scribed circularity that Jack/Ernest trumpets when he announces that all his life he has been speaking nothing but the truth. "I feel that you are sure to change," she responds (418).

Freedom and form define each other. Many nineteenth-century thinkers imagine them in a dialectical or productive relation. Wilde understands freedom, like form, in ways that are always political, personal, and aesthetic. In his works, anarchists and tyrants produce each other. Ungovernable desires are regarded as both personal failings and political threats. As Miss Prism remarks of Algernon's seemingly innocuous if extraordinary appetite, "To partake of two luncheons in one day would not be liberty. It would be licence" (388). This distinction, which is crucial in Wilde, is an excellent topic for class discussion. The very structure of society can be threatened by a hunger for muffins—that is, by idiosyncratic or antisocial needs.

So, I ask students if Wilde imagines, as with form, at least two different kinds of freedom. Students recognize the freedom of absentmindedness, the circumscribed freedom of the ignorant and the complacent. But this play gestures at a higher freedom in references not only to Bunbury but also to the limitations of all forms of dialogue. That realm of freedom is manifested in suggestions of pleasure and pain, being and nothingness, outside the immediate milieu of the stage, in experiences beyond the borders of the play. As I teach it, this play antic-ipates the works of Samuel Beckett, and Wilde, James Joyce, and Beckett serve as a wonderful threesome for a graduate seminar. Jack complains, "You never talk anything but nonsense," and Algernon replies, "Nobody ever does" (374). In *Earnest*, habitual behavior or, as Algernon puts it, "the hard work [of] doing noth-ing" (373) generally precludes the freedom of self-consciousness. But in the aes-thete one senses the liberating action of the self-knowing mind.

TEACHING *SALOMÉ*:
A TEST CASE FOR MODERN APPROACHES

Teaching Oscar Wilde's *Salomé* in a Theater History and Dramatic Literature Seminar

Eszter Szalczer

Oscar Wilde's *Salomé* is an important contribution to the evolution of symbolism, one of the first European avant-garde movements that spread across the boundaries of poetry, music, theater, and the visual arts at the turn of the nineteenth century. In this essay I share some of my experiences of teaching *Salomé* in a theater history and dramatic literature seminar that focuses on the symbolist theater of the 1890s. The same method can be incorporated in teaching comparative courses on naturalism and symbolism or courses dealing with the modernist period or avant-garde theater in a wider sense. The approach described here may be applied to upper-level undergraduate courses or graduate-level seminars (or to classes that, as in mine, include both senior undergraduate and graduate students). I draw attention to Wilde's relevance outside the scope of literary and English studies and point out his importance for the theater curriculum. I demonstrate how Wilde's *Salomé*, taught in the context of theater studies, allows for interdisciplinary and experiential ways of teaching and learning.

The study of the play as a piece for the theater calls for an interdisciplinary approach in several respects. *Salomé* can be studied by students as a quintessential example of symbolist aesthetics in its combination of a variety of media and sensory experiences in a unified work of art (the French symbolists' take on Richard Wagner's notion of the *Gesamtkunstwerk*). Furthermore, *Salomé* draws on an archetypal and at the same time thoroughly fin de siècle theme employed by several different art forms, including painting, graphic arts, music, literature, and theater. In turn, the play itself engendered numerous transpositions into other media: opera, dance, film. *Salomé* therefore accommodates a wide range of techniques in teaching, from textual analysis to multimedia demonstrations.

The seminar is conceived to explore symbolist drama, theory, and staging practices. In this framework, Wilde's *Salomé* is considered as a work with significant ties to the emerging independent theater movement of the times. Following the opening of the Théâtre Libre in Paris in 1887, little theaters— working on a subscription basis and thus free from mainstream commercial demands and to some extent from censorship—sprang up in rapid succession in Paris, London, Dublin, Berlin, Munich, and Stockholm. These were venues for experimentation, seeking alternative ways of expression as well as of staging. Their struggle revolutionized theater production and freed playwrights from the shackles of the theater industry that dominated the late nineteenth century. For them the theater became an art form once again, on equal grounds and in collaboration with poetry, music, and painting. It was one of these experimental, independent theaters, the Théâtre de l'Œuvre in Paris, that gave Wilde's *Salomé* its first hearing in 1896, after the original plans for a premiere with Sarah Bernhardt in London were frustrated by a ban on the play (Tydeman and Price 25–31).

At the early stages of the course, students explore through readings and discussions the historical and cultural context that produced the independent theater movement; they learn about concepts such as modernism and modernity, avant-gardism, urbanization, industrialization. Readings from Baudelaire, Verlaine, and Poe and slide shows of the works of impressionist, realist, symbolist, and Pre-Raphaelite painters help students understand the time period from the point of view of contemporaneous literary and visual responses. They also familiarize themselves with various approaches to social and cultural issues, artistic techniques, and aesthetic principles.

In the following sequence the class reads plays and theoretical writings by the symbolist playwrights (Maurice Maeterlinck, W. B. Yeats, Hugo von Hofmannsthal) and looks at how their radical dramatic techniques engendered new, innovative production practices in the context of the emerging independent theater movement throughout Europe. The sequence on *Salomé* is positioned in the study of symbolist theater, and it may take up to six class periods. It consists of five stages:

> the Salomé theme in literature
> textual analysis of Wilde's *Salomé*
> discussion of the play in the context of Wilde's theoretical writings, influences on and circumstances of its creation, its reception and afterlife, and Aubrey Beardsley's illustrations
> group projects
> summary, conclusion

The study of this play and surrounding issues is a centerpiece of the course, because it demonstrates the problematics of symbolism and antirealism on many complex levels: literary theme; dramatic-poetic and staging techniques; cross-cultural and cross-media transpositions; social, political, and cultural issues of the times reflected in the text; the play's reception; the play's adaptations in response to patriarchy, censorship, gender issues, orientalism.

First, the class explores the emergence and variations of the Salomé theme in literature, including the New Testament accounts in the Gospels of Mark and Matthew and nineteenth-century variants by Stéphane Mallarmé, Gustave Flaubert, Joris-Karl Huysmans, and Jules Laforgue. When students compare Wilde's take on the theme with the biblical and the nineteenth-century approaches (which they may read as a selection of excerpts), they discern the novelty of his approach as well as its embeddedness in the cultural and sociopolitical climate of his time.

The textual analysis of the play considers various aspects intrinsic to the dramatic text and how the text operates. The class looks at the dramatic structure (the dynamics of space, time, characters and their relationships), visual imagery, and sound effects implied in the dialogue as well as in the stage directions. We also consider the operation of the text on the level of musical structure, the development of themes by the use of leitmotifs and variations. The interplay of all these elements and levels of the text to create the world of the play is emphasized. Extratextual issues are considered, such as roots of the biblical quasi-religious theme and dramatic structure of medieval drama. The vertically layered stage, for example, is reminiscent of the simultaneous presentation in the mystery plays of heaven, Earth, and hell—though in *Salomé* the order is ironically inverted, John the Baptist being placed in an underground cistern and an infernal, foreboding moon in the sky. The heavy use of spoken decor harks back to the Elizabethan tradition: a minimal physical set, limited spatial and temporal dimensions, and the embedding of atmospheric qualities in the dialogue.

Proceeding further in textual analysis, students are encouraged to note the unique use of poetic language in the play. We look at how symbolist techniques such as synesthesia, correspondences, suggestions, similes, metaphors, specific rhythms, stresses, silences, and repetitions are used to endow the language with both visual and musical qualities. We explore how the dramatic-poetic techniques make the text of the play function as visual-musical performance involving sense perception. These considerations bring us back to the notion of the total work of art so dear to the French symbolists who inspired Wilde's *Salomé* project, to the extent even that Wilde chose to write the play in French.

Textual analysis thus effortlessly leads the class to consider the play in context. First, we look at *Salomé* in the light of Wilde's aesthetic views ("The Decay of Lying" and the preface to *The Picture of Dorian Gray*). Next, we look at the circumstances, inspirations, and influences surrounding the creation of the play (e.g., Wilde's affinity with the French symbolists and with decadent sensibilities). We look at the play and its reception in England and elsewhere (the ban, the political climate in England and on the Continent, its first production in France, etc.). Finally, we consider the play juxtaposed with Beardsley's illustrations in the first publication of the English translation by Lord Alfred Douglas (1894). Students observe text and drawings side by side and relate their experience of this nineteenth-century multimedia performance, which again ties back into the symbolist concept of the total work of art. For this reason we use in class the Dover paperback edition of *Salomé* (an affordable yet fine edition that students may own), which reproduces the original English edition complete with the drawings. Students discover that image and text often do not overlap or even directly correspond and that these discrepancies, in fact, give even greater room to suggestion and ambiguity and evoke a wider range of meanings. This approach helps students experience how symbols work and helps them see differences between symbol (in the symbolist sense) and, for example, allegory.

From here we proceed to the section where students present the research projects they have been working on in small groups. The *Salomé* Group Projects assignment is designed as a creative and at the same time research exercise that leads to experiential learning. The class is divided into five small groups, each focusing on a topic related to Wilde's *Salomé*. The five topics are:

the stage history of *Salomé*: the original production and famous productions such as Max Reinhardt's
nineteenth- and early-twentieth-century visual representations of Salomé
the Salomé dance: dancers and dance forms inspired by Wilde's play
opera and other musical versions of *Salomé*
Salomé on film

The work is collaborative in both research and creative ideas for the presentation. But it is recommended that the group select a leader responsible for coordinating the effort. The evaluation of the group projects is based on the depth and extent of research, the authenticity of the presented information, the clarity and ingenuity of presentation, and the appropriateness and affinity of the mode and tools of presentation with the subject.

The assignment has many purposes. It reveals Wilde's *Salomé* not as an isolated piece but as an integral part of a cultural and historical process; the play's creation, reception, production, and afterlife are embedded in cultural, political, and theater history. Exploring the issues historically attached to the Salomé theme and various responses and approaches to it, students discover and experience Wilde's *Salomé* as a prototypical symbolist work in which a plurality of sense perceptions and media intersect. From this intersection emerges the acoustic-visual-sensual figure of Salomé. Students learn that the symbolist nature of the play makes possible an elusive and metamorphic afterlife for this figure, manifest in the various transpositions into different media. Therefore, students are encouraged to let themselves be infected with the symbolist spirit and poetic impulse. At the same time, their research and presentations make them aware of the necessity of an interdisciplinary approach to the subject.

Students begin the assignment by reading the introduction and appropriate chapters with notes, and they study the bibliography of William Tydeman and Steven Price's *Wilde*: Salomé, a work that deals with the production history and different transformations of the play. Using notes and bibliography found in this book, each group generates a preliminary bibliography for its topic. The group leader then assigns group members to locate and study these sources and to extend the research. At group meetings, members report their findings. Finally, each group is asked to arrange all information and materials into a coherent, presentable form. Students are encouraged to combine verbal, visual, and musical media in their presentations to illustrate symbolist techniques and aesthetics and to demonstrate how *Salomé* has been looked at as a total work of art. In the spirit of symbolism, they are asked to convey an experience rather than just dry facts and rational explanations. At the time of presentation, each group distributes in class a detailed outline of the topic and an annotated bibliography of the research done. Each presentation may take thirty to forty minutes, depending on group size, class size, and class schedule.

The groups are free to focus selectively on aspects of their topic they find most significant or interesting. The group researching stage productions, for example, might include correspondence regarding production values Wilde had in mind for the unrealized production with Bernhardt. A comparison of Wilde's staging suggestions with the actual premiere of the play in 1896 in Paris by Aurélien Lugné-Poë at the Théâtre de l'Œuvre sheds light on the author's strong affinities with the French symbolists and their radical theatrical experiments. The inclusion of Reinhardt's production makes apparent multimedia and interdisciplinary aspects inherent in the play, as the class learns about the involvement of sculptors and painters in the design of the sets. A look at recent American and British productions reveals that Wilde's play is constantly revisited and reevaluated, both because of some still-relevant intellectual and political issues and because of inherent artistic challenges.

The group that deals with visual representations of the figure of Salomé discovers emerging images of the new woman in the late nineteenth century and the notion of the femme fatale. Students may also compare representations by male and female painters and discuss issues of gender, race, orientalism, and colonialism conveyed by these images.

The presentation of the third group, on the Salomé dance, ties into the themes explored by the visual group. The image of Salomé here is created by many ingredients: the narratives about and myths around such performers as Maud Allen, Mata Hari, "Colette" Wiley, and Ida Rubinstein; the settings and audiences of the dance; the elements of the performance, from costume and props to choreography. Through these dancers Salomé became a symbol of the emerging new woman who discovers her own power in the midst of a crumbling patriarchal edifice, who wields the very weapons by which she has been victimized.

An exploration of Richard Strauss's opera version further highlights how music, text, image, and acting work separately and together in conveying the atmosphere, the personalities, and the changing emotional and spiritual states of the characters. While each medium operates according to its inner logic and specific signifying system, the effects of all complement one another. But the music, already inherent in the structure of Wilde's text, takes the lead and provides a unifying principle.

The group recounting film versions of *Salomé* often comes to the conclusion that the cinema has been more interested in the possibilities for star acting and in the spectacular and sensational aspects of the story than in symbolist and artistic concerns. Ironically, the numerous film adaptations seem to take *Salomé* back to the world of entertainment industry, from which the nineteenth-century independent theater movement strove to break away. One exception perhaps is the 1922 silent film version directed by Charles Bryant with Alla Nazimova in the title role. Showing clips and stills from the film allows the group to analyze production elements and ideological and artistic implications of this experimental version.

The *Salomé* Group Projects have proved to be a challenging and highly motivating assignment and very effective in terms of the quality of learning. On the one hand, the class learns new and interesting information from each group, as pieces of the puzzle are gradually filled in. On the other hand, group members share both the work and the responsibility to effectively communicate information to their classmates. They learn to master and own a specific subject, and they pride themselves on their knowledge. I teach this course as a seminar that includes both senior undergraduate and graduate students. This combination inspires students to work together, and it develops skills of leadership, instruction, and organization on the one hand and of research and presentation on the other. The style of the presentations varies from casual dialogue to lecturing. The presenters ingeniously combine multimedia tools: computer-generated images, *PowerPoint* presentations, reproductions of set and costume designs, video and audio clips, and sometimes live demonstrations (if there is a piano available in the classroom, for example).

After the group projects, the class is asked to summarize themes and issues that consistently seemed to emerge from the presentations. These projects have shed light on Wilde's play as a symbolist total work of art and on the interdisciplinary nature of theatrical symbolism. Connections made among various aspects of Wilde's *Salomé* project guide the discussion toward conclusions regarding theater-historical and cultural-political circumstances. Questions such as why the Salomé theme became so popular in the late nineteenth century may provoke fierce debate, since students by now are able to argue on the basis of a wide range of information. At this point I bring up the wider notions introduced at the beginning of the course (e.g., modernity and the avant-garde, social crisis and patriarchy), thus returning Wilde's *Salomé* into the bloodstream of a culture in change.

Oscar Wilde and the Motif of Looking: An Approach to Teaching Gender Issues in *Salomé*

Joan Navarre

My approach to teaching *Salomé* introduces undergraduate students to gender issues that emerge from a reading of the play's dominant motif: looking and not looking. Salomé exists in the realm of the gaze. Her story deals with the dangers of looking and being looked at. Students analyze Wilde's motif and apply Laura Mulvey's theory that looking is gendered. The objectives of this approach are twofold: to develop analytical reading skills and to enhance historical understanding. With *Salomé*, Wilde's position as a playwright is unique. Wilde defies tradition by enhancing the characterization of Salomé. This is not the dutiful daughter of the Bible. Wilde's Salomé desires.

There are two parts to this approach. The first focuses on establishing the motif of looking and then questioning how it contributes to plot and characterization. The second part provides the theoretical and historical framework.

Before reading the play, students are asked to summarize the New Testament accounts of Salomé (Mark 6.14–29 and Matthew 14.1–14). When they read the play, they note the differences. At the first class meeting, I begin with a brief visual presentation (using transparencies or *PowerPoint*) and an oral reading of the Bible passages. This follows with a small group discussion of the differences between the biblical accounts and Wilde's play. We gather as a large group, share responses, and list the differences (see app. 1).

This exercise sharpens analytical reading skills and helps students understand Wilde's adaptation. They recognize that Wilde was conscious of the past but chose to differ from it. For the next class I ask them to select one of the differences—the motif of looking—and to question how it configures the plot and contributes to the characterization of Salomé. They track this motif using the elements of the traditional tragic plot: exposition, rising action, climax (recognition and reversal), falling action, and resolution. They quickly discover that Salomé is the catalyst for action. Her story is plotted in regard to being both an object of the gaze and a subject looking back.

This tracking exercise challenges students to identify and define the basic elements of the traditional tragic plot and to see how the motif illuminates the rise and fall of Salomé. The play begins and ends with men looking at Salomé. Debate regularly arises concerning the climax. Some students view Salomé's dance as the climax. Others believe that it is when she receives the silver charger and stares at the severed head. Still others point to an earlier passage: Salomé stares at the living prophet's body, hair, and lips. At this point, we discuss ambiguity and review the definition of climax, looking in particular for Salomé's recognition and reversal.

Wilde's dialogue provides cues. Students see that his language is repetitious and visually oriented. The word "look" and the phrase "Do not look at her" recur. While the play begins and ends with Salomé as the object of the male gaze, the encounter between Salomé and the prophet offers a striking variation. We focus on this section, tracking how she looks and looks again at Jokanaan. Salomé performs the equivalent of a close-up: she looks at the prophet, then approaches him, stating, "I would look closer at him. . . . I must look at him closer." The Young Syrian and Jokanaan interrupt, attempting to censor her. Jokanaan yells, "Who is this woman who is looking at me? I will not have her look at me" (589). A few lines later, she looks at Jokanaan three times: first at his white body, then at his black hair, and finally at his red lips (589–90).

This section is daring and full of contradictions. Salomé stares at the prophet. Although her desire waxes and wanes (she keeps changing her mind about what feature of his body she most desires), an idea and a motive emerge. Salomé wants the prophet to look at her.

I ask students to write a paper (three to five pages) defining Salomé. Is she a static or dynamic character? This question encourages them to review the structure of the play and to look, in particular, for dramatic reversals. We turn to Salomé's first entrance. When the play begins, she has left the banquet hall in an attempt to escape Herod's gaze. When she enters, she says, "I will not stay. I cannot stay. Why does the Tetrarch look at me all the while with his mole's eyes under his shaking eyelids?" (586). Herod comes out and looks at her, but she is still not willing to be an object of his gaze. It is only after she recognizes that she desires the prophet to look at her and after she sees that Herod has sworn an oath to give her whatsoever she desires that Salomé agrees to dance and make a spectacle of herself for Herod.

Wilde does not describe Salomé's dance; he simply states, "*Salomé dances the dance of the seven veils.*" Herod responds to the dance by exclaiming, "Ah! Wonderful! Wonderful!" (600). But it is Salomé who punctuates this passage. She presents an imperative: "Give me the head of Jokanaan" (602). She trumpets that she is not a dutiful daughter: "I do not heed my mother. It is for mine own pleasure that I ask the head of Jokanaan in a silver charger" (600).

We turn to the falling action and resolution (or the climax, falling action, and resolution—so much depends on how students diagram and defend their interpretations of the tragic plot). After reminding Herod that he has sworn an oath to give her what she desires and after refusing a parting gift from his long list of possible and exotic gifts (e.g., a great round emerald with mystical powers and white peacocks that are gilded and have feet stained with purple), Salomé once again asks for what she desires. She finally receives the head of the prophet. She stares, noting, "Thine eyes that were so terrible, so full of rage and scorn, are shut now. . . . Wherefore dost thou not look at me?" She repeats her close-ups of his body: "There was nothing in the world so white as thy body. There was nothing in the world so black as thy hair. In the whole world there was nothing so red as thy mouth." She speculates about the act of looking: "If thou hadst seen me thou wouldst have loved me. I, I saw thee, Jokanaan, and I loved thee" (604). The play concludes by censoring itself. Herod calls for the stage to fade to black: "Put out the torches! Hide the moon! Hide the stars! Let us hide ourselves in our palace. . . ." Finally he turns, sees Salomé, and orders, "Kill that woman!" (604–05).

After investigating how the motif colors the tragic plot and contributes to characterization, we discuss a theoretical approach to the theme of looking. I present excerpts from Mulvey's seminal essay "Visual Pleasure and Narrative Cinema."

For Mulvey, a feminist filmmaker and critic, looking is culturally coded. She identifies a gendered binary system that defines woman as other and partitions women from the privilege of seeing. She analyzes numerous cinematic texts and concludes that it is always men who look. Men look. Men act. Men make meaning. And woman? Woman is "still tied to her place as bearer, not maker of meaning" (15). Woman is image, a spectacle:

> The determining male gaze projects its fantasy on to the female figure which is styled accordingly. In their traditional exhibitionist role, women are simultaneously looked at and displayed, with their appearance coded for strong visual and erotic impact so that they can be said to connote *to-be-looked-at-ness*.   (11)

This kind of representation depends on a narrative that is not interrupted by exaggeration or incongruity (17). The text must not call attention to itself.

I ask students to write a short paper responding to the question, How does Wilde's *Salomé* adhere to and deviate from the basic rule that the female performs for the privileged male spectator? The purpose of this question is to prompt students to see that Salomé both signifies a spectacle and challenges this traditional exhibitionist role.

As a prewriting exercise, we review the structure of the play. The play begins and ends with Salomé performing for the privileged male gaze. Then we focus on the dialogue. Men, such as the Young Syrian and Herod, look at Salomé. The first line of the play is spoken by the besotted Young Syrian: "How beautiful is the Princess Salomé to-night!" The dialogue that immediately follows does not reveal what features make Salomé beautiful. Rather, the Page of Herodias and the Young Syrian turn to the moon. The Page states, "Look at the moon!," and the Young Syrian observes, "She has a strange look. She is like a little princess who wears a yellow veil, and whose feet are of silver" (583). These descriptions, directed toward and inspired by the moon, suggest a female figure adorned with costumes that have visual and erotic impact.

Students search for descriptions of how Salomé looks. One description is, "The Princess has hidden her face behind her fan! Her little white hands are fluttering like doves that fly to their dove-cots. They are like white butterflies" (585). When Salomé prepares for the dance of the seven veils, the reader learns that she has been wearing sandals. The slaves bring perfumes and the seven veils, and they take off the sandals (599).

Students note that the dialogue is both sparse and exaggerated. Salomé's costumes are never described, only suggested—for example, as a mirror image of the moon. Her dance of the seven veils remains a mystery. On the other hand, Wilde peppers his narrative with a significant gesture: Salomé looks, even stares. Her descriptions of John's body are detailed and colorful. White, black, and red ignite the dialogue with desire. Such details interrupt the narrative flow.

In concluding this approach, I review the reception of this play and encourage students to question why the play has been so controversial. (A handout with a historical overview of the reception of Wilde's *Salomé* and suggested readings is helpful. See app. 2.) I also ask students to consider Wilde's comments about the structure and stature of his play.

In 1897, just three years before his death, Wilde proclaims that his role as a dramatist revolves around *Salomé*. In a letter addressed to Lord Alfred Douglas, he calls attention to the structure of his tragedy in one act: "The recurring phrases of *Salomé*, that bind it together like a piece of music with recurring *motifs*, are, and were to me, the artistic equivalent of the refrains of old ballads" (*Complete Letters* 874).

The importance of the motif of looking has been recognized by readers of Wilde's play, among them Edward Burns, who notes that if male characters, such as Herod and the Young Syrian, look at Salomé, she in turn participates in "dangerous seeing, the desiring look" (32). Salomé desires to look at John the Baptist, and eventually does look at him. Burns concludes, "In the beginning was the word, but not for Salome, who exists in the domain of the look, and whose narrative is plotted by the hazards of looking and being looked at" (33).

Wilde was immensely proud of his artistic creation:

> If I were asked of myself as a dramatist, I would say that my unique position was that I had taken the Drama, the most objective form known to art, and made it as personal a mode of expression as the Lyric or the Sonnet, while enriching the characterisation of the stage, and enlarging—at any rate in the case of *Salomé*—its artistic horizon.   (*Complete Letters* 874)

As this approach to teaching *Salomé* suggests, the motif of looking enabled Wilde to enrich the characterization of the stage and enlarge the artistic horizon. His Salomé is unforgettable because she makes meaning by daring to stare. Finally, investigating the motif of looking challenges students to improve their reading and writing skills, to examine gender issues from a theoretical and historical perspective, and to discover that Wilde is not only a playwright and a poet but also a visionary.

APPENDIX 1:
DIFFERENCES BETWEEN THE NEW TESTAMENT ACCOUNTS AND WILDE'S *SALOMÉ*

New Testament	Wilde
The daughter of Herodias is not named.	The daughter of Herodias is Salomé, and the play is named after her.
The occasion of the dance is Herod's birthday party.	There is no mention of Herod's birthday.
Looking is not a motif.	Numerous characters look and are warned not to look.
The dancing daughter is an object, controlled by Herod and Herodias.	Salomé is an object, dancing for Herod, but she is also a desiring subject.
The daughter asks for the head of John the Baptist because her mother wants it.	The motive is revenge: Jokanaan refused to look at Salomé.
Herod does not present a list of possible and exotic gifts.	Herod presents a long list of gifts.
The daughter gives the head to her mother.	Salomé keeps the head, stares at it, and kisses the mouth of the prophet.
We do not learn what happens to the daughter.	Salomé is killed at Herod's order, crushed beneath the shields of his soldiers.
There is no moon.	The moon is a main character.

APPENDIX 2:
HISTORICAL OVERVIEW OF THE RECEPTION OF WILDE'S *SALOMÉ*

Oscar Wilde's *Salomé* was banned in 1892 and has a complicated publishing history. Because of the censorship, the play appeared first in French and then in English. This time line comes from *The Complete Letters of Oscar Wilde*:

> *1891, November–December.* Wilde writes *Salomé* in Paris.
>
> *1892, June.* A production of *Salomé*, with Sarah Bernhardt in the title role, is banned by the Lord Chamberlain.
>
> *1893, 22 February.* *Salomé* is published in French.
>
> *1894, 9 February.* *Salomé* is published in English, with illustrations by Aubrey Beardsley.

In 1892, Edward Pigott, Examiner of Plays for the Lord Chamberlain's Office, refused Wilde a license to produce his play. The refusal was warranted: Queen

Elizabeth's edict of 1559, still valid, banned biblical characters from appearing on the stage.

See *The Censorship of English Drama, 1824–1901*, by John Russell Stephens. In a chapter entitled "Religion and the Stage," Stephens discusses the various forms of prejudice against the theater. For centuries, English law upheld the belief that it was immoral to allow religious subjects onstage. Few dramatists dared write a play based on the Bible; but "one important exception of the early 1890s was Oscar Wilde" (112).

There are contemporary newspaper accounts of the censorship of Wilde's play. One is "The Censure and 'Salomé' "—an interview with Wilde published in the *Pall Mall Gazette* on 29 June 1892. Wilde addresses the banning of his play: "What I do care about is this, that the Censorship apparently regards the stage as the lowest of all the arts, and looks on acting as a vulgar thing" (1). He observes that painters, sculptors, and poets are quite free from this censorship. Playwrights, however, are restricted from presenting characters from the Bible. Wilde states, "I shall publish 'Salomé.' No one has the right to interfere with me, and no one shall interfere with me." Finally, he threatens to leave England and settle in France. "I will not consent to call myself a citizen of a country that shows such narrow mindedness in its artistic judgments" (2).

Viewing *Salomé* Symbolically

Beth Tashery Shannon

Salomé is Oscar Wilde's most puzzling play. Dramatizing a Bible story with necrophiliac eroticism; aestheticizing the revolting; addressing innocence, evil, desire, and depravity; yet making no easily definable statement, it leaves many students baffled. The first time I introduced a group of sophomore English majors to *Salomé*, the usually responsive students had little to say. When invitations for even gut-level responses produced only frowns and shrugs, I began to realize the difficulty was not verbalizing the play's elusive fascination and repulsion. My students were merely confused. This group's close-reading skills had progressed rapidly, but such skills depend on making certain choices—consciously or unconsciously—based on known points of reference. My students were not finding useful points of reference. They lacked a perspective from which to view *Salomé*.

Indeed, perspective may be the greatest challenge *Salomé* offers. Whereas Wilde's contemporary comedies feature sharply drawn characters, deft wit, and social issues, *Salomé* presents vague figures speaking in solipsistic images that nullify any possibility of social negotiation. The language (whether the original French or the English translation) is both too ornate and too spare for comfort. Furthermore, though Sarah Bernhardt was to appear in the title role, *Salomé* was not a success like Wilde's other plays: it was banned from the English stage before a performance ever took place. Because this text seems atypical, instructors may be tempted to ban it from their syllabi as well. Yet, the very qualities that make *Salomé* difficult make it especially rewarding to teach. It offers an excellent opportunity to shift students' attention away from learning a text toward teaching themselves to choose among alternative ways to read.

The following suggestions are intended for undergraduate courses, preferably those that have one and a half or two weeks to spend on *Salomé*. Typically, such courses are on fin de siècle literature or culture, Victorian or Irish drama, or the works of Wilde, but I have taught *Salomé* in sophomore surveys of British literature. I structure the schedule as follows. Students should complete their first reading before the first meeting (the text's brevity makes that feasible). The first week combines short presentations, writing prompts, and discussion. Each student's objective is to investigate perspectives from which to view *Salomé* and, during the last two sessions, to use one or more of those perspectives in discussions and finally a paper. Since the students select their perspectives individually and may get on diverse tracks, I find it helpful to require them to preface discussion comments by briefly identifying their working perspective. This protocol not only clues in others as to where a comment is coming from, it also enhances students' awareness of their ongoing selection processes.

As engagement with the text develops, its resistance to reductive readings—*Salomé*'s refusal to be possessed—may for some emerge as its most intriguing and transgressive aspect. To maintain focus and relieve anxiety, the instructor should repeatedly emphasize that success depends not on achieving a correct reading of *Salomé* but on rigorously considering how to read the play.

Two weeks may seem excessive for a minor text, but (questions of canon aside) *Salomé* can be as important as a so-called major work, because it is a good example of a text that inescapably centralizes questions about reading. Major texts that make a similar demand are Spenser's *Faerie Queene*, Blake's long poems, many of Yeats's middle and late poems, and Joyce's long fiction, to name a few. Some key films outside Hollywood norms similarly challenge how one reads or views (e.g., by Federico Fellini, Donald Cammell and Nicolas Roeg, Maya Deren, Kenneth Anger, David Lynch, Peter Weir). Admittedly, only majors in English and the arts usually recognize the importance of confronting how we read, but even students working off a humanities requirement often become interested in approaching *Salomé* through Aubrey Beardsley's drawings or Bernhardt, or in the cultural implications behind the transformation of the nameless, passive princess in the Bible into Wilde's transgressive figure.

To foreground the difficulties, I open the first session with the reminder that *Salomé* is a play. Staging it requires choices. Each student is asked to imagine being the director and to list decisions that must be made. For instance, is this play a tragedy, melodrama, or parody? Should it be presented as realism, recited poetry with stylized dance, over-the-top camp, or in some other way? As students address these questions, the challenges emerge: How do we view this strange work? What of its central figure? What about its peculiar dialogue?

Having identified these issues and any others the students raise, the class can begin exploring perspectives. Comparison with the Bible versions make an excellent initial writing or discussion prompt, since with this angle most students will find insights and develop confidence. For instance, they may notice resonances between biblical religion and Victorian culture, but also the counterenergies emerging in the 1880s and 1890s. The first session might end effectively with emphasis on *Salomé*'s position between opposing cultural forces.

Many teachers will want to use the angle of Beardsley's illustrations. For an instructor's or student's presentation comparing Wilde's words with Beardsley's images, Michael Patrick Gillespie's essay *Oscar Wilde and the Poetics of Ambiguity* provides a helpful verbal-visual intratextual analysis. In particular, Gillespie's remarks on the interchangeability of attributes between Salomé and Jokanaan (140–43) may provoke interesting discussion. Instructors who prefer issue-driven approaches will find a Wilde-Beardsley perspective useful for discussions of gender, sexuality, and censorship (of both Wilde's play and Beardsley's images).

Another perspective might be a focus on the play's censorship. John Russell Stephens's *The Censorship of English Drama* provides a useful background for the contrasting views presented by Kerry Powell in "Salomé, the Censor, and the Divine Sarah" and Richard Ellmann in *Oscar Wilde* (371–76). For the figure of Salomé, Bram Dijkstra's *Idols of Perversity* and Toni Bentley's *Sisters of*

Salome also set up intriguing contrasts, since Dijkstra reads the character (380–98) and the play (396–98) in terms of the misogyny of Wilde's era, while Bentley presents a positive feminist view of the figure of Salomé (19–32).

Yet, whatever the vantage point, students will be confronted with *Salomé's* most challenging obstacle: its style. Many are put off by what they call its flowery language. Sophisticated students may compare it unfavorably with the conciseness privileged by modernist influences, or, if approaching it as antirealism, they may find it excessive beside the minimalist surrealism characterizing certain strands in current fiction. From these reference points, sensory profusion belongs to mass-market romances and is bad writing.

But once identified, the excesses of language in *Salomé*, and—paradoxically— the sphinxlike restraint, open the way to an approach that is perhaps the most difficult of all yet the most potentially rewarding: the play's symbolist context.

Students can prepare for a symbolist view of *Salomé* with two brief readings from Ellmann's biography: "Mallarmé" and "Virgin Cruelty" (335–45) and "Overtures to *Salomé*" (371–76). This background material establishes Wilde's enduring fascination with the figure of Salomé and his admiration of treatments of her by certain painters and writers, especially Gustave Moreau, J.-K. Huysmans, and Stéphane Mallarmé.

Ellmann reports Wilde's fondness for quoting a certain passage from Huysmans's novel *À Rebours* (340). In this quintessentially decadent work (1884), Huysmans discusses two paintings of Salomé by Moreau. Wilde knew the pictorial iconography of Salomé (342). He admired Moreau's visual style and also the poetry of Mallarmé, whose unfinished "Hérodiade" treats the Salomé theme. Huysmans, Mallarmé, and Wilde were all in communication with one another (335–39). The Ellmann reading furnishes a concise introduction to Wilde's interest in the symbolists and the symbolist predilection for the Salomé theme. For many undergraduates this will be a first encounter with the symbolists.

Students discovering symbolism often find it at once outlandish and familiar. It stands in a peculiar relation to current literary studies, having been marginalized during the twentieth century by a canon heavily influenced by modernism yet at the same time having remained influential, directly and indirectly, on writers, artists, and pop culture. This dichotomy of influence and marginality was especially pronounced during the opening decades of the twentieth century and during the 1960s and 1970s; it is again pronounced at the opening of the twenty-first century. When my students discover the symbolists, some respond by making connections to recent subculture phenomena. Others respond to the fascination of decadence or to the symbolists' centralization of elements too often ignored in academic settings. Themes for discussion include subjectivity; rejecting logical analysis and embracing the intuitive and phantasmagoric; magic; the paranormal and death; physical and spiritual intoxication; sexuality outside mainstream norms; dreams and imagination as not merely psychological phenomena but powerful forces; and the transcendent potentials of art.

The influence of the symbolists on Wilde also offers a possible reason that the play was composed in French. He aspired (however ironically he expressed it) to become "a famous French author" (Ellmann, *Oscar Wilde* 374) and attributed the "curious effect" of Maeterlinck's plays to their being in French, which for Maurice Maeterlinck as well as for Wilde was an "alien" language (373). Writing (and reading) a foreign language foregrounds the sounds of the words, and word music was important to the symbolist poets. Reviewing his achievements from prison in *De Profundis*, Wilde describes *Salomé* in musical terms reminiscent of Mallarmé's descriptions of poetry. He calls his play "a piece of music" with "a note of Doom" that "binds it together like a ballad" (1026). The indications are strong that he intended *Salomé* as a bid to enter an international circle he had long esteemed, that of the French symbolists.

If Wilde intended Salomé as symbolist drama, is that relevant to us? Will it enhance our reading? That question launches the second week. Instructors (and students writing papers) looking for background reading on symbolist theory and technique will find a wonderfully tonal introduction in Arthur Symons's *The Symbolist Movement in Literature* (1908). Symons romanticizes as only a young convert can, but his interpretations understand the spirit of their subject, and he includes essays on Mallarmé and Huysmans. A handy collection of essays on symbolism by symbolists is T. G. West's anthology *Symbolism*; essays in it of particular relevance are Mallarmé's "Crises in Verse," W. B. Yeats's "The Symbolism of Poetry" and "A General Introduction for My Work," and Paul Valéry's "Remarks on Poetry."

The symbolist perspective on *Salomé* is most easily and effectively presented in this order: Moreau, Huysmans, Mallarmé. These writers already form a chain leading to Wilde's play; the lesson plan simply follows the links. Moreau's paintings of Salomé begin the sequence. Among his many representations of Salomé are the two that Huysmans will address, *Salomé Dancing before Herod* (see illus.) and *The Apparition*, both first exhibited in 1876.

Moreau's paintings do not reproduce well (either in print or online) because of their intricate detailing and dark colors, so using the best possible reproductions is important. An excellent source is Geneviève Lacambre's *Gustave Moreau: Between Epic and Dream*. Pierre-Louis Mathieu's *Gustave Moreau: The Watercolors* also contains many vivid reproductions, though *Salomé Dancing before Herod* is not there, being in oils. Instructors with computerized classrooms will find both *Salomé Dancing before Herod* and *The Apparition* on the Web. Here too, hunting for good reproductions is advised. Moreau painted several variants, which can be of interest since they reflect the symbolist painter's interest in Salomé's emotional states. For example, one version of *The Apparition* shows Salomé dismayed by the severed head, while in another she seems in sorcerous control of it. Moreau is interested in her internality as much as in the external spectacle of the femme fatale.

The difference between Moreau's and Beardsley's images is striking, but if a writing prompt is desired, a free-form response to one of Moreau's Salomés is

Gustave Moreau: *Salomé Dancing before Herod*, 1876. Oil on canvas, 56½×41¹⁄₁₆ in. The Armand Hammer Collection. Gift of the Armand Hammer Foundation, UCLA Hammer Museum

preferable to comparative analysis at this point. Sinking into Moreau's world, responding imaginatively rather than analytically, is the best way for students to begin to intuit symbolist constructs, which—like Wilde's play—resist linear logic and analytic rhetoric. Having tasted Moreau, students are now in a position to gain from Huysmans.

Huysmans was not a committed symbolist, but *À Rebours* (1884; *Against Nature*) treats symbolist dilemmas with astuteness. Wilde covertly (without mentioning its title) refers to *Against Nature* in *The Picture of Dorian Gray*. It may be the book with the yellow cover admired by Lord Henry and Dorian; it certainly influences chapter 11, in which Wilde halts his plot outright to give a description of Dorian's eccentric aesthetic pursuits, which reads more like an excerpt from Huysmans's novel than a chapter in Wilde's. In *Against Nature* the protagonist, Des Esseintes, purchases Moreau's *Salomé Dancing before Herod* and *The Apparition* (63–70). Huysmans's Salomé passage is neatly excerptable. During the discussion, it is useful to display one or both of Moreau's paintings.

Huysmans gives a knowledgeable account of the development of Salomé, "a figure with haunting fascination for artists and poets," from the Bible accounts of Herodias's obedient daughter to a figure possessing in her own right "maddening charm and potent depravity." She

> repelled the artistic advances of fleshly painters [of the Renaissance and seventeenth century and] passed the comprehension of the writing fraternity, who never succeeded in rendering the disquieting delirium of the dancer, the subtle grandeur of the murderess.   (65)

Huysmans sees in Moreau's paintings the first empowered Salomé. The passage also introduces other precursors for Wilde's play, Heinrich Heine's *Atta Troll* (1841), Gustave Flaubert's *Salammbô* (1862), and Mallarmé's "Hérodiade" (1887). It is difficult to find a more evocative or insightful introduction than Huysmans's to the development of the Salomé theme in art and literature. The excerpt also allows students to sample symbolist writing. This is the passage often quoted by Wilde (Ellmann, *Oscar Wilde* 342).

For Huysmans, only Moreau's paintings captured the essence of Salomé; the unattainable dancer had eluded the pen. The question I now pose to my class is whether the ambitious Wilde might have taken Huysmans's assertion as a challenge. Perhaps Wilde saw in Salomé at once the most esoteric, poetic, and conversely most popular of subjects, a figure of fascination for his era yet not exhausted or even completely achieved in words. Mallarmé, a poet Wilde admired, had come closest, but she had baffled Mallarmé; his "Hérodiade" remained unfinished.

The final link in the symbolist sequence is Mallarmé's "Hérodiade." Since Mallarmé's poems can be only approximately translated and rely much on the music of their sounds, students who read even a little French will benefit from a bilingual handout, such as from Henry Weinfield's translation, the *Collected Poems* of Mallarmé (25–37). Following an old tradition, Mallarmé gives Salomé her mother's name, Herodias. Parallels between his imagery and Wilde's will be spotted by students (orientalism, mirror, moon). Wilde's *Salomé* and Mallarmé's "Hérodiade" are also similar in their rejection of linear rationality. Attention might be called to Mallarmé's making his Salomé figure both gazer and the mirrored object of her own gaze, then students might be asked whether they find any parallels between Mallarmé's self-reflective gaze and Wilde's dialogue.

In the end, the symbolist perspective on Wilde's *Salomé* returns to our journey's beginning: *Salomé* is not a poem like the "Hérodiade" but a play. Huysmans implies that poetry cannot incorporate the visual power of the dance. But theater can incorporate both poetry and dance. Wilde knew he could entertain audiences with his comedies. Perhaps in the tragedy of Salomé as she is reconstructed by the symbolists, he saw potentials for combining poetic speech and dance in ways that had never yet been fully realized. From this perspective, *Salomé* is both a serious work of art and a comprehensible one. The morbidity of its themes, the dreamlike reflectiveness of its language, the ambiguous dialectic between Salomé and Jokanaan, and the phantasmagoria of its imagery can now be explored with new insight.

Close readings should notice that the dialogue works through subjective evocation rather than objective statement. The flowery language can be reconsidered in terms of imagery that pushes past the limits of logic into phantasmagoria, a method where exaggeration serves purposes having nothing to do with parody—though it is a method not without humor, as in the timing of Herodias's "the moon is like the moon, that is all" (592). From the symbolist perspective, Wilde's *Salomé* emerges as neither frivolous nor casually disjointed but as a controlled and patterned evocation of uncontrollable forces. Such a treatment opens its themes for exploration instead of wrapping them in tidy conclusions.

Related paper topics might include orientalism and the Victorian empire or a comparison of themes and imagery in *Salomé* (such as dancing) with similar themes and imagery in one of Wilde's most ambiguous fairy stories, "The Fisherman and His Soul." The Salomé fad of the late 1800s can, of course, be examined in the psychological terms of Victorian male fascinations and fears. (An amusing twist is provided by the question, Did Salomé die with the last gasp of Victorianism, or did she switch genders, becoming Mick Jagger, Jim Morrison, and other late-twentieth-century self-reflective male objects of the female gaze?)

Because the symbolist angle yields rich possibilities for viewing *Salomé*, in proposing that students consider the play from multiple perspectives, I have been urging an essentially symbolist reading. Approaching a text from alternate, equally valid angles is certainly a challenge. Students may—and often do—settle on a more reductive approach, finding a single perspective that appeals to them and becoming its proponent. Even so, they have still made an important stride: they have given thought to their approach to a text. If they are confronted with an ambiguous text again, the reward of that achievement will be considerable. If they have gone further, moving from blank puzzlement or frustration to an awareness as multifaceted as Wilde's "great round emerald," layered like sapphires where the "sea wanders within" (601, 602), that reward can be worth the effort of the entire course.

Salomé, C'est Moi? *Salomé* and Wilde as Icons of Sexual Transgression

Petra Dierkes-Thrun

> Moderation is a fatal thing, Lady Hunstanton. Nothing
> succeeds like excess.
> —Lord Illingworth, in A *Woman of No Importance*

Teaching Wilde's *Salomé* today presents a double challenge: while reconstructing the difficult historical and literary context of Wilde's least accessible play, we must also reckon with students' already established "knowledge" of Wilde, shaped by a whole century's worth of popular culture readings of him as an icon of sexual transgression. Although the twentieth-century reception of Wilde's work through the lens of his homosexuality now accompanies any Wildean text in the undergraduate classroom, acknowledging Wilde's symbolic status becomes particularly important for *Salomé*, a text that directly thematizes moral, aesthetic, and erotic excess. Like many readers before them, students tend to see the subversive Salomé as Wilde's alter ego, even as they are usually unaware of the various cultural clues that have contributed to this transgendered conflation since the 1890s. Judging from Wilde's own insistence on "the truth of masks" (1156–73), the play's homoerotic subtexts (the Page's love for Narraboth, Salomé's "little green flower" [588]), Aubrey Beardsley's androgynous illustrations or, later, the famously misappropriated photograph of Wilde as Salomé in Richard Ellmann's landmark biography (M. Holland, "Wilde as Salomé?"), many have viewed *Salomé* as Wilde's most intimate "closet drama" (Showalter, *Sexual Anarchy* 150).

The teaching sequence I propose strategically incorporates students' assumptions about Wilde into the study of *Salomé* in the undergraduate literature, film, or popular culture classroom, addressing both the play's history and the twentieth-century cultural imagination of Wilde, through three selected film adaptations. Alla Nazimova's silent *Salomé: A Pantomime after the Play by Oscar Wilde* (1922) emphasizes *Salomé*'s and Wilde's avant-garde qualities; Ken Russell's *Salomé's Last Dance* (1988) foregrounds Wilde's sexual and aesthetic censorship; and Suri Krishnamma's *A Man of No Importance* (1994) offers an empathetic melodramatic reading of Wilde as a historical gay martyr. Engaging students in recursive close readings of *Salomé* in comparison with these three interpretations, the two-week sequence moves students from *Salomé*'s historical literary and cultural circumstances to larger reflections on functions and mechanisms of the twentieth-century appropriations of Oscar Wilde as a queer icon.

The first session begins by engaging the students in a discussion of Wilde's biography and *Salomé*'s major themes. Asked what they already know of Wilde and his works, students typically mention his homosexuality and works that have dominated his twentieth-century cultural reception: *The Picture of Dorian Gray*, *The Importance of Being Earnest*, *An Ideal Husband*, or their respective film versions. Collecting students' answers on the board, I fill in basic information about Wilde's life and career, focusing on the period especially relevant to our topic, from the height of Wilde's playwriting in the early 1890s to his 1895 trials. If time permits, I show the Irish documentary *Oscar Wilde: Spendthrift of Genius*. Students can also be directed toward Richard Ellmann's and Barbara Belford's biographies and Brian Gilbert's 1997 biopic *Wilde*.

I start our analysis by asking students about the difficulties they experienced in reading *Salomé*: What seemed strange, different, or otherwise remarkable to them about the play's style, structure, or language? Responses can lead to the discussion of typical features of symbolist style: repetitions and leitmotifs, stylized language, elevated tone, nonrealistic portrayal of characters, a dreamlike atmosphere. To illustrate the play's symbolist affinities, I have students briefly look at the opening scenes of Maurice Maeterlinck's *La princesse Maleine* (similar to those of *Salomé*) and sections from Stéphane Mallarmé's "Hérodiade" ("Ouverture," "La scène: Nourrice—Hérodiade"). Tracing Wilde's approach to the theme, we then consider the synoptic Gospel accounts of John the Baptist's death in Mark (6.17–28) and Matthew (14.3–11) and Des Esseintes's hallucinatory descriptions of Gustave Moreau's Salomé paintings in Huysmans's *Against Nature* (ch. 5). Bram Dijkstra's *Idols of Perversity* is an excellent resource to illustrate the fin de siècle visual context of erotic Salomés by Franz von Stuck, Edouard Toudouze, Max Slevogt, Gustav Klimt, and others (379–401). Comparing and contrasting these texts with *Salomé*, I invite students to formulate their first impressions of Wilde's play, focusing on major themes, character constellations, style, and overall structural devices (like the white-red-black color and moon schemes symbolizing Salomé's gradual loss of innocence or the leitmotifs of the look and beating of wings signaling impending doom).

After this overview, students are in a good position to encounter *Salomé: A Pantomime after the Play by Oscar Wilde*, the first surviving film adaptation, directed, scripted, and produced by the Russian American Broadway and silent movie star Nazimova.[1] As with all the films in this sequence, I ask students to take screening notes on specific issues and scenes, which then serve as the basis for group work, class discussions, and written assignments. We examine Nazimova's film according to three main aspects: its innovative translation of Wilde's symbolist theatricality into visual language, specifically the treatment of his theme of the dangerous look by means of camera, acting, and editing techniques; Nazimova's portrayal of Salomé; and the film's striking gender-blurring qualities.

Students often note that Nazimova's slow-paced film, with its pantomimic acting style, extended close-ups, and Natacha Rambova's stylized sets and costumes freely adapted from Beardsley's 1894 art nouveau illustrations, feels just as artificial and removed from reality as Wilde's symbolist play. The silent film's acting technique of exaggerated gestures and facial expressions and the lengthy close-ups on Nazimova's—the star's—face echo the hypnotic effect of Wilde's verbal repetitions: they invite audiences to contemplate moments of beauty or mystery (while admittedly taxing some students' patience). At this point I introduce students to Wilde's original plans for the stage set, costumes, colors, and drifting perfumes (Tydeman and Price 45–51; Ellmann, *Oscar Wilde* 372) and explain the symbolist ideal of synesthesia, the simultaneous stimulation of multiple senses through aesthetic productions. Nazimova's visual allusions to Beardsley and the use of Richard Strauss's 1905 operatic music for the dance of the seven veils (which later sound editors added to Nazimova's original) are two additional ways in which the film approaches synesthetic evocation, while attractively placing Wilde's play in the context of 1890s sexual decadence and modernist avant-garde art (Tydeman and Price 159–61).

Focusing on the film's camera and editing techniques, students may discover Nazimova's interesting cinematic interpretation of Wilde's motif of the dangerous look. Good scenes to analyze in class are Salomé's enticement of Narraboth to hand over the prison key and the dance of the seven veils. The enticement scene shows the effects of Salomé's hypnotic femme fatale look, capturing first her eyes in an extreme camera close-up in iris-in frame and then, in an immediate countershot, Narraboth's mesmerized face. In the dance scene, the film even extends Wilde's theme of voyeurism to the cinematic audience: as Salomé seductively veils and unveils herself while staring directly into the camera, we too are transfixed and "look too much at her" (584).

The petite Nazimova portrays Salomé as a flapper-like teenager with the malicious cunning of a sphinx (the poem "The Sphinx" could be another Wildean text to accompany *Salomé*). Her overall faithful interpretation offers good opportunities for students to analyze the ambiguous *femme fragile*, femme fatale qualities of Wilde's Salomé. These qualities can be further illustrated by handout excerpts from Wilde's letters and interviews, in which Wilde variously called Salomé a virginal "mystic, the sister of Salammbô, a Sainte Thérèse who worships the moon," a "tragic daughter of passion," or a sensual orientalist princess (Ellmann, *Oscar Wilde* 376; Wilde, *Complete Letters* 556; Mikhail, *Oscar Wilde: Interviews* 192–95). Collecting passages and scenes in play and film that illustrate this essential ambivalence of Salomé, students can better approach the difficult interpretation of the end of the play. Is Salomé innocent or guilty, pure or perverse, or both—and what evidence does the text provide for either view? Whereas the film's last intertitle presents Salomé as the stereotypical vamp ("And the moon was hid by a great cloud . . . And the stars disappeared. And nothing in the world was as black as the name of SALOMÉ"), Wilde's thunderclap ending seems more open and ambiguous: did Salomé lose, or did she triumph? Does Herod's sudden command "Kill that woman!" reestablish moral law and order, or does it suggest an unsettling decadent coup d'état, since Salomé achieved what she wanted, and Herod fearfully retreats into his palace (605)?

Finally, in Nazimova's film students encounter first evidence of the influence of Wilde's sexual reputation on twentieth-century readings of *Salomé*. The camp-style "Ladies of the Court," played by male actors in drag and female make-up and Nazimova's androgynous appearance as Salomé strongly emphasize the gender-blurring and homoerotic subtexts of Wilde's play. Nazimova's own lesbianism sheds an interesting personal light on her project: besides carrying on an affair with the set designer, Rambova, Nazimova purportedly employed an all-gay male cast in posthumous honor of the transgressive Wilde (see Morris's useful chapter in *Madam Valentino*, 65–93). Fittingly, one of Nazimova's conquests immediately after *Salomé* was Dolly Wilde, Wilde's niece (Schenkar 145–47).

My teaching of *Salomé's Last Dance* and *A Man of No Importance* continues and extends these lines of inquiry, while offering students a chance to explicitly explore twentieth-century popular culture figurations of Wilde as a gay martyr. Narrated around fictional theatrical stagings of *Salomé* and studded with allusions to *Salomé's* 1892 ban and Wilde's 1895 trials, both films offer the chance to discuss the historical circumstances of *Salomé's* and Wilde's aesthetic and sexual censorship; they can thus be screened alternatively or, for contrastive analysis, in conjunction. Viewing questions like the following can help students decode the complex narrative and visual intertwinements of *Salomé* with Wilde's homosexuality in each film: Note the connections of the fictional stage production of *Salomé* with the framing narratives of each movie. How do Wilde's art and Wilde's/Byrne's life mirror and blend into each other? Pay special attention to scenes, dialogue, or visual cues suggesting a homoerotic reading of *Salomé*. How do these movies represent the historical Wilde's persona, verbally and visually?

Russell's gleefully ironic, sexually explicit historical fable *Salomé's Last Dance* restages almost the entire text of *Salomé* as a play within a play, performed for Wilde in a 1892 Victorian brothel, shortly after *Salomé's* ban. Art, sex, and censorship are intertwined, as *Salomé* quite literally crosses over from the stage into Wilde's life and life begins to mirror art: Wilde's lover Bosie (Douglas Hodge) takes on the role of John the Baptist and winks at Wilde from the stage ("It is through woman that evil has come into the world" [cf. 590 (*Salomé*)]), Salomé (Imogen Millais-Scott) sips champagne with Wilde and accepts a green carnation, Wilde has sex with the Page (Russell Lee Nash), and Wilde's arrest follows on the death of Salomé.

Considering Russell's ironic stylization of Wilde (played by Nickolas Grace), students should reflect on their own reactions to Wilde's verbal and visual manners and actions: what impression do they get of Wilde here? Russell's Wilde speaks in pseudo-quotes and bawdy witticisms ("There is only one thing worse than to be talked about, and that is not to be talked about"; "No sermons please . . . I'm not in the mood for the missionary position just now") and displays the provocatively carefree attitude of a drawing-room dandy. Asking students if they think the film simply spoofs Wilde and *Salomé*, I direct their attention to Russell's chosen setting (the anarchic-utopian space of a brothel, a trope also found in Arthur Schnitzler and Jean Genet) and his anachronistic twisting of historical events. Wilde's arrest for "gross sexual indecency" at the end immediately following *Salomé's* 1892 ban—when, in fact, Wilde was never arrested in a brothel and his trial did not take place until almost three years later—suggests a direct connection between Wilde's art and his sexual dissidence. Setting the action on Guy Fawkes Day in 1892, Russell's film also associates Wilde's *Salomé* with moral and political rebellion (in an early scene, Taylor explains that Guy Fawkes opposed "a parliament that he found oppressive . . . you have done the same with your play, *Salomé*"). The end of the film conjures up Wilde's tragic downfall as the camera pans out behind the bars of an iron fence, visually imprisoning the departing Wilde: Salomé's last dance, we are led to understand, was also Oscar's.

A Man of No Importance, too, interweaves a fictional staging of *Salomé* with Wilde's life, in a coming-out tale of Alfred Byrne (played by Albert Finney), a middle-aged bus conductor in 1963 who secretly pines for Robbie (Rufus Sewell), a younger bus driver whom he calls "Bosie" in allusion to Wilde's love Lord Alfred Douglas. An ardent Wilde fan who recites Wilde's works for his bus passengers, the closeted Byrne finds in Wilde his source of sexual and aesthetic redemption ("Wilde had no life aside from art. . . . He never descended into the sewer"). Eventually rehearsing *Salomé* with a ragtag drama group at the local parish hall, Byrne finds himself censored by moral zealots: like the historical *Salomé*, his production is nipped in the bud by the jealous butcher Mr. Carney (Michael Gambon) and religious watchdogs' outrage at *Salomé's* "immodest dancing" and "foul sexual language."

Students will notice that, like Russell, Krishnamma intersperses the *Salomé* plot with references to Wilde's trial, interlocking aesthetic censorship with sexual oppression by social and moral authorities. Allusions to Wilde's trials permeate the film throughout: the scary bus overseer's name is Mr. Carson, after Wilde's prosecutor; Byrne calls the jealous Mr. Carney "Queensberry," after Bosie Douglas's father; Byrne incessantly cites passages from Wilde's bitter prison letter to Douglas, using Wilde's words as a moral guide against hypocrisy ("If I can produce one more beautiful work of art I shall be able to rob malice of its venom, and cowardice of its sneer, and to pluck out the tongue of scorn by its roots" [1022 (*De Profundis*)]). Toward the end, Byrne stands up against his bullying homophobic overseer in Wilde's own words from his second trial: "Mr. Carson, the love that dare not speak its name, do you know what that is? It's fine. It's beautiful. It's the noblest form of affection. There's nothing unnatural about it!" (cf. Wilde's original passage in Hyde, *Trials* 201; Goodman 114).

Pointing to both films' critical indictment of sexual censorship, I ask students to examine the special bond established between Wilde and Salomé and to watch out for scenes that suggest a homoerotic reading of the play. In *Salomé's Last Dance*, two scenes poignantly illustrate the double reading of Salomé and Wilde: the beautifully choreographed dance of the seven veils and Salomé's moving final monologue. Through rapid crosscuts between the dancing Salomé and what turns out to be a male dancer in identical costume, Russell creates the illusion that Salomé is both male and female. Split into two bodies, two dancers whirl about synchronously side by side; in the climactic moment, the double Salomé removes the last veil to reveal first male, then female genitals, before quickly covering up. Presenting an orgiastic performance of gender (con)fusion, Millais-Scott's androgynous body (similar to Nazimova's) combines homoerotic and heteroerotic desire, like the attractive brothel scent that Wilde notices early on ("a blending of green carnations and the pubic hair of virgins," quips Taylor). During Salomé's love soliloquy to the severed head of John/Bosie, Russell also uses crosscuts between Salomé and a tearful Wilde to suggest a biographical connection between Salomé's words and Wilde's tragic love for a cruelly selfish Bosie ("If you had looked at me, you would have loved me. . . . Why did you not look at me, John the Baptist?" [cf. 604 (*Salomé*)]).

The same monologue plays a pivotal role in *A Man of No Importance*, as Byrne's Salomé—played by the secretly pregnant Adele Rice (Tara Fitzgerald), who is also scorned by her fittingly named lover John—breaks down when she stumbles over Wilde's lines: "What shall I do now, John the Baptist? Neither the floods nor the great waters can quench my passion. . . . I was a virgin, and thou didst take my virginity from me" (cf. 604). Undeceived about Adele's purity and realizing his own sexual naïveté, Byrne boldly approaches some young hustlers in a bar for his first homoerotic encounter, citing Lord Henry's words to Dorian Gray for encouragement ("The only way to get rid of temptation is to yield to it" [28 (*Picture of Dorian Gray*)]). When he is violently beaten and robbed instead of kissed and embraced, Byrne resigns himself with Wilde's words from *De Profundis*, "There is only one thing for me now, absolute Humility" (1018). As the film follows Byrne and Adele's growing friendship, it shows the two transgressive outsiders as intuitive allies. Like Wilde and Salomé, the film suggests, they mirror and understand each other.

A Man of No Importance focuses strongly on Wilde's status as a gay martyr. Students may soon notice that the film's entertaining, creative portrait of *Salomé* and Wilde is geared at making the audience identify and empathize. Krishnamma hints at Wilde's sexual innuendo and his reputation as the archetypal queer wit, continuously emphasizing his personal tragedy. While analyzing the film's use of textual selections besides *Salomé*—excerpts from "The Harlot's House," *De Profundis*, *The Ballad of Reading Gaol*, the preface to *Dorian Gray*, *The Importance of Being Earnest*—students can be asked to consider the strategic functions of such selections as well as of such visual clues as the green carnation (prominently figured in the film's opening scene), Byrne's dandyesque robe and makeup in the alley scene, and the Wildean mise-en-scène of Byrne's room (with Beardsley's "Dancer's Reward" *Salomé* print in the background). Ironically belying its own title (adapted from Wilde's 1893 society comedy), Krishnamma actually develops a genealogical line between the two men, Wilde and Byrne. Both *A Man of No Importance* and *Salomé's Last Dance* transform the historical Wilde and *Salomé* into allegorical stories for the present: the violent suppression of Wilde's/Byrne's aesthetic and sexual esprit is designed to convince contemporary audiences that homophobia has terrible effects on individuals as well as social groups and the power to destroy lives.

To contextualize the films' allusions to *Salomé*'s and Wilde's censorship with historical and critical materials in class, I bring in excerpts from interviews and letters in which Wilde and others discussed the play's ban as well as critics' notices concerning the 1893 French and 1894 English book editions (Beckson, *Oscar Wilde: The Critical Heritage* 132–43; Mikhail, *Oscar Wilde: Interviews* 186–91). When students identify the main issues of the controversy—*Salomé*'s subject matter, Wilde's artistic worthiness, and the institution of stage censorship itself—they can begin to gauge the play's powerful first impact on Victorians, in responses ranging from William Archer's defense of *Salomé* as "an oriental Hedda Gabler" and Wilde as an important modern dramatist; to Wilde's protest against the censorship and his announcement to leave England for Paris, "the centre of art, the artistic capital of the world"; to the censor's private view of *Salomé* as "a miracle of impudence," "half Biblical, half pornographic. . . . Imagine the average British public's reception of it" (Beckson, *Oscar Wilde: The Critical Heritage* 142; Mikhail, *Oscar Wilde: Interviews* 188; Stephens 112). For further information and research assignments on Wilde's stormy relationship with Bosie Douglas, students can usefully consult Ellmann's and Belford's biographies and relevant passages in *De Profundis*. For students interested in the implications of Wilde's trials for the legal and cultural discourse about homosexuality in Britain, H. Montgomery Hyde's (*Trials*), Jonathan Goodman's and now also Merlin Holland's (*Real Trial*) partial compilations of the historical trial transcripts, and Ed Cohen's and Michael Foldy's critical analyses of the materials and reactions are good resources for further research and writing, as is the first film adaptation of Wilde's trial in pre-Wolfenden Britain, *The Green Carnation* (1960), which used Wilde's case to argue "for an end to the legal persecution of British male homosexuals" (Stetz 106).

It is easy to see how in a larger literature or popular culture course on Wilde, the sequence could be expanded to include figurations of Wilde's life and trials in such recent texts as Terry Eagleton's *Saint Oscar*, Neil Bartlett's *Who Was That Man?*, Moisés Kaufman's *Gross Indecency*, David Hare's *The Judas Kiss*, and Tom Stoppard's *The Invention of Love*. A course focusing on Wilde's wider influence on popular culture might also consider late-1990s films that present Wilde as a signifier for full-fledged rebellion, like Todd Haynes's *Velvet Goldmine* (associating the birth of glam rock in the 1970s with Wilde's flamboyant dandyism) or Robert Altman's *Cookie's Fortune*, which includes in its narrative of small-town dreams and delusions a minor theatrical staging of Wilde's *Salomé*.

In analyzing these strategic conflations of *Salomé* and Wilde, students become gradually aware of *Salomé*'s adaptation as a process of critical interpretation. But instead of merely contemplating the distance between the original and its copies (would Wilde have agreed to Nazimova's reduction of Herod and Herodias to an orientalist sideshow, or would he have approved of Russell's and Krishnamma's turning his symbolist tragedy into an ironic comedy?), students should be encouraged to reflect on the mechanisms, functions, and effects of the films' appropriation of Wilde and *Salomé*. What interpretation of the author and his play do these adaptations suggest to a contemporary audience? And what ends do they pursue by presenting social critique in such forms of popular entertainment? Students usually take different positions about the success of these films as gay-friendly mainstream entertainment. This variety of opinion is also reflected in the film reviews that I bring to class (easily obtainable online through the *Movie Review Query Engine* [www.mrqe.com]). As some students are quick to point out, don't the directors reduce the whole play to the figure of its author, who is in turn reduced to Oscar Wilde the homosexual? And if we in the twenty-first century have inherited an already interpreted Wilde, how does our reading hold up against the historical Wilde and *Salomé*? Who and what are they for us today?

So at the end of this teaching sequence the circle closes: from a close reading of the play and its literary and cultural contexts we proceeded to the three adaptations' focus on Wilde's transgressions and are now back facing the problem of reading *Salomé* and Wilde. Hopefully students have come to realize that their images of Wilde rely on a complex tradition of literary, social, and cultural interpretation that has enlisted Wilde and his intellectual works for various purposes, among them the desire to forge a literary-cultural genealogy for the twentieth century's gay rights struggles. Complicating and enriching *Salomé* for students today also means showing them that Wilde's "is simply not a life which can tolerate an either/or approach with logical conclusions; it demands the flexibility of a both/and treatment, often raising questions for which there are no answers" (M. Holland, "Biography" 4).

The overall goal of teaching *Salomé* in the ways suggested here is to open up a pedagogical space for addressing intersections of Wilde's transgressive eroticism with his works, while deconstructing the narrowly predetermined contents of this space. Although some insecurity, skepticism, and even resistance are still to be expected in any discussion of homosexuality in the undergraduate classroom, students can find in Wilde and *Salomé* an important test case to negotiate the historical and cultural ideas influencing representations of (homo)sexuality and gender, in Wilde's times and our own. Teaching *Salomé* in conjunction with Wilde's twentieth-century intercultural reception, leading students from history to the present, from text to context and back to text, deeply engages them in Wilde's most challenging play, allowing in the process a more complex Wilde to emerge from behind the glamorous curtain.

NOTE

[1] The most widely available edition of Nazimova's film is the 38-minute one distributed in the United States by Grapevine Video. While this edition is useful for the pedagogical purposes outlined in this essay, readers should be aware that there are more

complete versions available for research and study purposes. I recently viewed a six-reel 35mm film held at the Library of Congress in Washington, DC, which at a length of 5,122 feet seems to be the longest surviving version in existence (another comparatively long print is at the Eastman Kodak House in Rochester, NY; see P. White 84n19). The Library of Congress also holds a shortened 16mm reedited version (68 minutes), which the silent-film collector Raymond Rohauer newly assembled with the textual assistance of Wilde's son, Vyvyan Holland, for a Beardsley retrospective in New York in 1967 (67–68). Intertitles vary significantly among these film editions, and the long 1922 Library of Congress print includes important scenes cut from later editions of the film. Further research is needed to sort all relevant archival materials, to establish genealogical relations among the different versions, and to produce reliable comparative analyses.

Unveiling *Salomé*:
The Word-Made-Flesh Undone

Samuel Lyndon Gladden

Overview

Teaching *Salomé* presents an opportunity to show students how Wilde's work engages artistic and historical traditions as well as how it intersects ongoing conversations about a range of cultural anxieties, chiefly those concerning bodies and beliefs, pleasures and faiths. Wilde's play anticipates late-twentieth-century debates about the social place and function of pleasure and about the borders demarcating two of pleasure's representational modes, the erotic and the pornographic. I draw on *Salomé* to show how Wilde's play charts a distinction between the erotic and the pornographic that may easily and exactly be mapped alongside another of *Salomé*'s binaries, the sacred and the profane, as aesthetic, discursive, and experiential realms.

I devote three one-hour periods to *Salomé*. My students and I spend the first day discussing representations of Salomé in other media, the second establishing connections to other works by Wilde, and the third reading the play through Aubrey Beardsley's drawings. Every time I teach *Salomé*, I stress the overlapping of matters religious and sexual: with undergraduates, I focus my energies on contextual links and close readings; with graduate students, I emphasize theoretical interpretations and applications to recent feminist and queer scholarship. What follows characterizes that theoretical argument. The proposed three-day plan, however, outlines a model for teaching these issues specifically to undergraduates.

I think it best to state my general argument about *Salomé* at the outset, so that my descriptions of textual and contextual materials will make better sense to readers seeking strategies for teaching that argument. For me, *Salomé* exemplifies three tendencies that mark much of Wilde's oeuvre: first, the incorporation of traditional Christian language and imagery in decidedly exotic, and erotic, contexts; second, the construction of a conservative frame narrative around a resolutely radical text; and third, the turn to ambiguity as a strategy for celebrating unlicensed ideas, experiences, and pleasures. In these ways, *Salomé* may be read alongside Wilde's better-known works, such as *Dorian Gray* and *Earnest*, as a text that exposes the underside of nineteenth-century life only in the end to discipline and contain such play, however ironically, however transparently. In *Salomé*, Wilde teases his readers, for while initially he seems to delight in subversion, he finally punishes subversion's agents, so that his readers are left with upright, uptight Victorianism—or at least with its highly polished veneer.

The Argument

Salomé explores a model of the erotic grounded in the following conditions: in the space of the erotic, all participants retain subjectivity, speaking for themselves and articulating their individual desires; anticipation gets privileged over completion; and cathexis, the overconcentration of thought, emotion, and energy, allows for the psychic heightening of an experience by way of which participants transcend the limits of self through an abundance of pleasure. The pornographic may be described by schematizing oppositions to the erotic. In the space of the pornographic, at least some participants are denied subjectivity; completion is privileged over anticipation, so that anticipation is employed not for its own end but in the service of completion; and what I call negative cathexis—horror, disgust, and death—limits, binds, and otherwise demarcates all experiences of pleasure. While these descriptions leave gaps and beg questions, they at least begin to differentiate the erotic from the pornographic, even if only to return both terms to a binary relation that constructs each in terms of the other.

The meanings *Salomé* offers for the spaces of the erotic and the pornographic may be linked to another scheme of tremendous cultural significance: the Christian belief in salvation through Jesus Christ as manifested in the doctrine of the Word-made-flesh. My model for understanding *Salomé* hinges on aligning the erotic with Christian doctrine or, more broadly, with the sacred. In such a model, the erotic signifies the Christian promise, the Word-made-flesh; the pornographic, on the other hand, stands as the undoing of that realm in its negation of Christianity. In this new model—exactly the one *Salomé* suggests—the erotic and the sacred occupy one space, the pornographic and the profane another. Ultimately, my reading of *Salomé* exposes the move from the erotic to the pornographic as exactly the same as the move from the sacred to the profane, a move coincident with Salomé's dance of the seven veils.

Christianity proceeds from the notion of incarnation, of God's Word taking physical shape, ultimately in Jesus Christ, himself the Word-made-flesh. Yet a central Christian sacrament, the Eucharist, might also be considered its most blatantly pornographic moment, for the Eucharist offers up the fleshy nature of the Savior as the object of desire. To non-Christians, Communion might seem oddly cannibalistic, and such a ritualistic devouring might well be coded as pornographic, for the consumption of the body of the deity by mere humans is not really very far removed from Salomé's blasphemous demand that Iokanaan be beheaded. In both Communion and *Salomé*, purely human flesh consumes and is consumed by its desire, its passion, for the body of (the representative of) the Lord. Thus, Wilde's play overcodes religion and sex, pornographizing Christian sacrament only in the end to (or at least to appear to) punish, to discipline, the figure who stoked desire.

The Christian doctrine of the incarnation of Jesus Christ—"And the Word was made flesh, and dwelt among us . . ." (John 1.14 [King James Vers.])—offers a key for understanding *Salomé's* demarcations of the erotic and the pornographic. The play's undoing of that covenant, the severing of Word from flesh, signifies the pornographic precisely because it signifies the profane. Demanding the head of Iokanaan on a silver charger, Salomé initiates the process of the undoing of Christianity, and her act of profanation—flying directly in the face of God and rendering his Word mute, dead—occupies the same moment in the play as does the turn from the erotic to the pornographic: Salomé's dance of the seven veils, through which power and control are transferred from man to woman, from Herod to Salomé, by way of the beautiful maiden's provocative display. *Salomé* thus suggests that two realms fundamentalist Christians fight so diligently to separate, religion and sex, constantly dissolve into each other, and the play locates an origin from which our cultural assumptions about the erotic and the pornographic emanate.

Christ *is* the Word-made-flesh, says the Bible; to reject the Christian doctrine of redemption and salvation is to profane. In Wilde's play, the separation of Word and flesh manifested in the beheading of the prophet signifies an act of profanation that renders Iokanaan representative no longer of the union of Word (God's message) and flesh (a human body) but, instead, of mere flesh devoid of word. Exploited, objectified, Iokanaan becomes the object of the play's now-pornographic gaze. The events in *Salomé* that culminate in his beheading thus establish a trajectory that moves the play out of the realm of the erotic (word-and-flesh, subjectivity, articulation/sense) and into the pornographic (mere flesh, objectivity, inarticulation/horror).

This Word-from-flesh notion of the pornographic may easily be charted alongside my description of the erotic. If the erotic is a space in which subjectivity is guaranteed, an area of anticipation rather than completion, and a vehicle for cathexis, then the living Iokanaan exemplifies that realm. Even imprisoned, he exhibits subjectivity in his unceasing assertions of his role as the messenger of God; he devotes his entire life to anticipation, prophesying the coming of Christ; he resists being profaned by insisting that his body is (nothing but) a temple of God. Wilde explicitly eroticizes Iokanaan through Salomé's speeches by drawing attention to the beauty and desirability of his body. Ultimately, though, the prophet gets destroyed by another manifestation of the erotic that Richard Dellamora finds embodied in Salomé, "a force . . . able to subvert the customary superiority of men" ("Traversing" 250), an unabashed display of what at least one of Beardsley's drawings suggests is the self-satisfying, masturbating female (*The Toilette of Salomé—II* [O. Wilde, *Salomé* (Beardsley) 58]). Like the play itself, Iokanaan moves from the space of the erotic to the space of the pornographic as *Salomé* climaxes in the dance of the seven veils, setting in motion the events that culminate in Iokanaan's beheading. At her request, he is reduced to pure object: symbolically castrated, he is denied subjectivity, rendered word-less by his reduction to mere flesh.

Quite interestingly, it is only by way of stage directions, not dialogue, that Wilde marks the play's climax: the explosion of sexual energy in Salomé's dance of the seven veils, which initiates a shift in representational modes from the sacred to the profane and from the erotic to the pornographic. The staging of this move, the fall from Word-made-flesh to pure flesh, Wilde thus envisions by means of a body (movement) without language (text). With Salomé's dance, he emphasizes the key element structuring this new pornographic-profane realm of experience, the body, over that which is left out of it, the Word (i.e., proper biblical attitudes toward desire and its containment); thus, Salomé's dance stages the Word-made-flesh undone.

The play's shifts in embodiments of power and representational mode grow increasingly complicated when Herod reasserts his kingly privilege by calling for Salomé's assassination, reinforcing and restabilizing a more conventional form of sexuality. Salomé's removal expels the incestuous, the profane, and the pornographic from the play's realm of desire. In the end, Herod upholds traditional sexual rules, silencing the one who has pushed the erotic too far, who has moved the atmosphere of play out of the realm of the sacred and into the realm of the profane. While Herod's erotic desire for Salomé's body may seem revolutionary in its disregard for the boundaries of incest, his call for her death ultimately appears reactionary: Salomé must die because she has frustrated his desire and thus irrevocably violated—profaned, so to speak—his authority.

In my reading, Herod stands as the play's moral center, and his insistence on Salomé's murder initiates a move out of the pornographic as well as a retreat from the profane, just as his ultimate command signifies a desperate attempt to recover what threatens to be lost: the sacred-erotic—that is, the Word-and-flesh space of pleasure, subjectivity, articulation. In direct contrast to the climax of the play in Salomé's wordless dance of the seven veils, Herod's desires are articulated through language as manifested directly on a body; thus, through Herod, Word and flesh are conjoined, and incarnation reigns as the model and phenomenon that structures the world of Wilde's play. Such a framing of the revolutionary within the reactionary typifies much of Wilde's work and can be seen in his other writings, *Dorian Gray*, *Earnest*, and "The Sphinx" chief among them.

In an odd way, though, Herod's move from a revolutionary-erotic space, in which sexual and familial roles blur, to a reactionary one, in which such differences reemerge, suggests that *Salomé's* ultimate gesture is not simply from the erotic-sacred to the pornographic profane and back again but, instead, from the erotic-sacred to the pornographic-profane and, finally, to a new configuration in which the erotic (Word-made-flesh) is reasserted even as the sacred (Iokanaan) fails truly to be recovered. Thus, *Salomé* may well end in the space of patriarchal certainty: in Herod's newly reorganized camp, an erotic utopia is no longer threatened by the wailings of God's mouthpiece from the dungeon; it is a world in which Herod's word once again guarantees the fleshy response

Herod desires, a secular-sexual Word-made-flesh world in which the power of incarnation belongs again, and now exclusively, to him.

Teaching the Argument

For the first hour of instruction, I introduce contextual documents that establish the various forms of *Salomé*'s appeal. I set the mood by greeting students with music from two operatic versions of *Salomé*, Jules Massenet's *Hérodiade* (1881) and Richard Strauss's *Salomé* (1905). I begin by pointing out the radically different versions of the story Massenet and Strauss offer. Massenet positions Salomé and John as faithful lovers and Salomé as a would-be matricide who finally turns a dagger on herself in despair over being denied the privilege of accompanying her lover in execution. Strauss, on the other hand, follows and borrows heavily from the language of Wilde's play. Two tracks from *Hérodiade* emphasize Herod's deep desire for Salomé ("Que m'oses-tu dire?") and Salomé's violent, self-destructive response to his refusal to give her, finally, what she desires ("Laissez-vous émouvoir!"). Strauss's "Dance of the Seven Veils" invokes the sultry context of the play's seduction scene—its climax, in my reading—where eroticism slips into pornography as the sacred gives way to the profane. Most students recognize Strauss's piece, which underscores for them the presence of *Salomé* in our collective cultural consciousness. Though different in their versions of the story, both operas emphasize Salomé's sexual appeal as well as the danger of her attractiveness, and both remind us of the story's deeply religious and political consequences, which leave Herod's patriarchal rule virtually untouched.

Next, I invite my students to consider representations of Salomé in another medium, and I turn to paintings by Gustave Moreau and Gustav Klimt that play up Salomé's exotic and erotic appeal as well as her fatal attraction. Moreau's *Salomé Dancing before Herod* (1876) introduces students to a visual alphabet that anticipates the stylized look of so-called decadence, and Klimt's *Judith and Holofernes I* and *II* (1901, 1909) depict a Salomé-like femme fatale wielding the head of the man she has vanquished. Together, these images cast Salomé (or a Salomé type) as a seductress whose beauty and appeal mask a frighteningly powerful avidity—apt images to compare to Wilde's Salomé as well as to the erotic-pornographic duality she embodies.

Two film versions of Wilde's play also offer students opportunities for constructing a visual sense of the drama and its cultural milieu. Alla Nazimova's 1923 silent *Salomé* draws inspiration from Beardsley's illustrations for costume and set design. Nazimova's film helps my students understand the powerful link between text and image, which makes them more attentive to, and more appreciative of, Beardsley's drawings when we return to them on the final day of discussion. A scene or two from Ken Russell's campy *Salomé's Last Dance* (1987) underscores the play's sudden shift from pleasure to horror (not only Herod's, as in the play, but also the presumably heterosexual male viewer's), for as the final veil falls, the youthful Salomé gets exposed as a young man. Russell thus moves from titillation to shock, from socially sanctioned eroticism (heterosexual) to something other (homosexual), and in so doing he cannily replicates *Salomé*'s shift from eroticism to pornography.

My students find particularly interesting a visual representation of Salomé in David Shenton's graphic novel *Salomé* (1986), and a careful selection of two or three pages from that volume effectively closes our first day's discussion of the play as well as demonstrates the continuing place of Salomé in late-twentieth-century imagery. Like Beardsley's drawings and Russell's *Salomé's Last Dance*, Shenton's *Salomé* situates the playwright as a character in the drama (the Cappodocian). Shenton's illustrations offer a particularly grisly rendering of Salomé's work, focusing on her associations with blood and illustrating vividly the sexually charged atmosphere her presence conjures. By the end of the first hour, my students have begun to think about *Salomé* in terms of three media—music, painting, and film—and they have begun to recognize in her and in the play that bears her name a constellation of concepts the following days' discussions will disentangle.

Throughout the second hour of study, I reemphasize the presence of Salomé in nineteenth- and twentieth-century art by inviting my students to consider two images. Franz von Stuck's shadowy *Sin* (1893) depicts a titillating yet threatening seminude woman who seems to dare the viewer to approach her even as an enormous black serpent surrounds her body, framing her breasts and covering her vulva, hissing at the viewer from over her right shoulder and thus warning us away from the dark lady's charms. Julius Klinger's *Salomé* (1909) picks up on the theme of the seductress's monstrosity as well as of her threat to patriarchal rule by showing a haglike woman, her huge breasts balanced by the phallus-like leg protruding from her skirt, holding before her a bloody, castrated penis. Both Stuck and Klinger emphasize Salomé's sexual potential, but where Stuck portrays Salomé as a femme fatale, finding in her the simultaneous nature of the erotic and the pornographic, Klinger's image focuses on Salomé as a pure monster bent on man's violent destruction, on his reduction to a now-useless body part.

My students and I close our consideration of contextual images by examining one more painting, Georges de Feure's *The Voice of Evil* (1895), a portrait of a stunningly Wilde-like writer whose shoulder-length hair and aesthetic costume invoke the Sarony-era Wilde and who seems to be plotting our temptation, staging our doom. Feure's striking work helps my students better understand the place of Wilde in late-nineteenth- and early-twentieth-century cultural consciousness, and it encourages them to see Wilde as a stand-in for the femme fatale, as yet another embodiment of the evil, threatening, feminine other so effectively depicted in the playwright's rendering of Salomé.

For the bulk of the hour, my students and I turn to other works by Wilde that illustrate two aspects key to the structure and content of *Salomé*. "The Sphinx" (1894) exemplifies Wilde's strategy of framing a revolutionary narrative within a reactionary one. Often, I refer to this doubling by other names to help my students better understand the tensions Wilde sets in competition, and so we discuss his decision to situate a homoerotic narrative within a homophobic frame or to contain a pagan celebration within a Christian repudiation.

In "The Sphinx," the first-person speaker envisions the title character's whole history, imaginatively returning to antique eras and fancying what knowledge of the eroticized male body the sphinx harbors. Wilde shields these ruminations from attacks of impropriety by displacing them onto the sphinx herself, a strategy not unlike Herod's displacement of responsibility throughout *Salomé*, first to Herodias, who calls for Iokanaan's incarceration, and then to Salomé, who demands his execution. Having distanced his first-person speaker from homoeroticism, if not from outright homosexuality, Wilde enjoys such pleasures from a safe remove. As the poem concludes, however, the speaker disdains the vision he has imagined, displacing it back onto the sphinx and rejecting such knowledge by turning from that embodiment of paganism to one of Christianity—the crucifix on the wall beneath which the speaker cowers, begging for forgiveness even as he curses the sphinx for her vision (which really, of course, is his). The speaker thus punishes the agent of his own transgression by repudiating her and clinging instead to a Christian symbol. In so doing, "The Sphinx" plays out the move from pleasure to faith, from flesh to Word-made-flesh, that *Salomé* stages.

Finally, we turn to Wilde's play *La Sainte Courtesaine; or, The Woman Covered with Jewels* (c. 1894), which offers a fascinating counterpoint to *Salomé*, not only in plot and setting but also in its stark staging and sparse language, which I encourage my students to see as a protomodernist alternative to *Salomé*'s highly decorated spectacle of excess, itself much more typically Victorian. In all these aspects, *Courtesaine* seems *Salomé*'s opposite, its other; but in the end, the message the play delivers remains *Salomé*'s, a parable about the tensions between faith and desire. The play's setting exactly reverses *Salomé*'s: no longer in the realm of Moreau-like decadence, Wilde offers nothing more than a crucifix, a cavern, and sand dunes, which in my reading represent faith, retreat-punishment, and transcendence, both geographic and chronological.

In *Salomé*, the action preceding the play's climax comes in the exchanges between Salomé and Iokanaan—she driving for erotic satisfaction, begging for a kiss, he denying her such knowledge and pleasure. In *Courtesaine*, Myrrhina (the Salomé figure) tempts Honorious (this play's Iokanaan), who stands resolved to deny the pleasures of the flesh both to himself and to Myrrhina, since to give in, he fears, would ruin them both. Myrrhina, acknowledging her impurity, convinces Honorious of the shortsightedness of his ways, of the price of his purity. Honorious finally acquiesces (a moment recalling, perhaps, the Garden of Eden's Eve-then-Adam sequence), but then, in a startling reversal, Myrrhina rebukes him, saying that she was pure all along, that she tempted Honorious only to test his inner strength and spiritual faith. As the play closes, Myrrhina bemoans her duplicity and the powerful lure of her erotic appeal, lamenting, "I have cursed my beauty for what it has done, and cursed the wonder of my body for the evil that it has brought upon you" (738), a phrase my students agree might well have been uttered by Salomé had Herod allowed her to live long enough to reflect on the chaos her actions wrought.

On day 3, we turn to the play proper, focusing on Beardsley's drawings to see his take on Wilde's play and to consider the larger theoretical argument about the play I have described. Beardsley emphasizes Salomé's vanity—her narcissistic awareness of the power of her beauty to sway others—in the twin images *The Toilette of Salomé I* and *II* (58), where her ablutions are undertaken to entice others (in the first) as well as to pleasure herself (in the second). Her sexiness reaches its zenith in what I consider the play's climax, given its coincidence with the double shifts in faith and pleasure, in *The Stomach Dance*, where Beardsley visually invokes Salomé's intention to overtake Herod's power by way of the phallic drapery rising from her crotch (54). Beardsley prefigures the darker side of her power in *The Peacock Skirt*, where she looms over and around a male figure (2), whose crown-of-thorns-like headpiece Beardsley gives to her in *John and Salomé* (20), subtly suggesting another moment of her appropriation of one of Beardsley's markers of masculinity and, thus, of power. *The Dancer's Reward* features Salomé, triumphant, receiving the bloody head of Iokanaan, and one could argue that the head and the slave's arm that supports it represent a displaced image of Salomé's phallic power (62). *The Climax*, originally printed in *The Studio* (and reproduced in the Dover edition of *Salomé*), includes a quote from the play's original French ("J'ai baisé ta bouche Iokanaan, j'ai baisé ta bouche"), and it depicts Salomé rising above the earth, celebrating her victory over the man who spurned her and thus claiming him by way of both language (word) and real, tactile possession (flesh, which, significantly, is severed, undone, pornographized [64]).

Finally, Beardsley's *Cul-de-lampe* offers an occasion for my students to return again to my interest in the play's narrative frame. The death of Salomé—which Beardsley pictures as an ironic effect of her beauty, burying her in another version of the powder boxes featured earlier on her dressing table in *Toilette I* and *II*—underscores the containment of the excesses of desire she has sanctioned and points to a turn away from the unbridled pagan lust she embodied, gesturing instead toward a faith-fearing, patriarchally dominated milieu. All's well that ends well—or so the play's patriarchal Word-made-flesh pose seems to suggests (67).

My approach to *Salomé* remains grounded in my argument about the play's double shifts, which conjoin a move from the sacred to the profane with a shift from the erotic to the pornographic. Finally and suddenly, realizing the effects of this double gesture, Herod seizes control in the only way he can. He exacts the power of his word on the flesh of an/other, by calling for the eradication of the play's embodiment of chaos. Thus Herod reincarnates his position, his privilege and pleasure, of rule and order. In this way, Wilde's *Salomé* stages the effects of Word and flesh, done and undone, by examining socially unlicensed pleasure through a narrative that, at its end, sports the shallow mask of Victorian earnestness and propriety.

TEACHING WILDE'S CRITICISM

Using Wilde's *Intentions*
to Help Students Establish Wilde's Intentions

Joe Law

Intentions, published in May 1891, is a curious collection of four prose pieces: "The Decay of Lying," a witty dialogue dealing with aesthetics; "Pen, Pencil, and Poison," a biographical sketch of Thomas Griffiths Wainewright, a painter, writer, forger, and poisoner; "The Critic as Artist," another dialogue about aesthetics; and "The Truth of Masks," an essay about historical accuracy in stage costume, ending with the declaration that that author does not necessarily agree with much of what he has written.

Although *Intentions* is much less likely to appear on the syllabus of an undergraduate literature course than, say, *The Importance of Being Earnest* or *The Picture of Dorian Gray*, this set of critical pieces should be a central document in any course that gives sustained attention to Wilde's life and works. These essays can be used as a lens to help students perceive the serious intent that Wilde's playful, aphoristic style does not always reveal at once. While such an approach will undoubtedly be of assistance to students coming to Wilde for the first time, it may be even more helpful for those already conditioned to regard him as merely the writer of mannered social comedies or gothic thrillers or the source of countless "wit and wisdom of" collections. In addition, because *Intentions* responds so pointedly to issues raised by earlier nineteenth-century literary and cultural critics (particularly John Ruskin, Matthew Arnold, and Walter Pater), these essays make an excellent culminating text in courses that address nineteenth-century criticism.

In a course devoted substantially to Wilde, *Intentions* makes an ideal starting point. Here, in concentrated form, are concerns addressed in many of his other works, and the repetition of these central themes from one essay to another provides a good opportunity for students to get a sense of them. One such theme is the fundamental importance of self-realization and the fully developed individual. These essays value the contemplative life above the productive one and stress the necessity of intensifying one's personality, neither placing restrictions on the means by which that intensification is achieved nor setting up expectations for a particular outcome or even a permanent outcome.

"The Critic as Artist" returns repeatedly to the theme of self-realization, but because it is cast in the form of dialogue rather than academic exposition, students may need to (re)construct the argument from the comments of the speakers. Gilbert, the dominant speaker, holds up as an ideal "the contemplative life, the life that has for its aim not *doing* but *being*, and not *being* merely, but *becoming*" (1138–39). The stress on becoming suggests that the process is dynamic, never completed. For that reason, the critic of whom Gilbert speaks will never arrive at a fixed, unchanging identity:

> Through constant change, and through constant change alone, he will find his true unity. He will not consent to be the slave of his own opinions. . . . The essence of thought, as the essence of life, is growth. . . . What people call insincerity is simply a method by which we can multiply our personalities.   (1144–45)

This multiplication or intensification of personality is essential for the work of the critic-artist:

> . . . it is only by intensifying his own personality that the critic can interpret the personality and work of others, and the more strongly this personality enters into the interpretation, the more real the interpretation becomes, the more satisfying, the more convincing, the more true. . . . If you wish to understand others you must intensify your own individualism.
>   (1131)

Furthermore, individual development should not be restricted in any way, particularly by conventional views of morality:

> What is termed Sin is an essential element of progress. . . . Through its intensified assertion of individualism it saves us from monotony of type. . . . Self-denial is simply a method by which man arrests his progress, and self-sacrifice a survival of the mutilation of the savage. . . .   (1121–22)

Gilbert later comments that "[i]t takes a thoroughly selfish age, like our own, to deify self-sacrifice" and suggests that those who insist on enforcing that version of conventional morality may actually "miss their aim": "For the development of the race depends on the development of the individual, and where self-culture has ceased to be the ideal, the intellectual standard is instantly low-ered, and, often, ultimately lost" (1140).

Extracting this argument from its context is, admittedly, reductive, but a sense of that argument may well enrich students' reading of the other essays in *Intentions*. Consider the way in which it informs Vivian's seemingly breezy dis-missal of Cyril's charge of inconsistency near the beginning of "The Decay of Lying": "Who wants to be consistent? The dullard and the doctrinaire, the te-dious people who carry out their principles to the bitter end of action, to the *re-ductio ad absurdum* of practice" (1072).

Asking students to summarize views set forth in "The Critic as Artist" may also help them find more intellectual substance in "Pen, Pencil and Poison." Wainewright is distinguished not only as a painter and writer "but also a forger of no mean or ordinary capabilities, and as a subtle and secret poisoner almost without rival in this or any age" (1093). With a grasp of the principles Gilbert sets out in the dialogue, it is easier to comprehend the approving judgment that Wainewright "sought to be somebody, rather than to do something" (1095), the bland conclusion that his forgeries and murders seem to have given "a strong personality to his style . . . that his early work certainly lacked" (1106), or the provocatively casual speculation that "[o]ne can fancy an intense personality be-ing created out of sin" (1106).

The witty language and light tone of *Intentions* may leave some students un-convinced of the seriousness with which these ideas are being advanced. At that point it may be useful to direct them to other places in which Wilde enter-tains similar ideas. They appear as early as the commonplace book he kept dur-ing his Oxford years (1874–78), where his seriousness is unquestionable. There he suggests, for example, that "Individualism, or the attempt to affirm one's own essence, is a late product of matured civilization" and that "progress in thought is the assertion of individualism against authority" (*Oscar Wilde's Ox-ford Notebooks* 117, 121). Still more telling is the observation that "the end of life is not action but contemplation, not doing but being: to treat life in the spirit of art is to treat it as a thing in which means and end are identified" (141), a statement that the editors of the commonplace book have traced to an essay by Pater (194–95) and a portion of which reappears in "The Critic as Artist" (qtd. above).

At the end of his career, Wilde continued to insist on the importance of self-development, identifying himself as an artist "the quality of whose work de-pends on the intensification of personality" (981). That description occurs early in *De Profundis*, the letter written to Lord Alfred Douglas during Wilde's im-prisonment. The letter is punctuated by a thrice repeated statement of princi-ple: "The supreme vice is shallowness. Everything that is realised is right" (981 and, in slightly varied form, 1002 and 1020). Wilde returns as well to the notion of individualism, writing that he is "far more of an individualist than [he] ever was" (1018) and later suggesting that his "ruin came, not from too great indi-vidualism of life, but from too little" (1041).

Between the chronological extremes marked by Magdalen College and Reading Gaol, students can find this same set of principles giving shape to many of Wilde's writings. Awareness of them as principles makes it easier to recognize *The Picture of Dorian Gray* as a novel of ideas. When Lord Henry Wotton addresses Dorian at their first meeting, he covers now-familiar ground:

> The aim of life is self-development. To realise one's nature perfectly—that is what each of us is here for. . . . The mutilation of the savage has its tragic survival in the self-denial that mars our lives. . . . Every impulse that we strive to strangle broods in the mind, and poisons us. . . . The only way to get rid of a temptation is to yield to it. Resist it, and your soul grows sick with longing for the things it has forbidden to itself. . . .   (28)

These principles may also clarify Lord Henry's curious compliment to Dorian near the end of the novel: "I am so glad you have never done anything, never . . . produced anything outside of yourself!" (155).

The same set of ideas is central to many of Wilde's other works. It is, for example, fundamental to "The Soul of Man under Socialism," where it appears for a final time in this form in the concluding paragraph:

> Man has sought to live intensely, fully, perfectly. When he can do so without exercising restraint on others, or suffering it ever, and his activities are all pleasurable to him, he will be saner, healthier, more civilised, more himself.   (1197)

Three of Wilde's plays with contemporary settings—*Lady Windermere's Fan*, *A Woman of No Importance*, *An Ideal Husband*—approvingly show self-proclaimed puritans relaxing the restraint they wish to exercise on others. At the end of *An Ideal Husband*, for instance, Mabel Chiltern pointedly avoids the error of her sister-in-law by rejecting the suggestion that Lord Goring be compelled to be "an ideal husband," saying instead that "[h]e can be what he chooses" (582). Also consistent with these views is the playwright's refusal to mete out conventional punishment to those who have yielded to temptation in their quest for self-realization. More than a century after the premiere of *An Ideal Husband*, some students are troubled that neither Mrs. Cheveley nor Sir Robert Chiltern suffers for past crimes and that the ultimate reconciliation of the Chilterns rests on a half-truth. Connecting this feature of the plot to the principles set out in Wilde's other writing may help students discover "the philosopher that underlies the dandy," to borrow Wilde's own description of Lord Goring (578).

The concern for self-realization is, of course, only one of the important notions introduced in "The Critic as Artist" and the other essays in *Intentions*. Among related topics that students may wish to pursue there and in other works by Wilde are the surprisingly postmodern claims that the self is fluid, not fixed ("The permanence of personality is a very subtle metaphysical problem,"

Wilde notes in "Pen, Pencil and Poison" [1104]); that truth is not absolute or even ultimately knowable; that language shapes thought; that criticism is a creative art, no less than painting, poetry, or fiction.

Several of the passages quoted above call into question the unified self, and one of Gilbert's assertions aligns the impossibility of knowing the self with the impossibility of ascertaining absolute knowledge:

> To arrive at what one really believes, one must speak through lips different from one's own. To know the truth one must imagine myriads of false-hoods. For what is Truth? In matters of religion, it is simply the opinion that has survived. In matters of science, it is the ultimate sensation. In matters of art, it is one's last mood.   (1143)

Students may find an echo of these sentiments in Lord Henry's contention that the value of an idea is unrelated to the sincerity of the man who expresses it and that the insincere man is likelier to express a "more purely intellectual" idea uncolored by "his wants, his desires, or his prejudices" (23). The catalog of Dorian's changing pursuits (ch. 11) might also be seen as a quest for the ultimate sensation—certainly his activities there (and elsewhere) might lead students to test Gilbert's declaration that "[e]ven a colour-sense is more important, in the development of the individual, than a sense of right and wrong" (1154).

To take only one other illustration, students might wish to examine Gilbert's view that language is "the parent, and not the child, of thought" (1121), a statement that anticipates both Martin Heidegger's pronouncements on language (e.g., "Humans speak only insofar as they co-respond to language" [25]) and the Sapir-Whorf hypothesis. Gilbert himself supplies several examples, of which this is perhaps the most telling: "Do you wish to love? Use Love's Litany, and the words will create the yearning from which the world fancies that they spring" (1149). Such a view has important connections to the seemingly willful paradox advanced by Vivian in "The Decay of Lying," that "Life imitates Art far more often than Art imitates Life" (1082). It gives more weight, too, to Vivian's claims that the nihilist was "invented by Tourguenieff, and completed by Dostoevski" and that "Robespierre came out of the pages of Rousseau" (1083).

This powerful notion about language is present in other works by Wilde. Dorian's reactions to Lord Henry's initial words—to say nothing of the fateful verbal expression of Dorian's own desire concerning the portrait and himself—are easily recognized instances of this idea, as is Dorian's sustained imitation of the "poisonous" book given him by Lord Henry. *The Importance of Being Earnest* spins variation after giddy variation on the same theme.

Although these aspects of *Intentions* are, from our own vantage point, forward-looking, Wilde's writings grow out of a centuries-long tradition and respond to the critical debates of his day. In a class in which students are not likely to have read widely in criticism, particularly nineteenth-century criticism, it would probably be worthwhile to set aside time to introduce some texts representative of those to which Wilde was responding. For example, a number of students probably will not recognize the significance of the word *lying* in the title of the first essay, even in the light of Vivian's pointed reference to Plato's view of lying and poetry as "not unconnected" arts (1073). So it may be helpful to provide brief readings from the *Republic*—perhaps from the passages in book 2 dealing with the role of fables in education (around section 377) or from the portion of book 10 that deals with the distance between mimetic art and truth (around sections 598–99). Another important point of contact with earlier ideas is Sir Philip Sidney's well-known response to Plato's charge that poets are liars ("Now, for the poet, he nothing affirmeth, and therefore never lieth") and his defense of the value of poetry in moving readers to virtue and his concession that poetry, when "abused," can do much harm (101–04). A class discussion in which students identify the shared assumptions and values of Plato and Sidney could prove especially useful in helping them see the underlying seriousness of Wilde's dialogue and the complexity of his relationship to his forebears.

It is equally important to recognize the complexity of Wilde's connections with his contemporaries, particularly Ruskin, Arnold, and Pater. Speakers in both "The Decay of Lying" and "The Critic as Artist" refer admiringly to Ruskin, with Gilbert in "Critic" valuing Ruskin's prose about J. M. W. Turner's paintings without being concerned about the soundness of the views expressed (1126). To demonstrate the radical way Gilbert's seeming compliment actually strikes at the heart of Ruskin's critical stance, students might well be given "Of the Real Nature of Greatness of Style" from the third volume of *Modern Painters*, which grew out of Ruskin's defense of Turner. In this often anthologized chapter, Ruskin articulates a set of criteria in which an artist's choice of subject matter, sincerity, truthfulness to nature, and moral purpose all rank high. He lays out these qualities all but schematically, so students might be asked to check Gilbert's and Vivian's comments against Ruskin's list. This simple but revealing exercise could lead to a fruitful exploration of Wilde's complex relationship to the earlier writer.

Arnold, too, is an important presence in *Intentions*. The original title of "The Critic as Artist" ("The True Function and Value of Criticism") identifies it as a response to Arnold's "The Function of Criticism at the Present Time," the logical starting point for looking at this particular connection. Gilbert himself begins by quoting a key idea that opens and underlies Arnold's essay (the familiar pronouncement that the "proper aim of Criticism is to see the object as in itself it really is"), but then he challenges that notion as a "very serious error" on the grounds that criticism "is in its essence purely subjective" (1126).

On this point, Gilbert's views echo and build on the work of Pater, the other major contemporary presence in *Intentions*. Two key passages are the introduction and conclusion of Pater's *The Renaissance*. After having read "The Function of Criticism at the Present Time," students will readily see the reference to Arnold in Pater's opening contention that the "first step towards seeing one's object as it really is, is to know one's own impression as it really is, . . . to realise it distinctly" (Pref. 71). That remark seems the starting point for much of *Intentions*, as does Pater's inclusion of "accomplished forms of human life" and an "engaging personality presented in life" among the artistic creations with which aesthetic criticism deals (71). Similarly, his concluding exhortations are strikingly consistent with Gilbert's agenda:

> What we have to do is to be for ever curiously testing new opinions and courting new impressions, never acquiescing in a facile orthodoxy. . . . The theory or idea or system which requires of us the sacrifice of any part of this experience, in consideration of some interest into which we cannot enter, or some abstract theory we have not identified with ourselves, or of what is only conventional, has no real claim upon us. (Conclusion 219–20)

Students will have no difficulty connecting the opening and concluding sections of *The Renaissance* with "The Critic as Artist" or, for that matter, with the rest of *Intentions* and Wilde's other works. They should also be encouraged to look for ways Wilde moves beyond Pater. For the earlier writer, an aesthetic critic "feels, and wishes to explain" the "special impression of beauty or pleasure" produced by some object of contemplation, and "his end is reached" when the explanation has been made with the greatest precision, much in the manner of a scientist (Pref. 72). Whereas Pater's critic as scientist still seems hopeful of somehow connecting the critic with the object of criticism, Wilde's Gilbert seems to embrace the impression itself. According to Gilbert, the "sole aim" of the critic should be to "chronicle his own impressions" (1125), an act that is creative in its own right and independent of the work with which it is associated: "To the critic the work of art is simply a suggestion for a new work of his own, that need not necessarily bear any obvious resemblance to the thing it criticises" (1128). Thus the accuracy of Ruskin's views on Turner or Pater's on the *Mona Lisa* is of no consequence. Ruskin's prose is "at least as great a work of art" as any of Turner's paintings or "greater indeed"; likewise, thanks to Pater's description, Leonardo da Vinci's painting "becomes more wonderful to us than it really is, and reveals to us a secret of which, in truth, it knows nothing" (1126). As Ernest sums it up (to Gilbert's satisfaction), "The highest Criticism, then is more creative than creation, and the primary aim of the critic is to see the object as in itself it really is not . . ." (1128).

The first part of Ernest's summary also points back to Arnold's "Function of Criticism," this time his assumption that no matter how high a form the critical power may take, it is inherently "of lower rank than the creative" (318). There are a good many other connections among Arnold, Pater, and Wilde that might be explored by means of *Intentions*. Asked to articulate the writers' positions on the role of criticism, for example, students might be surprised at the extent to which Wilde, who emphasizes the development of the individual, addresses the role of the critic in society in the final section of "The Critic as Artist." In other instances, the surprise may come from finding Wildean preechoes in Arnold's contention that that criticism has failed to accomplish "its best spiritual work" because it "has so little detached itself from practice" (327) and in his judgment that "the practical man is not apt for fine distinctions" (330). As even these few comments indicate, the connections between *Intentions* and the work of Arnold and Pater are significant. Introducing excerpts from their work in a class devoted to Wilde is essential in helping students place Wilde in the intellectual context of the late nineteenth century.

These brief comments should also suggest that *Intentions* (particularly "The Critic as Artist") would be an excellent culminating work in a course dealing with nineteenth-century nonfiction prose. Students who have studied other works by Arnold, for example, may see some hint of his wider influence in Wilde's allusive use of familiar Arnoldian language (e.g., "Philistine" [1139, 1146], "the free play of the mind" [1153], "the best that is known and thought" [1138]), which Wilde clearly expected readers to recognize. The wide-ranging conversation of Wilde's dialogues also takes in a good deal of what might be called "practical criticism," touching on a number of artistic and literary topics. The discussion of literary realism or naturalism in "The Decay of Lying" can provide a good illustration of the seriousness of these issues: shortly before this dialogue appeared in its original magazine form in 1889, the English publisher of Zola's *La terre* was sentenced to three months in prison for "obscene libel."

As suggested above, Wilde also touches on social issues, most notably a passage near the end of "The Critic as Artist" in which Gilbert discusses the way in which criticism leads to cosmopolitanism (1152–54). In bringing together art and social issues, Wilde is squarely in the tradition of Victorian social critics, including Ruskin, Arnold, Pater, and William Morris. In courses that devote much time to Victorian nonfiction prose, then, *Intentions* has a place.

A number of resources are available for anyone wishing to incorporate *Intentions* into a course dealing with Wilde or nineteenth-century prose writers. All four of Wilde's essays were revised significantly from their first published forms, and the original periodical versions are available electronically as part of Alfred J. Drake's *Victorian Text Archive*. A most helpful starting point for investigating the essays themselves is Lawrence Danson's brief overview of Wilde's criticism in *The Cambridge Companion to Oscar Wilde* ("Wilde"), which is in turn a good introduction to his book-length examination of *Intentions* and related critical works (*Wilde's* Intentions). Wendell V. Harris's discussion of the relationship of Wilde, Arnold, and Pater may be especially helpful for students unacquainted with the earlier writers. Finally, anyone wishing to pursue the postmodern implications of *Intentions* would do well to begin with Zhang Longxi's survey of Wilde's critical legacy.

Teaching Oscar Wilde:
"The Portrait of Mr. W. H." and the Crisis of Faith in Victorian England and English Studies

Jarlath Killeen

One of the problems encountered by teachers of "The Portrait of Mr. W. H." is its existence as two distinct texts. The short story published in *Blackwood's Edinburgh Magazine*, July 1889, is, in material and thematic terms, a very different text from the expanded novella, finally published in the 1920s. In formal terms the original short story can be classified with one group of Wilde's texts, composed of *"Lord Arthur Savile's Crime" and Other Stories* (1891) and his two collections of children's literature (*"The Happy Prince" and Other Tales* [1888] and *A House of Pomegranates* [1891]). The expanded version is a formal anomaly, divided between the literary "essays" in *Intentions* (1891) (where Wilde apparently intended to consign it) and *The Picture of Dorian Gray* (1891), to which it bears a strong resemblance. This textual confusion is heightened because, although the final version of the text should be considered the authorized version—in the same way as the revised version of *Dorian Gray* is preferred over its original version in *Lippincott's Magazine*—in this case the revised manuscript may or may not be complete. Moreover, this "final" version is less artistically satisfying than the original one.

In Wilde's canon then, "The Portrait of Mr. W. H." exists as a highly contested fugitive of material history. The extant versions of the narrative play off each other, deconstructing and reconstructing plot, sources, and style. Both short story and art-historical novella are widely available in relatively cheap editions. In editing collections of Wilde's prose, Ian Small (*Oscar Wilde: Complete Short Fiction*) and Isobel Murray (*Complete Shorter Fiction*) both chose, on aesthetic grounds, to print the short story, while Owen Dudley Edwards includes the expanded novella as the most authoritative version for the *Collins Complete Works*.

Having two versions of the text is important for a teacher of Wilde. Courses that center on Wilde invariably work with *Collins Complete Works*, while those that include Wilde as one of a number of authors use the cheaper Small or Murray editions. In my seminars, I have found it useful to distribute copies of the short story to my students as a Derridean supplement to the novella. Reactions to this supplement are quite interesting. Presenting students with two versions of the narrative, facing them with the material problems surrounding its existence, and asking them to come to terms with the notion of textual authority itself often unearth unexamined assumptions about such authority.

This challenge is highlighted by the textual conditions in which the two versions are presented. The longer version, unpublished in Wilde's lifetime and therefore theoretically more contentious, is in the *Collins Complete Works*, which claims to be "established as the most comprehensive and authoritative single-volume collection of Wilde's works available" (statement on the book jacket cover). But my students have found this version less appealing, complaining of its unnecessary length, pedanticism, and stylistic hyperbole. They consider Small's and Murray's decision to reprint the short story instead a good one. I ask them to wrestle with this theoretical question: If the better version of the text is not the "authorized" version and if the "authorized" version was unpublished in the author's lifetime and is unfinished and aesthetically inferior, what are we as students of Wilde's life and work to do in the interpretative process?

I find that this question allows students to recognize and grapple with the issues of interpretative authority that are not only integral to "The Portrait of Mr. W. H." but also lie at the center of English studies. The question brings to conscious light the hermeneutical problematic that generates theoretical debates in courses on literary theory. If students are supposed to undergo training in contemporary literary theory, they often appear to consume it with little or no reflection. Theory is approached as something to be assimilated and regurgitated rather than something to be engaged with and critiqued; theory has become a set of canonical texts and authors existing alongside, and sometimes replacing, the traditional canon of great writers. If Shakespeare and his canonical cohorts were spoken of as axiomatically establishing a tradition in the days before the theoretical revolution, then Roland Barthes, Jacques Derrida, and Eve Kosofsky Sedgwick have too often simply been added to the lists of set authors. Introducing students to two versions of one text puts them in the position of arbiters of textual authority, which, as participants in the elite practice of institutional English studies, they are anyway. This is a useful method of enabling them to develop critical positions from which theory can be demystified and interrogated, a process that should have positive implications for English studies. Once the issue of textual authority has been raised, it can be translated into a practical thematic debated in a specific narrative as well as in a modern humanities department.

My students usually notice that "The Portrait of Mr. W. H." appears to address directly issues that engage modern theorists. It is vital to get them to consider such a possibility, because one of the most persistent trends in Wilde criticism of the late twentieth century has been the attempt to make him our contemporary, often through readings of his work that appropriate it as an example of poststructuralism *avant la lettre*. Terry Eagleton has famously described Wilde as a "proto-deconstructionist" who "prefigures the insights of contemporary cultural theory" (Introduction vii, viii). In his creation of diffuse, provisional, and fluid characters who provoke multiple interpretations, Wilde refused to accept the policed boundaries of the Western logocentric myth and invested in his own marginal account of *jouissance* (see Kopelson, "Wilde"). "Oscar Wilde," writes Eagleton, "looms up for us more and more as the Irish Roland Barthes" (vii).

If the center of the debate over literary theory is the hermeneutical crux, the issue of interpretation, "The Portrait of Mr. W. H." too has most often been read as an attack on textual and historical authority. The narrative concerns the attempts by a group of characters (Cyril Graham, Erskine, and an unnamed narrator) to unlock the great literary secret of the identity of "Mr. W. H.," the dedicatee of Shakespeare's sonnets, but critics have usually argued that the story is an assault on the notion of authorial authority, as it undermines the belief that what Shakespeare intended his sonnets to mean can have any bearing on the reader response to them. For example, Michael Patrick Gillespie argues:

> In the equally plausible / equally unreliable accounts of the creation and vivification of Willie Hughes presented by several different characters, Wilde gives us a clear-cut strategy for reading: the efforts of numerous characters to offer their views of Shakespeare's creative motivations undermine the relevance of using a particular set of attitudes ostensibly held by Shakespeare as the basis for interpretation of the sonnets. Not only can we not know Shakespeare's intentions, we also cannot judge which of the alternatives should have interpretative primacy.   (*Oscar Wilde* 47)

The "clear-cut strategy" for reading provided by Wilde is a warning not to attempt to fix interpretation in the intentions of the author. This warning releases the reader into interpretive free play and liberty.

William Cohen believes that the novella is actually about itself and textuality rather than about reality and reference. He claims that W. H. is not a "real" person but only a graphic symbol so that "Wilde's theory of the sonnets becomes a determinably visual one, in the sense that it proceeds by reading—or more precisely, looking at—the printed words on the page" ("Indeterminate Wilde" 223). Linda Dowling claims that the absence of Willie Hughes is at the center of the text and that it demonstrates the wider absence of any determinate meaning to control interpretation.

In response to this critical position, I have found it useful to divide study of "The Portrait of Mr. W. H." into two classes. In the first, I have students read Barthes's essay "The Death of the Author" in conjunction with Wilde's story. They are given the job of debating the argument and implications of the essay, setting out their own theoretical stalls instead of passively ingesting chunks in theoretical anthologies. I try to ensure that the intellectual ambition of "The Death of the Author" is clear. Barthes has more in mind than the elimination of the realist author and attacks the "Author-God," believing the death of the author "liberates what might be called an anti-theological activity, an activity that is truly revolutionary, since to refuse to fix meaning is, in the end, to refuse God and his hypostases—reason, science, law" (147). Together, the death of the author and death of God undermine authority and liberate the world from monological obedience. Barthes sees the Author as derived from the monotheistic God, since both stand in relation to their creation as sole arbiter of meaning. Readers must start and end their interpretation with the Author-God, passively receiving and accepting his authority. This passivity is unacceptable to Barthes, who empowers readers to deconstruct this authoritarian Author-God. Debating the question of authorial authority usually gets the students heated up before they turn to Wilde, after which the parallels between Wilde and Barthes can be teased out.

The narrative appears committed to the same project as Barthes's. The characters in "The Portrait of Mr. W. H." see the sonnets as the "key that unlocks the mystery of [Shakespeare's] heart," as "poems of serious and tragic import, wrung out of the bitterness of Shakespeare's heart" (307). Having read Barthes, students are equipped to bring out competing discourses in the narrative, which undermine the investment in a straightforward reading of the sonnets. Killing the (A)uthor allows for the "birth of the reader." When the readers are English students studying Wilde's story, the plight of Cyril Graham becomes more acute. If the death of the Author dissolves authority into intertextuality, where a text is "a multidimensional space in which a variety of writings, none of them original, blend and clash" (Barthes 146), then "The Portrait of Mr. W. H." appears to endorse such interpretative acrobatics. As Cohen points out, it begins and ends in a library, its characters surrounded by the ubiquity of discourse (191–93). It is a text, moreover, that is about texts and about reading, containing extensive quotations from Shakespeare's sonnets and involving the interrogation of documents, papers, poems, and signatures. The story opens with a sentence declaring forgery to be the only authentic form of art, because of its self-evident, self-referential textuality, which means it is unable to refer to any extratextual reality except obliquely. Moreover, the theory put forward by Cyril Graham is textual rather than referential, dependent on the fact that the word "Will" is printed with a capital letter. The theory is based on purely internal evidence and will not yield to the call for extratextual verification from the rationalist Erskine. We have "wall to wall text" (W. Cohen, "Indeterminate Wilde" 227–30).

"The Portrait of Mr. W. H." thus appears to support the poststructuralist claim that canonical authority—the authority even of Shakespeare—is only a cipher. Reading is the primary activity of the text. The characters may peruse Shakespeare's sonnets to find out what they mean, but what they find are versions of themselves. A boy actor who plays the female role in Shakespearean drama finds that the sonnets were written to a boy actor who played the female role in Shakespearean drama. The narrator reads the sonnets and finds in them "the whole story of my soul's romance" (344). These examples confirm the poststructuralist claim that reading is not an objective but a theory-laden activity. The reader comes to the text from a particular cultural position determining the kind of interpretation that reader will posit. The reader is no mere passive receptor but an active constructor, "writing" the text. Choosing between readings is also a political rather than an objective act, as it depends on social authority rather than any access to objective truth. Deconstruction opens up the inherently political act of reading, demonstrating the institutionalized and culturally determined ways this activity is carried out. The deconstructionist thus frees interpretative practice, revealing that no one authorized interpretation is either possible or desirable (Derrida, *Acts* 56).

Students usually get these points from the text quite easily, having read Barthes, and this theory-in-practice exercise has the potential to transform the dynamic of the classroom (revealing, for example, the authority of the course instructor as a chimera!). As a primer in literary theory, the exercise has the effect of politicizing and theorizing interpretative activity to a degree that classes on pure theory rarely achieve.

Read in this way, "The Portrait of Mr. W. H." yields many of the theoretical arguments associated with names like Barthes, Derrida, Wolfgang Iser, and others. Students become excited about such associations, because although a poststructural reading can be performed on every text, poststructuralist concerns seem to be the motive of this text and indeed of Wilde. If one of the persistent complaints of students is that their teachers tend to be overinterpreters (a complaint articulated by students confronted for the first time with poststructural interpretation in all its hermeneutical varieties), here the very practice of multiple interpretation appears to be validated by the narrative. The text acts as literary evidence assuring students that authors as well as critics endorse the kinds of reading their department is forcing them to consider.

But those of us concerned with the often ahistorical nature of much Wilde criticism and who are suspicious of the need to fetishize Wilde as our contemporary have the opportunity, with this story, to historicize both contemporary theory and Wilde's text, because, as Ian Small points out, "past writers can indeed be relevant to contemporary issues and to contemporary debates about those issues, but the grounds of that relevance have to be determined by *their* concerns, not by *ours*" (*Conditions* 132–33).

This is the time to activate the expertise of the students whose study in other disciplines can be called on, and I have found it useful to historicize the novella in a second class. Students who have objected to the poststructural interpretation of the story for whatever reason also should be given an opportunity to make an argument. Unfortunately, the cultural information the objectors need is difficult to access. Many might recognize some of the references in the text—those with knowledge of Shakespeare's sonnets, Platonic theories of love, or Oxford Hellenism—but the decreasing knowledge of the Bible among students, and their relative ignorance of its interpretative history, means that few will make the link between the hermeneutical debate in the text and higher criticism's attack on the Bible in Victorian England and Germany. At this point I usually send many students off on a scholarly detective mission to report back to their colleagues. These reports galvanize the group, changing students from passive readers to members of an interpretative community.

Textuality, after all, meant something different to the Victorians from grammatology. The position of the word was certainly at stake when Wilde was writing his novella, but it was the biblical word of God and not Jacques Lacan's floating signifier. In Victorian England the Bible was fetishized by biblical literalists (Protestant sects who invested in the notion of plenary inspiration) but came under serious attack by the 1880s when the finding of the German higher criticism, that the Bible was a text much like others rather than the inspired word, began to filter through Victorian society. Authors often encoded the critical undermining of the Bible in their work, through what Joss Marsh has called "the trope of the [heretical] Book" (323). In this undermining, Shakespeare could be used. The King James Bible was considered analogous to Shakespeare's writings, because its translators had worked contemporaneously with Shakespeare. The translators and Shakespeare had constructed a language taken as authoritative because of its beauty and linguistic power (Norton 180).

That the Bible and Christianity are central concerns of "The Portrait of Mr. W. H." becomes clear when we examine the language of the narrative. The narrator compares Platonic love to a "dream of the incarnation of the Idea in a beautiful and living form, and of a real spiritual conception with a travail and a bringing to birth" (324); he suggests that "the true world was the world of ideas . . . [which] took visible form and became incarnate in man" (325). This is the language of the fourth Gospel rather than of pure Platonic theory. Students should be introduced to John's gospel at this stage, and the problematics of its historiographical position should be explained to them: this preliminary information can lead to an entirely new interpretation of Wilde.

The Protestant reformers argued that religious authority should be grounded on the reasoned interpretation of the word of God by the individual believer. Catholicism warned against this claim, arguing that such reasoned interpretation was likely to lead one astray. Instead, the First Vatican Council (1869–70) promoted faith rather than reason as the way to understand God, faith as

> a supernatural virtue by which we . . . believe that the things revealed by Him are true, not because the intrinsic truth of the revealed things has been perceived by the natural light of reason, but because of the authority of God Himself who reveals them.   (qtd. in Hick 13)

The council argued that doctrinal and theological propositions that appeared inscrutable by reason (virgin birth, resurrection, transubstantiation) were precisely those that required faith for acceptance, and faith could not be persuaded by force of logic. In faith there is and must be no logical compelling (13). Faith is the strict Catholic process. To give too much weight to reason is considered so dangerous by the First Vatican Council that "if anyone shall say that the assent of Christian faith is not a free act, but necessarily produced by the arguments of human reason . . . let him be anathema" (qtd. in Blanshard 31).

Wilde would have been aware of the Catholic attitude, both through his childhood excursions in the west of Ireland and through his reading of the pronouncements emanating from the council. Some students could be given the task of reading selections from the published work of Wilde's parents (Sir William Wilde's introduction to his *Irish Popular Superstitions* [1852] is a good place to begin); from Wilde's letters that demonstrate his knowledge of the First Vatican Council; or from the documents of Vatican I, which are available on the Internet. These students would inform the class of Wilde's rather Catholic notion of faith. For example, in a letter of 1879 Wilde writes that "Faith is . . . a bright lantern for the feet" (*Complete Letters* 25). Whereas Episcopalians highlight the rationality of God and claim that his reasonable revelation allows us, through scientific methodology, to reach the facts that save us, Catholicism highlights the impenetrability of God, who can be approached only symbolically to reach the truths that save us. "The Portrait of Mr. W. H." thus demolishes the language of empirical, reason-oriented science and insists on faith in the unprovable Willie Hughes theory.

Such student-conducted research historicizes also the questioning of authority in literary theory and demonstrates the situatedness of poststructuralism itself. After all, the breach between the authority of the author and the demands of interpretation was first created by the higher critical questioning of the relation between the Bible and God. The critic Hans Frei has shown how the higher critical collapse in trust that the Bible was the unambiguous word of God affected all hermeneutics. As biblical texts began to be judged on the basis of the interpreter's understanding of the world—instead of the interpreter's being an exegete explaining God's purpose—a skepticism about the trustworthiness of texts became an institutionalized stance. In other words, deconstruction originated in the eighteenth- and nineteenth-century attack on the "Book." For Derrida, who begins *Of Grammatology* with the chapter "The End of the Book and the Beginning of Writing," "the Book" is a closed unified totality demonstrative of logocentric metaphysics (18). The Bible is the "book of books," and such a "Book" requires an Author. When the higher critics buried the book of Scripture and effectively dispensed with the notion of its Author, the playful "text" emerged.

Scripture was now to be judged against either scientific fact (higher criticism) or the reader (poststructuralism). In "The Portrait of Mr. W. H." the grand lie of the forged portrait is not simply the flipside of truth; it is an ironic comment on what passed for truth in Victorian England: empirically verifiable, tangible fact. Erskine claims that Graham's theory needed "some independent evidence about the existence of this young actor," and he searches the registers of London's churches, the Record Office, the Lord Chamberlain's papers, "everything, in fact, that we thought might contain some allusion to Willie Hughes . . . [until his] actual existence . . . had been placed beyond the reach of doubt or cavil." Cyril Graham believes this obsession with scientific positivism evidence of a "philistine tone of mind" (309). He tells Erskine that "he himself required no proof of the kind" (310). What validates the theory for Graham is its spiritual completeness: it depends not on "demonstrable proof or formal evidence, but on a kind of spiritual and artistic sense" (308).

Two languages, scientific and religious, are being debated here. The philosophy of empirical analysis challenges the theological language Graham is using, rejecting it as meaningless. Unless Graham proves empirically that Willie Hughes existed, his theory is worthless. At stake is whether Willie Hughes can be spoken of and whether, in a deeper sense, religious language can be used at all.

Graham states that what the narrator calls a lie is actually the only truth, thus affirming the Catholic notion of faith. For the narrator, statements about Willie Hughes (and by implication, about God) fail the verificationist's test of meaningfulness. To talk about Willie Hughes (and about God) you must postulate the truth of his existence first, an a priori move unacceptable to the empiricists. Graham insists that Willie Hughes existed and that, despite any evidence to the contrary, this assertion must be accepted. That Willie Hughes existed is to him not a statement that can be falsified. What governs Graham is his personal relationship with Willie Hughes. Willie Hughes is a "presence" to him. For the scientific-minded to insist on verification through sense perception misses the point.

After the two classes, students can see the tensions between these two readings of "The Portrait of Mr. W. H."—one concentrating on Wilde as a protodeconstructionist, the other positing him as a proto-Catholic. The purpose is not that students be attracted to one or other of these readings or that they in part construct these readings themselves; it is that they be enabled to set up a real dialogue between interpretations and contribute in an original and personal way to the tradition of literary interpretation. In my experience, this exercise gives students a sense of ownership of the information they have personally excavated and also more confidence to engage critically with theoretical studies that have seemed daunting to them.

Tomorrow on Trial:
Wilde's Case in the Classroom

S. I. Salamensky

Oscar Wilde's dramatic impact extends far beyond the stage. While his works continue to astonish and delight, it is his performance on trial for "gross indecency" with men that remains foremost in the cultural imagination. Although scholars have long been taught that biography is off-limits to literary discussion, the trial materials may be investigated in the realms of performance and cultural studies as texts unto themselves.

Like the O. J. Simpson murder trial of the 1990s, Wilde's trials were a pivotal public event of the 1890s. And just as the O. J. trials became a public forum for issues of power, justice, and race, Wilde's trials served as a forum for issues of power, justice, and sexuality, questions of ethics and difference vital in their context as well as in our own time. Finally, the problems the trials raise of language, representation, truth, and the role of the artist in society remain meaningful and crucial to debates today.

Background on the Trials

Long before Wilde wrote a play, he was famed as an actor on the social scene. As early as his Oxford college days, he was known for his promotion of art for art's sake, elaborate raiment, and above all exquisite, epigrammatic speech. In his youth he published fairly derivative poems and mounted ponderous plays that failed after short runs. He garnered greater attention as a public speaker, object of parody, and general celebrity. By the time he was twenty-seven, several novel and play characters had been based on him. It was not until his mid-thirties that he found success with a number of playful, provocative works in varied genres. In essays, such as "The Decay of Lying," he praised artifice over the natural, worship of attractive surfaces over moral depth, imagination over reality, and the subjective inventions of the word over presumed objective, material truth. His philosophies combined a background in the thought of the ancients with a lively, modern sensibility. In his novel *The Picture of Dorian Gray* and his tragedy *Salomé*, he depicted characters driven by these tenets, along with rapacious sensuality. In his drawing-room comedies, such as *Lady Windermere's Fan* and *An Ideal Husband*, he exposed problems of moralistic hypocrisy, opposing to it a preferred ethos of tolerance, frivolity, and pleasure. All Wilde's works are distinguished by his signature wordplay. In his final theatrical hit, *The Importance of Being Earnest*, he elevated linguistic foolery to an absurd yet high and serious art.

Wilde's social, literary, and philosophical audacity delighted and scandalized stolid Victorian society. However, until the trials, his homosexuality was not a public issue. It may be that, being married and having two children, he escaped suspicion. Further, notions of homosexuality as a detectable social identity were only developing in Wilde's time and were less fully codified than are our own. In 1895, at the height of his career, Wilde—married, with two children—received a visiting card from the Marquess of Queensberry, father of Wilde's much younger male partner, Bosie, accusing him of "posing" as a "somdomite" (sodomite; the card is reproduced in Goodman 37)—of displaying inappropriate intimacy in public—with Bosie. Although Queensberry did not accuse Wilde and Bosie of committing sexual acts per se, he demanded that their public behavior desist at once. Queensberry's card, seen only by Wilde and the club employee(s) who delivered it to him, would likely have had little effect on Wilde's situation. His public exploits with Bosie, if not their private goings-on, were no secret; Bosie showed no sign of obeying his father; and Wilde held great cultural sway, while Queensberry was lesser known and widely disliked. Nonetheless, urged on by the rebellious Bosie, Wilde filed a libel charge against Queensberry. Under British law, Queensberry bore the burden of proving that the words in question were in fact not libelous, because true.

An extended, much-publicized trial, led by the examiner Edward Carson, an old Irish school rival of Wilde's, ensued. The first part of the proceedings concerned Wilde's epigrams, works, and philosophies and whether these indicated moral corruption. Wilde was in top form, tromping his cross-examiners with superior wit. Newspaper readers thrilled to blow-by-blow accounts, and the Old Bailey courtroom had standing room only. Wilde's fate, however, turned when the opposition introduced witnesses and material evidence that up to this point had been withheld, confirming Wilde's involvements with lower-class male prostitutes as well as with Bosie. Queensberry was cleared. Given the chance to escape to France, Wilde remained. Two more trials followed, this time with

Wilde as defendant, charged with criminal "gross indecency" with men. He was convicted and sentenced to two years imprisonment with hard labor. Not long after his release, in 1990, he died in self-exile and penury in France.

During the trials, Wilde's written works were withdrawn or republished without his name, and his plays were removed from the stage. His reputation in Britain was partially recuperated with a London revival of *Earnest* in 1909. Further rediscoveries of his oeuvre occurred through the twentieth century. Wilde is now remembered as a great artist and thinker and hailed as an inspiration and icon for not only queer but all human rights.

Key Texts and Materials

Until recently, H. Montgomery Hyde's *Trials of Oscar Wilde*, assembled years after the trials from eyewitness and newspaper reports, remained the standard record of events. While Hyde's authority has been questioned and his comments on Wilde's sexuality may seem dated to modern eyes, the work overall—rendered in narrative form interspersed with long excerpts of courtroom dialogue—is a gripping read and provides an excellent overview of the course of the trials. The greatest challenge to Hyde arrived with the publication of what appear to be privately recorded transcripts of the libel proceedings, in the form of *The Real Trial of Oscar Wilde*, a volume released with the help of Wilde's grandson, Merlin Holland. Although Holland has not disclosed the precise provenance of these materials, no overwhelming evidence has yet been presented to discredit their authenticity. As the Holland version covers only the libel trial, in any case, the Hyde remains a useful account of the second and third trials.

Supplementary materials surrounding the trials, useful for slides and handouts, may be drawn from Jonathan Goodman's *The Oscar Wilde File*, a collection of helpful photos and clippings, and Ed Cohen's *Talk on the Wilde Side*, which includes fascinating cartoons that show the ways in which Wilde's society employed the trials as a public forum for examination of the nature of male same-sex desire itself. In addition, Michael Foldy's *The Trials of Oscar Wilde* provides useful insight into other same-sex scandals of the era, particularly one involving Bosie's brother and Lord Rosebery, a British official.

For information on Wilde's life overall, Richard Ellmann's epic *Oscar Wilde: A Biography*, despite minor errors and misunderstandings, is unrivaled. Karl Beckson's *Oscar Wilde Encyclopedia* provides a helpful quick reference, offering detailed entries on notable aspects of Wilde's time and milieu. Among major critical works on Wilde, his socioeconomic context, and notions of same-sex desire in the period are Regenia Gagnier's *Idylls of the Marketplace*, Eve Kosofsky Sedgwick's *Between Men* and *Epistemology of the Closet*, Jonathan Dollimore's *Sexual Dissidence*, Alan Sinfield's *The Wilde Century*, and Joseph Bristow's *Effeminate England*.

Several plays and films have been based on Wilde's life and trials. The best-known recent play, Moisés Kaufman's *Gross Indecency*, might be used in a course but can seem overlong and didactic and adds little to the texts from which it is drawn. Further, as I have argued elsewhere, the play, while well-meaning, misunderstands everything for which Wilde fought. Brian Gilbert's *Wilde*—as of this writing, the most recent biographical film—takes liberties with the story but offers engaging direction and cinematography and fine performances by Stephen Fry, Jude Law, and others. The trial scenes in this film make useful classroom clips. Another recent film, Todd Haynes's *Velvet Goldmine*, reprises the trials in a scene in which characters based on 1970s "glam rocker" David Bowie (Jonathan Rhys Meyers) and Iggy Pop (Ewan McGregor) quote Wilde to defend their love before a hostile press. Monty Python's brief "Oscar Wilde Sketch" also echoes the trials, as Wilde (Graham Chapman) struggles to compose successful epigrams against a mocking mob of peers. These films provide graphic illustration of historic material that might otherwise feel remote to students, as well as great entertainment.

Using the Trials in Syllabi

I have used the trial materials in a variety of my courses, such as Late-Victorian Literature and Culture, World Theatre History, Modern Drama, Performance Studies, Shylocks and Salomés, and Language, Performance, and Culture. The readings I assign vary according to the level of the course and the degree to which I plan to concentrate on Wilde-related issues. But my focus in the trials is overwhelmingly on the libel trial: with its concentration on Wilde's words and works, it is the most literary and philosophical in orientation. Before the publication of the Holland volume, I assigned students to read the Hyde account of the first trials, or the Hyde in toto. As of this writing, I have not yet had the chance to assign the Holland version to students. But a future syllabus might well contain both the Holland and Hyde versions of the first trial, for comparison. I generally have my lower-level classes read only the libel trial transcripts; in an advanced class, I assign all three trials for reading.

While I prefer to synthesize key points from the critical and bibliographic sources myself into my lecture notes rather than assign secondary readings per se, I always place these sources on reserve for further student investigation and essay reference. When time permits, I show the trial scene from *Wilde*, the press scene from *Velvet Goldmine*, and the short Monty Python sketch.

Supplementary readings depend on the course. In Late-Victorian Literature and Culture, I generally include landmark pieces such as Wilde's novel *The Picture of Dorian Gray* and his plays *Salomé* and *The Importance of Being Earnest*, along with classics of the era such as Robert Louis Stevenson's *Dr. Jekyll and Mr. Hyde* and Bram Stoker's *Dracula*. In World Theatre History, Modern Drama, or Shylocks and Salomés, which are surveys of performance in cultural context, I assign the libel trial transcripts to follow readings of one or more of Wilde's plays. In Performance Studies, I assign the transcripts of all three trials as a case study in reference to courtroom process as quotidian drama and what it might mean to exhibit, or to be viewed in terms of, sexual identity. Comparable case studies might include a look at notions of performing race in African American minstrel performance or field research at a contemporary cultural site such as a beauty contest. In Language, Performance, and Culture, I have students examine Wilde's uses of language and the epigram, and reactions to them, in *Earnest* and the libel trials. Although Wilde's homosexuality was most obviously the central trial issue, questions of representation, particularly in the form of language, and truth were paramount. Other readings in this course are "The Decay of Lying," *The Importance of Being Earnest*, a vast array of materials involving language play—for instance, Dr. Seuss's *Green Eggs and Ham*, Eugene Ionesco's *La leçon*, Samuel Beckett's *Not I*, and robotics language programs—as well as philosophical and critical readings on the nature of language and its functions in society.

Teaching the Trials in Class

My courses vary in theme, size, and format, but a typical upper-level two-to-three-hour seminar meeting on the libel trial might run as follows. Students arrive with some background on Wilde's work and life, either from previous meetings' readings or from preparatory discussion, and they have read the Hyde or Holland versions of the first trial transcripts, or both, as assigned. There may be students from religious, national, or cultural backgrounds who feel that exposure to such materials violates their belief system or that they will be treated badly for expressing their opinions. Most can be persuaded to treat the material as simple historical documentation, and all are assured that they will be judged only on the rigor of their work. In one extreme instance, I allowed a student who contacted me before the reading was due to substitute an alternative assignment of equivalent length and import to the course. I do ask that such students remain present for class discussion if possible, emphasizing that understanding can arise only through exchange. In general, however, students find the courtroom drama exciting and have a great deal to say about it. Often the trial material, after it is covered, dominates the remainder of the course.

To focus students' energies, I begin with a brief ungraded in-class writing exercise, asking students to reflect on any aspect of the text or texts that has struck them as confusing, interesting, or unusual and to hold on to their exercise through class, as prompts for contribution. I then open class with a general overview of central problems and issues of the text or texts to be addressed in discussion. My first concern is to address the complexity of the case. For some students, the case is simple: Wilde was gay, in the sense that homosexuality is understood today; he tried to hide it, was found out, and was punished for breaking the law. Many will be outraged that such laws existed and feel empathy for Wilde's plight. Others will be upset that Wilde broke the law, betrayed his wife, paid youths from poorer classes for sex, or lied in court. I permit students to air these concerns but emphasize the divergence in Wilde's historical context from ours and shift the discussion from a right-versus-wrong debate to structural analysis.

The first complication lies in the wording of Queensberry's accusation, which said that Wilde was not a sodomite per se but merely that he had posed as one. Before the trials, Wilde was not commonly deemed homosexual, though his ethos of illusion and his flamboyant, fanciful dress and speech did stand out as divergent from Victorian norms for men. If he was thought queer, it was less in the sense of male-male desire than of general oddness. His behaviors enthusiastically stressed their own put-on quality. I ask students why pretending to be something that one was not thought to be might constitute an offense.

The libel case, I point out to students, had as its goal not only reinforcement of the appearance of sameness to the mainstream but also reinforcement of the appearance of the appearance of sameness. Technically, Wilde sought action against a claim of seeming, not being, different. Thus, until the introduction of the witnesses and material evidence, his essential sameness remained unchallenged through most of the libel trial. The mystery remains how he thought to establish nondifference through display of difference, if the wish was indeed wholehearted. I ask students, why did Wilde, if planning to win the case, answer serious, straightforward legal questions in a flippant, frivolous, disrespectful spirit instead of in the manner expected in court? Why did he choose to display a flamboyant, aberrant, subversive persona resembling the one Queensberry's note had described? Did Wilde hope to win the court's approval or display contempt of it? Did he hope to disprove Queensberry's characterization of him or display his difference as something to be accepted?

And if Wilde was posing in court, as what was he posing? As one not posing, a nonposing aesthete mistaken for a homosexual? As one posing in a different direction than accused, a posing aesthete mistaken for a posing homosexual? Was he posing as himself as a homosexual, but in so charming or clever a way as to defy the authorities to call him pernicious? Or was he placing posing, as an end in itself, in lieu of the far more serious charge of sexual engagement with men? Further, while Wilde is popularly recalled as lionizing homosexuality, he initiated the libel suit in the attempt to escape that charge. It is only late in the libel trial, when he is nearly beaten, that he begins to admit his affections for men and defends them. Overall, I ask students what Wilde's strategy was, if any. If he wished to celebrate a queer identity, why did he bring the case? If he wished to escape the charges, why did he not just simply "play it straight"? Scholars have puzzled over these questions for more than a century. But the questions continue to fascinate fans and students of Wilde, old and new.

Whatever Wilde's intentions, the libel trial stands to teach us a great deal about the nature not only of sexual identity but also of selfhood, representation, art, language, and truth itself. Although the trial was ostensibly focused on Wilde's private life, the opposition began by investigating his artistic career and philosophical premises. As the transcripts detail, Wilde was asked about the moral bases of certain literary works. He argued that no work was immoral or corruptive, only well or badly written. He was asked whether his epigrams, touting the virtues of artifice, wickedness, and lying, were true. He countered that not all that is written must be true and further denied that he found his own statements true. I have students take parts and read aloud the opening exchanges of the libel transcripts—Hyde's or Holland's alone or the two in comparison—to hear them as they might sound in a courtroom. Wilde continually hijacks the mode of discourse from that of jurisprudence to blithe salon chitchat and diverts the discussion from the realms of sex and body-based crimes to those of art and thought. Edward Carson engages heartily in this intellectual debate, which escalates to a pitched battle.

Certain major themes emerge in their conversation. One concerns the nature of language, of Wilde's epigrams in particular, which Carson quotes extensively. I have students each take a moment to choose a favorite among those quoted and break it down into component parts, investigating not just the content of the epigram but also its form: setup, break, turnabout, and so on. How, I ask, does the epigram function? Is it funny and, if so, why? Does it express a truth, and, if so, does that truth hold up under closer examination? I then assign students to groups to create three original aphorisms, on any topic, to present to the class, discussing the dynamics of their construction and the difficulties and pleasures of the format. I point out that the word *epigram* derives from the Greek *epigraph* and *epitaph* and seems to have originated as a short inscription on ancient gravestones. Why, I ask, does this immaterial linguistic form seem so concrete and unassailable? Another major theme is the social responsibility of the artist. Must art promote socially productive modes of behavior? Can art lead to social irresponsibility? Must the artist and the artwork be considered as one? How might art—for instance, Wilde's epigrams—seem, not only in content but also in form, to be socially threatening?

The most profound theme raised in the debates is the philosophical tension between the realms of reality and representation, body and thought, the material and the ideal. Is posing as something the same as being it? Is writing or saying something the same as meaning it? Must we always adhere to truth? Can words change truth? Can we know what truth is? Is sexual identity located in the mind or in the body? Is selfhood—human identity—located in our words, thoughts, or actions? What might be at stake, socially, in these philosophical conflicts? Where do we see related issues and tensions in our world today?

As the transcripts detail, Carson, after allowing these metaphysical problems great play, begins to work toward his final goal of proving Wilde's guilt, not only of posing but also of physical involvements with men. Although Wilde has argued, throughout his career, for imaginative alternatives to what is conventionally considered real and although this philosophy has been considered by the court, Carson proceeds to determine the reality, as commonly conceived, beneath Wilde's elaborate surface appearances. Wilde's art, words, philosophies, pretenses—poses—are stripped from him to reveal what is cast as a deeper truth of the body, which appears to emerge victorious over the less palpable, less locatable versions of truth identity that Wilde has celebrated. I show the trial clip from *Wilde*, the press clip from *Velvet Goldmine*, and the Monty Python spoof. In all, despite the humor of the third, is evident a violent dislike of Wilde that parallels Carson's determination to break him down—as artist, as philosopher, as thinker—as well as to simply prove him queer and win the suit. Why, I ask students, does Carson choose to prolong the philosophical investigation when, all along, the court has in hand witnesses and material evidence in what will prove to be an open-and-shut case?

Wilde lost and would go on to lose two ruinous cases more. But his legacy and his tenets live on. Notions of art, language, and illusion as challenging conventional structures of truth underlie modern movements across the arts and largely form the basis of our vertiginous, kaleidoscopic everyday experience in our postmodern existence. As a final question, I ask students to discuss how Wilde's insights seem false or true for their own lives and to imagine what Wilde would think if he were beamed into their world today.

From Discussion to Writing

I do not assign specific essay topics, preferring that students choose topics that interest them. I do, however, ask students to base all writings on close readings of limited materials, to avoid generalization in favor of in-depth exploration, and to bypass emotional reactions and moralistic judgments for rigorous structural investigation. For an essay, a student might examine a short series of Wilde's epigrams or other writings in rhetorical detail, analyze a short passage from the Hyde or Holland transcripts, contrast similar passages in Hyde and in Holland, compare a passage from the transcripts with one from one of Wilde's works, or investigate the trials through one or two works of critical theory from the course reserves or material otherwise approved in advance. Students often like to base creative or interdisciplinary projects on the trial materials. Depending on the nature of the course, I may grant credit for these when accompanied by a scholarly component. I may also leave extra time in the course for such projects to be shared.

Wilde's works—and in his works I include the trial transcripts, as his unfortunate cocreation—are few but endlessly rich and seem ever more apt for innovative uses. I have here suggested some uses regarding sexuality, identity, justice, art, language, representation, truth, and other problems central to Wilde's world and to our lives today. Different communities, individuals, and student generations will read these materials differently. All should be encouraged to make of them what they will. Wilde loved nothing more than the spirit of youth, with its bravery, inquisitiveness, and humor. His spirit can best be honored through fresh, new, bold, bright exploration.

The Love That Dare Not Teach Its Name: Wilde, Religious Studies, and Teaching Tolerance

Frederick Roden

In this essay, I discuss Oscar Wilde in a moral way: that is to say, how his art and the culture industry that has grown up around it can be used to teach. By *teaching* I mean not simply giving advice on using the Wilde canon in the classroom but also addressing the subject on a much larger level: how Wilde speaks to us today, if you will. I believe that the works and critical reception of Wilde have much to offer contemporary society—particularly with respect to a somewhat surprising category: religion. In recent years, approaches to Wilde studies concerning questions of Christianity have blossomed. Ellis Hanson's 1997 book *Decadence and Catholicism* is an excellent example of how we have reevaluated writers of the fin de siècle.[1] We are moving away from the question "Was he or wasn't he?"—religious, that is—which predominated critical studies that sought to either denigrate or celebrate Wilde's relation to Christianity as aesthetic. Perhaps his orthodoxy or heresy no longer matters. This general movement has mirrored the similar question, "Was he or wasn't he?" homosexual—in the sense of how useful modern categories of identity are in understanding the public space of the previous turn of the century.

I examine issues both religious and queer. How have the often antireligious sentiments of the secular academy—which typically wishes to construct capital-R Religion as a cultural artifact, as a hegemonic fossil—served to marginalize the study of religion and literature and made it more reactionary? I have heard statements at conferences on Christianity along the lines of the following: "This is like a retreat!" and "We couldn't do this at the MLA." The literary studies academy has sufficiently polarized the many (who reject religious studies for a variety of reasons, some perhaps because they simply reject religion) from the few (who at times construct themselves as staunch defenders of a capital-F Faith more than as serious critics of religion and literature). Is it easier to discuss Christianity in a queer studies context or to talk about queer studies in a religious studies one? I am not sure I have an answer to that question, although I can affirm that I have had sufficient experience of both. While LGBTQ studies can be seen in relation to various critical and theoretical paradigms—such as feminism and gender or identity politics—religious approaches to literature (except perhaps for the medievalists and early modernists, who cannot get away from Christianity) have fewer admirers in the secular academy.[2] Despite new-historicist approaches that emphasize so-called nonliterary texts, the study of devotional literature is for the most part out of fashion. Philosophical approaches to literature can claim some theological orientations, but those pertain almost exclusively to high culture; popular literature has little place there.

Finally, studies of spirituality run the risk of outright denouncement for being too personal, in an academy that otherwise has sought to validate individual experience.

The intersection of queer and religious discourses has obvious impact on contemporary critical and pedagogical positions. A perfect case in point, in the light of the recent upheaval in the Roman Catholic Church regarding pedophilia, is John Bloxam's 1894 short story "The Priest and the Acolyte," which Wilde was accused of having penned. I have taught this work in undergraduate and graduate courses on Victorian literature. Each time I teach it, the work is placed at the end of a long line of texts that interrogate the relation between gender, sexual identity, and the spiritual life. "The Priest and the Acolyte" requires a lot of classroom space for discussion. The obvious evocation of child abuse threatens to undermine the project of portraying the struggle to reconcile one's sexuality with one's devotional life. The student response (and my own) is to denounce the abuse of power found in the relationship in the story. Nevertheless, by this point in the course, students have already read too much Gerard Manley Hopkins and Christina Rossetti to fail to question how Christianity and the body intersect in literature.

The message of my pedagogical approach, in presenting different manifestations of the sexual self, is tolerance.[3] I seek to open up the minds and hearts of students to those whose experiences are different from their own. I believe that with respect to sexual difference, the best entry is through gender difference. In my Victorian courses I usually teach a large number of women writers. Sensitivity to and awareness of the different experience of the female author in the nineteenth century can open the door to a greater appreciation of the marginalized space of the sexual dissident. In my teaching, I am rarely preaching to the choir. While the majority of my students are familiar with the Christian tradition, few will speak freely in identification with LGBTQ cultures.

This reality places me, the teacher, in a challenging position: an out gay man, I run the risk of students' dismissal of "prohomosexual" work as important only because of their instructor's identity, not in and of itself. Thus my strategy calls on students to recognize the merits in Wilde's literary compositions and find value in his thought. My purpose is to create sympathy. By *sympathy* I mean not pity but rather feeling another's experience as one's own. The reality may be grim and the method not without problems, but I find the suffering expressed in Wilde's *De Profundis* useful in this regard. Its pain can then be balanced with the author's denigration of Christian suffering in "The Soul of Man under Socialism." If evocations of pity for the suffering homosexual are controversial in gay pedagogical practice, so too is my stance with respect to history. I suggest we accept the resonances of similar feelings (however different from our own) while still maintaining an awareness of our time and place in a world of socially constructed identities.

If I fail to convince because of homophobia, by using "The Priest and the Acolyte" in class I also risk the accusation that I am supporting pedophilia.

But how does one interpret—or explain, for that matter—a passage such as the following?

> Can you not see that people are different, totally different from one an-
> other? . . . One law laid down by the majority, who happen to be of one
> disposition, is only binding on the minority *legally*, not *morally*. . . . For
> me, with my nature, to have married, would have been sinful: it would
> have been a crime, a gross immorality, and my conscience would have re-
> volted. . . . I have committed no moral offence in this matter; in the sight
> of God, my soul is blameless.   (42–43)

This excerpt is taken from the young clergyman's defense of his relationship with an acolyte. It is at once a convincing homosexual apologia and a frighten-ing justification for the abuse of power and perhaps sexual misconduct. I sug-gest we consider this piece not because I believe that every discussion of homosexuality and Christianity should come down to pedophilia (or contempo-rary concerns, for that matter) but rather because it serves to demonstrate how very complicated questions of religion and literature can be—for us as scholars, and certainly for our students. While we may attempt to historicize the Greek ideal of *erastes/eromenos* love—that of the older lover and beloved youth—as it was presented in the 1890s, a relationship specific to its particular time and place, most of the recent, highly publicized cases of so-called priestly pederasty are in fact examples of ephebophilia—love of adolescents—not true pedophilia or child abuse, as that category is defined. We therefore confront the question of our own relationships with students: as figures of authority, as potential teachers of tolerance, and often simply as adults who are interacting with them in the emotionally charged space of the classroom.

The remainder of this essay considers the place of religion in the works of Wilde and how his prose can be employed pedagogically. What does his religious-philosophical aesthetic have to teach us and our students? His 1891 "The Soul of Man under Socialism" and the prison letter *De Profundis* form the basis of my discussion. Many critics—Isobel Murray, Norbert Kohl, and Hanson among them—have explored questions of Wilde's philosophy and religion. But I want to step away from the critical history of Wilde's ideas and consider instead what their effect may be on the novice reader when read in the classroom.

Teaching Wilde is always also staging Wilde. In my 2001 undergraduate course on Wilde, I included David Hare's play *The Judas Kiss*, the film *A Man of No Im-portance*, and Moisés Kaufman's *Gross Indecency: The Three Trials of Oscar Wilde*. I believe that such appropriations of the writer's story are extremely effec-tive in enabling students to move into his life. Playing Wilde, staging Wilde—like reading *De Profundis* or experiencing Christ, for that matter—means living his story, his suffering, and his sacrifice. Kaufman's *Gross Indecency*, which makes extensive use of texts from the trials, contains the famous "Love that dare not speak its name" speech. It is important for students to hear that dramatic monologue: not only for them to understand the historical construction of the pathology and crime of homosexuality that Wilde was a martyr to but also for them to experience more fully the speaker's pain.

In writing this essay, I mistakenly typed the title of that speech as "Love that dare not teach its name." On reflection, I believe the error results in a rather fitting phrase, given the anxieties many secondary-school teachers and even university professors experience about raising LGBTQ issues in the classroom. The playwright of *Gross Indecency* also wrote a work called *The Laramie Project*, based on interviews made in Laramie, Wyoming, after the brutal crucifixion-style murder of the gay college student Matthew Shepard in 1998 (Kaufman et al.). In spring 2002, I saw a production of this play staged by students at New York University. I cannot remember a time when I have been so moved by a theater experience. For undergraduates to perform a work exploring the execution of one of their own elicits the very kind of imaginative sympathy that I suggest may result from reading Wilde's works. In both teaching and scholarship, there is also the "Christianity that dare not speak its name." I urge readers and teachers alike to consider doing new work in the area of religion and literature; developing curricula in that area; and rethinking the place of the moral, religious, and sexual Wilde. Given the recent ecclesiastical scapegoating of the Catholic homosexual, there could be no better time than now (Roden, Introd.).

To begin with Wilde's works: Why should we single out "The Soul of Man" and *De Profundis* to be included in the courses we teach? What value do they have for current critical practice? On one level, they offer our students a different perspective on religion (popularly) and religious studies (more specifically). Many who have knowledge of Christianity fall into one of two polarized categories: either they reject religious studies as irrelevant and oppressive, or they embrace doctrine, Scripture, and faith without much critical examination. The study of Wilde's writings on Christianity offers the former an awareness that such literature can be much more complex, potentially subversive, and intellectually invigorating than they imagined, while it challenges the latter to interrogate the head rather than heart of their beliefs. In all cases, Wilde's religious writings provide students with a fine entry into these subjects. His works are concrete enough to provoke inquiry yet sufficiently complex to allow a great depth of exploration.

Similarly, for our colleagues, the study of Wildean religion can help reshape how the discipline of religion and literature has been constructed. It can encourage proponents of gender and performance theory to think more extensively about theology (as in Wilde's comments about liturgy, for instance) and can also offer alternatives to a particular kind of scholarship that limits itself to some semblance of Catholic orthodoxy found in Flannery O'Connor or Hopkins. Indeed, many studies of the Jesuit poet that do the theology well fail to take into account the place of the body in his works, while critical approaches that delve into Hopkins's sexuality often lack a proper understanding of his spirituality.

To return to a moral approach to teaching and reading Wilde: the fin de siècle aesthete has long been regarded as the grandfather of the twentieth-century gay rights movement. Wilde writes about individualism in "The Soul of Man" and suffering in *De Profundis*. Both these works have tremendous pedagogical potential at the secondary and undergraduate level for teaching tolerance. Although as scholars we must consider "The Soul of Man" in the light of its particular intellectual history, Wilde's text itself teaches students a respect for difference that is very much in keeping with the kind of diversity education that schools seek to promote. Indeed, despite current crises in Christian education (that include anxieties over who makes a safe and responsible mentor for "our children"), "The Soul of Man" seems ideally suited for the mission of religiously affiliated schools.

De Profundis likewise offers much in the way of education that addresses homophobia. As the letter of a man imprisoned for his sexual behavior (however much Wilde may fail as a "good queer," given his exploitation of rent boys and such), this work speaks out from the "voiceless world of pain," as Wilde named that space (*Complete Letters* 746). The text is an excellent example of how, historically, homosexuals have been oppressed and misunderstood in Western culture. Furthermore, the Christianity that Wilde explores in *De Profundis* deeply interrogates the relation between the erotic body—whether Bosie's or Christ's—and the self. Lord Alfred Douglas and Lord Christ substitute for each other throughout the text. No work in the Wilde canon more profoundly engages sex and spirit. In his letter, the consumable body of Christ in the Eucharist stands in juxtaposition to the sacrament of love to be received on bended knee from Bosie Douglas.

I present a brief outline of my approach to "The Soul of Man under Socialism" and *De Profundis* and comment on their use in the classroom.[4]

Wilde wrote to Charles Eliot Norton on 15 July 1882, "I can see no better way of getting rid of the mediaeval discord between soul and body than by sculpture. Phidias is the best answer to Thomas à Kempis" (*Complete Letters* 177). In "The Soul of Man," the relation between these two forces, Christian and Hellenic, is explored. Influenced by William Morris's socialism, this essay describes the goal of the contemplative life: the perfection of the individual soul. Wilde's notion of personal perfection can be attributed to several different models. The first is Christian contemplation, the soul's journey to God. Although traditionally this model implied an everyman's road that led all people to the same destination, Wilde modifies the ideal: perfection is based not on similarity but on complementarity. The Christian community operating harmoniously is the closest to perfection the world can achieve. His theory depends on the development of all the diverse aspects of an individual. Instead of emphasizing a uniformity of type, he advocates a Whitmanian composite community of individuals whose diversity recalls Hopkins's "Pied Beauty."

"The Soul of Man under Socialism" must be understood with respect to Christian socialism. The socialist movement in the late nineteenth century intersected with High Church, as is evident in the activity of many Anglo-Catholic parishes in urban slums. The Catholic emphasis on the doctrine of the Incarnation, stressing the inherent dignity of the human person, prepared the way for Christian socialism. The title of Wilde's essay suggests its religious spirit. Wilde seeks to secularize the domain of the sacred and make holy the secular. He follows the Victorian sage tradition, advocating a fluidity between material and spiritual worlds. The goal of the contemplative life is not to reinforce the dichotomies of soul versus body, sacred versus secular, but to find in the quotidian an element of the sacred, to avoid a separation between the life of the spirit and the life of the senses. This notion looks back; modernity emphasizes compartmentalization. "A place for everything and everything in its place" marginalizes the spiritual life as separate from rational reality. "The Soul of Man" combats this tendency.

I have taught Wilde's essay in several different classes: undergraduate British literature surveys, an undergraduate course on Wilde, an undergraduate course on religion and literature, and a graduate Victorian literature course. In all cases, students are provoked by Wilde's antimaterialist position. They comment on his use of Christianity. They are surprised that the witty and cultivated author of epigrams was also capable of thinking deeply about the spiritual life. Some even challenge his right to speak in a theological mode, given his worldly (read "homosexual") life. Some may never have encountered this sort of essay before. My graduate students read John Henry Newman's *Apologia*, but undergraduates typically have read religious debate only in poetry or fiction. All students, however, will have read the preface and conclusion to Walter Pater's *Renaissance* by the time they get to Wilde. Hence Victorian prose is not entirely new to them, although they may associate that genre with a particular privilege and elitism. As with the Bloxam reading, I rely on vigorous class discussion to tease out meaning, after a lecture pointing out the various pieces of background information I have sketched out here. I rarely insist that students write at length about certain texts, although I increasingly find myself expecting weekly short reaction papers. When given the choice, however, students seem as intrigued with Wilde as I am. Although I am sure my emphasis on his importance directs them in some ways, I do believe his works speak for themselves as well.

If "The Soul of Man" addresses the question of the place of the individual in the community, *De Profundis* is much more concerned with a particular soul's journey. It is a work of contemplative literature, as both Regenia Gagnier (*Idylls*) and John Albert have pointed out. The letter locates Wilde in the present moment, to which he brings a Paterian passion for capturing sensory experience. Outer senses fail; he must rely on inner sense. He accepts the Newmanian epistemology he had rejected in "The Critic as Artist." Only continued recollection of the past can serve as a sufficient reminder of what the future may hold. *De Profundis* is the fulfillment of the utopian theology of "The Soul of Man." Instead of going to heaven, the writer entered hell and must transform it through imagination. If in "The Soul of Man" the Hellenic—the life of the body—wins out, here the life of the spirit takes precedence.

Wilde no longer opposed religion to the sensual life. If Christ ultimately failed in "The Soul of Man" (by realizing his perfection through pain rather than pleasure), here he succeeds utterly. Wilde takes the trope of artistic creation and theologizes it: artistic production becomes a metaphor for the Incarnation; material creation is infused with Divinity. In *De Profundis*, Art is a form of sacrament. The dichotomy between spirit and matter that had troubled Wilde is not present in this text; art is fully incarnational, and Christianity can be reconciled with Hellenic aesthetics. This transfiguration at once elevates Christianity as an aesthetic and makes all art religious.

Wilde gives body to Christ's beauty. Religion can change society in a way that the secular humanity of "The Soul of Man" cannot. Wilde does not avoid the power of mystical transformation. "All who come into contact with [Christ's] personality . . . somehow find that the ugliness of their sins is taken away and the beauty of their sorrow revealed to them" (*Complete Letters* 742). In *De Profundis*, the magical conclusion of *Dorian Gray* is rewritten through the flesh's mystical connection with Divine Presence. Wilde finds in the Christ story a meaningful comparison to his life, a hermeneutic for spiritualizing his existence. He enacts the individual *imitatio Christi* that he had put forth in "The Soul of Man."

The theology of this letter is amatory. Christ is

> the leader of all the lovers. He saw that love was that lost secret of the world for which the wise men had been looking, and that it was only through love that one could approach either the heart of the leper or the feet of God. . . . [He is] the most supreme of Individualists.
>
> (*Complete Letters* 744)

> Christ took the entire world of the inarticulate, the voiceless world of pain, as his kingdom, and made of himself its eternal mouthpiece. Those . . . who are dumb under oppression and "whose silence is heard only of God," he chose as his brothers. He sought to become eyes to the blind, ears to the deaf, and a cry on the lips of those whose tongue had been tied. His desire was to be to the myriads who had found no utterance a very trumpet through which they might call to Heaven. And feeling . . . that an idea is of no value till it becomes incarnate and is made an image, he makes of himself the image of the Man of Sorrows, and as such has fascinated and dominated Art as no Greek god ever succeeded in doing.   (746)

If Wilde once advocated that Greek sculpture was the highest mode of expression, here he suggests that the image of Christ—the self-depiction of the artist, more perfect than the picture or body of Dorian Gray, for example—is superior in its Incarnation. He sums up his theological aesthetic: "For is not truth in Art . . . 'that in which the outward is expressive of the inward; in which the soul is made flesh, and the body instinct with spirit: in which Form reveals?' " (747).

Students arrive at *De Profundis* as the end of their road with me. In a Wilde course, I tend to proceed chronologically. Apart from "Reading Gaol," which I am surprised to find students approve of, there is little else to present from the Wilde canon. In the Victorian courses, students have reached the conclusion of the narrative: finding death, decay, Decadence. If they read "The Priest and the Acolyte," the message there is that transgression results in punishment and death, however much society's rules might be criticized or even subverted. In *De Profundis*, readers are summoned by a suffering man—a Job, if they recognize him—to reconsider meaning in their own lives. In my Wilde course, students may place these stories next to "The Ballad of Reading Gaol," a bid for mercy.

All the texts considered in this essay, Wildean and otherwise, work the reader hard in the area of sentimentality. They evoke strong emotion. Is it useful (or even ethical) to provoke these kinds of feelings in our students? As a humanist I believe it is. Studying the works of a bourgeois, social-climbing, Oxford-educated, Victorian dead white male may open students' eyes to other kinds of human rights abuses in their world.

To return to the purpose of this essay: how effective is my strategy in teaching Wilde—and in teaching tolerance? There will always be dismissals of Wilde's story, of his works, and of tolerance. I have found that this approach of heart over head has produced some of the best student papers I have read. I have also found it to produce tolerance, even in unlikely places. Reflecting on this question of sense and sensibility, I cannot help but wonder why I favor the sentimentality present in *De Profundis* and reject that of "Reading Gaol." When I once denigrated the style of "Reading Gaol" in class, a number of students leaped to its defense. Am I more willing to excuse raw emotion in the rather homiletic prose document that is *De Profundis* than in what I might want to call bad poetry? What is it in the combination of form and content that constitutes a work of literature that prompts me to reject or accept a text in my canon? As I contemplate my own critical prejudices in privileging certain kinds of writing over others, I invite readers, critics, and teachers to consider our own self-imposed limits to approaching Wilde's works. More broadly, I invite us to consider our limits in the relations between religion and literature, in the subject of pedagogy and homophobia, and finally in the resistance to tolerance and unconditional acceptance.

NOTES

[1] Continuing the theme of this essay, see also O'Malley.

[2] This phenomenon is changing in the academy, just as public perception of religion in popular culture is moving to the left. Liberal religious voices are "coming out."

[3] A body of work has emerged in both religious and queer studies that demonstrates the trouble with tolerance: its limits and limitations. See, for instance, Jakobsen and Pellegrini. For the purpose of this essay I maintain the value of tolerance, even if I hope we are moving beyond its usefulness. I continue to be impressed by my students' comfort with both homosexual and religious subjects, reflecting popular culture's transformation.

[4] For a more detailed critical analysis, see Roden, *Same-Sex Desire*.

Learning the Importance
of Being an Earnest Reader
through *De Profundis* and *Gross Indecency*

Heath A. Diehl

The Course

At Bowling Green State University, the Department of English annually offers a handful of sections of English 200, Introduction to Literature. Described in the undergraduate course catalog as "a general education course with emphasis on humanistic themes and basic literary concepts," English 200 is geared primarily toward first- and second-year nonmajors who need to fulfill their one humanities and arts general education requirement. Topics for the course vary from section to section, but generally the topics focus on broad thematic (e.g., black literature, women in literature, literature and psychology) or generic (e.g., short story, poetry, novel) concerns.

For the spring term of 1998, I was slated to teach one section of English 200 on the broad theme of growing up. To that point, those instructors assigned this particular section of English 200 typically had opted for one of two approaches: either they examined growing up as a thematic concern in young adult literature (e.g., Lois Lowry's *The Giver*, Katherine Patterson's *The Bridge to Terabithia*, or Judy Blume's *Then Again, Maybe I Won't*) or they explored growing up as a generic concern in bildungsroman novels (e.g., Charlotte Brontë's *Jane Eyre*, Charles Dickens's *Great Expectations*, or George Eliot's *The Mill on the Floss*). Since my training as a world drama and queer theory specialist had not adequately prepared me to teach either of these literary traditions, I chose instead to focus the course readings on a subspecialty of mine: gay and lesbian literature. At the time, the English department at BGSU did not offer (nor had it ever regularly offered) a course on gay and lesbian literature, despite the obvious student demand for such a course. As one of the only members of the department who had specific training in gay and lesbian studies, I took the initiative to fill this void in our curriculum.

The purpose of my Growing Up Gay/Lesbian class was threefold. First, as in all sections of English 200, we were required to survey major literary genres, literary movements, or critical reading strategies and to include in the course readings at least one literary work written before 1900. A second, more section-specific goal of the course was to explore the generic conventions and thematic concerns of coming-out narratives. A third goal of the course was to trace the sociohistorical evolution (or maturation, growing up) of gay/lesbian/bisexual/transgender liberation movements, both in England and in the United States, from the time of Oscar Wilde to the present. Organized chronologically, required readings ranged in period from late Victorian to modern (e.g., from Wilde's *De Profundis* to Jonathan Harvey's *Beautiful Thing*), and covered all major literary genres from drama (e.g., Jane Chambers's *Last Summer at Bluefish Cove*) to novel (e.g., Rita Mae Brown's *Rubyfruit Jungle*) to poetry (e.g., Hart Crane and Allen Ginsberg) to short story (e.g., John Weir's "Homo in Heteroland") and autobiography-memoir (e.g., Frank Decaro's *A Boy Named Phyllis*).

The Wilde Unit

During the initial four weeks of the semester, in-class discussions and out-of-class writing assignments centered on four related readings: Eve Kosofsky Sedgwick's "Epistemology of the Closet" (taken from *The Lesbian and Gay Studies Reader*), Neil Miller's chapter on Oscar Wilde from *Out of the Past: Gay and Lesbian History from 1869 to the Present*, Wilde's *De Profundis* (selections), and Moisés Kaufman's *Gross Indecency: The Three Trials of Oscar Wilde* (a contemporary play that re-visions Wilde's life and times). At first I chose to include Kaufman's play for pragmatic pedagogical reasons. On the one hand, because *Gross Indecency* so clearly and skillfully borrows the conventions of Brechtian epic theater, I hoped that the play would provide students with an introduction to one of the most influential forms of twentieth-century drama. On the other hand, because *Gross Indecency* consists of a montage of historical documents from Wilde's historical moment (e.g., personal correspondence, newspaper reports, trial transcripts), I felt that the play would provide students with some of the background information about late Victorian social norms and conventions that they would need in order to contextualize *De Profundis*.

The Method

While the juxtapositioning of disparate texts and contexts allowed me to achieve the pragmatic pedagogical goals that I identify above, it also facilitated a useful approach to reading literature critically. This comparative method encouraged students to trace lines of relation and discontinuity between and among a diverse collection of texts in order to gain a deepened understanding of the themes, ideas, and concepts central to the course (in this case, the emergence of the homosexual as a recognizable identity construct regulated and proscribed by a host of normative social and juridical practices specific to the late Victorian period). In many important ways, comparative pedagogy is similar to the specialization in English studies known as comparative literature. Both presuppose that critical engagement with literary history necessitates a juxtapositioning of literatures of different genres, nations, periods, or (sometimes) languages. This juxtapositioning of texts and contexts is intended to generate a dialogue of perspectives about a particular idea, theme, genre, or approach to representation. In this essay, I explain how I teach general education students the comparative method of analysis. The particular object of study here also brings into play some insights

from queer theory. My ultimate goal is to show how my approach not only eluci-
dates Wilde and a culturally specific set of attitudes about growing up and coming out but also leads to a more sophisticated understanding of the role of the
reader in constructing meaning out of comparison.

The comparative approach should produce earnest readers. *Earnest*, in its
simplest form, denotes sincerity or seriousness, two characteristics that are central to the type of reading that I promote in my classes. Too often students enroll
in general education literature courses believing that the purpose of literary interpretation is to connect the events and emotions conveyed in an assigned text
to their own life experiences. By contrast, earnest readers approach a text looking for the generic signals, cultural codes, and social markers that give it its ideological and interpretive force. Earnest readers are simply close readers, attuned
to the various ways in which a text is constructed as a text; they are readers who
can peel off the various layers surrounding a text to discover its deeper meanings
(both literary and social).

The Students

The comparative method asks students to interrogate the role of the reader, the
purpose of the text, and the operations of the reading process in a more critical
and systematic manner than most English 200 students have the opportunity to
do. Students enrolled in an English 200 course at BGSU are like students at many
state universities who are required to take general education courses in literature
and who have limited interest in and experience with analyzing literature. Typically they adopt a passive approach to the reading assignments. They view literary
works as self-evident, ideologically neutral texts that convey universal themes
about the human condition and that also offer the possibility of escape.

The only exposure to the study of literature for most of the students enrolled
in English 200 is high school classes where they read the great works of Western
literature (i.e., the canon as defined by often outdated textbooks) and are taught
that literary analysis consists of the memorization and regurgitation of biographical facts, plot details, and (less frequently) definitions of literary terms—much
as in history classes, where students memorize important figures and dates, or in
chemistry classes, where students memorize the periodic table. They were perhaps tested on plot details in multiple-choice questions. If evaluated at all, then
their skills at literary analysis were gauged by open-ended, often hypothetical
questions that encouraged a reader-response approach. In high school, little if
any systematic textual analysis is done.

The Method in Practice

During initial discussions of the four texts, my students were quick to point out
the most obvious similarities and differences among them. *De Profundis* is part

love letter and part philosophical treatise; *Gross Indecency* is a play. *De Profundis* was written by Wilde in the late Victorian period; *Gross Indecency* was written about Wilde in the contemporary period. *De Profundis* is a first-person account of Wilde's notorious relationship with Bosie; *Gross Indecency* constitutes a montage of historical documents and focuses on the historical and social implications of Wilde's relationship with Bosie.

As we progressed deeper into the unit, however, my questions became more probing and nuanced, to push students' thinking beyond these superficial generalizations. For whose consumption was *De Profundis* written? I asked. Was the letter written solely for the eyes of Bosie? Was it simply a private correspondence between two lovers that was not made public until many years later? Can any piece of writing—love letter, poem, novel, play, or otherwise—ever be marked as private only? Or is the act of writing, which presupposes an audience, a purpose, and a rhetorical context, always and already public? If we regard the letter as both private correspondence and public treatise, then who were Wilde's public audience? Friends? Family? Fans? Future generations? Or the reproving Victorian public? And why might Wilde have chosen the love letter, a very intimate form of correspondence, as the medium to explain (and justify) to a reproving Victorian public his aberrant relationship? Furthermore, why did he seek to place his relationship with Bosie not solely in the realm of feeling and emotion but also in the realm of philosophy? And why, more than a hundred years later, did a modern playwright (Kaufman) return to the selfsame historical documents that, at least to Wilde's contemporaries, condemned Wilde to the roles of deviant and social pariah? How were historical documents chosen for inclusion or exclusion in Kaufman's play? What does the order of their presentation reveal about Kaufman's take on Wilde's life?

One of the most interesting and insightful discussions centered on the topic of history. I began this discussion by asking the basic question, Whose (hi)story does each text record? I punctuate the term *history* as *(hi)story* to suggest the historical tentativeness of any document. Too often students have been taught to classify documents as either fictional (and thus made up) or historical (and thus absolutely truthful). I try to teach my students, to make earnest readers of them, that historical documents-circumstances and fictional narratives bear on each other, are mutually generative rather than mutually exclusive. In other words, texts are simultaneously histories of a particular cultural moment and stories, fictional accounts of either real or imagined events. I hope that my students will question the biases and circumstances that gave rise to historical documents (as well as the veracity of the documents themselves) as rigorously as they question the constructedness of fiction. *De Profundis* is a particularly useful text for teaching such a lesson, because generically it exists somewhere in between history and fiction. So with the question, Whose (hi)story does each text record?, I am asking students to consider the various assumptions that they (as readers) bring to the texts on the basis of how we (as a culture of readers) classify texts.

In response, most students uncritically pointed to difference in authors, but some were more discerning. A couple challenged the assumption that literary texts are part of our collective historical record; literature is fiction, they argued, while history is fact. In a further attempt to flesh out the murky relation between literature-fiction and history-fact, I reminded my students that *Gross Indecency* is founded on precisely the factual records to which history so often lays claim. The overlapping of literature and history, of fiction and fact, in this play confounded their hypothesis but at first did not force them to redefine the terms of debate. Instead, my dissenting students simply amended their responses, noting that since Kaufman bases his play on factual records, that *Gross Indecency* is more like history than like literature.

I sometimes capitalize *history* to indicate its revered place as a master narrative—as an all-encompassing, omnipotent, truthful account of past events. Many postmodern theorists contrast "History" with "history," to question the veracity of any account (historical, scientific, religious, or otherwise) that is regarded as a unified, coherent, truthful totality. If students are to enter into a productive discussion regarding literary texts, then they must understand the constructedness not only of the literary texts but also of the historical circumstances-texts surrounding their production.

At this point in the discussion, I began challenging my students' assumption that history is predicated on the factual and objective reporting of past events. I posed the question, How is history recorded? In the discussions that followed, I encouraged my students to respond using three of the assigned texts—Wilde's *De Profundis,* Kaufman's *Gross Indecency,* and Miller's *Out of the Past.* All three concern themselves centrally with Wilde's homosexual relationship with Bosie, yet each operates according to a different set of generic and historical presuppositions. Wilde's love letter / philosophical treatise is, in large part, written as an apologia, an "autobiographical form in which a defense is the framework for a discussion by the author of his personal beliefs and viewpoints" ("Apología"). The voice is Wilde's, and the intent is to explain and justify his relationship with Bosie to a critical Victorian public that regarded it as "the love that dare not speak its name."

Of course, earnest readers might wonder why I think Wilde is addressing the Victorian public, given that this text as private letter did not see print until years after his death and then only in censored form. My answer is based on one of the foundational tenets of Sedgwick's groundbreaking work *Epistemology of the Closet.* In a much-cited passage, she contends:

> [A] lot of the energy of attention and demarcation that has swirled around issues of homosexuality since the end of the nineteenth century, in Europe and the United States, has been impelled by the distinctively indicative relation of homosexuality to wider mappings of secrecy and disclosure, and of the private and the public, that were and are critically problematical for the gender, sexual, and economic structures of the

heterosexist culture at large, mappings whose enabling but dangerous incoherence has become oppressively, durably condensed in certain fig- ures of homosexuality.   ("Epistemology" 71)

Sedgwick makes clear that any discourse regarding homosexuality is simulta- neously marked both private and public. In simplest terms, the very act of com- ing out, an arguably private declaration of personal identity, must of necessity be rendered public knowledge through social discourse (e.g., "I am gay," "I am lesbian"), precisely because of the cultural construction of homosexuality as an unmarked identity category. In *De Profundis*, the compulsion to justify, in the form of a personal letter, a private (and consensual) relationship between two adult men was motivated by the Victorian norms that condemned it as an aber- ration and that confined Wilde to a jail cell. In other words, his need to write the private letter was always and already implicated in and produced by the very public historical and social conditions that rendered Victorian homosexu- alities as "the love that dare not speak its name."

By contrast, Kaufman's *Gross Indecency* is intended to clarify the normative social practices and cultural beliefs that proscribed same-sex intimacies in Wilde's historical moment.[1] Finally, Miller's *Out of the Past* (published in 1995), seeks to trace "the making of a gay and lesbian community over the last 125 years in the West. It moves from the period in which gay and lesbian identity was in embryonic form to the 'gay moments' of the first years of the Clinton ad- ministration" (xviii). From this abbreviated statement of the author's purpose, it is clear that Miller is a modern historian who regards gay and lesbian history as a linear progression from repression to acceptance.

The above discussion might lead some readers to conclude that my approach to the study and teaching of literature privileges the artist's or historian's inten- tion above all else, but it is a fallacy to privilege authorial intention. My ap- proach has two interrelated concerns: historicity and genre. On the one hand, I am deeply committed to historicizing the works that my students and I read, placing those works in their original contexts (as much as possible) by reading them alongside other works from or about their period. For *De Profundis*, I seek to tease out the wider cultural and social implications of the text (specifi- cally, of the text's construction of homosexuality) by reading it in relation to his- torical accounts of homosexuality in the Victorian period (i.e., Miller) as well as to modern dramatic re-visions of the events that led to the text's construction (i.e., Kaufman). Such historicizing allows my students and me to draw lines of relation between seemingly disparate pieces of knowledge and to arrive at a deeper understanding of the conditions of the text's production.

On the other hand, I seek to locate texts generically—often in several com- peting generic categories—in order to understand how the texts build on and expand literary history. In other words, how *De Profundis* both adheres to and deviates from the tradition of the apologia is as important to our class discus- sions as how the text constructs and responds to Victorian constructions of homosexuality. Again, locating works in a wider mapping of literary history allows us to arrive at a deeper understanding of how they came to be.

My students and I used charting to record the generic and historical presuppositions outlined above. Once the chart was complete, I continued my questioning. How is history shaped (or is it?) by the biases of the historians who look back? Why, for instance, does Miller champion Wilde as a pioneer of the modern gay liberation movement while Wilde is himself critical of his relationship with Bosie—and not of the Victorian mores that led to its infamous denouement? Furthermore, should we assume that Kaufman's play is factual and, by implication, ideologically neutral simply because the primary source of information is historical records?

Near the end of the unit, my students and I arrived finally at the basic question that had driven all our discussions: How do we reconcile historical records (or do we) that contradict or compete with one another? At the beginning of our discussions, many students regarded history as an objective discipline that produces facts that can be empirically verified and objectively reported. (Note here the similarity of this view to the view of literature as ideologically neutral.) After reading and discussing the four texts in the Wilde unit, however, most students had widened their views about history, literature, fact, fiction, and even homosexuality. To be sure, some still clung to the idea that literature exists solely for the purpose of personal escape and that it neither conveys attitudes professed by those who write nor alters beliefs and values held by those who read. But most had come to a newfound understanding of the relation between past and present, between history and literature, and between fact and fiction.

In class discussions, response essays, and conference settings, students began to acknowledge the complicated and mutually generative relation between each pair of these variables. They acknowledged that both historiography and literature are predicated on the careful selection of material and details—a process whereby authors implicitly or explicitly reveal their biases regarding the subject matter. They recognized that the presentation of any historical event is predicated on the subjective selection of important facts, details, and information rather than on an objective translation of that event into narrative form. And, perhaps most important, they saw that both history and literature are constituted by a multiplicity of perspectives—some complementary, some competing, and some contradictory. They learned that our goal as discerning readers is not to criticize and ultimately defeat all but one perspective, which we then hold up as the definitive historical record or literary interpretation. Rather, our goal is to read about, engage with, and finally reconcile these multiple perspectives with the knowledge, values, and beliefs that we bring to the reading process.

The implications of this newfound knowledge to students of literature are self-evident. The comparative method presented them with a dialogue of perspectives on Wilde's life and times and required them to engage with and ultimately reconcile those often competing perspectives. Once they were confronted with that dialogue, they could no longer easily or unproblematically give in to the pull of cultural or historical anachronism, leveling out real material differences between Wilde's historical moment and their own by romanticizing his relationship with Bosie (and thus championing Wilde as a trailblazing gay pioneer unconcerned with or untouched by social mores of the late Victorian period) or by drawing exact parallels between his oppressive circumstances and those operative in their own lives. Instead, students saw themselves as active creators of meaning about a text (or a series of texts), not simply passive receptacles waiting to be filled by an all-knowing author or authority. This sense of active reading was heightened by Kaufman's play precisely because of its resistance to teleological narratives and because of its insistence on blurring the boundaries between historical fact and literary fiction.

The Alternative Applications

Although my discussion of the comparative method derives from one specific application, the method is highly flexible and can be adapted to a variety of learning situations and subject matters. For a British literature survey course or a dramatic literature survey course, Wilde's plays could be assigned in conjunction with work by Noel Coward and Joe Orton in order to yield a heightened understanding of the generic conventions and evolution of social farce. Class discussions or essay assignments also could probe more deeply into the relation among social farce, sexual orientation, and political theater. For a single-author course on Wilde, a comparative analysis of several adaptations of one text (e.g., *The Importance of Being Earnest*) could generate a fruitful dialogue about what constituted normative gender and sexual behavior during the late Victorian period (especially if Wilde's play was read in the light of more modern and queer adaptations, like the most recent film version). In a gay and lesbian or gender studies course, Wilde's writings (perhaps *The Picture of Dorian Gray*) could be read in relation to contemporary re-visions of the Victorian period (e.g., Tom Stoppard's *The Invention of Love* or David Hare's *The Judas Kiss* or even the film *Urinal*) in order to understand better the regimes of social, cultural, and juridical power that proscribed same-sex relationships and intimacies during that historical moment.

In my classes, I do not use the term "earnest readers" with my students to talk about my aims for them. To be sure, I have tried in the past to directly address pedagogical aims and rationales with my students, telling them why they should acquire a particular body of knowledge or grapple with a set of challenging questions or issues. Because such discussions often seemed to bore my ever-practical students, who only want "to know what they need to know for the test," I now do not offer explanations of why my assignments are pedagogically sound; rather, I provide students with ways to apply the skills they learn in my class to other situations (academic or otherwise). The comparative method, for example, teaching them to draw lines of relation and discontinuity between different texts and contexts, is a skill that we use every day, both in our personal lives and in our work. Close-reading skills, fostered by the comparative method and used by earnest readers, will help students be more precise and accurate when writing reports, talking with teachers or employers, and so on. The process of contextualizing information and texts can help them understand the biases that underlie the construction of television or print news reports or the selection of one employee over another for a promotion.

Ultimately I'm trying to sell students not a set of academic or life skills but an ideology. Indeed, all pedagogical choices are ideological, in the sense that they put into practice theoretical beliefs about which knowledges matter and how they should be made to matter. The textbooks that we select for courses are invested with values and ideas that we deem crucial for the professional development and perhaps personal growth of ourselves and our students. How we translate those values and ideas and how we engage with the values and ideas that our students bring to the table reveal much about our attitudes toward intellectual curiosity, professional courtesy, and human compassion.

One of my primary responsibilities as an educator is to translate specialized bodies of knowledge to my students. In the English 200 course, students were taught the salient generic features that distinguish basic types of literature (e.g., the novel, poetry, drama, the short story, nonfiction) as well as ways of approaching and interpreting literature (e.g., theme, characterization, setting, plot, genre). A related and equally important responsibility is to transmit certain analytic-practical skills that allow students to apply their learning to alternative texts and contexts. In the English 200 course, students were encouraged to grapple with competing historical records and literary representations of the same event and then arrive at their own informed interpretation of the personal, social, cultural, and historical meanings of that event.

By teaching not only reading comprehension but also analytic skills, I try to convey to my students that correct answers often are less important than the process of questioning that prompts those answers. Students should realize that their interpretation of an assigned reading is as much determined by their commitments as by the values and beliefs invested in the text. I want to make students accountable for the unique group of experiences they bring to a text and to discussions about it. Students must put their bodies and beliefs on the line and not simply respond from the position of an objective, disinterested critic looking at themes, characterization, or setting. When they make that personal commitment to the production of knowledge, they will see that "ideas and what they can do have real meanings and real effects" (Dolan 144). This goal is the finest toward which we as educators can aspire, and the comparative method can help us achieve it.

NOTE

[1] As Kaufman explains in the introduction to his most recent work, *The Laramie Project*, "There are moments in history when a particular event brings the various ideologies and beliefs prevailing in a culture into sharp focus. At these junctures the event becomes a lightning rod of sorts, attracting and distilling the essence of these philosophies and convictions. By paying careful attention in moments like this to people's words, one is able to hear the way these prevailing ideas affect not only individual lives but also the culture at large. The trials of Oscar Wilde were such an event. When I read the transcripts of the trials (while preparing to write *Gross Indecency*), I was struck by the clarity with which they illuminated an entire culture" (Kaufman et al. v).

"All Men Kill the Thing They Love": Romance, Realism, and *The Ballad of Reading Gaol*

Joseph Bristow

If a line of poetry by Oscar Wilde has been preserved in cultural memory, then it is the one on which he rings a number of striking changes in *The Ballad of Reading Gaol* (1898)—the poem that he first published under not his own name but the number allotted to his prison cell, "C.3.3." (see fig. 1). The line occurs for the first time in the rousing sixth stanza: "The man had killed the thing he loved" (883). At this point, the "man" and the "thing" have specific referents. The "man" refers to Charles Thomas Wooldridge (known in the dedication by the initials "C. T. W."), a trooper in the prestigious Royal Horse Guards (Blue), who on 7 July 1896 became the fourth person to swing from the gallows since Reading Gaol opened in 1844. Wooldridge, in whose memory Wilde dedicated the *Ballad*, suffered the death penalty because three months earlier, in a frenzy of sexual jealousy, he slit three times the throat of "the thing he loved," his spouse, Laura Ellen Wooldridge, at the village of Clewer, near Windsor, Berkshire.

In this essay, I explain how students and teachers can grasp why Wilde chose to develop the particular reference to "the man" and "the thing" as a starting point for his broader—truly controversial—meditation on the intimate links between loving and killing. As the *Ballad* unfolds its 109 stanzas, this particularized line, "The man had killed the thing he loved," modulates into a strikingly sweeping statement. Soon afterward, Wilde asserts only to repeat that "each man kills the thing he loves" (884). Implicitly, in its shift from definite article to adjective the line broadens out from the execution of "C. T. W." to the scandalous events that eventually took "C.3.3.," whom most reviewers of the *Ballad* knew was Wilde,[1] to Reading Gaol in late 1895. Gradually, C.3.3. transforms this line so expansively that he is ultimately moved to make the following, startling assertion: "all men kill the thing they love" (899).

The contentiousness of Wilde's *Ballad* indubitably rests on this astonishing amplification. So extreme is the culminating line that it regularly faces classroom discussion with a number of demanding questions. How can Wooldridge's homicide legitimately serve as the ground on which a poet might elaborate the much disputed belief that all human beings, whether literally or figuratively, have murderous desires? In what respects might this immoderate proposition be true? Are we supposed to assent to the belief that brutal killing is the result of passionate loving? Such questions can prove disturbing and frustrating to address, because they move, as the poem moves, from the particular instance of Wooldridge's murder to a highly abstract, immensely debatable statement. One of the main perils in discussing this poem lies in readers' unsuspecting attitude toward its slow but sure movement away from the grounded example of C. T. W.'s crime to the general-

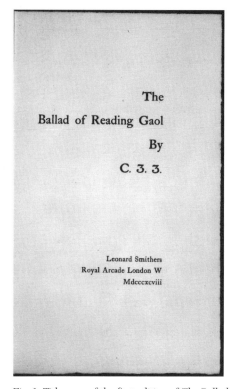

The

Ballad of Reading Gaol

By

C. 3. 3.

Leonard Smithers
Royal Arcade London W
Mdcccxcviii

Fig: 1. Title page of the first edition of *The Ballad of Reading Gaol*

ized principle that everyone, at some level, resembles the man who swung from the gallows.

Any reader coming to the *Ballad* for the first time is likely to ask why Wilde suggests that there is a definite, if not absolute, link between loving and killing. Is it because loving and killing are supposed to be equally intense? Is there a recognizable link between erotic desire and murderous rage? Can all who have loved also destroy the object of their passion? On what philosophical basis might we establish this view? The very fact that one is able to spin so many questions about the poem with such rapid immediacy implies that teaching it— the one work that became Wilde's most popular in his lifetime—says much about the stubbornness of such questions. As most instructors realize, instant discussion of abstract principles tends to do considerable disservice to our readings, since the more we attempt to start with larger matters, the less we engage with the textual details in which statements such as "all men kill the thing they love" are embedded. Before anyone engages with the ethical complications of this carefully modulated line, it therefore helps to have an informed understanding of the personal and political circumstances that brought its neatly paced monosyllables to such controversial articulation.

In what follows, I show that Wilde's carefully crafted *Ballad* is not limited to the idea that C. T. W exemplifies a murderous impulse shared by all passionate lovers. I begin by exploring how this poem was the product of Wilde's twenty-four months in jail, a period in which his spirit was almost broken, his health was ruined, and the appalling conditions of the three English prisons in which he was incarcerated filled him with despair. There is no doubt that he intended his poem to make a forthright contribution to debates that were raging, especially in Parliament, about prison reform. Thus I begin by outlining the conditions in British jails that Wilde takes pains to record here.

The *Ballad*, however, was not written exclusively in the name of political propaganda. Wilde wanted his poem to make a contribution to literary history as well. To show the kind of literary intervention he wished to make, I devote the closing part of this essay to an examination of the widely acknowledged literary antecedents on which he fashioned the outdated common meter—interlaced four-beat and three-beat lines—that drive his pounding stanzas toward their trenchant final statement.[2] By concentrating on the political and literary aspects of the *Ballad*, I address what Wilde called its "realistic" and "romantic" sides (*Complete Letters* 956). We can learn much more about the timing and execution of the poem by looking first at its realism and romance instead of attempting first to figure out whether the poem's most memorable line has any philosophical validity.

Charles Thomas Wooldridge's execution, both chronologically and politically, stood at the center of Wilde's brutal two-year sentence of solitary confinement with hard labor. In the *Ballad*, Wilde speaks in the first person to recall the terrible impact of Wooldridge's death not only on C.3.3. in particular but also on all the inmates who learned indirectly that the state would execute a fellow prisoner. One day, as he took the stipulated exercise of pacing silently in a ring, Wilde, like the other felons held at Reading Gaol, caught sight of the strange look of an unknown detainee who "walked amongst the Trial Men." At the risk of breaking prison rules, a fellow convict "whispered low" to Wilde, *"That fellow's got to swing"* (883).

The reasons for Wilde's imprisonment were notorious. On 9 March 1895, Wilde began hazardous proceedings against the Marquess of Queensberry, the volatile father of his male lover Alfred Douglas, for libeling him as a sodomite. Queensberry responded by obtaining evidence, including paid confessions from male sex workers and love letters that blackmailers had pilfered. In response, the director of public prosecutions took Wilde through two trials. On 25 May that year, Justice Wills jailed Wilde under the provisions of the Criminal Law Amendment Act (1885) whose eleventh section proscribed acts of "gross indecency" between males in private.

Readers can infer a link between C. T. W. and C.3.3. from the eighth stanza, where Wilde lists various murderers that include those who "kill their love when they are young" and those who "strangle with the hands of Lust" (884).

The connection, however, becomes plain when he later observes that he and Wooldridge "crossed each other's way" as if they were "two doomed ships that pass in storm." Thus the *Ballad* points to a resemblance between C. T. W. and C.3.3.: both men, though to very different ends, suffered greatly for their passion. At the same time, both belonged to a community of "outcast men" that an uncompassionate "world" had "thrust" from "its heart" (887).

Further, C.3.3. suggests that there is more than the analogy between himself and Wooldridge. From the seventh stanza onward, he declares that "each man," not just Wooldridge and Wilde, engages in acts of simultaneous loving and killing. The killing may not result in crime, but nonetheless it ends in destruction. "Some do it with a bitter look, / Some with a flattering word," he says. But "each man" who inflicts such harm, whether by look or word, "does not die" (884). Toward the end of the poem—in the light of its gruesome record of how the inmates "heard the prayer the hangman's snare / Strangled into a scream" (892)—the speaker widens this viewpoint further so that it acquires the status of a universal truth. Thus by drawing the confrontational conclusion that "all men kill the thing they love," Wilde seeks to strengthen the troublesome view that everyone, not solely the "outcast men," is linked, on the one hand, to the *crime passionel* that sent Wooldridge to the gallows and, on the other hand, to the sexual peril that incarcerated Wilde.

Wilde transformed this evocative line for political reasons as well. In many respects, he wished to draw on his solitary confinement and the state murder of Wooldridge when humanitarians and former inmates were campaigning for the overhaul of the British penal system. In the journal *Nineteenth Century*, for example, the Irish nationalist Michael Davitt deplored a "savage and vindictive" system that he knew well; he experienced nine years of solitary confinement because he smuggled arms for the Fenian cause. Such callous practices could scarcely "reform as well as . . . punish" if they sought to "reclaim" prisoners "by means which are directly meant to deaden every one of the common, not to speak of the higher qualities, of man," because they frequently led to "reconviction and insanity" (880).

In response to such incisive criticism, the Liberal administration appointed a departmental committee to investigate the demoralized condition of prisoners. At this stage, the aim was not to remove the death penalty, which remained on the statute books until 1983. Instead, the government-appointed committee was set the task of investigating the severe restrictions—relating to diet, visits, talking, and hard labor—imposed on inmates. During the prolonged passage of the resulting Prisons Bill, which gained its second reading soon after the *Ballad* was published on 13 February 1898, John Redmond of the United Irish Parliamentary Party would quote with approval Wilde's belief that the "vilest deeds like poison weeds / Bloom well in prison-air" (897); such lines upheld the view, one shared by Davitt, that Britain's debased penal system could only perpetuate the corruption that it purportedly aimed to eradicate. Since he, too, was raised in an Irish nationalist family, Wilde took pride in the fact that the parliamentarians who were "bringing about Prison Reform" were "Celtic to a man" (*Complete Letters* 1080).

Given the close involvement of the *Ballad* with this protracted political debate, the poem's stance in many respects appears different from the largely aesthetic poetry that Wilde started publishing, with mixed success, as an Oxford undergraduate during the mid-1870s. To some degree, the difference unsettled him. In October 1897, when he was completing his final draft, he informed Robert Ross, the loyal friend whom he chose as his literary executor, that the "poem suffer[ed] under the difficulty of a divided aim in style." "Some is realistic," he observed, "some is romantic: some poetry, some propaganda" (*Complete Letters* 956). In this formulation, the word "propaganda" is striking. To be sure, Wilde had written earlier poems that passed comment on newsworthy matters, such as his Republican protest at British imperialism in Afghanistan and his appalled reaction to the Turkish massacre of the Christians in Bulgaria.[3] But never before had he used poetry as a tool to sway public opinion.

By any account, the well-documented hardship that Wilde endured at three British jails—Pentonville (six weeks), Wandsworth (four and a half months), and Reading (eighteen months)—almost drove him insane. It is important to understand the specific types of suffering that he withstood, because they inform many of the macabre details and shape much of the bitter sentiment of the *Ballad*. During the first month of his sentence, he seemed to have escaped at least some of the prescribed forms of hard labor—working the exhausting treadmill, turning the crank ten thousand times a day—but he spent many tedious hours at the start of his sentence tearing "the tarry rope to shreds / With blunt and bleeding nails" (oakum picking provided caulking for ship's hulls) and "sew[ing] the sacks" (i.e., making mailbags for the post office) (888). After hours of such unproductive work, he underwent restless nights on his "three-plank bed" (891). The stringent prison regulations, which except in special circumstances permitted him only two visitors every thirteen weeks, wore down his mental and physical health.

During the first five months of his sentence, his condition worsened to such an alarming degree that the state took steps to ensure that it did not provoke outrage. Meanwhile the Liberal government was dedicating much energy to bringing backward British prisons in line with their modern Continental counterparts. Several people—some of them Wilde's friends, others state officials—reported Wilde's deterioration. The first noteworthy figure to seek out knowledge of his welfare was Richard Burdon Haldane, a respected Liberal MP who visited Pentonville in June 1895. Haldane had good reason to inquire into Wilde's condition, because he served on the Departmental Committee of Prisons, which would make recommendations to reform the severity of the Prisons Act of 1877. Haldane later recalled that the author asked for writing materials, together with books more interesting than *Pilgrim's Progress*—the only work, besides the Bible, that the authorities permitted him to read (166). But even if Haldane managed to secure a short list of titles that included works by Saint Augustine, John Henry Newman, and Walter Pater (made available in the prison library), he told him that a request for Gustave Flaubert's *Madame Bovary*, which the French state tried to ban in 1857, would be unrealistic.[4] Neither could Haldane secure Wilde pen and ink.

Just as Wilde's reading was strictly controlled, so was his diet. His thinness became the subject of much discussion soon after he entered Wandsworth, the London jail to which he may have been sent at Haldane's bidding, because the MP trusted the penal reformer W. D. Morrison, who worked as prison chaplain, to keep a close eye on the inmate there.[5] Even though a medical officer observed that Wilde was on an "extra diet," the additional portions of bacon, beans, skilly (austere rations of bread and oatmeal), and soup hardly enhanced the standard meager fare. By 18 September 1895, Wilde's weight dropped from 190 to 168 pounds (Hyde, *Oscar Wilde: The Aftermath* 26). News spread about his wasting body. H. W. Massingham, radical editor of the *Daily Chronicle*, informed a fellow journalist of the terrible news that he gleaned from sources close to Wilde: "Oscar Wilde is being slowly starved to death, [and] is now little better than an hysterical imbecile" (qtd. in Havighurst 67).

On 28 September 1895, Massingham published a letter from Robert H. Sherard, Wilde's dedicated friend who had recently visited him at Wandsworth, that the prisoner was "suffering greatly from sheer want of nourishment" (qtd. in Hyde, *Oscar Wilde: The Aftermath* 26). Wilde was among a number of public figures whose harrowing experience of British prisons caught Massingham's attention. Since joining the *Chronicle* in 1892, Massingham had turned the respected newspaper into a vehicle that led a mounting campaign for restructuring the antiquated prison system. The *Chronicle* proved especially vigilant of the Departmental Committee and the Prisons Bill. In 1895, the Departmental Committee made twenty-five recommendations, which included changes in the use of skilly, termination of unproductive labor, provision of books for prisoners, and redefinition of the age of juveniles from sixteen to seventeen. The 1898 Prisons Bill would absorb these proposed changes. In Massingham's view, however, the bill left "the whole structure of ignorance, cruelty, and efficiency untouched." Such reforms, Massingham asserted, were cosmetic touches that barely tempered a heartless regime that threatened to remain "the worst in the world": "It starves men, it crazes men, it makes brutes of them" ("Editorial"). Like Davitt, who told his parliamentary colleagues that the prison diet was "scientific starvation" ("Prisons Bill," col. 1182), he believed that the penal system was "a mere criminal factory" whose brutalities hardened inmates so much that they were driven toward reconviction.

It was not just the dire conditions of prison life—which Massingham recorded at length—that took their toll on Wilde's well-being. As Wilde's friends knew, the impact of bankruptcy proceedings that led Wilde back to court on 24 September 1895 could only further vitiate his mind and body. By the following week, he was so enfeebled that he fell and bruised himself in his cell. Later that day he fainted during the required chapel service. He awoke in the prison infirmary, sensing the pain of a perforated eardrum.

By late October, reports of Wilde's collapse reached the columns of Massingham's newspaper, prompting Evelyn Ruggles-Brise, chairman of the Prison Commission, to order yet another medical inquiry into Wilde's health, this time possibly under the apprehension that "there would be an extensive public outcry in the country, if Wilde was allowed to go mad or die in prison" (Hyde, *Oscar Wilde: The Aftermath* 33). The inquiry found that "no disease or derangement" could be detected in Wilde's "mental condition" (36). But, in contemplating "further treatment," it made further suggestions for improving the inmate's welfare: his removal to a prison outside London that would enable outdoor exercise; a larger cell than usual; employment, such as bookbinding, that would help pass the time more bearably; and a "freer range of books" in a "larger supply" (37). While the doctors maintained that Wilde should be permitted "association with other prisoners," they remained anxious that "his proclivities," his "avowed love for the society of males," might jeopardize prison security. Thus they advised that any "association" should be allowed only "*under the continuous supervision of a warder*" (37). Later, Haldane recommended Wilde's subsequent transfer to Reading Gaol, some thirty-five miles west of London.

Wilde's arrival at Reading Gaol, however, brought Wilde little relief. As the *Ballad* puts it, he was set beneath the thumb of a "Governor" (Major Henry B. Isaacson) who "was strong upon / The Regulations Act" (887). To add to his sorrow, his mother passed away in early February 1896. At the same time, attempts by his friends, including George Bernard Shaw, to collect signatures in France and England for petitions for his release resulted in failure. Few distinguished artistic contemporaries on either side of the Channel would lend their support. By the time Wilde witnessed Wooldridge's "wistful eye" (883), his prospects could not have been bleaker.

By 2 July 1896, five days before the executioner took the life of C. T. W., Wilde submitted the first of three petitions to the home secretary to ease the restrictions imposed on him. In this long document, he stated that he feared he might go mad:

> Dreadful as are the results of the prison system—a system so terrible that it hardens their hearts whose hearts it does not break, and brutalises those who have to carry it out no less than those who have to submit to it—yet at least amongst its aims is not the desire to wreck human reason.
> (*Complete Letters* 658)

For the preservation of his sanity, he needed better and more numerous reading materials. Even though he was now "allowed two books a week to read," the prison library still "hardly contain[ed] a score of books suitable for an educated man" (657). Apart from regretting the lack of adequate reading matter, he drew attention to his hearing and eyesight, both of which were waning. Once again, the prison authorities refused to listen.

Significant changes, however, were afoot. Soon afterward, Isaacson transferred to another post in the prison service. Meanwhile, Ruggles-Brise assisted in ensuring that the home secretary's office would look into Wilde's health while permitting Wilde "foolscap paper, ink and pen, for use in his leisure moments in his cell" (Hyde, *Oscar Wilde: The Aftermath* 77). Moreover, the home secretary advised that the rule of two books per week should be relaxed in Wilde's case. Under the merciful governorship of Major James Osmond Nelson, these concessions were increased even further, so that Wilde obtained a notebook in which, among other things, he could list the titles of books that he wished to read. Moreover, he took charge of the prison library, and by January 1897 he was allowed the privilege of white bread. Certainly, he had further pain to endure. On 12 February 1897 he lost custody of his two young sons, whom he would never see again. His wife filed for divorce seven weeks later. But, in the midst of such anguish, he could at last devote time to what the state had long denied him—the ability to write.

In early 1897, Governor Nelson provided Wilde with pen, ink, and paper. C.3.3. duly converted his "three-plank bed" into a desk. Soon, under Nelson's supervision, he began writing on the pale-blue prison foolscap that would become the document—ostensibly a retributive letter to his former lover, Alfred Douglas, but also a work that combines autobiographical reflection with meditations on sorrow and pain—that Robert Ross would publish, in carefully abridged form, as *De Profundis* in 1905.[6] Wilde drew this fifty-five-thousand-word document, which he wished to call "Epistola: In Carcere et Vinculis" ("Letter: In Prison and in Chains"), to completion by the end of March 1897, when he handed it to Nelson for inspection. In this document, he protested, "The prison-system is absolutely and entirely wrong. I would give anything to be able to alter it when I go out. I intend to try" (1038). It is to Nelson's credit that he refused to censor Wilde's strongly worded intention, which would be realized with the completion of the *Ballad*.

While he was finishing the long prison letter addressed to Douglas, Wilde established such good rapport with a newly appointed prison warder—Thomas Martin, a fellow Irishman—that he at last gained access to the types of publication that had not been sanctioned by the authorities. More than anything else, he wished to renew contact with current affairs, in the form of weekly journals and daily newspapers. Martin kindly fetched them from town. It was in the *Chronicle* that Wilde learned about Massingham's fierce criticism of the pending Prisons Bill.

Wilde's jail term ended on 19 May 1897. Immediately, Wilde left England for France as discreetly as he could, under a pseudonym to escape a scandal-mongering press. Within six weeks of settling at Berneval-sur-Mer in Normandy, he set resolutely to work on the *Ballad*. By 20 July that year, he declared that his poem was "nearly finished." "I like what I have done," he told a correspondent, "though it is a new style for me." His manner of characterizing the "new style" is revealing. "I am," he said, "out-Henleying Kipling" (*Complete Letters* 916). This remark requires careful consideration, because its competitive spirit has important bearing on not only Wilde's choice of the ballad form but also his vexed relations with two conservative journals, the *Scots Observer* (1888–90) and the *National Observer* (1890–97), which had done much to vilify him in the years leading up to his incarceration.[7] William Ernest Henley edited these periodicals until 1894; later issues bear the mark of his editorial style.

In May 1895, when the director of public prosecutions had proceeded to try Wilde, the *National Observer* told its readers that everyone should thank the Marquess of Queensberry for destroying "the High Priest of the Decadents." Then, as if such condemnation were not enough, the editor contended that Wilde should suffer more than "another trial at the Old Bailey." The best choice, in the words of this avowed imperial weekly, would be "a coroner's inquest" (Editorial).[8]

Dealings among Wilde, Henley, and Henley's followers had not always been acrimonious. In 1889, while editor of the *Woman's World*, Wilde wrote a sympathetic, though far from uncritical, review of Henley's recent *Book of Verses*, which reprinted the experimental "In Hospital" sequence of sonnets and free verse that first attracted critical attention in 1875. In particular, Henley's innovative vers libre depictions of the Edinburgh Infirmary, where Joseph Lister saved Henley from further ravages of tubercular arthritis during 1873–75, struck Wilde as possessing "new methods of expression" that displayed not only "a delicate sense of beauty and a brilliant, fantastic wit" but also "a real passion for . . . what is horrible, ugly, or grotesque" ("Note" 347).

In "Interior," for example, Henley recalls the infirmary's "gaunt brown walls," which "Look infinite in their decent meanness" (*Poems* 4). Similarly, in "Vigil" his speaker observes the interminable boredom when life is "Lived on one's back"; immobilized, the hospital patient experiences "a practical nightmare— / Hideous asleep or awake" (7). But much as Wilde admitted that it was "impossible to deny" the grim "power" of "In Hospital," he found the formal experimentation of Henley's sequence unsatisfactory. Such poems, he said, were "still in the twilight," because they were not "perfected." Their lack of perfection lay in Henley's "constant rejection of rhyme," since rhyme lent "architecture as well as melody to verse" ("Note" 348).

In the *Ballad*, Wilde intensifies Henley's grotesquerie but does so by restoring both internal and end rhymes to it. Each cell, he writes, "Is a foul and dark latrine," where "the fetid breath of living Death / Chokes up each grated screen" (897). Likewise, on the night before Wooldridge's execution "each man" in the prison "trembled as he crept / Into his numbered tomb" (889). Thus Wilde indulged in a type of "out-Henleying" insofar as he took some of his archenemy's arresting images of one unendurable institution and elaborated them through rhyme and meter for the purpose of reforming another.

But, as his letter of 20 July 1897 shows, his sense of competition with Henley relates to the work of yet another contemporary. In early 1890, the Anglo-

Indian Rudyard Kipling made his mark in the *Scots Observer* with the first of his *Barrack-Room Ballads*. As the title suggests, Kipling's ballads, which Henley's journal featured throughout that year, involve military subject matter. They articulate the rant of Tommy Atkins, the name that the armed forces used in official documents to denote the typical low-ranking foot soldier. In Kipling's opening ballad, "Danny Deever," Atkins recalls a conversation between Files-on-Parade and the Colour-Sergeant. "What are the bugles blowin' for?" the one asks the other in working-class cockney (line 1). "To turn you out," the Colour-Sergeant replies (2). "I'm dreadin' what I've got to watch," he adds (4). The reason is that the military is "hangin' Danny Deever" (5). Deever, we learn, "shot a comrade sleepin'" (22). Consequently, the "regiment's in column" and "the young recruits are shakin'" (31) as they hear the terrifying "Dead March" that presages the execution (5).

Kipling's articulation of a raucous working-class voice that chillingly chants "they're hangin' Danny Deever in the mornin'" betokened a remarkable revision of the ballad form, a form that proved popular with generations of nineteenth-century poets—such as Samuel Taylor Coleridge, whose famous *Rime of the Ancient Mariner* (1817) echoes in some of Wilde's grisliest lines.[9] The fresh emphasis that Kipling placed on the ordinary soldier's forthright perceptions of the military machine, however, hardly aimed at undermining the death penalty. Kipling took such brutalities for granted. By the time Wilde started work on the *Ballad*, Kipling's name was closely attached to upholding the prowess of Britain's empire, if with the "bouncing vulgar vitality" that would later appall George Orwell (186).[10] Henley, too, gained a staunch reputation for bellicose patriotism. Famously, in "The Song of the Sword" (1892), a long poem dedicated to Kipling, he evoked the rhythms and imagery of the Anglo-Saxon *Beowulf* to characterize a primordially English poetic voice that praised the Darwinian valor of empire in "Sifting the nations, / The slag from the metal, / The waste and the weak / From the fit and the strong" (*Poems* 35).

Wilde certainly did not seek to emulate either Kipling's or Henley's pugnacious tone. By "out-Henleying Kipling" he had two aims in mind. At one and the same time, he restored Kipling's balladic rhythms and regular rhymes to the "horrible" and "grotesque" imagery of "In Hospital" and transformed the subject matter of "Danny Deever"—who, like C. T. W., was an ordinary soldier—into a matter of political concern. Yet even though the *Ballad* sought to wrest its chosen poetic genre away from Kipling, it connected the incantatory rhythms of "Danny Deever" with a much earlier poem, one that also featured a horrific murder—and held an altogether more dignified place in the literary canon.

Even though, in a perceptive 1898 review, Arthur Symons acknowledged that parts of the *Ballad* might be "properly compared with Mr. Henley's 'In Hospital'" (365), he also recognized that both the form and theme of Wilde's six-line ballad stanzas were indebted to Thomas Hood's "The Dream of Eugene Aram, the Murderer" (1829). But Hood's poem, which became a favorite among Victorian anthologists and parodists, had much greater value than Symons would concede when he discussed the line on which much of the meaning of the *Ballad* hangs. To be sure, Symons understood that Wilde's conclusion—"all men kill the thing they love"—was "a central idea." Yet for him it remained only "half, but no more than half, a paradox" (365). Like many interpreters, he failed to see why the tale of eighteenth-century homicide Eugene Aram might help to elucidate an aspect of this difficult line.

Hood, like Edward Bulwer in his popular novel *Eugene Aram* (1831), based much of his understanding of this celebrated murderer on misleading sources that advanced the romanticized view that it was almost impossible to believe that a man who claimed to be a noble scholar could have participated in an atrocious crime motivated by material greed. On 3 August 1759, Aram, a schoolmaster at Knaresborough, Yorkshire, was convicted of murdering some fifteen years earlier Daniel Clark, a shoemaker who hatched a plan to defraud local people who kindly loaned him goods in order to help him with the preparations for his wedding. Together with a working man, Aram killed Clark and seized some of the property. Even though Aram was arrested for hoarding part of the stolen property at his home, he paid off his debtors and left town. Until 1758, the year when a laborer quarrying stone found human remains buried on a nearby hill, the townsfolk knew nothing of Aram's whereabouts. A search, however, tracked him down to the prestigious grammar school at Lynn, Norfolk, where he had served for eight months as usher. It was there that the authorities led him away to York Assizes.

While awaiting execution, Aram wrote an eloquent account of his scholarly accomplishments, which included amazing proficiency in numerous languages, such as Arabic, Chaldean, and Celtic ("in all its dialects") (*Genuine Account* 38). He left a parting note that stated that although he "was stained by malevolence," his "life was not polluted" and his "morals" remained "irreproachable" (41). Subsequent historians appear to have believed him. In the various editions of their *Newgate Calendar*, Andrew Knapp and William Baldwin described Aram's history as "perhaps . . . the most remarkable and extraordinary trial in our whole Calendar." "The perpetrator," they observed, "was a man of extraordinary endowments, and of high education; therefore little to be suspected of committing so very foul a crime" (2: 246).

Hood added to the myth by prefacing his poem with an anecdote gleaned from the late James Burney, brother of well-known novelist Frances Burney and a former pupil at Lynn Grammar School, that the kindly usher was "loved by the boys," to whom he related edifying tales about murderers.[11] In the poem, Hood's narrator records that Aram "told" the pupils "how murderers walk the earth / Beneath the curse of Cain" (66–67). It therefore comes as a shock to learn that Aram, who had grown "very lean, / And pale, and leaden-ey'd" from "much study" (29–30), might have committed the murder that he subsequently recalls from a terrible haunting dream. It was Aram's idiosyncratic position as the scholar guilty of the crime against which he warned his charges that contributed to Wilde's seemingly paradoxical "all men kill the thing they love." Aram's exaggerated legend exemplified the forceful paradox that no human being, not even a well-respected teacher, could escape the crime that he or she denounced.

Hood's poem has further bearing on how Aram's homicide ironically "kills" the moral that Aram allegedly "loves." Hood's rendition of Aram as a distinctive type of scholar-murderer became the focus of a tradition of nineteenth-century writings that elaborated what Joel Black terms "the aesthetics of murder." Black's main thesis is that in a famous 1827 essay, Thomas De Quincey was the first to consider murder as one of the fine arts. De Quincey jokingly fabricated the idea that in London there was "a Society for the Encouragement of Murder" whose members would "meet and criticize as they would a picture, statue, or other work of art" (112). "By treating murder as an art form," Black observes, "De Quincey demonstrated the aesthetic subversion of the beautiful by the sublime, and more generally, the philosophical subversion of ethics by aesthetics" (15). In other words, De Quincey gave the lie to the idea, central in much Romantic thought, that there was an indissoluble link between beauty and justice.

Wilde had long been responsive to the troubling idea that a murderer could convert a heinous act into an aesthetic masterpiece. In "Pen, Pencil and Poison" (1889), he drew on two well-known accounts of the dandyish Thomas Griffith Wainewright, an art critic connected with notable figures of the Romantic era such as De Quincey, who became "one of the most subtle and secret poisoners of this or any age" (1101, 1102). Wilde observes that in "one of his beautiful rings," Wainewright "used to carry crystals of the Indian *nux vomica*," a substance that is "nearly tasteless, difficult of discovery, and capable of infinite dilution" (1102). Thus Wilde discovered in Wainewright's history the type of paradox that shapes the key line from the *Ballad*. "There is," he concluded, "no essential incongruity between crime and culture. We cannot re-write the whole of history for the purpose of gratifying our moral sense of what should be" (1106).

Yet, as Karen Alkalay-Gut maintains, the *Ballad* shifts the tradition of aesthetic murder into a different register. She points out that De Quincey's 1827 essay does "not consider the confluence of murder and love" (355). Instead, as Alfred Douglas perceived (49), Wilde plays on the meaning of a well-known line from act 4, scene 1, of Shakespeare's *Merchant of Venice*, where Bassanio asks Shylock, "Do all men kill the things they do not love?" Shylock replies, "Hates any man the thing he would not kill?" (line 137). Thus by stating that "all men kill the thing they love," Wilde brings a challenging irony to bear on Shakespeare's two ostensibly rhetorical questions. By inverting the play's dialogue, the *Ballad* sounds a discordant note that invites its educated audience, one intimately acquainted with Shakespeare's comedy, to consider that there might indeed be a link between loving and killing.

Besides drawing on well-known literary precedents—Coleridge's "Ancient Mariner," Hood's "Eugene Aram," and Shakespeare's *Merchant of Venice*—to revise critically the imperial brutishness of Henley and Kipling, he echoed (as at least one reviewer detected)[12] some other poems that ensured that C. T. W.

became a far more dignified figure than Danny Deever. On Wilde's release, A. E. Housman sent Wilde (through Ross) a copy of his anonymously published *A Shropshire Lad* (1896), an exquisite collection of sometimes homoerotic lyrics that focus mainly on the loves and lives of young working men in rural England who endure the hardships of modern existence. Poem "IX" in Housman's collection features the voice of a country lad who recalls in quatrains written in common meter how a "hundred years ago" the "dead man stood on air" as he swung from "yon . . . gallows" that "used to clank" (14, 8, 3). Now, almost thirty years after public executions were ended because the state deplored spectators' bloodlust, the speaker thinks of the young man "in Shrewsbury jail to-night" who will wake to feel "the hangman's noose" around his "neck"—one that "God made for other use / Than strangling on a string" (13, 17, 19–20).

Even more potent for Wilde's political critique was Housman's poem "XLVII," also known as "The Carpenter's Son," which concentrates attention not on an ordinary Shropshire lad but on one of the most famous historical figures to have suffered execution. Here Housman shows Jesus Christ on the cross addressing a crowd, stating that had he "but left ill alone" by staying at his father's side, he might have done honest work by building "Gallows-trees for other chaps" instead of being led to his own (10). But since the authorities concluded that he created "ill" by shepherding his people toward God, they crucified him: "Here hang I, and right and left / Two fellows hang for theft; / All the same's the luck we prove, / Though the midmost hangs for love" (17–20). The stanza, with its deliberately jolting rhythms, makes it plain that the Roman Empire treated the Savior as a common thief when in fact he was, in the broadest sense, a lover. By inference, Housman's lyric asks his audience to question how society can permit capital punishment when the Son of God was killed because of his passionate devotion to humanity.

Housman's thoughtful poems, especially their reference to Christ's Passion, left a special mark on Wilde's *Ballad*. C.3.3. begins by vividly suggesting the intimacy between Christ's love and the murderer's sinfulness. The opening lines equate the "wine" that represents Christ's sacrificial "blood" in Holy Communion and the "blood" and "wine" that were found on Wooldridge's "hands" (883). The equating of these different forms of blood—the one lost to save humankind, the other taken in a fit of jealousy—is startling. Other details elaborate the proposed link between Christ and C. T. W. We are told how "the grey cock crew" and "the red cock crew" each morning before the unknown day of execution took place (890). Reminding us of how Peter betrayed Jesus Christ (Matt. 26.74–75), this line introduces a sequence of stanzas that shows that the supposedly Christian society that demands the daily attendance of prisoners at chapel has betrayed C. T. W.[13]

In Wilde's view, by murdering C. T. W. the regime at Reading Gaol also destroyed the Christian faith, to which faith it demanded prisoners' devotion: "The Chaplain would not kneel to pray / By his [Wooldridge's] dishonoured grave: / Nor mark it with that blessed Cross / That Christ for sinners gave"

(896). The unforgiving chaplain therefore stands as the most glaring example of the innumerable people who devotedly "kill the thing they love," not understanding that the pain that they feel they have the right to inflict on others is to some degree criminal.

Since his *Ballad* suggests that capital punishment amounts to the betrayal of Christian faith, Wilde knew he risked offending editors, especially when his scandalous imprisonment had already besmirched his name. John Lane, who issued five of Wilde's books before the trials, declined the *Ballad* for this reason (see J. Nelson 176; O'Sullivan 113). By August 1897, however, Wilde was in touch with the small press of Leonard Smithers, known for its exclusive list of pornographic titles and exquisitely printed volumes of decadent poetry. Smithers was unfazed by Wilde's sullied reputation. According to Smithers's son, Ross persuaded the publisher that Wilde's "notoriety would enhance sales enormously" (19). During the next six months, Wilde and Smithers tested each other's patience over the print run, profits, and typeface of the poem, which Smithers initially wished to bring out in a small edition of five hundred copies at the inexpensive price of two shillings. Wilde, since his bankruptcy meant he relied on a modest allowance from his spouse, wanted a much better return.

Smithers finally agreed to print eight hundred copies at two shillings sixpence, and he was taken aback by the immediate success of the *Ballad*. Within days, it sold out. Thus Smithers responded positively to Wilde's request that he advertise subsequent editions. By 19 March 1898, the publisher informed readers of the *Athenaeum*, a distinguished literary weekly that did not review the *Ballad* in 1898, that Wilde's poem had a turnover of three thousand copies (see fig. 2). Wilde joked that such promotion made him "feel like Lipton's tea" (*Complete Letters* 1043). By 1899 the poem's commercial success meant that the seventh edition could bear Wilde's name. Sales had more than doubled, making it not only "one of the most important successes in poetry publishing during the Nineties" (J. Nelson 202) but also the best selling of the sixteen books that Wilde published in English during his lifetime.

But from the moment it reached booksellers, the *Ballad* met with readers' misgivings. As one might expect, Henley's new journal *Outlook* took issue with the poem, which it thought a "patchwork of what is and what is not." In particular, the reviewer seemed confused by Wilde's assertion that "all men kill the thing they love." The poem, the critic remarked, "states the fact with gloom . . . yet it seems to approve, and it pleads passionately against the penalizing of such excesses of emotion." Little wonder *Outlook* perceived that the *Ballad* was "stertorous with sentimentalism."

Henley's paper was not alone in drawing such conclusions. Almost forty years later, as Leonard Nathan has shown, W. B. Yeats took the liberty of editing the poem's 109 stanzas down to thirty-eight, and in the process he removed all references to "the man," "each man," and "all men" who "kill the thing" that they "love." Yeats said that "even [these] famous lines," regardless of whether or not

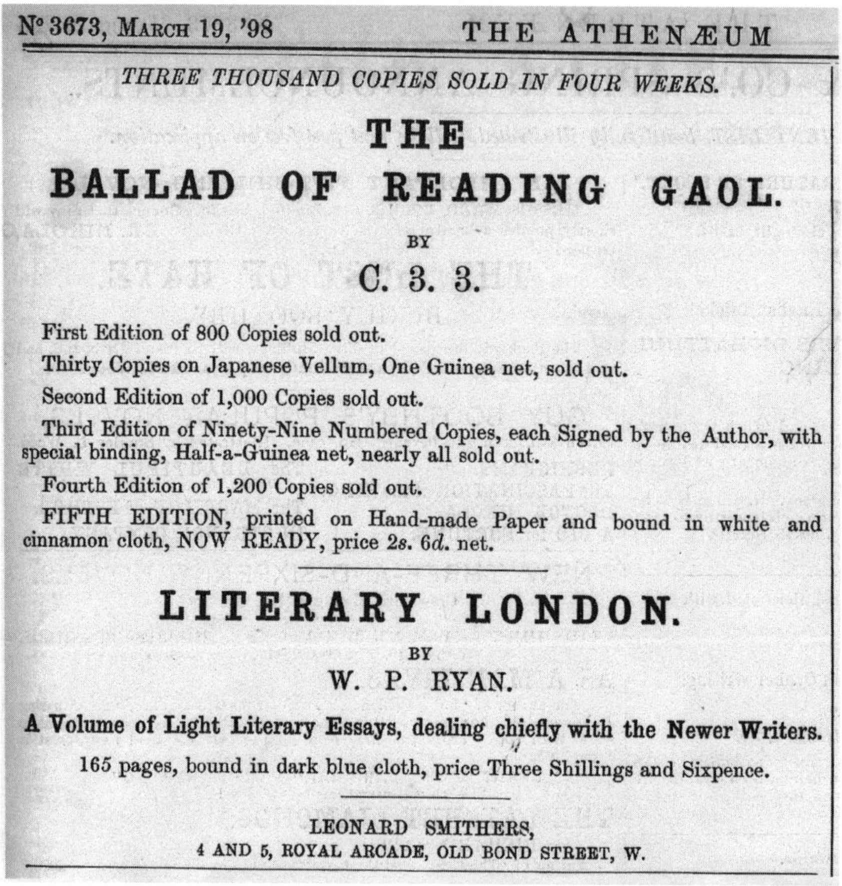

No 3673, MARCH 19, '98   THE ATHENÆUM

THREE THOUSAND COPIES SOLD IN FOUR WEEKS.

THE
BALLAD OF READING GAOL.

BY

C. 3. 3.

First Edition of 800 Copies sold out.

Thirty Copies on Japanese Vellum, One Guinea net, sold out.

Second Edition of 1,000 Copies sold out.

Third Edition of Ninety-Nine Numbered Copies, each Signed by the Author, with special binding, Half-a-Guinea net, nearly all sold out.

Fourth Edition of 1,200 Copies sold out.

FIFTH EDITION, printed on Hand-made Paper and bound in white and cinnamon cloth, NOW READY, price 2s. 6d. net.

LITERARY LONDON.

BY

W. P. RYAN.

A Volume of Light Literary Essays, dealing chiefly with the Newer Writers.

165 pages, bound in dark blue cloth, price Three Shillings and Sixpence.

LEONARD SMITHERS,
4 AND 5, ROYAL ARCADE, OLD BOND STREET, W.

Fig. 2. Smithers's advertisement of the *Ballad* in *Athenaeum*

they were "effective in themselves," looked "artificial, trivial, arbitrary" (vii). Since he had "plucked from the *Ballad* . . . its foreign feathers," Yeats presumed that he brought "into the light a great, or almost great poem" whose "stark realism" contrasted with what he terms the earlier "trick[ing] and clown[ing]" that Wilde supposedly exploited in his heyday in order "to draw attention to himself" (vii).

Many other readers have found much of the *Ballad* florid in its gestures and histrionic in tone. Not only that, the poem distorts some technical details. Wilde claims, for dramatic effect, that C. T. W.'s military coat was "scarlet" (883) when in fact it was blue with red trimmings. Similarly, he states that the inmates heard Wooldridge "scream" (892) on execution when the press reported that the man expired in silence. To some readers, such excesses may weaken the poem's advocacy for prison reform and stance against capital punishment.

In 1906, Robert Sherard, Wilde's earliest biographer, protested the statement that "each man kills the thing he loves": "The thing is not true; if it were true it is badly expressed" (*Life* 413). It is a hard statement to accept at face value. Moreover, to some ears the modulations of this line may be intolerable, because they strike a sexually contemptible note.[14] That the depersonalized "thing" initially refers to the body of a dead woman can make it appear that the heartlessness of "each man," if not "all men," stems from misogyny (Bristow, *Effeminate England* 48).

Wilde knew he had completed a work whose style and structure, as he self-mockingly told Ross, pulled in such opposing directions that it might as well be called "*Poésie et Propagande*" (*Complete Letters* 964). The *Ballad* was divided not only in aim. It also revised earlier Victorian ballads so strenuously that it took an increasingly antiquated genre to an extreme, even terminal, point. In the years anticipating modernism, any poems that indulgently personified such entities as "Fear" (889), "Hope" (892), "Justice" (891), and "Lust" (884) and that used thumping common meter would look distinctly outmoded.

Wilde acknowledged that the *Ballad*, in both its poetic form and its position in his career, marked an end point. Toward its completion, he told Ross that he no longer wished to "out-Kipling Henley" (*Complete Letters* 950). By the time it went on sale, the *Ballad*, as he informed a friend, had become his "*chant de cygne*" ("swan song") (1035). He would publish no more original writing, unless one considers his correspondence with the *Chronicle* on penal reform. In the last of his three letters to the newspaper (dated 23 March 1898 and signed "BY THE AU-THOR OF *THE BALLAD OF READING GAOL*"), he promotes the key points made in his poem, including the need to "Christianise the chaplains" (1049).[15] He seems to have felt that now he could only repeat what he said in the *Ballad*, which remained his last word on an unjust world that had driven him into exile.

Wilde's last word began a controversy of more than a hundred years about the poem's claim. In the light of the information provided in this essay, we can see more clearly why Wilde asserted that the whole of humanity stands convicted of the homicidal lust that led Wooldridge to his death. The assertion that "all men kill the thing they love" is not so much an alarming abstraction (and one that can mire us in philosophical debate) as a statement that stems from recognizable personal, political, and literary sources.

From a realistic perspective, the line is the result of Wilde's objections to how the penal system destroys the lives of the incarcerated. A Victorian prison metaphorically "loves" the prisoners it "kills," because it is in the business of punishing the people it has embraced within its walls. The poem is realistic also because it reveals that, in the face of a state-run killing machine, prisoners nonetheless share a common bond, one that enables them to experience compassion that not even the prison chaplain can express.

The line is romantic in that it reminds us of the powerful poems that it thoughtfully echoes and revises. On the one hand, the form of the *Ballad* evokes the morally complex story of Eugene Aram, which Hood immortalized, just as it reminds us of the spiritual poignancy of Christ's crucifixion, an extreme form of suffering that redeemed humankind and that Housman represented in "The Carpenter's Son." On the other hand, Wilde's poem takes issue with the imperialist appropriation of the ballad in jingoistic works by the immensely popular Kipling and his aggressive sponsor Henley.

With these points in mind, teachers and students will be in a better position to assess the degree to which Wilde's unforgettable line is justified. Likewise, they should be able to see how its rhetorical extravagance is the result of its rich literary allusiveness. Is there a politically and historically grounded belief beneath its haunting monosyllabic surface? Or does the finely crafted statement exemplify how rhetoric can override reason? Is the *Ballad* mostly *"Propagande"* or is it finally accomplished *"Poésie"*? Are we to judge these aspects of the poem apart from or together with each other? In the end, the answers will be yours and your students', not mine. My investigation into the realistic and romantic contexts of Wilde's *Ballad* is not to answer these kinds of questions but to raise them. At the very least, my account of this stirring poem should give readers a firmer grasp on the overdetermined forces that direct these much quoted stanzas toward the ethically troubling view that "all men," including you and me, "kill the thing they love."

NOTES

I wish to thank Josephine McDonagh for advice on aspects of Romantic aesthetics, Philip E. Smith for advice on earlier drafts, and Ian Small for alerting me to Wilde's knowledge of Wilfred Scawen Blunt's *In Vinculis*.

[1] The *Daily Chronicle*, for example, stated that the *Ballad* was a poem "whose authorship is not difficult to detect" (Rev. of *Ballad*).

[2] The sources on which Wilde drew have long been familiar to Wilde's readers, as Gagnier explains (*Idylls* 230).

[3] On Wilde's criticism of British imperial expansionism in Afghanistan, see "Ave Imperatrix" (851–54); for his attack on Muslim Turks massacring Bulgarian Christians, see "Sonnet" (771).

[4] Hyde points out that the governor of Pentonville found some of the books that Haldane secured for Wilde to be " 'of controversial character' and consequently contrary to the Local Prison Code" (*Oscar Wilde: The Aftermath* 26).

[5] The searing comments that Wilde makes in the *Ballad* on prison chaplains, which I discuss below, are obviously not aimed at Morrison, who was both on the staff of the *Daily Chronicle* and the author of a number of publications on prison reform, including "Prisons and Prisoners." Bobby Fong and Karl Beckson state that the chaplain at Reading Gaol was Rev. Martin Thomas Friend (Wilde, *Poems* 311).

[6] In 1905 Ross published a shortened version of *De Profundis* that excluded Wilde's recriminatory remarks on Douglas's behavior. The first complete text, with editorial apparatus, appeared in 1962; it is reprinted in *Complete Letters* 683–786.

[7] In the 1880s, both Wilde and Henley were employed at Cassell and Company, the publisher that funded *The Woman's World*, the largely feminist magazine that Wilde edited from 1887 to 1889. Henley edited Cassell's *Magazine of Art* from 1880 to 1886.

Both men published volumes with David Nutt. Henley's antipathy to Wilde might have been based in large part on literary rivalry.

[8] At this time Henley was no longer editor of the *National Observer*. The antipathy of the editorial toward Wilde, however, deepens the hostility that the *Scots Observer* expressed toward *The Picture of Dorian Gray* in 1890. During the summer of that year, Henley's weekly paper ran a forum that used Wilde's novel as the focus for a spirited, frequently offensive debate entitled "Art and Morality."

[9] Early reviewers and modern critics, including Ellmann (*Oscar Wilde* 533) and Fong and Beckson (Wilde, *Poems* 313), concur with Shaw that in the *Ballad* Wilde "borrow[s] form and melody from Coleridge" ("My Memories" 403), most notably the lines in the *Rime* that run "About, about, in reel and rout / The death-fires danced at night" (16.127–28), which Wilde reformulates as "About, about, in ghastly rout / They trod a saraband" when describing the "crooked shapes of Terror" (890) that preyed on the prisoners' nerves in the days leading up to Wooldridge's execution.

[10] In Wilde's "The Critic as Artist," which first appeared as "The True Function and Value of Criticism" in the *Nineteenth Century* in 1890, Ernest informs his interlocutor, Gilbert, that he is struck by the "superb flashes of vulgarity" that appear in Kipling's collection of stories, *Plain Tales from the Hills* (1889) (1151).

[11] Tyson suggests that Hood may have gleaned knowledge of Burney's time at Lynn Grammar School through Charles Lamb (49). When Hood's poem first appeared in *The Gem: A Literary Annual* in 1829, the information about Burney's schooldays was put in an endnote. Hood's preface was published in the first edition of "The Dream of Eugene Aram" in 1831.

[12] The *Daily Chronicle* stated that the *Ballad* echoed *A Shropshire Lad* but felt that the "thought" in Wilde's poem was more "mature" than that expressed in Housman's lyric on Shrewsbury jail (Rev. of *Ballad*).

[13] Not all men "feel upon" their "shuddering cheek[s] / The kiss of Caiaphas" (885)—an allusion to the high priest who funded Judas's betrayal of Christ (see, e.g., Matt. 25.3–16). The allusion to Caiaphas may derive from the opening sonnet in *In Vinculis* (1889) by the anticolonialist English poet Wilfred Scawen Blunt, who was imprisoned in Galway Gaol in 1887. He served two years with hard labor at Galway and Kilmainhaim prisons. Blunt, as Wilde knew, was actively involved in campaigns for home rule. He was jailed for giving a speech at the banned antivivisection demonstrations: "From Caiaphas to Pilate I was sent, / Who judged with unwashed hands a crime to me. / Next came the sentence, and the soldiery / Claimed me their prey" (1). Wilde was personally acquainted with Blunt. In "Poetry and Prison," a review that originally appeared in the *Pall Mall Gazette* on 3 January 1889, he observed that "*In Vinculis* . . . is a book that stirs one by its fine sincerity of purpose, its lofty and impassioned thought, its depth and ardour of intense feeling" (393).

[14] Alkalay-Guy writes that the "dehumanization is not an assertion of misogyny" (353). Students and colleagues may disagree with Alkalay-Gut on this point. In my contextual reading, I have not been able to discuss the incompatibility among various feminist and gay-affirmative approaches to Wilde's *Ballad*. For an exploration of how gay analysis can elucidate Wilde's poem, see Koestenbaum.

[15] In his exhaustive study of the 1898 Prisons Bill, McConville observes Wilde's "mixed motives" in this letter to the *Chronicle*. He senses that Wilde wished not only to be taken seriously as a commentator on penal reform but also to increase the sales of the *Ballad* (709).

NOTES ON CONTRIBUTORS

Alan Ackerman is associate professor of English at the University of Toronto. He is the author of *The Portable Theater: American Literature and the Nineteenth-Century Stage* (1999), coeditor with Martin Puchner of *Against Theatre: Creative Destructions on the Modernist Stage* (2006), and editor of the journal *Modern Drama*.

Jonathan Alexander is associate professor of English at the University of California, Irvine. His books include *Digital Youth: Emerging Literacies on the World Wide Web*; two edited collection, *Role Play: Distance Learning and the Teaching of Writing* and *Bisexuality and Transgenderism: InterSEXions of the Others*; and two coauthored books, *Argument Now* and *Finding Out: An Introduction to LGBT Studies*.

Bruce Bashford, author of *Oscar Wilde: The Critic as Humanist* (1999), is associate professor of English at Stony Brook University. He teaches courses in literary theory and the history of criticism, the art of rhetoric, and Oscar Wilde.

Joseph Bristow, professor of English at the University of California, Los Angeles, is the author of *Effeminate England* and *Sexuality* and has edited *Wilde Writings: Contextual Conditions* (2002) and *The Fin-de-Siècle Poem: English Literary Culture and the 1890s* (2005). His interests are Victorian and twentieth-century British literature, theories and histories of sexuality, and Oscar Wilde.

Francesca Coppa is associate professor of English and director of film studies at Muhlenberg College, where she teaches twentieth-century dramatic literature, sexuality theory, and performance studies. She is the editor of Joe Orton's early works and a collection of critical essays on his plays. She wrote an essay on Wilde and performance theory for *Palgrave Advances in Oscar Wilde Studies* and contributed to the forthcoming *Oscar Wilde and Modern Culture: The Making of a Legend* (ed. Joseph Bristow).

Heath A. Diehl is instructor of English at Bowling Green State University, where he teaches dramatic literature, literary and cultural theory (queer, feminist, postmodern, performance), gay and lesbian literature, and composition. He has written articles on Martin MacDonagh and Oscar Wilde.

Petra Dierkes-Thrun is assistant professor of modern British literature at California State University, Northridge. Her interests are interdisciplinary, comparative approaches to fin de siècle and modernist literature and culture; gender studies; critical and queer theory; film studies; and the pedagogy of literature and writing. She is currently working on a book analyzing adaptations and interpretations of Wilde's *Salomé*.

Sos Eltis is fellow and tutor in English, Brasenose College, Oxford. She is the author of *Revising Wilde: Society and Subversion in the Plays of Oscar Wilde* (1996). She is currently preparing a book on the fallen woman on stage from 1850 to the present. She teaches nineteenth- and twentieth-century literature and has a special interest in drama.

Nikolai Endres is associate professor of world literature in the English department at Western Kentucky University. He has published articles on Plato, Petronius, Wilde,

E. M. Forster, Mary Renault, and Gore Vidal and on gay and lesbian pedagogy. His courses include classics, mythology, British literature, critical theory, and queer studies.

Samuel Lyndon Gladden is associate professor and coordinator of Graduate Studies in English at the University of Northern Iowa. He is the author of *Shelley's Textual Seductions: Plotting Utopia in the Erotic and Political Works* (2002). His edition of Wilde's *The Importance of Being Earnest* is forthcoming. He teaches nineteenth-century British literature and culture, visual culture studies, gender and sexuality studies, and space studies.

Jarlath Killeen is lecturer in the School of English in Trinity College, Dublin, where he teaches Victorian literature. He is the author of *The Faiths of Oscar Wilde* (2005), *Gothic Ireland* (2005), and *The Fairy Tales of Oscar Wilde* (2007).

Melissa Knox is the author of *Oscar Wilde: A Long and Lovely Suicide* (1994) and *Oscar Wilde in the 1990s: The Critic as Creator* (2001). She has published essays on Oscar Wilde, Charles Maturin, Dorothy Parker, Henry Rider Haggard, Thomas De Quincey, Henry James, Edmund Wilson, Anaïs Nin, Shirley Jackson, Paul Monette, and (with Josef Raab) Tony Kushner. She lectures at the University of Duisberg-Essen in Germany.

Joe Law is assistant vice-president for Articulation and Transfer, coordinator of Writing across the Curriculum, and professor of English at Wright State University. He is both author and editor of material on writing centers, literature, opera, and writing across the curriculum. He has taught composition and literature and the seminar Oscar Wilde and His Age.

Joan Navarre, an independent scholar, is the author of *The Publishing History of Aubrey Beardsley's Compositions for Oscar Wilde's* Salomé and articles on Wilde. She has taught courses on Wilde and theater history. She is at work on the first biography of Wilde's friend, Edward Heron-Allen, FRS.

Robert Preissle is lecturer in the Department of Comparative Studies at Ohio State University and senior professor in general education at DeVry University, Columbus. He teaches courses in film, literature, nineteenth- and twentieth-century British and American literature, and the social impacts of science and technology. His interest is in *trans-* phenomena of all types.

Frederick S. Roden is associate professor of English at the University of Connecticut. He is the author of *Same-Sex Desire in Victorian Religious Culture* and *Love's Trinity*, a commentary companion to Julian of Norwich. He is the editor of *Palgrave Advances in Oscar Wilde Studies*, and coeditor of *Catholic Figures, Queer Narratives*. He is currently working on a book entitled "Jewish/Christian/Queer: Crossroads and Intersections" and a translation of Marc-André Raffalovich's *Uranisme et unisexualité* (1896).

D. C. Rose was director of the Oscar Wilde Summer School in Bray, Ireland, and edits the online journal *Oscholars*. His chief area of interest is fin de siècle Paris and Wilde's accommodation within it. He is now engaged in an extended study of *Pelléas et Mélisande* and also researching the construction of Paris in English fiction.

Nicholas Ruddick is professor of English, director of the Humanities Research Institute, and president's scholar (2002–04) at the University of Regina. He is the author of

Christopher Priest, British Science Fiction: A Chronology, 1478–1990 and *Ultimate Island: On the Nature of British Science Fiction.* He is currently writing a book on prehistoric fiction and editing a new edition of Jack London's *The Call of the Wild.*

S. I. Salamensky, a literary and performance scholar, is assistant professor of theater at the University of California, Los Angeles. She is author of *Wilde Words: Performance and the Proto-modernist Cultural Imagination* and editor of *Talk Talk Talk: The Cultural Life of Everyday Conversation.*

Neil Sammells is professor of English and Irish literature and dean of academic development at Bath Spa University. He is the author of *Tom Stoppard: The Artist as Critic* (1988) and *Wilde Style: The Plays and Prose of Oscar Wilde* (2000). He is the editor, with Paul Hyland, of *Irish Writing: Exile and Subversions* (1991) and has edited *Irish Studies Review* since 1992.

Beth Tashery Shannon has taught literature and writing at Georgetown College and the University of Kentucky. Her fiction is published in *Pushcart Prize, Women Write Erotica* (1984), the *Chicago Review,* and *TriQuarterly.* She is working on a study of the poetry of W. B. Yeats, *A Vision,* and the hermetic tradition.

Kirsten Shepherd-Barr is university lecturer in English and modern drama and fellow of Saint Catherine's College, University of Oxford. She is the author of *Ibsen and Early Modernist Theatre, 1890–1900* (1997) and *Science on Stage: From* Doctor Faustus *to* Copenhagen (2006).

Philip E. Smith II is associate professor of English at the University of Pittsburgh. With Michael S. Helfand he coauthored and coedited *Oscar Wilde's Oxford Notebooks: A Portrait of Mind in the Making* (1989). He has written on Wilde, Constance Naden, Robert Heinlein, Ursula Le Guin, Brian Aldiss, August Wilson, John Galsworthy, Charles Olson; on issues of curriculum, staffing, and teaching in the profession of English studies.

Eszter Szalczer is associate professor of theater at the University at Albany, State University of New York, where she teaches theater history and dramatic literature. Her research focuses on August Strindberg. Her book *Writing Daughters: August Strindberg's Other Voices* is forthcoming.

Shelton Waldrep teaches in the English Department at the University of Southern Maine. He has edited a special issue of *Studies in the Literary Imagination* entitled *Inauthentic Pleasures: Victorian Fakery and the Limitations of Form.* His most recent book is *The Aesthetics of Self-Invention: Oscar Wilde to David Bowie.*

SURVEY RESPONDENTS

The editor gratefully acknowledges the generosity of all who shared their approaches to teaching Wilde by answering the survey questions. Their descriptions of classes, readings, and assignments helped shape the contents of this volume. Many of the respondents also contributed essays to it.

Richard S. Albright, *Lehigh University*
Jonathan Alexander, *University of Cincinnati*
Stephen Arata, *University of Virginia*
Bruce Bashford, *Stony Brook University*
Joseph Bristow, *University of California, Los Angeles*
Ellen Miller Casey, *University of Scranton*
Francesca Coppa, *Muhlenberg College*
Petra Dierkes-Thrun, *California State University, Northridge*
Nikolai Endres, *Western Kentucky University*
Paul Fortunato, *University of Illinois, Chicago*
Samuel Lyndon Gladden, *University of Northern Iowa*
Piotr Gwiaza, *University of Maryland, Baltimore County*
Michael Helfand, *University of Pittsburgh*
Joan Navarre, *independent scholar*
Janice Neuleib, *Illinois State University*
Frederick Roden, *University of Connecticut, Torrington*
Nicholas Ruddick, *University of Regina*
S. I. Salamensky, *University of California, Los Angeles*
Talia Schaffer, *Queen's College, City University of New York*
Carol A. Senf, *Georgia Institute of Technology*
Beth Tashery Shannon, *University of Kentucky*
Clifton Snider, *California State University, Long Beach*
Shelton Waldrep, *University of Southern Maine*
Chris Willis, *Birkbeck College, University of London*

WORKS CITED

Abrams, M. H., et al., eds. *The Norton Anthology of English Literature*. 7th ed. Vol. 2. New York: Norton, 2000.

Adams, James Eli. *Dandies and Desert Saints: Styles of Victorian Masculinity*. Ithaca: Cornell UP, 1995.

Albert, John. "The Christ of Oscar Wilde." *American Benedictine Review* 39 (1988): 372–403.

Alkalay-Gut, Karen. "The Thing He Loves: Murder as Aesthetic Experience in *The Ballad of Reading Gaol*." *Victorian Poetry* 35 (1997): 349–66.

Allen, Grant. "The Celt in English Art." *Fortnightly Review* 1 Feb. 1891: 267–77.

Andersen, Hans Christian. *The Complete Stories*. Trans. Jean Hersholt. 1949. London: British Lib., 2005.

"Apología." *Merriam-Webster's Encyclopedia of Literature*. Springfield: Merriam, 1995.

Aristotle. *Aristotle's* Poetics. Trans. James Hutton. New York: Norton, 1982.

Arnold, Matthew. "The Function of Criticism at the Present Time." *Matthew Arnold*. Ed. Miriam Allott and Robert H. Super. Oxford Authors. Oxford: Oxford UP, 1986. 317–38.

Austen, Jane. *Emma*. 1816. Ed. Stephen M. Parrish. Norton Critical Ed. 3rd ed. New York: Norton, 1999.

Banville, John. *The Untouchable*. London: Picador, 1997.

Barker, Harley Granville. *The Voysey Inheritance*. New York: Dramatists Play Service, 2007.

Barr, Roseanne. *Quotes by Roseanne Barr*. Zaadz. 5 Oct. 2007 <http://quotes.zaadz.com/Roseanne_Barr>.

Barthes, Roland. "The Death of the Author." *Image—Music—Text*. Trans. and ed. Stephen Heath. London: Fontana, 1977. 142–48.

Bartlett, Neil. *Who Was That Man? A Present for Mr. Oscar Wilde*. London: Serpent's Tail, 1988.

Baselga, Mariano. "Oscar Wilde and the Semantic Mechanism of Humour: The Satire of Social Habits." Sandulescu 13–20.

Bashford, Bruce. *Oscar Wilde: The Critic as Humanist*. Madison: Fairleigh Dickinson UP; Assoc. UPs, 1999.

Baudelaire, Charles. *Œuvres complètes*. Bibliothèque de la Pléiade. Paris: Gallimard, 1961.

Beckett, Samuel. *Not I. Collected Shorter Plays*. New York: Grove, 1984. 213–24.

Beckson, Karl. *London in the 1890s: A Cultural History*. New York: Norton, 1992.

———. *The Oscar Wilde Encyclopedia*. Fwd. Merlin Holland. New York: AMS, 1998.

———, ed. *Oscar Wilde: The Critical Heritage*. 1970. London: Routledge, 1997.

———. "Wilde's Autobiographical Signature in *The Picture of Dorian Gray*." *Victorian Newsletter* 69 (1986): 30–32.

Beerbohm, Max. *The Happy Hypocrite*. 1896. *The Bodley Head Beerbohm*. Ed. and introd. David Cecil. London: Bodley Head, 1970.

Behrendt, Patricia Flanagan. *Oscar Wilde: Eros and Aesthetics*. New York: St. Martin's, 1991.

Belford, Barbara. *Oscar Wilde: A Certain Genius*. New York: Random, 2000.

Bentley, Toni. *Sisters of Salome*. New Haven: Yale UP, 2002.

Bergson, Henri. "Laughter." *Comedy*. Ed. Wylie Sypher. Baltimore: Johns Hopkins UP, 1956. 61–192.

Bird, Alan. *The Plays of Oscar Wilde*. New York: Barnes, 1977.

Black, Joel. *The Aesthetics of Murder: A Study in Romantic Literature and Contemporary Culture*. Baltimore: Johns Hopkins UP, 1991.

Blanshard, Brand. *Reason and Belief*. London: Allen, 1976.

Bloxam, John Francis [pseud.]. "The Priest and the Acolyte." *The Chameleon: A Facsimile Edition*. London: Eighteen-Nineties Soc., 1978. 29–47.

Blunt, Wilfred Scawen. *In Vinculis*. London: Kegan, 1889.

Booth, Michael, ed. The Lights o' London *and Other Victorian Plays*. Oxford: Oxford UP, 1995.

———. *Theatre in the Victorian Age*. Cambridge: Cambridge UP, 1991.

Booth, Wayne. "Preface to the First Edition." *The Rhetoric of Fiction*. 2nd ed. Chicago: U of Chicago P, 1983. xiii–xv.

Borges, Jorge Luis. "About Oscar Wilde." *Other Inquisitions, 1937–1952*. Trans. Ruth L. C. Simms. 1946. New York: Simon, 1965. 79–81.

Braby, Dorothea, illus. *Lord Arthur Savile's Crime*. By Oscar Wilde. London: Rodale, 1954.

Bram Stoker's Dracula. Dir. Francis Ford Coppola. American Zoetrope, 1992.

Bredbeck, Gregory W. "Narcissus in the Wilde: Textual Cathexis and the Historical Origins of Queer Camp." *The Politics and Poetics of Camp*. Ed. Moe Meyer. New York: Routledge, 1994. 51–74.

Bristow, Joseph. "Dowdies and Dandies: Oscar Wilde's Refashioning of Society Comedy." Joel Kaplan, Spec. issue on Wilde 53–70.

———. *Effeminate England: Homoerotic Writing after 1885*. Between Men–between Women: Lesbian and Gay Studies. New York: Columbia UP, 1995.

———. "Wilde, *Dorian Gray*, and Gross Indecency." *Sexual Sameness: Textual Differences in Lesbian and Gay Writing*. London: Routledge, 1992. 44–63.

———, ed. *Wilde Writings: Contextual Conditions*. UCLA Clark Memorial Lib. Ser. Toronto: U of Toronto P, 2003.

Brontë, Charlotte. *Jane Eyre*. Ed. Beth Newman. New York: Bedford, 1996.

Brown, Julia Prewitt. *Cosmopolitan Criticism: Oscar Wilde's Philosophy of Art*. Charlottesville: UP of Virginia, 1997.

Buckler, William E., ed. *Walter Pater: Three Major Texts*. New York: New York UP, 1986.

Burns, Edward. "*Salomé*: Wilde's Radical Tragedy." Sandulescu 30–36.

Callow, Simon. *Oscar Wilde and His Circle*. Character Sketches. London: Natl. Portrait Gallery, 2000.

Cave, Richard Allen. "Wilde's Plays: Some Lines of Influence." Raby, *Cambridge Companion* 219–48.

Certeau, Michel de. *The Practice of Everyday Life*. Trans. Steven F. Rendall. Berkeley: U of California P, 1984.

Chamberlin, J. E. *Ripe Was the Drowsy Hour: The Age of Oscar Wilde*. New York: Seabury, 1977.

Coakley, Davis. *Oscar Wilde: The Importance of Being Irish*. Dublin: Town House, 1994.

Cohen, Ed. *Talk on the Wilde Side: Toward a Genealogy of a Discourse on Male Sexualities*. New York: Routledge, 1993.

Cohen, Philip K. *The Moral Vision of Oscar Wilde*. Cranbury: Assoc. UPs, 1978.

Cohen, William A. "Indeterminate Wilde." W. Cohen, *Sex Scandal* 191–236.

———. *Sex Scandal: The Private Parts of Victorian Fiction*. Durham: Duke UP, 1996.

Coleridge, Samuel Taylor. *Coleridge's Shakespearean Criticism*. 2 vols. Ed. Thomas Middleton Raysor. Cambridge: Harvard UP, 1930.

———. *Poetical Works (Reading Text), Part I*. 2 vols. Ed. J. C. C. Mays. Bollingen Ser. 75. Princeton: Princeton UP, 1969. Vol. 16 of *The Collected Works of Samuel Taylor Coleridge*.

Cookie's Fortune. Dir. Robert Altman. Perf. Glenn Close, Julianne Moore, Liv Tyler, Chris O'Donnell, Charles Dutton, and Patricia Neal. Sony Pictures Classics, 1999.

Craft, Christopher. *Another Kind of Love: Male Homosexual Desire in English Discourse, 1850–1920*. Berkeley: U of California P, 1994.

Danson, Lawrence. "Wilde as Critic and Theorist." Raby, *Cambridge Companion* 80–95.

———. *Wilde's* Intentions: *The Artist in His Criticism*. Oxford: Clarendon, 1997.

Davitt, Michael. "Criminal and Prison Reform." *Nineteenth Century* 36 (1894): 875–85.

Deane, Seamus, ed. *The Field Day Anthology of Irish Writing* 3 vols. Derry, Ire.: Field Day, 1991.

de la Croix, Horst, and Richard G. Tansey. *Gardner's Art through the Ages*. 8th ed. San Diego: Harcourt, 1986.

Dellamora, Richard. *Apocalyptic Overtures: Sexual Politics and the Sense of an Ending*. New Brunswick: Rutgers UP, 1994.

———. *Masculine Desire: The Sexual Politics of Victorian Aestheticism*. Chapel Hill: U of North Carolina P, 1990.

———. "Traversing the Feminine in Oscar Wilde's *Salomé*." *Victorian Sages and Cultural Discourse: Renegotiating Gender and Power*. Ed. Thäis Morgan. New Brunswick: Rutgers UP, 1990. 246–64.

De Quincey, Thomas. "On Murder Considered as One of the Fine Arts." *The Works of Thomas De Quincey*. Vol. 6. Ed. David Groves and Grevel Lindop. London: Pickering, 2000. 110–33.

Derrida, Jacques. *Acts of Literature*. Ed. Derek Attridge. New York: Routledge, 1992.

———. *Of Grammatology*. Trans. Gayatri Chakravorty Spivak. Baltimore: Johns Hopkins UP, 1976.

Dijkstra, Bram. *Idols of Perversity: Fantasies of Feminine Evil in Fin-de-Siècle Culture*. New York: Oxford UP, 1986.

Dolan, Jill. *Geographies of Learning: Theory and Practice, Activism and Performance*. Middletown: Wesleyan UP, 2001.

Dollimore, Jonathan. *Sexual Dissidence: Augustine to Wilde, Freud to Foucault*. Oxford: Oxford UP, 1991.

Douglas, Alfred. *Without Apology*. London: Secker, 1938.

Dowling, Linda. *Hellenism and Homosexuality in Victorian Oxford*. Ithaca: Cornell UP, 1994.

Drake, Alfred J., ed. *Victorian Text Archive*. 31 Aug. 2003 <http://www.victorianprose .org/>.

Eagleton, Terry. *Heathcliff and the Great Hunger: Studies in Irish Culture*. New York: Verso, 1995.

———. Introduction. *Saint Oscar*. Derry, Ire.: Field Day, 1989. i–xii.

———. Saint Oscar *and Other Plays*. Cambridge: Blackwell, 1997.

Edwards, Owen Dudley. "Oscar Wilde: The Soul of Man under Hibernicism." *Irish Studies Review* 11 (1995): 7–13.

Ellmann, Richard. "Introduction: The Critic as Artist as Wilde." Wilde, *Artist* ix–xxviii.

———. *Oscar Wilde*. London: Hamish Hamilton, 1987; New York: Knopf, 1988.

Eltis, Sos. *Revising Wilde: Society and Subversion in the Plays of Oscar Wilde*. Oxford English Monographs. Oxford: Clarendon, 1996.

Endres, Nikolai. "*Panta Rhei*: André Gide's *Les nourritures terrestres*, Oscar Wilde's *The Picture of Dorian Gray*, and Walter Pater's 'Conclusion.' " *Romance Notes* 41 (2001): 209–21.

Ericksen, Donald H. *Oscar Wilde*. Twayne's English Authors 211. Boston: Twayne, 1977.

Felski, Rita. "The Counterdiscourse of the Feminine in Three Texts by Wilde, Huysmans, and Sacher-Masoch." *PMLA* 106 (1991): 1094–105.

Feure, Georges de. *The Voice of Evil*. Gibson 107.

Foldy, Michael S. *The Trials of Oscar Wilde: Deviance, Morality, and Late-Victorian Society*. New Haven: Yale UP, 1997.

Fone, Byrne R. S. *A Road to Stonewall: Male Homosexuality and Homophobia in English and American Literature, 1750–1969*. New York: Twayne, 1995.

Fortunato, Paul. *Modernist Aesthetics and Consumer Culture in the Writings of Oscar Wilde*. New York: Routledge, 2007.

Foucault, Michel. *The History of Sexuality: An Introduction: Volume 1*. Trans. Robert Hurley. New York: Random, 1978.

Franci, Giovanna, and Giovanna Silvani, eds. *The Importance of Being Misunderstood: Homage to Oscar Wilde*. Bologna: Pàtron, 2003.

Freedman, Jonathan, ed. *Oscar Wilde: A Collection of Critical Essays*. Series ed. Richard Brodhead and Maynard Mack. New Century Views. Upper Saddle River: Prentice, 1996.

Frei, Hans. *The Eclipse of Biblical Narrative*. New Haven: Yale UP, 1974.

Frodl, Gerbert. *Klimt.* 1990. Trans. Alexandra Campbell. New York: Konecky, 1992.

Fryer, Jonathan. *André and Oscar: The Literary Friendship of André Gide and Oscar Wilde.* New York: St. Martin's, 1998.

Gaastra, John, illus. *The Young King.* By Oscar Wilde. London: Folio Soc., n.d.

Gadamer, Hans-Georg. *Hegel's Dialectic: Five Hermeneutical Studies.* Trans. P. Christopher Smith. New Haven: Yale UP, 1976.

Gagnier, Regenia, ed. *Critical Essays on Oscar Wilde.* Critical Essays on British Literature. New York: Hall, 1991.

———. *Idylls of the Marketplace: Oscar Wilde and the Victorian Public.* Stanford: Stanford UP, 1986.

Geary, Robert, illus. *"The Canterville Ghost" and Other Stories.* By Oscar Wilde. Retold by John Davage. Penguin Readers Level 4. Harlow: Pearson Educ., 2003.

The Genuine Account of the Life and Trial of Eugene Aram, for the Murder of Daniel Clarke, Late of Knaresborough. London: Bristow, 1759.

Gibson, Michael. *Symbolism.* Köln: Benedikt Taschen, 1995.

Gide, André. *Oscar Wilde.* Trans. Bernard Frechtman. New York: Philosophical Lib., 1949.

———. *Si le grain ne meurt.* Paris: Gallimard, 1954.

Gilbert, W. S. *Patience; or, Bunthorne's Bride.* 1881. New York: Doubleday, 1902.

Gillespie, Michael Patrick. "Ethics and Aesthetics in *The Picture of Dorian Gray.*" Sandulescu 137–55.

———. *Oscar Wilde and the Poetics of Ambiguity.* Gainesville: UP of Florida, 1996.

Goodman, Jonathan, comp. *The Oscar Wilde File.* London: Allen, 1989.

Green, Stephanie. "Grave Desires: Sexual Alterity and Gothic Romance in Oscar Wilde's 'The Canterville Ghost.'" *Australasian Victorian Studies Journal* 3 (1997): 71–79.

Greenblatt, Stephen. "Fiction and Friction." *Shakespearean Negotiations: The Circulation of Social Energy in Renaissance England.* Berkeley: U of California P, 1988. 66–93.

Guy, Josephine. "An Allusion in Oscar Wilde's 'The Canterville Ghost.'" *Notes and Queries* 243 (1998): 224–26.

Guy, Josephine, and Ian Small. *Oscar Wilde's Profession: Writing and the Culture Industry in the Late Nineteenth Century.* Oxford: Oxford UP, 2000.

———. *Studying Oscar Wilde: History, Criticism, and Myth.* 1880–1920 British Author Ser. 22. Greensboro: ELT, 2006.

Hadley, Elaine. *Melodramatic Tactics: Theatricalized Dissent in the English Marketplace, 1800–1885.* Stanford: Stanford UP, 1995.

Halberstam, Judith. *Skin Shows: Gothic Horror and the Technology of Monsters.* Durham: Duke UP, 1995.

Haldane, Richard Burdon. *An Autobiography.* London: Hodder, 1929.

Hallett, Martin, and Barbara Karasek, eds. *Folk and Fairy Tales.* 3rd ed. Peterborough: Broadview, 2002.

Hamilton, Lisa. "Oscar Wilde, New Women, and the Rhetoric of Effeminacy." Bristow, *Wilde Writings* 230–53.

Hanson, Ellis. *Decadence and Catholicism*. Cambridge: Harvard UP, 1997.

Hare, David. *The Judas Kiss*. New York: Grove, 1998.

Harris, Frank. *Oscar Wilde: His Life and Confessions*. 1930. London: Panther, 1965.

Harris, Wendell V. "Arnold, Pater, Wilde, and the Object As in Themselves They See It." *Studies in English Literature 1500–1900* 11 (1971): 733–47.

Havighurst, Alfred. *Radical Journalist: H. W. Massingham, 1860–1924*. Cambridge: Cambridge UP, 1974.

Heidegger, Martin. "The Theological Discussion of 'The Problem of a Non-objectifying Thinking and Speaking in Today's Theology'—Some Pointers to Its Major Aspects." *The Piety of Thinking*. Trans. James G. Hart and John C. Maroldo. Bloomington: Indiana UP, 1976. 22–31.

Henley, William Ernest. Editorial. *National Observer* 6 Apr. 1895: 547.

———. *Poems*. London: Macmillan, 1926.

Henry, Maurice, illus. *"Le fantôme de Canterville" et autres contes*. By Oscar Wilde. Ed. Jean-Luc Steinmetz. Paris: Livre de Poche, 1988.

Hichens, Robert. *The Green Carnation*. Ed. Stanley Weintraub. Lincoln: U of Nebraska P, 1970.

Hick, John. *Faith and Knowledge*. London: Macmillan, 1967.

Holland, Merlin. "Biography and the Art of Lying." Raby, *Cambridge Companion* 3–17.

———. *The Real Trial of Oscar Wilde: The First Uncensored Transcript of the Trial of Oscar Wilde vs. John Douglas (Marquess of Queensberry), 1895*. New York: Fourth Estate, 2003.

———. *The Wilde Album*. New York: Henry Holt, 1998.

———. "Wilde as Salomé?" *Times Literary Supplement* 22 July 1994: 14.

Holland, Vyvyan. *Son of Oscar Wilde*. London: Hart-Davis, 1954.

Hood, Thomas. *Selected Poems of Thomas Hood*. Ed. John Clubbe. Cambridge: Harvard UP, 1970.

Hopkins, Gerard Manley. *The Poetical Works of Gerard Manley Hopkins*. Ed. Norman H. MacKenzie. Oxford: Clarendon, 1990.

Horan, Patrick M. *The Importance of Being Paradoxical: Maternal Presence in the Works of Oscar Wilde*. Madison: Fairleigh Dickinson UP, 1997.

Hornung, E. W. *The Collected Raffles*. Introd. Jeremy Lewis. London: Everyman's Lib., 1992.

Housman, A. E. *The Poems of A. E. Housman*. Ed. Archie Burnett. Oxford: Clarendon, 1997.

Hubbard, Thomas K., ed. *Homosexuality in Greece and Rome: A Sourcebook of Basic Documents*. Berkeley: U of California P, 2003.

Huysmans, Joris-Karl. *Against Nature*. Trans. Robert Baldick. London: Penguin, 1959.

Hyde, H. Montgomery. *Famous Trials 7: Oscar Wilde*. Rev. ed. Harmondsworth: Penguin, 1962.

———. *Oscar Wilde: The Aftermath*. London: Methuen, 1963.

————. *The Trials of Oscar Wilde*. New York: Dover, 1962. 2nd ed. 1973.

Ibsen, Henrik. *Four Major Plays: A Doll's House, Ghosts, Hedda Gabler, The Master Builder*. Introd. James McFarlane. Trans. McFarlane and Jens Arup. Oxford World's Classics. Oxford: Oxford UP, 1998.

————. *Pillars of Society*. Whitefish: Kessinger, 2004.

An Ideal Husband. Dir. Alexander Korda. Perf. Paulette Godard, Michael Wilding, and Diana Wynard. MGM, 1948.

An Ideal Husband. Dir. Oliver Parker. Perf. Cate Blanchett, Julianne Moore, Rupert Everett, and Jeremy Northam. Pathe, 1999.

Ionesco, Eugene. The Bald Soprano *and Other Plays*. New York: Grove, 1982.

Jackson, Holbrook. *The Eighteen Nineties: A Review of Art and Ideas at the Close of the Nineteenth Century*. 1913. Introd. Karl Beckson. New York: Capricorn, 1966.

Jackson, Russell, ed. *Victorian Theatre*. London: Black, 1989.

Jakobsen, Janet R., and Ann Pellegrini. *Love the Sin: Sexual Regulation and the Limits of Religious Tolerance*. Boston: Beacon, 2004.

Jay, Mike, and Michael Neve, eds. *1900: A Fin-de-Siècle Reader*. Harmondsworth: Penguin, 1999.

Jefferson, Thomas. Letter from Paris to Mrs. John Bolling. 23 July 1787. *Correspondence, 1786–1787*. Vol. 5 of *The Works of Thomas Jefferson* [1905]. 21 Dec. 2007 <http://oll.libertyfund.org/title/802/86667>.

Jenkins, Henry. "Television Fans, Poachers, Nomads." *The Subcultures Reader*. Ed. Ken Gelder and Sarah Thornton. London: Routledge, 1997. 506–22.

————. *Textual Poachers: Television Fans and Participatory Culture*. New York: Routledge, 1992.

Jerome, Jerome K. *On the Stage—and Off*. Phoenix Mill, Eng.: Sutton, 1991.

Jones, Henry Arthur. *The Case of Rebellious Susan*. New York: French, 1909.

————. *Mrs. Dane's Defence*. New York: Macmillan, 1905.

————. *Saints and Sinners*. New York: Macmillan, 1891.

Kaplan, Joel, ed. Spec. issue on Oscar Wilde. *Modern Drama* 37.1 (1994): 1–241.

————. "Wilde on the Stage." Raby, *Cambridge Companion* 249–75.

Kaplan, Joel, and Sheila Stowell. *Theatre and Fashion: Oscar Wilde to the Suffragettes*. Cambridge: Cambridge UP, 1994.

Kaplan, Morris B. *Sodom on the Thames: Sex, Love, and Scandal in Wilde Times*. Ithaca: Cornell UP, 2005.

Kaufman, Moisés. *Gross Indecency: The Three Trials of Oscar Wilde*. New York: Vintage, 1998.

Kaufman, Moisés, et al. *The Laramie Project*. New York: Vintage, 2001.

Kaye, Richard A. " 'Determined Raptures': St. Sebastian and the Victorian Discourse of Decadence." *Victorian Literature and Culture* 27 (1999): 269–303.

Keane, Robert, ed. *Oscar Wilde: The Man, His Writings, and His World*. New York: AMS, 2003.

Kerleroux, Jean, illus. *"Le crime de Lord Arthur Savile" et autres contes*. By Oscar Wilde. Trans. Claude Martineau. 1969. Paris: Érable, 1974.

Killeen, Jarlath. *The Fairy Tales of Oscar Wilde*. Aldershot, Eng.: Ashgate, 2007.

———. *The Faiths of Oscar Wilde: Catholicism, Folklore, and Ireland*. Houndsmill, Eng.: Palgrave-Macmillan, 2005.

Kipling, Rudyard. *Rudyard Kipling: A Critical Edition of the Major Works*. Ed. Daniel Karlin. Oxford: Oxford UP, 1999.

Kittler, Friedrich. "Dracula's Legacy." Trans. William Stephen Davis. *Stanford Humanities Review* 1.1 (1989): 143–73.

Klein, Alfons. "Motive und Themen in Oscar Wildes 'Lord Arthur Savile's Crime.' " *Motive und Themen in Erzählungen des späten 19 Jahrhunderts*. Ed. Theodor Wolpers. Göttingen: Vandenhoeck, 1982. 66–87.

Klimt, Gustav. *Judith and Holofernes I*. Frodl 76.

———. *Judith and Holofernes II*. Frodl 77.

Klinger, Julius. *Salomé*. Gibson 129.

Knapp, Andrew, and William Baldwin. *The Newgate Calendar; Comprising Interesting Memoirs of the Most Interesting Characters Who Have Been Convicted of Outrages on the Laws of England since the Commencement of the Eighteenth Century; with Occasional Anecdotes and Observations, Speeches, and Last Exclamations of Sufferers*. 2 vols. London: Robins, 1825.

Knox, Melissa. *Oscar Wilde: A Long and Lovely Suicide*. New Haven: Yale UP, 1994.

———. *Oscar Wilde in the 1990s: The Critic as Creator*. Rochester: Camden, 2001.

Koestenbaum, Wayne. "Wilde's Hard Labor and the Birth of Gay Reading." *Engendering Men: The Question of Male Feminist Criticism*. Ed. Joseph A. Boone and Michael Cadden. New York: Routledge, 1990. 161–75.

Kohl, Norbert. *Oscar Wilde: The Works of a Conformist Rebel*. Trans. David Henry Wilson. European Studies in English Literature. Cambridge: Cambridge UP, 1989.

Kohl, Stephan. "The Aesthetics of the Expressionless Face: Representation of Authority in Oscar Wilde's *An Ideal Husband*." *Word and Action in Drama*. Ed. Gunter Ahrends et al. Trier, Ger.: WVT Wissenschaftlicher, 1994. 107–17.

Kopelson, Kevin. *Love's Litany: The Writing of Modern Homoerotics*. Stanford: Stanford UP, 1994.

———. "Wilde, Barthes, and the Orgasmics of Truth." *Genders* 7 (1990): 22–31.

Kucich, John. *Repression in Victorian Fiction: Charlotte Brontë, George Eliot, and Charles Dickens*. Berkeley: U of California P, 1987.

Kucich, John, and Dianne F. Sadoff, eds. *Victorian Afterlife: Postmodern Culture Rewrites the Nineteenth Century*. Minneapolis: U of Minnesota P, 2000.

Lacambre, Geneviève. *Gustave Moreau: Between Epic and Dream*. Princeton: Princeton UP, 1999.

Ledger, Sally. "Oscar Wilde and the 'Daughters of Decadence.' " *Decadence and Danger: Writing, History and the Fin de Siècle*. Ed. Tracey Hill. Bath, Eng.: Sulis, 1997. 109–18.

Lewis, Jane, ed. *Before the Vote Was Won: Arguments for and against Women's Suffrage*. London: Routledge, 1987.

Longxi, Zhang. "The Critical Legacy of Oscar Wilde." *Texas Studies in Literature and Language* 30 (1988): 87–103.

Losey, Jay. "Disguising the Self in Pater and Wilde." *Mapping Male Sexuality: Nineteenth-Century England.* Ed. Losey and William D. Brewer. Madison: Fairleigh Dickinson UP, 2000. 250–73.

Maeterlinck, Maurice. *The Plays of Maurice Maeterlinck.* Trans. Richard Hovey. Chicago: Stone, 1894.

Mahaffey, Vicki. *States of Desire: Wilde, Yeats, Joyce, and the Irish Experiment.* New York: Oxford UP, 1998.

Malcolm, Ian. "Gilded Youth." *Fifty Years, Memories and Contrasts: A Composite Picture of the Period 1882–1932, by Twenty-Seven Contributors to* The Times. 1932. London: Keystone Lib., 1936.

Mallarmé, Stéphane. *Collected Poems.* Trans. Henry Weinfield. Berkeley: U of California P, 1994.

A Man of No Importance. Dir. Suri Krishnamma. Perf. Albert Finney, Brenda Fricker, and Tara Fitzgerald. Videocassette. Little Bird, 1994. Columbia Tristar, 1995.

Marez, Curtis. "The Other Addict: Reflections on Colonialism and Oscar Wilde's Opium Smoke Screen." *ELH* 64 (1997): 257–87.

Marsh, Joss Lutz. " 'Bibliolatry' and 'Bible-Smashing': G. W. Foote, George Meredith, and the Heretic Trope of the Book." *Victorian Studies* 34 (1991): 315–36.

Martin, Robert K. "Oscar Wilde and the Fairy Tale: 'The Happy Prince' as Self-Dramatization." *Studies in Short Fiction* 16 (1979): 74–77.

———. "Parody and Homage: The Presence of Pater in *Dorian Gray*." *Victorian Newsletter* 63 (1983): 15–18.

Marx, Karl. "Economic and Philosophical Manuscripts of 1844." *The Marx-Engels Reader.* 2nd ed. Ed. Robert C. Tucker. New York: Norton, 1978. 66–125.

Massenet, Jules. *Hérodiade.* 1881. Cond. Valery Gergiev. Perf. Renée Fleming and Placido Domingo. Sony Classical, 1995.

Massingham, H. W. Editorial. *Daily Chronicle* 24 Mar. 1898: 6.

Mathieu, Pierre-Louis. *Gustave Moreau: The Watercolors.* New York: Hudson Hills, 1984.

McConville, Séan. *English Local Prisons, 1860–1900: Next Only to Death.* London: Routledge, 1995.

McCormack, Jerusha, ed. *Wilde the Irishman.* New Haven: Yale UP, 1998.

McKenna, Neil. *The Secret Life of Oscar Wilde: An Intimate Biography.* New York: Basic, 2005.

Meyer, Susan. *Imperialism at Home: Race and Victorian Women's Fiction.* Ithaca: Cornell UP, 1996.

Michie, Elsie. "White Chimpanzees and Oriental Despots: Racial Stereotyping and Edward Rochester." *Jane Eyre.* By Charlotte Brontë. Ed. Beth Newman. Boston: Bedford, 1996. 584–98.

Mikhail, E. H. *Oscar Wilde: An Annotated Bibliography of Criticism.* London: Macmillan, 1978.

————, ed. *Oscar Wilde: Interviews and Recollections*. 2 vols. New York: Barnes, 1979.

————. "Self-Revelation in *An Ideal Husband*." *Modern Drama* 11.2 (1968): 180–86.

Mikolyzk, Thomas A., comp. *Oscar Wilde: An Annotated Bibliography*. Bibliographies and Indexes in World Literature. Westport: Greenwood, 1993.

Miller, Neil. *Out of the Past: Gay and Lesbian History from 1869 to the Present*. New York: Vintage, 1995.

Moers, Ellen. *The Dandy: Brummell to Beerbohm*. New York: Viking, 1960.

Moreau, Gustave. *Salomé Dancing before Herod*. 1876. *Gustave Moreau*. By Julius Kaplan. Greenwich: New York Graphic Soc., 1974. 34.

Morris, Michael. *Madam Valentino: The Many Lives of Natacha Rambova*. New York: Abbeville, 1991.

Morrison, W. D. "Prisons and Prisoners." *Fortnightly Review* 69 (1898): 781–89.

Mulvey, Laura. "Visual Pleasure and Narrative Cinema." *Screen* 16 (1975): 6–18.

Murray, Douglas. *Bosie: A Biography of Lord Alfred Douglas*. New York: Hyperion, 2000.

Murray, Isobel. Introduction. Wilde, *Complete Shorter Fiction* 1–17.

Murray, Raymond, ed. *Images in the Dark: An Encyclopedia of Gay and Lesbian Film and Video*. Philadelphia: TLA, 1994.

Nassaar, Christopher S. *Into the Demon Universe: A Literary Exploration of Oscar Wilde*. New Haven: Yale UP, 1974.

Nathan, Leonard. "The Ballads of Reading Gaol: At the Limits of the Lyric." Gagnier, *Critical Essays* 213–22.

Nelson, Claudia. "Sex and the Single Boy: Ideals of Manliness and Sexuality in Victorian Literature for Boys." *Victorian Studies* 32 (1989): 525–50.

Nelson, James G. *Publisher to the Decadents: Leonard Smithers in the Careers of Beardsley, Wilde, Dowson*. University Park: Pennsylvania State UP, 2000.

Ní Chuilleanáin, Eiléan, ed. *The Wilde Legacy*. Dublin: Four Courts, 2003.

Nietzsche, Friedrich. *On the Genealogy of Morals [and] Ecce Homo*. Ed. and trans. Walter J. Kaufman. Trans. R. J. Hollingdale. New York: Vintage, 1989.

Nordau, Max. *Degeneration*. Introd. George L. Mosse. 1895. Lincoln: U of Nebraska P, 1993.

Norton, David. *From 1700 to the Present Day*. Cambridge: Cambridge UP, 1993. Vol. 2 of *A History of the Bible as Literature*.

Nunokawa, Jeff. "Homosexual Desire and the Effacement of the Self in *The Picture of Dorian Gray*." *American Imago* 49 (1992): 311–22.

————. "The Importance of Being Bored: The Dividends of Ennui in *The Picture of Dorian Gray*." *Studies in the Novel* 28 (1996): 357–71.

————. *Oscar Wilde*. Gen. ed. Martin Duberman. Lives of Notable Gay Men and Lesbians. New York: Chelsea, 1995.

————. *Tame Passions of Oscar Wilde: The Styles of Manageable Desire*. Princeton: Princeton UP, 2003.

O'Malley, Patrick. "Wilde's Religion." Roden, *Palgrave Advances* 167–88.

Orton, Joe. *The Complete Plays*. New York: Grove, 1990.

Orwell, George. "Rudyard Kipling." *My Country Right or Left, 1940–1943*. Ed. Sonia Orwell and Ian Angus. New York: Harcourt, 1968. 184–97. Vol. 2 of *The Collected Essays, Journalism, and Letters of George Orwell.*

Oscar Wilde: Spendthrift of Genius. By Richard Ellmann. Prod. Radio Telefís Éireann. Videocassette. Films for the Humanities and Sciences, 1994.

The Oscar Wilde Collection. 40 microfilm reels and guide. Woodbridge: Primary Source Microfilm, 1999.

"The Oscar Wilde Sketch." *Monty Python's Flying Circus*. Episode 39. 18 Jan. 1973. 20 Oct. 2007 <http://orangecow.org/pythonet/sketches/oscarwil.htm>.

O'Sullivan, Vincent. *Aspects of Wilde*. New York: Henry Holt, 1936.

Paglia, Camille A. "Oscar Wilde and the English Epicene." *Raritan* 4 (1985): 85–109.

Pater, Walter. Conclusion to *The Renaissance*. Buckler 217–20

———. Preface to *The Renaissance*. Buckler 71–75.

———. *The Renaissance: Studies in Art and Poetry*. Ed. Donald L. Hill. Berkeley: U of California P, 1980.

Pearson, Hesketh. *The Life of Oscar Wilde*. 1946. Harmondsworth: Penguin, 1988.

———, ed. *Oscar Wilde's Plays, Prose Writings and Poems*. London: Dent; Everyman's Lib., 1930.

The Picture of Dorian Gray. Dir. Albert Lewin. Perf. George Sanders, Hurd Hatfield, Donna Reed, and Angela Lansbury. MGM, 1945.

Pine, Richard. *The Thief of Reason: Oscar Wilde and Modern Ireland*. New York: St. Martin's, 1995.

Pinero, Arthur Wing. *The Cabinet Minister: A Farce in Four Acts*. London: Heinemann, 1892.

———. *Dandy Dick: A Farce in Three Acts*. London: Heinemann, 1893.

———. *The Magistrate*. Pinero, Trelawny 1–70.

———. *The Notorious Mrs. Ebbsmith*. Project Gutenberg. 14 Mar. 2005. 14 Feb. 2008 <http://www.gutenberg.org/etext/15357>.

———. *The Profligate*. Boston: Baker, 1892.

———. *The Second Mrs. Tanqueray*. Pinero, Trelawny 141–212.

———. *The Times: A Comedy in Four Acts*. London: Heinemann, 1891.

———. Trelawny of the "Wells" *and Other Plays*. Ed. J. S. Bratton. Oxford: Oxford UP, 1995.

———. *The Weaker Sex: A Comedy in Three Acts*. Boston: Baker, 1894.

Plato. *Republic*. Trans. Paul Shorey. *The Collected Dialogues*. Ed. Edith Hamilton and Huntington Cairns. Princeton: Princeton UP, 1961. 575–844.

Powell, Kerry. *Oscar Wilde and the Theatre of the 1890s*. Cambridge: Cambridge UP, 1990.

———. "Salomé, the Censor, and the Divine Sarah." Powell, *Oscar Wilde* 33–54.

Price, Jody. "*A Map with Utopia*": *Oscar Wilde's Theory for Social Transformation*. Amer. University Studies, ser. 4: English Language and Literature, vol. 162. New York: Lang, 1996.

"Prisons Bill." *Parliamentary Debates*. 4th ser., vol. 55. London: HMSO, 1898.

Proust, Marcel. *Sodom and Gomorrah*. Trans. John Sturrock. New York: Viking, 2004.

Raby, Peter, ed. *The Cambridge Companion to Oscar Wilde*. Cambridge Companions to Literature. Cambridge: Cambridge UP, 1997.

———. Introduction. Wilde, Importance [ed. Raby] vii–xxv.

———. *Oscar Wilde*. British and Irish Authors: Introductory Critical Studies. Cambridge: Cambridge UP, 1988.

———. "Wilde's Comedies of Society." Raby, *Cambridge Companion* 143–60.

Reade, Brian, ed. *Sexual Heretics: Male Homosexuality in English Literature from 1850 to 1900*. New York: Coward, 1971.

Redmond, James. *Melodrama*. Cambridge: Cambridge UP, 1992.

Renan, Ernest. *The Life of Jesus*. Trans. of *La vie de Jésus*. Project Gutenberg. 22 Aug. 2005. 30 July 2007 <http://www.gutenberg.org/etext/16581>.

Renier, G. J. *Oscar Wilde*. London: Nelson, 1933.

Rev. of *The Ballad of Reading Gaol*, by C.3.3. *Daily Chronicle* 15 Feb. 1898: 6.

Rev. of *The Ballad of Reading Gaol*, by C.3.3. *Outlook* 5 Mar. 1898: 146.

Rev. of *An Ideal Husband*, by Oscar Wilde. *Pick-Me-Up* 13 (1895): 246–47.

Robb, Graham. *Strangers: Homosexual Love in the Nineteenth Century*. New York: Norton, 2004.

Roberts, David, illus. *"Lord Arthur Savile's Crime" and Other Stories*. By Oscar Wilde. Adapt. Bill Bowler. Oxford: Oxford UP, 2003.

Roden, Frederick S. Introduction. *Catholic Figures, Queer Narratives*. Ed. Lowell Gallagher, Roden, and Patricia Juliana Smith. Basingstoke: Palgrave-Macmillan, 2007. 1–18.

———, ed. *Palgrave Advances in Oscar Wilde Studies*. Houndmills, Eng.: Palgrave-Macmillan, 2004.

———. *Same-Sex Desire in Victorian Religious Culture*. New York: Palgrave-Macmillan, 2002.

Rowell, George, ed. *Nineteenth-Century Plays*. Oxford: Oxford UP, 1972.

Ruskin, John. *Modern Painters*. Ed. E. T. Cook and Alexander Wedderburn. 5 vols. New York: Longmans, 1904.

———. "Of Queens' Gardens." *Sesame and Lilies*. London: Allen, 1892. *Bartleby.com*. 16 June 2008 <http://www.bartleby.com/28/7.html>.

———. "Of the Real Nature of Greatness of Style." Ruskin, *Modern Painters* 3: 44–69.

Russo, Vito. *The Celluloid Closet: Homosexuality in the Movies*. New York: Harper, 1987.

Saki [H. H. Munro]. *The Complete Short Stories of "Saki."* London: Bodley Head, 1930.

Salamensky, S. I. "Re-presenting Oscar Wilde: Wilde's Trials, *Gross Indecency*, and Documentary Spectacle." *Theatre Journal* 54 (2002): 575–88.

Salomé. Dir. Charles Bryant. Perf. Alla Nazimova, Rose Dione, and Mitchell Lewis. Videocassette. Nazimova Productions, 1923.

Salomé's Last Dance. Dir. Ken Russell. Perf. Glenda Jackson, Stratford Jones, Nicholas Grace, Douglas Hodge, and Imogen Millais-Scott. Videocassette. Jolly Russell Company, 1988.

Sammells, Neil. *Wilde Style: The Plays and Prose of Oscar Wilde*. Studies in Eighteenth- and Nineteenth-Century Literature. Harlow, Eng.: Pearson Educ., 2000.

Sandulescu, C. George, ed. *Rediscovering Oscar Wilde*. Princess Grace Irish Lib. 8. Gerrards Cross, Eng.: Smythe, 1994.

Sato, Tomoko, and Lionel Lambourne, eds. *The Wilde Years: Oscar Wilde and the Art of His Time*. London: Barbican Centre, 2000.

Schenkar, Joan. *Truly Wilde: The Unsettling Story of Dolly Wilde, Oscar's Unusual Niece*. New York: Basic, 2000.

Schmidgall, Gary. *The Stranger Wilde: Interpeting Oscar*. New York: Dutton, 1994.

Schöllkopf, Günter, illus. *Zwei Novellen: Das Gespenst von Canterville und Lord Arthur Saviles Verbrechen*. By Oscar Wilde. Fwd. Annemarie Hofmann. Stuttgart: Riederer, 1967[?].

Schroeder, Horst. *Additions and Corrections to Richard Ellmann's* Oscar Wilde. Rev. 2nd ed. Braunschweig, Ger.: Schmidt, 2002.

———. "Oscar Wilde, 'The Canterville Ghost.'" *Literatur in Wissenschaft und Unterricht* 10 (1977): 289–92.

Scream. Dir. Wes Craven. Dimension Films, 1996.

Scribe, Eugène. *A Glass of Water*. Trans. Robert Cornthwaite. Lyme: Smith, 1995.

The Secret of Dorian Gray. Dir. Massimo Dallamano. 1970. Videotape. Allied Artists Entertainment, 2000.

Sedgwick, Eve Kosofsky. *Between Men: English Literature and Male Homosocial Desire*. Gender and Culture. New York: Columbia UP, 1985.

———. *Epistemology of the Closet*. Berkeley: U of California P, 1990.

———. "Epistemology of the Closet." *The Lesbian and Gay Studies Reader*. Ed. Henry Abelove et. al. New York: Routledge, 1993. 45–61.

Seuss, Dr. [Theodor Seuss Geisel]. *Green Eggs and Ham*. New York: Random, 1960.

Shakespeare, William. *As You Like It*. New Variorum Ed. of Shakespeare. Ed. Richard Knowles. New York: MLA, 1977.

———. *The Merchant of Venice*. Ed. John Russell Brown. London: Methuen, 1964.

Shaw, George Bernard. *Major Barbara*. Harmondsworth: Penguin, 1945.

———. *Mrs. Warren's Profession*. Project Gutenberg. 11 Feb. 2002. 14 Feb. 2008 <http://www.gutenberg.org/etext/1097>.

———. "My Memories of Oscar Wilde." *Oscar Wilde: His Life and Confessions, Including the Hitherto Unpublished Full and Final Confession of Lord Alfred Douglas and My Memories of Oscar Wilde by Bernard Shaw*. By Frank Harris. New York: Covici, 1930. 387–406.

———. "An Old Play and a New One." *Our Theatres in the Nineties*. Vol. 1. London: Constable, 1932. 41–48.

———. "Two New Plays." Rev. of *An Ideal Husband*, by Oscar Wilde. *Saturday Review* 12 Jan. 1895: 44–45.

———. *Widowers' Houses. Plays Unpleasant*. New York: Penguin, 2001. 29–96.

Shenton, David, illus. *Salomé*. By Oscar Wilde. London: Quartet, 1986.

Shepherd-Barr, Kirsten. *Ibsen and Early Modernist Theatre, 1890–1900*. Westport: Greenwood, 1997.

Sherard, Robert Harborough. *The Life of Oscar Wilde*. London: T. Werner Laurie, 1906.

———. *The Real Oscar Wilde: To Be Used as a Supplement to, and an Illustration of* The Life of Oscar Wilde. London: Laurie, 1916; Philadelphia: McKay, n.d. [c. 1916].

Shewan, Rodney. *Oscar Wilde: Art and Egotism*. New York: Barnes, 1977.

Showalter, Elaine, ed. *Daughters of Decadence: Women Writers of the Fin-de-Siècle*. New Brunswick: Rutgers UP, 1993.

———. *Sexual Anarchy: Gender and Culture at the Fin de Siècle*. New York: Viking, 1990.

Sidney, Philip. "A Defence of Poetry." *Miscellaneous Prose*. Ed. Katherine Duncan-Jones and Jan Van Dorsten. Oxford: Clarendon, 1973. 71–121.

Sinfield, Alan. " 'Effeminacy' and 'Femininity': Sexual Politics in Wilde's Comedies." Joel Kaplan, Spec. issue on Wilde 34–52.

———. *The Wilde Century: Effeminacy, Oscar Wilde, and the Queer Moment*. Between Men—between Women: Lesbian and Gay Studies. New York: Columbia UP, 1994.

The Sins of Dorian Gray. Dir. Tony Maylam. Perf. Anthony Perkins, Belinda Bauer, Joseph Bottoms, and Olga Karlatos. Rankin-Bass Productions, 1983.

Sloan, John. *Oscar Wilde*. Oxford World's Classics: Authors in Context. New York: Oxford UP, 2003.

Small, Ian. *Conditions for Criticism: Authority, Knowledge and Literature in the Late Nineteenth Century*. Oxford: Clarendon, 1991.

———. *Oscar Wilde: Recent Research, a Supplement to* Oscar Wilde Revalued. 1880–1920 British Authors. Greensboro: ELT, 2000.

———. *Oscar Wilde Revalued: An Essay on New Materials and Methods of Research*. 1880–1920 British Authors. Greensboro: ELT, 1993.

Smith, James L. *Melodrama*. London: Methuen, 1973.

Smithers, Jack. *The Early Life and Vicissitudes of Jack Smithers*. London: Secker, 1939.

Snider, Clifton. "Eros and Logos in Some Fairy Tales by Oscar Wilde: A Jungian Interpretation." *Victorian Newsletter* 84 (1993): 1–8.

Søderman, Sven. " 'The Canterville Ghost' and 'The Portrait of Mr. W. H.' " *Stockholm Dagbladet* 23 Mar. 1906: n. pag.

Stephens, John Russell. *The Censorship of English Drama, 1824–1901*. Cambridge: Cambridge UP, 1980.

Stetz, Margaret. "Oscar Wilde at the Movies: British Sexual Politics and *The Green Carnation* (1960)." *Biography* 23 (2000): 90–107.

Stewart, Garrett. "Film's Victorian Retrofit." *Victorian Studies* 38.2 (1995): 153–98.

Stoker, Bram. *Dracula*. Ed. Nina Auerbach and David J. Skal. New York: Norton, 1997.

Stokes, John. *Oscar Wilde*. Writers and Their Work 264. Harlow, Eng.: Longman for the British Council, 1978.

———. *Oscar Wilde: Myths, Miracles, and Imitations*. Cambridge: Cambridge UP, 1996.

Stoppard, Tom. *The Invention of Love*. New York: Grove, 1997.

Strauss, Richard. *Salomé*. 1907. Cond. Kurt Böhm. Perf. Leonie Rysanke and Eberhard Wächter. Allegro, 1999.

Stuck, Franz von. *Sin*. 1893. Gibson 25.

Symons, Arthur. Rev. of *The Ballad of Reading Gaol*, by C.3.3. *Saturday Review* 85 (1898): 365–66.

———. *The Symbolist Movement in Literature*. 2nd ed. London: Constable, 1908.

Tanitch, Robert. *Oscar Wilde on Stage and Screen*. London: Methuen, 1999.

Tatar, Maria, ed. *The Classic Fairy Tales*. New York: Norton, 1999.

Taylor, George, ed. Trilby *and Other Plays: Four Plays for Victorian Star Actors*. Oxford: Oxford UP, 1996.

Thomas, Ronald R. "Specters of the Novel: *Dracula* and the Cinematic Afterlife of the Victorian Novel." Kucich and Sadoff 288–310.

Tydeman, William, and Steven Price. *Wilde:* Salomé. Cambridge: Cambridge UP, 1996.

Tyson, Nancy-Jane. *Eugene Aram: Literary History and Typology of the Scholar-Criminal*. Hamden: Archon, 1983.

Ulrichs, Karl Heinrich. *The Riddle of "Man-Manly Love": The Pioneering Work on Male Homosexuality*. 2 vols. Trans. Michael A. Lombardi-Nash. Buffalo: Prometheus, 1994.

Urinal. Dir. John Greyson. Walter Bearer Films, 1988.

Varty, Anne. *A Preface to Oscar Wilde*. Preface Books. New York: Longman, 1998.

Velvet Goldmine. Dir. Todd Haynes. Perf. Ewan McGregor, Jonathan Rhys Meyers, Christian Bale, and Toni Colette. Videocassette. Miramax, 1998.

Verlaine, Paul. *Selected Poems*. Bilingual ed. Trans. and introd. Joanna Richardson. Harmondsworth: Penguin, 1974.

Vicinus, Martha. "The Adolescent Boy: Fin de Siècle Femme Fatale?" *Journal of the History of Sexuality* 5 (1994): 90–114.

Von Eckardt, Wolf, Sander L. Gilman, and J. Edward Chamberlin. *Oscar Wilde's London: A Scrapbook of Vices and Virtues, 1880–1900*. Garden City: Anchor-Doubleday, 1987.

Waldrep, Shelton. *The Aesthetics of Self-Invention: Oscar Wilde to David Bowie*. Minneapolis: U of Minnesota P, 2004.

———. "The Uses and Misuses of Oscar Wilde." Kucich and Sadoff 49–63.

Walkley, A. B. Rev. of *An Ideal Husband*, by Oscar Wilde. *Speaker* 11 (1895): 44.

Warner, Alan. *A Guide to Anglo-Irish Literature*. Dublin: Gill, 1981.

West, T. G., ed. *Symbolism: An Anthology*. London: Methuen, 1980.

White, Chris, ed. *Nineteenth-Century Writings on Homosexuality: A Sourcebook*. London: Routledge, 1999.

White, Patricia. "Nazimova's Veils: Salomé at the Intersection of Film Histories." *A Feminist Reader in Early Cinema*. Ed. Jennifer M. Bean and Diane Negra. Durham: Duke UP, 2002. 60–87.

Whitman, Walt. Leaves of Grass *and Other Writings: Authoritative Texts, Other Poetry and Prose, Criticism*. Ed. Michael Moon. New York: Norton, 2002.

Wikoff, Karin. "The Many Pictures of Dorian Gray." *Horror-Wood*. Aug. 1998. 16 Jan. 2003 <http://www.horror-wood.com/doriangray.htm>.

Wilburn, Lydia Reineck. "Oscar Wilde's 'The Canterville Ghost': The Power of an Audience." *Papers on Language and Literature* 23 (1987): 41–55.

Wilde. Dir. Brian Gilbert. Perf. Stephen Fry, Jude Law, Vanessa Redgrave, and Jennifer Ehle. DVD. Sony Pictures Classics, 1998.

Wilde, Oscar. *The Artist as Critic: Critical Writings of Oscar Wilde*. Ed. and introd. Richard Ellmann. New York: Vintage, 1970.

———. *The Canterville Ghost*. Illus. Lisbeth Zwerger. Natick: Picture Book Studio, 1986.

———. "The Censure and 'Salomé:' An Interview with Mr. Oscar Wilde." *Pall Mall Gazette* 29 June 1892: 1–2.

———. *Collins Complete Works of Oscar Wilde: Centenary Edition*. Ed. Merlin Holland. Glasgow: Harper, 1999.

———. *The Complete Letters of Oscar Wilde*. Ed. Merlin Holland and Rupert Hart-Davis. New York: Henry Holt, 2000.

———. *Complete Shorter Fiction*. Ed. Isobel Murray. Oxford World's Classics. New York: Oxford UP, 1998.

———. *Criticism:* Historical Criticism, Intentions, The Soul of Man. Ed. Josephine M. Guy. Oxford: Oxford UP, 2007. Vol. 4 of *The Complete Works of Oscar Wilde*.

———. *De Profundis: A Facsimile*. Introd. Merlin Holland. London: British Lib., 2000.

———. *De Profundis [and] Epistola: In Carcere et Vinculis*. Ed. Ian Small. Oxford: Oxford UP, 2004. Vol. 2 of *The Complete Works of Oscar Wilde*.

———. *The Fairy Stories of Oscar Wilde*. London: Gollancz, 1976.

———. *Fairy Tales*. London: Bodley Head, 1960.

———. *Fairy Tales of Oscar Wilde*. Illus. P. Craig Russell. 4 vols. New York: NBM, 1994–2004.

———. *The Happy Prince*. Long Crendon, Eng.: Sator, 1983.

———. *"The Happy Prince" and Other Tales*. London: Nutt, 1888.

———. *The House of Pomegranates*. London: Osgood, 1891.

———. *The Importance of Being Earnest*. 3rd ed. Ed. Russell Jackson. New Mermaids. London: Black; New York: Norton, 1990.

———. The Importance of Being Earnest *and Other Plays*. Ed. Richard Allen Cave. Penguin Classics. New York: Penguin, 2001.

———. The Importance of Being Earnest *and Other Plays*. Ed. Peter Raby. Oxford Drama Lib. New York: Oxford UP, 1995.

———. The Importance of Being Earnest *and Related Writings*. Ed. Joseph Bristow. Routledge English Texts. London: Routledge, 1992.

———. *Lady Windermere's Fan*. Ed. Ian Small. 2nd ed. New Mermaids. London: Black; New York: Norton, 1999.

———. *The Letters of Oscar Wilde*. Ed. Rupert Hart-Davis. London: Hart-Davis, 1962.

————. *The Literary Criticism of Oscar Wilde*. Ed. Stanley Weintraub. Regents Critics. Lincoln: U of Nebraska P, 1968.

————. *More Letters of Oscar Wilde*. Ed. Rupert Hart-Davis. New York: Vanguard, 1985.

————. "A Note on Some Modern Poets." *Woman's World* 2 (1889): 108–12. Rpt. in *The Collected Works of Oscar Wilde*. Ed. Robert Ross. Vol. 13. London: Methuen, 1908. 347–65.

————. *Oscar Wilde: Complete Short Fiction*. Ed. Ian Small. Harmondsworth: Penguin, 1994.

————. *Oscar Wilde's Oxford Notebooks: A Portrait of Mind in the Making*. Ed. Philip E. Smith and Michael S. Helfand. New York: Oxford UP, 1989.

————. *Oscar Wilde's* The Importance of Being Earnest: *A Reconstructive Critical Edition of the Text of the First Production*. Ed. Joseph Donohue and Ruth Berggren. Princess Grace Irish Lib. 10. Gerrards Cross, Eng.: Smythe, 1995.

————. *Oscar Wilde: The Major Works*. Ed. Isobel Murray. Oxford World's Classics. Oxford: Oxford UP, 1989.

————. *The Picture of Dorian Gray*. Ed. Donald Lawler. Norton Critical Ed. New York: Norton, 1987.

————. The Picture of Dorian Gray: *The 1890 and 1891 Texts*. Ed. Joseph Bristow. Oxford: Oxford UP, 2005. Vol. 3 of *The Complete Works of Oscar Wilde*.

————. *Plays, Prose Writings, and Poems*. Introd. Terry Eagleton. New York: Everyman's Lib.; Knopf, 1991.

————. *Poems and Poems in Prose*. Ed. Bobby Fong and Karl Beckson. Oxford: Oxford UP, 2000. Vol. 1 of *The Complete Works of Oscar Wilde*.

————. "Poetry and Prison." *Pall Mall Gazette* 3 Jan. 1889: 393–96. Rpt. in *The Collected Works of Oscar Wilde*. Ed. Robert Ross. Vol. 13. London: Methuen, 1908. 393–96.

————. *Salomé*. Adaptations of Pelleas and Melisande, Salomé, Ein Heldentraum, Cavalleria Rusticana. By P. Craig Russell. New York: NBM, 2004. 107–56. Vol. 3 of the P. Craig Russell Lib. of Opera Adaptations.

————. *Salomé*. Illus. Aubrey Beardsley. Trans. Alfred Douglas. 1894. New York: Dover, 1967.

————. *The Selfish Giant*. Illus. Lisbeth Zwerger. New York: Simon, 1991.

————. *The Selfish Giant*. London: Macdonald Young, 1996.

————. *The Selfish Giant*. London: Walker, 1986.

Wilde, William R. *Irish Popular Superstitions*. 1852. New York: Sterling, 1995.

Williams, Linda. "Melodrama Revised." *Refiguring American Film Genres: History and Theory*. Ed. Nick Browne. Berkeley: U of California P, 1998. 42–88.

Willoughby, Guy. *Art and Christhood: The Aesthetics of Oscar Wilde*. Rutherford: Fairleigh Dickinson UP, 1993.

Wordsworth, William. "My Heart Leaps Up When I Behold." *Selected Poems*. Ed. John O. Hayden. Penguin Classics. New York: Penguin, 1994. 38.

Worth, Katharine. *Oscar Wilde*. Grove Press Modern Dramatists. New York: Grove, 1984.

Yeats, W. B., ed. *The Oxford Book of Modern Verse*. New York: Oxford UP, 1937.

Zhou, Xiaoyi. *Beyond Aestheticism: Oscar Wilde and Consumer Society*. Beijing: Peking UP, 1996.

Zipes, Jack. *Fairy Tales and the Art of Subversion: The Classical Genre for Children and the Process of Civilization*. London: Heinemann, 1983.

———. Introduction. *Spells of Enchantment: The Wondrous Fairy Tales of Western Culture*. 1991. New York: Penguin, 1992. xi-xxx.

Zwerger, Lisbeth, illus. *The Canterville Ghost*. By Oscar Wilde. Salzburg: Neugebauer, 1986.

INDEX

Modern Language Association of America

Approaches to Teaching World Literature

Joseph Gibaldi, series editor

Achebe's Things Fall Apart. Ed. Bernth Lindfors. 1991.

Arthurian Tradition. Ed. Maureen Fries and Jeanie Watson. 1992.

Atwood's The Handmaid's Tale *and Other Works*. Ed. Sharon R. Wilson, Thomas B. Friedman, and Shannon Hengen. 1996.

Austen's Emma. Ed. Marcia McClintock Folsom. 2004.

Austen's Pride and Prejudice. Ed. Marcia McClintock Folsom. 1993.

Balzac's Old Goriot. Ed. Michal Peled Ginsburg. 2000.

Baudelaire's Flowers of Evil. Ed. Laurence M. Porter. 2000.

Beckett's Waiting for Godot. Ed. June Schlueter and Enoch Brater. 1991.

Beowulf. Ed. Jess B. Bessinger, Jr., and Robert F. Yeager. 1984.

Blake's Songs of Innocence and of Experience. Ed. Robert F. Gleckner and Mark L. Greenberg. 1989.

Boccaccio's Decameron. Ed. James H. McGregor. 2000.

British Women Poets of the Romantic Period. Ed. Stephen C. Behrendt and Harriet Kramer Linkin. 1997.

Charlotte Brontë's Jane Eyre. Ed. Diane Long Hoeveler and Beth Lau. 1993.

Emily Brontë's Wuthering Heights. Ed. Sue Lonoff and Terri A. Hasseler. 2006.

Byron's Poetry. Ed. Frederick W. Shilstone. 1991.

Camus's The Plague. Ed. Steven G. Kellman. 1985.

Writings of Bartolomé de Las Casas. Ed. Santa Arias and Eyda M. Merediz. 2008.

Cather's My Ántonia. Ed. Susan J. Rosowski. 1989.

Cervantes' Don Quixote. Ed. Richard Bjornson. 1984.

Chaucer's Canterbury Tales. Ed. Joseph Gibaldi. 1980.

Chaucer's Troilus and Criseyde *and the Shorter Poems*. Ed. Tison Pugh and Angela Jane Weisl. 2006.

Chopin's The Awakening. Ed. Bernard Koloski. 1988.

Coleridge's Poetry and Prose. Ed. Richard E. Matlak. 1991.

Collodi's Pinocchio *and Its Adaptations*. Ed. Michael Sherberg. 2006.

Conrad's "Heart of Darkness" and "The Secret Sharer." Ed. Hunt Hawkins and Brian W. Shaffer. 2002.

Dante's Divine Comedy. Ed. Carole Slade. 1982.

Defoe's Robinson Crusoe. Ed. Maximillian E. Novak and Carl Fisher. 2005.

DeLillo's White Noise. Ed. Tim Engles and John N. Duvall. 2006.

Dickens' David Copperfield. Ed. Richard J. Dunn. 1984.

Dickinson's Poetry. Ed. Robin Riley Fast and Christine Mack Gordon. 1989.

Narrative of the Life of Frederick Douglass. Ed. James C. Hall. 1999.

Early Modern Spanish Drama. Ed. Laura R. Bass and Margaret R. Greer. 2006

Eliot's Middlemarch. Ed. Kathleen Blake. 1990.

Eliot's Poetry and Plays. Ed. Jewel Spears Brooker. 1988.

Shorter Elizabethan Poetry. Ed. Patrick Cheney and Anne Lake Prescott. 2000.

Ellison's Invisible Man. Ed. Susan Resneck Parr and Pancho Savery. 1989.

English Renaissance Drama. Ed. Karen Bamford and Alexander Leggatt. 2002.

Works of Louise Erdrich. Ed. Gregg Sarris, Connie A. Jacobs, and James R. Giles. 2004.

Dramas of Euripides. Ed. Robin Mitchell-Boyask. 2002.

Faulkner's The Sound and the Fury. Ed. Stephen Hahn and Arthur F. Kinney. 1996.

Flaubert's Madame Bovary. Ed. Laurence M. Porter and Eugene F. Gray. 1995.

García Márquez's One Hundred Years of Solitude. Ed. María Elena de Valdés and Mario J. Valdés. 1990.

Gilman's "The Yellow Wall-Paper" and Herland. Ed. Denise D. Knight and Cynthia J. Davis. 2003.

Goethe's Faust. Ed. Douglas J. McMillan. 1987.

Gothic Fiction: The British and American Traditions. Ed. Diane Long Hoeveler and Tamar Heller. 2003.

Grass's The Tin Drum. Ed. Monika Shafi. 2008.

Hebrew Bible as Literature in Translation. Ed. Barry N. Olshen and Yael S. Feldman. 1989.

Homer's Iliad *and* Odyssey. Ed. Kostas Myrsiades. 1987.

Ibsen's A Doll House. Ed. Yvonne Shafer. 1985.

Henry James's Daisy Miller *and* The Turn of the Screw. Ed. Kimberly C. Reed and Peter G. Beidler. 2005.

Works of Samuel Johnson. Ed. David R. Anderson and Gwin J. Kolb. 1993.

Joyce's Ulysses. Ed. Kathleen McCormick and Erwin R. Steinberg. 1993.

Works of Sor Juana Inés de la Cruz. Ed. Emilie L. Bergmann and Stacey Schlau. 2007.

Kafka's Short Fiction. Ed. Richard T. Gray. 1995.

Keats's Poetry. Ed. Walter H. Evert and Jack W. Rhodes. 1991.

Kingston's The Woman Warrior. Ed. Shirley Geok-lin Lim. 1991.

Lafayette's The Princess of Clèves. Ed. Faith E. Beasley and Katharine Ann Jensen. 1998.

Works of D. H. Lawrence. Ed. M. Elizabeth Sargent and Garry Watson. 2001.

Lessing's The Golden Notebook. Ed. Carey Kaplan and Ellen Cronan Rose. 1989.

Mann's Death in Venice *and Other Short Fiction*. Ed. Jeffrey B. Berlin. 1992.

Marguerite de Navarre's Heptameron. Ed. Colette H. Winn. 2007.

Medieval English Drama. Ed. Richard K. Emmerson. 1990.

Melville's Moby-Dick. Ed. Martin Bickman. 1985.

Metaphysical Poets. Ed. Sidney Gottlieb. 1990.

Miller's Death of a Salesman. Ed. Matthew C. Roudané. 1995.

Milton's Paradise Lost. Ed. Galbraith M. Crump. 1986.

Milton's Shorter Poetry and Prose. Ed. Peter C. Herman. 2007.

Molière's Tartuffe *and Other Plays*. Ed. James F. Gaines and Michael S. Koppisch. 1995.

Momaday's The Way to Rainy Mountain. Ed. Kenneth M. Roemer. 1988.
Montaigne's Essays. Ed. Patrick Henry. 1994.
Novels of Toni Morrison. Ed. Nellie Y. McKay and Kathryn Earle. 1997.
Murasaki Shikibu's The Tale of Genji. Ed. Edward Kamens. 1993.
Nabokov's Lolita. Ed. Zoran Kuzmanovich and Galya Diment. 2008.
Poe's Prose and Poetry. Ed. Jeffrey Andrew Weinstock and Tony Magistrale. 2008.
Pope's Poetry. Ed. Wallace Jackson and R. Paul Yoder. 1993.
Proust's Fiction and Criticism. Ed. Elyane Dezon-Jones and
    Inge Crosman Wimmers. 2003.
Puig's Kiss of the Spider Woman. Ed. Daniel Balderston and Francine Masiello.
    2007.
Pynchon's The Crying of Lot 49 *and Other Works.* Ed. Thomas H. Schaub. 2008.
Novels of Samuel Richardson. Ed. Lisa Zunshine and Jocelyn Harris. 2006.
Rousseau's Confessions *and* Reveries of the Solitary Walker. Ed. John C. O'Neal
    and Ourida Mostefai. 2003.
Shakespeare's Hamlet. Ed. Bernice W. Kliman. 2001.
Shakespeare's King Lear. Ed. Robert H. Ray. 1986.
Shakespeare's Othello. Ed. Peter Erickson and Maurice Hunt. 2005.
Shakespeare's Romeo and Juliet. Ed. Maurice Hunt. 2000.
Shakespeare's The Tempest *and Other Late Romances.* Ed. Maurice Hunt. 1992.
Shelley's Frankenstein. Ed. Stephen C. Behrendt. 1990.
Shelley's Poetry. Ed. Spencer Hall. 1990.
Sir Gawain and the Green Knight. Ed. Miriam Youngerman Miller and
    Jane Chance. 1986.
Song of Roland. Ed. William W. Kibler and Leslie Zarker Morgan. 2006.
Spenser's Faerie Queene. Ed. David Lee Miller and Alexander Dunlop. 1994.
Stendhal's The Red and the Black. Ed. Dean de la Motte and Stirling Haig. 1999.
Sterne's Tristram Shandy. Ed. Melvyn New. 1989.
Stowe's Uncle Tom's Cabin. Ed. Elizabeth Ammons and Susan Belasco. 2000.
Swift's Gulliver's Travels. Ed. Edward J. Rielly. 1988.
Thoreau's Walden *and Other Works.* Ed. Richard J. Schneider. 1996.
Tolstoy's Anna Karenina. Ed. Liza Knapp and Amy Mandelker. 2003.
Vergil's Aeneid. Ed. William S. Anderson and Lorina N. Quartarone. 2002.
Voltaire's Candide. Ed. Renée Waldinger. 1987.
Whitman's Leaves of Grass. Ed. Donald D. Kummings. 1990.
Wiesel's Night. Ed. Alan Rosen. 2007.
Works of Oscar Wilde. Ed. Philip E. Smith II. 2008.
Woolf's To the Lighthouse. Ed. Beth Rigel Daugherty and Mary Beth Pringle.
    2001.
Wordsworth's Poetry. Ed. Spencer Hall, with Jonathan Ramsey. 1986.
Wright's Native Son. Ed. James A. Miller. 1997.

RETURNING *to* CEREMONY

RETURNING *to* CEREMONY
Spirituality in Manitoba Métis Communities

CHANTAL FIOLA

UNIVERSITY OF MANITOBA PRESS

25   24   23   22   21   1   2   3   4   5

University of Manitoba Press
Winnipeg, Manitoba, Canada
Treaty 1 Territory
uofmpress.ca

Cataloguing data available from Library and Archives Canada
ISBN 978-0-88755-962-4 (PAPER)
ISBN 978-0-88755-935-8 (PDF)
ISBN 978-0-88755-964-8 (EPUB)
ISBN 978-0-88755-937-2 (BOUND)

Cover image: Detail of beaded tikinaagan. Photo by Chantal Fiola.
Cover Design by Frank Reimer
Interior design by Karen Armstrong

Printed in Canada

This book has been published with the help of a grant from the
Federation for the Humanities and Social Sciences, through the Awards
to Scholarly Publications Program, using funds provided by the
Social Sciences and Humanities Research Council of Canada.

The University of Manitoba Press acknowledges the financial support for
its publication program provided by the Government of Canada through
the Canada Book Fund, the Canada Council for the Arts, the Manitoba
Department of Sport, Culture, and Heritage, the Manitoba Arts Council,
and the Manitoba Book Publishing Tax Credit.

Funded by the Government of Canada | Canadä

This book is dedicated to my daughter, Mireille, and to all Red River Métis children. It is a reminder of where you come from and who your communities are. It is a path to the spiritual lodges of our ancestors—may you always feel welcome there.

CONTENTS

Note on Terminology

Many Red River Métis people in Manitoba are reclaiming the older term *Michif* (our endonym, the name we call ourselves), though this is not yet reflected in the literature or in common vernacular outside our communities; therefore, I use this term interchangeably with *Métis* (except when referring to the Michif language). I utilize the double vowel writing system and the endonyms *Anishinaabe* (plural: *Anishinaabeg*; language: *Anishinaabemowin*), or less frequently *Ojibwe*, and *Nêhiyaw* (plural: *Nêhiyawak*; language: *Nêhiyawawin*) rather than their exonyms (Saulteaux/Chippewa and Cree, respectively). Just as there are regional and dialectical differences within the Anishinaabe nation (i.e., Saulteaux, Ojibwe, Chippewa), these also exist within the Cree nation (i.e., *Nêhiyaw* or *Ininiw* for "Plains Cree," and *Omushkeego* for "Swampy Cree"). Exceptions occur when I reproduce exonyms and the phonetic writing system used in texts that I discuss. The Métis participants in this study all used the term "Cree" (except for one mention of "Nêhiyawak"); therefore, I use this term when discussing participant stories and findings. Moreover, I distinguish between *spirituality* and *religion*. I believe the former more accurately describes the spiritual ways of Indigenous peoples, and the latter connotes an institutionalized approach to faith with a heavier emphasis on dogma and hierarchy. While dogma and hierarchy may be present within some Indigenous spiritual practices, they are not defining characteristics as they are within religion.

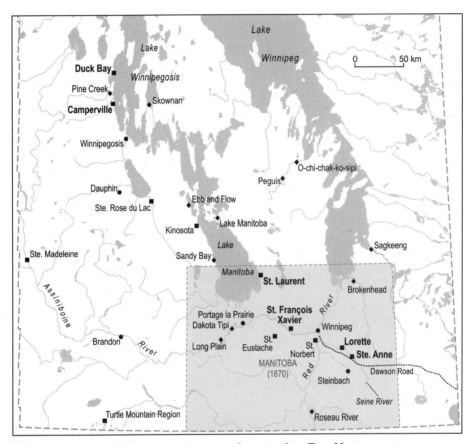

Figure 1. Six featured Métis communities, and surrounding First Nations reserves and urban centres. Also illustrated, other Métis communities and regions of interest noted in the book.

Métis Spirituality: Confronting Stereotypes

For fifteen years, Indigenous ceremony—and the spiritual, cultural education found within—has guided my life. I am Michif (Red River Métis) and grew up in my father's rural, French farming community of Ste. Geneviève, Manitoba. Before I moved away from home at age seventeen, my family and I regularly visited my mother's Métis community of St. Laurent, Manitoba (Figures 2 and 3).[1] Both my parents were raised Catholic, as were my sisters and I. I was first introduced to ceremony far from my prairie home while pursuing a master of arts degree at the University of Toronto and taking Indigenous-specific courses. For the first time in my formal education, I had a Métis professor. Through Dr. Judy Iseke's courses, I began learning about smudging with plant medicines, sharing circles and talking sticks, and colonization and decolonization from Indigenous perspectives. I was starving for cultural education and was eager to learn more; Dr. Iseke saw this in me and began inviting me to participate in ceremonies. Thanks to her, I participated in my first women's drum circle, women's full moon ceremony, and two-spirit sweat lodge[2]—in downtown Toronto, of all places!

Indigenous spirituality became increasingly important in my life. I began actively seeking out spiritual teachers, elders, and ceremonies, especially when I moved back to my ancestral land of southern Manitoba. Over the years, I would pass tobacco to Mizhakwanagiizhik (Charlie Nelson of Roseau River First Nation, who would adopt me as a daughter)[3] and learn *Zaagaate Kwe n'dizhinikaaz* (I carry the spirit name Sunrays Shining through the Clouds Woman) and *biizhew n'doodem* (I belong to the lynx clan).[4] I would be initiated as first-degree Midewiwin (Figure 4) in the Three Fires Midewiwin Society, and later begin my journey as a Sundancer (Figure 5).[5] I also began focusing on

Figure 2. The Guiboche sisters, c. 1951. Left to right: Patricia, Suzanne, Julie, Dorothée (author's maternal grandmother), and Bernadette. Author's photo.

Figure 3. Author's maternal grandfather, Robert Normand with a woman believed to be his grandmother Marguerite Laliberté, before 1953. Author's photo.

Figure 4. Author with Midewiwin relatives after initiating into the Three Fires Midewiwin Society at Bad River Indian Reservation, Wisconsin, 2011. Author's photo.

Indigenous spirituality where possible in my graduate studies, including in the research for my PhD in Indigenous Studies at Trent University. Eventually, I published my dissertation as a book titled *Rekindling the Sacred Fire: Métis Ancestry and Anishinaabe Spirituality* (2015). The book you are now reading is a follow-up to that early exploration of Métis spirituality.

Through my personal, academic, and spiritual journey, I have come across many false stereotypes surrounding Métis identity and

Figure 5. Author's completion of second year of Sundance at the Blacksmith Sundance, Manitoba, 2018. Author's photo shared with permission from Sundance Chiefs David and Sherryl Blacksmith.

spirituality. Stereotypes regarding Métis identity include the following:

- *Métis equals mixed;*
- *Métis refers to any mixture of Indigenous and non-Indigenous blood/ ancestry;*
- *Métis people are more mixed than other Indigenous peoples;*
- *Métis people are not truly Indigenous;* and
- *Métis people are less Indigenous/authentic than First Nations people.*[6]

Stereotypes regarding Métis spirituality include these notions:

- *all Métis people are Christian (especially Roman Catholic);*
- *Métis people only go to church (and First Nations people only go to ceremonies);* and
- *Métis people do not smudge, use hand drums, participate in sweat lodges or other ceremonies.*

Unfortunately, these stereotypical views are widely held by First Nations, by non-Indigenous people, and even by some Métis people themselves.

Early on in this study, I approached a Métis person in a position of authority, hoping for support with my research; instead, this person likened ceremonies to "sacrificing chickens" and then gave me the run-around. Whether this was their attempt at an offensive joke or merely ignorance, I still do not know. Such confusion and contradictory views can be found among other Métis people as well. For instance, people continue to hold the views outlined above while at the same time, rumours circulate about Métis leaders using the services of traditional medicine people. I personally know Métis people in leadership positions who participate in ceremony; however, some do so secretly and do not want others to find out. When asked why they are not open about their participation in ceremony, these individuals respond with statements like "Oh, we don't talk about that." Have they internalized the misinformation and stereotypes about Métis spirituality and worry they will be perceived as not fitting the mould of what a Métis person is "supposed" to be?

These stereotypes stubbornly persist and are most harmful and disappointing when perpetuated by Métis leadership and Métis elders. Our leaders and elders are supposed to be role models for our people, and when they spread misinformation about our spirituality (and discourage us from going to ceremonies) it confuses, silences, and misdirects Métis people who are trying to heal our ancestral dispossession and find our way back to our ancestral lodges (such as Sundance and the Midewiwin). The personal healing that can come from ceremonies, indeed the healing of our ancestral wounds, is threatened by these stereotypes that inhibit Métis participation in ceremonies. My purpose here is not to discourage Métis people from having a relationship with Christianity; rather, it is simply to encourage the understanding that some Métis people participate in ceremonies instead of (or alongside) Christianity.

The stereotyped beliefs listed above do not reflect many Métis people's lived realities, contemporarily or historically. In my previous book, I explored some of the reasons why these stereotypes persist; I argued that they are also partially a result of the rights-based agenda Indigenous peoples have been forced to fight for (since our sovereignty is questioned at every turn). For example, for Métis people to have our constitutionally protected section 35 rights legally recognized and upheld[7]—indeed, for our identity as Métis to be recognized at all[8]—we must prove that we are *wholly distinct from other Indigenous peoples.* This creates a situation where Métis are discouraged from having, and admitting to, shared characteristics with First Nations cultures, languages, and spirituality. Métis people have had to fight so long for recognition from the Canadian government that we are an Indigenous people because the government did not want to recognize and honour our rights. As a result of this (and many other colonial pressures to assimilate), many Métis people have internalized the need to prove we are completely distinct from First Nations in the hopes of receiving Métis-specific rights. Consequently, commonalities and familial relationships that exist among Michif (Métis), Anishinaabeg (Saulteaux/Ojibwe/Chippewa), and Nêhiyawak (Cree) on the prairies, today and historically, are downplayed, denied, silenced, and erased.[9] Of course there are differences between us; we form distinct Indigenous nations and are entitled to section 35 rights—that is not up for debate. Rather, I seek to caution against forgetting that we are also relatives and share (sometimes considerable) cultural overlap. Highlighting the commonalities in Métis, Anishinaabe, and Nêhiyaw spiritual beliefs and participating in ceremonies together again is one way to counter this forced forgetting, remember our kinship obligations, and heal our relationships and spiritual traumas resulting from colonization. I offer both my books as a contribution to our collective healing.

Rekindling the Sacred Fire

In *Rekindling the Sacred Fire*, I examined Métis relationships with traditional, Indigenous spirituality and how this affected self-identification. My aim was to begin a conversation about Métis people who participate in Indigenous ceremonies—that book remains one of the only sources ever published on the topic. I continue to believe that Métis people can play an important role in the resurgence of Indigenous ways of life, including spirituality. To this end, I crafted what I called a Métis Anishinaabe research design and methodology and interviewed eighteen Métis individuals (mostly in Manitoba) who participate in Indigenous ceremonies. I asked the participants about their family history, personal identification and experiences, and relationship to spirituality. I found that most of their families had extensive, multi-generational relationships with Roman Catholicism and few individuals had had relationships with Indigenous ceremonies while growing up. This was not surprising, given the long history between Red River Métis people and Catholicism. However, I also uncovered evidence that historically, despite the best efforts of clergy, some Red River Métis people participated in ceremonies that we had learned from our earliest maternal relations—notably, Anishinaabe and Nêhiyaw (Chapters 1 and 2).[10]

The Métis participants shared stories about disconnection factors that had inhibited their relationship with Indigenous ceremonies over time; these included Christianity, residential and day schools, addiction, and government-imposed divisions between Métis and First Nations people (which we ourselves came to internalize). Connection factors that enabled and nurtured relationships with Indigenous spirituality also emerged, including key people and places (e.g., elders and reserves), ceremonies themselves (e.g., one's first sweat lodge, or the first time hearing a water drum), the Red Power Movement of the 1960s and '70s (including the American Indian Movement [AIM] and its Canadian chapters), and higher education (via access to elders, cultural teachings, and ceremonies). My research also revealed that colonization continues to impact Métis lives and relationships with ceremony, and that some Métis people are overcoming barriers and having transformational experiences that lead to an adherence to Indigenous spirituality (some-times singularly, sometimes alongside Christianity).

Stoking the Fire

While my first book examined the relationships of Métis individuals with Indigenous ceremonies, *Returning to Ceremony* explores such relationships at the community level. More specifically, I focus here-in on Métis relationships with ceremony in the following six Métis communities in Manitoba: Duck Bay, Camperville, St. Laurent, St. François-Xavier, Lorette, and Ste. Anne (see Figure 1). These com-munities were selected because they are each recognized as important historic Red River Métis communities that date back to early Métis nationhood. Over the years, these communities have experienced vary-ing degrees of pressure to suppress their Métis identity and assimilate into mainstream Canadian (often French-Canadian) communities. Such pressures to assimilate can be heard in the participants' own stories.

With funding from the Social Sciences and Humanities Research Council of Canada (via the Manitoba Research Alliance), I hired six Métis community researchers (CRs) to assist me. Each CR was already connected to one or more of the Métis communities highlighted in this study via childhood residence, adulthood residence, or familial connection (such as having relatives who live there), or a combination thereof. The CRs proved invaluable in many ways, including by helping to ensure the study remained community centred.

This time, rather than a Métis Anishinaabe research design and methodology, I have attempted to fashion a Métis-specific approach, relying upon a Métis methodology and Métis-specific ethical consid-erations. Toward this goal, I worked collaboratively with the Manitoba Metis Federation (MMF) throughout my research. I hope to continue contributing to the development of Métis methodologies by offering this study as one such example. The CRs and I spoke with thirty-two Métis people who go to ceremonies and are connected to at least one of the six Métis communities in this study. Building on my previous research, we listened to what these folks had to say about their family histories, self-identity and experiences, and relationships with spiri-tuality; we studied the stories for patterns within the context of each community as well as across the six Métis communities. When both my studies are combined, a total of fifty Red River Métis people who participate in ceremonies have shared their stories.

I have organized this book in the following way: Chapters 1 and 2 explore oral history and new scholarly and community-based literature that has been published since *Rekindling* (or that I learned of since then) on the topic of Métis spirituality, especially historical and contemporary relationships with Indigenous ceremonies. In Chapter 1, I offer an update on my efforts to learn more about the possibility that Louis Riel was adopted by a Midewiwin family while in exile in the United States, as shared with me by the late Bawdwaywidun Banaiseban (Grand Chief of the Three Fires Midewiwin Lodge, Edward Benton-Banai) and mentioned in my first book. And, thanks to time I was able to spend with esteemed Métis Elder Maria Campbell, I expand this discussion to include another famed historic Métis leader, Gabriel Dumont, and his relationship with Indigenous ceremony. In Chapter 2, I conduct a deeper dive into the archives, looking for Métis participation in ceremonies in the earliest days of the Métis Nation. I also explore new literature regarding Métis spirituality, Indigenous Christianity, and syncretism (the blend of traditional Indigenous spirituality and Christianity). Taken together, evidence from the archives, literature, and oral history proves that Métis people participated in Indigenous ceremonies historically; this is no longer up for debate—it is a fact. It is also a fact that some Métis people participate in ceremonies today, as is illustrated by the Métis participants in *Rekindling* and the present book. For some Métis people, this is a historical continuation of the relationships our communities have had with ceremonies since time immemorial; and for others, it is a homecoming—a return to ceremonies after some time away.

A detailed explanation of my efforts to craft a Métis-specific research design and methodology can be found in Chapter 3. I track my evolution from the Métis Anishinaabe approach I took in my first book to the Métis-specific approach in this study and highlight similarities between the two (including ongoing use of plant medicines and ceremony), differences (including criteria for participation and ethics), as well as motivations for maintaining some aspects and modifying others. I detail my efforts to honour a more community-based approach this time, including concentrating on Métis communities, collaborating with six Métis CRs, and delivering presentations of findings in each of these communities. Moreover, I share my experiences of working with the MMF's new Manitoba Metis Community Research Ethics Protocol (MMCREP) as drafted by the MMF's Tripartite Self-Government Negotiations (TSN) Department. Also in Chapter 3, I discuss the problematic practice of *raceshifting* occurring in Eastern and Atlantic Canada, whereby White (often French-Canadian) people suddenly adopt a "métis" identity. This practice threatens Métis self-determination and sovereignty over our identity and culture, including spirituality.[11] These threats were, in part, my motivation to adhere to a more Métis-centred approach in this study.

In Chapter 4, I offer a brief history of each of the six Red River Métis communities that are the focus of this study. More specifically, I identify the geographic location of each community and attempt to highlight when each community was established and by whom, as well as when the church arrived in the community—the latter was usually Roman Catholic, given the close relationship between Métis and French-speaking people. I also look at demographics for each community based upon historic census records as well as the most recent Canadian census statistics and comment upon potential pressures to assimilate, such as the size of the non-Indigenous population in each community and the proximity of nearby White townships, urban centres, or First Nations reserves. In Chapter 5, I introduce the participants themselves and comment on the demographics of the group overall and by community—including age, gender, level of education, and occupation. These two chapters, along with the oral history and literature from Chapters 1 and 2, help set the context for understanding the community-specific findings in the remaining chapters of the book.

The bulk of the findings emerging from this study are shared in Chapters 6 through 10. In Chapter 6, I focus upon Métis family relationships with Métis communities and/or territory, Métis scrip, Indian status, Indigenous languages, and family self-identification over time. In the next chapter (7), I explore participants' family relationships with Métis, First Nations, and Euro-Canadian cultures, as well as with spirituality. Themes surrounding self-identification and personal experiences with racism and discrimination form the basis of Chapter 8. In Chapter 9, we hear about participants' own relationships with spirituality, including ways that they describe their spirituality, the types of Indigenous ceremonies they participate in, and factors that have inhibited their connection to ceremony. I continue this discussion in Chapter 10, where participants discuss factors that have nurtured such a connection as well as reactions from others as a result of their participation in ceremonies. Throughout, I take care to present themes that emerged within specific communities as well as across all six Métis communities.

Métis Sovereignty

At this point, I would like to specify who I am referring to when I say *Métis*. To avoid any misunderstanding, I want to clarify that I uphold the definition adopted by the Métis National Council (MNC) in 2002 (a definition that had been true in practice since the late eighteenth century): "'Métis' means a person who self-identifies as Métis, is distinct from other Aboriginal peoples, is of historic Métis Nation Ancestry and who is accepted by the Métis Nation."[12] The MNC is the national government of the citizens of the Métis Nation; at the provincial level, the Governing Members representing the MNC are the Manitoba Metis Federation (MMF), Métis Nation-Saskatchewan (MN-S), Métis Nation of Alberta (MNA), Métis Nation British Columbia (MNBC), and Métis Nation of Ontario (MNO). In turn, these provincial bodies represent Métis citizens in their respective provinces: "To be registered as Métis, you must apply to the Métis Registry operated by the MNC Governing Member in the province in which you reside. Each registry has its own application forms and application process."[13] The provincial Governing Members are expected to adhere to the MNC's definition of Métis and, beginning in 2002, each Governing Member was supposed to undertake a review of their existing membership to ensure that all members met the criteria for membership in the national body. All Métis citizens had to reapply for their citizenship and were issued new membership cards (Figure 6).[14] Any individuals and families who failed to meet the criteria were not reissued a membership card and are not recognized as citizens of the Métis Nation.[15]

I distinguish between legitimate Métis without a citizenship card, First Nations with and without registered Indian status who have a legitimate kinship connection to the Métis (Chapter 6, note 9, and

Figure 6. Métis Nation boundaries. Adapted from Métis National Council map. Map shared with permission from Housing Minister, Will Goodon, Manitoba Metis Federation.

Rekindling) and those who do not, and White settlers who co-opt an Indigenous identity (self-Indigenization). Herein, my discussion of raceshifting centres only upon the last group. Especially at a time when raceshifting is becoming increasingly problematic, we must protect the integrity of the Métis Nation and its citizenship. Although raceshifting was occurring when I published my first book, it was not nearly as prevalent as it is today, nor had it hit mainstream awareness—we have Chris Andersen, Darryl Leroux, Adam Gaudry, Jennifer Adese and Darren O'Toole, among others, to thank for exposing this threat (Chapter 3). Nonetheless, in retrospect, I worry that I did not take a firm enough stance on this issue in my previous book and do not want raceshifters to use my work to promote their own agenda; for these reasons, I am taking an unequivocal stance against raceshifting this time, as I explain in Chapter 3.

Reasons for *Returning to Ceremony*

I have several motivations and goals in writing this book. Building on my previous study, I aim to examine Métis spirituality, especially relationships with ceremonies, at the community level. I hope to narrow the gap that continues to exist in the literature regarding this neglected topic. In so doing, I tackle persistent stereotypes about Métis identity and Métis spirituality. My research illustrates that an increasing number of Métis people are returning to ceremonies—and that some Métis families have maintained ceremonies within their spiritual practice since the birth of our nation in the late eighteenth and early nineteenth centuries.

In focusing on Métis spirituality, I spend much time discussing the Métis people and communities themselves to provide context. As a result, this book also contributes to the study of Métis people and Red River Métis communities with regard to identity, kinship and belonging, culture, and shared community histories as they relate to this study's central theme of spirituality.[16] Métis orality, oral history, and storytelling shine through the stories and experiences shared by the Métis people within these pages. A more nuanced understanding of Métis identity emerges as a result of the examination of Métis spirituality (as inclusive of ceremonies) presented herein.

To accomplish this, I have modified my approach from a Métis Anishinaabe research design and methodology to a Métis-specific one. Indigenous methodologies remain relatively new additions to academia, breaking into the colonial ivory tower with increasing frequency from the 1990s onwards[17]—though Indigenous methodologies have existed outside academia for as long as Indigenous people have existed. By comparison, Métis-specific approaches within academia are nearly brand new (Chapter 3). I wish to contribute to this emerging field and offer *Rekindling* and *Returning* as examples of Métis-specific research design and methodology.

I intend to create space for Métis people to find their way back to ceremonies and encourage them not to give up. I want to let Métis people know they are not alone if they feel anxious about approaching

ceremonial spaces, or worry they are "not Indigenous enough" to participate. As the stories shared by the folks in this book (and the previous
one) illustrate, internalizing those particular self-doubts is not an uncommon Métis experience and is a legacy of colonization, one aspect
of the larger dispossession of Métis people. Stories shared by Métis
people herein illustrate how barriers to ceremonies can be successfully
overcome, and how the beauty, peace, and healing that come from
walking this path in life can be recovered. In this way, we contribute to
our larger collective healing. I believe that honouring Métis self-determination includes honouring our spiritual empowerment. Those of
us who feel called to ceremony should be nurtured to pursue this; the
healing we receive will also benefit our families, communities, and the
Métis Nation. Returning to participate in ceremony together, as we
did historically (and as some of us have sustained all this time), Métis
and First Nations people will remember we are related; repairing our
kinship bonds and honouring our obligations to each other will help
heal our peoples.

Finally, I continue to find guidance and inspiration in the Niizhwaaswi
Ishkodekaan (Seven Fires Prophecy) and the Oshkibimaadiziig
(New People) it speaks of.[18] Briefly, a very long time ago—before
Europeans arrived on these continents—spiritual prophets visited the
Anishinaabeg (one of the parent nations of the Métis) and predicted future events, including the newcomers' arrival and a time when
Indigenous people would all but forget Gizhe-Manido's (Creator's)
original instructions for *mino-bimaadiziwin* (a good, healthy, balanced
life). In the time of the seventh fire, the Oshkibimaadiziig would retrace
the steps of their ancestors and pick up what they had left behind; if
they remained steadfast in their task, Indigenous ways of life would
come to thrive again. I am more convinced than ever that Métis people
can play an important role in the resurgence of Indigenous ways of life,
including spirituality. Métis elders, traditional knowledge holders, and
people who live a ceremonial life have much to offer in our collective
efforts to reassert Métis sovereignty.

CHAPTER 1

Searching for Our Stories in Oral History

Publications that focus on Métis relationships with Indigenous ceremonies remain few and far between. In the following two chapters, I offer an overview of the existing landscape in terms of oral history (this chapter), and written texts and publications (Chapter 2). I briefly review the oral history and literature I shared in *Rekindling* and then present fresh information on the subject. In terms of oral history, I offer additional details regarding the story Bawdwaywidun Banaiseban, the Grand Chief of the Three Fires Midewiwin Lodge, shared with me about Louis Riel potentially being adopted by a Midewiwin family during his time in exile. I am also eager to share what I learned during a multi-day visit with respected Métis Elder Maria Campbell at her home near Batoche, Saskatchewan, during the summer of 2018, as it has led me to a more nuanced understanding of both historical and contemporary Métis relationships with ceremony. Taken together, the oral history and written record eliminate the question of whether Métis people have participated in ceremonies historically and contemporarily; this is an irrefutable fact. As more people become aware of this, we can correct harmful misinformation and stereotypes about us and our spirituality.

Highlighting Sources from *Rekindling*

When I wrote *Rekindling*, I struggled to find oral and written sources pertaining directly to Métis relationships with Indigenous spirituality. I did find archival evidence of Métis participation in ceremonies in the correspondence of priests, as well as in sources documenting the Christianization of the Métis (more on this in the next chapter). For these reasons, I found it important to provide context regarding colonial legislation influencing Métis spirituality (e.g., treaties, the Indian Act, the Constitution Act, court cases) and colonial systems (residential and day schools, child welfare system). Such legislation and systems enabled the differential treatment of First Nations and Métis people by the Canadian government and church officials and created divisions between First Nations and Métis relatives that were not there previously.

Similarities across language, culture, values, and spirituality among the Anishinaabeg (Saulteaux, Ojibwe), Nêhiyawak (Cree), and Michif have been ignored and silenced,[1] for instance, by refusing to allow Métis to enter into treaty as a collective.[2] A similar approach was taken by the federal government regarding the exclusion of Métis from the 1876 Indian Act,[3] including a series of amendments to strengthen such exclusion.[4] Differential treatment between First Nations and Métis can also be seen in the government's preference for pushing Métis to take scrip for money or land and for First Nations to enter treaty.[5] A continuation of this differential treatment can be seen in more recent history in the unequal application of section 35 of the 1982 Constitution Act and in court cases.[6] In order to enjoy Métis-specific section 35 rights, individuals must prove they are wholly distinct from other Indigenous peoples, as I mentioned above. In yet another example, *Alberta v. Cunningham* (2011),[7] the Supreme Court of Canada upheld an Alberta Métis settlement's right to remove a Métis family from the settlement for obtaining registered Indian status;[8] this reiterated the federal government's long-standing view that one cannot be both status Indian and Métis.[9]

The argument I made in *Rekindling* (and am reinforcing in these pages) is that colonial legislation and systems have failed to honour Métis self-determination, have unfairly excluded Métis from special rights accorded to other Indigenous peoples, and have created false divisions between Métis people and our First Nations relatives. After generations of having to prove our Indigeneity and having to fight for our rights to be recognized and honoured, it is no wonder many Métis people have internalized the message that we are wholly distinct from our First Nations cousins, resulting in a distancing of Métis people from Indigenous identity, culture, spirituality, and rights.[10] Despite these pressures to assimilate, some Métis have continued to participate in ceremonies throughout the generations; I turn now to oral Métis history to provide additional examples of this.

Building on Oral History: Listening to More Stories

The late Grand Chief of the Three Fires Midewiwin Lodge, Bawdwaywidun Banaise-ban (Edward Benton-Banai) shared a story with me about Louis Riel's adoption by a Midewiwin family during his time in exile in the United States, and questions about whether Riel himself became Midewiwin as a result. In *Rekindling*, I discussed how surprising this information is, since Riel is portrayed, and appears in his own writing, as a staunch Roman Catholic, albeit with strong critiques of the Catholic Church and suggestions on how to reform it, prompting clergy to accuse him of heresy.[11] Maggie Siggins, author of *Riel: A Life of Revolution*, has argued that while Riel was a devout Catholic, his "heart-felt religion was laced with Indian spiritualism."[12] I elaborate upon this, as well as syncretism, or blending Christianity and Indigenous spirituality historically and contemporarily, a little later.

With the publication of *Rekindling*, readers became interested in this story about a Riel-Mide connection and asked for more details than I could provide. Everywhere I went, I inquired whether anyone else had ever heard the story, and no one had. I even asked Jean Teillet, well-known Métis lawyer and author of *The North-West Is Our Mother: The Story of Louis Riel's People, The Métis* (2019) who is also Riel's great-grandniece. In April 2018, Teillet and I were both invited speakers at the "Ways of Knowing: Promising New Directions for Métis Research" conference hosted by the Métis Nation of Ontario and the University of Ottawa. I asked Teillet if she knew anything about Riel's being adopted by a Midewiwin family while in exile in the United States; she had no knowledge of this story and reminded me about Riel's Catholicism.[13]

Four months after speaking with Teillet, one of my spiritual mentors and friends, Rainey Gaywish, and I packed the car and drove nine hours from Winnipeg, Manitoba, to Wisconsin to visit Uncle Eddie (Benton-Banai). At that time, Uncle's health was failing him (he was in his late eighties) and he was living in a care home. We brought him coffee, tea, and strawberry cream-cheese strudels because he liked pastries. Following protocol, I passed him *asemaa* (tobacco), solid-coloured cloth, and gifted him a copy of my first book and asked if he would share more about the Riel-Mide story with me. He told me he did not know many more details but accepted my tobacco and gave me permission to share our conversation with others.

Figure 7. Late Elder Edward Benton-Banai at Lac Courte Oreilles Reservation, Wisconsin, n.d. Photo by (and shared with permission of) Rainey Gaywish.

According to Uncle Eddie, the family who took in Riel (i.e., adopted him) was from Rocky Boy, Montana, and carried the family name Ozawaa Makwaa, which translates to "Yellow Bear." (Or this might have been the name of a chief; Benton-Banai was unsure.) Uncle explained that the Midewiwin influence persists in the Rocky Boy area to this day. He related that about ten years earlier, a family from Rocky Boy had travelled to Wisconsin to participate in Three Fires Midewiwin ceremonies (where Uncle Eddie—with help from many—hosted ceremonies at least four times a year). This family shared with Uncle that they still participate in ceremonies but were quiet and secretive about it. Bawdwaywidun told them, as he told us all, that we do not have to hide anymore.[14]

I explained to Uncle that some Métis people feel they "aren't Indigenous enough" to participate in ceremonies. He laughed and said, "That's ridiculous, of course Métis people are welcome at ceremonies."[15] He smiled and nodded when I said I want to clear space for Métis people to come home to the ceremonies our ancestors had participated in before the government made them illegal and the churches helped to suppress them. Uncle encouraged me to keep doing my research and uncovering our knowledge and memory that had been nearly extinguished; he said we all have a responsibility to recover these. He told me, "I give you every encouragement. You may feel you walk alone now but you will attract like-minded people. Put your notes together; do your research. Stay the course."[16] As we parted, we hugged and he told me he loved me; I told him I loved him too (Figure 7).[17]

On the long drive back to Winnipeg, Rainey and I had much to ponder about our visit with Bawdwaywidun. Since then, she has tried to help me locate the family from Rocky Boy that Uncle Eddie spoke of. Rainey, herself an upper-degree Midewiwin, has reached out to other Mide people, including posting on Three Fires Midewiwin boards online, asking if anyone recalls the family from Rocky Boy who came to ceremonies ten years ago. Although people remember this family's visit, no one seems to have maintained contact with them, and the family does not appear to have returned to Three Fires ceremonies since. The search continues for Riel's possible Midewiwin relatives.[18]

My search for oral history regarding the historic participation of Métis people in ceremonies also led me to a meaningful discussion with well-regarded Métis Elder Maria Campbell. In 2018, I was among a handful of delegates invited by the President of the University of Winnipeg to travel from Winnipeg to Maria's home at Gabriel's Crossing near Batoche, Saskatchewan, to award her with an Honorary Doctor of Letters. After driving for eight and a half hours, our caravan pulled onto Maria's property—I knew we had found the right place because award-winning Métis actress and Member of the Order of Canada, Tantoo Cardinal, was pulling out as we were pulling in! From 22 to 25 July, some of us stayed in nearby hotels, others stayed in Campbell's guest cabin, and still others, like me, chose to pitch tents on her land and listen to the coyotes howling in the night. This land along the mighty South Saskatchewan River (Figure 8), takes its name (Gabriel's Crossing) from the days when Gabriel Dumont, the renowned Métis leader and military advisor to Riel himself, used to operate a ferry along the river. It was surreal to sit on the porch and drink tea with Maria (whose great-grandmother was Dumont's niece) and listen to stories about Gabriel living here and planning "the war" (that was how Maria referred to the Northwest Resistance of 1885). Maria shared that at that time, there were 500 (mostly) Métis people here planning around a fire (fires were few to avoid detection), strategizing against General Middleton and his army, right where we were having our tea! Maria also treated us to a Métis soirée with fiddling, jigging, square dancing, and spoken-word poetry in an arbour in her yard. I was especially excited to notice that not far from the arbour were the wooden frames of two sweat lodges. I would learn from Maria that she has lived on this land for fifty years and has held fasting camps here for twenty of those years. She does not invite people to her lodges or camps—those who come have been doing this work with her for decades.

During that time, I had the opportunity to visit one-on-one with Maria, sitting on the couch in her cabin and talking about Métis spirituality. Earlier, I had prepared a tobacco tie and gifts for her—a copy of my book (which I learned she already owned and was next on her reading list, but she asked me to sign this copy) and copies of the Métis issue of *Red Rising Magazine*[19]—a magazine prepared and published by a collective of Indigenous youth from Winnipeg, Manitoba, that features works mainly by Indigenous youth. I was not surprised when Maria declined my tobacco because I was on my moontime,[20] but she also encouraged me to do more "homework" before offering her tobacco. Despite this, we continued our conversation. Afterwards, I asked if she would be comfortable if I wrote about our talk in my next book and she said, "I don't care as long as you write the truth."[21]

Maria has piercing light-blue eyes with two parallel black lines under each, a traditional Indigenous tattoo representing water (as per her vision) tattooed by well-known Métis artist Christi Belcourt, using the hand poke and hand stitching technique (Figure 9). Maria has a beautiful, soft, soothing voice that you want to listen to for days—she is a gifted storyteller. She also has a no-nonsense, tough-love way about her and will bluntly tell you exactly what she thinks. In this way, after listening to what I had to say and asking me some questions, she gave

Figure 8. South Saskatchewan River, Saskatchewan. Author's photo.

me heck. She said, "I'm not a living legend; I'm a cranky old woman. I might seem like a bitch, but many come here wanting a lifetime's knowledge in a snippet. Though, I might be being harder on you because you're Métis."[22] She helped me realize my Riel myopia and told me: "Stop looking in priests' journals for our [Métis] people's ceremonies; you won't find it there. Talk to the Old Ones who still know. And look in archeology and anthropology texts and in the works of Métis historians like Brenda Macdougall."

With the anticipation of finally getting to speak with a matriarch of our nation about something I am so passionate about (precisely because I feel it is so important to the resurgence of our nation), my emotions were high and I had to hold back tears when Maria said these things. It was a very humbling conversation for me, especially since I felt I had been "doing my homework" on the subject for so long! By that time, I had spent more than a decade poring over old books, approaching Métis historians (including Brenda Macdougall, but this is not one of her areas of specialization), speaking with Métis people of all ages about their family's relationship with ceremonies or oral history about Métis spirituality, and had even published what may be the only book in existence on this particular subject. Ironically, eight months later, Maria Campbell would deliver the keynote address at the "Rising Up: Graduate Students' Conference on Indigenous Knowledges and Research in Indigenous Studies" at the University of Manitoba, in which she talked about her three years of studying Jesuit journals in

Figure 9. Author with Elder Maria Campbell at Gabriel's Crossing, along the South Saskatchewan River, Saskatchewan, 2018. Author's photo.

search of historic Métis lifeways. I still wonder how our conversation would have gone had she already read my book.

Nonetheless, Maria shared with me her view that "there are different types of Métis people [in the Métis Nation] who carry different names (*Michif, Bois-Brulées, Otipemisiwak* [the people who own themselves], Mountain Men, etc.) and have different relationships to ceremonies, different spiritualities."[23] She continued, "Métis people have had sweat lodges in our communities for as long as Métis people have been around—except in communities with a dominant hold by the Catholic Church [or other denominations]." Maria explained that some Métis families, like her own, have kept their ceremonies alive this whole time. She shared that "those who call themselves *Otipemisiwak* (notably, bison hunters) participated more in ceremonies historically and held onto them for longer" than others in the Métis Nation, despite colonization and pressures to assimilate. She also told me that Louis Riel and Gabriel Dumont were both pipe carriers, and that Dumont's pipe is currently held in Alberta (she knows the family that carries it);[24] Maria understands the significance of this, as she is herself a pipe carrier and so is her family.[25] She also said that Riel had been adopted by a Lakota family. She cautioned me not to believe everything I am told, including by elders, and not to take people at face value, including herself. Maria then suggested several books for me to review regarding Gabriel Dumont. As our conversation concluded, I thanked her for talking with me and encouraging me to dig deeper. She replied warmly, "You're always welcome here," invited me to visit again, hugged me, kissed my cheek, and said, "I'll see you again soon."[26] Interestingly, this was not the first time I had come across a story shared orally that associated Riel and Dumont with ceremonial pipes. I turn now to stories shared orally but converted to text.

Oral Stories Recorded on Paper

In addition to Maria Campbell, Michif Elder Barbara Bruce and Cree Métis traditional knowledge holder Louis Soren—both long-time ceremony conductors themselves and participants in this study—shared with me that they had heard Riel was a pipe carrier. They could not offer any details, but Soren sent me an article by David McCrady titled "Louis Riel and Sitting Bull's Sioux: Three Lost Letters." Two of the three letters in McCrady's piece had never been published before. According to McCrady, Riel had been trying to get Sitting Bull and his people to leave the Canadian-American borderlands in order to secure his own position as leader of a Métis community in Montana during his time there. Riel wrote the letters in question to Colonel Henry Moore Black, a commanding officer at Fort Assiniboine, in early 1880. Riel appears to be an intermediary between Sioux in the area and Colonel Black, who was tasked with getting the Sioux to settle in one place and accept terms imposed by the American government. In one letter, Riel speaks of his attempts to convince Bull Dog, leader of fifty-seven lodges (approximately 300 people) to surrender. McCrady explains, "As symbols of their intentions, Bull Dog and Red Elk gave Riel a pipe and knife to give to Black. But, not having instructions from Washington to deviate from standard policy, Black could not accept the gifts. He told Riel to inform Bull Dog and Red Elk that the surrender had to be unconditional. Talks then broke down."[27] In Riel's own words, "The 'Bull Dog' chief of the Brulees Sioux and his first soldier 'Red Elk' send the Calumet [pipe] and Knife to fort Assiniboin and ask for peace."[28] In another letter to Black, Riel explains:

> The Brulés [Sioux], a party of fifty seven lodges amongst them have entrusted me with a pipe and a knife which I bring, in their name, to you as to commanding officer of this post: the pipe is a demand of reconciliation and the knife a mark that they want no more fighting with the Americans. At the same time, they address the government through you; and they say: give us good reservations on our lands which you have conquered. . . . We want you to feel good in seing [*sic*] this pipe and this knife: take them: if you take them, it will be to prove that you are going to act with us, according [to] our demands.[29]

These letters illustrate that Riel was familiar with Indigenous diplomacy and the importance of traditional pipes (i.e., ceremony) in securing alliances and agreements. They do not indicate whether Riel himself was a pipe carrier; rather, the letters show he was entrusted to bring a pipe from the Sioux to a colonial official. Lawrence Barkwell, Darren Préfontaine, and Anne Carrière-Acco also wonder about Riel's and Dumont's Indigenous spirituality: "It is our belief that Riel's spiritual vision was similar to those obtained through the 'Thirst Dance' ('Sun Dance') and other spiritual practices of the various Plains First Nations. . . . Maria Campbell supports this hypothesis by noting that Gabriel Dumont was extensively involved in the spiritual practices of the Plains Indians and carried two medicine bundles: one of Sioux origin and the other of Plains Cree. More research should be conducted to link Riel to the numerous spiritual beliefs of his Dene ancestors, [and to] the Plains First Nations."[30] While delving deeper into Riel's and Dumont's Indigenous spirituality is fascinating (and validating for contemporary Métis who adhere to Indigenous spirituality), evidence exists that other Métis people, beyond these famous leaders, also pursued such spirituality historically (Figure 10).

Figure 10. Cree and Métis men participating in a pipe ceremony at Waterhen, c. 1931. Provincial Archives of Alberta, Paul Coze fonds, PR 2006.0508/32. See Ferris, "Blurred Lines and Kinship Tales."

Mary Weekes's *The Last Buffalo Hunter* was first published in 1939; it is an oral autobiographical account shared by Norbert Welsh with Weekes in 1931 when he was eighty-seven years old and blind. Welsh is described as a prominent Halfbreed trader and buffalo hunter who was born in Red River (near St. Boniface) in 1845.[31] His mother was "a Swampy Cree Halfbreed" and his English father worked for the Hudson's Bay Company, like his father before him. Welsh's "Indian name" was Wa-ka-kootchich (no English translation is given).[32] Like many Halfbreeds and Métis in Red River at that time, Welsh was not formally educated but was multilingual; he could speak Nêhiyawawin (Cree), Assiniboine, Sioux, Blackfoot, Stoney, English, and French. In at least three instances in the book, Welsh describes in considerable detail "Indians and Halfbreeds" participating together in Indigenous ceremonies.

In the first instance, Welsh describes "a Giving Away Dance" hosted by Chief Moon-e-ash (White Man), a brother to Kah-payuk-wah-skoonum (Chief One Arrow, signatory to Treaty 6 in 1876). According to Welsh, "In the old days on the plains, the buffalo hunters and traders [who were often Métis or Halfbreeds] were expected to take part in these dances. We were all wintering together in Indian Territory, and were surrounded by Indian lodges. The Indians were our customers and we had to be sociable."[33] He continues, "Altogether, there must have been thirty or forty men in the lodge, Indians and half-breeds. Moon-e-ash told the crowd that he was going to begin the dance, and that it would last for five days and five nights."[34] Welsh shares many details about the ceremony and the songs (along with their English translations), including the importance of praying to "the Manitou" (Spirit, possibly Gichi-Manitou/Gizhe-Manido, the Great Spirit or Creator) and the custom of sharing "marrow fat mixed with crushed dried choke cherries and packed into a bladder," whereby each person in attendance took one bite, then passed it to his neighbour. An account is also given of the extremely generous gift giving that occurs as part of the ceremony. Moon-e-ash gave Welsh and his wife seven shaggannappis (long ropes of buffalo hide), seven horses, five buffalo robes, two bags of pemmi-can, and two bales of dried meat; in return, Welsh and his wife gifted Moon-e-ash and his wife a Red River cart, six horses, sixty pounds of tea, twenty pounds of sugar, and plugs of tobacco![35] At the conclusion of this ceremony, held in Round Plain (Saskatchewan), Welsh and his hunting brigade travelled directly to another ceremony, this time held in Red Deer Lake, Alberta, at the camp of Chief Shash-apew (Spread Sitter).

While still at the dance at Round Plain, Welsh had received a mes-sage from Chief Shash-apew warning "the half-breeds not to hunt buffalo in his territory unless they were willing to pay a duty on every buffalo they killed."[36] Adhering to diplomatic custom, Welsh sent the messenger back to the chief with a gift of tea, sugar, and tobacco, and said they would come speak with him about this matter. Upon his arrival with the hunting brigade, Welsh estimated that between two and three hundred Cree people had assembled there for the dancing ceremony. He describes a huge dancing tent that "held about two hundred danc-ers. It was formed by combining the buffalo-skin coverings of several other lodges, and covered over an acre of ground."[37] Chief Shash-apew, referring to himself as their uncle, invited the three principal men of the hunting brigade (Welsh, Charles Trottier, and Isadore Dumont— Gabriel's father) to enter the dancing tent and thanked them for the gift they had sent in advance of their arrival. In this way—responding to the chief's warning, offering a gift, accepting the invitation to participate in the ceremony, travelling there, calling the man uncle (and being aware of the kinship obligations this entails)—Welsh, Trottier, and Isadore

Dumont were able to secure Chief Shash-apew's blessing to hunt buffalo in his territory. Over the next two days, they killed 250 buffalo.[38]

Welsh also describes Halfbreeds participating in Sundances (having attended many himself), including in what he believed to be the last Sundance held on the plains; it was hosted by Chief Starblanket on the File Hills Reserve (around 1884). It was around this time that Canada began outlawing Indigenous ceremonies in order to force assimilation.[39] There are oral stories of resistance that describe ceremonies held in secret, while the Indian agent was away, sometimes with the assistance of Métis or Halfbreeds. This is precisely what happened in Welsh's account of the Sundance at File Hills Reserve—Indian agent John Wright had gone away and asked Norbert Welsh to "keep an eye on the Indians" for him.[40] During his absence, a Sundance was held.

Welsh describes the Sundance ceremony in considerable detail over several pages; to do so, he speaks as though he is the chief sponsoring a Sundance and pronounces, step by step, what is done to undertake the complex ceremony. Interestingly, he says that in those days, there were always "hundreds" of White men who would gather to watch the Sundance; to attend, they were made to pay "one dollar in money or in goods."[41] Around 10 June, Welsh explains, is when the Sundance usually occurred—this remains true to this day (at least at the lodge where I dance).

Other accounts exist specifically regarding Michif participation in the Sundance. Just as Mary Weekes assisted Norbert Welsh in putting pen to paper while telling her his life stories, Tom Spaulding and Nicholas Vrooman each wrote a short article in the 2004 *Métis Voyageur*, a publication of the Métis Nation of Ontario (MNO), detailing a story about the Sundance that has been passed down orally since the early 1800s and confirms contemporary continuity of this ceremony among the Métis. Barkwell, Préfontaine, and Carrière-Acco corroborate by discussing this same Sundance with Métis participation and include a section written by Vrooman in their own chapter.[42]

According to historian Nicholas Vrooman, an alliance was forming in the early 1800s between the Cree, Assiniboine, Chippewa (Saulteaux/Ojibwe), and Michif (Métis) in order to create a unified front to deal with the Hudson's Bay Company (HBC), as well as their Indigenous enemies such as the Sioux-Cheyenne alliance. When the HBC and the North West Company (NWC) merged in 1821, there was a need to formalize the alliance. For these reasons, a "Thirsty Dance" (Sundance) was called by Many Eagle Set, a Cree Assiniboine leader, at Buffalo Lodge Lake (in present-day North Dakota). Another reason for the ceremony was to formally welcome the newest comers to the area, the Ojibwe and the Michif; there, "the [Sun]dance would be given to the newcomers."[43] Vrooman explains, "The Ojibwe were Mdewin [Midewiwin], from the woodlands, who now needed to have the Medicine of the plains. The Michif were Romish (Roman Catholic), but *some were to take on both traditions*, just as many Ojibwe maintained their Mdewin."[44] According to oral tradition, it was the largest Sundance ever to occur on the northern plains, with fourteen centre poles and 1,500 dancers from these nations (including the Michif). Vrooman continues, "Many Eagle Set received a song from Gishay Manitou [Creator] to commemorate the 'Unity of the People' and symbolize the alliance."[45] The song was given to the people and today is carried by Francis Eagleheart Cree, great-grandson of Many Eagle Set and spiritual leader of the Turtle Mountain people. Vrooman concludes, "This song is sung every year at the Sun Dance on the Turtle Mountains commemorating the alliance between the Assiniboine, Cree, Ojibwe and Michif, which has remained intact since the dance at Buffalo Lodge Lake."[46]

In the same 2004 issue of *The Voyageur*, Tom Spaulding writes about this ongoing relationship and Sundance. In 2003, the song carried by Elder Francis Eagleheart Cree was gifted to Tony Belcourt, who was the founding president of the MNO, serving from 1994 to 2007. Belcourt had been searching for a song to commemorate the nation-to-nation relationship between the Michif and the Anishinaabeg; previously, Elder Gordon Waidebence "had recommended that this relationship be developed in a traditional way through song, smoke, feast and dance."[47] Vrooman suggested using the song that had been sung in forming the alliance between the Métis (Michif) and the Ojibwe (Anishinaabeg) in the 1820s in North Dakota. After consulting Elder Francis Eagle Heart Cree, a sweat lodge was held in Belcourt, North Dakota, and it was decided that the song would be transferred to Tony Belcourt in a ceremony during the Traditional Elders and Youth Circle held in Elder Francis Cree's roundhouse at the Turtle Mountain Reservation near Belcourt in August 2004. The ceremony was attended by members of the community and delegations from the MNO and the Manitoba Metis

Federation. Elder Francis Cree, hoping to help preserve the song and our cultures for future generations, asked that the ceremony be filmed.[48]

~

In summary, much evidence can be found in oral history regarding historic Métis participation in ceremonies, including intriguing stories such as the ones shared with me by Elders Bawdwaywidun Banaiseban and Maria Campbell. Some oral accounts have been committed to paper, as with Norbert Welsh's life experiences.[49] In 2004, stories about the Iron Confederacy re-emerged through the singing of the Sundance song gifted to the Michif and Anishinaabeg commemorating the alliance from the early 1800s. The oral record indicates that participation in Indigenous ceremonies was a customary and regular part of the bison and fur trade and that Michif (Métis) people actively participated. Despite the forced forgetting of our relationships with ceremony, some Michif families have carried these stories into the present day and have continued to participate in ceremonies all this time. In the next chapter, I turn to a more in-depth discussion of recent sources available in the written and published record regarding past and present Michif relationships with ceremony.

CHAPTER 2

Combing the Written Record for Our Stories

The written record provides additional proof of Métis participation in Indigenous spirituality, both historically and in the present day. With Elder Maria Campbell's guidance, I located publications regarding celebrated Michif leader Gabriel Dumont's participation in ceremonies. Building on my work in *Rekindling*, I offer a closer examination of archival records, specifically priests' correspondence that mentions Michif people in ceremony in the early days of Métis nationhood in Red River and surrounding regions. I discuss the establishment of Roman Catholicism in Manitoba—especially itinerant and sedentary missions, and the establishment of infrastructure such as churches and schools—to illustrate its impacts upon Métis identity and spirituality. I conclude by exploring publications confirming the cultural continuity of Métis spirituality that includes ceremonies.

Gabriel Dumont's Participation in Ceremonies

Charles Duncan Thompson's *Red Sun: Gabriel Dumont, The Folk Hero* (2017) deals most comprehensively with Dumont's spirituality; I am indebted to him for much of what follows.[1] George Woodcock's *Gabriel Dumont* (2003) and Darren Préfontaine's *Gabriel Dumont: Li Chef Michif in Images and in Words* (2011) are also useful. According to Thompson, there is no proof of where or when Dumont was born—his educated guess is 1837 in Fort Garry (present-day Winnipeg), where Dumont's father had a farm.[2] The Dumonts were aligned with the Plains Cree (Nêhiyawak); the men spoke Cree and other Indigenous languages and had Cree names.[3] Gabriel's father was named Isadore dit Ecapow Dumont and his mother was Louise Laframboise, a Nakoda-Métis. Ecapow (Ai-caw-pow)[4] was a third-generation Brayroo (Michif for "badger"; *blaireau* in French)—the term referred to a "helper (perhaps one who is too confident) and one who is also a caller of buffalo." These were men who did not back down from adversity.[5] Gabriel also carried the names Red Sun—gifted by a Piikani (Piegan) in Montana whose life had been spared by Gabriel when he was a boy[6]—and Buffalo Child—as he belonged to the buffalo clan.[7] As was customary among the Métis, each bison hunt began with the democratic election of a Captain of the Hunt. Once he reached the age of twenty-five, Gabriel would be elected captain repeatedly—he was recognized as a permanent chief of the Métis and would also broker peace treaties for First Nations chiefs.[8] He was also a member of the Society of Generous Ones—a traditional Métis organization whose members ensured that those who were old, sick, young, or had disabilities received bison meat after a hunt; in addition, he adhered to the Nêhiyaw-Pwat (Iron Confederacy) and to Indigenous spirituality.[9]

Gabriel's spirituality was influenced by the men in his life, including his father, his uncle Skakastaow, who was a sacred pipestem holder of the Cree,[10] and his father-in-law Nakawiniuk ("Jock," Jean-Baptiste Wilkie), who succeeded Cuthbert Grant Jr. (the first Métis leader) as Captain of the Hunt[11] and founded the Brayroo Nation.[12] Gabriel's father put him out on a four-day vision quest ceremony before puberty. He was visited spiritually by White Buffalo Woman, who taught him "sacred songs and told him what amulets [like sweetgrass] to wear and where to dig for medicinal roots" before turning into a bison and walking away.[13] Consequently, Gabriel gained the power and ability to call the bison, and perform doctoring rites.[14] He married Madeleine Wilkie, a recognized medicine woman.[15]

The Dumonts would have been around plant medicines regularly, including on the bison hunt, as were most Michif at that time.[16] Thompson relays Father Albert Lacombe's writing on the bison hunt in 1850, explaining that priests disapproved of the presence of "'heathen' sorcerers" (medicine people), especially because they usually had more followers than the "black robes" (priests).[17] Thompson details many instances of Gabriel's use of medicines, sacred bundle items, smudging, and pipe ceremonies. Dumont appears to have used sweetgrass and tobacco often.[18] He smudged with sweetgrass and wove a braid of it into the shape of a cross, carrying it with him everywhere[19]—an excellent example of syncretism. Upon crossing the international border to retrieve Riel from exile, Gabriel and Michel Dumas dismounted their horses

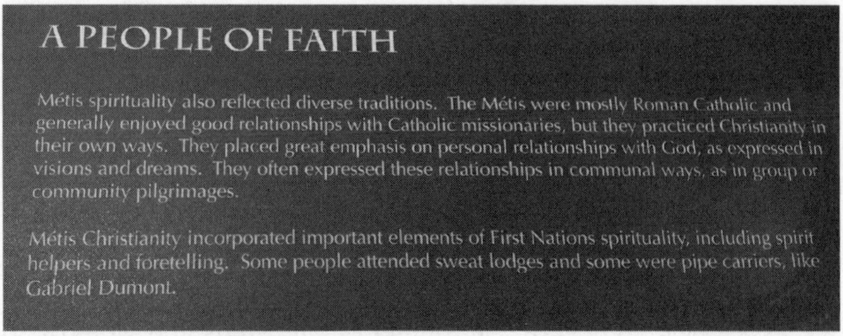

A PEOPLE OF FAITH

Métis spirituality also reflected diverse traditions. The Métis were mostly Roman Catholic and generally enjoyed good relationships with Catholic missionaries, but they practiced Christianity in their own ways. They placed great emphasis on personal relationships with God, as expressed in visions and dreams. They often expressed these relationships in communal ways, as in group or community pilgrimages.

Métis Christianity incorporated important elements of First Nations spirituality, including spirit helpers and foretelling. Some people attended sweat lodges and some were pipe carriers, like Gabriel Dumont.

Figure 11. Plaque at Batoche National Museum identifying Gabriel Dumont as a pipe carrier and describing Métis spirituality as syncretic and inclusive of sweat lodges. Author's photo.

and "burned sweetgrass to cleanse themselves, and perform the sacred pipe ceremony."[20] Later, Gabriel lit sweetgrass and smudged Riel's grave as his grieving followers gathered nearby.[21] He put tobacco down [in prayer] when his father-in-law died.[22] Before he passed away, Gabriel's uncle Skakastaow gifted him the sacred pipestem to carry.[23] There is also evidence that Gabriel carried a pipe that was previously carried by Cree Chief Mistahimaskwa (Big Bear).[24] The Batoche National Historic Site Museum has a plaque that identifies Gabriel Dumont as a pipe carrier and Métis spirituality as a syncretic blending of Indigenous and

Figure 12. "Dumont, Gabriel, Smoking Peace Pipe," 2003. Illustration by Peter Myo. Gabriel Dumont Institute's Virtual Museum of Métis Culture and History.

Figure 13. Gabriel Dumont's grave in the cemetery near his church (the old Sundance grounds) at the site of the Battle of Batoche, Saskatchewan. Author's photo.

Christian elements (Figures 11 and 12).[25] Dumont was familiar with being gifted sacred bundle items and with gifting them—he gifted an eagle rattle to the grieving widow of the Sioux Chief Wahnaton.[26] Use of medicines, bundle items, and smudging would have been familiar to many Métis of the past.[27]

Among all the references to Dumont's spirituality in Thompson's book, the sweat lodge and Sundance are mentioned most frequently.[28] Gabriel was a firekeeper for sweat lodges, built sweat lodges himself (including for funerary rites), and participated in them.[29] He assisted in brokering peace and attended to important matters at Sundances and on sacred Sundance grounds,[30] including while pursuing his goal of securing a Métis–First Nations alliance.[31] Dumont once declined an invitation from the Dakota to participate in a Ghost Dance because he would be attending a Sundance at that same time at Carrot River and encouraged Indigenous nations to retain their distinct spiritual practices.[32] Gabriel would sell his ferry and use the money to construct a church (St. Antoine de Padoue, which still stands) on former Sundance grounds, where his syncretic religion could be practised (Figure 13).[33]

Historic Métis Spirituality: A Shifting Syncretism

According to Thompson, "since before 1800, the Elders had discussed the need for a non-sectarian spirituality, which melded all beliefs," and they chose Louis Riel to lead it.[34] Riel, whose Cree name was *Uneeyen*,[35] had the gift of prophecy, perhaps inherited from his grandmother Marie-Anne Gaboury—"a famous seer [who] could predict the future to an amazing degree."[36] Most Métis had this ability, "which made many people assume that all Métis were superstitious. In fact, if one wasn't able to prophesize the future, that person wasn't Indigenous!"[37] On 15 March 1885, during the Northwest Resistance, Riel was democratically chosen at Gabriel's Crossing as the religious leader of the Métis (after they were denied the sacraments by Father Fourmond for participating in the Resistance).[38] Riel (recognized as a prophet by now) urged fasting and prayer and predicted that if there was an eclipse of the sun the next day, their efforts would be a success. Indeed, as Thompson writes, "an eclipse happened shortly after noon, March 16."[39] During the Resistance, Riel called the Métis to the little church in Batoche and denounced the pope; "now St. Francis of Assisi and the Sun Dance as well as Riel's God or Walcantanka or Manitou were equal and approved."[40] Riel believed that "an Indigenous religion, combining elements of all, could go a long way to end the conflict between people of other cultures."[41] Riel and Dumont strived to create a Métis and First Nations confederacy using spiritual, political, and economic efforts to unify the people.[42]

In *Riel's People: How the Métis Lived* (1992), Maria Campbell confirms Métis spirituality as syncretic—the book's inside cover depicts a Métis person seated in front of a Red River cart holding a sacred pipe (Figure 14). Describing family life, Campbell writes that "the Métis were religious, the majority of them being Roman Catholic, Anglican or Methodist, but they also respected Indian taboos and beliefs. Consequently, their religion was sometimes a mixture of Indian beliefs and Christian practices, and not always what the missionaries wanted."[43] In Métis homes, there were usually many kinds of dried herbs and roots used for medicine and cooking, and "always on one wall hung a fiddle and, if the family were Roman Catholic, a crucifix. No home was complete without them."[44] Campbell's assessment that missionaries were displeased when Métis people maintained Indigenous beliefs and ceremonies is confirmed by the priests themselves. Let us examine

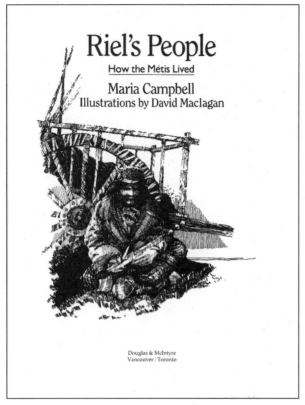

Figure 14. Inside cover, depicting a Métis person holding a sacred pipe, from Maria Campell's *Riel's People: How the Métis Lived.* Illustrated by David Maclagan, published by Douglas and McIntyre, 1992.

writings of the earliest priests to arrive in the Red River region as the Catholic Church was establishing its grip on this part of the world.

Catholicism Arrives in Red River

After the Battle of Seven Oaks in 1816 (in present-day Winnipeg), HBC Governor Miles Macdonnell requested assistance from religious officials to keep the peace with the Métis. Also, some Métis and local French Catholic freemen who had settled in Red River wanted access to the religion of their fathers and prepared a petition requesting a priest.[45] Lord Selkirk granted land within the settlement along the east bank of Red River to establish a permanent mission and the Bishop of Quebec, Joseph-Octave Plessis, sent the first missionaries to Red River in 1818: priests Joseph-Norbert Provencher and Sévère Dumoulin, and seminarian William Edge. Bishop Plessis instructed the missionaries "to draw the Indian nations of this vast country 'out of barbarism and the disorders which result from it'. . . and to look after the French-Canadians and Métis Christians who had adopted the customs of the Indians and lived 'licentiously and forgetful of their duties as Christians.'"[46] Provencher built a house-chapel on the bank of the Red River and by 1822 had been consecrated as Bishop of the North West, with his mission receiving the name of St. Boniface.[47] Dumoulin built a church and priests' quarters in Pembina (present-day North Dakota) for the Métis there, but by 1823–24, Provencher had moved the mission (called St. François-Xavier) north of the forty-ninth parallel to White Horse Plains in the Red River Settlement along the Assiniboine River. Some Métis refused to move; those who followed the priest established a new community headed by Cuthbert Grant Jr. (the first Métis leader) called Grantown. Grant had recently become a Christian and many of the Métis in Grantown (referred to today as St. François-Xavier—one of the selected communities in this study) were also Christian.[48]

The missions at St. Boniface and St. François-Xavier were the only two sedentary missions in Red River until 1833. Itinerant missions, when priests visited Métis communities but did not live there, were the norm until 1870; *missions ambulantes* (mobile/travelling missions) took place when visiting priests accompanied Métis hunters *à la prairie*, preaching to them on bison hunts and wintering with them.[49] In 1833, Provencher established a third mission west of St. François-Xavier and named it St. Paul des Saulteaux (Baie St. Paul); Father Georges-Antoine Belcourt was sent from Quebec to run this mission. Belcourt often left his sedentary mission station to pursue itinerant missions around Lakes Manitoba and Winnipegosis and throughout the Lake Winnipeg area to Rainy Lake.[50] In 1845, he accompanied the Métis (numbering 309 people) on their fall hunt, catechized to sixty-nine children, and said mass daily for families;[51] he did so again in 1846. In 1849, Father Jean Tissot accompanied the Métis summer hunt, which numbered 1,500 people (including 200 Saulteaux) with 700 Red River carts, 1,000 horses, and 400 dogs.[52] In 1851, Father Louis Richer Laflèche accompanied Métis from White Horse Plains, Red River, and Pembina (again including some Saulteaux); the Battle of Grand Coteau with the Sioux that occurred on this hunt is well known.

For many Métis hunters, itinerant or bison hunt missions were the only time they saw a priest; they favoured priests who preached in Saulteaux, which they understood better than French.[53] Belcourt preferred the sedentary approach but Bishop Provencher thought that was expensive and encouraged itinerant missions, so Belcourt combined both methods.[54] Belcourt would eventually initiate the missions of Duck Bay (another community in this study) at the south end of Lake Manitoba, and Fort Alexander (Sagkeeng).[55]

When a location had enough inhabitants living there year-round, a sedentary mission would develop into a parish, as occurred in Ste. Anne des Chênes[56]—yet another community in this study. By 1845, Red River had six priests, four Grey Nuns, and several Oblates; ten years later, there were thirty priests, and by the end of the nineteenth century, the Diocese of St. Boniface (in present-day Winnipeg) had sixty priests, 350 nuns, and 140 Oblates—it had become the "gateway to the Catholic Northwest."[57] According to McCarthy, "through these missions, the Church maintained contact year-round with at least some of the Métis, and some relationship with the hivernants [winterers], who spent most of the year far from any priest or parish."[58] By the 1860s, many itinerant missions had been replaced by settled parishes, as southern Manitoba became predominantly parochial and sedentary in preparation for incoming White settlers from the east.[59] The infrastructure of Catholic schools also helped Christianize the Métis.

By the time of Manitoba's confederation in 1870, the Catholic Church had constructed two schools in St. Boniface, and one each in St. François-Xavier, St. Vital, St. Norbert, Lorette, St. Charles, Pointe Coupée (St. Adolphe), Baie St. Paul, Fort Garry (Winnipeg), and Ste. Anne des Chênes.[60] Others had begun at St. Laurent and Oak Point on an irregular basis, and by the end of 1871, seven more schools had commenced, bringing the combined enrollment to 639 children.[61] Manitoba's confederation triggered a massive influx of settlers from the East; these shifting demographics boded poorly for the Métis.

The arrival of White settlers caused a rise in racial discrimination and increased segregation between Métis and French Canadians. Métis communities such as St. Pierre-Jolys were physically split along racial and ethnic lines, with Métis concentrated on the poorer side of town and most French Canadians on the wealthier side. Métis abandoned other communities and founded new ones like Richer and Lorette.[62] As the Métis were pushed out by newcomers, the Catholic Church became the biggest landowner in the new province. Louis Riel accused the clergy of growing rich on Métis misery[63]—Alexandre-Antonin Taché (who arrived in Red River in 1845 and became the first Archbishop of St. Boniface in 1871) grew extremely wealthy from his land transactions, as did Father Joseph-Noël Ritchot (who arrived in Red River in 1862).

Between 1818 and 1870, the Roman Catholic Church vastly expanded throughout Manitoba, and "the Métis, Cree, Saulteaux, and Chipewyan [Dene] were instructed, baptized, and integrated into the Church."[64] By 1879, the residential schooling period would officially commence. Considerable efforts were also made to develop an Indigenous clergy.[65] As a result, the Métis were not completely independent of the church, but neither were they wholly subservient to it.[66]

Digging into the Archives: Priests' Correspondence

As an Indigenous people with an oral language, Michif people were rarely literate in the early days of our nationhood. Those who were usually had a Western Catholic education and were involved with the Catholic Church, as was the case for the Nolin sisters and Sara and Louis Riel.[67] As faithful Christian converts, these individuals would not have been writing about Indigenous ceremonies. Rather, it was Métis bison hunters, fisherpeople, and trappers who remained closer to Indigenous spirituality and to their First Nations kin—often indistinguishable from Métis to missionaries.[68] They did not leave a written record; even writing from literate Métis in the early 1800s is uncommon.

Le Centre du patrimoine de la Société historique de Saint-Boniface (the St. Boniface Archives) houses the largest collection of francophone archives west of Ottawa and specializes in Métis genealogies.[69] When I inquired about the earliest writing by Métis people, the archivist brought me a single one-inch-thick white binder.[70] He tried to think of early Métis who could write and mentioned the Nolin sisters but did not think much of their writing survived.

The correspondence of Catholic priests—exceptional record keepers but deeply biased—offers insight from a colonial religious perspective into the earliest days of Métis nationhood. Priests tried to convert as many Indigenous people as possible and increasingly discouraged Indigenous spirituality. Jacinthe Duval states that "the indigenous aspects of Métis culture were seen as a threat to this goal [of creating a new Catholic French-Canadian prairie society and] had to be excised."[71] Missionaries described Métis and First Nations nearly identically as "inferior" and "condemned their customs as savage or pagan," along with their refusal to exchange their semi-nomadic lifestyle for an agrarian one.[72] Duval notes that missionaries appreciated the religious devotion of the Métis but "worried that they would not abandon certain Native traditions including what they termed *médecine sauvage* [savage medicine], the belief in the immortality of the soul and of some form of the body, and marriage rites."[73] Priests' correspondence in the archives confirm this.

What follows are excerpts from letters written by Father Georges-Antoine Belcourt, Bishop Joseph-Norbert Provencher, and by later comers such as Fathers Charles Camper and Laurent Simonet, held in Le Centre du patrimoine in Winnipeg. The letters are handwritten in French and occasionally hard to decipher. Missionary views of Indigenous people as uncivilized are apparent in terminology used to describe us, including "néophites" (neophytes), "infidèles" (infidels), "la civilization des infidels" (civilization of infidels), "peuple barbare" (barbarians), and "les plus boeufs du globe" (the biggest oxen/cows on earth).[74] Their main subjects include confession, communion, and conversion of Indigenous people. Earlier correspondence does not always distinguish between Michif and First Nations people, using the term *sauvages* (savages) generally. Later letters distinguish Michif people from First Nations with names such as "Bois-Brulées," "Métifs," and "Métis."

Priests exaggerated their conversion successes and downplayed their struggles; not surprising, since they were writing to their superiors in Montreal who were responsible for funding their operations. The letters must be read critically for biases; despite these, evidence of Métis participation in Indigenous ceremonies can be found in such early correspondence.

Even when First Nations and Métis are recognized as distinct, similarities between them are noted, including ways of life, language, and resistance to conversion (sometimes openly mocking priests). In a letter written to the secretary of the bishop in Montreal in 1839, Father Belcourt discusses the difference between Christian Indigenous individuals and "infidels," and comments on the similarities between Métis and First Nations:

Un chrétien est peiné qu'on ne l'ai pas reconnue et un infidèle se moque de nous en nous virant le dos. Je ne parle pas de tous mais de tous ceux que je viens de visiter. Ils sont les plus bœufs du globe. . . . Msr. Thibault restant à la Fourche et Msr. Mérand à la Prairie du Cheval Blanc (août 1841). . . . J'ai confessé à la Baie des Canards 7 métis dont trois ont communé; donc 6 conf. Sauvages; je n'ai baptisai que des sauvages. J'aurais peut être dû observer que je ne baptise que les enfants au dessous de 7 ans. Mais cette année il sera facile de les préparer au baptême en grande partie parce qu'ils sont fort avancées dans leurs prières. . . . *La proportion est moitié metis moitié sauvage mais tous élevés à la façon sauvage et ne parlent que sauvage.*

(A Christian is pained when we do not recognize them as such and an infidel makes fun of us and turns their back on us. I'm not talking about all of them [Indigenous people] but all of the ones I just visited. They are the biggest oxen/cows on earth. . . . Monseigneur Thibault is staying at The Forks and Monseigneur Mérand is staying at White Horse Plains [St. François-Xavier] (August 1841). . . . At Duck Bay, I heard confession from seven Métis individuals of which three received communion; whereas I heard confession from six Indian individuals; I baptized only Indian individuals. I should have realized that I was baptizing only children under seven years old. But this year, it will be easier to prepare them collectively for baptism since they have come so far in their prayers. . . . *The proportion is half Métis and half Indian but all of them were raised as savages and speak only savage.*)[75]

The themes of similarities between Métis and First Nations, poor conversion rates, and mocking priests can be read in another excerpt by Father Belcourt; this time, he is recounting his recent canoe travel to Fort William (Thunder Bay, Ontario):

Le compagnon de ce simple [illegible] qu'on venait de passer était hiverné là. Il avait d'abord été écouté mais ayant voulu rire de la confession et des prêtres (c'est un sauvage qu'ils instruisaient) *tous les métifs comme les sauvages se retirèrent et n'y retournèrent plus.* Le commis en charge du poste se fâcha et voulu les forcer de venir aux instructions au moins une fois mais ils se moquèrent de lui comme du ministre et n'y allèrent [illegible] *il n'en baptisa pas un seul.*

(The companion of this simple [illegible] that we just passed was wintering there. He was listened to but he just wanted to laugh at confession and at priests (it was a savage that he was instructing), *all the Métis like the Indians are withdrawing and do not return.* The clerk in charge of the fort got angry and wanted to force them to come listen to Christian instruction at least once but they made fun of him as well as of the minister and do not go [illegible]; he was unable to baptize even a single person.)[76]

These same themes can be found in letters penned by Bishop Joseph-Norbert Provencher. Provencher was higher than Belcourt in the Catholic hierarchy and had less direct contact with Indigenous people. He gave frequent updates to the bishop in Montreal regarding the activities of priests in and around Red River including Fathers Belcourt, Darveau, and Thibault (who interacted directly with Indigenous people). Bishop Provencher was aware of struggles to convert Indigenous people who seemed non-committal, and he sometimes exaggerated their requests for priests in their communities. He refers to Indigenous peoples as "sauvages" and often does not attempt to distinguish between Métis and First Nations, or between specific nations among the latter, such as "Sauteux" (Saulteaux) or "Cris" (Cree) the way other priests did. Bishop Provencher occasionally gives an honest account of the challenges, indicating that even after years of instruction by a priest, some Métis and First Nations people refused Catholicism. We glimpse these struggles beneath Provencher's sugar-coated exaggerations here:

> Il est cependant vrai de dire et j'ai l'indicible satisfaction de vous en informer, Mgr., que l'opinion générale des Sauteuses est merveilleusement changé en faveur de la religion [Catholique]. . . . J'ai fait faire le jour de Pâques la première communion de Sauteuse *ils n'étaient que cinq qui étaient à l'épreuve depuis trois ans.*

> (It is certainly true to say that I have the unspeakable satisfaction of informing you, Monseigneur, that the general

opinion of the Saulteaux [Ojibwe] has marvellously changed in favour of the Catholic religion. . . . On Easter Day, I conducted the first communion for the Saulteaux but *there are only five people that have been participating for the last three years.*)[77]

Provencher indicates the Saulteaux opinion of Catholicism had marvellously improved despite only (the same?) five people participating in Easter Mass for three years. If this was a marvellous improvement, one wonders what the Saulteaux opinion of Catholicism had formerly been.

In a letter to Pierre-Flavien Turgeon, Bishop of Sidyme in Quebec, dated 1847, Bishop Provencher more honestly laments the lack of progress among "les sauvages" of White Horse Plains (recall that the population was mainly Red River Métis who had moved there from Pembina, North Dakota), despite Father Belcourt's incessant efforts. Provencher writes, "Les sauvages ont oubliés l'instruction des enfans mise de coté. Je lui ai entendu dire devant nous tous qu'il avait dit à ses paroisiens que leurs enfans ne savaient rien pas meme faire le signe de la croise." (The savages have forgotten the Catholic instruction of their children and put it aside. I heard him say in front of all of us that he said to his parishioners that their children did not know any Catholic teachings, not even how to perform the sign of the cross.)[78] The priests' lack of success was due to the persistence of Indigenous spirituality and Indigenous people's refusal to uphold Whiteness and settler colonialism.

The theme of ongoing adherence to Indigenous spirituality can also be found in early priests' correspondence. These instances are infrequent because clergy emphasize and embellish their successes with conversion in order to continue receiving funding. Between accounts of their activities, finances, and infrastructure, one can read the priests' disappointment.[79] In a letter written by Father Camper (while stationed in St. Laurent) to Archbishop Taché in 1868, we read of a large gathering of Indigenous people that he had hoped was for the purpose of hearing Catholic instruction but was, in fact, for Indigenous ceremony in the region of Duck Bay. He writes at length:

La plupart des catholiques de la Baie des Canards y étaient déjà rendus. J'y ai trouvé aussi un grand nombre de Sauvages. Les uns venaient de la Rivière aux Castors. . . . Dans quel dessein y étaient-ils venus? Était-ce pour se faire instruire dans la religion catholique? C'était leur moindre souci.... *Le principal but de leur passage à la Saline, était, je pense, de faire la Grade Médecine. Ils battaient le tambour et la nuit et le jour. La veille de leur départ une grande loge fut dressé. La médecine se fit en grand. Tous les Sauvages avaient la face vermillonnée. Ils en étaient tous fiers....* Les autres Sauvages que j'ai trouvés à la Saline, errent continuellement çà et là dans les environs de la Baie des Canards. N'étant pas catholique eux-mêmes, ou du moins ne l'étant que par leur baptême, ils aiment cependant à faire baptiser leurs enfants et à les faire instruire lorsqu'ils se trouvent dans l'occasion de voire le prêtre. A mon arrivée à la Saline, l'un d'eux nommé Wunswano, a été chercher ses enfants qu'il avait laissés derrière lui. La plupart de ses enfants ont été baptisés par le Révérend Père Simonet. Ils sont généralement assez bons catholiques. J'ai marié l'une de ses filles à un des garçons du view Napakisit. Ce vieux qui, je crois bien, n'a jamais été bien fort dans la pratique de la religion catholique, aujourd'hui y a renoncé complètement. Ces pauvres Sauvages font vraiment pitié. *Lorsqu'on leur parle de religion, ils semblent écouter volontiers, ils semblent convenir de tout, et cependant ils ne font pas le moindre effort pour abandonner leur sauvagerie.... Mais au milieu des faiseurs de médecine, tantôt ils prient et tantôt ils se mettent de connivence avec les faiseurs de médecine. La foi n'est pas bien vive dans les cœurs des Sauteux.*

(The majority of the Indigenous Catholics in Duck Bay had already arrived. There were also many "savages" [non-Christian Indigenous people] who had arrived. These ones had come from Beaver River.... For what purpose had all these Christian and non-Christian Indigenous people gathered here? Was it to be instructed in the teachings of the Catholic religion? This was the least of their concerns.... Their principal goal for converging on the Salt Springs was, I believe, to participate in *"la Grade Médecine"* [the Midewiwin Lodge]. *They beat their drums day and night. The evening before they departed, a grand lodge was dressed. The complex ceremony unfolded. Every savage had their face pained with ochre. They were all very proud....* The other savages that I found at the Salt Springs were continually here and there in Duck Bay and the surrounding regions. They were not Catholic, or they were only Catholic by virtue of their baptism; however, they are fond of having their children baptized and instructed in Catholicism whenever they have occasion to be visited by a priest. Upon my arrival, the one who goes by the name Wunswano was looking for his children, whom he had previously left behind. Most of his children had been baptized by Father Simonet and were generally good Catholics. I married one of his daughters to one of the sons of Old [Elder] Napakisit. This elder who, I believe, has never been strong in the Catholic religion, today renounced it completely. These poor savages are really to be pitied. When we speak to them about Catholicism, they appear to listen, they appear to agree with all this instruction, and yet, they do not make the slightest effort to abandon their savagery.... Rather, amidst their ceremony-makers, they pray, and they conspire with them. The [Catholic] faith is not strong in the hearts of these Saulteaux.)[80]

Father Camper's disappointment in Indigenous people's apparent ambivalence toward Christianization and their pursuit of Indigenous ceremonies is unmistakable. Despite his reference solely to Saulteaux people, Duck Bay was a known gathering place for Saulteaux, Métis, and some Swampy Cree people.[81] Individuals from these nations (especially the Métis) were likely also in attendance at the ceremony, as can be seen in the next excerpt.

The persistence of Indigenous spirituality, including among the Métis, can also be observed in an 1866 letter by Father Simonet, who congratulates himself for converting a Métis spiritual leader. Father Simonet describes travelling on the west side of Lake Manitoba to Duck Bay in the company of Métis guide Pierre Chartrand, when they encounter a Métis spiritual leader on his deathbed:

> Le malade était *un vieux métis, mais qui avait passé toute sa vie en véritable sauvage, croyant et pratiquant toutes les superstitions des sauvages. Il a même toujours passé pour un grand faiseur de médecine.* Il n'avait pas vu de prêtre depuis que le prêtre

[illegible] avait quitté le poste Manitoba, on ne savait même pas faire le signe de la croix. Quoi qu'il eût toujours dit qu'il voulait mourir come il avait vécu, en sauvage, il parut heureux de me voir. Je lui fis connaître en quelques mots, des principales vérités de notre religion. Il parut touché en apprenant que le Bon Dieu était prêt à lui pardonner toutes ses folies. Il renonça devant tout le monde à ses pratiques superstitieuses, fit un acte de joie sur toutes les vérités qu'il venait d'entendre et après sa confession, je lui donnai l'extrême onction.

(The sick person was *an old Métis [elder] but one who had lived his life as a veritable savage, believing and practising all the superstitions of savages. He has always been recognized as a powerful ceremony maker* [spiritual leader]. He had not seen a priest since the priest [illegible] left the Manitoba post; he did not even know how to make the sign of the cross. Despite always having said he wanted to die the way he lived, in savagery [according to Indigenous spiritual beliefs and customs], he appeared happy to see me. With a few words, I taught him some of the principal truths of our religion. He appeared touched when he learned that the Good Lord was ready to pardon all his sins. In front of the whole world [i.e., Father Simonet and his Métis guide], he renounced his Indigenous spirituality, out of joy at having just heard the truth about Catholicism, and, after his confession, I performed his last rites.)[82]

This Métis spiritual leader adhered to Indigenous spirituality all his life and only converted to Catholicism on his deathbed. When imminently facing the eternal unknown, it must sound appealing to hear your sins will be forgiven and you will be cared for in the afterlife if you renounce Indigenous spirituality for Catholicism—talk about getting people at their most vulnerable!

Contemporary Métis Adherence to Ceremonies

Pressures to assimilate Métis to Christianity were not always or wholly successful. Despite some people's insistence that Métis have only ever been Catholic (and do not smudge, sweat, etc.), some Métis individuals and families have always participated in ceremonies, and others, like

Figure 15. Author's wiidiigewin (union of souls) wedding ceremony, Lorette, Manitoba. Author's photo. Photo shared with permission from Midewiwin chief Ron Indian-Mandamin, Michif elders Charlotte Nolin (L) and Barbara Bruce (R), and Madix Photography.

my family, have more recently (re)committed to the spiritual ways of life of our ancestors (as hinted to in the priests' correspondence above).

My Michif wife and I had our *wiidiigewin* (union of souls) Midewiwin wedding ceremony on her family's land in their Métis community of Lorette (Figure 15). After our daughter was born, we buried the placenta and had a feast incorporating *asemaa* (tobacco), smudge, and a spirit dish on that same land. Likewise, we had a ceremony to bury our daughter's umbilical cord in my mother's Métis community of St. Laurent (Figure 16). We had a "Feet Touch the Earth" ceremony for her with earth that had been gathered for us by relatives from our communities (Figure 17). As a baby, our daughter spent time in a beautiful *tikinaagan* (cradleboard) made by my Anishinaabe Midewiwin Aunties Hilda Atkinson and Barb Smith (with help from Shannon and Ryan Gustafson). Our Michif friend, David Heinrichs, added stunning contemporary Métis-style beadwork with heavy influence from old-style Métis beadwork (Figure 18 and book cover). When our daughter first learned how to walk, we had a "Walking Out" ceremony at Normand Creek (named after my mother's family) in a park in St. Vital to honour her first steps upon the earth (Figure 19). Most recently, my wife and daughter came to greet me when I emerged from the Sundance arbour after completing my fourth year in August 2021.[83] We are now planning our daughter's (spirit) naming ceremony and look forward to other rites of passage ceremonies in the future—hopefully with our community now that COVID-19 vaccinations are available. These ceremonies ensure that our daughter remains connected to the land of her Métis ancestors and to her communities so she never forgets where she comes from, that her people love and support her, and that she is an important part of Creation with kinship responsibilities.

The importance of such ceremonies to my Michif family is not an anomaly among Métis people.[84] Written sources beyond priests' correspondence also confirm Métis participation in ceremonies historically and in the present. Below, I discuss texts highlighting the cultural continuity of Métis participation in ceremonies, especially in contemporary times.

Chapter 17 in *Metis Legacy II* (2006), published by Pemmican Publications and the Gabriel Dumont Institute, is dedicated to Métis spirituality. Chapter authors Lawrence Barkwell, Darren Préfontaine, and Anne Carrière-Acco note that Métis spirituality is "an important but neglected area of study" and that "most of the literature on Metis spiritualism . . . relates to the Metis' embrace of various forms of Christianity rather than to their Aboriginal spiritual practices."[85] They call for "a more in-depth explanation of the Metis peoples' traditional religion."[86] The chapter features guest author Nicholas Vrooman discussing Métis and Saulteaux (Anishinaabe) admission into the Iron Confederacy [Nêhiyaw-Pwat] via the gifting of the Sundance ceremony in the early 1800s, and a renewal of this alliance via the gifting of the "Unity of the People" Sundance song in 2003 (see Chapter 1).[87] Barkwell, Préfontaine, and Carrière-Acco also touch upon other Indigenous ceremonies that Métis people practised historically and into the present day, including birthing ceremonies, feasting and the preparation of spirit dishes, and mourning ceremonies. They state that "many Metis families still follow the First Nations' post-partum practice of taking the baby's placenta and burying it at the base of a young tree (usually cedar). If the birth occurs in winter, the placenta is kept frozen until spring and then the ritual is performed. Once the umbilical cord separates, this is placed in the branches of a tree for boys, and in the crotch of a tree or buried on a small rise for girls. This is so that boys

Figure 16. Burying the umbilical cord, author and daughter, St. Laurent, Manitoba. Author's photo.

will become good hunters and girls will be fertile."[88] On the topic of feasting ceremonies and spirit dishes, they note: "It is a Metis custom that during the large holiday meals an extra plate would always be set at the table with the best of everything—foods, cutlery and dinnerware. After the meal, the food was put into the fire for 'those who went before us."[89] Red River Métis researcher Carol Leclair agrees that "feasting is a fine old Metis tradition."[90] Barkwell, Préfontaine, and Carrière-Acco also highlight Métis participation in Indigenous mourning ceremonies: "Some Metis people cut their hair as a sacrifice in honour of the one who has died."[91]

In her dissertation on Métis environmental knowledge, Leclair discusses her participation in birthing ceremonies which include plant medicines, smudging, singing, and drumming.[92] She shares the story of when her grandchildren were born: "I carried my drum into the labour and delivery room of the hospital. A little smudge of sweetgrass was allowed. I sang a birth song to each of these babies, a few hours after they took their first breaths, a special song meant only for each of them. I knew by the tears in their parents' eyes that together we had rightly

Figure 17. Author's wife and their daughter during a Feet Touch the Earth ceremony. We modified our postpartum ceremonies as a safety precaution against COVID-19. Author's photo.

Figure 18. Author's daughter in her tikinaagan (cradleboard). Author's photo. For a close up of the Métis-style beadwork, see book cover.

Figure 19. Author, her wife, and their daughter during her Walking Out ceremony.
Photo credit: Andrea Clarke.

honoured these new spirits."[93] Leclair goes to ceremonies wearing her
"Métis clothing" and follows protocol.[94] While she indicates that she
finds "strength in contemporary expressions of Anishinaabe spirituality,"[95] she discusses feasting, gifting, and tobacco as an offering[96] as
aspects of her Métis culture and approach to research.[97]

The ceremonies and spiritual identity illustrated above can be
found among other contemporary Métis people (Figures 15–19).[96] For
example, Elmer Ghostkeeper's *Spirit Gifting: The Concept of Spiritual
Exchange*, includes his Métis Cree world view.[98] Another example is
found in "Métis Spiritualism," wherein authors Darren Préfontaine,
Todd Paquin, and Patrick Young claim that "it is impossible to discern
a common Métis religion and spiritualism. For instance, many Métis
orient themselves toward traditional Aboriginal spiritualism, while
others are adherents of Roman Catholicism and various Protestant
denominations; and still others blend Christianity with Aboriginal
spiritualism."[99] According to the authors, the Métis historically adhered
to either "Aboriginal spiritualism" or to a denomination of Christianity,
with Michif-speaking Roman Catholics having a more favourable
opinion of Aboriginal spiritualism than the "Country Born" or English
Métis.[100]

Cultural continuity of Métis participation in ceremonies is also evident in the 2006 Aboriginal Peoples Survey and its Métis supplement.[101] According to the survey, many Métis adults are "very or moderately spiritual" and have "combined traditional Aboriginal spiritualism and Roman Catholicism."[102] The results found that the spiritual and religious practices of Métis are diverse, with some maintaining their well-being "through prayer (36%), attending church (30%), meditation (20%), talking with elders (15%), participating in pilgrimages (5%), or attending sweat lodges (4%). Just over 20% of all Métis used some 'other' means of maintaining religious/spiritual wellbeing."[103]

The results of a research study published in 2020 also illustrate cultural continuity of Métis participation in ceremonies. In their article "Métis Women Gathering: Visiting Together and Voicing Wellness for Ourselves," Métis authors Anna Flaminio, Janice Cindy Gaudet, and Leah Dorion discuss their study wherein fifty-four Métis women learned about Métis women's knowledge. The women participated in cultural activities and ceremonies, including "(a) two Métis women's full moon ceremonies; (b) Métis women's firebag [pouch/bag for holding pipe, tobacco, flint, medicines, etc.] teachings; (c) Métis sewing teachings; (d) Métis buffalo teachings; and (e) Métis tea teachings as shared by [Leah Dorion]."[104] While acknowledging the "maternal Métis ancestral connections to Cree and Saulteaux ceremonies and teachings from within the prairie region,"[105] the authors identify the events and ceremonies as "*Métis-specific* teachings."[106]

~

Alongside the oral history (described in Chapter 1), the written accounts detailed in this chapter leave no doubt that Métis spirituality included ceremonies historically and continues to do so. Correspondence of the earliest clergy to arrive in Red River provide evidence of this—despite their dogged pursuit of Métis conversion from birth (baptisms) until death (last rites). The priests' inability to distinguish between Métis and First Nations, similarities across Anishinaabe, Nêhiyaw, and Michif cultures, resistance to conversion, and ongoing adherence to Indigenous spirituality are evident in this correspondence. These letters also illustrate syncretism: Métis (and First Nations) people adhering to a blend of Indigenous spirituality and Catholicism, favouring one or the other when it suited them (e.g., Catholicism when a priest was available, and Indigenous spirituality when ceremonies were underway).[107] The arrival of Catholic missionaries in and around Red River resulted in unprecedented growth in the church's infrastructure from 1818 to 1870 and ensured that Catholicism became a dominant colonial force in the lives of many Métis.[108]

Despite the increasingly overwhelming influence of the church, some Métis continued to participate in ceremonies—and still do today. This is confirmed in contemporary sources, including publications by the Manitoba Metis Federation in collaboration with the Gabriel Dumont Institute.[109] While the evidence is indisputable, a gap in knowledge regarding Métis participation in ceremonies remains in the archives, literature, and oral history. The topic is misunderstood by many, including by some Métis and First Nations people. In the following pages, I hope to close this gap and correct harmful misinformation with findings from my study. I begin by outlining my research design in the next chapter.

CHAPTER 3

A Métis-Centred Study and Approach

When I conducted my doctoral research, I could not find publications or templates for Métis-specific methodologies regarding a topic remotely like mine that I could draw upon. A growing field of Métis scholars had been emerging, but as far as I could tell, many were adhering to existing methodologies used in specific disciplines such as history. I found examples of culturally specific approaches to research used by other (non-Métis) Indigenous researchers and learned much from them. I tried to create an approach that resonated with my topic, the Métis participants, and myself. I have refined my methodological approach in this study. Together, my efforts in *Rekindling* and in this book result in a Métis-specific research approach; I offer this methodology as an example for other (Métis) scholars to build upon.

Below, I briefly summarize the approach I crafted in my first book before sharing more recent publications in the development of Métis methodological approaches. I also discuss my experiences with the research ethics protocol developed by the Manitoba Metis Federation (MMF). Next, I highlight changes to my approach, which I now refer to as a *Métis-specific* research design and methodology. I explain choices I made in my earlier approach and my motivations for modifying it, including an effort to counter *raceshifters* and *self-Indigenization*. By this I am referring to White settlers (especially along the eastern seaboard of North America) newly identifying as Indigenous, often specifically Métis—so-called Eastern metis and Acadian metis.[1]

Methodological Approach in *Rekindling*

Unable to locate Métis-specific methodologies when designing my approach in *Rekindling*, I learned from non-Métis Indigenous researchers, who remind us that the strongest Indigenous approaches are nation-specific and place-specific.[2] I listened when they spoke of the importance of obtaining community direction, ensuring our research will benefit our communities and lands, and countering harmful messages about us by highlighting the positive in our communities.[3] I crafted what I called a Métis Anishinaabe research design and methodology that incorporated teachings I learned in ceremony to help me examine Métis relationships with Indigenous spirituality.

In an effort to be accountable to all my relations, I situated myself in the research by naming my ancestors, teachers, and relationships to community and land, and shared my spirit name, clan, and kinship connections at every opportunity, including in my previous book.[4] I approached Métis and First Nations community members in my life and invited suggestions for research topics, and heeded my cousin Chubby's call to focus on the Métis.[5] I also offered *asemaa* (tobacco) in prayer and asked for guidance from Spirit and participated in a four-day fast in Hollow Water First Nation. I was gifted with a dream that helped me realize that one of my roles was to support Métis in finding their way back to ceremonies.[6] In these ways, I came to my research topic, which aimed to "uncover experiences and factors that influence people with Métis ancestry to pursue Anishinaabe spirituality and explore how this relationship influences identity."[7]

In fashioning my research design, I combined Western research tools with Métis Anishinaabe world views, protocols, teachings, and values. I identified selected concepts and teachings that influenced my world view (ontology), relationship to knowledge (epistemology), values and ethics (axiology), and approach to research (methodology).[8] These concepts included the Niizhwaaswi Ishkodekaan (Seven Fires Prophecy) and the Oshkibimaadiziig (New People) and my belief that Métis people have much to contribute to this important work.[9] I was also drawn to the concepts of *mikwayndaasowin* and *mino-bimaadiziwin*,[10] and to the importance of decolonizing our minds and lives. I took seriously the responsibility to conduct research that benefits the greater good,[11] that incorporates relational accountability and the ethic of reciprocity.[12] I understood that knowledge can come from texts and people, from dreams, prayer, plant medicine, and ceremony.[13] As Midewiwin, I began every day with an *asemaa* (tobacco) and *nibi* (water) ceremony to set the course of my day, and try to live in gratitude and balance even in research.[14]

Western elements rounded out my approach, including quota sampling,[15] semi-structured interviews, thematic coding,[16] and NVivo qualitative research software. Eighteen people with Red River Métis ancestry who participate in Indigenous ceremonies shared their stories with me.[17] I also mobilized "prayerfully intuitive" analysis to make sense of the data by remaining open to guidance through prayer, petitions to Spirit, sacred medicines, and participation in ceremony.[18]

Developments in Métis Methodology

A few trailblazing Métis scholars have put forth excellent examples of Métis-specific methodologies since *Rekindling* came out. I have also become aware of a handful of other relevant approaches, especially in health studies, and some to be avoided;[19] together, these texts are helping to build a canon on Métis methodologies. The MMF has also been hard at work in designing a Métis research ethics protocol for researchers working with the Manitoba Métis community.

I am excited about several Métis research models that came out after *Rekindling*.[20] In her doctoral research, Amanda LaVallee collaborated with Métis Nation-Saskatchewan's Health Branch Director Dr. Tara Turner and Assistant Director Cheryl Troupe in examining tuberculosis in Saskatchewan Métis communities. The team combined a Euro-Western computer science–based participatory methodology with Métis research methods, ethics, and knowledge. Focusing on Métis communities, they aimed to be culturally responsive and used a reflexive practice involving their stakeholders to analyze their data. Highlighting the challenges and rewards of Métis community-based research, Troupe and Turner admit to pushing LaVallee "harder than we might have pushed other researchers because she is a Métis woman, a Métis researcher, and we knew that her work would impact our Métis communities."[21] The pair encouraged LaVallee to confront her unconscious desire to privilege Western methodological aspects over Métis ones. LaVallee realized she did this out of insecurity: "feeling as though *I was not Métis enough to engage in Métis methods* . . . as though my fair skin and education disenfranchised me from my Métis knowledge and culture."[22]

Métis scholar Janice Cindy Gaudet offers another valuable example of a community-based research methodology that privileges Métis (and Cree) world view, knowledge, and communities. Her approach, *keeoukaywin* (the visiting way), emerged in relationship with Omushkego (Swampy Cree) people of Moose Cree First Nation, with the support of Métis (and Cree) elders, scholars, and her family during her doctoral research. She explains, "With relationality at its core, keeoukaywin re-centres Métis and Cree ways of being, and presents a practical and meaningful methodology that fosters milo pimatisiwin [*mino-bimaadiziwin*], living and being well in relation."[23] *Keeoukaywin* ensures wellness in Métis families and is connected to Indigenous resurgence and relationship with the land. The term was gifted to her in the Cree language and led her to "the visiting way as a Métis way of life."[24] Gaudet's "visiting way" places importance on self-reflexivity as a decolonizing approach to research methodologies. Characteristics of this concept, way of life, and approach to research include hospitality, teaching, reciprocity, "sharing emotions, knowledge, ideas, food from the land," laws of visiting, and responsibility.[25] She elaborates: "The way of visiting is part of a land-based society's way of life," and "visiting may seem on the surface to be a passive and apolitical activity, but it is, in fact, political, re-centring authority in a way of relating that is itself rooted in a cultural, spiritual, and social context."[26] Gaudet explains that visiting as a way of being is gendered, often being taught by women who are "responsible for the governance of their households"[27] and whose authority is often overlooked as a "key factor in the transmission of knowledge."[28] She states that this "visiting way" illuminates "special times and spaces in which connections are strengthened, stories are heard, remembering occurs, and we are reminded of who we are and of our responsibility for the well-being of the whole."[29] Gaudet cautions that *keeoukaywin* should not be confused with the notion of relationship building in other community-based and participatory action research methodologies, because the latter focus on problems and solutions or outcomes, while the former trusts in a "process with unforeseen or unscripted outcomes,"[30] leaving room for unpredictability, empathy for all beings, and gender balance.[31]

Métis scholars Anna Flaminio, Janice Gaudet, and Leah Dorion put forth an exciting Métis-specific research methodology via their study on Métis women's wellness in the St. Louis region of Saskatchewan. Their approach is community-engaged, uses "visiting" as a methodology along with mixed methods such as participant engagement, evaluation forms, ceremony, gatherings, semi-structured interviews, and learning-by-doing,[32] and recognizes that transmission of knowledge is gendered. The researchers located fifty-four Métis women known to them to participate in their study (thirteen are interviewed). They created a tree diagram with their objectives written into the roots, branches, leaves, and trunk prior to meeting the Métis women community leaders; then, together with the women, they filled in the research activities.[33] Their approach relies heavily on concepts such as *wahkotowin* (kinship roles, responsibilities, and behaving in culturally appropriate ways) and *kiyokewin* (visiting responsibilities).[34] As mentioned in the previous chapter, Flaminio, Gaudet, and Dorion "focused on Métis conceptions of kinship relationships" while also acknowledging their "intertwined maternal Métis ancestral connection to Cree and Saulteaux ceremonies and teachings from within the prairie region."[35] The research team began their meetings with prayer and conducted their data analysis in multiple readings, then validated their findings by revisiting the women. They "included the names of the participants as part of an Indigenous methodology to honour the lives of the women and their kinship system."[36]

These Métis researchers all use ceremonies as part of their approach; for example, they figure prominently in Flaminio, Gaudet, and Dorion's methodology. Elsewhere, Gaudet has shared that when she approached Moose Factory Cree Nation for research purposes, a community member respectfully told her she knew nothing about his people and invited her to a sweat lodge ceremony.[37] In the sweat lodge, she received the message that she must ask the community to help her with her research, since she needed their help more than they needed hers. Gaudet also participated in a fasting ceremony during her research process.[38] Métis researcher Carol Leclair also discusses ceremonies as part of her approach to her doctoral research; she notes that Métis researchers may choose to include multidisciplinary approaches in their research, including "traditional methods, such as gatherings, Elders' knowledge, stories, celebrations, and ceremonies."[39] She states that Métis researchers can employ "storytelling, rituals, dances, music and songs, ceremonies and many invisible protocols."[40] She used a model of a dreamcatcher to organize her research approach and refers to the dreamcatcher as a "Saulteaux/Metis tradition."[41] Rather than relying on a lone researcher, she explains, her model of inquiry includes "ancestors, Elders, traditionalists, dancers, singers, language teachers, artists, in fact the whole of creation."[42] She elaborates that "smudging with sage, a women's medicine, is always part of my research practices," and that in her work, "ceremony and ritual are not subject to explication, rather they are allowed to shine through, woven in without analysis, not disrupting the text but acting as a condition which allows the text to be produced."[43] Moreover, Leclair uses feasting, gifting, and tobacco as an offering as part of her Métis-specific research.[44]

Health studies are also contributing to Métis-specific methodologies. In 2009, the Prairie Women's Health Centre of Excellence (PWHCE) published a paper titled "Métis-Specific Gender-Based Analysis Framework for Health."[45] The paper details the methodology used to develop the framework—including a multi-method community review process with Métis community women to review and comment on an early draft of the framework. This culturally relevant framework is meant to be used by Health Canada, the federal government, Métis governments and people, and others more broadly, and highlights the need for a Métis-specific gender-based analysis.

In 2010, the National Aboriginal Health Organization (NAHO) released a document titled "Principles of Ethical Métis Research" that resulted from a think tank hosted by the Métis Centre that targeted Métis researchers, students, and organizations across Canada in a dialogue about Métis-specific research ethics. The document includes six Métis-specific principles of health research.[46] It is encouraging to see gender- and sexual identity–based analyses being promoted in Métis-specific research frameworks and ethics such as these.

Another Métis-specific research framework can be found in the *Citizen Engagement in Health Casebook* of the Canadian Institutes of Health Research (CIHR); specifically in Case 8, "The Use of a Holistic Wellness Framework and Knowledge Networks in Métis Health Planning."[47] This case study describes an effort by the MMF and scholars to mobilize a framework for interpreting chronic diseases research and adapting programs and services for Métis citizens.[48]

One more health-specific example, published by the University of Manitoba, is titled *Framework for Research Engagement with First Nation, Metis, and Inuit Peoples*.[49] The framework offers a set of objectives, principles for collaboration, and areas for action which amount to a systemic process for engagement to ensure that Indigenous knowledges are incorporated and valued by researchers. Among the document's appendices are distinct research protocols for collaborating with First Nations, Métis, and Inuit peoples. Appendix 4 of the document, "Metis Research Protocols," offers a list of ethical principles for Métis research (Ownership, Control, Access, and Stewardship) and a "Metis Algorithm"—a step-by-step process for researchers interested in collaborating with the MMF to conduct health-based research with Manitoba Métis people. Together, the successful applicant and the MMF decide upon one of three levels of engagement: full (MMF is a co-researcher); partial (letter of support, and MMF facilitates contact with Manitoba Métis); or minimal (letter of support from MMF). The Metis Research Protocols were influenced by the Métis-specific casebook produced for CIHR, discussed above.[50]

Lastly, while it is not Métis-specific, *Sources and Methods in Indigenous Studies*, edited by Chris Andersen and Jean O'Brien (2017), contains three chapters written by Métis scholars. Chris Andersen (with Tahu Kukutai) examines developments in quantitative research (especially statistical analysis) that make space for Indigenous agency. Sherry Farrell Racette (with Alan Corbiere and Crystal Migwans) questions whether there is something inherently or uniquely Indigenous about how Indigenous historians approach material culture research. And Brenda Macdougall (with Nicole St-Onge) concentrates on historical texts describing Métis societies that transcended the U.S.–Canada international border and suggests connecting the history of these Métis societies to a transborder narrative of the northern plains within a framework of borderlands theory and methodology.

Métis-specific developments pertaining to research methods and methodologies are arising across diverse subject areas and disciplines. Health research is making a notable contribution to Métis-specific methodologies, as seen in the work done by NAHO, PWHCE, and CIHR described above. In addition to my own research, other Métis researchers such as Flaminio, Gaudet, and Dorion are incorporating ceremonies into their methodologies.[51] In addition to NAHO's "Principles of Ethical Métis Research,"[52] the MMF has also put forward protocol regarding Métis research ethics.

The Manitoba Metis Federation's Research Ethics Protocol

The MMF has been promoting Métis self-determination on several fronts, including via the development of the Manitoba Metis Community Research Ethics Protocol (MMCREP). The Tripartite Self-Government Negotiation (TSN) Department of the MMF began implementing the MMCREP in late 2016. Scholars wishing to undertake research involving Manitoba Métis citizens and communities were encouraged to submit a Request for Research Engagement application via the MMCREP.[53] Successful researchers received a Letter of Support from the MMF and could proceed to develop a Memorandum of Collaboration (MoC) signed between the researcher, their institution (if affiliated with one), and the MMF. The MoC outlines the roles, responsibilities, obligations, and rights of each party, as well as the expected level of involvement of the MMF in the research study itself. While the MMCREP did not exist when I was conducting research and writing *Rekindling*, I was one of the first two researchers to apply to the MMCREP when I began work for *Returning*.[54]

I embarked on the MMCREP journey with the hopes of being more Métis- and community-centred in my methodology for my current study. I contacted the TSN Department responsible for MMCREP and began forming a research relationship with the then-director, which I continue to find valuable. My "Request for Research Engagement" form was reviewed by the TSN Steering Committee and the MMF Caucus/Cabinet;[55] my research study was approved. The TSN contacted the vice-president (VP) for each of the MMF regions in Manitoba that would be impacted by my study to inform them of who I was, where I work, what my study was about, the community researchers (CRs) I hoped to hire, and my goals. This provided an opportunity for the VPs to ask questions and obtain clarification from the TSN. Next, the TSN Director arranged for an in-person meeting at the MMF Head Office between herself, the VPs, and me. Two of the four VPs in question opted for this meeting; I met the remaining two VPs at the next MMF Annual General Assembly.

Each VP asked me additional questions about my study and made suggestions. One suggestion was to split the communities of Duck Bay and Camperville and study them separately, assigning each their own

CR; I had originally planned to study these two communities together (see Chapter 4). A Métis community member from Duck Bay was suggested by one of the VPs (since the CR I had originally suggested was from Camperville). I contacted this person and she agreed to be the CR for Duck Bay; she became an invaluable asset to the study. Once their questions and suggestions had been addressed, each VP welcomed me to begin my fieldwork in the Métis communities in their region and helped identify potential participants.[56]

Unfortunately, in 2019, after thirty-one years in operation, the TSN Department was discontinued because of funding cuts by Manitoba's Conservative government. At the 2019 MMF Annual General Assembly, the former director of the TSN shared with me that the MMF wanted to maintain existing relationships with the (approximately eighteen) researchers who were in varying stages of the MMCREP process.[57] She encouraged me to continue sending researchers to the MMF who are interested in conducting research in Manitoba Métis communities. It is unclear how the MMF will continue this work given the closure of the TSN. I hope they are successful, because the MMCREP facilitates ethical research, ensures benefits, rights, and obligations are respected and enjoyed by all stakeholders, and promotes Métis-centred research.

It is important to be welcomed into community and to meaningfully collaborate with community members; this is also true of Métis researchers conducting research in Métis communities. Leclair asserts that Métis researchers must be "known and accepted" in Métis communities and that "becoming known and trusted takes years, family connections, cultural knowledge, gas money and a good car!"[58] She explains that as insiders, Métis researchers enter into research relationships with humility and responsibility, "since we do not usually get to leave the field once our project is completed" and Métis researchers should report back to the people understanding that "sharing knowledge is rarely a one-time event, as in delivering a document. . . . [I]t is a continuous process which can last for years."[59] Collaborating with the MMF and the six Métis CRs has helped ensure that I work within Métis communities in an ethical way.

I turn now to a detailed discussion of my own ongoing efforts to develop a Métis methodology to examine Métis relationships with ceremony. I hope the approach I offer will benefit other Métis scholars and be adapted to suit the needs of other research projects that enhance quality of life among the Métis.

Refining My Métis Methodology

In offering an example of a Métis methodology, I want to highlight what has changed in my approach since my first study and what has remained consistent. Importantly, the changes reflect my desire to create a more Métis-specific and community-centred approach. I also identify the motivations for the decisions I have made.

I called my previous process a "Métis Anishinaabe research design and methodology." I began my *Midewit* (Midewiwin initiate) journey at the same time as I was undertaking the doctoral research that formed the basis for *Rekindling*. I had been adopted as a daughter by Midewiwin Chief Mizhakwanagiizhik, Charlie Nelson.[60] The adoption meant that I belonged to the *biizhew doodem* (lynx clan).[61] I had also been taking Anishinaabemowin (Ojibwe language) courses. My spiritual and cultural education led to concepts that underpinned my methodology (e.g., Niizhwaaswi Ishkodekaan and Oshkibimaadiziig). Viewing these concepts from a Métis perspective, I listened for what they might have to say to Métis people. This made sense on personal (ancestral), historical, and cultural levels given the intermarriage between the Métis and Anishinaabeg (Saulteaux) on the prairies, the fact that the Anishinaabeg are a parent culture of the Métis,[62] and that the Métis were (are) multilingual and spoke Anishinaabemowin.[63] This approach was strengthened as I uncovered evidence that historically, Métis had participated in the Midewiwin lodge (Chapters 1 and 2). These concepts and values continue to resonate in my life and in my research methodology; however, my approach has evolved with new experiences and motivations.

One important new experience has been my journey, begun in 2017, as a Sundancer with the Blacksmith Sundance, which is carried by Chiefs David and Sherryl Blacksmith. The lodge has been passed down through Sherryl's Anishinaabe family (Swan Lake First Nation), but David is Ininiw (Cree) from Cross Lake First Nation and a fluent Cree-speaker; therefore, many of the teachings are Cree. This has enabled me to feel closer to a part of my own identity and ancestry, as my maternal great-grandparents were Cree speakers (who also spoke

Michif and Saulteaux [Anishinaabemowin]). I have a responsibility to ensure the Sundance and Midewiwin continue into the future; I hope my books motivate others (especially Métis) to return to these lodges.

My aim for a more Métis-specific and community-centred approach is reflected in the new description of my research design and methodology as "Métis-centred." The evolution of my approach reflects my ongoing journey of learning what it means to be Métis and my growing understanding of Métis spirituality. I now understand that Métis identity and Métis spirituality include participation in ceremonies in their own right. I am also motivated by the new publications by Métis scholars discussed in these pages, and by a desire to counter raceshifting.

Raceshifting is the process whereby White settlers discover (or fabricate) a long-ago Indigenous ancestor in their family tree and begin identifying as Indigenous—literally settler self-Indigenizing. They identify as "métis" because they use the incorrect and harmful "Métis = mixed (race)" definition.[64] This phenomenon is centred in eastern Ontario, Quebec, and the maritime provinces (the so-called Eastern metis and Acadian metis), where there were no Métis communities historically. Métis and settler scholars have been exposing this phenomenon and the deceptive tactics used to enable and justify White settler claims to Indigeneity.[65]

Raceshifters fail the Powley Test for determining Métis identity, community, and Métis-specific section 35 rights.[66] They fail to prove the existence of a historic and contemporary Métis community in eastern Canada—one judge went as far as saying it would be "easier to nail Jell-O to the wall."[67] Instead of community evidence, raceshifters rely entirely upon purported relationships with Indigenous individuals (often from nations without a historic or contemporary relationship with the Métis Nation) who have been dead for hundreds of years—they are literally "communing with the dead."[68] These settlers lack relationships with living Métis people, and the Métis Nation does not accept them.[69]

Raceshifting represents a threat to Métis identity, self-determination (including regarding spirituality), and to the Métis Nation. If anyone can claim to be Métis, then Métis identity, citizenship, and rights become meaningless. Specifically, Métis history, culture, language, our homeland, and communities all become minimized, erased, and replaced by random individuals unconnected to us. Raceshifting exemplifies White supremacy and White privilege: a blinding sense of entitlement justifies (in their own minds) White settlers' theft of Métis identity and rights (along with jobs, awards, scholarships, etc.).[70] Moreover, by gaining intervenor status in Supreme Court cases, raceshifters are attempting to negotiate Métis rights in a way that benefits White settler colonialism. Tuck and Yang explain that co-opting Indigenous identity and rights are examples of "moves to innocence"[71]—tactics mobilized to absolve settler guilt, mask White privilege, and promote White supremacist colonization.[72]

When I wrote *Rekindling*, raceshifting had not hit mainstream awareness, Leroux's ground-breaking book, *Distorted Descent*, had not yet been released, and the Métis Nation was just beginning to intensify its resistance to this threat.[73] At the time I was more concerned about narrow definitions of "Métis" that ignored the complexity of Métis, Anishinaabe, and Nêhiyaw relationships (by holding to the criterion that one must be wholly distinct from other Indigenous nations) and did not honour ongoing relationships across our nations.[74] For the reasons described above, I am now taking an unequivocal stance against raceshifting and have tried to refine a Métis methodology that honours Métis Nation self-determination.

My efforts to be Métis-centred and community-centred in my current research design and methodology can be seen, for example, in my criteria for selecting participants and communities, my choice of ethics protocols and community researchers, and in sharing of findings in the communities. In the research for my previous book, one criterion for participation was simply to have "Métis ancestry," which I thought left room for the overlap in culture and intermarriage among Métis, Anishinaabe, and Nêhiyaw in Manitoba. In the research for this book, the criterion for participation was Métis identity as defined by the Métis National Council (MNC): *"Métis" means a person who self-identifies as Métis, is distinct from other Aboriginal peoples, is of historic Métis Nation Ancestry and who is accepted by the Métis Nation."*[75] While the cultural overlap between Métis and other Indigenous identities still exists (and can be seen in the lived experience of some of the participants), I honour the MNC definition of Métis to counter raceshifters and uphold Métis sovereignty.

The second criterion for individuals to participate, linked to the first, was to have a connection to one of six historic Métis communities chosen for this study: Duck Bay, Camperville, St. Laurent, St.

François-Xavier, Lorette, and Ste. Anne. These selected communities emerged as Métis in the early days of Métis nationhood.[76] Connection to the community could be in the form of childhood and/or adult residence, having relatives who reside there, or through an historic familial connection such as having relatives buried in the cemetery or familial Métis scrip for land in the community. The final criterion for participation was taking part in Indigenous ceremonies. I did not define ceremonies or a time frame for being involved in them, since this can vary considerably (Chapter 10). These three criteria for selecting participants ensured that the research design was centred on citizens of the Métis Nation connected to legitimate historic Métis communities.

In another effort to refine a Métis- and community-centred approach, I hired six Métis community researchers (CRs): Gloria Campbell (Duck Bay), Ron Richard (Camperville), Jacinthe Lambert (St. Laurent), Julia Lafreniere (St. François-Xavier), Nicki Ferland (Lorette), and Amanda Burton (Ste. Anne). These individuals are Métis citizens and are themselves connected to at least one of the six Métis communities in the ways described above. The CRs had varying levels of experience as researchers (from none to graduate-level experience) and all are active members of their Métis communities. Their participation in this study has resulted in knowledge mobilization, both through their own research experience as well as through working with other Métis citizens to learn more about Métis spirituality and debunk stereotypes. The CRs provided invaluable assistance throughout the study: they helped modify interview questions, developed a recruitment strategy specific to each community, conducted interviews, collaborated on data analysis, helped organize and deliver presentations of findings in the six Métis communities, and facilitated ongoing communication and feedback.

In the beginning, I had personal connections to only half of the Métis communities selected for this study (St. Laurent, Ste. Anne, and Lorette). The CRs' pre-existing community relationships (especially to the other three communities—Duck Bay, Camperville, and St. François-Xavier) were crucial. They introduced me to community members, suggested potential participants from their community who met the criteria for participation, and advertised the presentations of findings, ensuring their success. Their personal experiences and intimate knowledge of their Métis community enabled them to provide culturally sensitive and community-specific insights throughout the study.

Together with the MMF's MMCREP process, the Métis CRs helped ensure that I adhered to Métis-specific ethics and remained accountable by obtaining permission from the Métis government, and by respectfully engaging with Métis citizens from their communities. I agree with Leclair that Métis research should reflect Métis ethical conduct via a practice that "recognize[s] Metis people as the guardians of their customary knowledge; accepts that they have the right to protect and control dissemination of that knowledge; understands that they have the right to create new knowledge based on cultural traditions; [and] acknowledges that the first beneficiaries of Metis knowledge must be Metis people."[77] I aspire to these ethical standards throughout my research endeavours.

As with my previous research, I aimed for semi-structured interviews with participants; however, my understanding of our encounters has grown.[78] While the CRs and I approached the Métis people in this study with a list of questions, what emerged were dialogic conversations, with both parties sharing personal stories and experiences "off script." Together, the stories shared across these six Métis communities illustrate Métis orality, oral history, and storytelling on personal and community levels. Métis scholar Jennifer Adese reminds us of the "importance of reading localized Métis stories"[79] and of recognizing "Métis life stories as teachings for contemporary Métis."[80] She notes "the value of remembering stories, of recording stories to reflect Métis realities to the wider world, and also of recording them for future generations of Métis," and that Métis folks who share their stories in print "form relationships with their readership, entrusting their stories to them. They enable a re-knowing, re-claiming of Métisness."[81] Adese points out that such stories "contribute to the collective memory of Métis":[82] Métis storytellers "bridge the generations, weaving in stories of their ancestors and allowing their words to stand as the collective hopes and dreams for the future of Métis."[83]

Similarly, Leclair discusses the importance of Métis people telling their own stories and notes that Métis stories are "evidence of the ways we relate to the world around us. Producing this evidence is part of the process of decolonization."[84] She continues, "Metis people are great talkers. The ability to persuade the heart and mind has always been our gift. Oration comes easily to us, within our homes, at ceremonies, traditional dances, and seminars held in church basements," and "the words we use in song, ceremony and sharing give life to our personal and communal aspirations for our children."[85] Leclair comments on gathering Métis stories within a research context, noting that "those who share their stories most often place great value on extended conversations, on the quality of interaction between the teller and the listener. The relationship between storyteller and Metis researcher is primary."[86] She reminds us that "developing an atmosphere of trust [and] openness can take a few days or a few years, depending on the individual.[87] Oral traditions still exist in Metis life. Telling stories and personal histories is still a part of our day-to-day realities."[88]

Cree scholar Maggie Kovach adds the notion of "'collaborative storying' which positions the researcher as a participant. As both parties become engaged in a collaborative process, the relationship builds and deepens as stories are shared."[89] She elaborates: "When used in an Indigenous framework, a conversational method invokes several distinctive characteristics: a) it is linked to a particular tribal epistemology (or knowledge) and situated within an Indigenous paradigm; b) it is relational; c) it is purposeful (most often involving a decolonizing aim); d) it involves particular protocol as determined by the epistemology and/or place; e) it involves an informality and flexibility; f) it is collaborative and dialogic; and g) it is reflexive."[90] This resonates with the approach I have taken in this study, including founding it upon a Métis world view, aiming to decolonize views of Métis spirituality and contribute to a resurgence in Métis participation in ceremonies, adhering to Métis-specific ethics (such as the MMF's MMCREP), and being community-centred and collaborative (especially with the help of the CRs) as well as relational and reflexive. Most of the Métis people in this study opted to use their real names. Adese notes that this is "an important practice within Métis oral traditions; people need to identify themselves and their family, 'community and place, before continuing on to speak to issues of interest to contemporary Métis.'"[91]

Regarding sampling (the method for selecting participants), I knew it would be difficult to fill quotas (e.g., for age and gender) in small communities that might have few people who participate in ceremonies. Therefore, instead of quota sampling, I began with convenience sampling (selecting participants known to me or the CRs), then used snowball sampling (asking participants to suggest additional contacts). Regarding data analysis, I sent interview transcripts and quotes to every participant who wanted to review these for accuracy and addressed any modifications they requested.[92] Then, I used thematic coding with NVivo qualitative research software along with prayerful/intuitive analysis to understand the data. The latter involved ongoing participation in ceremonies, guidance from Spirit, listening to dreams, and use of sacred medicines.[93] I also met with the CRs to discuss the data and listened to their insight, given their intimate knowledge of their home community (and across all the communities).

My participation in ceremonies remained consistent across both studies as I strive for *mino-bimaadiziwin* and hope my books promote this in others. I began both projects with a four-day fast in Hollow Water First Nation, seeking guidance from Spirit. And just as I was Midewit (Midewiwin initiate) during my first study, I began my Sundance journey during this new study. My research is inextricable from my spiritual/ceremonial life and vice versa—both are strengthened as a result. I have continued to begin every day in gratitude with an *asemaa* and *nibi* (tobacco and water) ceremony (Figure 20). I (or the CRs) approached each potential participant with an *asemaa* (tobacco) tie (Figure 21), which was accepted prior to the consent form being signed. Before beginning the interview, each person was offered smudge with *mashkodewashk* (sage that I had harvested; Figure 22). Again, I made medicine bundles (Figure 23), among other small gifts to say

Figure 20. *Asemaa* (tobacco) and *nibi* (water) ceremony. Author's photo.

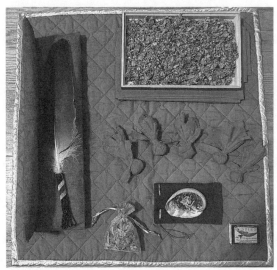

Figure 21. *Asemaa* (tobacco) ties made by the author. Author's photo.

Figure 22. *Mashkodewashk* (sage) harvested by the author. Author's photo.

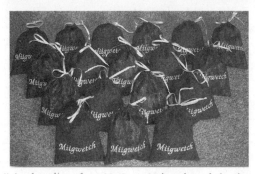

Figure 23. Medicine bundles of *mashkodewashk* (sage) made by the author. Author's photo.

miigwetch to the to the CRs and to the participants at the community presentations of findings (or I gave the gifts to relatives in attendance to pass on to them). Most importantly, I now understand that participation in ceremony, guidance by Spirit, and use of plant medicines in these ways are also Métis-specific practices (not just "First Nations practices") that inform a Métis methodology.

One final way that I aimed for a more Métis- and community-centred methodology with this research was by delivering a presentation of findings in each of the six selected Manitoba Métis communities. The CRs were instrumental in helping me organize the presentations, advertising in the communities (including in local newsletters, electronic billboards, and postering), making arrangements for a venue (local community centre, school), and assisting me in delivering the presentations. Attendance ranged from four attendees (in Ste. Anne) to thirty-four (in St. Laurent). I provided light refreshments, and one CR (Julia) treated us to homemade bannock and jam at the St. François-Xavier presentation. Reception at these presentations was very positive overall with lots of engaged discussion, and St. François-Xavier and St. Laurent ran stories about the event in their local newsletters.[94] There was no shortage of potential participants across most of these Métis communities. Going back to the (Métis) communities to share what has been learned is important in Indigenous methodologies.[95]

~

In this chapter, I have presented a detailed description of my research design and methodology. I explained the approach I took in *Rekindling* before discussing new developments in Métis research and methodology that have emerged since then (or that I have learned of since then). Few examples of Métis-specific methodologies exist, but there have been some notable developments.[96] Lastly, I explained the evolution of my own approach, which aims to be Métis-specific and community-centred by adhering to the MNC's definition of Métis, focusing on six historic Red River Métis communities, working with six Métis CRs, and collaborating with the MMF via their research ethics protocol to help ensure accountability. I hope my efforts will be useful to other Métis researchers as one example of a Métis-centred research design and methodology.

CHAPTER 4

Six Red River Métis Communities

In this chapter, I offer an overview of the six Red River Métis communities that are the focus of this study: Duck Bay, Camperville, St. Laurent, St. François-Xavier, Lorette, and Ste. Anne (see Figure 1). All six predate confederation of the province of Manitoba (1870) and of Canada itself (1867). They were selected because they had emerged as important Métis communities at the time of the birth of the Métis Nation,[1] and though some may look different today because of changes in population and pressures to assimilate, they continue to be recognized as (historic) Métis communities.[2]

These Métis communities originated between the 1820s and the 1850s, if not earlier. Métis families lived in this region prior to the 1820s, probably since the late 1700s and certainly predating the Métis Victoire de la Grenouillère (Victory at Frog Plain, or the Battle of Seven Oaks) in 1816; this time period and location are recognized by many as the birth(place) of the Métis Nation.[3] Métis people, like our First Nations relatives, were multilingual but had low literacy rates and rarely left written records from that time period. In addition to oral history, we must rely on (biased) records left by the fur trade explorers, company men, and the first White settlers and clergy to settle in the region.

Pierre Gauthier de La Vérendrye and his sons are credited with being the first White men to "stake a claim" in these regions, including establishing Fort Rouge in 1738 in present-day Winnipeg and another post in present-day Portage la Prairie—these are considered to be "the oldest communities established by white men in the Northwest."[4] In 1811, Thomas Douglas, fifth Earl of Selkirk (Lord Selkirk) purchased 116,000 square miles of land from the Hudson's Bay Company (which considered itself owner of all of Rupert's Land under its charter of 1670) to establish the Red River Colony; the following year, the first permanent settlers began arriving. The boundaries of the Red River Colony—also known as Assiniboia, or the Selkirk Settlement—stretched west beyond the present-day Manitoba-Saskatchewan border, north to halfway up Lake Winnipeg, east almost to present-day Thunder Bay, Ontario, and south into present-day North Dakota,[5] including Pembina, the first capital of the Métis Nation.[6] On 15 July 1870, Manitoba joined Confederation as the fifth province of Canada (due in large part to the actions of Métis people in the 1869–70 Red River Resistance). At 13,928 square miles, the area of Manitoba, nicknamed "the postage stamp" province (see Figure 1),[7] was much smaller than that of the Red River Colony; Manitoba's boundaries would be extended in 1881 and again in 1912 to reach its present-day size.

All six Métis communities in this study fell within the boundaries of the Red River Colony, with Duck Bay and Camperville located at the northern boundary. However, these two communities found themselves beyond the northern boundary of the postage stamp province of Manitoba in 1870; St. Laurent was situated at the northernmost boundary of the new province.[8] Métis inhabitants of these communities continued their relationships with their Métis kin across the new arbitrary borders.

In the following pages, I offer a brief introduction to each of these six historic Red River Métis communities. I begin by identifying their geographic location, including distance to the nearest other communities (reserves, towns, urban centres). I touch upon the history of each community, including the arrival of Christian clergy (notably Roman Catholics). I also comment on the earliest available historic population statistics for each community before outlining their current population statistics according to the 2016 Canadian Census. I conclude by noting changes in population, pressures to assimilate, and their potential impacts on Métis inhabitants. I discuss the communities in order from the oldest, or earliest to be established, to the most recent.[9]

St. François-Xavier (Grantown)

St. François-Xavier is situated thirty kilometres west of Winnipeg along the Assiniboine River and sixty-one kilometres southeast of Portage la Prairie; the nearest First Nations reserves are Long Plain (Anishinaabe) (70 km away) and Dakota Tipi (70 km). Originally named Grantown (or Prairie du Cheval Blanc/White Horse Plains), the settlement was established by Cuthbert Grant Jr. in 1823; its name changed to St. François-Xavier in 1854.[10] The community was composed mainly of Métis people who had followed Grant from Pembina when Father Sévère Dumoulin closed his ministry there on the orders of Bishop Joseph-Norbert Provencher in 1823 (after 1818, Pembina found itself located south of the Canadian border).[11] At that time, the new HBC Governor George Simpson made an arrangement with Grant (who had recently married Marie McGillis and converted to Christianity) to create the new Métis settlement and encourage agriculture and cattle-rearing; approximately eighty to 100 Métis families joined him. By 1850, the White Horse Plains bison hunt had separated from that of Red River, and the community was thriving in the construction of Red River carts, thanks to an abundance of oak wood and the skilled hands of people like François Ridland, Michel Chalifaux and Michel Paenaude.[12]

Grantown was the earliest and for a long time the only extension of the Catholic Church outside St. Boniface. According to Martha McCarthy's *To Evangelize the Nations: Roman Catholic Missions in MB 1818–1870*, Grant himself "was godfather to many Indian boys and his house served as the priest's residence for many years."[13] Father Thomas Destroismaisons held church services in Grant's house from 1823 to 1827. In 1828, a log chapel was built; then in 1834, the Catholic mission community was designated as a parish.

There was a steady but revolving presence of Catholic missionaries who visited or resided at Grantown. Jean Harper, a young seminarian from Quebec, preached to the Métis at Grantown while on bison hunt missions in 1824 and 1827; he resided there during winters until 1831. Upon his departure, Father François Boucher was responsible for the ministry (including on bison hunts) until 1833, at which time, Bishop Provencher recorded the total population at 424.[14] That year, Charles-Edouard Poiré took over; he knew the Saulteaux (Anishinaabemowin) language well enough to hear confessions and teach Christian doctrine but not enough to preach. McCarthy explains that "this was a considerable handicap, since Sauteux, rather than French, appeared to be the usual language of the Métis of White Horse Plains."[15] In 1834, the parish of St. François-Xavier began its own register separate from that of St. Boniface; that year, the population was recorded at 503, with fifty-eight baptisms, fourteen marriages, and thirteen burials.[16] In 1838, Poiré was replaced by Father Jean-Baptiste Thibault, who stayed until 1839, followed by Joseph Mayrand, who stayed for three years. Mayrand was succeeded by Father Jean Edouard Darveau in 1843; he had learned Saulteaux from Provencher and undertook missions to Duck Bay—he died on one such mission.[17] By 1844, several Métis moved to St. François-Xavier from the north, boosting its population.[18]

Bishop Provencher sent the Grey Nuns of St. Boniface to St. François-Xavier to deliver religious instruction to the children in the community. On 5 November 1850, three sisters arrived to fulfil this purpose. (After 118 years, the Grey Nuns departed from the parish in June 1968.)[19] After Darveau, there was no permanent priest in St. François-Xavier until Father Louis-François Laflèche arrived in 1855 to continue the bison hunt missions. In 1860, the Earl of Southesk visited the community and noted about 200 people "more or less of French-Canadian blood" coming out of the church.[20] In contrast, in 1862, Father Jean-Baptiste Petitot visited and reported that all the Métis were at Mass before going on the summer hunt but that none could speak French.[21]

By 1872, the population of Métis at White Horse Plains (1,804 inhabitants) was higher than that of any other parish of St. Boniface, but the population was changing, as Métis were dispossessed (after the confederation of Manitoba) and moving west while immigrants from Ontario settled in their place.[22] Many Métis moved to Father Jules Decorby's new mission near "Lake Qu'Appelle"; and by 1882, some Métis families from St. François-Xavier had joined with others from nearby Baie St. Paul to form a small settlement at Fort Ellice.[23]

In these ways, St. François-Xavier has had extensive relationships with Roman Catholicism since its inception. Clergy records are among the few in existence for the community at that time. As I stated in Chapter 2, we must read such records critically and with an understanding that missionaries were biased by their goal of converting as many Indigenous people as possible and reporting their progress to their superiors. Therefore, these documents are not a good indication regarding whether Métis inhabitants also participated in Indigenous ceremonies.

Locating historic population counts for these communities has proved challenging. In the paragraphs above, McCarthy is useful for establishing an initial population of eighty to 100 families in the 1820s, rising to 841 people after additional Métis moved there in 1844.[24] I located census records for Grantown for the years 1827, 1849, and 1870 held at the Manitoba Archives. The 1827 census notes a total population count of 112 for Grantown: twenty-two families, twenty women (i.e., wives), thirty-nine sons, and thirty-one daughters are recorded.[25] Of the twenty-two families, twenty are recorded as Roman Catholic and two as Protestant. Country of origin is also stated, with ten families from Rupert's Land, nine from Canada, two from Scotland, and one from the Orkney Islands. In the 1849 Red River Census, Grantown is listed as having 169 families, with country of origin identified mostly as Rupert's Land and Canada (and one from Italy); all except one (Protestant) identified as Catholic. The number 169 seems to refer to heads of households (usually males, with the occasional widowed female); another column includes family members and totals 914. The latter number more closely reflects the total population for Grantown in 1849.[26] The 1870 Red River Census includes population statistics for the parish area of St. François-Xavier (Grantown) along with several other parish areas.[27] Of the 1,850 inhabitants, 1,801 are listed as *Métis Français* (French Métis), one as *Métis Anglais* (English Métis), and one person is listed as both *Métis Français* and *Métis Anglais*; all are Catholic except the *Métis Anglais*, who is recorded as Protestant.[28] There are also forty-two people listed as *Blanc* (White—all Catholic except one Protestant), and seven as *Indien* (Indian—five are listed as Catholic, and two as Protestant).

The population of St. François-Xavier has decreased since 1870 and today the non-Aboriginal population greatly surpasses the Aboriginal population.[29] In the 2016 Census, the total population for the community was 1,411.[30] Of these, 185 identified as Aboriginal, including 140 as Métis and twenty as First Nation; twenty individuals identified with multiple Aboriginal categories.[31] The non-Aboriginal identity population is listed as 1,180. The census classifies St. François-Xavier as a "rural municipality."[32]

St. Laurent (Fond du Lac)

St. Laurent, formerly called Fond du Lac, is eighty-seven kilometres northwest of Winnipeg on the southeastern curve of Lake Manitoba, eighty-eight kilometres northeast of Portage la Prairie, and sixty-eight kilometres northwest of St. François-Xavier. The nearest First Nations reserves are Lake Manitoba (Anishinaabe) (92 km away), Peguis

(Anishinaabe and Nêhiyaw) (144 km), and Sandy Bay (Anishinaabe) (157 km). The origins of St. Laurent are similar to those of St. François-Xavier: it was established in 1824 by a group of Métis who had been pushed out of Pembina after it became American territory.[33] More Métis arrived in Fond du Lac in 1826 when flooding of the Red River forced them to winter there; some of the earliest Métis families in the community were the Pangmans, Chartrands, Sayers, Lavallées, and Carrières.[34] According to Hourie, by 1850 twelve Métis families lived in the vicinity, including Charles Lambert, Norbert Larance (from North Dakota), a Chartrand (from Duck Bay), the Lavallées, and the Ducharmes—they were drawn there by the abundance of lumber, fish, wild game, and wild berries and fruit.[35] Most Métis, like the Saulteaux, Cree, and Assiniboine who preceded them in the area, spent winters hunting and trapping in the forest to the north.[36] There was frequent visiting and travel (by Métis themselves as well as by Catholic priests) between Fond du Lac and St. François-Xavier, and between Fond du Lac and Duck Bay.[37] According to McCarthy, "each missionary visiting the Lake missions left from Fond du Lac and spent some time with the people there, because it was the main transfer point between the lakes and the Red River Settlement."[38] Since Fond du Lac had no resident priest, some Métis chose to travel from there to St. François-Xavier or Duck Bay for mass; many Fond du Lac residents buried their relatives in the cemetery at St. François-Xavier.[39] Before the 1860s, itinerant missionaries visited Fond du Lac, including Father Destroismaisons in 1826.

In the late 1850s, Fond du Lac was chosen as a base for Catholic missionary activity which included efforts to convert Indigenous people to Christianity, and to curb free trade, American traders, and the selling and consumption of alcohol.[40] Father Jean-Marie Lestanc spent the winter of 1856–57 there and supervised the initial construction work on a chapel. The next year, missionary Zéphérin Gascon moved there to preach to the thirty or forty Métis and White families who lived in the area and to continue building the chapel; he left in 1859. In 1861, St. Laurent received a resident priest, Father Laurent Simonet; he was also the priest for Notre Dame du Lac at Manitoba House, and Duck Bay. According to Bishop Alexandre-Antonin Taché (Provencher's coadjutor bishop), the total population of these missions at the time was "several hundred Catholics and *a greater number of 'infidels'* [Indigenous people who had not converted]."[41] In 1895, a convent was built for the Order of the Franciscan Missionaries of Mary—nuns who would arrive in 1897.

Father Simonet had begun a small school in 1862 before leaving the community in 1870; by that time, he had been joined by Father Charles Camper and missionary Jeremiah Mulvihill who, with the help of the nuns, would operate the first school. In 1869, a building was constructed for the Pères Oblats de Marie Immaculée with an extension that served as the first school beginning in 1870.[42] Upon their arrival, priests and nuns delivered French Catholic education in St. Laurent; however, (Protestant) English education became the norm after the provincial government decreed in 1890 that all schools in the province fell under the authority of the Department of Education.[43] Priests and nuns continued to teach in the St. Laurent school until the late 1970s, when they would be replaced by non-clergy.[44]

According to McCarthy, "St. Laurent became an important regional headquarters for the Oblates of Manitoba. In the early twentieth century, many future Oblates were trained at the novitiate in St. Laurent."[45] By 1881, the rural municipality of St. Laurent had been created and had its own local government. At that time, the community had thirty-two Métis families and a school population of fifty.[46]

St. Laurent was populated by Métis and First Nations families and the languages spoken there were Michif French, Saulteaux, and Cree.[47] In the early 1900s, Breton families arrived from France; they were followed by French-Canadian families in the 1930s. Mennonite families moved to the area in the 1950s, and since the 1960s, lake-front cabins have drawn many non-Métis (often White) city dwellers to the area.[48] Hourie notes, "French Michif survived the pressures from the church, the nuns, and the 'Bretons' who attempted to replace Michif French with the new French language. The Saulteaux language did not survive as few people now speak it."[49] It appears Saulteaux and Cree were no longer spoken fluently by the Métis of St. Laurent by the 1950s.[50]

With the changes in population, Father Lavallée notes that many Catholic ritual practices all but disappeared, including "the family rosary, daily catechism, Catholic Action, parish processions, most of the Lenten observances, the month of Mary [May] and some sacramental observances such as confessions."[51] Other rituals remain to the present day, such as the use of "holy water, holy pictures and crucifixes," but to a lesser degree.[52] Father Lavallée believes secularization has occurred and that the church no longer exercises the influence it once did, but that Catholicism continues to play a significant role in the lives of the Métis of St. Laurent.[53]

As mentioned earlier, there were an estimated twelve Métis families in St. Laurent by 1850,[54] growing to thirty or forty families by 1857.[55] I located the 1857 census records for Fond du Lac, which list the following: sixty-five individuals (heads of households), 173 husbands, 161 wives, 238 sons, 202 daughters, and 165 "followers" (extended family members such as grandparents).[56] The column titled "total" shows the number of individuals associated with each head of household or family; when these numbers are tallied, the total 1857 population for Fond du Lac amounts to 939.[57] The parish of St. Laurent does not appear in the 1870 Red River Census.

In 2016, the population of St. Laurent was 1,338 residents.[58] Of these, 855 identified as Aboriginal, including 750 as Métis, eighty-five as First Nation, and ten identifying with multiple Aboriginal categories. Non-Aboriginal identity was reported by 480 people. Like St. François-Xavier, St. Laurent is identified as a "rural municipality."

Duck Bay

The community of Duck Bay is 452 kilometres northwest of Winnipeg on the northwestern shore of Lake Winnipegosis; of all the communities in this study, it is the furthest from Winnipeg. It is seventy-two kilometres northwest of Winnipegosis, 129 kilometres north of Dauphin, and 295 kilometres north of Brandon. The nearest First Nations reserves are Pine Creek (Anishinaabe) (14 km away), Skownan (Anishinaabe) (15 km), O-chi-chak-ko-sipi (Anishinaabe) (146 km), and Ebb and Flow (Anishinaabe) (198 km).

Locals call their community Zhiishiibi-Ziibiing (literally, Duck River) and Lake Winnipegosis by the name Lake Pittowinipik.[59] In the 1800s, Duck Bay became a wintering area for Métis hunters, fishermen, and traders; and in 1839, the first sustained mission in this region began with Father Belcourt at Duck Bay.[60] The HBC established Duck Bay House at the south end of the bay—the fort existed from 1859 to 1887.

McCarthy offers an extensive write-up of Roman Catholic history in Duck Bay, noting that the Duck Bay mission was originally called St. Norbert, then St. Edouard. In 1839, Father Belcourt visited Lake

Winnipegosis, Duck Bay, and surrounding communities for the purpose of evangelization and was met with a cold reception from local First Nations people.[61] He also visited 200 Saulteaux families near Manitoba House who had gathered for a Midewiwin ceremony (Chapter 2).[62] Father Darveau also preached in these communities, and in 1843, he estimated the population of Duck Bay to be about sixty.[63] He would eventually baptize Mizi-Epit, the Saulteaux Chief of the Duck Bay Mission.[64] As mentioned earlier, Father Darveau seems to have met an untimely death.[65]

Divisions between locals interested in Catholicism and those who preferred Indigenous spirituality were evident when Father Belcourt visited Duck Bay in 1844, and when Henry Youle Hind visited in 1858. By the time Father Simonet spent the winter in Duck Bay in 1861–62,[66] he could preach to an estimated nine Métis families who lived there but described the population as a mixture of Métis, Saulteaux, and some Swampy Cree. He lamented that "nearly half of them had abandoned their Catholic religion and renewed their Native beliefs and practices," but he persisted and baptized many Indigenous people, including a well-regarded "*jongleur* or Native prophet."[67] In the winter of 1862–63, Simonet counted only six First Nations families and eleven Métis families who planned to stay the winter.[68] Also, recall Father Camper's visit to Duck Bay in 1868, when he encountered many Indigenous people gathered there for Midewiwin ceremonies (Chapter 2).

In 1871, a treaty was signed at Manitoba House creating the Pine Creek reserve nearby.[69] The Duck Bay reserve (9,620 acres) was created when the Duck Bay Band entered Treaty 4 (1874); many Métis band members later withdrew.[70] Beginning in 1883, Father Camper, then Father Dupont, lobbied for a new reserve for the remaining Duck Bay Band at Pine River and the government agreed. Barkwell explains that "subsequently, the Duck Bay reserve was surrendered by Headman Jean Baptiste Napakisit signing on behalf of the band, in 1899."[71] The Métis who had withdrawn regretted doing so and petitioned to return to Treaty in 1993, but the government refused.[72]

The Pine Creek Residential School (located in Camperville) began in 1890 for First Nations and Métis children in the region. In 1894, Fathers St. Germain and Adelard Chaumont began construction of a larger building to house the school.[73] The school and surrounding farmland covered 632 acres; it closed in 1969.[74] When the Roman Catholic mission could no longer finance the school, they turned it over to the provincial government who continued its operation but as a day school.[75] The St. Thomas Aquinas day school, run by Oblate priests and nuns, provided a Catholic education to the children of Duck Bay historically.

I struggled to find historic population statistics for Duck Bay. Thanks to Father Darveau, we have an estimated population count in 1843 at sixty families; then Father Simonet estimated nine Métis families in 1862, and the following winter, he counted eleven Métis families and six First Nations families (as mentioned above). McCarthy notes that by the late nineteenth century, most of the people of Duck Bay had moved south to the Pine River reserve, where they formed a population of "323 Catholic Métis Indians."[76] The Manitoba Archives only has census records for Duck Bay dating back to 1987.[77] The 2016 Canadian Census identified a total of 349 people living in Duck Bay. Individuals who self-identified as Aboriginal numbered 390;[78] of these, 235 were Métis, 155 were First Nations, and no one self-identified with more than one Aboriginal identity category. The non-Aboriginal identity population was enumerated at ten individuals. Duck Bay is classified as a "northern community" in this census.

Camperville

Camperville is located 429 kilometres northwest of Winnipeg and sits on the northwestern shore of Lake Winnipegosis; it is fifty kilometres northwest of Winnipegosis and 107 kilometres north of Dauphin. The nearest First Nations reserves are Pine Creek (Anishinaabe) (7 km away), Skownan (Anishinaabe) (111 km), O-chi-chak-ko-sipi (Anishinaabe) (123 km), and Ebb and Flow (Anishinaabe) (176 km). Camperville and Duck Bay are twenty-two kilometres apart.

Camperville and Duck Bay are inseparable in their history, religion, and society.[79] Swampy Cree and Saulteaux inhabited the region before the arrival of the Métis. Hunting, fishing, and trading were common on these inland waterways; eventually, canoes would be replaced by York boats steered by Métis from Red River, St. Laurent, and St. Ambroise.[80] Nearby salt deposits were used to make salt to trade with the HBC; the area was nicknamed "La Saline."[81] The first permanent settlements at Camperville and Duck Bay resulted from marriages between Cree and Saulteaux women and Métis men, and from Métis families who previously lived in St. François-Xavier, St. Laurent, and St. Ambroise.

Later, missionaries continued promoting settlement in Camperville and Duck Bay to Métis from St. Laurent. An HBC post was established in Camperville before 1867.

The residents of Camperville also appear to be tied to the history of the creation and dissolution of the Duck Bay reserve mentioned above. After Pine Creek reserve was created, missionaries and government encouraged First Nations people to settle in Pine Creek, and Métis to settle in Camperville and Duck Bay. However, participants from both communities in this study insist the matter was not cut and dried. Today, there are divisions in these communities regarding whether Camperville and/or Duck Bay should pursue reserve status, and whether residents are mainly non-status Indians or Métis. Pine Creek reserve is a mere eight kilometres from Camperville and fifteen kilometres from Duck Bay, sitting in between these two communities.

Early ministries in Camperville and Duck Bay were Roman Catholic, but Anglican missions would later be established at Pinaymootang (Fairford) First Nation to the east in 1842, and at Shoal Lake to the north in 1855.[82] Camperville and Duck Bay were visited by itinerant missionaries in the early 1840s, namely, by Fathers Jean Edouard Darveau and Georges-Antoine Belcourt. The town is named after one of the first itinerant Catholic missionaries, Father Charles Camper, who preached at the Pine River Mission and built a wooden church-school.[83] The name Camperville begins appearing on maps as of 1914; prior to that, it was known as Pine Creek.[84] The first resident priest was Father J.A. Dupont, followed by Fathers St. Germain and Adelard Chaumont. Father Joseph Brachet resided at the Camperville mission from 1912 to 1938; he was fluent in English, French, Cree, and Saulteaux; he wrote a Cree hymnal and translated scripture into Cree. Camperville was a Catholic parish community.

Recall that in 1890 the Pine Creek Residential School in Camperville began offering Catholic education to the children of the region including those from Duck Bay. The residential school closed in 1969 and was converted into day schools, including Christ the King School in Camperville, and St. Thomas Aquinas School in Duck Bay, as mentioned earlier. Provincial education was delivered in English as of 1890 but priests and nuns spoke to each other in French in these schools (clergy was replaced by secular teachers by the mid-1970s); altar boys had to learn Latin.[85]

I have been unable to locate early historic population statistics for Camperville. According to Barkwell, a 1958 census enumerated 655 Métis living at Camperville.[86] The Manitoba Archives census records for Camperville only dated back to 1987.[87] In 2016, Camperville was home to 820 residents.[88] The number of individuals self-identifying as Aboriginal is recorded as 885;[89] of those, 290 identified as Métis, 585 identified as First Nation, and ten individuals identified with multiple Aboriginal categories. Forty people identified as non-Aboriginal. Camperville is listed as a "northern community" in this census.

Ste. Anne (Grande Pointe des Chênes)

Ste. Anne (or Ste. Anne des Chênes), formerly called Grande Pointe des Chênes, is forty-eight kilometres southeast of Winnipeg and eighteen kilometres north of the city of Steinbach. The nearest First Nations reserves are Brokenhead (Anishinaabe) (96 km away), Roseau River (Anishinaabe) (102 km), and Sagkeeng (Anishinaabe) (138 km). Swamp and forest land—called *l'épinettière* by the Métis—can be found to the east of Ste. Anne, stretching to Lake of the Woods. Large oak (*chênes* in French) groves along the Seine River provided good lumber and game hunting for early Métis inhabitants. Lumber was retrieved from the area to build infrastructure in Red River since at least the 1830s, and was used to build the St. Boniface Cathedral. According to Barkwell, some animosity seems to have existed between early Métis and Saulteaux, who considered this region their hunting territory.[90] The area was purchased by Métis and French settlers in 1852 from Na-sa-kee-byness (Flying Down Bird), also known as Grands Oreilles, the Chief of the Roseau River Band.

Most Métis families who established a permanent community here were bison hunters who had been dwelling in the region. Documentation about individual inhabitants is sparse but it seems the population increased after the flood of 1852, when other Métis arrived in search of higher ground.[91] Métis from Red River began establishing new communities along the Assiniboine River between 1850 and 1860 for the same reason; increased population pressure on river lots provided another incentive for relocation.[92] Early families in the area included those of François and Charles Nolin, Jean Baptiste Sapoint, August Harrison, and Jean Baptiste Perrault *dit* Morin.[93] By 1860, the families living in Ste. Anne were all Métis who made their living from hunting,[94] with agriculture as a secondary subsistence base.[95] The flood of 1861 brought White farmers to settle in Ste. Anne. By 1868, the mission at Ste. Anne had grown to about forty families.[96]

Like the other Métis communities in this study, Ste. Anne became a Catholic parish community soon after its establishment. The first parish was established in 1856; itinerant visits from priests occurred infrequently, including by Father Simonet in 1858 (possibly the first visit by a priest in the region). The substantial marsh sometimes made it impossible for the inhabitants of Ste. Anne to travel to St. Boniface for Catholic mass. Then, in 1861, Bishop Taché founded the Mission of St. Alexander at Pointe des Chênes. In 1866, a chapel was opened and a church was built the following year. Within six months, Father Joseph Lefloch renamed the mission Ste. Anne after the patron saint of the Bretons.[97] Itinerant visits by priests stationed at St. Boniface would continue: by Lefloch himself (once a month), and occasionally by Fathers Lestanc, Tissot, and St. Germain. In 1869, the twenty-eight heads of households petitioned Taché for a resident priest; the following year, Father Louis Raymond Giroux was assigned to Ste. Anne.[98] Prior to this, Father Giroux had been chaplain to Louis Riel's Provisional Government until Taché stationed him in Ste. Anne; he was also responsible for the surrounding settlements of Lorette, Richer (formerly Thibaultville), and Ste. Geneviève.[99] Giroux would remain at Ste. Anne for forty-one years until his death in 1911. These priests concerned themselves with providing Catholic education to the children of the community; by 1888, there were 200 children enrolled across three schools in Ste. Anne.[100]

Reports from the 1857–58 Dawson and Hind exploratory survey of the West (on behalf of the Government of Canada) offer the oldest documentary evidence of settlement in this region. Among other tasks, Dawson and Hind were searching for a connecting route to Canada and thought the German River (the Seine River) might be such a route to Lake of the Woods. This expedition would build Dawson Road from Lake of the Woods to the Red River Colony, passing through Ste. Anne along the way. Construction of the road began in 1868; local Métis were the main labourers. The road increased the White settler population in Ste. Anne and, in 1870, the Red River Expeditionary Forces were sent by Canada down this road to punish the Métis for the Red River Resistance and for confederating Manitoba.

John Snow was hired to supervise construction of Dawson Road; he hated the local Métis residents and they disliked him in return.[101] Barkwell explains that Snow ignored local Métis residence patterns and property boundaries (previously laid out by Roger Goulet for the Council of Assiniboia) and claimed to have bought the land on which they lived from the Saulteaux. The residents of Ste. Anne evicted Snow and he was charged with two counts of selling liquor to the Saulteaux for land at Pointe des Chênes;[102] he soon returned and continued construction of the road. To make matters worse, Snow hired Orangemen (Catholic antagonists)—including the infamous Thomas Scott—from Ontario to come work on Dawson Road (he also hired some locals). Tensions increased because wages were too low and workers were not given cash; rather, they were given provisions from a new store opened by John Christian Schultz, who was abhorred by the Métis.[103] Charles Mair, a friend of Snow also employed in Ste. Anne, published insulting letters about the Métis in the Toronto *Globe*.

With good reason, the Métis grew increasingly worried about their land. Snow described the Métis in Ste. Anne in the following way: "The French halfbreed population are particularly very troublesome and no doubt the sooner a strong [White settler] force is organized here the better."[104] Lieutentant-Colonel John Stoughten Dennis was also sent by Canada to survey plots of land; he stayed with John Schultz in Ste. Anne, which heightened Métis suspicions. McCarthy notes that Dennis and "his men were accused of marking out private claims of land in the settlement of Ste. Anne and he was expected to choose the best land for the people from Ontario who would move west the next spring. This was a well-founded suspicion."[105] Dennis recommended that a town plan be laid out and "not a lot granted except to an actual [White] settler."[106]

In terms of historic population counts for Ste. Anne, as mentioned earlier, McCarthy notes approximately forty families by 1868, and twenty-eight heads of households (amounting to approximately 200 people) the following year. The parish of Ste. Anne was enumerated in the 1870 Red River Census, in which a total of 323 individuals are listed. Of those, 256 are identified as *Métis*, 63 as *Blanc*, and two as *Indien*. Every Métis individual is recorded as *Métis Français* and Catholic; the "Indians" are also listed as Catholic. The White inhabitants are also identified as Catholic, except for six Protestants.[107] According to the Canadian Census, the total population of Ste. Anne in 2016 was 2,114.[108] Of these, 495 individuals self-identified as Aboriginal, with 420 identifying as Métis and fifty-five as First Nation; in addition, twenty-five respondents self-identified across multiple Aboriginal identity categories. The non-Aboriginal identity category is recorded at 1,520 individuals. In the 2016 Census, Ste. Anne is identified as a "town."

Lorette (Petite Pointe des Chênes)

The community of Lorette (formerly Petite Pointe des Chênes[109]) is located thirty-one kilometres southeast of Winnipeg and thirty-five kilometres northwest of the city of Steinbach. The nearest First Nations reserves are Brokenhead (Anishinaabe) (83 km away), Roseau River (Anishinaabe) (96 km), and Sagkeeng (Anishinaabe) (133 km). Lorette is a mere twenty kilometres northwest of Ste. Anne; they are geographically close to each other and their histories are also linked. Historically, when travelling from Lake of the Woods along Dawson Road, one would first pass through Grande Pointe des Chênes (Ste. Anne), then through Petite Pointe des Chênes (Lorette), before finally arriving in what would become the city of Winnipeg.

Lorette was first settled in the 1850s by Métis bison hunters, freighters, traders, and farmers whose cattle grazed along the Seine River—they had come from St. Boniface, St. Norbert, and St. Vital.[110] The first families who established themselves in the community (by 1860 or earlier) were Métis; they included François Bériau (who later moved to Ste. Anne), Toussaint Vaudry, Roman Lagimodière and Elzéar Lagimodière (Louis Riel's cousins), André Gaudry, Maxime Dumais, Norbert Landry, Collin McDougall, and Francis Flamand.[111] The first French-Canadian family to arrive was that of Jean-Baptiste Gauthier (from Ste. Scholastique, near Montreal) and Rosalie Germain (from Verchères, Quebec); they lived in Lorette from 1861 to 1866, and returned in 1873 to 1895, having stayed intermittently in Ste. Anne and LaBroquerie.[112] The second French-Canadian family to arrive was that of Jean-Baptiste Desautels, in 1869, but they too moved to Ste. Anne the following year. Desautels was the mail carrier from Ste. Anne to Winnipeg every week for thirty years; the round trip took two days.[113] Other individuals and families soon moved to Lorette, including Agenor Dubuc, Camille Henri, Joseph Gendron, François Phaneuf,

Basile Laurin and Joseph Laurin, Norbert Plante, Rémi Manaigre, the Mousseaus, the Grégoires, the Remillards, the Désorcys, and the Landrys.[114] In 1880, the Taché Municipal Council was organized there.

The Gautiers' home served as the first Catholic church room (when itinerant priests would visit Lorette), schoolhouse, and post office.[115] The first Roman Catholic baptisms in the community were performed by itinerant missionaries in 1870.[116] Father David Fillion visited on 12 October 1873, delivered mass, and recorded the collection amount as fifty-one cents.[117] In 1874, the Episcopal Corporation of the St. Boniface diocese bought 289 acres (River Lot #54) in Petite Pointe des Chênes from Louis Thibault for $300,000—this would become the heart of the parish of Notre Dame de Lorette.[118] The first pastor, Father Thomas Quévillon, was appointed in 1877; he was followed by Father Jules Comminges, who built the first church in Lorette in 1879, then by Father Joseph Dufresne in 1892.[119]

The first school instruction in Lorette occurred in the home of the first French Canadian family (Mr. and Mrs. Jean-Baptiste Gauthier), then, in 1877, the first resident priest (Father Quévillon) had a two-storey building erected which served as rectory, school, and church. The first standalone building used as a schoolhouse was built in 1880; ever larger school buildings would be constructed in 1888 and 1899, and so on. As of 1901, the Sisters of St. Joseph provided a French Catholic education to the community in a day school; they left in 2007.[120]

I was unable to locate any historic population statistics for Petite Pointe des Chênes or Lorette in the Manitoba Archives. However, according to the Lorette History Book Committee, a census was conducted in 1874, wherein Father Fillion entered twenty-seven Catholic families in Petite Pointe des Chênes: twenty-two Métis and five French Canadian (146 individuals in total).[121] The 2016 Canadian Census lists the total population count for Lorette at 3,208, with 840 people self-identifying as Aboriginal; of these, 665 self-identified as Métis, 145 as First Nation, and fifteen individuals self-identified using multiple Aboriginal identity categories.[122] The non-Aboriginal identity category records 2,520 individuals. In the 2016 Canadian Census, Lorette is identified as a "local urban district."

~

This chapter has given a brief overview of the six Métis communities in this study. These communities share many commonalities, including being preceded in the region by First Nations inhabitation (especially Cree, Saulteaux, and Assiniboine). Other shared characteristics include Métis kinship relationships, and movement from one community to another (or back and forth) across these communities. Especially close relationships are noted between St. François-Xavier and St. Laurent, between Camperville and Duck Bay (and St. Laurent), and between Ste. Anne and Lorette. The communities also share a long history with Roman Catholicism and can be identified as early Catholic parishes in what would become Manitoba. However, these parishes were usually preceded by Métis settlement and habitation. Itinerant missionary work or occasional visits by priests characterized the presence of Roman Catholicism in these communities before any priest took up residence permanently.

Catholic clergy established schools in each of these communities and taught in French first, then in English as per the Manitoba School Act of 1890. The Pine Creek Residential School was in operation from 1890 to 1969 in Camperville and served the communities of Camperville, Duck Bay, and Pine Creek First Nation; clergy continued to teach in the three-day schools (one in each community) that replaced the residential school. Day schools were also present historically in St. Laurent, St. François-Xavier, Lorette, and Ste. Anne. Day schools operated with the support of the federal and provincial governments and religious organizations and instructed First Nations, Métis, and Inuit children daily; unlike in residential schools, the children lived with their parents and remained in their community.[123] Catholic clergy taught in these schools until the late 1970s; thereafter, the teachers would no longer be clergy. Later, participants explain how day schools and being taught by clergy impacted their family's relationship with religion (Chapter 7), and their personal relationship to spirituality (Chapter 9).

As I explained earlier, we are reliant almost entirely upon church records for historic information in these regions—and this writing is biased, male-centred, and emphasizes colonial goals, including Indigenous conversion to Christianity. Other records include documentation by fur trade companies, but these often worked hand in hand with religious officials and suffer from the same biases. Therefore, it is not surprising that we rarely find mention of Indigenous spiritual practices and ceremonies in this early historic documentation, though exceptions to this do indeed exist.

Notable examples, from this and the previous chapter, come to us from Fathers Belcourt, Simonet, and Camper. In 1839, Father Belcourt visited the region of Lake Winnipegosis, Duck Bay, and surrounding communities and was met with a cold shoulder from local Indigenous inhabitants.[124] Around this time, he visited 200 Saulteaux families in nearby Manitoba House who had gathered for a Midewiwin ceremony.[125] It is likely there were Métis families present as well, given that the makeup of this and surrounding communities was Métis, Saulteaux, and some Swampy Cree.[126] In 1861, Father Simonet took over the mission of Fond du Lac (St. Laurent), Duck Bay, and Notre Dame du Lac at Manitoba House; at that time, Bishop Taché described the combined population of these mission areas as "several hundred Catholics and *a greater number of 'infidels'* [Indigenous people who had not converted]."[127] In 1861-62, Father Simonet was wintering at Duck Bay and preaching to the Métis and Saulteaux (and some Cree) families who lived there but lamented that "nearly half of them had abandoned their Catholic religion and renewed their Native beliefs and practices."[128] And, in a letter written by Father Camper (while stationed in St. Laurent) to Archbishop Taché in 1868, we read of a large gathering of Indigenous people that he had hoped was for the purpose of hearing Catholic instruction but was, in fact, for *la Grade Médecine* [Midewiwin ceremonies] in the region of Duck Bay. He wrote, "La plupart des catholiques de la Baie des Canards y étaient déjà rendus. J'y ai trouvé aussi un grand nombre de Sauvages." (The majority of the Indigenous Catholics in Duck Bay had already arrived. There were also many "savages" [non-Christian Indigenous people] who had arrived.)[129] There, Camper tried to baptize the children of the Catholics, but the families continued their participation in the "medicine" lodge.[130] Significantly, even inhabitants identified by priests as "Catholic" living in and around Duck Bay (which included Métis people) participated in the Midewiwin lodge historically.

Where possible, I also offered historic population statistics for these communities; these were available for St. François-Xavier, St. Laurent, and Ste. Anne. In the cases of Duck Bay, Camperville, and Lorette historic census records were unavailable; however, other sources (usually priests' records) offer the occasional population count. Sixty families were enumerated in Duck Bay in 1843, falling to seventeen families in 1863 [eleven Métis and six First Nations] as most families moved to

Pine Creek reserve where, by the late nineteenth century, 323 individuals were recorded there as "Catholic Métis Indians."[131] Father Fillion enumerated twenty-seven families in Lorette in 1874.[132] The earliest record I could find for Camperville was 655 Métis individuals recorded in the 1958 census.[133] On the other hand, historic census records were available from 1827, 1849, and 1870 for Grantown (St. François-Xavier); census statistics for St. Laurent (Fond du Lac) were available from 1857 (but not from the 1870 Red River Census); for Ste. Anne, these statistics were available from 1870. The total population count is recorded at 112 individuals in Grantown in 1827 (then 914 in 1849, then 1,959 or 1,850, depending on how the columns are calculated in 1870), 939 individuals in St. Laurent in 1857, and 323 in Ste. Anne in 1870. Historically, in every community, the Métis segment of the population far outnumbered any other segment, and they are all (almost without exception) recorded as French Métis and Roman Catholic.

I also offered population statistics from the 2016 Canadian Census. The total 2016 population count for these communities, in decreasing order, is as follows: Lorette, 3,208; Ste. Anne, 2,114; St. François-Xavier, 1,411; St. Laurent, 1,338; Camperville, 820; and Duck Bay, 349. The Aboriginal population continues to outnumber the non-Aboriginal population in Camperville (885 to 40), St. Laurent (855 to 480), and Duck Bay (390 to 10). Conversely, the non-Aboriginal population has surpassed the Aboriginal population in Lorette (2,520 to 840), Ste. Anne (1,520 to 495), and St. François-Xavier (1,180 to 185). In five of the communities, the Métis population outnumbers the First Nations population, in some cases by a large margin: in St. Laurent, 750 Métis individuals to 85 First Nations individuals; in Lorette, 665 to 145; in Ste. Anne, 420 to 55; in Duck Bay, 235 to 155; and in St. François-Xavier, 140 to 20. Camperville is the only community in this study with a larger self-identified First Nations population than Métis population in the 2016 Census, with 585 First Nations individuals and 290 Métis individuals recorded.

It is also interesting to note that Lorette and Ste. Anne have comparable overall population sizes, and non-Aboriginal and Aboriginal population counts; however, while Lorette is recognized by many as a Métis community today, Ste. Anne tends to be viewed as French Canadian. Perhaps this has to do with varying pressures to assimilate to a Catholic French-Canadian identity; after all, Ste. Anne was

historically the centre for Roman Catholicism in the region and served
the spiritual needs of all the neighbouring parishes, including Lorette.
In addition, Ste. Anne was also the home base for the Dawson-Hind
expedition and the crew who built Dawson Road—as a result, White
settlers coming from Ontario would access this community first, and
many chose to remain there. Moreover, Lorette seems to have enjoyed
a resurgence in Métis pride over the last decade or so, as can be heard
in the participants' stories in the upcoming chapters; such a resurgence does not seem to have occurred to the same extent in Ste. Anne
beyond the participants. Unsurprisingly, pressures to assimilate to non-
Aboriginal values can also be heard in the stories and experiences from
some of the St. François-Xavier participants—this is the oldest Métis
community in this study with the longest Catholic parish presence, and
the only other community whose non-Aboriginal population now also
outnumbers the Aboriginal population.

In spite of increasing White settler presence, and the fact that the
2016 Canadian Census does not identify these communities as Métis
communities, they remain Métis communities in the hearts and minds
of Manitoba Métis (and others). In the next chapter, I introduce the
Métis participants themselves and note their relationships to these
communities. As we will see in subsequent chapters, despite long-
term Catholic presence, Métis residents of these communities are
returning to the ceremonies that, historically, some of their ancestors
participated in.

CHAPTER 5

Meeting the Participants

The thirty-two Métis participants in this study are all role models; they have overcome stereotypes and misinformation about Métis people and spirituality and found their way back to the ceremonies that some of our ancestors participated in historically (Chapters 1 and 2). As we will see in the coming chapters, some faced greater struggles to reconnect with ceremony than others; indeed, some speak about ongoing pressures to assimilate to mainstream culture coming from within their own families and communities. For these and other reasons, ten people did not use their legal names; of these ten, those who did not use their spirit name chose (or had me choose) a first-name pseudonym. Nonetheless, they all generously agreed to be part of this study. Many spoke of the importance of unlearning harmful misinformation about the Métis and our spiritual practices, and of the beauty and peace that can come from a life of ceremony; others spoke of wanting to help more Métis people learn about ceremonies and places to participate if they feel so inclined.

Below, I introduce the participants themselves. I begin with a brief overview and summary of their combined demographics, including the number of participants by community, and a breakdown in terms of gender, age, level of education, and occupation. I also explain each participant's connection to their Métis community (including residential and familial connections), as well as their residence today. Following this, I discuss each of the six communities introduced in the previous chapter in terms of the participants and their demographics—including a brief personal introduction for each participant—to give a sense of how each community compares to the overall summary this chapter begins with. I conclude by highlighting interesting demographic patterns across the six Métis communities. These demographics provide additional context for understanding the findings that are discussed in Chapters 6 through 10.

Ceremony and cultural protocols practised among the Métis (and other Indigenous nations) were adhered to at every stage of this study as part of my effort to mobilize a Métis methodology (Chapter 3). *Asemaa*, in the form of a tobacco tie that I made, was offered to each person upon first being approached about the possibility of participating in this study. If the person was unfamiliar with me, this was an opportunity to introduce myself, my family, and my connections to Métis communities (and First Nations communities, when relevant), and to explain the nature of my study and my goals. Most people accepted the tobacco at this point, and we proceeded to sign a consent form. They were then given the option of smudging with *mashkodewashk* (sage that I had harvested myself) so we could clear our minds and the air around us, and let the spirit of the medicine help us focus our minds and hearts on the work we were about to do together.[1] The six Métis community researchers (CRs) who helped me locate potential participants also had the option of conducting interviews.[2]

Demographic Summary

The thirty-two Métis participants in this study were distributed across the Métis communities as follows: six each from Duck Bay, Camperville, St. Laurent, and St. François-Xavier, and four each from Ste. Anne and Lorette. Nine were male and twenty-three were female, including two transgender women. At the time of interview, they ranged in age from eighteen to eighty-three.[3] There was a wide range of educational attainment among participants: three people did not have a high school diploma (having left school in grades six, ten, and eleven, respectively); nine had a high school diploma (six were pursuing higher education); seven had a college or university certificate or diploma; another seven had received an undergraduate degree (one has two undergrad degrees, and three were pursuing a master's degree); and six had obtained a graduate degree (four have master's degrees, one has two master's degrees, and one holds a doctorate). The participants also had diverse forms of employment or occupation: eight were in social services (such as child and family services worker, outreach worker, foster parents, and counsellor/advisor), six were retired, four were in business (small business owners and a project manager), three were in education (consultant/support teacher, service-learning coordinator, and assistant professor), two each were in blue collar jobs (school bus driver and security guard) and administration (office manager and receptionist), two more were unemployed, two others were undergraduate students, two are elders, and one was a research analyst.

The most common type of connection to a Métis community was familial. Nine participants either had ancestors who had been given scrip for land in one of the Métis communities in this study, or their relatives live(d) in that community; in one case, the participant and their children frequent the community daily because it is the nearest community to their home that offers services such as school and a bank. Six people were born and grew up in their Métis community. Five people were born elsewhere but grew up in their Métis community, which was also their adulthood residence. Another five lived in their community only during their childhood. The most extensive personal connection existed with four people who were born in their Métis community, lived there as children, and continue to live there in adulthood. Lastly, three people are connected to a Métis community in this study because it is their adulthood residence. Most participants now live in Winnipeg (sixteen), but twelve continue to live in their Métis community: five in St. Laurent, three each in Duck Bay and Lorette, and one in Ste. Anne. Three people live in urban locations other than Winnipeg (Dauphin, Manitoba; Tucson, Arizona; and Montreal, Quebec), and one lives in a different rural community than those featured in this study (Ross, Manitoba). None of the participants presently lives in Camperville or St. François-Xavier.[4]

Demographics by Community

Duck Bay

The six people from Duck Bay who agreed to be in this study included three females and three males, ranging from thirty-two to seventy-two years old.[5] Two do not have a high school diploma, two have a high school diploma, one has a college certificate, and one has a university diploma. In terms of occupation, two work in administration, two work in social services, one was unemployed at the time of interview, and one was retired. Three of these individuals were born and raised in Duck Bay, two grew up in Duck Bay and live(d) there as an adult, and one lives there in adulthood (though he also lived there for a year or two after birth). Today, three of these people live in Duck Bay, and three live in Winnipeg.

When we spoke, George Munro was seventy-two and retired from the fisheries and boxcar freight industries. He went to school until grade five or six; then, later in life, he went back to school to obtain his General Education Development for grade ten in order to get a job. He was born in Duck Bay and lived there until age twelve or thirteen. He spoke of being an altar boy at the nearby Pine Creek First Nation residential school (which was located in Camperville). George moved to Winnipeg from Duck Bay and continues to live there today.

Ray Delaronde was fifty-one when I interviewed him; he was on employment insurance and shy one credit of graduating from grade twelve through an adult education program. He was born in Dauphin and lived in Duck Bay until age one or two, when he entered the child welfare system. Ray was adopted out to the United States at age five, then moved back to Duck Bay at age eighteen. He was still living in Duck Bay when we spoke.

Lightning Rattle Woman was thirty-two years old when we met for this study. She holds a grade twelve diploma and works in the social services. She was born in Dauphin (the nearest urban community) and raised there for her first few years. She moved to Duck Bay while still a child and has lived there ever since.

Betsy was thirty-three years old at the time of being interviewed and worked in administration. She holds a college certificate. She was born and raised in Duck Bay, then moved to Winnipeg before she was a teenager and continues to live there today.

Maryanne was forty-five when we spoke regarding this study. She has a university diploma and works in social services in an educational setting. She was born in northwestern Ontario and lived there as a child until she and her family moved to Duck Bay (her parents' community). She lived in Duck Bay until graduating from university, then moved to Winnipeg, where she currently resides.

At the time of being interviewed, Whistling Eagle Child was thirty-three years old. He has a high school diploma and has pursued some college education. He works in administration. He was born and raised in Duck Bay and has lived there all his life.

Camperville

The six people connected to Camperville who participated in this study consisted of five females and one male between the ages of thirty-six and seventy-three. One person has a college diploma, three have an undergraduate degree (one of these has two undergraduate degrees, and the other two took master's degree courses but have not graduated), and two hold a master's degree. At the time of being interviewed, three were employed in the social services sector (as foster parent and as student advisor/counsellors in an education setting), one held a blue-collar job (in security), one was working in research (analysis), and one was retired. Four of these individuals grew up in Camperville, another was born and raised there, and one has a familial connection to the community, with family members having lived there. Today, all six of them live in urban areas: five in Winnipeg and one in Dauphin.

When we spoke, Karen Church was fifty-five years old and a full-time foster parent for an adult with disabilities. She holds two undergraduate degrees. Karen was born in Dauphin and raised in Camperville, where she lived until she was nineteen years old, at which time she moved to Brandon for higher education. She currently lives in Winnipeg.

Ahnungoonhs was sixty-one years old when we conducted the interview. She works in social services in an educational context and has obtained a master's of education degree. Born in Winnipegosis and raised in Camperville until age fifteen, Ahnungoonhs then moved to Winnipeg, where she lives to this day.

When I interviewed Jason McKay, he was forty-five years old. After graduating from high school, he obtained a college diploma. He works as a security guard in a health facility in Dauphin. Jason was born in Swan River and raised in Camperville until age eighteen, at which time he moved to Pine Creek First Nation. After getting married and having children, Jason and his family moved to Dauphin, where they continue to reside.

Brenda Lee Lafreniere was sixty years old when she shared her experiences for this study. She obtained a master's degree and works in social services in a higher education setting. Brenda was born in Winnipegosis—she pointed out that it is not uncommon for people from Camperville and Duck Bay to be born in Winnipegosis, since it has the nearest hospital. She was raised in Camperville until age four or five, then moved to Winnipeg until age seven or eight. From there she moved back to Camperville and resided there until she was sixteen years old. At that point, she moved to Winnipeg and still lives there today.

Louise Chippeway was seventy-three years old when we spoke together. She holds an undergraduate degree and has completed two years of a master's program. She used to be employed in equity and diversity in the Manitoba government and is now retired. Louise continues to be active in the community and does contract work as an elder, delivering cultural workshops for regional health authorities and colleges. She was born and raised in Camperville and shared with me that the community was and still is called Minegoziibe, or Negoziibe for short, in Anishinaabemowin (the Ojibwe language). Louise lived in Camperville until she was twenty-two, then moved to Winnipeg where she continues to reside.

Julia Lafreniere was thirty-six years old at the time of being interviewed. She has an undergraduate degree and has completed some coursework toward a master's degree. She was employed as a market research analyst for the Aboriginal Peoples Television Network (APTN). Julia was born in Portage la Prairie and lived there until age three, when she moved to The Pas. She lived in The Pas until she was seven, when she and her family moved to Winnipeg, where she has lived ever since (except for living in Ottawa for six months). Julia's father and his fifteen brothers and sisters were all born in Camperville, and all moved to Winnipeg or Alberta after leaving school. Her grandparents are buried in Camperville, and her father continues to hunt in the area and enjoys spending most of his time there. Julia was the CR for St. François-Xavier, where she also has a familial connection: some family members lived in St. François-Xavier and some are buried in the cemetery, including her mother. Her father lives in the neighbouring community of Cartier.

St. Laurent

There were also six participants from the Métis community of St. Laurent: five females and one male ranging in age from forty-two to eighty-three.[6] Three of these individuals have a high school diploma, two have an undergraduate degree (one of these has also met all the requirements for a master's degree except for the thesis component), and one holds a college diploma. Two people work in the business sector (small business owners), two are retired (from the health sector and a blue-collar job, respectively), one is employed as an elder for a health authority, and one works in education (as a consultant and support teacher). In terms of connection to the community, three people were born and raised in St. Laurent and continue to live there as adults, one was born and raised there, another was raised there and lives there as an adult, and one moved there as an adult. Five of these individuals continue to live in St. Laurent, and one lives in Winnipeg.

Debbie Lavallee was sixty years old at the time of our interview. She holds a college diploma and was employed as a practical nurse but has since retired. She was born and raised in St. Laurent and continues to live there to this day.

Lucille Ducharme was fifty-two and has a high school diploma. She works in the business sector as a paraprofessional in an educational context. In addition, she co-owns a couple of businesses with her husband. Lucille was born in St. Boniface but raised in St. Laurent. She continues to reside in St. Laurent today.

Barbara Bruce was sixty-seven years old when we spoke for this study. She pursued two and a half years of a university education and is employed in the business sector as an event planner and consultant. She was born in St. Laurent via midwife and raised there. Today, Barbara lives in Winnipeg.

When we spent time together for this study, Gripette was sixty-five years old. She obtained an undergraduate degree and has completed the requirements for a master's degree except for the thesis. Gripette is employed as an elder in the health field. She was born and raised in St. Laurent and resides there to this day.

Bobbie-Jo Leclair was forty-two years old at the time of interview. She has an undergraduate degree and is employed as an education consultant and as a support teacher. She was born in Edmonton and raised in Lorette. The community of St. Laurent has been her place of residence as an adult.

Jules Chartrand was eighty-three years old when he shared his experiences for this study. He has a high school diploma and was a jack-of-all-trades, working as a farm hand, railway telegraph operator, and in train traffic control. Despite retiring, he continues to do contract work for Statistics Canada, the Court of Queen's Bench, and as

a long-haul truck driver. Jules was born and raised in St. Laurent and
has lived there all his life.

Ste. Anne

I was able to speak with four Métis individuals connected to the
community of Ste. Anne. Two participants were female and two were
male; they ranged in age from twenty-five to sixty-seven. Two of the
participants have obtained a master's degree (one of these also holds a
university graduate certificate), one has an undergraduate degree, and
one holds a college diploma. All four individuals have been employed
in the field of social services, though one is now retired. Each of these
people has a familial connection to Ste. Anne; for example, ancestral
scrip for land, and, in one case, visiting the community regularly as it is
their nearest access to services. Ste. Anne is the adult residence for one
of the participants and her children. Two of the others call Winnipeg
home today, and another resides in the rural community of Ross (which
neighbours Ste. Anne).

Amanda Burton was thirty-seven years old when she shared her
experiences for this project. She has obtained a master's degree and
works in the field of social services. She was born in Winnipeg and
raised in Kelwood (a small rural community thirty minutes north of
Neepawa). Amanda also lived in Lorette for five years before moving
to Ste. Anne, where she currently resides with her children. She was
the CR for Ste. Anne.

At the time of being interviewed, Charlotte Nolin was sixty-seven
years old. She has a college diploma and has worked in the field of
social services for nearly thirty years, specializing in services and support for women struggling with addictions and/or working in the sex
trade, and their children. She was born in Winnipeg and entered the
foster care system when she was a baby. As a result, Charlotte has lived
all over southeastern Manitoba, including in Richer (near Ste. Anne)
and Lorette (as a young person, and for two years as an adult after she
bought a house there). Today, she calls Winnipeg home. Charlotte
has a familial connection to Ste. Anne through ancestral family scrip
for land in the community; her ancestors, the Nolins, were among the
first Métis families to live in the historic Métis community of Ste.
Anne. Her ancestors include Marguerite and Angélique, the Roman

Catholic–educated Métis sisters who ran the first school for Indigenous children in Red River from 1829 to 1834 (Chapter 2).

Justin L'Arrivée was twenty-five years old when we spoke on the topic of this study. He has an undergraduate degree and works in the social services field, helping provide cultural programming for Indigenous youth in the child welfare system, including taking them to sweat lodges and other ceremonies. He is a talented graphic designer on the side. Justin was born in Winnipeg and raised in Prairie Grove (an urban community just outside Lorette) until grade five, when he and his family moved to Winnipeg. He continues to reside in Winnipeg today. Justin's connection to Ste. Anne is familial: his grandmother, her father, and her grandfather all lived in Ste. Anne. His ancestors were also offered scrip; however, he is unsure of the land's location (as is the case with many Métis, owing to the legacy of colonial dispossession).

When I spoke with Louis Soren, he was fifty-seven years old. He obtained a university graduate certificate as well as a master's degree. He used to work in social services and is credited with helping co-create the Brighter Futures Initiative (a national initiative to address the suicide crisis impacting Indigenous people); he was also a community director and patient advocate for the Winnipeg Regional Health Authority. After retirement, Louis spent some time as the CEO for End Homelessness Winnipeg; he now works freelance. He was born in Ste. Agathe along the Red River and today lives in Ross, a small rural community near Ste. Anne. All of Louis's children attended the French school in Ste. Anne until graduation; he also frequents the community regularly to access services such as banking and for community service and board work. For a time, his cousin was the parish priest in Ste. Anne.

St. François-Xavier

As with Duck Bay, Camperville, and St. Laurent, six Métis people from St. François-Xavier appear in this study. Four are female and two are male; they range from forty to seventy-five years old. One person did not obtain a high school diploma, two others did (one has taken some college courses and the other some undergraduate courses), one person has a university certificate, another has two master's degrees, and one person has a doctorate. As with the participants from the other communities, these participants represent a diverse set of occupations:

one works in the business sector, one in a blue-collar job, another is a cultural advisor within the field of child welfare, another is an assistant professor, one is retired, and another was unemployed. The most common type of connection to the community for this group was familial, with five individuals having land scrip for the area and ancestors and relatives who lived there. The sixth person was born and raised in St. François-Xavier. Today, all six individuals live in urban areas: four in Winnipeg, one in Montreal, Quebec, and one in Tucson, Arizona.

At the time of our interview, Nancy was fifty years old. She has taken some community college courses and was unemployed when we spoke. Nancy was born in Selkirk and raised in Lockport, living there until age twenty or twenty-one. At that point, she moved to Winnipeg, where she still resided when we did the interview. She has a familial connection to St. François-Xavier: her ancestors lived there historically, her relatives lived there in recent history, and her family has scrip for land in the community. Nancy shared with me that she is a direct descendant of Cuthbert Grant Jr., the Métis leader who founded of the community of Grantown, or St. François-Xavier (Chapter 4).

Denise Miller was fifty-eight years old when we spoke for the purpose of this study. She has obtained two master's degrees and is a small business owner in the field of alternative health. She was born in Denver, Colorado, moved to Libya at age two, then to Long Island, New York, then to Indiana. Presently she resides in Tucson, Arizona. Denise's connection to St. François-Xavier is familial, with ancestors and relatives having lived there. Her family has scrip for land in the community; she shared that their land was directly behind the cemetery and the church but was sold in the 1960s. She is a direct descendant of Cuthbert Grant Jr. and is related to Louis Riel, on his mother's side. Most of her family reside in Winnipeg today.

Linda Chisholm was sixty-two years old when we spoke. She has a high school diploma and has taken some university courses. She works as a cultural advisor for an organization connected to the child welfare system; the organization provides culturally appropriate programming for children and families. Linda was born and raised in Winnipeg. Five of her siblings were adopted out in 1971; she herself grew up in the child welfare system from age twelve to eighteen. She continues to reside in Winnipeg today. She has a familial connection to St. François-Xavier, with her ancestors having resided in the area.

Her family genealogy records indicate that her ancestors had scrip for land in the region, including in the "Saulteaux Village," also known as Baie St. Paul (present-day St. Eustache in the municipality of St. François-Xavier).

At the time of our interview, Ronnie was seventy-two years old. He did not complete high school and left school in grade six. He is now retired. He was born and raised in St. Vital, Winnipeg, and continues to live in Winnipeg today. Ronnie also has a familial connection to St. François-Xavier, with scrip for land in his ancestors' names.

Vern Henry was seventy-five years old when he shared his experiences for this study. He holds a certificate in theology from a university in Winnipeg. He is employed as a school bus driver. Born in Brandon, Vern lived there until age six then moved to Winnipeg. He also grew up in the child welfare system. He has lived in Winnipeg since he was a small child. Like others in this group, his connection to St. François-Xavier is through his family: his ancestors have scrip for land in this community. Vern is also a direct descendant of Cuthbert Grant Jr.

Elizabeth Fast was forty years old when we spent time together for this study. She has a doctorate degree and is an assistant professor at a Canadian university. She was born in St. François-Xavier and lived there until she was five or six years old. At that point, she and her family moved to Winnipeg, where she stayed until age eighteen. She then moved to Montreal to pursue post-secondary education and has lived there on and off ever since. Elizabeth visits Winnipeg every year.

Lorette

As with Ste. Anne, I was able to locate four individuals connected to Lorette who participated in this study. All four are female; they ranged in age from eighteen to fifty-three. Two hold a high school diploma (both are now pursuing undergraduate degrees), one has a college diploma, and one has obtained an undergraduate degree and is currently pursuing a master's degree. Regarding occupation, two people are full-time university students, one works in post-secondary education, and another is employed in the business sector. Two of these participants grew up in Lorette and continue to live there as adults, one lived there as a child, and the other was born and raised there and continues to reside in Lorette to this day. Today, three of the individuals live in Lorette and one lives in Winnipeg.

Nicki Ferland was thirty-three years old when we spoke for the purpose of this study. She holds an undergraduate degree and was working on her thesis for a master's degree. She was also employed in the post-secondary education system. Nicki was born in Winnipeg and was raised in Lorette until age nine, when she moved to Winnipeg. She continued to spend weekends in Lorette until age fourteen and spent a year in Lorette at age twenty. As an adult, Nicki has lived in Winnipeg.

At the time of our interview, Janice was fifty-three years old. She has obtained a college diploma and was employed in the business sector as a project manager. Born and raised in Lorette, Janice continues to live in the community today.

Andrea Clarke (Nicki's older sister) was thirty-six years old when we spoke. She has a high school diploma and was then completing her final year in an undergraduate degree as a full-time student. Andrea was born in Winnipeg and raised in Lorette until age sixteen, at which time she moved to Winnipeg, where she continued to reside into adulthood. Ten years ago, Andrea moved back to Lorette and has been living there ever since.

Bethany (Janice's daughter) was eighteen years old when we spoke together about this study. She has a high school diploma and was pursuing an undergraduate degree. In addition to being a full-time student, she was also picking up summer employment at a Métis National Historic Site. Bethany was born in Winnipeg but raised in Lorette. She has continued to live in Lorette as an adult except when living out of province during the academic year in order to attend her university.

Demographic Patterns

With assistance from the CRs, it was relatively easy to locate people who met the criteria for participation for the Métis communities of Duck Bay, Camperville, and St. Laurent. More Métis people wanted to participate in this study than we were able to accommodate, notably in St. Laurent. That we were able to find more people in St. Laurent may be explained by the fact that the CR herself was from that community and resides there. Also, my maternal family comes from that community—even if folks in St. Laurent do not know me personally, they know my grandmother and late grandfather, my mother and her six brothers, and my cousins. This may have helped to create a sense of familiarity that facilitated rapport and trust, especially given the potentially sensitive topic of ceremonies.

Conversely, I had a hard time (even with assistance from the CRs) locating six participants in the Métis communities of St. François-Xavier, Ste. Anne, and Lorette. While I ended up with six in St. François-Xavier, we found only four participants in the other two communities. This was the case even though the CRs who assisted with Ste. Anne and Lorette had both lived in those communities, in adulthood and childhood, respectively. Perhaps an explanation can be found in the overall demographic patterns for these communities. Unlike in Duck Bay, Camperville, and St. Laurent, the non-Indigenous community in St. François-Xavier, Ste. Anne, and Lorette now outnumbers the Indigenous population. As discussed in Chapter 4, the resulting pressures to assimilate may have taken their toll over the years; subsequently, these communities offer fewer opportunities to participate in ceremonies—and there are fewer potential people in the community to connect with and go to ceremonies together.

Also note that there are many more female than male participants in this study—twenty-three and nine, respectively. Because of the effects of colonization, the population of Métis people in Manitoba who attend ceremonies is likely small (but steadily growing); therefore, I was unable to ensure equal gender representation (including transgender individuals) with the additional criterion of having a connection to one of the six Métis communities. More women than men can often be found in Indigenous ceremonies themselves. This has been the case in ceremonies I have attended—on the "women's side" of the sweat lodge we are usually packed like sardines while the "men's side" is spacious in comparison. Remarks can be heard about women outnumbering men at different types of ceremonies whether they be in Manitoba, Ontario, or elsewhere, and it is not uncommon to hear the question "Where are the other men?" This gender dynamic can also be seen at the Sundance I dance at, as well as at the Sundance my wife dances at.

There exists a wide age range among the Métis people in this study, from eighteen to eighty-three years. It is exciting to see that Métis people of all ages are interested in and, in some cases, committing to a life of ceremony. The most common age decades among participants in this study were thirties, fifties, and sixties, which indicates an older demographic. Many people in this study were suggested to me from the personal and ceremonial networks of the CRs, who themselves ranged in age from thirties to sixties. Also, the age limit to participate in this study was eighteen (to steer clear of the added ethical issues that arise when including teenagers and children in a research study). In addition, teenagers often go through a period of exploration and experimentation when they are susceptible to peer pressure and might think going to ceremonies with their parents is "uncool." Indeed, I have noticed fewer people at ceremonies in the teenager to young adult age range.[7]

The level of educational attainment among the Métis folks in this study is balanced. On one end of the spectrum are twelve people who do not have a high school diploma or have not graduated from grade twelve, and on the other end are thirteen people who have obtained a university degree (seven undergraduate, five master's, and one doctorate). It is interesting to note that Métis people without higher education as well as those with post-secondary and graduate education are participating in ceremonies.

Another noteworthy demographic factor was the degree to which participants had close personal connections to the community with which they identified. St. Laurent had the most participants who were born and raised there and who continue to reside there in adulthood. On the flip side, St. François-Xavier was the Métis community with the fewest number of participants who were born and/or raised there, and/or continue to live there in adulthood. At the same time, this was the community with the highest number of participants with familial connections (ancestral connections via scrip for land, or relatives who lived there historically or more recently). As in other small rural communities, retention has been a growing issue, with an increasing number of people moving away from their home community in pursuit of educational and employment opportunities in larger rural and urban locations. While this may help to explain the situation in St. François-Xavier, it is also true that most participants in this study are now living in urban areas (especially Winnipeg). This residence pattern of urbanization can also be found among Indigenous populations in general.[8]

Several people in this study were born in the nearest urban area to the Métis community that they were raised in. This was particularly noticeable for participants in the communities of Duck Bay and Camperville, who were born in Dauphin and Winnipegosis, since those are where the nearest hospitals are located. Similarly, while Ste. Anne has a small hospital, people from that community (and from nearby Lorette) are often born in Winnipeg hospitals—as was the case for some folks in this study. Unsurprisingly, the participants connected to St. François-Xavier had the widest array of birthplaces and locations of adult residence for the reasons noted above.

One final demographic pattern I want to highlight is that the Métis people in this study were connected to multiple Métis communities. These connections can be understood in terms of ongoing historic kinship and residence patterns, with ancestors and relatives moving from one Métis community (sometimes not by choice) to another—recall the discussion in Chapter 4 about historic migration patterns between many of the Métis communities in this study. Evelyn Peters, Matthew Stock, and Adrian Werner illustrate how Métis families who experienced pressures from outside forces to leave their communities often chose (as recently as the 1950s) to move to another Métis community, usually where they had kinship relationships, to maintain a sense of Métis-specific community and values.[9] This occurred when Métis in Winnipeg were pushed out of their homes by incoming White settlers and formed the Métis road allowance community of Rooster Town, only to be evicted from that community in the 1950s and early 1960s by the City of Winnipeg as urbanization expanded and the Grant Park Shopping Centre, Grant Park High School, and Pan Am Pool were built.

Métis scrip for land is another reason that Métis people have connections to multiple Métis communities. Sometimes the land designated to the name-bearer on the scrip coupon was located in a different Métis community, and they were expected to move from the Métis community they currently resided in (Chapter 6). Métis families are often aware of these historic patterns and know they have relatives who continue to live in other Métis communities. Examples of connections to multiple Métis communities can be heard in stories shared by Amanda, Charlotte, and Justin, who each mentioned familial connections to Ste. Anne and Lorette (recall that these historic Métis communities are only twenty kilometres apart), by Bobbie-Jo, whose family is connected to St. Laurent and Lorette, and by Julia, whose family has connections to Camperville and St. François-Xavier.

~

In this chapter, I have briefly introduced the participants and discussed demographic patterns within and across the six historic Métis communities of this study in terms of the participants' gender, age, education, employment, and relationship to community. These demographics provide useful context that helps to understand the stories and experiences shared by the Métis people in this study. The remaining chapters of this book offer an in-depth exploration of such stories shared across the overarching themes of family history, self-identification and personal experiences, and relationship to spirituality.

CHAPTER 6

Métis Family Relationships with Land, Language, and Identity

In the pages to come, I explore participants' family histories to illuminate intergenerational Métis relationships with Indigenous spirituality. Even if Métis families were disconnected from ceremonies while growing up, there may be shared experiences in family histories among those who have found their way to ceremonies later in life. More specifically, the people who contributed to this study shared stories about their families' connections to Métis communities, Métis scrip, registered Indian status, Indigenous languages, and family self-identification. Excerpts from the participants' accounts bring to life their lived experiences, emotions, and perspectives, and illustrate themes that emerged across all six Métis communities, as well as interesting patterns within each community.

Family Connections to Métis Communities

Participants shared stories about family relationships with Métis communities; their families are connected to multiple Métis communities beyond those featured in this study. Moreover, multiple generations—at least up to their grandparents—have lived in at least one of these communities. Interestingly, when discussing family relationships with Métis territory and communities, several people mentioned registered Indian status as well as "living on the land"; I discuss both of these points later in the chapter (and in Chapter 7).

Everyone from Ste. Anne and Lorette spoke of family connections to multiple Métis communities; people from St. Laurent spoke least about these—long-term residence can be seen in the latter. This is noteworthy, given that the St. Laurent participants had the highest degree of direct, personal connection to their community and continue to live in their community in the greatest number (Chapter 5). Recall that greater pressures to assimilate were experienced in Ste. Anne and Lorette as the White settler population came to outnumber the Indigenous one. Consequently, some Métis inhabitants of these communities, including their ancestors or older relatives, moved away. Also recall that in the early history of these Métis communities in Manitoba, residents moved between them for varying reasons over time (Chapters 4 and 5).

The list of Métis communities that participants' families were connected to is extensive.[1] People from Camperville spoke of their grandparents first living in the Métis communities of St. Laurent and Ste. Madeleine, then moving to Camperville for various reasons (including economic) and, in the case of Ste. Madeleine, being forced to move when the community was destroyed by the Province of Manitoba. Karen shared painful family memories of being evicted from Ste. Madeleine: "We used to hear a lot of stories about that—where all of our relatives came from, and what happened when the Métis houses were burned. It upset my mom that a lot of them were . . . like the graves were turned over; they had no respect for the graves. So, she always went back there and she—I don't even know if there's a monument there now for the names? We've always heard that side of the story."[2] Some participants from Camperville also mentioned having relatives who live in St. François-Xavier.

In the neighbouring Métis community of Duck Bay, a couple of people talked about ancestors having first lived along the Red River before moving to Duck Bay, or having come from St. Laurent and then moving to Duck Bay (after accepting scrip money). Maryanne has one parent from Camperville and one from Duck Bay; she also has relatives in the Métis community of St. Lazare.[3] Similar patterns can be found among the people from St. Laurent: for example, Gripette's family history goes back to the Red River Settlement before St. Laurent existed. She also mentioned other Métis communities: "We have connections to St. Eustache, and my brother married into St. Ambroise; so, St. Laurent, St. Ambroise, and St. Eustache are very connected." Bobbie-Jo was raised in Lorette before moving to St. Laurent (her maternal family's community) as an adult. Janice and Bethany, mother and daughter from Lorette, have family who originally lived in St. Laurent before moving to Lorette. Andrea and Nicki (sisters), also from Lorette, had ancestors who first lived in the Métis community of Ile des Chênes (mother's community) before moving to Lorette (father's community). Nicki recalled that her maternal ancestors lived in St. Vital in Louis Riel's family home: "At times, the Poitras, who were my great-grandmothers, actually lived in [the Riel family] home as well and raised their families there and spent a lot of time in the Riel House—which is now a historic museum."

St. François-Xavier and Ste. Anne participants also mentioned several other Métis communities that their family is directly connected to. Those from St. François-Xavier described historic family connections to the site of the Battle of Seven Oaks (Red River Settlement) and other communities with a strong Métis presence in what became Winnipeg, including St. Norbert (formerly Rivière Salle) and St. Boniface. Other Métis communities were also identified, such as Baie St. Paul (St. Eustache), Ashern, Ste. Rose du Lac, Eddystone (formerly Cayer), San Clara (formerly Ste. Claire), Boggy Creek, and the Roblin area. Nancy illustrated these extensive kinship connections across Métis communities:

> My grandparents lived [in St. François-Xavier] for many, many years. And for over ten years, I used to go there every summer. We used to go to my grandparents' house because they were actually married in San Clara, but they ended up staying and had a house in Ste. Rose du Lac. They were firmly [did not finish sentence]—everyone was related to each other [around] there. I'm related to many people in Ste. Rose du Lac. My grandparents are buried there. . . . We travelled through that area and we used to go—my mother was going to cemeteries . . . [to visit] some of our relatives. . . . And, we would drive through Eddystone and those areas, and the Manitoba Narrows—my aunt lived there. We were all over those places because we had relatives at every one of those [Métis] towns.

People from Ste. Anne also mentioned family connections to several Métis communities (or communities known for having a large Métis population). These included St. François-Xavier, Prairie Grove,[4] San Clara, Lorette, Ste. Agathe (formerly Petit Point au Roches, Pointe à Grouette, or Petite Pointe à Saline), St. Boniface, and Ross. Charlotte's

ancestors are also connected to the Battle of Seven Oaks (Red River
Settlement), to the Métis community of Duck Lake in Saskatchewan,
and to the Turtle Mountain region in southwest Manitoba. As a result
of being in the foster care system, Charlotte herself has lived in many
Métis communities (or communities with large Métis populations),
including St. Norbert, St. Pierre-Jolys, St. Malo, Lorette, and Richer
(formerly Coteau de Chênes, then Thibaultville). In addition to Ste.
Anne, Louis's family also has connections to the Métis communities of
Ste. Agathe, St. Boniface, and Ross. Louis discussed the fact that Métis
land and communities were extensive before the shifts in demographics
brought about by incoming White settlers:

> Ste. Agathe Parish is where Louis Riel hid on his way, after
> the rebellion, he had to make his way to the States. But he
> spent time in Ste. Agathe because he was Catholic; Louis
> Riel spent time there, so there's a lot of Métis alliances with
> that community. The whole territory was Métis land; St.
> Boniface, it was all Métis land. It was Métis until someone
> "better" [in the eyes of the government] came to own the
> land; [we had to give] up the Métis land to French people
> there. But, for a long time, it was Métis land, [until] "good
> Catholics" got the land; so, there's a lot of Métis roots in
> Ste. Agathe and in the area. Those roots were not allowed to
> thrive [or] show themselves.

Louis continued:

> We discovered that Ross, Manitoba, is one of those commu-
> nities that's Métis land [and has] a lot of Métis families. The
> Lagimodière [family] had a strong connection to the Métis
> Nation, [through] Louis Riel. [Ross] was part of that family
> of land, and [Bishop] Taché had a parish down the road in
> Ste. Geneviève. So, Ross is a Métis family there; Ross is a
> very well-known Métis family name. And they were settled
> here because they were instrumental in building the aqueduct
> for the Winnipeg water district railway to bring water from
> Shoal Lake to Winnipeg. They were the people willing to
> work, usually in bad conditions and tough environments as
> far as marshy lands, bush lands. And they weren't afraid of

working in the wilderness kind of area, because this is the last [Métis] settlement before you almost get to, it's all bush and wild before you get to, Shoal Lake from here. So, they were the ones that, the crews were settled here. There used to be a school here, there used to be all kinds of things here.

In addition to being connected to several Métis communities, many participants' families reported intergenerational connections to Métis communities.

Many participants shared that their families have been living in their Métis community for generations, at least since their grandparents' generation—and some continue to live there.[5] This was the case for more than half the people in each of the communities in this study except St. François-Xavier. Camperville interviewees commented on their families' long-standing and ongoing connections to the community. Louise explained, "That would be Camperville. I mean, it was there from time immemorial. We were always there. That's my connection to my homeland. That's my homeland. That's where I come from." Likewise, Julia shared, "That's where my roots are. That's where my grandparents are buried and my family that passed on. We have a lot of ties to that community. My dad [who was raised in St. François-Xavier along with his fifteen brothers and sisters, still] goes hunting or fishing [there]; that's where he likes to spend most of his time." George's family has been living in Duck Bay since they moved there from St. Laurent, when scrip was being distributed in the late 1800s. Similar sentiments were expressed by people from St. Laurent. For example, Jules said, "My father, Aimé Chartrand, was from St. Laurent and so was my grandfather and great-grandfather and other people in our family, grandmothers and great-grandmothers and all that. We were descendants of the Red River Métis buffalo hunters and voyageurs. We're from the Manitoba Métis community, Red River." Gripette had this to say: "This is our Métis territory. St. Laurent is a historic Métis community. I was born here, both my parents were born here, their parents were born here, and we go all the way back to the Red River Settlement. From there, they came here, and we've been here ever since." Family relationships to multiple Métis communities, as well as across multiple generations, can be further understood when considering the impacts of Métis scrip.

Métis Scrip

Nearly three-quarters of the participants were aware of having Métis scrip in their family (Figure 24).[6] Of those, just shy of half knew some detail about what happened; for example, whether the scrip was for land or money, where the land was supposed to be located, or what happened to the land. The communities with the highest number of people reporting scrip in their family were (in decreasing order): Camperville and St. François-Xavier, St. Laurent, Lorette, and Ste. Anne.[7] Only two people from Duck Bay indicated their family had Métis scrip. This may have to do with the creation of the Duck Bay Band, which entered Treaty 4 in 1874—even though many Métis members subsequently withdrew from treaty (Chapter 4). A few participants explained that they were aware of their family's scrip because they had done extensive family history research—for example, to obtain citizenship in the Manitoba Metis Federation. Moreover, the history of scrip is intertwined with the history of treaties and registered Indian status; as some participants share below, when status was lost and the individual subsequently removed from treaty and their reserve, they sometimes had the option of taking Métis scrip.[8]

In Camperville, Anungoohns knew that her paternal grandfather was supposed to receive land in the Camperville area. Brenda learned that ten ancestors on her father's side were supposed to receive scrip (some in the St. Boniface area) and that most accepted money instead of land. She said, "I think most of them did it for the money because they were poor, eh. I was able to read some of them this morning that it was [for] $160 which is kind of sad." Likewise, Louise shared that her ancestors "got scrip but somehow, they lost it, or they sold their land and when they tried to get it back, they weren't able to get it back. It became—the land that we lived on in Camperville—it became Crown land. [But, at] one time it was Métis lands around there."

People connected to St. François-Xavier indicated that their family's scrip was issued in locations such as St. Boniface, St. Norbert, and possibly Kinosota, in addition to St. François-Xavier. Elizabeth explained, "There were [scrip] lots in St. Boniface and St. Norbert. I know the actual numbers; I found them. My great-great and my great-great-great grandparents were also on record for being at the signing of the Manitoba Act. . . . [I also found] their lot numbers and

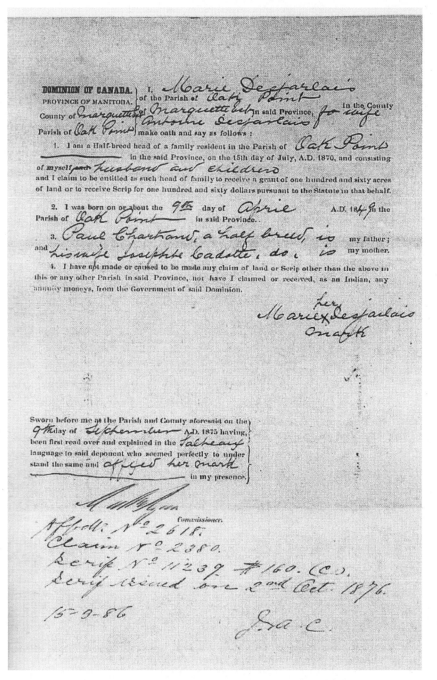

Figure 24. Example of Métis scrip issued to author's ancestor Marie Desjarlais, 2 October 1876.

I cross-referenced it with their dates of birth and their exact names. I have probably ten or fifteen pages of history that I've been able to piece together in addition to the scrip." Nancy was aware that copies of scrip in her family were explained to her ancestors in the languages of French and Cree; she also hinted at some of the problems of the scrip system: "It was kind of interesting because they couldn't sign their name at that time because it was very early scrip; they indicated [their signatures] with the mark X." Vern brought up additional challenges associated with trying to uncover scrip details (on his maternal side) because of being adopted out of his Métis family: "I'm even further away because 'I don't have family' [air quotes]. I have a half-sister who won't talk to me, and I have another half-sister who I've met, and we've talked [but] she's from my father's side."

Three of the people from St. Laurent were aware of some of the details regarding their family's scrip. Jules had perhaps the most extensive knowledge:

> I looked up in my genealogy there, some people signed for scrip. Pierre Chartrand claim[ed lot] #2366 in 1876 and, apparently, he did get a piece of land. The one that my father and his brothers and sisters had there in the south end [of St. Laurent], that was part of the land that he got as scrip. But nobody else did; like my grandfather, all his brothers and sisters [did not get scrip] as compared to all the immigrants that were coming in here. All the Mennonites and Ukrainians, they would get, the man would get free land—"homestead" they called it. And, the wife, I think they would get something like 240 acres each or 100 acres and something each. And, each child that was twenty-one, they would all get so many acres each. [The Mennonite families] would register the other ones, the younger ones, and when they got to be twenty-one, they got handed land [too]. But, the Métis were here already, so they couldn't do it that way. My brother wrote a book on it and 80 per cent of the Métis—and I think it was worse in St. Laurent, the majority of Métis—never got any land, no land whatsoever. There was also Norbert Laurence, that's my grandmother's father, in 1828, he signed for scrip at the same time as his wife, Josette Parenteau. Yeah, [in] 1828 they both signed for scrip. Whether they got land or

not, I don't know, but they might have. But, none of their children got any.[9]

Barbara echoed this, stating that most Métis never received the land promised to them via scrip:

B: [The community of] St. Laurent was offered scrip. In fact, I have the books with the genealogy, the names of people that were offered scrip. And, you know this, most of the scrip was lost in that community, like [along] all of the shores of Lake Manitoba. In St. Laurent, around St. Laurent, was scrip land.

Where all those cottages are now?

B: Yeah, so it's from the lake back 120 acres, and around the community.

Everyone connected to Lorette knew that their ancestors were supposed to receive scrip. However, they struggled to piece together details of this scrip and what became of it, as can be heard in Nicki's comments:

Both sides [of my parents' ancestors] had farmland. However, we do know that generally Métis families who got the acreage as opposed to the dollars [from scrip] were put in much more northern areas like in the rough [land unsuitable for agriculture]; and, it is more likely that settlers would [get] farmland close to Winnipeg. So, I doubt that the farms that my father's family had in Lorette, and the farms that my mother's family had in Ile des Chênes, would have been those 160 acres [from scrip]. If I had to guess or make an assumption, I would say they probably took the dollars [then bought land], but it's a guess. I don't know how it shook out for people [like my ancestors] who were on the Provisional Government that established Manitoba, because we do know that André [Beauchemin]'s son, Léon, was the one who farmed that land in Ile des Chênes. So, perhaps those members of the Provisional Government got better acreages of land, like in more southern places; but again, I'm just guessing here.

Similar challenges are evident in the following statement by Janice, who is discussing scrip for land in St. Laurent that her ancestor was supposed to receive:

After Great-great-grandfather passed—we don't know all the details—but once he passed, [my great-great-grandmother] did still have a few of the children with her, and gave up her treaty rights to get scrip, to get some of those scrip benefits, in terms of, I think, the money. Did she actually get the land? We don't think so. There's nothing, there's no history of that yet or proven continuation of that to this day. So, we believe she took scrip because she needed the money; she no longer had a spouse and she still had some children that she needed to support and provide for.

Janice added intriguing details regarding the switch from treaty to scrip:

> J: When Great-grandmother gave up her treaty rights and took scrip, they had a two-page little interview, like it was questions. . . . There's actually these two additional pages where they ask her a whole bunch of detailed questions: How many children does she have? Where do they all live? There's a whole bunch of things. . . . And, she specified exactly where they lived, for all the periods of time.
>
> **Do those papers ask what her reasons were for leaving treaty to take scrip?**
>
> J: No. That's a key one but, of course, they wouldn't be asked. I don't think they'd be asking that; they just ask that she's giving it up, and she says "yes."

Likewise, in Ste. Anne, all but one person was aware of scrip in their family but knew few, if any, details. Amanda knew the names of two of her ancestors who were supposed to receive scrip in St. François-Xavier. Charlotte was aware of two dozen scrip issued to her ancestors. Louis was the only participant connected to Ste. Anne who was unsure of whether any of his ancestors had been offered scrip. He discussed Métis families being forcibly removed from their communities across the plains and "forgetting" their connections (including their relationship with scrip) after the Red River Resistance of 1869–70 and the Northwest Resistance of 1885 (in Saskatchewan). He also spoke of added challenges in piecing his family history together because of the complication of his mother being born out of wedlock (as a result of rape) and therefore not being allowed to marry in a church. In Louis's own words:

It's a complicated thing when you're trying to reclaim some of this history—beginning with my mom's history of being born out of wedlock. We'll have to go [research scrip in] Chitek Lake, and Saskatchewan, north of Saskatoon, north of Spiritwood. Her family was involved in the Métis rebellion at Batoche, is deeply rooted there as Métis. But, if you think it was bad [for Métis] along the Red River [after 1870], it was really bad around Batoche [after 1885], so we don't know [about family scrip]. [The] Métis Nation is kind of like a dandelion where the wind blows all the seeds everywhere. So, we don't know that we come from the same plant because we're all over the place. We were forced against the winds of colonization, and all these things that force us to scatter rather than stay together. So, reclaiming our relationships is an ongoing thing.[10]

Finally, only a few people from Duck Bay were certain that their ancestors had been offered scrip. Whistling Eagle Child spoke of his maternal great-grandfather and great-great-grandfather being offered scrip in Winnipeg. He described his family talking about this scrip as "outstanding," and therefore assumes they never got land or money. George spoke of his relatives, the Chartrands, receiving scrip in St. Laurent; he said they took money instead of land and moved north to Duck Bay. George also pinpointed challenges and corruption in the scrip system itself: "All those scrip—we did the research—are all illegal. Because, in order for a scrip to be enforced it had to be sworn in front of a justice of the peace with two witnesses. It never happened because [instead] the Indian agents signed it right there on the spot and [they] got a [fraudulent] witness here. They stole the land [from us Métis]." The issue of scrip becomes a little clearer (or murkier!) when we also take into consideration treaty and registered Indian status.

Registered Indian Status

One-quarter of participants indicated they had at least one family member with registered Indian status (historically or contemporarily). Moreover, several mentioned a female family member who had lost status because of "marrying out" (marrying a non status man);[11] three people explained that status was lost by an ancestor when they married a Métis man. Other reasons for losing status included moving away from the reserve and giving up treaty or status to take scrip (as mentioned above with Janice's widowed great-great-grandmother). Some folks discussed family members who obtained status after amendments to the Indian Act, such as Bill C-31, which has enabled some women and their children to regain status after having lost it for marrying out. A handful of people were unsure if anyone in their family ever had status, and one person was certain none of their ancestors had Indian status. Only three participants have status themselves (two in Camperville and one in Duck Bay).

Everyone from Camperville and Duck Bay indicated that at least one person in their family has or had registered Indian status, and seven of these (four in Camperville, three in Duck Bay) lost status for marrying out. In Camperville, Anungoohns, Louise, Brenda, and Julia all spoke of female family members losing status for this reason. Julia's grandmother lost her status when she married her Métis husband. She spoke about divisions in her family over whether they should pursue regaining status. Similarly, Brenda explained, "My great-grandmother lost her Treaty [Indian status] when she married Alex Chartrand [a Métis man whose family originated in the Red River Settlement but had moved to Duck Bay]." Brenda described her family history as a blend of Métis and First Nations communities: "My mom's side have Métis and Treaty status from St. Boniface, Shoal River, Key Reserve, Duck Bay, Red River Settlement, and Qu'Appelle, Saskatchewan."[12] She has been unable to get status herself—her father tried to get it fifteen years ago and became angry when he was unsuccessful. Jason's grandmother was raised by her grandparents in the community of Mafeking; he spoke of her being "signed out" of the reserve at Sapatoyak Cree Nation (i.e., she lost her status) but was unsure of why this happened. Jason was the only one in his family to have status, though he was raised by a Métis stepfather. Anungoohns has obtained Bill C-31 status, as has Louise's mother.

Folks connected to Duck Bay also spoke of family members with Indian status. Betsy's father's side of the family all have registered Indian status with Pine Creek First Nation, but no one on her Métis mother's side has status. In this community, it was more common for participants to talk about their ancestors losing status, especially for marrying out—as was the case in Maryanne's family. The loss of status was additionally complex for George's mother. As he explained, "My mom lost her status because the priests forced the marriage on my mom. That only lasted one week.... The priest brought people from up north, and married people against their wishes.... [They became] non-status."

People in Duck Bay also spoke of regaining status, including Ray. Several of Lightning Rattle Woman's relatives have now regained status, though she herself does not have status. Whistling Eagle Child's father has obtained status, but he himself does not have it. Several people on Maryanne's maternal side of the family have obtained status, but she and her mother have not. George obtained Bill C-31 status in 1995, as did many of his family members (excluding one family line). He spoke extensively about trying to regain reserve status for Duck Bay and the fact that many Chartrands from Duck Bay have reinstated status. He insisted that the Duck Bay reserve was surrendered illegally: "[In] Pine Creek, they moved out of a reserve there—there was about eighteen people at that meeting or twenty people [who supposedly surrendered the Duck Bay reserve]. And the people who signed that leave of surrender, not one of those people who signed that surrender is an original person from Duck Bay.... Well, the church got involved.... See, what the church done, they eliminated Duck Bay's and Camperville's Treaty 4 [and] Treaty 2 [relationship] and made one INAC [Indian and Northern Affairs Canada] reserve in 1905: Pine Creek."[13] However, not everyone in Duck Bay supported the idea of Duck Bay as a reserve; there seemed to be a lot of division in the community regarding this subject. This can be heard in an excerpt from Maryanne's interview:

> [My dad] said that someone came around and was trying to get him to sign on to suing the Manitoba Metis Federation and saying that Duck Bay was once a reserve. There were some forms and my dad's just so old school, he was like "bullshit" [and refused to sign it]. . . . People went around and they were trying to tell people that Duck Bay used to be a reserve, similar to Pine Creek. But that way back when, the Métis took it over and it became a Métis settlement when all the priests and the mission came there.... [MMF] President Chartrand came [to Duck Bay] and he was talking to the community about—it was when they won their Supreme Court ruling. So, was it 2016? He came around to the communities and was talking to community about winning the Supreme Court ruling, and [asked] what the community

wanted to do with the money. So, it was more like a consultation for all the communities. And I happened to be there, so
my kids and I and my dad went to go listen to what they were
talking about, about this ruling and money that they won.
And there were people in the room, like I know everybody
there, it's a small community. But I was surprised because, it
was weird, you could see the visible divide. . . .

**In that meeting were they also talking about the whole
reserve thing?**

M: There was some talk of it but not too much. It was more
about the scrip and what was [MMF President] David
[Chartrand] going to do with those families that had scrip?
And "How dare he speak for all of the people in community?"
That type of thing.

While Maryanne's family does not have status, her story highlights a
rift in the community regarding whether blame is to be laid with the
MMF for the surrender of Duck Bay. It seems the church, government,
and Indian agents were responsible for the original surrender; however,
some community members feel the MMF has exacerbated the situation
and is preventing talks of potential reserve status in favour of continuing
to recognize the community as Métis.[14] There are no easy answers in
this situation, and it is obvious that the community has a long history
of First Nations and Métis inhabitation, intermarriage, and cultural
overlap. It is not surprising that these (primarily government-imposed)
divisions and strong feelings continue to be felt.

In St. Laurent, all but one participant mentioned having at least one
family member with registered Indian status. One side of Bobbie-Jo's
family is Cree and has status; both Barbara and Gripette spoke of individuals with status marrying into their family and having nieces and
nephews with status as a result. Some also spoke of family members
regaining status, including Lucille's mother and her mother's siblings.
Only Jules discussed ancestors who had lost status for marrying out.
He indicated that both his father's grandmothers lost status for this
reason; however, he later admitted that he was unsure of this: "Both of
my father's grandmothers were treaty Indians and they lost their treaty
status because they married Métis. I see in certain papers and books
and stuff they say that Indian women would lose their treaty status if

they married White men. Well neither of [my grandmothers] married White men; my dad's two grandmothers, they married Métis guys. Now, these Métis guys, their mothers were treaty Indians, but these women still lost their status. Really, I think we should be Indians. I don't think we should have lost status, but we did. So, we're Métis." Later Jules shared: "In my family, like I mentioned, nobody in my immediate family [has status]. . . . My grandfather's mother was a pure Indian, she was Blackfoot and my grandmother's mother was Saulteaux. So, they must have had Indian status, but I'm only assuming that. I don't know for sure." None of the people from St. Laurent has status themselves.

Of the participants connected to Ste. Anne, Justin, Charlotte, and Louis mentioned a family member with status. Justin's mother is Cree from Peguis First Nation and has status, and he himself is eligible for it; none of his father's Métis side has status. Charlotte talked about an uncle who moved to the United States and joined treaty in the Turtle Mountain area, and her maternal grandparents who were from White Dog First Nation (and presumably also had status). Louis spoke of an uncle who he believes has status but again mentioned the difficulty and secrecy surrounding his family history owing to tensions stemming from sexual abuse, having a child out of wedlock, and issues with alcohol.

In Lorette, Janice and Bethany spoke of status in their family. As mentioned above, their female ancestor gave up status to take scrip after being widowed. Janice was aware that her great-grandmother and great-grandfather had status in Treaty 2 and received treaty monies. Bethany, Janice's daughter, gave a different explanation for her great-great-grandmother's loss of status, saying it was due to marrying a non-status Métis man. She also said that her grandmother has no interest in trying to regain status. Bethany explained: "My grandma could technically be a status Indian per se, but she doesn't feel the need to do that, because she was raised Métis. She's just not that interested in that side of it. . . . There was talk of [trying to regain status], but it just never, they never went through with it. They never felt that they were that identity [First Nation]. So, they just kept their Métis [citizenship] cards and their Métis status, and they were content with that." Andrea and Nicki do not know if anyone in their family ever had status.

Of those connected to St. François-Xavier, only Ronnie and Elizabeth spoke of having a family member with registered Indian status; the rest were unsure. Ronnie's grandson has status through his parent, who married into Ronnie's family. Elizabeth's aunt married a Mi'kmaq man with status.

As illustrated by the participants in this study, Métis people have a complex relationship with registered Indian status. Despite offering people a choice between identifying as Métis and taking scrip, or identifying as Indian and taking treaty, the government increasingly encouraged (pushed) an ever-greater number of individuals to take scrip, since this was economically more efficient for the government. Following this, a stereotype developed that only First Nations people have status and Métis people do not. This stereotype is exacerbated by the fact that the federal government, the Métis National Council, and First Nations' band councils all say that one cannot be both status Indian and Métis. This leaves families with long histories of having both First Nations and Métis family members in a confused state. Indeed, some individuals have a status parent and a Métis parent, yet they are told they "cannot be both."[15] Overlap between Métis and First Nations cultures, as well as conflicting messages coming from Indigenous and colonial governments and institutions alike, merit additional examination and discussion—including consideration of how such conflicting messaging impacts identity, relationships (and exaggerated divisions) between Métis and First Nations relatives, and access to section 35 Aboriginal rights.

Indigenous Languages

More than half of the participants indicated that one or more people in their family can speak an Indigenous language. The most frequently cited language was Michif,[16] followed closely by Anishinaabemowin (Saulteaux/Ojibwe) and Nêhiyawawin (Cree). More than half of the respondents also shared that one or more family member could speak multiple Indigenous (and non-Indigenous) languages. Historically, Métis people were multilingual,[17] and this characteristic of Métis culture persists for some today. Eight participants indicated that they themselves are fluent in an Indigenous language: four identified Michif, three mentioned Anishinaabemowin, and one Nêhiyawawin. Thirteen individuals reported understanding a bit and being able to speak at least a few words in an Indigenous language but did not identify as an

Indigenous language speaker, while the remaining eleven people do not understand or speak an Indigenous language.

When taking a closer look at each of the communities, it is noteworthy that everyone in St. Laurent, Duck Bay, and Ste. Anne indicated that one or more of their family members could speak an Indigenous language: Michif, Anishinaabemowin, and Nêhiyawawin, respectively. The following comments by Jules, from St. Laurent, highlight the fact that the Michif French dialect has been spoken in that community for generations and that residents also know standard French and use it strategically: "Me and my dad spoke Michif, and a majority of the Métis people in St. Laurent [do too]; so, all my brothers and sisters grew up speaking Métis dialect of French, which we all call Michif. As opposed to the other Michif; there's two forms of Michif. There's another Michif, farther north and farther west, that originated there—it's a combination of Cree and Michif." He continued: "[My paternal grandfather] spoke Michif French but wrote in standard French. But, the majority of them, people in St. Laurent, did [this too] at that time. I saw some records, they used to have a school board at that south end there and the guys used to take turns being the chairman and it's all written in standard French. Yeah, all written in very good standard French. But, none of them would have spoken like that; they would have spoken Michif."

Several people also discussed ways in which their families, at least the older generations, were multilingual. Gripette, from St. Laurent, explained: "My dad spoke English, French, Michif, Cree, Ojibwe, and Icelandic. Well, they had to, right? To survive. And my mother was brought up by a Cree uncle and an Ojibwe auntie. So, my mother understood Cree, Ojibwe, English, and French, and Michif. That's [the case for] most of the people in St Laurent." In Camperville, Louise shared that "we speak three languages, or maybe even four. For sure there's the Michif, the Cree, Ojibwe, and English. I grew up with those languages." Echoing this, Brenda (also from Camperville) explained: "My dad speaks Michif, Cree, Ojibwe, and English. My mom speaks Cree, Ojibwe, and English. The first language of my parents is Cree. They speak Cree amongst themselves, their siblings, and so I refer to myself as Métis Cree and Ojibwe." Julia, also connected to Camperville, had this to say: "My grandma spoke five languages: she spoke Cree, and Saulteaux, and English, French, and Michif. . . . My older aunties will talk Cree to each other. And my dad, we were talking about this recently, he said that until he went to school, they spoke all five languages in the home; they couldn't differentiate between the languages." Another recollection from Jules (St. Laurent), the oldest participant in this study, highlights this theme:

> My grandfather Chartrand, he could speak, read, and write four languages. I saw myself, when I was four, five years old; I went to his place and he was writing, handwriting. He had papers on his table, he explained to me he was writing to two of his brothers; he had more than that but this particular day he was writing to a brother in Camperville and a brother in The Pas. He was writing in Cree, in the syllabics—he was explaining to me how some of those syllabics work, the sounds they make, and some of that. And he could speak Cree, he could speak Saulteaux, French, and English. He spoke Michif French but wrote in standard French.

While older generations were multilingual, this was not the case for younger generations, unfortunately. Participants in each of the communities discussed Indigenous language loss and pressures to assimilate. Several reasons for this loss emerged, including the education system and clergy enforcing a hierarchy of French dialect and "proper French" (especially in day schools via corporal punishment); being shamed for speaking an Indigenous language; urbanization; being discouraged by French-Canadian family members; older generations not teaching younger generations, in an effort to escape discrimination; and internalized linguistic assimilation. George (Duck Bay) observed, "No one speaks the languages [in Duck Bay anymore]. Only the old people. There's only a few old people in Camperville that speak Michif. There's one that's trying to train people but it's hard to train them."[18] Nancy (St. François-Xavier) and Charlotte (Ste. Anne) pinpointed the education system, particularly day schools, and corporal punishment as reasons for present-day language loss:

> [My mom] grew up in Ste. Rose du Lac. Their school was run by nuns. When she went and started school, she knew no English. I remember my mom telling me this story, and her sisters can verify it: when they went to school if they spoke

their Native language, they were punished. My mom said they used to get the ruler on the knuckles. . . . She couldn't understand why the nuns were hitting her on the knuckles because she was speaking French and Michif. That's when she refused to talk about Michif because she was getting reprimanded. . . . It took me a long time to get that information from my mom because it was too many bad memories.

Charlotte also mentioned corporal punishment in schools run by clergy:

My brothers, when they were younger, they used to speak Michif—so did I. [But,] the schools that we went to back then, they were Catholic schools, and you could not speak Michif. When they spoke, they had to speak French, and it had to be Parisian French. That was taught by the nuns and the priests. And if you didn't speak "properly," you had your knuckles rapped with a yardstick or the ruler. It's like with handwriting; everyone says I have really nice handwriting. I says: "Back then, you had to have [nice handwriting]. Otherwise, you had your knuckles rapped."

Charlotte's story also illustrates the hierarchy of French dialects. Louis (also connected to Ste. Anne) echoed this:

We were mocked. I still have a pet peeve with St. Boniface because we were the bottom; Métis were the bottom of the ladder when it comes to hierarchy of French-speaking communities and French speakers. If you were Métis and spoke [with a] Métis accent or vocabulary, or colloquialism and stuff, we were laughed at. . . . My dad's French was higher because there was a European influence there, colonial kind of French. My mom had—we spoke pretty good French. But still, I affiliated myself with some of the Métis people who came from rural Métis communities [and] we were told to go learn French, by professors, because we couldn't write or speak, because we had Métis accents, because we were Métis. We were bottom. [The highest form was considered] colonial French, which came from elsewhere, Europe. Then there was Quebec French, and in the '70s there was the era where a lot of French people started studying outside of Quebec. They

were better than Manitoba French. And then, Métis French
was really [low in the hierarchy].... You had to learn French;
it was really awful.

Finally, internalized linguistic assimilation could also be heard in some
of the participants' own views and in the views of their children. For
example, Ronnie (St. François-Xavier) said he and his siblings did not
understand English until age six; they only spoke Michif, which he
described as "a broken French." That is strikingly similar to the way
clergy described Michif in colonial day schools. Lucille (St. Laurent)
shared that "when my grandkids come [over], I speak to them in the
Métis culture [Michif]. I don't try and change that because we have a
different dialect than being French or English. Everyone comes from a
different dialect, and we use it, and we practise it. [But,] my kids always
say, 'Mom! Quit talking like that because now my kid talks just like
you!' We have that same dialect [laughing]. But it's nice. It's different."
With generations of Métis people experiencing multiple pressures to
assimilate to French or English, it is not surprising that some of the
participants may have internalized messages about Michif being an
inferior language. These messages persist even today, with some participants' children actively avoiding having their own children learn
Michif. Given that, it is heartening to know that nine participants
are actively trying to learn an Indigenous language (especially Michif,
Cree, and Anishinaabemowin), and some are taking classes. Louis
(Ste. Anne) shared that he has been learning Cree for thirty years in a
ceremonial context so that he can conduct ceremonies in Cree: "I speak
Cree enough for ceremonies because I conduct traditional ceremonies.
[I've been] doing that for thirty years. As a young adult, I kind of
immersed myself in the Cree language and had access to good elders
and people who would teach me my prayers and teach me songs. And
[I] know how to function because as a conductor of sweat lodge, and
pipe carrier, and leading people in fasts and stuff [I need to] function.
I have a spiritual vocabulary." Research has shown that such language
revitalization efforts promote individual and community healing and
can be a buffer against suicide.[19] It is interesting to note connections
between Indigenous languages spoken in participant families and the
way their families self-identified while growing up.

Family Self-Identification

When asked, "How did your family self-identify while you were grow-ing up?" just shy of three-quarters of the participants indicated that one or more of their family members used the terms "Métis" and/or "Michif."[20] Six people said their family identified as French while they were growing up, another four mentioned Roman Catholic, three sim-ply said White,[21] and another three indicated that their family avoided self-identifying.[22] For example, Amanda (Ste. Anne) said, "I remember identifying religiously maybe, like Christian, but not a racial identity."

Folks also reflected upon their family's feelings about self-identifi-cation and indicated a lot of mixed or contradictory feelings. Half of the participants discussed internalized racism and shame. Most of these individuals noted that they had family members who avoid self-identi-fying as Métis and any discussion around this because of internalized shame. Causes of this shame that were named included Catholicism, residential/day/mission schools, nuns as teachers, the church creating divisions in the community, racial hierarchy, racism from French immi-grants, racism at (Manitoba) Hydro, and internalized Euro-Canadian values (e.g., "Indian is bad," "Louis Riel was a traitor") and language (and not passing on Indigenous languages intergenerationally). There were also a handful of people who said their family never discussed being Métis, but this was not due to shame; rather, being Métis was simply a lived reality that did not come up in conversation. This was especially the case in communities with a dominant Indigenous pop-ulation, because "everyone was the same." For example, Gripette (St. Laurent) shared, "I don't know how to answer that because . . . we were just Michif people; we never discussed being Michif. We never had any conversation [about it], not like today. It was just a non-subject." Ronnie (St. François-Xavier) echoed this but indicated that "Halfbreed" was also used as an insult, including by some Métis children themselves: "We all sort of blended in because where we were from, we were all considered Halfbreeds. . . . All of our neighbours were—outside of a couple of families that were Scottish or something else—but everybody [was the same], and when they swore or get mad at you, you say, 'You're nothing but a Halfbreed!'" Ten people talked about their family's pride in being Métis, and a few of these discussed mixed emotions among family members—including internalized racism and shame.

Regarding change to their family's self-identification over time, several indicated that more family members were now identifying as Métis or Michif (especially among those who previously only identified as French or avoided self-identification altogether). When the latter are included, all but three people indicated that their family currently identified as Métis or Michif.[23]

Only the folks from St. Laurent indicated that all their family self-identified as Métis or Michif while growing up. Five people each from Camperville and Duck Bay mentioned family members who identified as Métis while growing up. The sixth person in Camperville spoke about her family being similar to and different from the people living in nearby Pine Creek First Nation; and the sixth person in Duck Bay said their family identified as Native. Anungoohns explained: "I really didn't have any sense about [Indian] status and Métis when I was growing up when I lived back home in Camperville. We spoke the same language, Anishinaabe, and we ate the same food, lived the same way.... Except, I kind of sensed a distinction between us and Pine Creek [First Nation]; I don't know if it was because they lived there [on reserve] and we lived here [in the Métis community], or if that was because they were status and I was not ... I didn't understand the difference until I moved away." The community with the most varied family self-identification was St. François-Xavier; folks mentioned the following identity categories in decreasing order: Métis/Halfbreed, French, White/English/WASP, Mennonite, and American. Interestingly, of all the communities in this study, people from St. François-Xavier also collectively indicated some of the highest levels of internalized racism and shame among their family members. Variation in family self-identification also appeared in stories shared by folks connected to Ste. Anne (in decreasing order): French, Catholic/Christian, Métis, and White. One person spoke of their family not self-identifying because it was simply a lived reality. Lastly, two people from Lorette talked about their family members identifying as Métis, another indicated French, and one said her family did not self-identify because of internalized racism.

With regard to family feelings toward self-identification, people from Camperville indicated a balance between pride and internalized colonization owing to the influence of the Catholic Church, with several also stating that these feelings have remained consistent over time. This balance or contradiction in feelings is illustrated by Louise:

They [my family] were proud Métis people. If there was any kind of shame, it came from the Roman Catholic Church who were our community leaders for a long, long time. . . . When I was growing up in Camperville, we were taught by Roman Catholic Oblates. One of the things I remember very distinctly is they would call us "savage" or "lazy, drunken Indians." That's what we were to them. But our family was a proud Métis [family]. My grandfather on my dad's side was a very proud and well-respected elder in our community, a Métis elder. He used to tell long stories and legends, mostly stories about Métis people or [First Nations] people of long ago. Especially Louis Riel, because Louis Riel was like a long distance relative. There was a residential school in Pine Creek, right adjacent to it. [Camperville and Pine Creek are] only about half a mile [apart], maybe not even that. The church separates us. But our community was [at] one time called Duck Bay. It was relocated to Camperville because of the churches again; they separated us.

In St. Laurent, people discussed high levels of internalized racism and shame as a result of the Catholic Church and French people who immigrated into their community and brought stereotypes and hierarchy with them. Jules explained that "the teachers—which were Franciscan nuns, most of them were from Quebec, there were a couple from Saskatchewan—they talked to us as if we were French Canadians." Likewise, Barbara shared, "The community, at one time, was mostly Michif. But then Li Bretons [people from France] started migrating into that community. Then there were more French people, all French people from Quebec and Manitoba, living on the north side of the community where there was economic development, stores, the train stopped there, the hotel was there." She also commented on the negative impact that the Catholic Church had upon Métis identity in St. Laurent: "Nobody wanted to say that they were Métis. I remember that, even though we were all Métis. Don't forget the nuns and priests controlled that community. . . . St. Laurent was called La Mission du St. Laurent (The Mission of St. Laurent) . . . 'La petite sauvage de St. Laurent' [the little savage from St. Laurent]—honest to god, [they called us that]; that's absolute archival documents!"[24] In contrast, several people also spoke about pride in their family, and two said that being

Métis was not discussed in St. Laurent (before French people arrived), since everyone was the same.

As mentioned above, folks from St. François-Xavier also expressed high levels of internalized racism, but two people also mentioned family pride in Métis identity. Two people also indicated having family members who had begun to identify as Métis in recent years. Folks from both Lorette and Ste. Anne discussed family pride and shame (Ste. Anne), or pride and a lack of discussion about identity because of lived reality (Lorette) in equal numbers. Like Barbara and Louise, above, Charlotte (Ste. Anne) also recalled being referred to as "savage": "We knew who we were as Métis people, but a lot of pride that we should've had wasn't there because of society. . . . They wouldn't call us Métis; they would call us *savages*." Likewise, Louis's family (Ste. Anne) identified as Catholic and French instead of Métis:

> It was survival to identify as French; there was no benefits to identify yourself as Métis. Already as kids, we were discouraged from doing anything that could expose us [as Métis]. No [speaking an Indigenous] language; we couldn't even go outside in the summer without a shirt on for the risk of getting dark, to further highlight our features or our black hair. We had to hide and [this] was overlaid with strong Christian, Catholic [messages]. We had to be proper and had to prove we were not *le savage*, [especially] because Roseau River [First Nation] was down the road.

Half the participants from Lorette and Ste. Anne indicated that some family members currently identified as Métis (especially those who formerly identified as French). Andrea (Lorette) believed this shift was a result of Métis success in the court system as well as changes in public perception toward Métis people in general: "Growing up, [people said], 'Louis Riel, he's a traitor, he's this negative person.' Then, all of a sudden, it was like, 'Wait a second, he's the father of Manitoba!' There was sort of that flip. . . . [I]t was okay now to say ['I'm Métis']. I think, maybe somewhat, we started learning more. . . . I think for my parents too, when I talk to them, there was sort of a shift in the way that people started to look at Métis and other Indigenous peoples." Likewise, Janice shared that when her parents were thirty or forty years old, they "got very involved with the Métis community. . . . They were Métis and they were strong and proud of that part. . . . They continue to be very, very involved, more to the other extreme now."

No obvious patterns arose regarding family feelings toward self-identification in Duck Bay, but a clear pattern emerged regarding change over time: one or more family members having obtained Indian status and now identifying with that as well as with being Métis (except for George, who said his family now solely identified as status, with the exception of one family line). Recall that some community members were actively trying to obtain reserve status for Duck Bay. George also discussed the terms "Halfbreed," and "Apitowgoshaanuk"[25] being used by his family, and Duck Bay residents more broadly, until the 1970s, at which time "Métis" became the preferred term. Debbie and Gripette said this was also true in St. Laurent. According to Gripette, "We were all Michif people. When I went to the city, they called me 'Métis,' and I didn't know what Métis was; nobody around here knew what Métis was." In this way, prominent themes of pride and shame—sometimes existing within the same family or individual—were present for many Métis families across each Métis community.

~

In the pages above, participant experiences with family history have been shared. Most people had a direct, personal connection to their Métis community, and their family had a direct, intergenerational connection to multiple Métis communities (in and beyond those in this study). Moreover, a majority were aware of Métis scrip within their family; however, most do not know whether their ancestors received the land, or money, or whether it was swindled from them, as was the case for so many Métis. While most people spoke of at least one person in their family having registered Indian status (including via marriage), only three had status themselves. When it came to Indigenous languages, more than half indicated that one or more family members could speak multiple Indigenous languages, with Michif, Anishinaabemowin (Saulteaux/Ojibwe), and Nêhiyawewin (Cree) being the most frequently cited. Finally, most participants' family members self-identified as Métis or Michif while growing up; only a handful identified as French, Catholic, or White. Despite external and internalized racism, most participants' families continued to self-identify as Métis, and others have begun to identify as Métis (despite lingering shame in some cases).

CHAPTER 7

Métis Family Relationships with Culture and Religion

In this chapter, I continue the discussion on participant family histories. Participants described common experiences regarding family relationships with Métis culture, with First Nations cultures, and with Euro-Canadian cultures. Participants also shared stories about their family's religious and/or spiritual expression while they were growing up. As with the previous chapter, I begin with an overview of major findings, followed by a closer look at the individual communities, and include people's own voices to illuminate their shared experiences.

Family Relationships with Métis Culture

When asked about their family's connections to Métis culture, many participants spoke about on-the-land subsistence activities, social gatherings, music and dance, cultural values, and traditional foods. More specifically, twenty people described their family's relationship with Métis culture in terms of subsistence activities, including (in decreasing order) hunting (deer, moose, geese, ducks, and rabbits), fishing (rarely commercial), harvesting (wood, blueberries, hazelnuts, saskatoons, medicines, Seneca root, mushrooms), trapping (family traplines and muskrats were mentioned), and farming (almost all on a small scale and usually involving beef cattle and horses, and sometimes making one's own milk, cream, and butter). Social gatherings were mentioned as a connection to Métis culture by almost as many people as subsistence activities, with the most popular being extended family gatherings, Métis Days celebrations in Métis communities, and winter carnivals (including Festival du Voyageur). Just as many people described their family's relationship with Métis culture as involving music and dance, with fiddling and jigging being the most frequently identified.

Cultural values were mentioned by several folks, including community participation, sharing, helping, generosity, and close-knit communities and families. Finally, many also spoke about traditional Métis foods or "Métis dishes," such as *beignes* (frybread), *gallet* (bannock), *boulettes* (meatballs), and wild meats (goose, duck, rabbit, and moose meat sausage).[1] When contemplating whether their family's relationship with Métis culture had changed in any way over time, one-third of participants cited involvement with the Manitoba Metis Federation (MMF), such as getting a citizenship card, increased participation in the MMF, or being dissatisfied with the organization. An equal number also discussed increased pride in being Métis, including an expanded understanding of what it means to be Métis, internal acceptance, efforts to maintain the Michif language, and recognition that Métis spirituality includes ceremonies. Several people spoke of a decrease in their family's subsistence activities over the years for a number of reasons, including children being sent away for school, the depletion of fish, overexploitation by the logging industry, the death of a grandparent, and moving to an urban location.[2] Four individuals indicated no change in their family's relationship with Métis culture over time.

The communities whose participants mentioned subsistence activities most frequently were Camperville, St. Laurent, and Duck Bay. Louise, in Camperville, explained: "They lived it. They hunted, they fished, they lived the Métis way. That was the tradition. That's how they made a living.... Hunting and fishing was always an important part of our culture. And sharing was part of that culture—like if you went hunting, you shared with the community. If you caught a deer or moose, you would share it with the community or with your extended family." Similarly, Gripette (St. Laurent) explained, "Everybody fished, everybody hunted; we needed to do that to survive. That was just part of survival. Just part of your way of life." George talked about a fish processing plant in Duck Bay in the 1950s: "[That is] where I learned how to cut fish as a kid. And trapping and hunting."

On a related note, a few people also spoke of plant medicines as part of Métis culture. Maryanne (Duck Bay) shared, "We followed whatever my grandmother was teaching us, like about medicines. She had medicines; if we were sick, there was no pills in the house. Everything was from the trees, from the sap, from the ground, from the cedar." Likewise, Louis (Ste. Anne) said, "Sometimes it was in the medicines, like when

we were sick. I had an uncle who would come; he was a smoker—I
don't know if he was smoking tobacco or if it was a mix of things. But,
every time I had an earache, he'd come and blow smoke in our ears.
Like traditional kind of healing approaches." In St. Laurent, Gripette
mentioned that there was always someone in the community who was
a medicine person: "In my family, the aunt that raised my mom was a
medicine woman and she taught my mom all the medicines." Barbara,
from the same community, shared the following: "My father used to
go to communities around St. Laurent to pick Seneca root. Burlap
bags, I remember the burlap bags, coming back. I guess they sold it to
pharmacies or something because it was used in all kinds of medicinal
products." Barbara also spoke of a midwife in the community: "A friend
of my mother's, who was a midwife—I think she was a Champagne—
she delivered me. And they, at the house, they used the wood stove door
and put me there, close, as an incubator, because I was four and a half
pounds." Gripette shared a similar story: "I was born at home, the one
[sibling] next to me was born at home, the one next to him was born
at home. [Then in the] mid to late 1950s, they started to have hospital
births and less midwifery. I don't know why."

In addition to subsistence activities, music and dance were also
identified by many participants across the communities as an important
connection to Métis culture. People from St. Laurent spoke about music
the most, but almost all participants mentioned dance as an important
Métis cultural trait in their family. Barbara shared the following: "Music
was really big in our family. I remember my mom and dad having gatherings where people were square dancing all night. And, the broom
dance, and the jigging. And, there was a full band in our house: guitar,
drums, violin, fiddle—I should say fiddle." In Camperville, Karen said,
"The guitar was famous in Camperville. My mom played. She used to
tell us when she was about seventeen, eighteen, nineteen [years old],
she'd play in barn dances around Pine River and Camperville. She
said the guys would come and get her. She said, at one time, she knew
forty-one songs." Similarly, Denise (St. François-Xavier) recalled,
"My mom's brother was a Western Canadian fiddling champion, so
he was a big fiddler. I grew up with a lot of fiddling in the house. My
grandmother's brother was actually, at one time, the Canadian fiddling
champion." Ste. Anne appears as an exception here, since no one mentioned music or dance.

Folks from Duck Bay and Lorette discussed social gatherings more than those from other communities—even though Duck Bay, St. Laurent, and Camperville host their own Métis Days celebrations. Nicki (Lorette) shared the following:

> I remember growing up and in my mother's family—she has a massive family, there are fourteen children in her immediate brothers and sisters. . . . Then there are six other great-aunts and uncles in that family with their own family sizes ranging from about . . . seven to fourteen children. Growing up, we would always have these huge family celebrations and there would be like 200 of us and we would get together in a hall around winter or New Year's [Eve], and then, in the summer, we would have these great big outdoor parties on my grandparents' farmland. I remember there was always this super Métis undercurrent at those events.

Participants also considered whether their family's relationship with Métis culture has changed over time. Stories about this were most noticeable in Ste. Anne and Duck Bay. In Ste. Anne, everyone identified an increased participation in Métis culture, an expanded understanding of being Métis, and acceptance of Métis identity occurring within their family over time. In Duck Bay, most people mentioned the MMF usually to express their family's dissatisfaction over wanting to obtain reserve status for Duck Bay and feeling that the MMF is actively preventing this, or from having approached the MMF for assistance and support but received none. Some individuals connected to Ste. Anne also brought up the MMF but with regard to family members obtaining citizenship cards and increased involvement in Métis politics.

Family Relationships with First Nations Cultures

In discussions with participants about their family's relationship to First Nations cultures while growing up, the largest patterns to emerge were "no relationship," or having one or more First Nations family members (including via marriage into the family). Several people also compared First Nations and Métis cultures, highlighting more similarities than differences. These similarities included values, everyone knowing everyone and feeling equally at home in Métis and First Nation communities; these folks insisted that there were few differences between First Nations and Métis until Euro-Canadians forced divisions between them. By contrast, some folks talked about not being accepted by First Nations people, being separate but respected, as well as finding it difficult to fit in with First Nations kids when they were children themselves. Internalized racism was emphasized as existing within some families in relation to First Nations cultures. Examples of this included racism directed toward First Nations and other Métis people, an internalized racial hierarchy (with Métis being supposedly superior to First Nations), as well as "racism" (or perhaps more accurately, discrimination or lateral violence) perpetrated by family members.[3] Interestingly, the largest pattern to emerge was with regard to improved relationships with First Nations cultures over time, specifically through increased participation by family members in First Nations cultures, increased awareness and connections, an openness to learn more, as well as better working relationships (especially now that the Catholic Church no longer dominates these communities the way it did historically).[4]

Upon closer examination of each community, perhaps what stands out the most is that participants' families generally seem to have had very few collective relationships with First Nations cultures while growing up. This seemed to be the case even when the Métis community bordered a First Nation reserve, as with Duck Bay and Camperville. This does not mean that individual families did not relate to First Nations cultures at all; instead, people described aspects of these relationships that were unique to their own family. Notably, those with families connected to St. François-Xavier indicated no relationship with First Nations cultures while growing up. Half the people from this community also shared stories about racism perpetrated by their own family members.[5] Denise recalled, "My grandmother wanted nothing to do. She called them *les maudits sauvages* [those damn savages]. I mean she hated Indians so there was a lot of that kind of mentality about Indians or Native, First Nations." Similarly, Elizabeth said, "One of my aunts worked in the prison system and she's really racist. I can't even talk to her. We don't even have a relationship." Elizabeth clarified that this was the only "blatant racism" she'd heard coming from her own family. Vern was adopted by a White family and regularly heard them make racist remarks against Indigenous people while he was growing up. He explained, "[My adopted family were] totally against Aboriginal culture.

That goes to my grandparents on both sides. As my one grandmother would say: 'If any of my children or grandchildren marry anybody with a -ski on the end of their name, they're going to be taken over to the well.' So, bad enough being Ukrainian, being Aboriginal would have just been frosting on the cake. I imagine they're all rolling over in their graves" [now that Vern knows he is Métis].

Half the participants from Camperville said they had at least one First Nations family member, and two people referred to the nearby reserve of Pine Creek, saying they also felt at home there. This can be heard in the following comments by Karen: "Pine Creek [First Nation] is right there. The church was there between Camperville and Pine Creek. We all got along with First Nations. The way my dad worked, and because everybody knew each other so well, and my mom worked in the public school system; they both knew how to get along with people.... [This was true] overall, I'd think, between all eight of us and my mom and dad. It's like home; being with First Nations and Métis, it's like being at home."

In Ste. Anne, Charlotte and Justin also discussed having one or more First Nations family members; and, Justin and Amanda emphasized shared values between First Nations and Métis cultures. Justin's mother's family is from Peguis First Nation, and Charlotte has family from White Dog First Nation. Justin noted similar values across Métis and First Nations cultures with respect to residence patterns, being on the land, and hunting:

> In my house, we had a lot of our cousins and exchange students. Even now that I've moved out, they always have people rooming there. They rent out a room. My cousin, who's my family from Peguis, he lived in Edmonton and moved here so he's living there now. So, in terms of that, for sure on my mom's side the values were there. Same with my dad's [Métis] side. Going hunting and being on the land. That's something that's always been a part of his and my relationship.... Everything about him, too, the relationship to family and having people live with us.

Amanda also spoke of shared First Nations and Métis values:

> A: I thought about this a lot over the past two years—nothing explicit was ever talked about with First Nations. But,

in retrospect, a lot of the values around family, community, childrearing, things like that, I would say were conducted in our family but not spoken of [explicitly]. . . . Or [not] identifying them as being Métis or First Nations or anything really. But then looking back, I can see where those values came in too like the importance of family—we have lots of extended family around where we lived. And with childrearing, like the non-interference and letting kids explore and do their own thing. . . . The freedom of being in nature and spending a lot of time in the bush and all those things are aligned with First Nations but it was never acknowledged as such. . . .

Do you see those values as just First Nations values, or do you see them as Métis as well?

A: Also [as] Métis.

Folks from St. Laurent generally indicated "no relationship" with First Nations cultures. However, Gripette argued that First Nations and Métis cultures in the region were historically similar and the divisions that can be seen between the two groups today are a result of government oppression and influence. She explained this at length:

It didn't really make a difference, I think, between Métis and First Nations; we were just a bunch of people doing our thing and along came treaty, or you gotta take scrip. And that created the divisions. And then, from what I can gather, there were Indian people, and Métis people. And, as time went on, there was more and more division between us, more things to push us apart, more things to make us different from each other. And then, here in this community, I think that the people in St. Laurent never had issues with the First Nations people until those people from France came over. And then when they came here, they were told the stories of "Indian people," and what it was like with Indian people. And so, they brought that with them and that came to become part of our life [too]. They would tell us to be afraid of the "Indians" and that kind of stuff. Here, in [Michif] French, they would say: *lii sauvages* [the savages], right? Now, that's very different than Indian people, the way they used it, because they used it very derogatorily. It further created division. And if there was any talk about practising Indian ways, or Indian medicine, or any of that kind of stuff, then that was "the way of the devil." So then people like my mom just moved away further back home from that kind of stuff, to the point where that wasn't practised hardly [anymore].

Andrea and Nicki, from Lorette, specifically mentioned their family's relationship with powwow while growing up. Andrea shared that "[My mom] used to say, 'Grandma used to love to go to powwows so we would take her sometimes." Nicki explained: "Growing up, my father was a photographer and I think he was always drawn to the beauty of powwow dance and regalia. I remember that when we were kids, we would always go to communities that were relatively close, like Roseau River [First Nation], in the summer and he would take photographs of community members and we had them blown up and they were [on display] in our home."

Most of the participants connected to Duck Bay mentioned tensions in their community regarding whether or not they should seek reserve status, as discussed in the previous chapter. In addition, folks shared unique stories about First Nations family, friends, intermarriage, poverty, and ceremonies existing in the community historically. A few folks from Duck Bay identified an increase in openness to learning about First Nations cultures in their family today. In fact, an improved relationship was also mentioned by everyone from Lorette and Ste. Anne, as well as by people in every other community except St. Laurent (which indicated no change in relationship). Regarding her family's relationship to First Nations cultures, Brenda (Camperville) said: "It's stronger, definitely. I became more aware of my First Nations' roots when I was about thirteen, and as a young teenager, through my aunties. My aunties are very strong Anishinaabe women. They're the ones that influenced me to become more proud of my First Nations' [ancestry rather] than shame as well as Métis." From the same community, Louise identified improved First Nations and Métis relationships, especially with regard to economic development:

Today, it's improved a bit. I think that they [First Nations and Métis] work with each other on common projects. Maybe on housing, and I think trade, economic development, and things like that. One of the things that's still common with our three communities, I always say—Duck Bay, Pine Creek, and Camperville—is the church. The church is still central. It doesn't dominate the people anymore but we're still all Roman Catholics in our communities. So that's a commonality between all our three communities. More of a team building relationship almost, on common projects. Like maybe building the highways and paving the roads, et cetera.

Several families' relationships with First Nations cultures seem to have improved as a direct result of participants' personal relationships with First Nations people and cultures, including their participation in cultural events and ceremonies. Consequently, some of their immediate and extended family members had begun to join them in this participation over the years. This is illustrated in the following excerpt by Andrea (Lorette) about her sister Nicki: "My sister participated in a Sundance this year. There were a lot of people in our family who were like, 'Wow, that's so cool. So interesting!' We've been going to some sweats and doing this. There's certain family [members] who are like, 'I'd love to do that.' I guess they just don't have that connection and, thankfully, my sister got in with these people who opened up and allowed her to find that." The discussion about family participation in ceremonies is continued later in this chapter as well as in Chapter 10. For now, let us move onto a discussion about family relationships with Euro-Canadian cultures.

Family Relationships with Euro-Canadian Cultures

The two most prominent areas of family relationships with Euro-Canadian cultures were French culture, specifically, and Christianity. Racism was also a frequent theme, including feelings of distrust, dislike, and purposely keeping separate from White people; White supremacy; and internalized racism. Some people spoke about assimilation and family members trying to "pass as White." Finally, the education system was identified as a significant aspect in family relationships with Euro-Canadian cultures.[6] While nine people said that their family's relationships with Euro-Canadian cultures had not changed over time, eight explained that they have one or more family members who now identify as Indigenous (as opposed to previously identifying as French or White).

When listening to stories across the six Métis communities, it became apparent that French culture was significant within participant families while growing up, notably in St. Laurent, Ste. Anne, and Lorette. Gripette explained why this was the case in St. Laurent:

> The church had a strong hold on St Laurent, and the church wanted to "civilize" us so they would bring people in from France, different parts of France. I think the first group that came from France was in the late 1800s, and then in the early 1900s, and then in the 1920s and 1930s. The last batch came in 1930 or 1940. They brought [over] those people in [order] to ... "take the Indian out of us" .... The goal of that was to civilize the Métis community, to take the Indian out of us so we would be more like them, I guess .... When those people came over, they didn't know how to live on the land, but we did, so we taught them how to live on the land. And then once they began to know how to live on the land, then they ... created a store [and] a post office. [They] created a rural municipality. Those ways came with them and then they made themselves the elite [in St. Laurent]. There were no divisions before that. Everybody was just the same before that.... [T]hen you had an elite group, and the elite group were those White people, those French people, those people that we had taught how to live on the land. Then along with that came the discrimination where those people were not, they didn't want to mix [with us].

In Lorette, Nicki talked about what it is like to also be descended from French settlers, and the impact of French culture upon Métis identity:

> [It] is really interesting to be also descended from French settler people.... We spoke French at home, which is both my parents' first language. We spoke French at home until I started school, roughly. Yeah, my sister [Andrea] was in grade two, I guess. We spoke the language and I guess, when I was younger, I identified more as Franco-Manitoban than I did as a Métis and again that might have been because we didn't discuss that too much at home. I didn't really understand the difference, but I just identified that way mainly because of the [French] language. And, I always also thought that Lorette

and Ile des Chênes were French Manitoban communities
and it wasn't until later in life, like in my late teens, early
twenties, that I realized that both Ile des Chênes and Lorette
are Métis communities.

A strong connection between Euro-Canadian (especially French)
culture and Catholicism (or Christianity, more broadly) was also
apparent; this arose most frequently with people from Duck Bay but
was also raised by people from every other community featured in this
study. Betsy, from Duck Bay, said: "My aunties and that didn't really like
the White culture. My grandmother also really didn't like them. But I
was confused as to why they liked the [Catholic] Church and all that,
and did the Church thing, but didn't like the White people. I always
questioned that from a very young age." Next door, in Camperville,
Louise explained the influence of Catholicism upon Métis people: "The
Roman Catholic Oblates, that was part of their mission: to change, to
Christianize, and to civilize Aboriginal people—including the Métis.
To make us more like them. They were our community leaders for a
long, long time. The nuns and the priests were the community leaders
until, I would say, the 1970s. Maybe even a little bit earlier, maybe late
'60s." For his part, Louis (Ste. Anne) highlighted hypocrisy regarding
Catholicism. Although his family was Catholic, they would not help
Indigenous people in need because of an internalized racism. He questioned his family members:

> Why don't you help [First Nations people]? What's wrong
> with them? Was it because they were Indigenous that it
> was okay to discriminate against [them]? I found that hard
> because I could see myself a little bit in "those people." There
> was sadness in what I saw as incongruent, when I look at
> the behaviour [of my family]: Why won't you help? You're
> Catholic; why won't you help? We're Christian, why won't
> you help them? There was a stigma. . . . [Even though] my
> mom's family, she had jet black hair and she kind of looked
> like them a bit. But that was the rule: we never helped. If
> someone stopped at our house, and they were Indigenous
> [First Nation]—[for example] because someone['s car] broke
> down on the road—if they were Indigenous, [my mom]
> wouldn't help them.

We will return to a discussion of family relationships with religion shortly.

Half the people in Duck Bay talked about their family's dislike or distrust of Euro-Canadians and Euro-Canadian cultures and how they purposely avoided Euro-Canadians when possible. Lightning Rattle Woman said: "As for White [people] though, it was kind of standoffish, [they were] different, and [we] didn't blend . . . . We don't mix." Betsy's comment, above, also touched on her family's discomfort with White people. Maryanne shared similar sentiments: "My dad still is very leery of [White people] because he doesn't understand a lot. He only went to grade four, and he got pulled out and then had to work with my grandfather on the farm. . . . So, he has a very limited understanding of like English language even, and writing. He gets very, he feels uncomfortable around non-Indigenous people and White society. He doesn't trust them. He doesn't trust the White man. If he were sitting here, that's what he would tell you [laughs]."

The theme of racism emerged most clearly in responses from Camperville, but internalized racism in particular was mentioned in responses from Duck Bay, St. François-Xavier, and Ste. Anne as well. Karen (Camperville) shared a story about her father returning home from the war and facing discrimination by the Canadian government. Anungoohns identified racism in the Winnipegosis school. She explains:

> I didn't really know that I was different from anybody else until I started going to school in a White town when I was in grade eight. . . . Until then, we went to school in Camperville and everyone was the same. But then we started going to elementary school, grade eight, in a White town back then. Now, they're mostly Métis or a number of them identify as Métis. At that time, they were a White people, and it was at that time that I started to realize that I was being treated differently and I was more on the periphery . . . I realized that I was being looked down upon. I don't know where that came from. I mean, in my family we worked hard and so I didn't understand the racism. Back then, I didn't have that knowledge that there is racism, I just knew that I was being treated differently because of how I looked, who I was, where I came from.

With experiences of racism like these, it is not surprising that folks also discussed internalized racism in their families, which included some family members trying to "pass as White" people. Louis (Ste. Anne) said, "My father's mom [who was Métis] was always so wrapped up in being French because her husband was French and [being Métis was] not something they would acknowledge." Similar family stories were shared by Justin and Charlotte. Charlotte said, "Back then, Métis people really didn't come out [self-identify]; they really stayed low key because of the stigma. They would try to blend in as much as they could. I know my sisters, they used to call themselves *French*, they wouldn't call themselves *Métis*. They both married White guys. Their daughters were being raised not in a Métis tradition or Aboriginal tradition; it was in White society." Likewise Ray, in Duck Bay, observed:

> You see a lot of Métis people that try to follow that lifestyle of the White people.... I think some of the Métis people are too proud of even themselves, they look down on people. It's almost like they're ashamed to be a Métis or an Indian or Native. They'd rather sit with the Whites and live the White way and be ashamed of their [own] people. And I've seen that and heard that through my relatives, through listening to their stories. A lot of them are ashamed of their culture to be recognized because of the way people categorize Indian people as poor and drunk and pill poppers.

Louise, in Camperville, had this to say: "White people, we saw them as superior and smarter than we were. There weren't any White people living in Camperville except maybe for two families. But the White culture—we went to Winnipegosis High School. That was about 30 miles south of Camperville and there was a lot of conflict, a lot of name-calling. So, we didn't like each other, and I think there was sometimes a sense that the White people were more superior than we were."

The Euro-Canadian education system was highlighted by half the people from Camperville and Ste. Anne. We have already heard some participants (especially from Camperville) comment on the Euro-Canadian education system and the perpetuation of racism against Indigenous people. Charlotte (Ste. Anne) echoed that her family was "Métis, and they knew that.... [B]ack then, it was a lot different than what it is today. Métis people lived in shame because of what was being taught in schools."[7]

Most participants, especially in Duck Bay and Camperville, said there has been no change in their family's relationships with Euro-Canadian cultures over time. Some folks indicated that one or more family members now identify as Indigenous instead of French or White. For instance, Charlotte (Ste. Anne) said her family members no longer consider themselves French: "Today, all of them [my family members] have their Métis cards. Which is good. There's a bit more pride in our family." Justin (Ste. Anne) noted: "My Uncle Louis embraces the Métis identity [now]. . . . My Auntie Denise, she actually started embracing Métis identity too; she doesn't necessarily do Métis cultural stuff but she's an advocate for Métis and First Nations stuff." In Lorette, both Nicki and Andrea shared stories about family members no longer iden-tifying solely as French Canadian; instead, they have embraced their Métis identity. In the following excerpt, Andrea admits to becoming disillusioned about Canada:

> Growing up, it was like, "I'm so proud to be Canadian and Canada is so wonderful! We're such a good country!" For the last ten years, I've just been like, "Okay, it's better than being American." I'm ashamed of my country because of some of the things that they've done and are still doing. You think, "How come not everyone knows or cares about this?" Definitely, in the last ten years, I have been disillusioned by Canada. Yeah, okay, we're still an alright country compared to some but you're still like, "Own up and actually do some-thing." I'm kind of not as proud, as [I was] growing up, to be Canadian.

Denise (St. François-Xavier) also talked about family members who now admit they are Métis: "My cousins own it that they are Métis, but they are not active in Métis community events; they're not active in anything. They [still] live a pretty White life." Similarly, Bobbie-Jo (St. Laurent) has recognized a shift in her family and community whereby people now identify as Métis instead of French Canadian: "A lot of people when I was growing up who denied that they were Métis are now very proud to be Métis so that's changed, and I see a lot more of that now in the Franco-Manitoban culture."[8] The elements of family history discussed thus far—including community, scrip, status, and Métis, First Nations, and Euro-Canadian cultures—have all impacted family relationships with religion and spirituality.

Family Relationships with Religion and Spirituality

The Métis people who participated in this study recalled their family's relationship with religion and spirituality while they were growing up, including among their grandparents' generation, and whether this had changed over time. All but one person identified their family's religion while growing up as Roman Catholic, and nearly one-quarter said this had been the same since their grandparents' generation or earlier. This represents the strongest pattern that emerged in the study.[9] The exception was Vern's adopted White parents, who were United Church Christians.[10] One-quarter of participants also discussed Indigenous spirituality (in the form of traditional ceremonies and medicines) within in their families; a handful said this had also been present in their grandparents' generation. Several people pointedly identified day schools as directly impacting their family's relationship with religion and spirituality.[11] Interestingly, half the participants noted a decline in their family's adherence to the Catholic Church, and the same number described their family's relationship with Indigenous spirituality in terms of increased awareness, openness, learning, and participation (often as a result of the participant's own spiritual journey).[12]

Many people shared stories about their family's strict adherence to Catholicism. I would like to share a few excerpts from across the six Métis communities to illustrate this:

> When I was a kid, we had to go to church every Sunday. If you didn't go to church, you were committing a mortal sin especially [on] Sunday. You would go to hell if you didn't go to church. You went to confession every first Friday of the month and then communion the next morning. We were staunch Roman Catholics in our community. (Louise, Camperville)
>
> We were Roman Catholic. I was born in 1963. I remember everybody going to church. We all grew up running to the church, and the church was in between Camperville and Pine Creek [First Nation]. It was a mile from our house. We'd run there each Wednesday night, and there'd be kids in the church

and the priest, and we'd have to do catechism. . . . That's where the nuns would come and teach us every day after school. (Karen, Camperville)

[At age 9, I moved in] with my *kookum* [grandma] and papa [grandpa], who both were *very* religious. It was shocking to have to sit on my knees and pray during Lent, every night for forty days. After we were done supper and I was done the dishes, just before seven [o'clock], it was on your knees praying. Well, they did the rosaries; he would say it in French and she would say it in Saulteaux. I could still recite that by rote memory; just listening, I could do both languages and say the full rosary. (Maryanne, Duck Bay)

Religion for us was taught in the school. So, you were taught everything about Catholicism, about the Bible in school, and we were encouraged to follow Catholicism and do all the sacraments. We were taught that the Catholic God was a very punishing God; and, in the Bible, it [says] that you're gonna fear the Lord. There was all that negativity along with all that Catholicism. Then we were encouraged, forced to follow that and to believe in that. (Gripette, St. Laurent)

Roman Catholicism. What did that look like? We went to church most Sundays. . . . *Ma tante* [my aunt] Aline who was [my dad's] great aunt, his father's sister, would insist that we went every Sunday. My sister [Andrea] was baptized, went through communion, and confirmation. I am baptized, did the communion or whatever it is when you are twelve, and I was an altar girl. (Nicki, Lorette)

The way to kind of rise above the poverty, to rise above the discrimination, is to show how devout you were as Catholics. That was your *Métishood*; that was who you were. It had to do with being a choirboy. It had to do with being altar boys from a young age. It had to be showing up for church and having twelve people [from your family] fill up two pews, and then you were proud. . . . If you weren't Catholic, you would not, could not elevate yourself. You could not find work; there was going to be no hope out of your poverty and misery. (Louis, Ste. Anne)

These are a fraction of the stories shared that illustrate a strong relation-ship with Catholicism among many families.

In addition to talking about Catholicism, folks from every community (except Lorette and Ste. Anne) mentioned Indigenous spirituality, in one form or another and to varying degrees, as present in their families or community while they were growing up. Louise and Brenda from Camperville and George from neighbouring Duck Bay indicated that while growing up, they were aware of Indigenous ceremonies in their community historically (specifically the Sundance, Midewiwin, shake tent, and sweat lodge). Louise explained, "I got a really big book about land surrendered here in Métis land scrip called *Pine Creek First Nation and Duck Bay Surrender*. That's part of our community and what hap-pened. Also, it goes into [great] length about Camperville and practising the Midewiwin ceremonies and Sundance ceremonies [historically]." George said the same about Duck Bay:

> There were ceremonies held in my community. The shake tent was brought there by the elders. There's a certain part there, if you drive, across the lake there, they used to hold ceremonies there. In the 1800s, all the tribes from all around [went] there, [to] have a powwow in September or August, for two weeks. Well, I don't know if "powwow" is what they called it [but] all the elders and chiefs came together.... They brought shake tents there twice because two twin brothers drowned and they wanted elders to help them, wise men to find where the bodies went down, where they'd be.... [That] was in the 1950s.

Brenda shared that her grandfather had been interviewed "a long, long time ago, and he talks about shaking tent in Camperville"—she believes this occurred within her lifetime. An undercurrent in stories like these was that Indigenous spirituality (and ceremonies in particular) had been outlawed by government and church and suppressed via punishment, and that it was dangerous when some community members continued to participate in secret. When discussing ceremonies in Camperville and Duck Bay, Brenda explained that it was "taboo. You'd get punished. You'd get beaten.... [My brother's mother-in-law said to me] 'Oh, you offer tobacco?' And I said, 'Yeah, I do.' And she says, 'I do that too, but nobody knows.' It was kind of sad. And I'm sure most of the old people in Camperville, and Pine Creek [First Nation], and Duck Bay did that in secret [too]. And they won't even talk about it [today] because it's just so ingrained in them." Gripette (St. Laurent) also spoke of how Indigenous spirituality was present among the older generations but that any discussion or practice had to be done quietly because of colonization and persecution by the church and government. She said, "Spirituality, to me, and religion are not the same thing. When I was growing up ... there was [Indigenous] spirituality that was talked about, but only in hushed voices. Like people talked about spirits way back when in St. Laurent; that was a way of life. Spirits, and seeing things, and somebody who is dead coming back. That was life; that was our life. That was spirituality. As a kid, there was, for me when I looked back, there was less and less and less of that spirituality" (because of forced Catholicism, as she noted above). On a related note, Barbara (St. Laurent) mentioned Michif storytelling that warned children about *ruugaruus* and covert talk in the community about "bad medicine" while she was growing up.[13] Likewise, Denise and Nancy, connected to St. François-Xavier, noted that when they were young, the practice and discussion of Indigenous spirituality was surrounded by secrecy and fear, a legacy of colonial repression of Indigenous ceremonies.

Participants specifically identified day or residential schools as having directly contributed to the separation of Métis people from Indigenous spirituality and ceremonies.[14] This can be seen in the following comments by Brenda (Camperville): "I was brought up in [the Camperville] day school. My parents were in day school. There was a residential school in Pine Creek. My grandmother worked there. So, Roman Catholic religion was really, really strong and it was really invasive. Although a lot of people will not admit to that, eh. There was abuse in the residential school as well as in the day school; and I was in the day school and so were my parents." No one from Ste. Anne or St. François-Xavier mentioned day schools in connection with Indigenous spirituality.

All participants from Camperville, Duck Bay, Lorette, and all but one from St. Laurent identified Catholicism as significant in their grandparents' generation, and their comments convey a sense of the severity of this religious practice. Sometimes folks believed this stretched back for generations before their grandparents. This was the case with Charlotte (Ste. Anne): "[My grandparents] would have been Catholic because the church had played a huge role in our family through the years. Even when Archbishop Provencher wanted Angélique and Marguerite to

come out here [to Red River to teach in the first Catholic school]."
Jules indicated that most of the Métis community of St. Laurent was
Catholic when he was growing up: "A majority, like 95 or 98 percent
of people in St. Laurent were Catholic. You could count on one hand
your family members who weren't going to church at the time. . . .
Everybody, including my parents, grandparents, as far as we know, they
all came from Catholics/Christians." Maryanne (Duck Bay) described
the strictest observance of Catholicism in sharing what the practice
looked like for her grandmother and in her family:

> My *kookum* [grandmother] prayed three times a day. All the
> time. Morning, noon, and before she went to bed; she did
> the full rosary three times a day. I would know, as a kid, when
> she was doing it not to come inside or to be noisy and inter-
> rupt. We'd have lunch, I'd do dishes and then we were sent
> outside, and she would pray. Then same within the evening,
> after supper: do the dishes, or we'd do our homework, or read
> while she'd go in the bedroom and pray. . . . And we couldn't
> turn on the TV; we would have to be quiet in the house. She
> was very, very, very, very, very, very strict. . . . [My dad] came
> home from fishing this one time, and it was during Lent. I
> thought it was just us kids that had to sit on the floor and
> kneel [to pray]. They were older so they had chairs that they
> sat on during Lent. And my dad came home from fishing
> this one evening, and we were just starting [to pray]. He
> pulled up from off the lake, and he came in. I remember being
> totally shocked because he came in, took off his stuff . . . and
> he knelt down, and I remember looking like "Oh! Okay!"
> Because, you know, it hurt to [kneel] down—that was like a
> half hour on your knees on a hardwood floor. And you had to
> sit up; there's no, "Okay, half an hour, [then] sit down." No,
> you had to [kneel with proper posture]. If [I] didn't, she'd
> give me a kick. And I'd have to sit up straight, and straighten
> my posture like that, for the whole thing. . . . [H]er praying
> was every day right until the day she died.

Participants in St. François-Xavier also mentioned grandparents who
were Catholic, Methodist, or Baptist; and Catholic, Anglican, or "not
Catholic" in Ste. Anne.

Some people also talked about Indigenous spirituality in their grandparents' generation. This often went hand in hand with the use of plant medicines. Half the folks connected to St. François-Xavier discussed Indigenous spirituality in connection with their grandparents. For instance, Nancy had this to say: "My grandfather was spiritual; he was Indigenous spirituality. . . . I'm sure he did go to church, but he didn't go every Sunday. He preferred to. . . . He called it 'the old ways.' He embraced the old ways, and he told me as a child: 'You don't need to go to a church or a building to worship.' He said, 'That's nonsense, you come out to the bush, the spirits are everywhere.' And he would tell me stories of Windigo and what to watch [for]."[15] In Camperville, Louise and Brenda spoke of their grandparents and Indigenous spirituality. Louise commented, "As far as I know [my grandparents were Catholic way back] until the Midewiwin disappeared, I guess in 1846. Around that time, the Midewiwin ceremonies were practised. They say in one of the books, the Midewiwin ceremonies was central to—it didn't say Manitoba, but the Midewiwin ceremonies were central to all the communities and in [this] surrounding area. People would come from far and close to attend the Midewiwin ceremonies." Brenda said, "I wish I could have met my great grandmother. I remember my mama, which is on the Lafreniere side, Chartrand. I remember finding a medicine [tobacco cloth offering] in the backyard, and she goes, 'You go put that back where it belongs. You can't take that from there.' It was buried. . . . I was always taught to respect the traditional ways." The theme of Indigenous spirituality—and use of medicines by grandparents or older generations in particular—also arose in stories from Duck Bay and St. Laurent. George (Duck Bay) shared, "My mom was a medicine woman, my grandmother was a medicine woman; they were healers. As a kid, I went with my mom and dad to go pick medicine in the territories, 100 miles up north to go pick medicines." Also, recall Gripette's discussion above, regarding Indigenous spirituality.

In describing changes over time in their family's religious or spiritual practices, the largest pattern to emerge was a decrease in family participation in the church, and sometimes a complete cessation.[16] In Duck Bay, George explained, "I don't think as many of them go to church because a lot of them are realizing the abuse that's starting to come [to light]. I think the church is dying in my community. There's no one that goes to church anymore, [not] even the young people." From the same community, Lightning Rattle Woman shared, "I would say since more of the grandparents [are] passing [away], then my mom and aunts and uncles don't force [church] on their kids [anymore]. Since the elders passed, more like you could [go to church only] if you want." A similar sentiment was expressed by Janice in Lorette: "My parents, you know, some younger than that generation that were brought up, were forced to practise or attend—married in that realm, had us baptized in those realms, in that spirituality. But we're not practising [anymore], basically it just kind of fell away. That's the best way to say it." In Camperville, Karen shared, "None of my brothers or sisters go to church [anymore] ... but they still believe in Jesus. Some of them have a difficult time because the way we grew up. They have a difficult time with the church. You can't really blame them." From St. François-Xavier, Elizabeth stated, "My brother doesn't go to church [anymore] and he never went back. My dad doesn't go anymore. But the rest of my family, like his brothers and sisters, all go to Mennonite Church. On my mom's side, I don't think anybody goes to church, on the Métis side. I don't think, of the eleven of them, any of them go [anymore]." And from Ste. Anne, Louis offered another possible explanation for the decrease in attendance at Catholic Church in his family and in general:

> It's interesting because none of us are really devout Catholics [anymore]. And maybe that's a generational thing, a cultural shift that occurred in our communities, regardless if we're Métis or not. There's no [longer] a strong adherence; it's not [even] in Quebec where the church ruled the state kind of thing. Things [have] changed in the French community. . . . In the 1950s, the Catholic Church in Quebec went through a change where the church lost all its power. In the 1970s, it happened in Manitoba. So, the Catholic Church lost its grip on lots of young people, our generation basically.

In addition to a decrease in their family's participation in Catholicism, several people spoke of an increase in their family's involvement with Indigenous spirituality over time. This increase happened specifically in terms of acceptance, learning, and/or participation.[17] Gripette noticed an increase in awareness and openness regarding Indigenous spirituality in her family and in St. Laurent generally: "A lot of people in the community believe more in [Indigenous] spirituality today than they did before. People don't blink at me having a sweat lodge [in my yard]. It's nuts, some people will approach me and speak in hushed tones [chuckles] and say, 'Next time you have a sweat can you let me know?' But they [do] approach and they [do] talk [now]. So, it's more accepted today than [it was even] five years ago." In Lorette, Nicki observed a generational change in her family's participation in Indigenous spirituality: "People, more in my generation, so myself and my sister and my cousins, we are searching for something else and in that way finding their way back to ceremony. My mother too potentially, because I know my mother has her own, maybe doubts isn't the right word, but has her own questions about Christianity. And, I think that maybe her curiosity is a bit piqued about Indigenous spiritualties." We hear about a similar acceptance of Indigenous spirituality in Nancy's family (St. François-Xavier):

> I've had a renewal of my [Indigenous] spirituality in the last maybe fifteen years. And I can tell that my parents are being more open to the possibility. Before, when I said, "I got to pick up some sage," they would look at me like, "What do you need a weed [for] in your house?" Now, they realize what I'm doing because I've explained it to them. [They say,] "Oh okay, I understand." They are more maybe accepting of it, and they realize that a lot of people are doing this. That it's just not some kind of screwball thing.

Finally, in Duck Bay, Whistling Eagle Child had some ideas about why his relatives and many community members are no longer going to church the way they used to, and instead are becoming increasingly interested in Indigenous spirituality:

> I don't think any of them go to church [anymore]. And I like to think of it as part of that awakening. The reintroduction of the Native culture, you know, to our people. It was pretty visible a few years ago when you would go to church and see maybe five people there. [For those that still go,] I call that the "residential school effect" because these people are still so ingrained in that religion. . . . They don't understand that this [Indigenous] spirituality is a part of who they are as a person, and that was taken from them by the church and the school. So, they still think that [church is] where they're supposed to be.

It is interesting to note that people from St. Laurent indicated the lowest decrease in their family's participation in church but the highest increase in their family's relationship with Indigenous spirituality. Perhaps this is an indication that family members in St. Laurent do not see Catholicism and Indigenous spirituality in opposition to one other or as mutually exclusive. This raises questions about the nature of syncretism in spirituality—the phenomenon by which practitioners blend aspects of Christianity and Indigenous ceremonies into a spirituality that resonates with them as individuals and families (Chapter 11).

~

In the pages above, people shared stories about their families' relationships with Métis, First Nations, and Euro-Canadian cultures. Particularly prominent themes associated with Métis culture included subsistence activities, social gatherings, music, and dance. When it came to relationships with First Nations cultures, a noticeable trend was a lack of collective relationship between Métis and First Nations. One reason for this is the forced divisions between Métis and First Nations peoples that resulted from an agenda of assimilation imposed by church, government, and the education system.[18] Folks also talked about their family's relationships with aspects of Euro-Canadian culture, including French culture, Catholicism, racism (including internalized racism), and the education system. Several people noted one or more family members who now identify as Métis (as opposed to French or White). In-depth stories about family relationships with religion and spirituality were also shared. All but one participant reported Roman Catholicism as the dominant religious influence in their family while growing up. At the same time, many also spoke about a decline in their family's participation in church and an increase in their openness and desire to learn about Indigenous spirituality. The influence of these family relationships can be seen in the participants' own self-identification, as I consider in the next chapter.

CHAPTER 8

Exploring Self-Identification

In Chapters 6 and 7, I discussed family relationships across several dimensions—including with Métis, First Nations, and Euro-Canadian cultures—because culture is passed down through the family (among other avenues). The experiences we have during our formative years—and the implicit and explicit values and teachings we learn from them—help shape who we are and how we live and function in the world. In the pages to follow, we see the influence of these family relationships upon participants' own self-identification. Experiences outside the family context also shape the way we understand our identity in relation to family and others. This chapter begins to illustrate some of the participants' personal experiences. I highlight patterns of self-identification (including whether self-identification is context specific and whether it has changed over time) and explore how experiences of racism and discrimination impact identity. As in the previous chapters, we see that the ongoing impacts of colonization upon Métis identity cannot be understated.

Participant Self-Identification

Whereas slightly less than one-quarter of participants indicated they have one or more family members who self-identify as Métis or Michif (Chapter 6), nearly all participants identified themselves in that way. Of these, most used the term "Métis," and five used "Michif." In addition to Métis or Michif, more than half of the participants also chose the following terms to self-identify (in order of decreasing frequency): Cree (one person used "Nêhiyawak"), Anishinaabe, Saulteaux, and Ojibwe.[1] The combination of terms participants used to self-identify was unique to the individual: no two participants self-identified in the same way.[2] This should not be interpreted to mean that Métis people do not have a cohesive collective identity; rather, we emphasize selected aspects of our identity based on our family makeup and personal experiences but nonetheless share common traits and acknowledge a collective identity. Stability of identity also comes across in the fact that for nearly three-quarters of the participants, identity is not context specific (i.e., they do not self-identify differently depending on where they are). The remaining folks said that the way they self-identify depends on audience (especially Indigenous vs. non-Indigenous), location (e.g., ceremonies, international border crossing, job interview), and/or safety (e.g., level of racism). In addition, most of the Métis participants in this study acknowledged that the way they self-identify has changed over time. This included changes in their relationship to identity or to the act of self-identifying (e.g., receiving a spirit name, learning how to say their spirit name in an Indigenous language, or also acknowledging their First Nations roots)—as opposed to a change in terminology and/or proper noun.

Everyone from Duck Bay, St. Laurent, St. François-Xavier, Lorette, and Ste. Anne self-identified using the terms "Métis" or "Michif" (or used to), and in George's case (Duck Bay), the names "Halfbreed" and "Apitowgoshaanuk" when he was younger.[3] In St. Laurent, Lucille responded simply: "I self-identify as a Michif." The response Amanda (Ste. Anne) gave was also straightforward: "I identify as Métis." For his part, Jules (St. Laurent) stated, "I self-identify as a Métis. Or, I might sometimes say 'Michif,' which is the way we pronounce Métis in our Métis dialect, which is [also called] Michif." Likewise, Charlotte (Ste. Anne) said: "I'm a Michif, which is also the language our people had." Debbie, from St. Laurent, explained, "I've always said 'Métis.' . . . I can remember when the government finally put the little box on their forms [for] 'Métis,' because before that it was all under 'Aboriginal.' And, finally, I think it was in the 1980s, I noticed [the Métis option on government forms], and [thought,] 'Oh good,' because we could [now] classify ourselves as Métis." Barbara, who is also from St. Laurent, said, "I identify as a member of the Métis Nation [from] St. Laurent." Similarly, Nicki (Lorette) said, "I identify as a citizen of the Métis Nation." Linda, who is connected to St. François-Xavier, explained, "I am a Métis woman who follows the Red Road [traditional Indigenous spirituality]." And, in one more example from Lorette, Bethany shared: "I self-identify as a Michif. . . . I try not to [use the term] Métis anymore because I feel like when I say 'Métis,' it's just like calling yourself 'Ojibwe' [instead of Anishinaabe], right? It's not the worst thing, but it's always good to go back to your own [Indigenous] language. And, from what I've seen just with other elders, they always introduce themselves as a Michif person. I really like that because then it's like, we're all from an Indigenous group [the Métis Nation], and we have our own language [Michif]—we're not just what[ever] you call us." In Camperville, most people identified with the term Métis, half used the terms Anishinaabe and/or Ojibwe, and a couple identified with the term Cree; however, only two used multiple terms to self-identify.

In comparison, most of the people connected to Ste. Anne, Duck Bay, and St. Laurent used several terms to self-identify. This was also the case for half the folks from St. François-Xavier and Lorette. The most frequently cited identity categories (in addition to Métis/Michif) were Cree and Anishinaabe/Saulteaux/Ojibwe.[4] For instance, Brenda (Camperville) said, "Now, today, I self-identify as Métis-Cree and Ojibwe or Anishinaabe." In St. Laurent, Bobbie-Jo explained: "I self-identify as Métis and Cree, not just one; I identify myself as somebody who walks in both worlds." Barbara (St. Laurent) elaborated, "I identify as a member of the Métis Nation [from] St. Laurent. And, if it's appropriate, in certain circles, I will identify my two First Nation[s], my ancestors, which are Saulteaux and Cree." Bethany, from Lorette, said: "I self-identify as a Michif but sometimes people are like, 'Michif? What's that?' So, then … [I explain:] Anishinaabe, Cree [ancestry]. I still struggle sometimes with saying which European backgrounds I come from because I feel like a lot of [First Nations] people are very anti-White. So, sometimes it feels shameful to say ['I'm Métis'], but I'm getting better."[5] Here, Bethany grapples with internalized racism and the stereotype that Métis people are somehow less Indigenous than First Nations people, or that Métis people are essentially White. Justin (Ste. Anne) identifies as

> Cree and Métis. Sometimes I do the whole list: I'm Cree, Métis, Scottish, German, and Icelandic. Just to talk about how people are mixed in so many different ways. It's important to look into those histories. I really like my Scottish history. In Peguis [First Nation], that's why my mom was born a redhead. And a lot of my great-aunts were born

redheads, but the other ones were brown[-haired]. And my grandma would occasionally pop out a ginger baby. The community used to gossip about it, and they would say that she was sleeping with a Northern Store worker [chuckles]. Knowing my Scottish heritage is good for understanding my [mother's] First Nation side. . . . But, mainly, I just identify as Cree and Métis.

While variations of "Cree" and "Anishinaabe" were the most frequently mentioned identity terms after "Métis" or "Michif," some people also used other terms, including "treaty" and "Canadian."[6] The greatest variation occurred among Duck Bay residents, and the least variation was seen in those from St. Laurent. In one example from Camperville, Louise explained that she also identified with Indian status upon getting married: "By marrying into Lake Manitoba First Nation, I became a status Indian or treaty Indian. But I don't identify with the band, Lake Manitoba. I more identify with my nation or the Cree-Ojibwe Métis. That's what I am. I don't say Métis [only]; I just say this is what I am, Cree-Ojibwe—so, I acknowledge all of my ancestries. . . . Because I married before 1985, I got treaty status. I didn't even know I got treaty status until a couple years after that." Additional reasons for the use of multiple identity terms can be learned from people's discussions on identity and context.

Participant Identity and Context

Two-thirds of the Métis people in this study said they self-identify in the same way no matter where they are or who is around. Some of those for whom context does matter said audience (especially non-Indigenous people) was a significant factor in determining how they choose to identify in a given context.[7] As mentioned, Bethany (Lorette) sometimes has trouble admitting she is Métis because she perceives anti-Whiteness from some First Nations folks who view Métis people as "mostly White." She elaborated: "Sometimes I'll say I'm Michif/Anishinaabe; sometimes I'll just say I'm Michif. It really depends on the context and who I'm with because some people still know me from when I was introducing myself as Anishinaabe. So, I feel like if they heard me [say] 'Oh, I'm Michif,' they'd be like, 'What?' [laughs]. I have yet to break that to them. But I'm sure they probably already know, right? So, yeah [it] depends on the context but I definitely recognize my Indigeneity; it's never a shameful thing to me." While Bethany is learning to acknowledge that she is Métis, instead of First Nation, this is part of a larger process for her.

Other shared stories highlight more dramatically the role that audience and, to a lesser extent, location, play in terms of self-identification. Whistling Eagle Child (Duck Bay) said: "It depends on the situation and where I'm at. If I'm at a Métis meeting then I'm Métis; if I'm at a non-Métis meeting, I'm a non-status [person]." Gripette (St. Laurent) gave an extensive list of types of people with whom and places where she identifies differently:

> When I'm in St. Laurent, I'm a Michif woman, or we use the word "Métis" more now. When I'm describing myself to most people—so, if I'm at a job interview, I'm an Aboriginal person, or Indigenous. When I'm with friends—most of the time the friends that I'm with are people who [also] go to ceremonies or people who identify as First Nation or Anishinaabe—so we call each other *neechie* [friend]. . . . If I'm talking to mainstream [non-Indigenous] people, I'll use the word "Aboriginal." I'll use the word "Indigenous" when I'm describing [myself] to a [mixed company] group. [And,] "Métis" when I'm with Métis people; or, around the community [of St. Laurent], we're "Michif." When we're speaking the [Michif] language, we use the word "Michif" more often. When I'm talking to kids, like my grandkids, we use the word "Michif" most of the time.

Gripette is not the only one who emphasized that when she is in the presence of non-Indigenous people, especially White people, she adjusts the way she typically self-identifies. For example, Jason (Camperville) downplays his Indigeneity and sometimes fibs about his identity when he is speaking with Roman Catholic people. In his own words: "You have to [modify how you identify]. You can't let them—some of the guys expect you to go to church every Sunday. I don't. I just tell them, if they ask me, [that] I'm Roman Catholic and that's when they leave me alone. Because, I had one friend who tried to make me go to his church. Nope, sorry my friend!" Later in this chapter it will become clearer that experiencing racism (especially from White people) is a strong influence in how these Métis people self-identify. Elizabeth (St. François-Xavier) also simplifies how she identifies when she is around non-Indigenous people, as many carry false assumptions about Métis identity; she also explicitly identified safety as an important consideration:

> I self-identify—depending on the group I'm in, and how much information [I share], and how safe I feel—as Métis and Mennonite. Often, I'll go into a longer explanation of introducing myself in Michif and then saying where I was born and all of the different kinds of ancestors that I have. . . . It's mostly with non-Indigenous audiences; I guess it's hard for them to wrap their heads around "Well, are you Indigenous or not?" Or, like, "What amount?" And, "Duh-duh-duh." Sometimes, I just say I'm Métis and that's simpler, like if I'm not going to go into a big explanation. But if I'm doing a relational introduction, and it feels okay to do that and there's space and time to do that, I'll be more explicit about exactly every part of who I am. I've done presentations about this before because my whole area of research is identity but around all the different reactions that you have when you say who you are. . . . Earlier on, when I was just starting to do my PhD work and some of the first relationships I was building with the urban Indigenous community here, people [were] like, "Well, why do you need to say you're Métis and Mennonite? Just say Métis because that encompasses everything." Or, other people being like, "You seem like you're kind of European, and you're kind of Métis; just be who you are." And, "You're an Indigenous woman!" And everybody having their kind of like [reactions]. . . . Like, "What does that [being Métis and Mennonite] even mean?" Or, my brother, for example, [saying] "You should really just do one of these ancestry tests because, do you really have the right to claim this [being Métis]?" And, I'm like, "No! Don't do that [laughs]. Don't make your kids do that. You're not going to get the answers that you're looking for; that's not going to clarify anything for you!" Yeah, just everybody having their own like: "You're claiming too much"; "You're not claiming enough"; "This is how you should identify"; "No, it should be like that."[8]

Justin (Ste. Anne) also self-identifies differently when speaking with White people; he takes the opportunity to encourage them to investigate their own ancestry, history, identity, and culture instead of fixating on Indigenous culture and spirituality:

> For sure. Like, when I open it up [i.e., a conversation regarding my identity] to be everything along with Icelandic. Like here [at this Indigenous gathering], I wouldn't do that. But, with White people, I'll do that. Just so they talk about being mixed. I like to encourage people to be open to their own cultures and identities. I have lots of non-Indigenous friends and we've had conversations about identity, and my best friend was talking about being on the land. He was like, "I love being in the bush and everything, but somewhere deep down I don't feel like I belong here because it's not my land." [And, I replied,] "That's a really good insight. It's important to look at your history and how you got here. Because you should feel comfortable in your place as a settler." We were talking about his heritage and the ancient "Indigenous" heritages that European people have too. Like the pagan traditions and stuff. He's really into First Nations spirituality, too. He really wants to learn about it. "You have your own stuff too; look into that as well. You'll have this feeling that I'm having, of having your history really connected [to you]." So, with White people, I open it up, and I think that's the reason why.

For others, acknowledging the Euro-Canadian element(s) of their identity is also context specific. Vern (St. François-Xavier) had this to say:

> It depends on who I'm with. Not that I'm trying to hide one from the other. I certainly identify as Métis. I quite often have a Métis flag flying outside my house, which ticks off my neighbours. But, then again, I also have a flag of Israel that flies out there every once in a while, and a flag of Scotland. It depends on the time. I guess [in terms of] self-identifying, I would be Canadian initially. . . . It's not that I'm trying to protect [myself] from one thing or another. I found the Swedish Club; there's a Scandinavian Club; I'm definitely [also] Swedish. If I'm wearing my kilt, I'm probably

[identifying as] Scottish. [If] I'm wearing my tam, and this is, by the way, a Grant tartan—there's another story to that. You know, it depends. I don't go out flaunting one [identity] over the other.

Finally, a couple of people said they try to avoid self-identifying entirely—one dislikes labels in general, and the other hopes identity does not come up but says she is "proud/vocal" about being Métis in certain contexts. Louis (Ste. Anne) explained: "I don't profess it [my identity]; I don't declare who I belong to. Because again, I don't come from a place of politics or wherever. It's really more a matter of spirituality for me, and so part of me doesn't care who you think I am. I'm not looking to have someone say, 'You belong to me,' or 'You belong to us.' That kind of thing. Because I had too many experiences—people can exploit that 'you're one of us' kind of stuff." Janice (Lorette) had this to say: "I just hope that self-identification doesn't come up because it's just like, do we need to go there all the time? Is it relevant? I guess it is for some people, depending on what the conversation is, and the context, in terms of wanting to have an understanding of the person, and maybe some of those struggles. Or, you know, where they are coming from. But we need to know what a person is [and how they identify] to help them." Despite not wanting to talk about self-identity with others, Janice acknowledges there are times when those conversations are important. Considerations such as location and audience were also emphasized by folks as reasons for changing their self-identification over time.

Participant Self-Identification over Time

Most of the Métis people in this study indicated that the way they self-identify has changed in some way over time. For instance, half the people from Camperville said their sense of identity has changed as a result of going to ceremonies (Chapter 10). Brenda now also identifies with her First Nations roots; she notes that "before, I used to self-identify as Métis. I now refuse to say that I am only Métis. I am very proud of my First Nation roots and that is why I started self-identifying as Métis-Cree-Ojibwe, because that's who I am." Louise explained why Métis people were reluctant to acknowledge they were Métis:

When I was growing up [in Camperville], there was still shame in being Métis because the way the churches and the

nuns and the priests made us feel. Also, [because of] the
White communities surrounding Camperville. We were
"savage and lazy," "drunken Indians." They didn't like us,
and we didn't like them. [Things changed] I guess probably
[as] part of that revolution in the late '60s and early '70s that
was occurring across Canada among Métis people, among
First Nations, among the Aboriginal people. And what was
happening here in Winnipeg, that Red Power Movement,
and being part of the Indian and Metis Friendship Centre.
. . . That helped me find who I really was and what I was
comfortable with.

Jason grew up identifying as Métis but began identifying as First
Nations after the age of eighteen when he moved to Pine Creek First
Nation to live with his girlfriend (now wife).

In St. François-Xavier, Ronnie identified as Métis from birth
until his twenties; once he reached his fifties, he began to identify as
Canadian.[9] Nancy began acknowledging she is Métis fifteen years ago
and was upset when the Daniels decision was announced because she
thought it meant the courts were forcing Métis people to give up their
distinct identity:

[My identity is] evolving still as I see things in the news
about fighting for the rights of Métis peoples and [I have]
become more vigilant because [of] that Supreme Court
[Daniels] decision where they were going to lock the three
(Inuit, status Indians, and Métis people) together and call all
of us "Indian." I remember I was in the airport in Winnipeg
and I was actually very, very upset that they would do that
because no, I am not an Indian! I guess it was easier for the
government to just lump you in[to] one category: "You're an
Indian." No. I had just found my [Métis] identity and now
the government of Canada was going to take it away from
me. I think being Métis is a unique, separate Indigenous
group from Inuit or status Indian; we're different. . . . There
is only one place in the world where a Métis person exists,
it is technically in the Red River area of Manitoba—the
origin[al birthplace].

I explained to Nancy that the Daniels decision has to do with section 91(24) of the Canadian Constitution, which identifies "Indians and lands reserved for Indians" as falling under federal jurisdiction—this is the reason that the federal government offers (limited) financial assistance for post-secondary education and health benefits to people with registered Indian status. Previously, the federal government had insisted that non-status Indians and Métis people fell under provincial jurisdiction and were, therefore, excluded from the benefits described above. However, in *Daniels v. Canada*,[10] the Supreme Court confirmed that non-status Indians and Métis are included in the term "Indians" in section 91(24) of Canada's Constitution, meaning that legally, these groups should receive similar benefits to folks with Indian status. Nancy understood and said that this hadn't been explained properly by the media.[11] Another person connected to St. François-Xavier, Vern, was told by his White adopted family that he was "a dumb Swede" but learned later in life that he is Métis and has since obtained his Manitoba Metis Federation (MMF) citizenship card. Linda, who was also adopted out, grew up calling herself French and learned later in life that she is Métis and got her MMF card as well.

Everyone connected to Ste. Anne had experienced a change in the way they self-identify. Like Vern and Linda above, Charlotte was adopted out and only learned she is Métis as an adult; she began embracing this identity and proudly identifying as such at the age of forty: "Since the '70s, I knew I was Métis. I've been involved in the Métis organizations here in Winnipeg. There was a certain pride to that too, that we were learning more and more about the history, [and] that the history we learned in school was bullshit [regarding] who Riel was. Here [in Manitoba], all of our ancestors were a part of the rebellion and that it was good." Though she was raised in her birth family, Amanda only learned she is Métis at age seventeen; while she now identifies as Métis, she still sometimes struggles with internalized assimilation and being White-coded (perceived by others as White because of her lighter skin tone). In her own words: "I struggle with it sometimes. I don't look Indigenous. If you look at me, I look White. . . . I [felt I] didn't belong to a Métis community. I wasn't raised in an explicitly Métis way, even knowing that I was [Métis]. There were times that I felt like I shouldn't even be saying that I am [Métis], or that I even had the right to say I was." Amanda shared that confidence in her Métis identity has improved because of her participation in ceremonies (Chapter 10). Justin used to say he was French, a result of internalized racism, but now identifies as Cree and Métis. Louis formerly identified as a "pale-skinned Cree" and now also identifies as Cree and Métis; however, he avoids proper nouns (especially "Métis," since he believes this term has become too political) and prefers the terms "traditionalist, leader, helper, and Indigenous."

As in Ste. Anne, everyone in Lorette indicated that the way they self-identify has changed over time. Janice used to avoid self-identifying in general until her late thirties; she has since obtained her MMF citizenship and also identifies with her First Nations ancestry. She began openly self-identifying as Métis, thanks to affirmative action in the workplace. When she came across job applications and government forms asking if she identified as Aboriginal, she thought: "Should I say [I am]? Because you'll get preferential treatment, or you could in terms of when they fill their mandate of how many [minorities] they need to hire. If you self-identify, you'll be in that [group]. [But,] I never thought of it as 'preferential treatment'; I never viewed it as that. It was almost just like, okay it's there [on the forms], we can do this and why wouldn't I? From that [point], I did identify in that fashion." Andrea went from identifying simply as Canadian to Métis. She explained, "More than half of my life [I said I] was 'Canadian' and never 'Métis.' Now, I would say [I'm Métis], even my husband [would say]: 'My wife is Métis.' I remember my cousin, a couple years ago [when] we were going to a social . . . [said to me,] 'You're a White girl.' I was like, 'Don't call me a White girl!' But people look at me and they see a White girl. . . . I told her, 'I'm Métis. . . . You're Métis as well but you can identify how you want . . . I don't want you to call me a White girl anymore.'" Andrea explained that her cousin had not been trying to insult her but that she felt insulted nonetheless. Similarly, Nicki (Andrea's sister) used to identify as French and now also proudly identifies as Métis. Nicki said, "In my twenties, when I started learning more about who my [Métis] people were, I started identifying more as a Métis person. And, I guess in the last few years, I have used the language of 'Métis Nation citizen.'" Janice's daughter Bethany (the youngest participant in the study) has benefitted from her mother's growing pride as a Métis woman. Whereas her mother did not want to acknowledge her Indigeneity when she was younger, Bethany's experience has been the opposite: when she was younger, she did not want to acknowledge that she is Métis, preferring instead to identify as Anishinaabe. Later, she identified as mixed and Métis, and today she identifies solely as Michif.

In Duck Bay, George spoke of a change in popular terminology over the decades that has impacted Métis people. He discussed how people (himself included) used the terms "Halfbreed" and "Apitowgoshaanuk" until the 1970s, then "Indian," then "Anishinaabe." Now he acknowledges his Nêhiyaw/Cree, Michif/Métis, and Sioux roots and languages. Betsy went from identifying simply as "Native" to calling herself "Métis." Ray used to call himself a "treaty French-Canadian Indian" while living in the States because that is what he was called there; today, he explains that his mom is Cree, his dad was (Saulteaux) Métis, and he himself is "treaty" (status Indian).

Finally, in St. Laurent, Gripette said she used to identify solely as Michif but over time, she has also become comfortable with the term "Métis," especially because of hearing it frequently during her visits to Winnipeg. She clarified, "When we were kids growing up in the community [of St. Laurent], we were Michif people. When we moved to the city [of Winnipeg], they told me I was Métis. I didn't know what 'Métis' was. Then when they described what Métis was, it didn't fit me because when they were describing Métis, there was discrimination in their descriptions. It took me years before I would use the word 'Métis' to describe [myself], and I would only use it [when] talking about the MMF membership." Bobbie-Jo shared that learning more about her Cree culture has made a difference: "As I come to learn more and more about my First Nations Cree culture, I've identified more with First Nations than anything, although I still practise a lot of my Métis culture."

As can be heard in the excerpts above, several factors influence self-identification over time, including experiencing racism. Folks shared many stories about the ways in which racism and discrimination impacted their self-identification.

Participant Experiences with Racism and Discrimination

When participants talked about experiences of racism and discrimination, the largest pattern to emerge was having to navigate harmful stereotypes about Métis people. The range of stereotypes mentioned was extensive, including the belief that all Métis people are thieves and dangerous, uneducated or unintelligent, liars, cheaters, addicts, and unclean. Several people discussed being White-coded and therefore spared the brunt of racism. Nearly one-quarter of folks mentioned resisting racism and trying to protect themselves and their loved ones, for example through student activism; enrolling their children in multicultural schools and taking care to dress them nicely; showing bravery in racist confrontations; adopting an attitude of not being bothered by racism; and specializing in the academic study of racism and its effects upon Métis people. Schools were mentioned by the most participants as sites where they experienced racism, followed by urban areas, then places of employment. Some people mentioned name-calling and verbal abuse, including at the hands of nuns, foster and adopted family members, in public schools, as well as within their own marriage. Folks also described experiencing lateral violence at the hands of First Nations people, and a few spoke of suffering racism specifically at the hands of White perpetrators. After listening to these stories about racism and discrimination, it was not surprising to hear many folks also talk about internalized racism.[12]

Racist Stereotypes

People from St. Laurent spoke the most about racist stereotypes; in particular, stereotypes about Métis people from St. Laurent and about Métis people as thieves and alcoholics. For instance, Jules said, "Some of my nephews and nieces are darker, so I know they face discrimination in stores and jobs, looking for work and stuff like that—being followed around in stores." In Duck Bay, Whistling Eagle Child offered an example of the stereotype of Métis people as addicts: "I was eighteen or nineteen [years old] at the time and it was cheque day; I was on welfare. I didn't get my cheque in the mail, so I called my worker in Swan River and she says to me, 'Why do you need your cheque so badly? So you can pay your drug bill?'" Nancy (St. François-Xavier) shared an example of the stereotype that Métis people are alcoholics and unclean: "In my first marriage, my ex-husband would call me a 'dirty, filthy, Indian.' When he found out that I was Métis, him being uneducated and not knowing what a Métis person was [he would say to me,] 'You're just a dirty, drunk Indian.' Well, I don't drink but thanks." The stereotype of Métis people as liars and cheaters came up in a story shared by Charlotte

(Ste. Anne): "In grade three, I had written an essay, a summer holiday essay, in French. I would use words that a grade twelve or university student would use. I read a lot; I knew how things fit in the world—nobody helped me to develop that. [But,] I was always [just] 'that damn little Indian.'" While several people discussed various examples of stereotypes directed at Métis (and other Indigenous people in general), many also spoke of being spared the brunt of racism.

On Being White-Coded

People from St. François-Xavier discussed their lighter skin as a buffer against racism more than folks from the other Métis communities did. Denise said, "I don't normally have that experience just because I look so White; I don't think that people even think I look Native." Elizabeth stated that while she does not experience racism as a result of her skin colour, she feels it peripherally: "I wouldn't call it 'racism' because I'm pretty White-looking. I think that definitely when I've been in places like advocating and educating, I've experienced strong resistance which I would call racist—maybe not toward me directly, but certainly like racist attitudes that come out when people feel threatened or unsettled." Two people each in Lorette and St. Laurent also raised this issue, as did one person connected to Ste. Anne. Andrea, in Lorette (like Denise from St. François-Xavier above), said: "When someone looks at me, if I didn't say I identify as Métis, they're just going to think I'm a White girl." Nicki's response echoed Elizabeth's in terms of experiencing racism only indirectly: "I have [experienced racism and discrimination] mostly indirectly. Mostly [by] people who 'White me out' or mis-identify me as a non-Indigenous person, making [racist] comments about First Nations or Métis people to me because, you know, they don't realize that I am Métis. Or they may realize that I'm Métis but still think that I am a safe space to make those kinds of [racist] comments." Barbara, from St. Laurent, spoke similarly about her own experiences of discrimination: "Probably not as an Indigenous person unless I tell them that I'm Indigenous, then people react differently. But, [I've] certainly [experienced discrimination] as a woman and as a two-spirit [person]. And, because of my fair colour, I will be able to, I can escape that bigotry and racism. It's when you tell somebody you're Indigenous and what background you are, then [the discrimination] creeps out." Jules, also from St. Laurent, talked about unequal experiences of racism within his own family that depended on skin colour: "I'm very lucky that I didn't [experience racism] because, you know, when in a Métis family, some of them [look] White, some of them are in between, some of them look like Indians. And I happened to look more White than anything else, I think. And most people didn't know I was Métis, so that probably did make a difference. I don't think I faced any discrimination. I was very lucky. It was different for some of my family, like nephews and nieces that are darker." In contrast, Louise (Camperville) spoke specifically about *not* being spared the brunt of racism despite having fair skin. In her own words, "Sometimes some people would say to me, 'But you're fair, how could you feel discrimination?' That's such a fallacy; it's so wrong. It's so inaccurate because we feel discrimination as much as [my brother] does because [he's] dark. I come from a family of seventeen with my mom and dad and nine brothers [and five sisters]. There's three of us that are fair and everybody else is dark. I felt discrimination in many places in the city of Winnipeg, and in Camperville, or [in] Winnipegosis." No one from Duck Bay indicated that they have been spared the brunt of racism because of having lighter skin or being perceived as White.

Resistance Efforts to Curb Racism

Resistance efforts in the face of racism were mentioned most frequently by folks from Camperville. Julia made a deliberate choice in the type of school where she enrolled her son, whom she described as visibly Indigenous, in the hopes of lessening his exposure to racism and discrimination. She said, "He goes to a really multicultural school. I'm so happy about that. I would never have him go to somewhere where he is the only person of colour or Indigenous person. He hasn't told me about anything directly that he's experienced. But he must have. I think that he sees racism, he sees other Indigenous people experience racism and he talks about that. But he's never talked about himself experiencing it, other than people are afraid of him [he's over six feet tall]. He said that, so I guess that would be racism." When her son was small, she also took care to ensure his clothes were nice in the hopes of avoiding stereotypes and sparing him racist experiences.

> I had him when I was nineteen, so I was young. I remember experiencing [racism] the most when he was a baby and I

would be out with him. People would definitely treat me differently and I noticed it right away. So, I made a pointed effort of making sure when we left the house, we always looked [good]; we never went out in sweat [pants], or we always looked our best regardless of where we were going. I made sure that he looked his best and that I looked my best just to sort of curb some of that judgement. That's fucked up. But yeah, I remember thinking that and realized that they don't treat me the same if I dress like this, or if I look like this, they treat me a little bit better. So, [I tried] any little thing that I can do to be treated better.

Brenda shared perhaps the most pointed example of fighting back against racism in the form of student activism:

[I experienced] racism when we started going to the all-White school in Winnipegosis. From Camperville, we were bused from grade seven. We experienced really a lot of racism from the Winnipegosis school, as well as from the community [of Winnipegosis]. We actually had a sit-in; [I'm] very proud of that and that's my days of activism. We had a sit-in in 1973, in March because of all the racism that was going on. The Camperville students all got in a circle, where we got that idea from, I can't remember, but we all got in a circle and we sat in the gymnasium and asked for the principal to come up to us. She came once and she ordered us back to our school; she wouldn't listen to our, we had a list of grievances about almost twenty or seventeen, and then, in the afternoon, she expelled all of us. I was deemed the associate leader or whatever, the secondary leader; my auntie [name retracted] was deemed leader. Although, we said we were in a circle [and] we are not going to have a leader, but they deemed us both leaders. I was expelled for six months, I think; and my auntie was expelled for life. We were all scared. We went back to Camperville and we were all scared to tell our parents; and, wouldn't you know it, the whole community backed us up! Ron Richard was actually one of the ones who spoke up; they all spoke up about that racism that they endured throughout the many years [at Winnipegosis school]. Then teachers were brought to Camperville because our parents refused to send us back [to Winnipegosis school]. The whole, all the school, all the students. And then we had teachers brought into the community centre and that's where we were taught. Eventually, I think in the fall or I don't know, after a year, then the students went back [to Winnipegosis school]. But I never went back; that's when I left, when I was sixteen [years old]. I came to Winnipeg and went to school, and my auntie never went back [either]. We also filed a human rights complaint; we were on TV. . . . But, [there] was insufficient evidence to support overt racism but there was institutional evidence for institutional discrimination. As a result, there were recommendations made and the Department of Education recommended Native Studies supplements to be added to the Social Studies curriculum. They recommended [Indigenous] adult role models to serve as examples to instill motivation and success with mature [Indigenous] students. . . . I believe that's where the first ACCESS Programs came about to train community members to be teachers and professionals; these teachers still teach in Camperville. My mom was one of them.[13]

One person each from Duck Bay, St. Laurent, St. François-Xavier, and Ste. Anne also talked about strategies for resisting racism or attempting to minimize its effect upon themselves and their loved ones. No one from Lorette mentioned efforts to resist racism, nor did they mention experiencing racism in specific locations.

Racist Hotspots

Participants mentioned schools, urban areas, and workplaces most frequently as sites of racism. In Camperville, half the respondents indicated they have experienced racism in urban cities like Vancouver and in the affluent, predominantly White Winnipeg suburb of Charleswood. Racism and discrimination in similar locations were also mentioned by individuals in each of the other communities. Like Brenda's story about racism in the Winnipegosis school, Lucille (St. Laurent) spoke of school as a site of racism, specifically around linguistic assimilation:

I remember teachers saying [not to] speak our Michif language between [our] friends, because it was an English school we attended. You'd be on your break, or recess time, and you'd be talking to your friends; and we all spoke Michif French. I guess it wasn't accepted or they didn't want us to speak that language because they couldn't understand so they'd often tell us, "Do not speak that language. We don't understand you. You're not allowed to speak that [Michif] French or whatever you're talking." To me, that was a big part of discrimination. It stayed with me. It's scarred [me]. You never forget [experiences like that].

In another story, Nancy (St. François-Xavier) shared an example of discrimination in the workplace:

[When] the Louis Riel holiday first came into play where it was a stat[utory] holiday [in Manitoba in 2008], I was standing by the photocopier, and there was a person there saying, "Why are we getting a holiday for a traitor that was hung?" And I just stood there and was just flabbergasted. I [thought to myself,] "Okay, you're uneducated; you don't know what you are talking about." I turned around and said, "Well, if you don't want to take the day off, just come to work." It took everything in my power to restrain myself [and not] to say what an ignorant, uneducated response from a businessperson. That was fairly recent[ly].

Ray, from Duck Bay, also said he has experienced racism in the work-place: "I've experienced it yeah. I think everybody has. There's a lot of racism.... Some people don't take it well and don't know how to deal with it like in the workplace. They're targeted; I can see it. It's a form of bullying what they do to people. You have to deal with it right away to stop it. It's too bad. It's the hate, the hate those people carry in their hearts toward others." Exceptions to these patterns were found among folks from Ste. Anne, who did not mention racism in the workplace; also, no one from Lorette spoke about racism in any of these sites (urban settings, schools, workplaces).

Name-Calling and Verbal Abuse

Name-calling and verbal abuse were raised by one or two people each in Ste. Anne, Camperville, Duck Bay, St. François-Xavier, and Lorette. Betsy, from Duck Bay, spoke of experiencing racism and other forms of discrimination (such as transphobic violence) regularly; she shared a frightening encounter that she experienced as a Métis trans woman:

> Oh yes! They literally, yes, almost every other day I get hit with racism. Somebody following me around. I remember when I was younger, people used to call me a "dirty fucking rez [reserve] Indian." As recently as two weeks before I came here ... I was celebrating [my recent graduation at a local pub] and this guy—while I was standing and waiting for a taxi—he was saying, "Fuck those squaws. Don't worry about those fucking squaws, man. Fuck that. Don't chase after those bitches." And then he goes, "There's a tranny squaw trying to pick you up and likes you." And then I said, "Thank you!" I said, "Thank you so much." And he said, "What the fuck are you trying to do here? Why are you jumping into our conversation?" I was like, "You were referring to me, so obviously I'm going to respond." And I said, "Thank you. If you feel that way about me, that's fine. That's totally fine, just keep that away from me. Stand over there a little bit." "No, you fucking stand over there!" And I was like, "Alright, definitely, I will." And the taxi driver was like, "Are you okay? Do you want to get in? That shouldn't be said. That shouldn't be happening around here; let's go." So, I said, "Yeah, definitely, thanks." It just reminds me that racism is alive and well and still out there.

In this story, Betsy also illustrates bravery in the face of racism, of standing one's ground, and of survival tactics. Charlotte (Ste. Anne) also discussed regularly experiencing racism:

> Oh God, yes [laughs]. Growing up, full-fledged [racism]; even today. Some people are still not comfortable with Aboriginal people. Some people aren't comfortable with Métis people. And some people aren't comfortable with themselves, so they throw it on everybody else. I grew up being called *maudit sauvage*, "damn Indian." [And], being told by the nuns that I would never amount to anything; and [the] same with the foster parents. [They told me] I was no good. So, growing up, that's why I had that hatred for so many years because how could they not see who I [really] was?

Lateral Violence by First Nations People

As part of their experiences of racism and discrimination, some folks in this study identified specific groups of people as perpetrators. Stories about experiencing lateral violence at the hands of First Nations people were shared by one or two people each from Ste. Anne, St. François-Xavier, Lorette, and St. Laurent. For instance, Louis (Ste. Anne) shared a story about racial hierarchy among Indigenous people[14] and being the perpetual "helper" at ceremonies—to the point of exploitation—because he was Métis:

> For a long time, it was okay to be the helper but I was never going to be the equal. They could exploit me, if they wanted; in the beginning, that's what it felt like. That if you really wanted to be a part of this [ceremonial] circle then you couldn't say no [to what they asked of you]. . . . I've been witness to people that were so strong, adamant traditionalists in a sense that, that person [would tell others they] cannot be in the lodge because they are "not Indigenous enough." Make them the fire keeper forever [never the conductor]. . . . You can exploit people in that way, right? Make them work hard and they never get the benefits of it. . . . I've had people who were very strong leaders in the spiritual circle, traditional, who've talked about the "purity of their blood," basically, in their family. The purity of their lineage; they were elitists. Until their daughter had a red-haired, green-eyed child. [This spiritual leader] had married a status Indian from up north so, in the lodge, this spiritual leader is crying because she didn't know what to do now that she had a grandchild that didn't fit her dogma. That put everything into question, because that's the thing with racism—it eventually comes back to bite you.

No one from Duck Bay indicated that they had experienced lateral violence at the hands of First Nations people.

Racism Perpetrated by White People

Some folks spoke specifically about suffering from racism at the hands of White perpetrators. This theme appeared most prominently in talking with people from St. Laurent but was also raised by participants in Camperville and in St. François-Xavier. Barbara discussed racism against Métis inhabitants of St. Laurent at the hands of White cottage owners along the beaches that St. Laurent is known for. She said, "If you say you're from St. Laurent, people say, 'Oh.' You know that they're thinking, 'those people.' [This happens with] anybody that knows about [or has a cottage at] Twin Beach. . . . It's White people [who behave like that]." Gripette discussed a long history of racism in St. Laurent resulting from White French immigrants and clergy moving to the community. In her own words:

> Racism and discrimination have been built into this com-
> munity for years from when those French people came, and
> when the priests were here, and when the nuns were here.
> I think everybody in St. Laurent has been victimized with
> racism and discrimination. . . . From the Métis end, it was not
> an issue with us and our folks; it was an issue with the French
> and their folks. One of the practices that they [the French
> people] did was they would send their [French] boys to high
> school outside of the community so they didn't mingle with
> the [Métis] girls in the community. And, the [French] girls,
> they would pull them out of school at a certain time when
> they felt there were some things going on that shouldn't
> be going on. . . . When I was sixteen, I was going out with
> a boy, he was in grade twelve, and he was a French boy. . . .
> Him and I did go out together, and then he graduated in
> June and his family told him that if I went to grad with him,
> that they weren't going to the ceremonies. . . . But he had a
> car that his parents had given him, so he would come, and
> he would pick me up. When his family found out about it,
> they took his car away. But, that's only one story; there are
> tons of stories about that. There's some babies that were born
> [in St. Laurent], they were [born to Métis] women that got
> pregnant and their families, the French people, would make
> sure that they sent that [French] boy away somewhere. Or,
> that they couldn't marry; couldn't have anything to do with
> each other.

Louise, from Camperville, shared that she does not believe racism perpetrated by White people is decreasing: "I don't think things have gotten any better between Aboriginal people, or Métis people and White people. I don't things have improved. I think there's still a lot of racism coming from the White people, from the dominant society toward Aboriginal people. What I mean by 'Aboriginal people,' I mean First Nation, Métis, and Inuit. There's a lot of discrimination toward them." Given all the racism and discrimination experienced across the Métis communities in this study—whether when folks were younger or ongoing as adults—it is not surprising that internalized racism also emerged as a key theme.

Internalized Racism and Shame

People from Ste. Anne, Lorette, St. François-Xavier, and Camperville spoke about internalized racism. Recall the story shared by Andrea (Lorette), above, about self-identifying as Canadian until adulthood because of hearing only negative things about Métis people in the school system and among the general public. Another example of internalized racism and assimilation can be heard in a story told by Justin (Ste. Anne):

> I always knew that I was brown. When I was asked when I was a kid, "What are you?" I was always asked that for so long when I was a kid. It was in school where I learned shame. It wasn't from my family; it was at school. I don't know why it happened. I don't know if it was what I was learning in school—the treaties were taught so poorly in school. It might have been that, or the racism coming out at an early age. Whenever people asked me what I was, I would just say I was French. . . . I didn't know what I was doing or what that meant, or what shame like that really was [about]. I just really didn't want to say [I was Métis]. I was scared people would find out.

Another heartbreaking example of internalized racism and shame at a very young age was shared by Brenda (Camperville). Even though she experienced racism at the Winnipegosis school, as told in her story about resistance above, Brenda indicated that the racism she experienced later in Winnipeg was even worse. She said, "I moved to Winnipeg and then that's when I experienced racism, direct racism.

I remember as a little girl, in grade one, trying to wash the brown off my skin. And why? Racism, I guess. What other reason [could it have been]? ... And then we moved to Vancouver where I experienced more [racism] the following year." No one from St. Laurent or Duck Bay mentioned struggling with internalized racism.

~

Unlike the preceding two chapters on family history and relationships, this chapter has focused squarely upon participants' own self-identification and experiences. Almost everyone reported identifying, at least for a period in their lives, as Métis or Michif and continue to identify in this way today. This represents a marked increase in self-identification as Métis or Michif in comparison to their parents' and grandparents' generations. One consistency between many participants and the older generations in their families is the use of multiple identity categories, especially "Cree" and "Anishinaabe/Ojibwe/Saulteaux" in addition to Métis/Michif. Most people indicated that the way they self-identify has changed over time, for reasons including changes in public perception of Métis people, family history research, participation in ceremonies, and gaining registered Indian status. One-third indicated that the way they self-identify is context specific and depends especially upon audience (Indigenous vs. non-Indigenous); level of safety (especially level of racism) was also raised as a factor that influences the way some folks self-identify in a given moment. Many of the Métis people in this study have experienced racism and discrimination at one time or another in their lives. Some continue to have these experiences regularly in adulthood. The most frequently cited forms of racism included stereotypes; racism experienced in schools, urban areas, or the workplace; name-calling and verbal abuse; lateral violence at the hands of First Nations; and racism perpetrated by White people. Some people spoke of being spared the brunt of racism as a result of their lighter skin; still others talked about internalizing racism and feeling ashamed of their Indigeneity. Stories were also shared about resisting racism individually and collectively in community (as in Camperville), and sometimes through survival tactics (e.g., nonchalance or standing one's ground in racist confrontations).

CHAPTER 9

Spirituality, Types of Ceremonies, and Disconnection Factors

Family history and relationships with community and identity (Chapter 6), and with culture and religion (Chapter 7), as well as the participants' own self-identification and experiences with racism and discrimination (Chapter 8) have all influenced the participants' own relationships with spirituality, as will become apparent in pages of this chapter and the next. Below, we hear how the participants describe their own spirituality and discuss the types of Indigenous ceremonies they take part in. They also share stories highlighting factors in their lives that threatened to inhibit their personal connection to Indigenous spirituality and ceremonies over the years.

Describing Spirituality

The Métis people in this study described their spirituality in terms of characteristics such as commitment and a sense of purpose, as well as values such as interconnection and relationships, respect, and a commitment to being non-hierarchical.[1] Many people also mentioned Christianity (usually Roman Catholicism), especially to say they are no longer practising Christians; some described syncretic blends of Christianity and Indigenous spirituality. A few people indicated that traditional Indigenous elements outweighed Christian ones in their spiritual practice, and a couple spoke of a balanced blend. Several folks noted that Indigenous ways of life are grounded in ceremonies. Importantly, some people stated that Métis spirituality includes ceremonies, that ceremonies are open to all Métis people, and mentioned Métis (and First Nations) knowledge holders and teachers and that Louis Riel was a pipe carrier. Challenges with regard to spirituality, including discrimination resulting from patriarchy, sexism, dogma, policing women's bodies, and homophobia, were also discussed.[2]

People from each Métis community described their spirituality in terms of certain characteristics. The importance of making a concerted, ongoing, daily commitment to spiritual practice was raised by Bobbie-Jo and Barbara (St. Laurent), Vern and Nancy (St. François-Xavier), Janice and Bethany (Lorette), and Whistling Eagle Child (Duck Bay). Nancy said, "For me, it's a part of my everyday life. It's been encompassed in my everyday life." Likewise, Bobbie-Jo stated, "I'm a ceremonial person. I attend a lot of ceremony on a bi-weekly basis; I smudge daily. . . . So, [I'm] very immersed into a ceremonial life." Whistling Eagle Child discussed the importance of fully committing to spiritual practice and not being distracted by alcohol: "I believe that we don't just pick [spirituality] up and put it down. If you're there, you're committed. They always tell us 'you meet Creator halfway.' And I'm not meeting Him halfway [if I get distracted]; I'm not going to pretend like I am. If I pick it up and put it down and a couple days later I pick up a beer, then I'm not doing my halfway; I'm just lying to myself. I am fully traditional; I will be traditional for the rest of my life." Barbara spoke of using bundle items as part of a regular, ongoing commitment: "This man said: 'You can't just put your drum on a wall and think it's going to give you messages. You have to use your sacred objects. You have to use your pipe; you have to use your rattle. You have to use those to help you to be stronger. Trust in those things to give messages to your ancestors so they can help you on this earth.'"

A strong sense of purpose also emerged as a defining characteristic of spirituality. This was articulated by Karen and Brenda in Camperville, Betsy in Duck Bay, Bethany in Lorette, and Charlotte and Amanda in Ste. Anne. Role modelling and raising one's children in ceremony were identified within this larger sense of purpose. For example, Amanda spoke of smudging with her children and the fact that they both want to learn their spirit names. Brenda shared, "My children are aware of [ceremonies] and they have come to the odd ceremony with me, but they are not as strong [committed] as I'd like. But I do believe I've planted the seed with all of them. Once they have that seed, they always have that [spiritual] home to come to. And that home is here, and that fire is lit within us. I've lit that [fire] and I'm very proud of that.

If they stray, that's fine. I know in my heart that they will come back."
Charlotte also spoke of her efforts to raise her children in ceremony:
"[An elder] said, 'Your kids are more traditional than the kids on our
reserve. They are growing up with their culture. That's sad that our
kids can't be raised that way.' I said it was important for me to have my
children know who they are. . . . I let my children make their choices.
They went to different churches with their friends, but they were raised
in a traditional [ceremonial] manner." Bethany also talked about the
importance of role modelling, including building kinship connections
through participation in ceremonies: "I brought one of my co-workers
into ceremony; and so, he's now my 'little brother' . . . . I have the responsibility where I should be going to ceremony so that he can also
see that. Like: '[Here]'s this older figure going to ceremony—I should
keep going to ceremony [too].'" Betsy has learned there is more to life
than makeup and attention from men; instead, she realizes a greater
purpose in helping others: "Before, I didn't feel like I had a purpose. I
felt like it was just about face value: doing makeup, being pretty, getting
attention from guys, dressing up in nice clothing, having that attention.
It was all false. . . . I know that when I hear people's stories now, *that* is
the kind of attention that should be [sought]—the attention of helping
somebody, of people coming toward you and seeking that help."

Characteristics were not the only way that participants described
their spirituality. Folks from every community, most notably Ste.
Anne and St. Laurent, described their spirituality in terms of values.
Interconnection and honouring relationships were particularly important for Debbie, Bobbie-Jo, and Gripette (St. Laurent), Linda and
Elizabeth (St. François-Xavier), Andrea and Bethany (Lorette), and
Justin and Charlotte (Ste. Anne). Debbie spoke about interconnection
and relationships extending beyond humans to include the land and
the earth: "I feel very grounded even with Mother Earth. We're rich in
that way because we know that there's a higher power. . . . You have to
respect the land, and Mother Earth, because they're the boss. . . . I feel
very blessed with that." Similarly, Linda shared: "I'm connected to the
earth. I have a garden. I talk to my flowers, plants. . . . That's what helps
me connect with spirituality: the land. . . . Spirituality means the land
and the connection to the universe and the Creator." Andrea echoed
this: "I believe in some sort of connection in the universe and that we
all have this part to play." Likewise, Charlotte said: "My spirituality is

the universe, being part of the universe and the universe being part of me," and "Spirituality connects me to everything—every blade of grass, every plant, every tree, every rock. It's being in touch with everything; the water, the land."

In addition to interconnection and relationships, the value of respect and rejecting hierarchical thinking was also mentioned by Andrea and Bethany (Lorette), Amanda and Charlotte (Ste. Anne), Brenda (Camperville), Betsy (Duck Bay), and by Gripette (St. Laurent). The importance of extending respect to all cultures, religions, and beings was discussed. On this topic, Betsy described her spirituality as "very embracing [of] everything. I learned that you can't ... be accepting of [just] one culture. . . . I will respect everybody as a human. It doesn't matter who you are, what colour you are, what gender [you are]." Brenda said, "I do respect all cultures. I do respect my family's Roman Catholic[ism]. . . . I say to them, 'I respect you; you respect me; and we will be okay.' I do not believe in forcing Indigenous spirituality on anybody." Bethany echoed this belief: "All prayers are sacred. I really respect that part and I don't support people who are like 'F—— the church.' I understand where it's coming from but it's also not really respectful [laughs]." Amanda spoke of respect for all life forms: "I say nature's a big part of it—like respecting all beings. In the past few years, I don't even like to kill anything in my house [including] if there are spiders everywhere. Just being aware of life and having that sanctity. Respecting all life even though there's such a hierarchal culture in mainstream culture with humans and animals. I just moved away from that." Characteristics and values such as the ones shared above were the most common ways that folks described their own spirituality.

Métis people from each community, especially from Ste. Anne and Lorette, mentioned Christianity when describing their spirituality. Many stated they are no longer practising Catholics (Betsy and George in Duck Bay; Andrea, Janice, and Bethany in Lorette; Louis, Charlotte, and Justin from Ste. Anne); or that they felt that they never "fit in" with Catholicism (Louise and Brenda in Camperville). When asked if she identifies with Roman Catholicism today, Janice unequivocally replied "no." George said, "I don't believe in any church today. Any church. Even though some do good work for the people." Charlotte elaborated as follows: "We don't need to go into a building, a church that somebody controls, locks the doors. We don't need to

pay for the privilege of sitting in that church. We don't get [shamed]
because we didn't pay enough money to the church. I remember the
bulletins being handed out each year: this family gave this much; this
family gave this much. It was disgusting. People were being put down
[shamed] because they didn't have any more to give." Brenda never
felt like she belonged at church: "I never felt I fit the Roman Catholic
religion. Although I respect it, I never felt I fit it. I did not believe in
hell. I was taught that if I was bad, I would go to hell. I was groomed
to be in that, by the way—by sister Ste. Rose. She took me under her
wing, and I was supposed to be a nun. We were all taught if you are bad
you will go to hell, so I grew up fearing death." Louise also spoke of not
fitting in and how her feelings toward the church have changed over
time: "I used to really dislike or hate the church at one time. In the '60s
and '70s, I hated the church so much. I was disgusted and I just felt a
lot of revulsion toward the church. But I came to a good place where
I feel much more at peace about the churches now. I've forgiven them
and I understand what their mission was or what their intention was.
I understand it differently, so I've reconciled with the church, with the
Roman Catholic church." In contrast, Jules and Debbie (St. Laurent)
and Ronnie and Vern (St. François-Xavier) continue to identify with
Christianity. When describing their spiritualty, they said the follow-
ing: "Christian actually, specifically Catholic" (Jules); "I'm a practising
Catholic" (Debbie); "I self-identify as Christian" (Vern); and "I still say
I'm a Catholic" (Ronnie).

Some people spoke of a blend of traditional Indigenous spirituality
and Christianity (syncretism) when describing their spirituality. Those
who said that the Indigenous elements outweighed the Christian ones
in their spiritual lives were Lightning Rattle Woman, Whistling Eagle
Child, Maryanne (all from Duck Bay), and Denise (St. François-
Xavier). Denise indicated that she sometimes goes to the Native
American church in her area. Maryanne revealed a change in her
participation in church and in the way she prays: "I don't go to church
every Sunday, but I do pray—differently than I did back then when I
was a kid, and I was forced to go to church. . . . I'm not [praying] per se
to God, or the Virgin Mary. . . . I'm praying for people and for humanity
because it brings me comfort." Lightning Rattle Woman mentioned
going to church infrequently, and only for the sake of her family: "[I

identify as] just more so traditional. More than Catholic. I don't bless my house with holy water; we more so just smudge and stuff." When asked if she found it difficult to blend traditional Indigenous spirituality with Catholicism, she replied, "Yeah, it's like you pick and choose which way is best for you; you can't hold onto [both]. We just basically [keep] church in our lives out of respect for our parents and for our kids whatever our kids plan to do for their lives; we still introduce[d] church in a Catholic way." Whistling Eagle Child reported a similar challenge: "It's very difficult for me; it's a great challenge. I'll give you an example, at [our child's] baptism, I did second reading in the church. In the Catholic religion they are very proper: you kneel before you get up, before you sit down. It was kind of shameful or painful for me to do that when I was in church. I just don't know if that respect [for Catholicism] is there anymore."

Other participants—Lucille (St. Laurent), Karen (Camperville), and Vern (St. François-Xavier)—described a balanced blend of Christianity and Indigenous spirituality and did not express concerns about adhering to both. Lucille said, "I use both; I practise both." Karen has been greatly influenced by an Indigenous woman Sundancer who rediscovered Jesus: "When I Sundance, I pray to that. I remember that Jesus went to her. So, [Christianity] does come into [the way I Sundance]. I don't go there with my rosaries and my crosses or my Bible—I don't do that. I have more respect for their way, but to me, I know that there's one God. You can respect Him in both religions, all religions." When Vern was asked if he had ever experienced any tensions in trying to adhere to both Christianity and Indigenous spirituality, he simply said "no." Like Karen, he shared a story about syncretism: "I went to Moose Factory; I was there for Christmas one year and went to four church services in twenty-four hours. I went to the Mass at the Anglican Church and it was—Oh, [I was] so impressed: real wine and bannock for communion. Then, at the very end, the priest said, 'We're going to sing "Amazing Grace" and we're going to sing it in Cree.'" Vern enjoyed that very much.

In contrast, several people described their spirituality as living "traditional Indigenous ways of life." This was the case for three people in Duck Bay (Ray, Lightning Rattle Woman, and Whistling Eagle Child), two people in Ste. Anne (Louis and Charlotte), and one each in St. Laurent (Gripette), Camperville (Brenda), St. François-Xavier

(Elizabeth), and Lorette (Janice). We have already heard from Whistling Eagle Child and Lightning Rattle Woman in this regard. Ray, also from Duck Bay, had this to say:

> That's what I walk: the Sweetgrass Road. It's a spiritual awakening that came to me seven years ago. As I was being woken up, I was being shown things. This is happening with a lot of people: when they're being woken up, they're being shown things in the world that are coming, in the future. People in Indian Country all over are starting to be woken up. . . . Things are happening. When you walk the Sweetgrass Road, you walk in two worlds. You are in the physical world here but [you] also have to find the balance of the spiritual world.

Brenda said, "I follow the traditional Aboriginal Indigenous ways. I describe myself as a traditional woman." Likewise, Louis simply stated, "I describe it as: I am very traditional." Elizabeth explained that she is "not religious, not church-religious; more Indigenous spirituality from a Cree or Métis perspective." Charlotte said, "It's a way of life. I get up in the morning, and I pray. I go to bed, and I pray. When things get difficult, I will go for a walk and I'll pray." Unlike in the past, Gripette can now talk openly about her Indigenous spirituality: "I started walking this way over thirty years ago. But my first sweat wasn't thirty years ago, it was twenty years ago or something. It wasn't that common then; like now, you can go to sweat almost anywhere, right? Everyone talks about it as if it's nothing. It's like Sundance, you can talk about that anytime now. Even five years ago, you didn't talk very much about Sundance; ten years ago, [you] never said the word in public."

On a related note, a few people specifically mentioned the importance of participating in ceremonies: Julia, Louise, and Brenda (Camperville), Justin and Charlotte (Ste. Anne), and Bethany (Lorette)—more will be said on this later in the chapter. Five people explicitly stated that Métis spirituality includes Indigenous ceremonies. Debbie (St. Laurent) shared her belief that Métis people can access traditional Indigenous spirituality: "We can [go to ceremonies]—with being Métis, the doors are so open." Charlotte had no qualms about identifying as a Métis person who goes to ceremonies: "I'm Métis, and my wife [was] Métis [before she passed] and our children are Métis. We live traditional lives. We live spiritual lives." The following exchange between Brenda and me illustrates her belief that ceremonies belong to Métis as well as First Nations people:

> B: I believed there was no Métis religion. There is Roman Catholic[ism]. . . . But then there's the Aboriginal spiritual way—and that's our way. I want to honour that Métis blood that runs in me. And, I'm part First Nation, so I'm going to honour that Métis and that First Nation part.
>
> **Do you see ceremonies as being strictly a First Nations, not a Métis, thing?**
>
> B: No. . . . That's our [Métis] way too; although, some people may say differently. But I know who I am and what I do and what my thoughts and beliefs are.

Nicki mentioned the stereotype that Métis spirituality means Roman Catholicism: "Because of misinformation we have about Métis people's form of spirituality historically, we make the assumption that Métis people are pretty much all Roman Catholic or some other denomination of Christianity [today]. I don't know that that's accurate. In fact, [my elder] told me a story that Louis Riel carried his fire bag, or an octopus bag, filled with tobacco [and] that he used to smoke it in his pipe but also [to] make offerings to Creator. I kind of love that. . . . [My elder said] he wasn't only smoking that in his pipe; he was making offerings." Nicki has rejected this stereotype. She and Elizabeth specifically discussed having traditional Métis elders as spiritual teachers. Nicki said much about "my elder, Barbara Bruce [a participant in this study], who identifies as Métis with Cree and Salteaux ancestry." Elizabeth said, "Most of my teachers, or elders, or people I've formed relationships with have been Cree or Métis."

Types of Ceremonies

In addition to describing how they understand their own spirituality, the Métis people in this study shared stories about ceremonies. Knowing the potential for increased health and wellness that can come from participating in ceremonies, I was particularly excited to hear about the kinds of Indigenous ceremonies they engage in. The strongest pattern to emerge is that these Métis folks participate in multiple types of ceremonies—between two to sixteen distinct ceremonies per participant, with an average of seven.[3] The most frequently mentioned ceremonies, in decreasing order, were sweat lodge; Sundance; smudging; ceremonies involving traditional medicines (e.g., plant medicines); pipe ceremonies; receiving a spirit name and naming ceremonies; ceremonies associated with a particular nation (or region);[4] fasting and/or vision quests;[5] drum ceremonies;[6] singing ceremonies; being on the land harvesting medicines for ceremonies; ceremonial feasts; powwows; Midewiwin ceremonies; shake tent ceremonies; and sharing circles.[7] Participating in several types of ceremonies makes sense, given the understanding that each of the ceremonies listed above exists to fulfill one or more specific purposes—no one ceremony can fulfill all purposes or goals. Also, some ceremonies are very elaborate (such as Midewiwin and Sundance) and contain several different ceremonies within them that occur over a period of four or more consecutive days, while fundamental ceremonies (such as tobacco and water ceremonies, and smudging) are a necessary part of many other ceremonies. Rather than this being a new phenomenon, these Métis people demonstrate cultural and spiritual continuity with (some of) their (Métis) ancestors who also participated in these ceremonies historically (Chapters 2 and 3).[8]

Across the six Métis communities, people from Ste. Anne indicated participating in the highest number of distinct ceremonies.[9] However, the individual who indicated participating in the highest number of distinct ceremonies (sixteen) was Linda (St. François-Xavier).[10] In the following excerpt, Barbara (St. Laurent) describes participating in multiple ceremonies: "The seven sacred teachings, like the pipe, the sweat, and the Sundance, witnessing a kind of a birth, blessing on a tree, all those teachings, I have done. I haven't completed my vision [that was given to me] yet, about this shaking tent, so I'd like to do that. I've fasted several times, like a vision quest, plus community fasting, and individual fasting." Louis (Ste. Anne) also explained that he has participated in many different types of ceremonies: "I've done lots of pipe [ceremonies]. I've done Sundances [in] Pipestone, Minnesota, [as part of the] American Indian Movement. I've never made a pipe, but I've carried pipes for different things, for different people. We've had lots of camps here [on my property], lots of teaching lodges, spring camps, fall camps, Sundances." Louis has received a teaching about not purposely seeking to expand one's bundle:

> It comes from my teaching that I got a long time ago
> from an elder in Maniwaki, the wampum belt keeper for
> the Algonquin Nation. . . . He told me, "My boy, don't go
> looking for what I have. I've been carrying this wampum
> belt my whole life. Don't go looking for what I have. Don't
> go looking for what I was looking for. . . ." So, [he means,]
> "Don't . . . [say,] I got to have a pipe, and an eagle feather,
> and I got [to have] a fan, and an eagle whistle, and I gotta
> have a buffalo hide, and I got to have regalia because I got
> to dance. And, I have to have all these things!"

This elder reminds us that bundle items should be earned and gifted
instead of actively sought.

People from Camperville identified (in decreasing order)
Sundance, spirit name, naming ceremony, sweat lodge, and pipe
ceremonies most frequently. Louise spoke of using medicine to learn
her spirit name and clan: "I gave tobacco to Mary Roberts. She was
an elder from Roseau [River First Nation]; an Ojibwe elder. She's
gone now but I gave her tobacco to find out what my Indian name
is, which is Pitaaycommigook ndizhinikaaz. That means "I am called
Thunderbird Woman." Charlie Nelson gave me my clan identification
which is the Marten clan—it's part of the warrior clan. That means
you would advocate for your people—you're part of the warrior clan
and you would fight for your people in an advocacy kind of way." In
another example, Karen shared a dream that led her to become a
Sundancer:

> As far as Sundance, I started going around 2010, and I've
> been going ever since. I went as a helper. I went to observe.
> I went to learn the first few times at Sundance. And I
> didn't know if I fit in there. I was very fearful. I felt, "Am I
> supposed to be here?" The year later, I got onto the ground;
> it was a sacred place [the Sundance arbour]. You give your-
> self to God. "Okay, let me learn whatever I'm supposed
> to learn." And I purified myself. . . . Next thing you know,
> you're getting answers. . . . I was given this dream, "Now,
> you're going to dance." They showed me the circle, and
> they showed me the south door, and it was just like there
> was a white chalk and the Sundance chief was pointing.

He brought me to go into [the arbour]. And he's pointing:
that's where I have to stand. And I was wearing white. I
had to wear white. [Later,] I went to [the Sundance Chief]
and I told him [my dream] ... I offered [him] tobacco ...
I've been [Sun]dancing [ever] since.

Everyone from Duck Bay has participated in sweat lodge ceremonies. In that community, the next most frequently enjoyed ceremonies
(in decreasing order) were smudging, ceremonies using traditional
medicines, fasting/vision quests, naming ceremonies, spirit names,
and drum ceremonies. Ray spoke about fasting in this way:

When we fast, we're fasting for the Creator, the sun, mother
earth, and grandfathers. We're fasting for all the people in
Indian Country. . . . We pray for the ones that are sick in
the hospitals, the ones in the jail, the orphans that don't
have parents. We fast for the homeless on the street that
have no food, nothing to eat, or anywhere to go. We fast
for the children, the grandchildren; everyone. . . . That's
how we have to walk when we come home from the lodge
and the fast. You don't stop there—you have to come home
and live that life.

In St. Laurent, folks talked most often (in decreasing order) about
sweat lodge, smudging, Sundance, and traditional medicines. Gripette
shared the following significant story about sweat lodge:

G: When we built the sweat lodge [in my yard], the priest
came. Father Michel was Métis; he would talk to me about
spirituality and ceremony. He'd have sage in the house
where he lived. I went and cleaned the sage for him one
time, and I did some teachings about sage. He always said
he wanted to know more, and he wanted to participate in
ceremony. So, on the day that we were building the lodge,
I had invited him. He came and dropped by with his holy
water, and he's doing his holy water on the sweat lodge
[laughs], on the ground. . . .

**When the priest came and blessed your [sweat] lodge with
holy water, was he doing it in a friendly and encouraging
way?**

G: Oh yeah.

Okay, because I've heard other stories about them doing it in a "remove the devil" kind of way, but I didn't get that feeling from your story.

G: It was neat because that same summer that we did that, there was a woman that came to the lodge. She's very Catholic and she felt really good being in the [sweat] lodge because Father Michel had blessed it with holy water; so, she felt it was okay [chuckles].

People connected to St. François-Xavier reported participating most often (in decreasing order) in sweat lodge, Sundance, smudging, and using traditional medicines. In Lorette, everyone participates in Sundance and sweat lodge ceremonies, and the following were also mentioned frequently (in decreasing order): pipe ceremonies, naming ceremonies, spirit names, feast, drumming, singing, and smudging. Nicki shared a story about cedar and eagle fan brushing (which often involves smudging):

> One of the ceremonies that I have found the most impactful for certain events or periods in my life has been the cedar brushing or eagle fan brushing as a cleansing ceremony. I always requested that kind of ceremony when I worked in the Truth and Reconciliation Commission national events because they were really heavy. I stage-managed the Commissioner sharing circles. Those were huge public events with a thousand, two thousand people in the audience. [Each] person got fifteen minutes to tell their story, and it was from 9 [o'clock] in the morning until 4 [o'clock] in the afternoon.... They would often talk about some of the most vicious violence perpetrated against them [in residential school]. By the end of the day, you would have to go stand by the sacred fire and just like let it all out. [Cedar or eagle fan brushings] were always a great ceremony to help in the aftermath of those events and even [at] the end of those days.

Lastly, everyone connected to Ste. Anne reported participating in sweat lodge and pipe ceremonies. They also frequently mentioned (in decreasing order): "Cree ceremonies," Sundance, Midewiwin, fasting,

"Anishinaabe/Ojibwe ceremonies,"being on the land/harvesting, medicines, and singing. Amanda shared a moving story about the power of sweat lodge ceremonies: "In September, I was at a sweat [lodge ceremony] at the university and came out for a break between rounds. I laid on the grass with my eyes closed, feeling the sun shining down on me. And, even though I knew my face was red and sweaty, and my hair was a puffy mess, I have never felt more beautiful and at peace than I did in that moment." As illustrated in the pages above, Métis people across each of the six Métis communities shared touching stories about the powerful impact that various ceremonies have in their lives.

Factors That Inhibit Connection to Ceremony (Disconnection Factors)

Participants identified several factors that have prevented their connection to Indigenous ceremonies at various times throughout their lives. The church was the most frequently cited disconnection factor, with many people specifically mentioning Catholicism. Linked to the church, day and residential schools were also discussed as disconnection factors. Also mentioned were fear, anxiety, and self-doubt, including internalized self-doubt about whether Métis people have the "right" to go to ceremonies, and having a panic attack in a sweat lodge, which led to long-term anxiety about whether to participate again.[11] Some folks identified divisions between Métis and First Nations people as causing or exacerbating the internalization of fear, anxiety, and self-doubt surrounding ceremonies.[12] Stories about having a bad experience in ceremony were shared by a few people, for reasons including dogma stemming from patriarchy, sexism, homo/transphobia, policing women and two-spirit people's bodies (especially "skirt shaming" and menstruation taboos), and hierarchy.[13] All of these disconnection factors can be understood as impacts of colonialization.

Catholicism (or in two cases, the Christian church in general) was cited as a factor that has inhibited connection to Indigenous spirituality and ceremonies by people from every Métis community except Lorette.[14] Louis (Ste. Anne) unequivocally stated, "I don't like the Christian/Catholic thing. It's oppressive, it's colonial; I don't fit [there]." Karen noted the link between the church, government, and the suppression of Indigenous spirituality: "When we grew up in Camperville and Pine Creek, there was no such thing as Sundance . . . [or] sweat lodge.

That was all gone. The Church and the Government knocked that all down and it was frowned upon." Similarly, in St. Laurent, Gripette shared: "Since I was a kid—well because my mom, still in those days, was kind of involved with [Indigenous] spirituality so I liked that part. There was a lightness to it. When Christianity became such a big thing in the community, that was kind of a heavy thing. It was heavy and dark, and more sinister, and that was [the Catholic] religion." Charlotte identified toxic Catholicism in the foster homes she grew up in: "When I was young, [Indigenous] spirituality was not being talked about, growing up in the Catholic [foster] homes. Those were 'pagan' things, and they are all going to go to hell and burn." She continued, "I stopped going to church because for me the church was evil. Everything that they professed was a total lie. They were all supposed to be spiritual people and yet they would swear at us and put us down for who we were [as Indigenous people] and tell us that we were going to burn in hell." George (Duck Bay) also expressed dissatisfaction with the Catholic Church, especially its obscene accumulation of wealth, abuse (especially pedophilia), and protection of perpetrators: "The church is all about money. The Pope is one of the richest heads of the mafia in this world and he's being taken to court now. He's lost cases; he's lost to judges. The biggest Bishop in New York City just got charged with child molestation last week. I mean it continues, the priests have been doing this and nothing is being done [to stop them]. They [just] move these priests from different—they transfer them to different places."

People from Duck Bay, St. Laurent, Camperville, and Ste. Anne identified day and residential schools as elements that have inhibited a connection to Indigenous spirituality.[15] Louis (Ste. Anne) spoke of how residential and day schools (and Catholicism generally) exploited Métis people's beliefs, teaching them to fear Indigenous spirituality and dividing them from other Indigenous peoples:

> Not every Métis is Catholic. It's much deeper than that. Why were we [Métis] attracted to Catholicism in the beginning? What is it that resonated in the beginning that we already knew? But, also that they [Christians] could inadvertently exploit? In the beginning, this fear that we had of power, the power of spirituality and our relationship to all of it, was exploited; [and], we were taught about fear, taught about hate, taught about all the negative stuff, taught about

discrimination and racism. We were divided [as Indigenous peoples]. I believe that because that was the role of the residential schools.

Lucille (St. Laurent) commented on large-scale intergenerational impacts of residential and day schools upon Métis people, and the efforts of the Catholic Church to prevent Indigenous people from gathering in ceremony: "Hearing the stories about Aboriginal people, residential schools, and little families on their own. How people have been sent by governments, placed here and there, to be on the outside and disconnected from the rest of the world is such a sad story. . . . How could you not all come together? I thought that's what it was all about. . . . When they have these [Indigenous] ceremonies, it's because they come together and be[come] stronger." Also from St. Laurent, Bobbie-Jo's father went to residential school; she spoke of the resulting disconnection to her Métis Cree culture and of traditional elders and spirit guides helping her find her way back: "Elders started to show themselves to me and I was told my name is "Walk with the Wind Woman." Part of that is because I was separated from my father who was a residential school survivor and separated from his community and, ultimately, my own Cree community. [But,] the wind would take me to all the elders that I need to learn from, and the wind has now taken me back to my home and my [spiritual] teachings." George (Duck Bay), who is himself a residential school survivor, discussed the devastating impacts of residential schools and abuse upon Indigenous well-being and disconnection from spirituality:

> Well they didn't like that [Indigenous spirituality] because of residential schools in the '50s, while I was growing up. Residential school was big, and we were being treated the same way [other] residential school people were being treated: abused at the schools. And we couldn't talk about it because the Church was so involved in the community. They go to every house and talk to the parents. No matter what you said, they believed the priests. So, you'd get beaten up by your parents, for lying, when you're telling the truth—but they believed the Church. How can the man in the cloth lie, when he's the man abusing you? How can I ever forget someone who's beaten me up and raped [me]? That's a scar

on my brain for the rest of my life. I went to a lot of these residential [school] meetings, and [heard] "Oh, I forgive them. Yeah, but they forgive them because they were never abused. It's different. If you were ever in residential school, you might have got[ten] beaten up but you were never [sexually] abused. That's different. You can take a beating and a week later [say], "Oh, we got in a fight and that's it." But you get raped? That'll never leave you. A lot of these people say, "Oh, get past it." You can't. [Like when] a woman is raped today; they turn to drugs, suicide. Why are people killing themselves? It's because of stuff like this. [But], they use that catch phrase "mental illness."[16]

Christianity and the day and residential schools have deeply impacted some of the participants' Métis identity, well-being, relationship with First Nations relatives, and with Indigenous spirituality.

Fear, anxiety, and self-doubt came up as disconnection factors for people in St. François-Xavier, Lorette, Ste. Anne, Duck Bay, and in Camperville.[17] Some folks expressed self-doubt about being Métis and having internalized the stereotype that ceremonies belong to First Nations people only. This can be heard in what Maryanne (Duck Bay) said: "I'm getting a chance to meet a lot of different elders. But, like I said, I'm so scared to ask some of those questions because I feel like I'm being rude. Because I do feel I'm Métis. I'm not First Nation; I'm not traditional, so I shouldn't be challenging or saying anything. I feel very: but, part of me is [Métis and ceremonial]!" Andrea (Lorette) shared something similar:

> I want to go to ceremonies more . . . but again, it's all the thoughts in my head like, "You're not Indigenous enough; you're not Métis enough." People are going to be like, "Tell me about this and that," and I'm going to be like, "Um? . . ." This past Sunday, I thought, "I can't go by myself to that sweat lodge. People are going to be like, "Who are you?" And, I'm going to be like, "I know nothing!" I talk myself out of it; I want that crutch like my sister, or you, or someone there so I don't feel so alone. . . . It's that working [myself] up where I'm like, "I have so many questions; what questions am I going to ask that [are] stupid?"

The sentiment of self-doubt was echoed by Linda (St. François-Xavier): "[An elder] was doing a sunrise ceremony at a gathering. I remember going there, and that's exactly how I felt: 'Am I worthy enough to offer prayer?' I remember she says, 'Why wouldn't you be worthy enough? Everyone can pray. Creator loves everyone.' I thought, 'Wow, how mixed up is that? That I felt I wouldn't be wanted. Where did I get that belief from? To me, that would be part of the upbringing that I got from the catechism probably—the way that system works is like a hierarchy.'"

Sometimes people's self-doubt stemmed from concerns about not appearing stereotypically Indigenous enough. When Lightning Rattle Woman (Duck Bay) first began attending ceremonies, she nervously thought, "We look a little bit White; we don't look Native enough." Denise (St. François-Xavier) shared a story where she felt she was not accepted by First Nations people at ceremony: "As far as not being accepted, I think that was [me] being the [appearance] of White." Elizabeth (St. François-Xavier) spoke at length about Métis-specific challenges regarding participation in ceremonies, especially now that she lives outside the recognized Métis homeland. She struggles with seeing herself as both a Métis person with the right to participate in ceremonies and as an ally who should make space for people who are more racialized than she is:

> It's not easy being Métis living here in Quebec. There's a lot of misunderstanding and not as much opportunity obviously to connect with other Métis. And there's other things that I think prevent me. . . . [Like] not wanting to take up space from people that are more racially classified. So just understanding the history and my role also as an ally. And [wondering], "How much am I an ally? And how much am I an Indigenous person? Can I be both?" And always wanting to make space for other people. . . . [I'm] still trying to allow myself to be like, "No, this is my spirituality and I need this and it's okay for me to do it too. It doesn't take away from anybody else." [I'm] still coming to terms with that.

Elizabeth (St. François-Xavier) also talked about tensions in her family life regarding when to include her son and her non-Indigenous husband in ceremonies.

Additional reasons for fear, anxiety, and self-doubt were also raised by other folks. Linda (St. François-Xavier), for example, shared stories about lingering fear from when the government outlawed Indigenous ceremonies in Canada:

> What has stopped me from ceremony is—and I've heard many, many stories of [this from] others: they've had their tipis burnt down, or taken down, lodges taken down. . . . In 1996, it was the beginning of Wahbung Abinoonjiiag [an Indigenous organization in Winnipeg] . . . and there was [still] such a fear of smudging. I remember we smudged and [worried] we were going to set off the [fire] alarm. I remember we smudged right underneath the thing, so we did set the alarm off. But that would be the one block: fear. People didn't want to smudge and that was in the late '90s. We couldn't smudge in buildings the way we do now.

Amanda (Ste. Anne) has anxiety around pronouncing her spirit name in Cree: "I still don't feel comfortable pronouncing my [spirit] name. It's not that I don't want to, but I haven't gotten the emphasis of the certain syllables right. I feel really stupid trying to say it. I need to practise more with someone who speaks Cree. Because I've said it [in public] before, [and] then they will, not correct me rudely but, say it the way it should be said. Then I feel sheepish because I don't know how to say it." For Nicki (Lorette), a chronic headache condition that is exacerbated by heat caused her to worry about going into a sweat lodge when she first started going to ceremonies. She happily reported, "Now, when I go into the lodge, it's never bothered my headache." Justin's (Ste. Anne) anxiety stems from a lack of time and worrying about how to balance all of life's commitments; he gave this as the reason he has not yet pursued Midewiwin ceremonies despite wanting to.

Divisions between Métis and First Nations people (which can also worsen fear, anxiety, and self-doubt) were raised as another disconnection factor among participants in Camperville, Duck Bay, St. François-Xavier, and Ste. Anne.[18] Whistling Eagle Child (Duck Bay) spoke of divisions between Métis people who are Christian and those who practise Indigenous spirituality: "The stereotypes [about Métis people and ceremonies] are still there. We were talking to someone not too long ago and they said, 'Well, even the president of the MMF has his own medicine man.' What's wrong with that? Is he not allowed to see a medicine man?" Some Christian Métis negatively judge Métis people who adhere to Indigenous spirituality, which can inhibit some Métis from seeking out ceremonies. Denise (St. François-Xavier) worries that many Métis have internalized a White, Catholic world view; she believes it would be beneficial for more Métis to go to ceremonies: "I think that maybe having the Métis work more with the [First Nations] communities to try to figure out who our relations are, I think that would be really good. I think that any kind of teachings that the First Nations can bring to the Métis that helps them connect [would be good]. I really do feel that [Métis] world view is very White. They may have Native blood . . . but [their] religion is, for the most part, Catholic." Here, Denise seems to characterize ceremonies as strictly First Nations instead of also belonging to Métis spirituality. Louis (Ste. Anne) also spoke of divisions existing within spiritual communities: "We have had divisions in our community whereby, [some say] 'I'm taking my part of this fire [i.e., spiritual community] and we're leaving.' It happens." Recall that Louis spoke earlier (Chapter 8) about being exploited in ceremonies as a Métis person by First Nations spiritual leaders perpetuating a racial hierarchy. Brenda (Camperville) raised concerns about divisions between First Nations (and others) and Métis, and among Métis people themselves resulting from intermarriage, status differences, and jurisdictional infighting:

> The intermarriage . . . back home [in Camperville], there's a lot of First Nation–Métis blood. I don't know how much there would be in other places like St. Ambroise and St. Laurent; I'm not sure if it's more Métis. But, I know intermarriage impacts that and if you were to say "Mohawk Métis" [didn't finish her thought]. . . . Unfortunately for one young person that I know, she's a very proud Métis, but because she's mixed with another ethnicity, I think she's going through a lot of identity [crises]. . . . I'm just concerned about all that jurisdiction boundaries and identity and how people can get so lost in it. . . . Although she is proud, I think she has been feeling from other Métis that "you're not Métis because you are partly of another ethnicity." I really feel for her because I went through some of that stuff, so I want to be there to help.

Karen (Camperville) also pointed out divisions as existing within and among Métis people themselves: "That's another thing—politics. I don't like the idea of tribalism now. . . . These Métis in Ontario are fighting the Indians. There's the French Métis, the Michif, they want things one way. And then there's ones like [MMF President] David Chartrand who doesn't know Michif. [The language he speaks], it's more Saulteaux and English than it is French and Saulteaux, or French and Cree. The tribalism is—you can get in trouble with that. I hope more people see that, because if you stop doing that you can do a whole lot better for the youth." Elizabeth (St. François-Xavier) shared a story about divisions between First Nations and Métis people as having long-lasting impacts on confidence and pursuing ceremonies:

> There was a woman who came into our class, I'm pretty sure she was from Kahnawake. And I kind of, in my stumbling way, was trying to explain to her who I was in my journey a little bit. And she was kind of harsh. And I get it. But she said something like, "I hate it when people who are barely Indigenous try to claim they are. . . ." I'm still really affected by that; [I] shut down totally. That lasted I think 10 years before I went back again. And that shame, it's like: I guess I don't have a right to ask these questions, or maybe I didn't do it properly.

Now, Elizabeth herself tries to create safer spaces in her own classrooms for students to explore these issues. She acknowledges that it is true that "there's a lot of appropriation happening, but there's also a lot of lateral violence happening around identity." Experiencing divisions like the ones discussed by the Métis people in this study can result in confusion, shame, a lack of confidence in identity, and subsequently, an avoidance of ceremonies when one feels one is not welcome there.

Another disconnection factor can be heard in shared stories of negative experiences at ceremonies, including being subjected to dogma resulting from patriarchy, sexism, and homo/transphobia—as was the case for some folks in Lorette, St. Laurent, Duck Bay, Ste. Anne, and St. François-Xavier.[19] Both Maryanne and Nicki have had difficult experiences in a sweat lodge. Maryanne (Duck Bay) said, "I honestly felt like I totally had a panic attack and I'm almost scared to go back in." Nicki (Lorette) had a similarly challenging experience but pushed herself to go back in and finish the sweat:

It really was the most intense sweat lodge of my life. In fact, in the third doorway it got so hot that [it felt like] my skin was on fire and when they opened the doorway, I bowled Barbara—my elder, she was sitting right next to the door and I was [at] the west doorway—I bowled her over to get out because I literally thought my skin was going to catch fire and blister with third-degree burns. In hindsight, I look back and it was really funny but at the time, I remember, I was so embarrassed because I was like, "Out of my way!"—like sacrificed my elder to get out of the lodge [laughs]. It's so funny now but, at the time, I was so mortified. I don't know how I picked myself up to go back in for the fourth door.

Nicki continues to sweat regularly. Lucille (St. Laurent) mentioned menstruation taboos as one element that prevents participation in ceremonies: "The only reason that you can't do the sharing circle is when you're on your moontime, but you're still sitting on the outside of it, experiencing it." Barbara (St. Laurent) raised the issue of "skirt shaming" (forcing or forbidding people to wear skirts based on their perceived gender) as another potential deterrent for some people who may otherwise want to participate in ceremonies. In her own words:

I respect others who wear skirts. That's their choice and is expected by most leaders of ceremonies. However, I believe that wearing a skirt or not you are still connected to Spirit. No matter what anyone tells me about a skirt, it's not going to connect me more to Spirit than I am now. No matter what their beliefs. I do wear skirts and sweat gowns in the lodge. That's what I've been wearing all my life, and I'll probably continue to wear this. But my belief is that I try to listen and to honour and to acknowledge. I don't like men telling women things about spirituality because I think women know who they are as spirit beings. Further, I will respect two-spirit people to wear what they want to wear at ceremonies. It is interesting that people say that two-spirit people are gifted, and they should be honoured, but at the same time, we are often not respected for who we are.

In another difficult experience, Andrea (Lorette) shared a story about being harshly corrected while at a Sundance:

When I was there, I was helping in the lodge and this woman was like, "Light the smudge." And, I was like, "Okay! [blows]." She said, "NEVER do we blow on it!" I [thought to myself], "Oh my god, for a year, I've been blowing on it." But, it's stuff like that. I'm like, tell me, don't yell at me! I get that sometimes people think, "Here comes this person who wants to be a part of this culture when they don't belong." I get that sometimes people might have that, "Oh, she's blowing on the smudge, she knows nothing. Oh, they're trying to appropriate; they don't belong here." I get that people don't know what your background is or whatever.

A few other people identified problematic experiences with a spiritual community, or with specific elders and knowledge holders. Bethany (Lorette) alluded to this when she said, "Certain ceremonies, like, you just don't feel safe with the people, so I don't go back to those." Denise (St. François-Xavier) had a bad experience at a Sundance, and it took her several years to reconnect to ceremonies. She shared, "That summer, they invited me to go to a Sundance and my mom and I went to the Sundance together out in Pine Ridge [Reservation] together. So, we went there and met with a medicine man and had a pretty disappointing experience, actually. Because of that experience, it was so bad that I never wanted anything to do with it again—it took a long time before I reconnected, about seven years ago." Louis (Ste. Anne) shared a story about being exploited and taken advantage of as a Métis *shkaabewis* (helper) in a ceremonial context by First Nations spiritual leaders and, shockingly, having his first pipe thrown at him. He had just completed a four-day fast on his own property when everyone showed up for a sweat lodge and expected him to do all the work to prepare it, as usual (not knowing he had just completed a fast):

> They expect me to pick the rocks, pick the wood, light the fire, and clean the lodge, and bring the water, set it up, because that's always the way it was. It was my land, this is where I live, therefore, it was expected that it was like a 7-Eleven where they could drive up, go into the lodge, and I'd be the firekeeper and all that stuff. . . . So on the Sunday [they arrived] . . . I'm at the lodge already, after four days of no eating, no nothing, except I had four days of beard growth.

I'm walking all dishevelled, I'm doing everything like I usually do. I started at 7 a.m.; I was a lot slower—I was like an old
man. . . . [My wife was] the one that kind of scolded them:
"Did you know he's been fasting for four days? Can't you see
anything? Didn't you notice? Didn't you notice he hasn't said
anything all morning? Didn't you notice he's done everything
for you?" She scolded them: "Grow up, do your part!" That
was the teaching of the day. So, one of the pipe carriers had
like four pipes. . . . He took the pipe and said, "Next time you
do that [fasting ceremony], you need that [pipe]." And he
just literally threw the pipe at me. And that's how I got my
pipe. And they were all mad at me, [saying] "you could have
died." It was all kind of guilt, it was like a Christian, colonial
thing . . . I've had a lot of those experiences.

Maryanne and Barbara both had negative experiences regarding
homophobic elders. Maryanne (Duck Bay) shared the following story:

Sometimes, I find I'm conflicted because I don't necessarily
agree with what [the elders are] saying. It makes me uncomfortable . . . I was brought up by my *kookum* [grandmother]
to very much respect elders all the time. . . . I found myself a
couple of times that I've been listening to an elder and I'm
like, "Oh my gosh, I can't believe they just said that!" It's so
totally not what I agree with. But I don't say anything and
then I just sit there conflicted with those thoughts and those
feelings. . . . One time, I was actually with a student, and [an
elder] was talking about homosexuality [in a homophobic
way]. And I'm trying not to look [at the student]. I felt so
uncomfortable; I put my head down. I remember almost like
it was yesterday. I couldn't even look at [the student]; it was
awful. I talked to my co-worker later and I'm like "I don't
want to go back there again; I feel so uncomfortable. I feel
so bad for [the student]. I don't know what to say to her; I
don't know how she felt about that."

Maryanne went on to talk about the fact that even elders have been
impacted by colonization and have internalized harmful messages such
as homophobia. She raises the important point that the teaching about
respecting elders and not talking back or asking questions leaves people

unable to address the toxic messaging that some elders perpetuate. Barbara (St. Laurent) also had difficult experiences with homophobia at ceremonies. In her own words, "I suffered at the ceremonies because I was Métis and because I was two-spirit; they didn't accept me. They made all kinds of jokes in the tipi, during a Sundance, really, really dirty jokes about gay people. I was [also] questioned about my identity; I wasn't helped by the First Nations people I was with [either]. I suffered a lot, but it didn't deter me. Well, no, I shouldn't say that; it kind of discouraged me. At moments I said, "I can't do this anymore, forget it." But, then the next day, I went back to it." Barbara told a story about an elder who may have disliked her sexuality and assumed she was non-Indigenous because of her lighter skin. Twice, the elder tried to throw her off during a sweat lodge ceremony, but he had a spiritual reaction and vomited when the door was opened. She continued:

> The next day, we get up and I'm like, "I'm leaving. If you guys want to come with me, you're welcome to, but I've been mistreated." I said, "It's not right." So, I saw [the elder] coming, from way out there, walking, walking, walking. And I went, "Oh my god, he's coming toward me!" Then he sits in front of me. "I'm sorry," he said. "I didn't know," he said. "Barbara, I'm wondering if you could come back." Then he calls me, while I was in Toronto, on my cellphone and asks me to come to his Sundance. I said, "I have to think about it." I didn't go. But those are the type of things that I suffered because of the colour of my skin [and my sexuality].

Elders have not been spared the impacts of colonization, patriarchy, sexism, and homo/transphobia. With all these disconnection factors inhibiting Métis connection to ceremony, it may seem surprising that folks return to ceremonies at all. Yet almost without exception, all the Métis people in this study continue to participate in various ceremonies today.

~

In this chapter, the Métis participants' own relationship with spirituality was highlighted. Folks described their spirituality in terms of characteristics and values. Many mentioned Roman Catholicism, a significant decrease in their participation in church, or that they no longer identify as Christian, while a handful explained syncretic blends of Christianity and Indigenous spirituality. Several people described their spirituality as "traditional Indigenous ways of life." Almost without exception, the Métis folks featured in this study participate in multiple types of ceremonies, especially sweat lodge, Sundance, smudging, and pipe ceremonies. Finally, folks also identified several factors that have discouraged their connection with Indigenous ceremonies over the years; however, this has not stopped them from going to ceremonies. Thankfully, as the participants themselves explain in the next chapter, there are also many powerful factors that have encouraged their reconnection with ceremonies.

CHAPTER 10

Spiritual Connection Factors, Impacts upon Identity, and Others' Reactions

Building on the stories shared in the previous chapter, the Métis people in this study continue to discuss their own spirituality highlighting factors that have encouraged or nurtured their connection to Indigenous spirituality. They also consider whether their self-identification has changed as a result of participating in ceremonies. Finally, they discuss how people in their lives—especially family and other members of their spiritual communities—have reacted to their involvement in ceremonies.

Factors That Encourage a Connection with Indigenous Ceremonies

When reflecting on factors that may have encouraged and nurtured their connection to Indigenous ceremony, most folks shared stories about people who have positively influenced this relationship. Friends, family,[1] elders, and other members within their spiritual community were specifically highlighted.[2] Several people spoke about the education system (especially universities), as well as particular places and events (especially conferences) as having significantly encouraged their connection to ceremony.[3] Difficult catalysts—such as a serious health issue, a death, or trauma (especially sexual abuse)—were identified as powerful connection factors. Finally, folks' own motivations, as well as "blood memory," Spirit, and ancestors were noted as factors that have nurtured their relationship with ceremony.[4]

Specific people were identified as an important connection factor within each Métis community in this study.[5] Friends and family were most frequently mentioned here, followed by elders and members of one's own spiritual community. Justin (Ste. Anne) indicated that friends were very important to his introduction to ceremonies: "Friends; big time—[the] *Red Rising* [*Magazine*] group." Amanda (Ste. Anne) said something similar: "Having friends to go with, like you and [a mentor/friend], [and another friend] who moved away. I have a few contacts that would let me know if [ceremony] is going on. That's helpful." Likewise, Lightning Rattle Woman spoke of a group of fifteen women friends with whom she first became involved in ceremonies in Duck Bay. Louise (Camperville) shared a story about Barbara (St. Laurent), and a friend with whom she first got involved in ceremonies: "[Barbara] and I went to our first sweat lodge together many, many years ago. That was our first and we were a little bit nervous about going into the ceremonies, but somebody gave us some medicine to hold or to put under our tongue. It helps you, they said. I've been going to Sundance [and] mainly doing a lot of sweat lodges, since that time." Gripette (St. Laurent) spoke of a friend, whom she also identifies as a spiritual teacher, as instrumental in her early journey with ceremonies: "Mae Louise [Campbell][6] and I started out together way back when. I always say she was my first teacher, but we were each other's teacher. . . . I always say she was my teacher for about eleven years. And the reason I say that is we were together for eleven years' time doing the same [ceremonial] things, going to the same places, exploring the world, and that kind of stuff."

In addition to friends, family members were identified as crucial in people's early spiritual journeys. Andrea (Lorette) shared a story crediting her sister, Nicki, with being the one who helped her first get involved with ceremonies:

> My sister, she knew [the spiritual teacher] through Barbara and her work, her ex-boss. She knew them and had been going to ceremony [with them]. . . . Then, in October, she went to go get her [spirit] name so I went with her. That was the first time that I went to the sweat lodge. That was pretty much how that all started [for me]. I know for years I'd been wanting to go to drumming circles, singing, and all this stuff. I'd been wanting and wanting but it's like, I don't know who to talk to. I don't know how to do that. So, when my sister was like, "I'm going back. I've done some work and I'm going back now to get [my spirit] name," I was like, "Okay, I'm going to come with you. . . ." That's sort of how

that started. My sister pretty much, I guess I would say, she brought me along.

Mother and daughter Janice and Bethany (Lorette) identified each other as influential in their connection with Indigenous spirituality—Bethany for her interest and participation in a cultural and spiritual program at her high school that Janice was able to participate in as well, and Janice (and her mother) for going to ceremonies and bringing Bethany with her. Whistling Eagle Child (Duck Bay) acknowledged that it was his wife who first helped him begin going to ceremonies: "My wife was already going at night having little sessions of drumming and smudging and stuff. She kept telling me, 'You should come with us; you should come with us.' I was a little bit nervous about it because you hear stories about [bad] medicine this and medicine that. It's never anything positive; it's always negative: 'You got to watch [out for] this; you got watch [out for] that.' Then I went and checked it out one time for myself, then I went back, [and] then I went back [again and again]." Jason (Camperville) also identified his wife as instrumental in his early journey with Indigenous spirituality: "[My wife] was starting in it and I was just helping her out. Slowly, I went into it and—because they needed people to help them with the burning of the wood, watching the fire while they're heating up the stones for the sweat lodge. They always had to have somebody there. That's when I slowly watched her do it. Then I slowly followed [her]." In addition, Jason said that his Métis stepfather encouraged his connection to ceremony and participated alongside him: "[For] a long time, he'd come out with us when [we'd go to ceremonies]; he [even] received [the right to host] a Sundance."

Specific elders were also identified as influential in helping participants first attend ceremonies. Jason (Camperville) identified Elder Frank Nepinak in this way. Barbara (St. Laurent) and Linda (St. François-Xavier) both spoke of Elder Barbara Daniels as influential in their early journey because she would invite them to ceremonies. Linda credited Elder Peter O'Chiese: "An elder that helped name my children called Peter O'Chiese; he named two of my children. One, she was on her [moon]time [and could not receive her name then]. So, two of my children were named. We had a gathering. The ceremonies influenced the beginning of my journey." In another example, mentioned previously, Nicki (Lorette) credits her Elder Barbara with helping her get started on her spiritual path: "[My first] sweat lodge was led by Barbara who became a great mentor [to me] and is still my elder. I'm still her helper now, whenever possible; [she] was [also] my employer at the time."

Interestingly, the education system was highlighted as both a disconnection and a connection factor. While day and residential schools were identified as extremely detrimental to Métis identity and relationships with traditional Indigenous spirituality historically, contemporary places of learning (especially universities) were noted as sites where people can find out about their culture, access elders and cultural events, and sometimes even participate in ceremonies. Folks from St. François-Xavier and Ste. Anne mentioned this most frequently; however, it was raised by one or two participants in every other community as well except for Duck Bay. The importance of higher education as a connection factor can be heard, for instance, in this comment by Julia (Camperville): "Being at the university and being around other Indigenous peoples and being encouraged to learn and to ask questions; that definitely fostered [my connection to ceremony]." Likewise, Justin (Ste. Anne) said, "That first year of religion and culture [in university], I read about Sundance and read about everything and Mide[wiwin]; I'm so interested and I want to find a Mide elder. I didn't even know there was a Mide elder. I just wasn't connected; I thought it was like this thing that was gone forever." Bobbie-Jo (St. Laurent) shared a story crediting university with helping her begin her spiritual path when she was younger: "When I was twenty-one, I started university. My first course was "Indigenous Peoples of Canada" with Dr. Fred Shore. . . . After my first class, I went home and I was crying and when I was asked why I was crying, my answer was that my [Métis] people were awesome. It opened up that doorway for me to want to know more and to start feeling proud of who I was. So, it's been a twenty-two-year journey of participating in ceremony." The first time Denise (St. François-Xavier) attended a sweat lodge was at a university: "I was living in Indiana and I was working on my master's degree and I found out that some people from AIM [American Indian Movement] were going to be at the University of Indiana, so I went down there to meet them." Amanda (Ste. Anne) also identified university and the sweat lodge on campus as instrumental in her spiritual journey: "At the university, there's a lot of opportunity to be a part of ceremonies through MSW-IK [Masters of Social Work–Indigenous Knowledges] built into the program. . . . [There's a sweat lodge on campus and] I feel comfortable there; I've been going to that university for a long time. I feel comfortable being in that space." Vern (St. François-Xavier) spoke about his certificate in theology as opening the doorway to his participation in Indigenous ceremony: "I took some of my courses at Dr. Jesse Saulteaux Centre. I took about a third of my theology courses for my certificate at Dr. Jesse Saulteaux. That involved smudges, and sweat lodges, and so forth." Bethany (Lorette) identified a cultural program in her high school as helping her to attend her first sweat lodge ceremony. Afterwards, she asked the group leader about other opportunities to sweat and if she could bring her mother, Janice—they began going to ceremonies together from that point on. Bethany said, "To this day, the group leader is like, really close to my mom and I both now. She's one of my elders, I would say—a really good auntie. She helped me get into my first ceremony, she helped me with my skirts for Sundance [and] my moccasins."

Besides educational institutions, several other places and events were highlighted as significant connection factors. Conferences and Indigenous-specific places of employment (or Indigenous-specific jobs within non-Indigenous workplaces) were particularly noted by people in St. Laurent, St. François-Xavier, Lorette, and Ste. Anne. For the most part, however, unique responses were given regarding spaces that encouraged a connection to Indigenous spirituality. Linda (St. François-Xavier) shared a story about learning about smudging and sunrise ceremony at a conference she participated in in 1990:

> It was an abuse conference. . . . There was so much negative energy going on with this conference. You hear nothing but abuse, even while we were eating. There was this woman who was talking about poetry and she talked about violence that women go through in a poem, and it got out of hand. There were people yelling, "Shut up!" Next thing, people were upset. Then Barbara [another participant in this study] came to me and she was like, "Come on, all of the red women need to gather. . . ." This woman says, "We have to help the other women because they don't know what to do when they're hearing all of this [negativity]. You've got to have a smudge." That's where I discovered about a smudge, the strength of the women, and sunrise ceremony.

Linda also spoke of the importance of Indigenous-centred organizations and places of employment as helping her first get connected to ceremonies: "Working at North End Women's Centre gave me that stepping stone because I went to a pipe ceremony and learned about prayer, smudge, and I started bringing it into work." Nicki (Lorette) also credits working for All My Relations (an Indigenous event-planning organization founded by Barbara and her niece) as influential in helping her get involved with ceremonies. Louis (Ste. Anne) recalled the importance of the first Indigenous organizations to emerge in Winnipeg and their role in making space for Indigenous culture and ceremonies in an urban environment: "Ma Mawi [Chi Itata Centre] was just born [then]; it's a big organization now. But that was the first generation of Aboriginal organizations. There was [a] reclamation, a conscious, the-eagle-has-landed kind of mindset, things are going to change. We [were the] first generation to open the doorway as Indigenous people [to] those teachings, in a sense." Similarly, Louise (Camperville) remembers first moving to Winnipeg and finding the Indian and Metis Friendship Centre: "Ever since I came to the city and found the Indian and Metis Friendship Centre, they always encouraged us. Just being part of the Indian and Metis Friendship Centre, and other Aboriginal people, and taking part in ceremonies—it just made you feel good. It made me feel good. I found my identity at the Indian and Metis Friendship Centre." Denise (St. François-Xavier) shared a touching story about another landmark Indigenous location in Winnipeg as significant in the early days of her spiritual journey:

> Whenever I go to Winnipeg, I always go to Thunderbird House. I've attended sweat lodge ceremonies there. I was recently there—they were making moccasins for the babies and I went to that and that was a powerful ceremony. . . . I've always felt very welcome there and that's really healing for my heart. I went there [for] the first time after my mom passed [away]. I went to Winnipeg to lay my mom to rest and they happened to have a sweat lodge ceremony out there the day before we were going to lay my mom to rest. So, I went there, and I don't know who the man was, it was an elder, I offered tobacco and some medicines from the southwest . . . [I] brought that to him and when he closed the [sweat lodge]

door he said, "We have a daughter who's come home to us."
And, I was just bawling.

In an example of a significant place outside Manitoba, Gripette spoke excitedly about being involved with the Métis of St. Laurent exhibit featured at the National Museum of the American Indian in Washington, DC: "They phoned me 1998, they were doing the museum [exhibit] right in Washington.... We had four exhibits; one exhibit was called *Our Lives*. In the *Our Lives* exhibit, there were nine communities and we [St. Laurent] were one of the communities. We were followed by the media . . . I did interviews for Japan, for China, for *National Geographic*, [for] New Zealand. We were on the front page of [the] *Winnipeg Free Press*, and [the] evening story of CBC six o'clock news three days in a row in 2000 when we did the grand opening." A common thread among the stories shared by the Métis people in this study is that these places and events were Indigenous-focused and helped to foster a sense of pride of identity among Indigenous people, in addition to providing opportunities to connect with ceremonies.

Significant catalysts, such as serious health issues, death, and trauma resulting from sexual abuse, were also identified as connection factors that encourage a relationship with spirituality. Health issues and death were mentioned most frequently among people from Duck Bay but were also noted by participants in Camperville and Lorette. People in St. Laurent and St. François-Xavier identified healing from the trauma of sexual abuse as motivation for connecting with ceremonies. Recall the earlier story related by Andrea (Lorette) about first finding ceremonies through her sister, Nicki, who had been struggling with a chronic headache condition and searching for relief in ceremony and medicines. Others discussed illness resulting in death as a catalyst for getting involved with ceremonies. Brenda (Camperville) shared this difficult story: "My son does give me permission to speak about that; that's one of the reasons why I turned to medicine people. We tried, I tried everything, nothing was working. He was about thirteen years old and then [his medical condition] affected his emotional and his spiritual [health]. So, I took him to a medicine man and the medicine man healed his spiritual and his emotional [health]. But, his physical [health was] still—unfortunately, he went on to the spiritual world. And after he passed, I devoted my life to these [spiritual] ways." Lightning

Rattle Woman (Duck Bay) also shared a story about her and her family turning to ceremonies to deal with the death of a family member and to assist with a family member's mental health issues:

> We had a passing in the family. A sudden death. And, I guess, there was some of the family that went to that, followed that [Indigenous spiritual] path before the passing of the relative. And they kind of show[ed] some of the relatives [these ways]. One of the relatives had kind of a nervous breakdown and they needed to sweat or fast. And she bettered herself [in that way]. And, after all that, it took me a while, but I saw it. I was drawn into the healing of it.... I just saw the healing that the whole smudging and fasting did for a lot of family members. And, that's what kind of drew me into it. After that, then I sadly lost my brother, and that was the [spiritual] path I stayed on and it helped me.

Similarly, Ray (Duck Bay) talked about a cousin who died but had led other family members, including Ray, to find ceremonies before he passed away: "There's others that went [to ceremonies] first. My cousin, the one that passed away, he searched all over. A lot of people will go look all over; there's lots of medicine men, different lodges, a lot of people that go looking for somebody, a teacher. This place [a lodge in Alberta], my cousin went there first so that's why we didn't have to look; we went there [too]."

In addition to turning to ceremonies to heal from illness and death, some people have also done so to heal from sexual abuse. Denise (St. François-Xavier) spoke about abuse in her life when she was younger and said, "The biggest thing that encouraged me was trying to heal from all the ill of my life. Nothing else worked. Ceremony is what helped me heal more than anything." Barbara (St. Laurent) also shared that she "searched and searched for the meaning of life, because I was so severely abused, sexually abused." She said that going to the six o'clock morning mass at the convent helped her survive childhood sexual abuse and Indigenous ceremonies have led to her lifelong healing. Like Denise and Barbara, Debbie (St. Laurent) turned to ceremonies to heal from abuse: "It was when I was going through a difficult time. Prayers were not enough. It was like a reconnection. It was during a time when I was dealing with sexual abuse, and I went to a healing centre in Fort

Frances. That's when I was first introduced to the Native culture, and the ceremonies." In these ways, turning to Indigenous spirituality has benefitted several Métis participants in their greatest time of need and nurtured their connection to ceremonies.

At least one person from each community credited their personal motivation as nurturing their connection with Indigenous spirituality.[7] Anungoohns (Camperville) shared this sentiment: "I think the biggest [connection] factor was that it was who I am, and I wanted to connect with that part of me [as a person who participates in ceremonies]. Before, I didn't have that opportunity to do that. I wanted to take that back; I wanted to connect with that part of who I was." Charlotte (Ste. Anne) said, "When I learned who I was as an Aboriginal person, a Métis person, that sparked something in me to learn as much as I could learn about our spirituality. The more I learned about myself, the more I learned about life." Amanda (Ste. Anne) explained it simply in this way: "It's something I feel in myself that I want to do. It's not someone inviting me out [to ceremonies]." Likewise, when Jules (St. Laurent) spoke of his connection to ceremonies, he said it was "my own view of it; I was in favour of it. I don't see anything wrong—there's nothing wrong with participating in First Nations ceremonies like smudging, sharing circles, prayers, stuff like that."[8] Vern (St. François-Xavier) spoke of the strength of his own interest and motivation in seeking out Indigenous spirituality: "I've attacked [my interest in Indigenous spirituality] quite aggressively. . . . I've attacked it this vigorously so that it surrounds me." Elizabeth (St. François-Xavier) had this to say, "There's been an enormous amount of growth [in me]. . . . There's this very strong like—I need to know more; I need to do more. I need to build relationships, to pray, and make space in my life for this." A couple of participants linked this self-motivation to a desire to help others. Recall the personal sense of responsibility for bringing a younger friend to ceremonies described by Bethany (Lorette), and as a result, her coming to recognize him as a little brother whom she encourages on his spiritual journey. Ray (Duck Bay) spoke about it like this: "As long as there's one person that hasn't given up [ceremonies] in your family, your family benefits from you. I always think of my kids; I don't think of myself. People are quick to judge, but because I go and fast, I've never given up. Because if I gave up, not only would I be giving up on Creator, Mother Earth, and Grandfathers, I'd be giving up on my children. I'd be turning my back on all the ones I've prayed for." The participants' self-motivation, interest, and a sense of responsibility to help were additional factors encouraging a connection to Indigenous spirituality.

Lastly, some people spoke of "blood memory, Spirit, and ancestors" as important elements in their own connection to Indigenous spirituality and ceremonies.[9] Brenda (Camperville) shared a story about her mother feeling powerfully drawn to the sound of the drum and attributed this to blood memory:

> My mother when she first heard the drum, she heard the drum in Camperville at a funeral. . . . My mom heard the drum outside the church and then she said it just struck her. And she looked at me and she said, "I want that at my funeral." And I said, "Really?" Because she didn't follow [Indigenous] spiritual ways. She said, "yes." That's that blood memory connection, that spirit memory connection that they don't understand because it hasn't been taught to them. But I understand it because I have some of the teachings and [blood memory] is like that: it will never leave you. I've been told by my aunt, my grandmother, different people walk with me, so I know the Spirit. I talk to the Spirit; I talk to the Creator.

Linda (St. François-Xavier) felt the importance of blood memory after growing up in foster care and then learning of her Métis identity as an adult, at a time when she had begun working in an Indigenous-centred job and participating in cultural events. She said, "That is what really helped identify that Indigenous [identity] in me. That's what we call 'blood memory.' The pipe ceremony—so, the spirituality: when you start smelling those medicines and feeling that sense of belonging." Karen (Camperville) described a similar concept without using the term "blood memory": "That's where I started learning the Anishinaabe way. The old way. How people kept their families together before colonization. They always say if you have one drop of Indian blood then it'll come to you. And that's what it did. It came to me in dreams. It came to me in things people would ask me to do. 'You want me to do that? Can't you find someone else?' 'No, you're the one who's supposed to do this.' I learned a lot." Denise (St. François-Xavier) expanded this discussion when she said that intergenerational trauma is also felt via blood memory and that ceremonies can be used to heal this: "We have a lot of addiction in my family including alcoholism. . . . I've struggled with addiction, not so much with alcohol but [with] codependency. I feel that really learning about intergenerational historical trauma [is important] and understanding [that] its impact on us is still there. I also believe in blood memory. That the trauma of our ancestors is in our blood and we need to heal that and so that is the kind of work I focus on doing." Some folks talked about Spirit and ancestors guiding them to connect with Indigenous spirituality and ceremonies. Janice (Lorette) said, "They give you your direction. That is what spirituality is to me: giving you directions. . . . I mean, like Spirit; that is very strong. Grandmothers, grandfathers, guiding [you]." Bobbie-Jo (St. Laurent) put it this way: "I learned a long time ago that, as hard as I try to stop doing ceremony or deny it because it caused problems or it was difficult—because ceremony means facing yourself and your own issues and your own healing—that every time I walked away, the elders pushed [me] back onto this [spiritual] path. I've come to realize I can't run away from it. What I'm trying to say is that my ancestors encourage me to do ceremony." Barbara (St. Laurent) also highlighted the importance of ancestors in her spiritual life: "I gave up drinking. I started reaching out to go to ceremonies. I started reaching out to go to sweats. I started doing all those things to try to reconnect to who I really was, ancestrally. I was trying to reconnect to my ancestors . . . I can put that in those words now, because I didn't know how to connect it [back] then. But I was reading books and I was looking for things. . . . I started attending ceremonies, smudging, and gathering medicines, attending Sundances, and having more visions, and just helping people as well. That's how I found myself." Blood memory and guidance from Spirit and ancestors were revealed as powerful elements of connection in the spiritual journeys of the Métis people in this study.[10]

Self-Identification and Indigenous Spirituality

More than three-quarters of the Métis people in this study indicated that their self-identification has changed because of their participation in ceremonies.[11] Of these, only one person discussed a change to their proper noun (the term they use to self-identify). Instead, folks talked about change with respect to a reinforcement of their identity (especially as Métis); a deeper connection to their identity and culture, especially a sense of belonging and to the way they introduce themselves (notably by including their spirit name once they have learned it); and overcoming self-doubt and increasing confidence.[12]

In Duck Bay, all but one person shared that they "think differently" as a result of participating in ceremonies. They each provided a unique view of what this meant for them. For instance, George now understands himself to be a messenger for the people: "Yes, I think different; I think different. Change is coming but it's just slow. See, what I was told, according to an elder [is that] I'm just a messenger. I tell that to the people. And yet, in my clan, if I followed the clan, the loon clan is leadership for the people. So that's what I'm doing. People ask me [about this and I say], 'Well, I'm just the [messenger]; I'm trying to wake the people up and I've been to ceremonies.'" Likewise, since participating in ceremonies, Ray recognizes a spiritual awakening within himself and tries to encourage others to see this in themselves as well.

Everyone from Lorette talked about their growing understanding that some Métis people do participate in Indigenous ceremonies, which has increased their confidence and sense of belonging as Métis women. Bethany clearly illustrated this when she said, "It definitely makes me more confident especially [in] our [ceremonial] circle because it's very inclusive. I can go there, and I can feel safe and say, 'Oh, I'm a Michif [person].' And, it's like, 'Oh, would you look at that, there's like ten other Michif [people here].' That definitely helped [me] with that confidence and also that reassurance that, yes, Michif people/Métis people can participate in ceremonies. That's one of our inherent—like that's an ancestral right, basically. We were always doing that; so, why can't I?" Similarly, Andrea shared, "It gives you a little more confidence in—I don't want to say 'if you don't go to ceremony, then you're not this or that.' But it gives you a little more confidence in saying to yourself: 'I belong here. I'm Métis. This is who I am.' I think that's probably [true] for a lot of different cultures—once you start learning more about stuff, you start feeling more like, 'This is who I am.'" On a related note, half the folks from St. François-Xavier indicated an increase in their Métis pride and a couple of people spoke about receiving their spirit name as impacts upon their identity resulting from ceremonies. Nancy said, "It's heightened—it's given me more of a sense of drive and pride. It's just made me more aware of how great we are as Métis people." Elizabeth shared: "In terms of having had that [spirit] name given to me, and the way that I did get a teaching to go tie a tobacco tie in the woods here and honour the name. . . . I'm very proud and really honoured to start having these experiences . . . it hasn't changed the way that I self-identify, but it has absolutely changed me as a person." In these ways, ceremonies have affected participants' self-identification in terms of an increase in Métis pride and an understanding that some Métis people do go to ceremonies; indeed, that going to ceremonies is part of a Métis identity.

Half the people from St. Laurent spoke of having a deeper understanding of self, and two people indicated a deeper connection in life resulting from their participation in Indigenous ceremonies. Bobbie-Jo said, "I just have a deeper understanding of who I am because of ceremony. I've always been Métis and Cree and I've self-identified as Métis and Cree for twenty-two years. I just now understand what that means." In Camperville, two people now include their spirit name when introducing themselves (where appropriate). While they both continue to identify as Métis, Karen now also identifies as Anishinaabe and Julia now introduces herself in Saulteaux in ceremony.

In Ste. Anne, a couple of people described feeling "more connected" because of going to ceremonies, and two others spoke of ongoing internalized self-doubt regarding their Indigenous identity. Charlotte had this to say: "The only change I have noticed is that I am more aware of the universe around me, and all of my relatives and their connection to me. I will always be a Métis [person] and carry that knowledge in all the work I do within Aboriginal communities and non-Aboriginal environments. Being a spiritual being has afforded me a broader view of humanity and its slow process in evolution." Amanda explained, "It hasn't changed how I self-identify but it's changed how I feel about myself as an Indigenous person. I feel more connected, more of that connection to a community. It's not necessarily a Métis community but an Indigenous community. More friends and acquaintances." Recall that Amanda continues to struggle with the pronunciation of her spirit name in Cree and with her identity as a Métis person: "I find it interesting that I had to go to university to learn about my heritage and learn about identity. You shouldn't have to do that, [or] to feel that, at almost forty [years of age], to feel weird about—not weird but still trying to get a solid sense of myself as Métis and Indigenous [and] not feeling awkward if someone thinks I'm White." In a similar vein, while ceremonies have helped, Justin continues to question his identity as Métis and First

Nations (since he has one Métis and one First Nations parent):

> Just being able to accept that I'm First Nation [as well as
> Métis] because I'm always questioning that still. Having
> that doubt just from the guilt and whatever. I've always had
> the issue of feeling not Native enough. Being at ceremony,
> everyone is so welcoming and reaffirming and then you see
> all their faces too. Like, my mom's White-coded. She's full
> status but she's White [in appearance]—her skin is white.
> To see a whole bunch of people [at ceremonies] and be like,
> it's not just about skin colour, or how much you know, or
> where you grew up. There's more to it than that. People are
> willing to acknowledge that and teach it. It has been huge
> for my identity.

In summary, among the Métis folks for whom participating in
Indigenous ceremonies has resulted in changes to their self-identity,
most have not changed the proper noun by which they identify (e.g.,
Métis); rather, these changes reflect the way they understand themselves
in relation to self-confidence, pride in being Métis, and with regard to
a deeper connection to community and within Creation.

Others' Reactions

Finally, the Métis folks featured in this study reflected upon reactions
from their families and from members of their spiritual communities regarding their participation in ceremonies. Slightly more than
one-quarter indicated that their family was supportive and accepting
of their participation in ceremonies. The same number also spoke
about family members' own participation in ceremonies or their desire
to do so. Other folks indicated that one or more family members have
been unsupportive of their participation in ceremonies; in particular,
that they are uncomfortable because of a lack of understanding about
ceremonies.[13] In terms of reactions from the participants' Indigenous
spiritual communities, more than half spoke of feeling supported,
accepted, and welcomed. A few said they felt unwelcomed or shamed
by others at ceremonies; of these, two people expressed internalized
shame.[14]

People from St. Laurent reported the greatest number of positive
family reactions to their participation in ceremony. More than half

spoke of one or more family members participating in ceremonies as well, and a few people indicated general support and acceptance. Barbara listed several family members who participate in ceremonies: "[My sister] does. [My other sister] is a Catholic but also has eagle feathers and smudge bowls and a medicine bag and she's attended different ceremonies. My younger sister has been in sweats. My nephews have [too]. And, some of my nieces in Manitoba and Alberta. The one in Alberta is a principal of an Indigenous school—she's practised the way. My sister who has passed on lived on a reserve and practised the way [as well]." Lucille also noted positive reactions from some of her family members: "I think it was on a positive note because everyone wants to experience something new and I think they as well have done so [i.e., participated in ceremonies]. More so, the younger generation, like our kids. My siblings, our children are more outgoing and more free-spirited to join these things and go check it out themselves. They don't hold back to the strict traditions of one culture over another. I think they're more open-hearted." Stories about positive family reactions were also notable in St. François-Xavier, with a couple of people discussing family participation in ceremonies and supportive reactions; pride, respect, and curiosity were also mentioned. Like Barbara, Linda listed many family members (especially her grandchildren) who have participated in ceremonies with her: "I have seven grandchildren. They've sat with me with my pipe, helped me. I've had them come to ceremony, full-moon ceremonies I conduct. My granddaughter was just mentioning to me, 'Remember Grandma, I was the first one up to go to the sunrise ceremony at the Forks?' At four [o'clock] in the morning, she got up; and, she remembers [that]." Denise shared a story about her family participating in Indigenous ceremony during the funeral she led for their mother: "When my mother passed, we did her funeral. I led the funeral. I did a full out ceremony, very traditional, and I brought my *chanupa* [pipe] with me and we did a *chanupa* ceremony with my family. My dad—they had never done anything like that before. So, I think it [i.e., my participation in ceremonies] has kind of shifted them a little bit."

However, not everyone's family has been supportive. Unsupportive family reactions were reported by participants in Lorette, with folks indicating a lack of support and understanding, or family that "does not believe in ceremonies." Janice described her experience: "There's the challenges [of] others not participating—because we have that in our family currently with my husband and my son. They have both been invited to come many, many times, but it's not something they would like to participate in and that's fine. . . . From the beginning [my husband] really made [it] known [that] he was not coming in this [spiritual] way or interested in that for himself. So, that can be challenging; [it's] scary for [some] people." Echoing this, Janice's daughter Bethany said: "My sibling doesn't participate in ceremony. He doesn't not believe in ceremony, but he also doesn't believe in ceremony. Like, he kind of has this little bit of disconnection and he's just finding his own path." However, folks in Lorette also mentioned supportive family reactions, or reactions that were unsupportive when the participant first started going to ceremonies but have since ameliorated. Janice illustrated this: "There are definitely others [in my family] that are okay with it, like my mom. [It] is really special to have us, three generations [together at ceremonies]; it's very powerful, very blessed. In terms of the support, that's what I mean by that: for me, having both my mother and my daughter [there with me in ceremony]. It's very supportive for me—really supportive to have one on each side of me. Really, I am very, very blessed." In another example, Nicki shared the following: "Maybe some incredulity from aunts and uncles, or family friends of that age group, who are still very Christian. I don't know that they see it as, not blasphemous but it's like it goes against Christianity, I guess, in their view. But I don't give a shit about what they think, so that's been easy. I think that, at the beginning, my parents made some jokes because they didn't really understand it. But when I likened it to making jokes about Christianity, they started being more like, 'Oh okay, it's not a religion but a spirituality to be respected.'" Discomfort arising from lack of understanding was also mentioned by a couple of people in St. Laurent and Ste. Anne. In St. Laurent, Bobbie-Jo discussed her family's discomfort with her participation in ceremonies although for some, this seems to be lessening over time:

> Family, it makes them uncomfortable because they don't know, and they don't understand [ceremonies]. My husband has been incredibly supportive. Although he's really against organized religion, he has strong beliefs in Indigenous spirituality. So, he's always supported me in my healing and

my journey and made it possible for me to be able to do the things I needed to do. Although, he doesn't always participate in it because that's his journey and [he] has his own healing to do. My parents no longer question why I do it, they don't ask a lot of questions anymore and they support me in it [now]. They just don't really want to participate in it with me. So, I think for my parents it's been discomforting for them.

Debbie (St. Laurent) described how her family's internalized belief that they are French instead of Métis (and that only First Nations people go to ceremonies) has impacted their responses to her participation in ceremonies: "It was like, 'What, you [participate in ceremonies]?!' And, 'I thought you were more French,' and all that. I had to laugh because where do you divide the line [regarding] who I am [between] French or Native? I am who I am. I said to these family members, 'Don't you realize how rich we are that we can practise and look into our cultures? We have cultures within us as Métis people. . . .' It kind of made me angry but, at the same time, for them, they didn't understand." Justin (Ste. Anne) shared that his mother has some concerns (especially about Justin piercing at Sundance) that also stem from a lack of understanding: "Some of my family are worried. My mom just gets worried all the time. She didn't see me pierce [at Sundance]. She came afterwards and was like, 'Oh, my God!'" If one has not been educated about the purpose and meaning behind piercing at Sundance, witnessing a piercing (or seeing the aftermath) can be unsettling—especially for loved ones who might only see pain, not the beautiful, honourable sacrifice that has been made and the blessings brought to one's family as a result.

In describing how their own spiritual community reacted to their participation, people across each Métis community in this study reported generally supportive responses. Particularly positive responses were noted by those in Lorette, Duck Bay, and St. François-Xavier. Janice (Lorette) explained, "I've got that circle that is so beautiful and wonderful; I'll be forever grateful. . . . There's been some beautiful connections with people, and people being around you that you didn't even know, and some long-term friends that you can share with." Denise (St. François-Xavier) said, "My experience at Thunderbird House has always been 100% completely positive. Absolute welcome. I never had to prove myself there. I just came and was welcomed completely."

Going to ceremonies with people you know and feel comfortable with increases the chance of having a positive experience, as Elizabeth (St. François-Xavier) notes: "I had pretty safe experiences because the two sweats that I've been involved with were mostly all people that I knew or had some connection to." Likewise, Nicki (Lorette) said, "I'm somewhat lucky in the early days of when I was first introduced to the sweat lodge, and then started going more often during those first few years, because I was in Barbara's lodge with mostly co-workers and her family members. So, those people knew me as Métis and were all Métis themselves with one or two exceptions here and there with either a non-Indigenous person or a First Nations person. So, there was never really like [a] negative reaction at all." Maryanne (Duck Bay) has been asked about her Métis identity at ceremonies but does not consider this to be a negative reaction:

> Very respectful, yeah, very respectful. And, very inviting and welcoming. Every year, when I go and I introduce myself before we go into the community, I say, "I'm Métis." Sometimes, I'll get asked, "Well, what division [percentage] are you of Métis? Are you Scottish and this? Are you da-da-da-da-da?" And, I'll explain. It's always been very good because I can say things in Saulteaux, and I can say things in Cree. I give them that background a little bit more. Like "Excuse me, I grew up in a Métis community, but I grew up with a *kookum* [grandmother] who spoke to me only in Saulteaux."

Lightning Rattle Woman (Duck Bay) used to worry that she would be questioned about her Métis identity at ceremonies but that has never actually happened: "I thought, like nervous[ly], 'Oh, we look a little bit White; we don't look Native enough.' But, it's not like that." Participants in Camperville were split in terms of the reactions they experienced from their spiritual community, with three people feeling accepted at ceremonies, and three others feeling shamed by others (or internalizing shame) in a ceremonial context. Brenda said, "It's fair to state there is no division of Métis and First Nation [people at ceremonies]; they don't see that." Louise has never had her identity questioned at ceremonies despite having lighter skin; like Maryanne, she attributes this to being able to speak Ojibwe (among other reasons): "I've never felt that where my identity [was questioned at ceremonies because of my appearance] ... because I could speak Ojibwe as well as they could. So, that made a lot of difference. But [I] have nine brothers that are dark and I'm fair. No, I've never felt uncomfortable. I was always made to feel welcome and people would take me under their wing." Julia has also felt very welcomed at ceremonies: "Welcoming; it's always been welcoming. Even when I first started and had never gone before. I was nervous [but] people are always welcoming. They were always welcoming, and they never shamed [me]. I felt ashamed [though] because I never knew about this stuff, and I should know about [ceremonies] but they never shamed [me] for that." However, Julia has heard of others being shamed at ceremonies.

Encountering negative reactions in a ceremonial context was mentioned by people connected to Ste. Anne, St. François-Xavier, and St. Laurent. Charlotte (Ste. Anne) shared a story about hosting a fasting camp on her property and her neighbours reacting out of ignorance:

> It was funny because I had told everybody, I'm going to be putting up red [prayer] flags at the four corners, the directions, to come to our place. So, they all found the place easily. ... There was about 300 people that showed up. [After the fast ended,] I went to take down the flags to burn them [in a sacred fire]. And here they were all gone. So, I thought because I had put them at road signs that the municipality picked them up. So, I went to the municipality and said, "Did you guys pick up four red flags at four different intersections?" He says, "Yeah. One of your neighbours came to us and told us there was going to be an Indian uprising, all these Native people heading to your place." And I burst out laughing! I says, "Oh my god, next time you talk to him, tell him to come over for tea and ask [me about it]." See the fear that people have—because this was two years after the Gustafsen Lake standoff and that's what he feared.[15] I says, "If he would have had tea and bannock with us, we would have helped him understand what this was about." And they all chuckled after that, gave me the flags, and I brought them home. .... See, people fear things because they don't understand [them].

In a different example, Julia (Camperville) noted having heard that gay and transgender people have been shamed in ceremonies: "Yeah, in Sundance. [People have been shamed] not for being unfamiliar with ceremony but for being transgender, or gay, or [for] not wearing [a skirt]. It depends on the elders too. Some are very strict, like: you have to wave the medicine this many times or do this [in this particular way]. And, I can understand why: they want to protect it. But yeah, I've heard of elders shaming different people coming to ceremony, but I've never experienced it, luckily." Also, recall the story Barbara (St. Laurent) shared about being shamed at a Sundance for being a two-spirit woman, and for having lighter skin and assumed to be White (Chapter 9). Elizabeth (St. François-Xavier) faced an intense response in ceremony and was told that women are not allowed to drum: "What I felt was the most violent reaction was when I brought my drum to Edmonton and was with one of my older sisters who plays her drum—she's an elder-in-residence at the university here. . . . I don't know why that's still fresh in my mind. It felt really like, 'You should not be doing that here on this territory.'" This brought up self-doubt and made Elizabeth worry that "I don't have the right to be here and they're all thinking that about me." On a related note, Amanda (Ste. Anne) described poor treatment in a ceremonial context on account of her Métis identity:

> The only thing I have noticed is if someone. . . . If it's a group of people that look stereotypically First Nations, Indigenous or whatever you want to say, and I'm there, they'll say something rude about White people [then] they will apologize to me. I feel super awkward when they do that. Because it's like, no, I'm Métis. . . . Sometimes I pretend like I didn't hear it. Or, it depends on the context of it. If it's in a group of people I don't know . . . I feel really uncomfortable when that happens. Because I do feel that they are looking at me like, "Why is that White person here?" Most of the time when I'm in ceremony, people know that I am Métis. So, it's usually with [my spiritual teacher] or people that I have worked with at the university, and they just know that. . . . That's another reason why I am careful which sweats I go to because I feel uncomfortable if it's a lot of First Nations people that don't know me—they assume I am White. Then I feel like I'm in a position where I have to defend myself almost. I never like

to feel like that. Whether it's being Métis [or some other aspect of identity]. No one wants to feel defensive especially when you're trying to go [to ceremonies] for healing or to feel better about yourself.

Also, recall how Louis (Ste. Anne) spoke about being exploited as a Métis person in ceremonies (Chapters 8 and 9) as a result of a perceived racial hierarchy among some First Nations spiritual leaders who view themselves as superior to Métis people and who do not believe Métis people can be recognized as spiritual leaders themselves. Ironically, Bethany (Lorette) has come across the stereotype that Métis people do not go to ceremonies while attending ceremonies:

> It's very interesting to reconnect to more Michif way[s] of ceremony, and having more Michif people in ceremony, because often, a lot of people see spirituality as First Nations' only and not [also belonging to] Métis people. It leads me to wonder why they think that. . . . We have to explain to them—the Métis, this particular Métis family was a practicing Catholic family but that doesn't mean all Métis families are practicing Catholic families traditionally. With that they [ask], "Oh, what did they [i.e., Métis people] do [traditionally]? So, then it's like, "they did different ceremonies like sweats and things like that [too]."

Other participants from Camperville and St. Laurent were confident in their understanding that Métis people can participate in ceremonies. For Brenda (Camperville) this was an unshakable truth:

> I know the Spirit; I talk to the Spirit—I talk to the Creator. And I offer that tobacco. He sees that spirit, that beautiful, beautiful spirit and that's what I share with people. You do good, you walk that healthy life even though you fall off [sometimes]. I am the first one to say I've made lots of mistakes in my life, but I'm going to acknowledge those mistakes. My two older children have been hurt by my partying in the past, and I always say I'm sorry but now they know that I've tried to change my life. I know they will be with me at Sundance one of these days soon.

That Métis people legitimately participate in ceremonies was also clearly illustrated by Gripette (St. Laurent) as she described building the sweat lodge on her property: "[My mother] helped build it. She helped with the tobacco in the holes for the poles. I made sure that she gives some of the time. There's little Métis sashes that tie some of the [sweat lodge] ribs together, and she tied that." I am struck by the symbolism here: the sash which has become an iconic representation of Métis culture has been woven into the frame of a sweat lodge—literally holding it together—built by a Métis sweat lodge conductor on her land in what is arguably one of the most recognizable historic Métis communities anywhere: St. Laurent. This is a beautiful image of how some Métis people do indeed (continue to) participate in ceremonies in the present day.

~

This chapter took a closer look at the Métis participants' own relationship with spirituality. People shared stories about factors that have nurtured their own connection with Indigenous spirituality over the years, including specific people (friends, family, and elders), the education system, specific events and places (conferences, urban locations, Friendship Centres), traumatic catalysts, and the Indigenous sovereignty movement, among others. Most indicated that their self-identification had changed because of participating in ceremonies, especially in terms of increased confidence about their identity and their relationships (as opposed to a change in the term/s by which they identify). Lastly, participants reflected upon reactions from family and from members of their Indigenous spiritual community regarding their participation in ceremonies. Across the board, supportive reactions outweigh unsupportive ones—and the occasional negative reaction has not deterred their ongoing participation in ceremonies.

CHAPTER 11

Métis Spirituality Today

With this book, I seek to bring attention to the often ignored and misunderstood topic of Métis spirituality. I laid the groundwork in *Rekindling the Sacred Fire: Métis Ancestry and Anishinaabe Spirituality*, wherein I noted that colonial pressures have resulted in many Métis families forgetting our ancestors' historic participation in ceremonies. Ironically, evidence for our participation in ceremonies is found in writings of the earliest Catholic priests to settle in what became Manitoba. Church and government made concerted efforts to assimilate and Christianize Métis and First Nations peoples via colonial legislation and policies (the Indian Act, treaties), systems (day and residential schools, child welfare), and the widespread dispossession of Métis from our lands, identity, and culture after the Red River Resistance (1869–70) and the Northwest Resistance (1885). Some Métis chose to pursue Christianity—many did so strategically as a survival tactic, as one participant in *Returning* pointed out (Louis, Ste. Anne). Still other Métis who adhered to Indigenous spirituality were increasingly and forcibly disconnected from it. Using a Métis Anishinaabe research design and methodology, *Rekindling* examined the experiences of eighteen Red River Métis people who had found their way back to the ceremonies of their ancestors. *Returning to Ceremony* resumes this conversation.

I have continued my search for oral and written evidence of historic Métis participation in ceremonies (Chapters 1 and 2). For example, Métis Elder Maria Campbell pointed to biographies of Gabriel Dumont that depict the importance of ceremonies in his life;[1] she also shared with me that some Métis families, including hers, have continued to participate in ceremonies to the present date. I also returned to the archives and have presented additional accounts describing historic Métis and Halfbreed participation in ceremonies found in the correspondence of early nineteenth-century clergy living in what would become "Manitoba" (e.g., Fathers Belcourt, Camper, Provencher, and Simonet; Chapter 2). Missionary struggles to convert the Métis can be heard, for instance, in an 1866 letter written by Father Simonet discussing his conversion of a Métis spiritual leader to Catholicism only upon the latter's deathbed, because he had steadfastly adhered to Indigenous spirituality throughout his life.[2]

In the present book, I have aimed for a more Métis-specific and community-centred research design and methodology guided by ceremony. This included commencing the research with a four-day fast and beginning my Sundance journey (Chapter 3). Adhering to the Manitoba Métis Community Research Ethics Protocol set out by the Manitoba Metis Federation (MMF), I hired six Métis community researchers (CRs) and selected six recognized historic Manitoba Métis communities as focal points for this study (Chapter 4). The criteria for individuals to participate in this study included meeting the Métis National Council's (MNC) national definition of Métis,[3] and having a connection to one of the following six Métis communities: Duck Bay, Camperville, St. Laurent, St. François-Xavier, Ste. Anne, and Lorette. In adopting these criteria, I honour Métis Nation self-determination and take a stand against raceshifters.[4] Another buffer against raceshifting can be found in the detailed histories and contemporary profiles of each of the Métis communities that highlight Métis identity, kinship and belonging, and culture, in addition to Métis spirituality at the community level. Across both my books, I have helped share the experiences of fifty Métis people who participate in ceremonies today. Where *Rekindling* proved that some Red River Métis individuals practise Indigenous spirituality, the present book demonstrates that this is also increasingly the case at the level of Métis communities.

Comparing Findings across *Rekindling* and *Returning*

In the following paragraphs, I touch upon patterns in demographics, residence, family history, self-identification, and relationship with spirituality across both studies.[5] The level of educational attainment was higher in the first study, with more than half the Métis participants having obtained one or more university degrees. Educational attainment was balanced in the current study, with thirteen individuals holding a university degree and twelve having a high school diploma or less.[6]

While most people in the former study worked in the tertiary sector (especially education, justice, human resources, and social work), jobs in social work, in particular, were most prominent among participants in this study.

Folks in both studies reflected upon registered Indian status within their family. In *Rekindling*, nine people had status, while this was true for only three people in this study, though twenty-four individuals spoke of someone in their family having status including folks who married into their family (Chapter 6).[7] Stories about enfranchisement (loss of status) were shared in both studies—and some family members could technically be classified as Métis *and* as status Indian, including a few participants themselves. Overlap between Métis, Anishinaabe, and Nêhiyaw cultures in Manitoba can be seen in the fact that most of the people across the two studies reported having one or more family members who speak an Indigenous language or who speak multiple Indigenous languages,[8] while also reporting low levels of intergenerational linguistic transmission (as a result of colonization). Some participants are taking Indigenous language courses.

In the present study, twenty-three people were born in one of the six featured Métis communities, and/or that community was their childhood and/or adulthood residence.[9] While connection to a specific historic Métis community was not a criterion for participation in *Rekindling*, seven people nonetheless identified one as their childhood residence, and three were born in one. Most of the Métis people in both studies currently live in a city (especially Winnipeg).[10]

Family History

Participants in this study shared stories about multiple generations in their family (at least to their grandparents and likely earlier) who lived in their Métis community and being connected to several Métis communities. Most have knowledge of their family being offered Métis scrip but do not know what became of it. Folks in *Rekindling* were not asked about their family's connection to Métis land and territory; however, more than half mentioned having scrip in their family and similarly having no idea what became of it.[11]

In comparison with *Rekindling*, more people in the current study indicated that their family self-identified as Métis or Michif while they were growing up.[12] One or more family members were reported to self-identify as French, Roman Catholic, or White in this book, and as Indian or Anishinaabe in *Rekindling*.[13] Internalized racism and inter-generational shame (as a result of colonization) came up in both studies, including one or more family members who avoid self-identification as Métis, prefer to remain unnamed, or try to pass as White. Nevertheless, family pride in Métis identity also emerged across both studies. Nearly one-quarter of participants in this study mentioned at least one family member who now identifies as Métis or Michif; reasons for change in family self-identity over time included overcoming internalized shame from day or residential schools and increased pride stemming from the Red Power Movement of the 1960s and '70s.[14]

Participants in this study described their family connections to Métis culture as including subsistence activities (hunting, fishing, harvesting, trapping), small-scale farming, social gatherings, music and dance, cultural values (sharing, humour, kinship), and traditional Métis foods (*beignes, gallets, boulettes*, wild meats, and berries). In *Rekindling*, folks were asked simply about their family's relationships with "Aboriginal cultures," so direct comparisons cannot be made; nonetheless, the following similarities can be noted: holding Indigenous values (importance of family/kinship, intergenerational cultural transmission, respect for elders), practising cultural subsistence activities (living on the land, holistic education/modelling, hunting, traditional foods, fishing, trapping, harvesting) and cultural activities (jigging and fiddling, powwow, drumming and singing).[15] Family relationships with Métis (or "Aboriginal") culture as a lived and embedded reality were evident in both studies. In the previous study, half the participants indicated their family's relationship with Indigenous cultures had improved over time (notably, through increased understanding and participation); here, participants spoke about their family's relationship with the MMF, an increase in pride in Métis identity, and a decrease in subsistence activities over time.

Family relationships with First Nations cultures were either non-existent, or folks mentioned having at least one First Nations family member (including via marriage) in this study. Several people highlighted similarities between First Nations and Métis cultures, a few discussed differences, and many shared stories about internalized racism. Nearly half reported an improvement in relationships with First Nations cultures over time.[16]

In discussing family relationships with Euro-Canadian cultures, participants described close connections through French culture, Roman Catholicism, racism, and the education system. One-third indicated no change in these relationships over time, while a few shared stories about a family member who now identifies as Indigenous (instead of French or White). These responses were similar to those in the first study (*Rekindling*), where participants mentioned Euro-Canadian education, employment, languages, control,[17] desire to fit in/blend in/try to pass as White, and Indigenous rights and resistance. Half of the participants in *Rekindling* indicated no change over time, while a few described a slight improvement, and two people said the situation had worsened.

Intergenerational family relationships with Christianity (especially Roman Catholicism) emerged in both studies. In addition, nearly one-third of interviewees in this study spoke of Indigenous ceremonies in their family or Métis community historically or practised in secret (with some indicating this was the case intergenerationally). This was also noted in three families in *Rekindling*, but in those cases the relationships were marked by secrecy or conflict. Across both studies, Métis people shared stories about church and government repression of Indigenous spirituality in their families (especially through internalizing harmful messaging in day and residential schools).

A decrease (or complete cessation) in family participation in church over time was noted by half the people in the current study, compared to a few family members no longer identifying as Christian in the first study. Moreover, half the people here shared stories about their family's relationship with Indigenous spirituality in terms of increased acceptance, learning, and participation in ceremonies. In the previous study, five people shared that Indigenous spirituality is now their family's primary faith.

Self-Identification and Personal Experiences

There were noticeable differences between the two studies in self-identification patterns. In the present study, all but two people self-identify today as Métis, Michif, or rarely, Halfbreed. In contrast, half the people in *Rekindling* self-identified as Anishinaabe, and slightly fewer as Métis or Michif. More than half the people in both studies identify using multiple terms.[18] Also noted across both studies was a change in the way folks have identified over time, usually reflecting a shift in self-perception and relationships (including in the act of self-identifying) as opposed to a change in terminology (i.e., proper noun). However, in *Rekindling*, participants noted a decrease in their use of the term "Halfbreed"[19] and an increase in use of the term "Anishinaabe." The differences in people's self-identification between the two studies can be explained by the more relaxed criteria for participation in the first study ("Métis ancestry," as opposed to MNC criteria for Métis identity used here).

Across both studies, most people reported that their self-identification is not context specific.[20] Only one-quarter of participants across both studies change the way they self-identify depending on audience (Indigenous vs. non-Indigenous), location (e.g., job interview, border crossing, ceremony), and safety (perceived level of racism). Depending on such context, some participants emphasize, elaborate, downplay, or conceal aspects of their identity, including relationship to First Nations, settler, or Catholic identity. Rather than changing their proper noun (i.e., Métis or Michif), a few people opt for the generalized descriptor of "Indigenous" when speaking with White settlers, for example. Only two people (the two youngest in the first study) change the proper noun they use to identify themselves depending on such contexts.

Common themes from people's experiences of racism and discrimination emerged in both studies. This was particularly notable around feeling the effects of racist stereotypes about Indigenous people (e.g., as thieves, unintelligent, addicts) and identifying racist hotspots such as schools, cities, and workplaces. Stories about internalized racism, racism perpetrated by White people, lateral violence perpetuated by First Nations people, intersectional discrimination (including racism, sexism, misogyny, sexualized violence, and trans/homophobia), overt racism (including name-calling and verbal abuse),[21] and agency and efforts to resist racism were also shared across both studies. In this study, some people spoke of being spared the brunt of racism because of being perceived as White.

Relationship with Spirituality

The participants in this book described their spirituality in terms of characteristics (commitment, powerful/strong, personal/individual), values (interconnection and relationships, respect, rejection of hierarchical thinking), and a sense of purpose or responsibility (especially to share these ways with others, and to raise their children with these ways). Many people also mentioned Christianity (usually Roman Catholicism), particularly to note that they were no longer practising Catholics, and a few spoke of practising a blend of Christianity and Indigenous spirituality (syncretism), usually indicating a preference for the Indigenous elements. More than one-third of the people in this study adhere solely or primarily to traditional Indigenous spirituality, and a few people took care to explicitly state that Métis spirituality includes participating in ceremonies. Participants in *Rekindling* described their spirituality in terms of giving back (highlighting various communal values and a sense of purpose/responsibility, and recognizing that Indigenous spirituality and giving back are lifelong commitments), gaining a stronger understanding of one's identity, and emphasized relationships and connections, especially with Creation, Creator, their ancestors, all beings, and the land. In this first study, folks also shared stories highlighting the phenomenon of searching or feeling that something was missing in their lives, then finding the answers or fulfillment in Indigenous spirituality.

The Métis people in the present study reported participating in many types of Indigenous ceremonies, including (in decreasing order of mention): sweat lodge, Sundance, smudging, pipe, traditional medicines, spirit name and naming ceremony, fasting/vision quest, drumming and singing, harvesting, feast, powwow, Midewiwin, shake tent, sharing circles, dreams/visions, clan, and sunrise ceremony. The number of distinct types of ceremonies people reported engaging in ranged from two to as many as sixteen. In the previous study, folks were not explicitly asked about the types of Indigenous ceremonies they participated in; however, ceremonies themselves were identified as an important factor that encouraged their connection to Indigenous spirituality. These ceremonies (in decreasing order) were as follows: sweat lodge, spirit name, clan, lodge affiliation (Midewiwin, Grandmother Moon Lodge, Red Willow Lodge, Camp Manitoo), traditional medicines, smudging, pipe, drumming and singing, dreams/visions, and experiences with non-human beings.

Participants in the present study shared stories identifying factors that have prevented or inhibited a connection to Indigenous spirituality and ceremony. These included (in decreasing order): Christianity (especially Catholicism and day/residential schools); fear, anxiety, and self-doubt (including internalized doubt about whether Métis people have the right to participate in ceremony); having had a bad experience at ceremonies (resulting from dogmatic beliefs or homo/transphobic elders); divisions between Métis and First Nations people, and among Métis people themselves (including the internalized stereotype that Métis people only go to church, not ceremonies); lack of opportunity or connection to ceremonies; unsupportive family; and drugs and alcohol.

Folks in *Rekindling the Sacred Fire* were not explicitly asked to identify factors that disconnected them from Indigenous spirituality; however, the following emerged unsolicited (in decreasing order): Christianity (fear-mongering, demonizing Indigenous ceremonies as a control tactic); day and residential schools (their ongoing impacts, including a lack of intergenerational cultural transmission); government-caused divisions between Métis and First Nations people (a hierarchy of Indigeneity perpetuated by registered Indian status and the differential treatment of Métis and First Nations people by the government); and addictions (in self, family, community). People across both studies also noted Canadian laws that had historically criminalized Indigenous ceremonies, including laws against potlatch, Sundance, sweat lodge, and pipe ceremonies; some folks also mentioned that in addition to fines or imprisonment, individuals caught participating in ceremony were at risk of being excommunicated by the church.[22] Also highlighted across both studies were the effects of forced divisions between Métis and First Nations people becoming internalized, with some family members using "us and them" language, and that such divisions discourage Métis families' connections to Indigenous spirituality and ceremony.

Everyone also reflected upon factors that have encouraged or nurtured their connection to Indigenous spirituality and ceremony. In the present study, the stories shared highlighted the following connection factors (in decreasing order): key people (friends, family, elders, spiritual community members, teachers and mentors, other Indigenous people); educational institutions (access to elders, cultural events, and sometimes ceremonies in high school and university); key places and events (conferences, reserves, Friendship Centres); traumatic catalysts (illness, death, abuse); personal motivation; blood memory, Spirit, and ancestors; places of employment (especially Indigenous companies, organizations, and positions); and the Indigenous sovereignty movement

(Red Power Movement, American Indian Movement). Similar stories were shared in *Rekindling*; the following connection factors were mentioned (in decreasing order): the power of participating in Indigenous ceremonies; key people (elders, medicine people/healers, teachers, family); key places (reserves, rural locations, provincial parks, and to a lesser extent, urban areas); spiritual and political movements (Red Power Movement, American Indian Movement); Indigenous organizations and programs (powwow groups, Friendship Centres); and the education system. Strikingly, all the older participants in the first study identified the Indigenous sovereignty movement as a powerful factor that connected them to Indigenous spirituality, whereas all the younger folks spoke about higher education as a powerful factor.

Most people across both studies felt that their self-identification had changed as a result of participating in ceremonies. In the present study, these changes included reinforcing their identity, deepening their connections and relationships, receiving their spirit name, increasing their confidence/overcoming self-doubt, and clarifying their purpose in life. In the previous study these changes similarly included deepening their connections and relationships, increasing their pride, stabilizing their identity, and encouraging group solidarity. A change in terminology (i.e., the proper noun used to describe oneself) did not emerge as a theme in either study.

Finally, folks reflected upon other people's reactions to their participation in ceremonies. In the current study, several people shared stories about supportive and accepting family reactions, and family members who participated in ceremonies themselves (or wanted to); a few people mentioned unsupportive reactions stemming from lack of understanding or internalized negative messaging about Indigenous spirituality perpetuated by Christianity. Remarkably similar family reactions were shared by participants in the first study, including support, acceptance, and pride; participation in ceremonies (or the desire to); as well as some unsupportive reactions (disapproval, judgement, ridicule, fear, suspicion) resulting from lack of understanding and internalized harmful messages coming from Christianity. Reactions from members of one's spiritual community were notably positive, with feelings of acceptance and welcome identified most frequently across both studies. Likewise, only a handful of people across both studies noted negative reactions to their participation in a ceremonial context, such as being made to feel unwelcome or shamed, or being questioned about their identity (especially for those not presenting as stereotypically Indigenous in appearance). The Métis people in both studies remain committed to Indigenous spirituality because they recognize that the positive and healing benefits of ceremonies outweigh any negative reaction or experience.

Truths about Métis Spirituality

I have gathered evidence of Métis participation in ceremony from oral history, from a close scan of existing literature including primary and secondary sources, from personal experience and observation, and from primary research across two studies in which fifty Métis people shared their experiences. As a result, I have learned some truths about Métis spirituality.

Having immersed myself (academically and personally) in this topic for over a decade, I have come to view Red River Métis spirituality on a continuum, with Indigenous spirituality on one end and Christianity (in all denominations, but especially Roman Catholicism) on the other; infinite variations of syncretic blending can be found in between the two. By "Indigenous spirituality," I mean Métis-specific expressions of and relationships with the spiritual ways of life found among the Métis and our First Nations relatives that can include ceremonies such as the sweat lodge. Likewise, by "Christianity," I mean Métis-specific expressions of and relationships with Christianity. Both ends of the continuum have room for endless expressions, though patterns in characteristics can be observed. Perspectives such as atheism and agnosticism can be found in the centre of the continuum.

When we recognize the varied and nuanced Métis-specific expressions of and relationships with religion and spirituality as encompassed by the continuum described above, we actively avoid a simplistic and unhelpful dichotomy between Christianity and Indigenous spirituality—a continuum is by definition not a dichotomy.[23] Of course, as with all things, there are exceptions—there may be Métis people who practise Buddhism or have converted to a Muslim faith, for example. I am less concerned with individual exceptions; instead, I am interested in larger patterns among Métis as a collective. Also, just because I have not come across any Métis family or Métis community collective relationships beyond the ones described above does not mean they do not exist—especially beyond southern Manitoba. I am excited for other

Métis researchers to contribute to the study of Métis spirituality and add their truths. With that added knowledge, we can re-evaluate the concept of a continuum and determine whether it remains useful; perhaps the concept of constellations across our homeland might become a more accurate reflection of Métis family and community relationships with religion and spirituality.

My purpose here is not to provide a one-size-fits-all definition of Métis spirituality; rather, I offer the concept of a continuum as one way of understanding Red River Métis spirituality in southern Manitoba. These expressions of Métis spirituality and religion are not new truths; rather, these are truths that too many Métis have been forced to forget. The complex and beautiful relationships that Métis people have with Indigenous spirituality and Christianity have existed since the early days of the birth of our people and of the Métis Nation, and persist to this day.

Many Métis people have forgotten these truths because of forced assimilation by the church and government, as well as through widespread dispossession after the Red River Resistance in 1869–70 and the Northwest Resistance in 1885. Fluent Michif language speaker and respected Métis Elder Norman Fleury commented on the consequences of Métis being forced off their land and out of the Métis community of Ste. Madeleine: "It was 250 people losing that connection, but also losing their community, their connection to one another. If your stories are in the land and your community, and that all gets uprooted and scattered, how do you continue telling your stories?"[24] Sadly, there are many such examples of the forced dissolution of Métis communities and subsequent disbanding of inhabitants. Given the legacy of dispossession among Métis, it is no wonder so many of us have forgotten our own (ancestors') stories and have become disconnected from ceremony. As a result of colonization, one end of the Métis spirituality continuum became obscured and hidden from us collectively; however, Métis people returning to ceremony today are helping to reveal and re-illuminate that end of the continuum. Because of this renewed clarity regarding Métis spirituality, a more nuanced and accurate understanding of Métis identity also emerges. Indeed, for some, participation in Indigenous ceremony is one characteristic of Métis identity.

In this book, I have thoroughly disproved the stereotypes that all Métis people are Christian (especially Catholic) and express their spirituality only by going to church, and that ceremonies only belong to First Nations people. It is true that, especially in our early history, we were blessed to learn these ways from our First Nations parent cultures; for this, we express ongoing gratitude. It is also true that historically, ceremonies became an integral part of our own Métis spirituality. In other words, historically, Métis spirituality in its own right included ceremonies. For some Métis, this has always been the case and such cultural and spiritual continuity persists into the present.

However, ceremony generally remains understood solely as an expression of First Nations spirituality by many First Nations folks, non-Indigenous folks, Métis folks who have internalized these false stereotypes, and even by some of the Métis people in this study. One might wonder whether some ceremonies, or the way they are practised, are Métis-specific[25] or only appear in Métis communities. These are challenging questions and were not specifically discussed with the participants. I respectfully refrained from asking for details about ceremonies (bundle items that are used, how the ceremonies are conducted and unfold, etc.) because this is sacred knowledge and not often shared in print, video, or audio for many good reasons.[26]

While some of my spiritual teachers are Métis and I participate in ceremonies with them, these ceremonies have not been identified to me as Métis-specific, nor do they only appear in Métis communities. Rather, they are ceremonies, such as sweat lodge, that are also practised among other Indigenous nations and were taught to them by teachers from other nations (e.g., Cree, Anishinaabe, Lakota). On the other hand, recall that Flaminio, Gaudet, and Dorion have identified certain ceremonies and teachings—"Métis women's full moon ceremonies," along with "Métis women's firebag teachings, and "Métis women's buffalo teachings," among others—as Métis-specific,[27] even as they acknowledge their "intertwined maternal Métis ancestral connection to Cree and Saulteaux (Anishinaabe) ceremonies and teachings from within the prairie region."[28] Indeed, Métis people are just as likely to practise ceremonies in Métis-specific ways as First Nations people are likely to practise ceremonies in ways specific to their nations. A beautiful example of Métis-specific practice that I shared earlier is how Gripette ties the ribs of her sweat lodge with mini Métis sashes.

Perhaps, then, the origin of a ceremony is significant in determining whether a particular ceremony is "Anishinaabe," "Cree," or "Métis." In which nation did sweat lodge emerge, and how was it then shared with other nations? What modifications were made by the nations that were gifted the ceremony? While the question of origins goes beyond the scope of this book (and may not be an appropriate topic for publication), I want to remind readers about the Sundance ceremony gifted by the Cree to the Métis (and Anishinaabe) in the early 1800s (in present day North Dakota) along with the "Unity of the People" song commemorating this ongoing alliance in 2003.[29] When a ceremony is gifted in such a manner, it comes with an expectation and responsibility to ensure that the ceremony will continue to be practised by those who received it (including their community and descendants) into the future.

There are variations in the way a ceremony is practised from nation to nation and even from community to community within a single nation. When the Métis were gifted with or adopted a ceremony, they may have slightly modified it in ways that made sense for them—as in the case with Gripette above. This is also the case in First Nation–to–First Nation transmission. Such adaptations are usually minor and do not alter the essence of the ceremony as it was originally taught to the ceremony conductor, because high importance is placed on intergenerational transmission of sacred knowledge. Individuals can make minor changes (or major ones if they have been instructed to do so via Spirit, dream, vision[30]). One could dig deeper into whether there are Métis-only ceremonies that do not appear in other Indigenous communities.

The legacy of colonization and forced dispossession from our spiritual traditions has meant that for generations many Métis (and First Nations people) have had to leave their community and travel (sometimes a great distance) to participate in ceremonies. The research conducted for this book, and the stories shared by the Métis people in these pages confirm that this is the case for many Métis people in southern Manitoba who travel from their own Métis community to access ceremonies elsewhere (especially First Nations reserves, provincial parks, private property in urban and rural locations, and even as far away as Alberta) and to be with their chosen spiritual community. However, in some cases, Métis people have resumed participating in ceremony in their Métis community (or in another Métis community). Examples of this were shared by Gripette who conducts sweat lodges in her yard in St. Laurent, and by Louis who does the same in his yard near Ste. Anne—he has conducted fasting camps and hosted Sundances there too. In another example, Gloria, the CR for Duck Bay, gave me a tour of her community, including the Sundance grounds. She explained to me that Sundance had returned to the community a few years prior, but that a non-Indigenous man had bought the land adjacent to the grounds and has been threatening to cut off community members' access to the grounds (ceremony-goers must drive down a dirt road through "his property" to get to the Sundance arbour). We spent some time on the grounds and, together, we prayed and made an offering of *asemaa* (tobacco) at the arbour. Thankfully, as more Métis people are returning to ceremony—and some are being given the right to conduct ceremonies themselves, ceremony is becoming increasingly available in Métis communities, thereby enabling more Métis people to find their way back.

Given that the topic of Métis practice of ceremony has been ignored for so long, that so little has been written about it, and that so many misconceptions about it persist, at this point it is significant to have debunked the myth that Métis people do not participate in ceremonies. It is important to state that *Métis spirituality includes ceremonies (sweat lodge, smudging, etc.) in its own right.* I would like to go a step further and suggest there is no need to say, "Métis people participate in *First Nations' spirituality/ceremonies*," as this delegitimates Métis spirituality. Likewise, I want to caution against viewing Métis participation in ceremonies as "appropriation of First Nations ceremonies," since we did not take these ways of life without permission. Rather, we were taught, gifted, adopted, or given the right to conduct them by our relatives (including our Métis ancestors and our First Nations kin) and Spirit historically, and in some cases, contemporarily.[31] It is sufficient, and accurate, to simply state that *Métis spirituality includes ceremony.*

Having said that, it remains important to establish lineage (pedigree) in the spiritual community as a way of safeguarding ceremonies and protecting their adherents. By this, I mean that ceremony conductors should be able to share who they have learned from—sometimes this may be an Anishinaabe teacher, a Nêhiyaw teacher, or a Métis spiritual teacher. Ideally, ceremony conductors would also know who their teacher's teacher was, and so on. After all, not just anyone can conduct a sweat lodge, for instance: one must first dream it, apprentice under a sweat lodge conductor for years, then/or be given the right to conduct the ceremony (the latter often itself occurring in a ceremony attended by community, as occurred with the gifting of the Sundance ceremony by the Cree to the Métis and Saulteaux in the early nineteenth century to solidify the Nêhiyaw-Pwat/Iron Confederacy). I might say: "My Métis spiritual teacher learned this sweat lodge ceremony from her Métis spiritual teacher, who, in turn, learned it from her Métis spiritual teacher" (and name the teachers). Or one might say: "My Métis spiritual teacher was given the right to conduct this Sundance ceremony from her Cree teacher, who learned it from her grandparents" (again naming the teachers). This communicates that our spiritual teachers have not only received important instruction on how to safely conduct ceremonies but also remain accountable to their teachers, to their community, and to all their relations.

Today, lineage often includes teachers who are not from one's own nation; this is, in part, a result of colonization. The Métis are not the only ones who have been disconnected from their teachings; the same thing has happened among many First Nations people and communities. Many of us are relearning the teachings and ceremonies, and sometimes we must travel to find teachers before bringing the ceremonies back to our families and communities. Then again, even historically, nations gifted ceremony to other nations, as mentioned above.

Métis people continue to learn from our First Nations relatives—and they can learn from us as well. Collectively, we can heal the wounds and false divisions that have made us forget our kinship relations and obligations to each other. As we did historically, we can do this healing work and ceremony together while honouring our nations as distinct and celebrating our cultural overlap. It is time for Métis (and First Nations) people to decolonize our thinking and nurture a fulsome resurgence of our spirituality and ceremony. Here, I call upon Métis Nation leadership in particular, as they have a responsibility to correct harmful stereotypes about Métis spirituality and help clear a path for Métis who feel called to reconnect with ceremony.[32] From now on, I hope that when people think of Métis spirituality, they think of a nuanced continuum and recognize that Métis individuals, families, and communities express these relationships in many ways that sometimes include ceremonies, such as sweat lodge.

I am confident in these truths as a result of the research conducted in *Rekindling the Sacred Fire* and *Returning to Ceremony*, and the family and community stories shared with me by Métis people. While I have begun to address the literature gap on this topic, there is still much to be unlearned, untangled, and (re)learned. I encourage others, especially Métis people, to take up this work. Now that the stubborn stereotypes have been debunked and replaced with the truth that Métis spirituality includes ceremony, perhaps we can further explore (with sensitivity and respect) the existence of Métis-specific ceremonies and/or ceremonies that are only found in Métis communities. My books have concentrated on Red River Métis from and in southern Manitoba; what do Métis relationships with ceremony look like beyond this region? Exploring Métis spirituality in Saskatchewan might be particularly fruitful, given the glimpse of Métis families who have held on to ceremonies there, as shared earlier by Métis Elder Maria Campbell. What can be learned about Métis spirituality in other areas of the Métis homeland (including the northcentral United States), or from diasporic Métis families forced to move away from our homeland after 1870 and 1885? My research has also focused upon Indigenous spirituality among Michif people with French Catholic ancestry in historic Métis communities with a long Catholic parish presence. Are there similarities or differences in expressions of Métis spirituality in historic Métis communities without a long-term Catholic (or other church) presence? What about specifically in Anglo-Protestant "Halfbreed" communities? Examining syncretism in its various forms in the lives of Métis people would open the way to an even richer understanding of Métis spirituality. What factors influence the degree to which Métis spirituality in a family or community falls closer to Christianity or to Indigenous spirituality? Still other Métis researchers could study intersectional implications of Métis spirituality: Are there unique or shared experiences of Métis spirituality among women? Youth? Elders? Elsewhere, I have noted interesting relationships between 2SLGBTQ Indigenous people, creation stories and prophecies, our gifts and responsibilities regarding ceremonies, and the well-being of our families, communities, and nations.[33] What unique insights can be learned by studying the relationship between 2SLGBTQ Métis people and Métis spirituality? Or by exploring Métis and First Nations relationships within spiritual communities and in a ceremonial context historically and contemporarily? How might Métis and First Nations people participating in ceremonies together reignite and strengthen the Nêhiyaw-Pwat (Iron Confederacy) in modern times?

Together with *Rekindling the Sacred Fire*, *Returning to Ceremony* helps restore an obscured but integral piece of the narrative of Métis history and collective experience that had been incrementally and intergenerationally taken from us by church, government, and then sometimes by Indigenous people ourselves. With this labour of love, Métis participants, community researchers, and I gift our collective memories back to our people, the descendants and citizens of the historic Métis Nation. I hope this creates space for more Métis people to find their way back to the spiritual ways of our ancestors. To those Métis who worry they are "not Indigenous enough" to go to ceremonies, I hope you draw confidence and find peace in the knowledge that some of your Métis ancestors participated in these ways. When you crawl into the sweat or enter a teaching lodge, an initiation lodge, or a sacred arbour—and especially when you commit your life to these healing ways—you are reconnecting your family line and strengthening the bond between your ancestors, your living relatives, and your descendants. When you participate in ceremony, even if you are the first one in your family to find your way back home in this way, you are not alone. The elders tell us that whenever we participate in ceremony here in the physical realm, our ancestors join us and participate in the spiritual realm. They remind us that we have responsibilities to fulfill to our ancestors seven generations past and to our descendants seven generations into the future. For instance, we can feast our ancestors in ceremony; the ancestors of many Métis people are starving and have not been fed in generations. We lovingly address and correct this when we participate in ceremony.

Returning to ceremony has perhaps never been more important than it is now. Extractive capitalism has resulted in toxic waters, clearcut forests and desertification, barren wastelands left by oil and gas companies, species extinction, and ever-greater rates of mental and physical health challenges across the globe. As I write this, my wife and I have been self-isolating for a year and a half in our home with our infant daughter, as per Health Canada's guidelines, to try to slow the spread of the COVID-19 coronavirus during this global pandemic.[34] Globally, we are also suffering the deadly results of intergenerational White supremacy and settler colonialism, with near daily reports of Black and Indigenous people being murdered (often by police officers) without consequence or justice. Humans are negatively altering the earth and jeopardizing our children's future, and possibly the earth itself. In writing these books, I encourage us to collectively exchange deadly capitalist and White settler colonial ways for the teachings and values of our ancestors who walked lightly upon the earth. Listening to the teachings and values within Indigenous spirituality can remind us how to treat all our relations with respect and can provide us with solutions to ensure modern science and technology are ethically utilized to promote *mino-bimaadiziwin* (balance in Creation). We may be living in times of unprecedented environmental and social upheaval, but we also have options—including returning to ceremony—that can help correct our collective course and bring about a brighter and healthier future for all beings.

Miigwetch, Niikaanigaana! (Thank you, all my relations!)

Gichi-Miigwetch (Acknowledgements)

This labour of love has been a community effort and I have many to thank. I honour the six historic Red River Métis communities that are the focus of this study—Duck Bay, Camperville, St. Laurent, St. François-Xavier, Lorette, and Ste. Anne; despite the legacy of colonization and pressures to assimilate, the strength, perseverance, and collectivity of the Métis spirit lives on in their inhabitants and descendants (some of whom may now live elsewhere). I am eternally grateful to the thirty-two Red River Métis people from these communities who agreed to be part of this study and shared their time, stories, experiences, and knowledge; this book would not exist without your trust, honesty, and faith.

This endeavour was larger than I could undertake alone, and I humbly recognize the significant assistance I received from six Métis community researchers—Gloria Campbell, Ron Richard, Jacinthe Lambert, Julia Lafreniere, Nicki Ferland, and Amanda Burton—your skills and effort have bettered every aspect from conception to selection of participants, interviewing, data analysis, community presentation of findings, and everything in between. To the fifteen Métis and First Nations University of Winnipeg and University of Manitoba undergraduate and graduate students I hired: thank you for all the hours of transcribing interviews you dedicated to this project. I acknowledge that any errors appearing in this book are my own.

I rely heavily on guidance and support from my spiritual community and elders to help me live (and research) in a good and ethical way. *Miigwetch* to my Midewiwin family, especially *nibaabaa* Mizhakwanagiizhik (Charlie Nelson), Uncle Bawdwaywidun Banaise-ban (Eddie Benton-Banai), Rainey Gaywish, and Ron Indian-Mandamin. *Kinanâskomitin* to my Sundance family, especially David and Sherryl Blacksmith, Cecil Sveinson, and Shelley Girardin. *Maarsii* to Michif Elders Barbara Bruce, Charlotte Nolin, and Maria Campbell.

A heartfelt *miigwetch* to my brilliant wife, Nicki, for challenging me and holding me accountable, for your insightful editing and feedback, for offering the occasional evocative subheading and sentence (including one that made it onto the book jacket!), and for loving me and believing in me especially when my confidence falters. *Miigwetch* to our precious daughter, Mireille (and to our future children, should we be so blessed), for teaching me about unconditional love, and for reminding me of my responsibilities to our ancestors and to our descendants.

I am grateful for the love and encouragement I receive from my biological family (Donna, Renald, Sylvie, Gina), my extended family, including niblings, and relatives from St. Laurent and Ste. Geneviève—you keep me grounded and secure in my identity. *Miigwetch* to my wonderful in-laws for their support and for loving their grandbaby so much.

Maarsii to the Manitoba Metis Federation (MMF), especially the (now-defunct) Tripartite Self-Government Negotiations Department and former director Georgina Liberty for assisting me through the Manitoba Metis Community Research Ethics Protocol (MMCREP) and reviewing sections of my manuscript, and to MMF Minister of Housing and Property Management Will Goodon for answering all my Métis Nation governance questions and for being a supportive friend.

A special thank you to genealogist Gail Morin and historian Dr. Nicole St-Onge for helping me make sense of historic census data, and to the archivists at the Manitoba Archives and the St. Boniface Archives, especially Julie Reid. *Maarsii* to Dr. Chris Andersen for being a friendly and supportive mentor and for your time and generosity in chatting with me about all things Métis. *Miigwetch* to *nishiime* Anna Parenteau for your assistance with Anishinaabemowin translations and spelling.

I express my gratitude to the superb team at University of Manitoba Press—David Carr, Glenn Bergen, Jill McConkey, David Larsen, Ariel Gordon, Nicole Haldoupis, and Barbara Romanik—for guiding me through this process once again, for your patience and expertise, and for helping me bring this second book to life. Thank you to Maureen Epp for your careful copyediting, and for improving my precision. I also thank the anonymous peer reviewers for their thoughtful feedback which resulted in a stronger book. I say *miigwetch* to Auntie Hilda Atkinson and Barb Smith (construction) and to my friend David Heinrichs (beadwork) for our daughter's beautiful tikinaagan featured on the book cover. Thank you to Frank Reimer for the lovely cover graphic design, and to Weldon Hiebert for masterfully creating the map of Métis communities I envisioned.

This book has been published with the help of a grant from the Federation for the Humanities and Social Sciences, through the Awards to Scholarly Publications Program, using funds provided by the Social Sciences and Humanities Research Council of Canada (SSHRC). The research underpinning this book was made possible with a SSHRC Partnering for Change—Community-Based Solutions for Aboriginal and Inner-City Poverty grant through the Canadian Centre for Policy Alternatives via the Manitoba Research Alliance.

There are many other people who have influenced me along the journey that resulted in this book; you are too many to list, but your contributions are greatly appreciated.

Gichi-miigwetch Gizhi-Manido Kwe, Gizhe-Manido, Mide Manido, Mishtikonaabe for the spiritual gifts and strength that help me walk a path of *mino-bimaadiziwin* in this physical realm.

GLOSSARY

Anishinaabe(g)	Ojibwe/Saulteaux/Chippewa person (people)
Anishinaabemowin	Ojibwe language
Âpihtawikosisân(ak) (Apitowgoshaanuk)	Half-son(s); Métis person (people) (Nêhiyawawin)
Asemaa	Tobacco
Beignes	Frybread (Michif)
Bimaadiziwin	Life
Biizhew	Lynx
Boulettes	Meatballs (Michif)
Brayroo	Badger (Michif)
Chanupa	Pipe (Lakȟótiyapi)
Doodem	Clan
Gallet	Bannock (Michif)
Gichi-Miigwetch	Thank you very much
Gizhe-Manido (Kwe)	Creator (female); Great Spirit (Gichi-Manido)
Inipi	Sweat lodge (Lakȟótiyapi)
Ininiw(ak)	Plains Cree person (people) (Nêhiyawawin)
Jiibay	Ghost, spirit
Keeoukaywin (Kiyokewin)	The visiting way; visiting responsibilities (Nêhiyawawin)
Kiimooch	Secret (Nêhiyawawin)
Kinanâskomitin	Thank you (Nêhiyawawin)
Kookum	Grandmother

Li Bretons	People from France (Michif)
Maarsii	Thank you (Michif)
Manido	Spirit
Michif	Métis person/people; Métis language (Michif)
Mide Manido	Mide Spirit
Midewit	Midewiwin initiate
Midewiwin	Way of the heart (Mide for short)
Mikwayndaasowin	Recalling, remembering that which was there before
Mino-bimaadiziwin	Good, healthy, balanced life
Mishomis	Grandfather
Mishtikonaabe	Tree of Life (Nêhiyawawin)
Miskâsowin	Finding one's sense of origin, belonging, self (Nêhiyawawin)
Miskwaadesiins	Little red turtle
Miigwetch	Thank you
Mashkodewashk	Sage
N'dizhinikaaz	I am called (my name is)
N'doodem	My clan
Neechie	Friend
Nêhiyaw(ak)	Plains Cree person (people) (Nêhiyawawin)
Nêhiyawawin	Plains Cree language (Nêhiyawawin)
Nêhiyaw-Pwat	Iron Confederacy; Iron Alliance (Nêhiyawawin)
Nibaabaa	My father
Nibi	Water
Nishiime	Younger sibling

Niikaanigaana	All my relations/relatives
Niizhwaaswi Ishkodekaan	Seven Fires Prophecy
Omushkeego(wak)	Plains Cree person (people) (Nêhiyawawin)
Oshkibimaadiziig	New People
Otipemisiwak	People Who Own Themselves; Métis people (Nêhiyawawin)
Ozawaa Makwaa	Yellow Bear
Ruugaruus (rugarus, roogaroos)	Werewolves (Michif)
Shaggannappis	Long braids of buffalo (bison) hide (Nêhiyawawin)
Tikinaagan	Cradleboard
Wahkotowin (Wahkootawin)	Kinship roles, responsibilities; culturally appropriate behaviour (Nêhiyawawin)
Windigo	Cannibal spirit/person
Windigokaan	Contrary person/ceremony
Wiidiigewin	Union of souls; wedding
Yuwipi	Tie-up ceremony (Lakȟótiyapi)
Zaagaate	Sun is coming out, shining; sunrays through clouds
Zhiishiibi-Ziibiing	Duck River

Note: Terms are in Anishinaabemowin (Ojibwe language) unless parentheses denote Michif (Métis language), Nêhiyawawin (Cree language), or Lakȟótiyapi (Lakota language).

NOTES

INTRODUCTION – Métis Spirituality: Confronting Stereotypes

1 On my mother's side, we have Métis-Métis ancestry for seven generations. My Michif ancestor, Pierre "Bostonnais" Pangman Jr. and his wife, Marie Wewejikabawik, were one of four Michif families to establish the historic Métis community of St. Laurent in the early nineteenth century (St-Onge, *Saint-Laurent, Manitoba*). My relatives continue to live there today.

2 *Two-spirit* is an umbrella term for Indigenous people who identify on the lesbian, gay, bisexual, transgender, queer (2SLGBTQ) spectrum; it recalls Indigenous nation-specific conceptions of gender identity and sexuality inextricable from culture, spirituality, and relationship to land. Two-spirit people were targeted for eradication by colonial religion and government through forced assimilation to the Christian binaries of male/female and heterosexual/homosexual. Two-spirit people, knowledge, and ceremonies were forced underground, and homo/transphobia became commonplace in some Indigenous communities (and ceremonies). Today, it is rare to encounter elders and traditional knowledge holders who carry two-spirit teachings and ceremonies. As a two-spirit person, I am amazed (and grateful) that my first sweat happened to be a two-spirit sweat. Two-spirit resistance to colonization and reclamation of gender and sexual diversity has intensified over the last few decades. To learn more about two-spirit people and the two-spirit movement, see Cameron, "Two-Spirited Aboriginal People"; Two-Spirited People of Manitoba, Welcome page; and works by A. Wilson and by Fiola in the bibliography. For more on the impacts of colonization on two-spirit people, see Ristock, Zoccole, and Passante, *Aboriginal Two-Spirit*; NAHO, "Suicide Prevention"; Passante, "Aboriginal Two-Spirit and LGBTQ Mobility"; Passante, "Becoming Home"; Egale Canada, "The Just Society Report"; Hunt, "An Introduction to the Health of Two-Spirit People"; and Ristock, Zoccole, Passante, and Potskin, "Impacts of Colonization."

3 At the time, he was Chief of the Western Doorway of the Three Fires Midewiwin Lodge; he later became Chief of the Minweyweyigaan Midewiwin Lodge.

4 I also carry the spirit name Miskwaadesiins (Little Red Turtle) and have a close connection to the turtle clan, as told to me by the late Elder Gary Raven of Hollow Water First Nation.

5 The Midewiwin is an ancestral spiritual way of life practised among the Anishinaabeg and other Indigenous peoples that involves elaborate ceremonies during specific times of the year. Sundance is also a complex ceremony (containing ceremonies within ceremonies) evoking an ancestral spiritual way of life practised among the Dakota, Nêhiyawak, Anishinaabeg, and other Indigenous peoples. I would learn that some Métis people also participated in the Midewiwin and Sundance historically (and contemporarily), as I explain in this book. For more on my personal journey, my family history, my traditional teachers and elders, and my relationships with territory (and specific Métis communities and First Nations reserves), see Fiola, *Rekindling*, especially Chapter 1 and the Acknowledgements.

6   Métis scholars have devoted much time and energy to debunking these harmful
     views about Métis identity. For example, see Chris Anderson's *"Métis": Race,
     Recognition, and the Struggle for Indigenous Peoplehood.*

7   Canada, *R. v. Powley.* Section 35 of the Constitution Act (1982) identifies Aboriginal
     peoples of Canada as Indian, Inuit, and Métis, and recognizes and affirms existing
     (and future) Aboriginal and treaty rights.

8   Métis National Council, "Métis Nation Citizenship." More on the definition of
     Métis shortly.

9   Fiola, *Rekindling.* Dr. Rob Innes explains how historically, the treaty-making process
     and the accompanying differential treatment of First Nations and Métis by treaty
     commissioners and government officials resulted in an exaggeration of supposed
     sharp differences between our nations; this is perpetuated by contemporary scholars.
     According to Innes, the effect of this is to "erase the actual close relations that
     existed between the Métis and Plains Cree, Assiniboine, and Saulteaux. . . . The
     cultural boundaries drawn between Aboriginal groups through the tribal history
     approach is a fiction that has served scholars and government officials well, *but has
     little direct relevance to the actual lives of the people*" (*Elder Brother and the Law of the
     People,* 20; emphasis added). He argues that, in obscuring the close relations between
     the Métis, Plains Cree, Assiniboine, and Saulteaux, scholars, politicians, and the
     general public have "created and perpetuated a racialized view of the Métis that
     acts to ignore their kinship links and cultural similarities with First Nations people"
     ("Multicultural Bands on the Northern Plains," 125). Innes agrees with Métis scholar
     Brenda Macdougall that "the weight given to Métis European-ness has unfairly
     overshadowed First Nations culture in the emerging Métis cultures" (Ibid., 137). He
     adds that, in so doing, "scholars have erased the significance of First Nations culture
     and the role of First Nations and Métis women on Métis cultural development"
     ("Challenging a Racist Fiction," 106). Innes also agrees with French-Canadian
     scholar Nicole St-Onge, long-time scholar of the Métis, that despite scholars'
     acceptance (since the 1980s) of supposed Métis endogamous practices, there was a
     high degree of intermarriage across Métis and Saulteaux [and Cree] groups (Ibid.,
     137). In "Challenging a Racist Fiction," Innes explains that many Métis and First
     Nations people have also internalized these misinformed views. He asserts that such
     racist fictions "benefitted the government's aim to undermine Indigenous rights,
     primarily Indigenous land rights, and to keep government costs for Indigenous
     People to a minimum," and that "though the Métis, Plains Cree, Saulteaux, and
     Assiniboine were culturally different from one another, they were not culturally
     distinct from their relatives" ("Challenging a Racist Fiction," 109–110). In his book,
     Elder Brother and the Law of the People, Innes offers historic and contemporary
     examples of cultural overlap, intermarriage, and resulting kinship obligations, for
     instance, the "multicultural composition" and the "flexibility and inclusiveness of
     the Cree, Saulteaux, Assiniboine, and Métis" in Cowessess First Nation (20). The
     Iron Confederacy (also known as the Iron Alliance or the *Nêhiyaw-Pwat*)—a
     confederacy among the Plains Cree, Assiniboine, Saulteaux, and Métis existing on
     the plains from the early 1800s to approximately 1870—is a particularly powerful
     example. (In "Multicultural Bands on the Northern Plains," Innes includes "English
     Halfbreeds" as a distinct category in this confederacy [123].) I return briefly to the
     Iron Confederacy in Chapter 1, note 46.

10   See also McCarthy, *To Evangelize the Nations*; Huel, *Proclaiming the Gospel*; Widder,
     Battle for the Soul; and Fiola, *Rekindling.*

11   Gaudry and Leroux, "White Settler Revisionism"; Gaudry, "Communing with the
     Dead"; Leroux, "Self-Made Métis"; Leroux, *Distorted Descent*; Leroux, "'Eastern
     Métis' Studies"; Leroux and O'Toole, "An Analysis of the MNO's Recognition"; and
     O'Toole, "Wiisaakodewininiwag ga-nanaakonaawaad."

12   Métis National Council, "Métis Nation Citizenship."

13   Ibid.

14   In 2018, the MNC Annual General Assembly passed a resolution putting the MNO
     on probation for one year while its citizenship was reviewed for compliance, and
     demanded that the MNO formally retract its recently unilaterally identified six "new
     historic Métis communities" in Ontario (Mattawa/Ottawa River Métis Community,
     Killarney Métis Community, Georgian Bay Métis Community, Abitibi-Inland
     Métis Community, Rainy Lake/Lake of the Woods Métis Community, and
     Northern Lake Superior Métis Community). Another resolution passed identifying
     the boundaries of the recognized historic Métis homeland, which centre the three
     prairie provinces (Manitoba Metis Federation, "Protecting the Citizens"; see
     Figure 6). Drs. Darryl Leroux and Darren O'Toole, in "An Analysis of the MNO's
     Recognition," examined the six communities and the MNO's supporting research
     and determined that most were not historically part of the Métis Nation; in most
     instances, the "root Métis ancestors" legitimizing the "Verified Métis Family Lines"
     were non-status Indians repurposed as Métis to further the MNO agenda of
     identifying more Métis section 35 rights holders. Only Rainy River/Lake of the
     Woods is accepted by the MNC as part of the historic Métis Nation homeland; in
     fact, this community is regarded as the only historic Métis community in Ontario.
     See Narine, "Claims of 'new' Métis communities in Ontario rejected by MMF's
     research document." In January 2020, the MNC suspended the MNO for failing to
     comply with these resolutions. See Stranger, "Métis of Ontario Suspended." In June
     2019, "self-government agreements" were signed by the federal government with
     the MNO, MN-S, and MNA, who have begun referring to themselves as the "Tri-
     Council." The MMF refused to sign a "self-government agreement," critiquing these
     agreements for failing to truly represent self-government, and (together with the
     MNC) has accused the MNA and MN-S of supporting the MNO in disregarding
     MNC criteria for citizenship and homeland boundaries, thereby compromising
     the integrity of the Métis Nation and leaving it vulnerable to raceshifters. See
     Lamirande, "Three Metis Nations"; Chartier, "The Case against the Tri-Council."
     Unlike these agreements, which identify the MN-S, MNA, and MNO as "Métis
     organizations," the MMF signed a Self-Government Agreement with the federal
     government (in July 2021) which recognizes the MMF as a "Métis government"
     with its own Constitution. See Manitoba Metis Federation, "MMF and Canada
     Sign Historic Self-Government Recognition Agreement."

15   Some Métis people dissatisfied with the governance of a provincial Governing
     Member or the MNC have not reapplied for the new membership card, or have
     never applied for one. These are nonetheless legitimate Métis people if they can
     prove they are descendants of the Métis Nation through genealogy and connection
     to one or more MNC-recognized historic Métis communities—for example, via
     Métis scrip for land. For instance, while most members of L'Union Nationale
     Métisse Saint-Joseph du Manitoba (2020), founded in 1887, are citizens of the
     MMF, some feel that the MMF is not doing enough to meet the needs of French-
     speaking Métis citizens in Manitoba and therefore refuse to get an MMF citizenship
     card. A note on scrip: Métis living in Manitoba during the province's confederation
     in 1870 (which occurred thanks to Louis Riel's provisional government and largely

Métis efforts) were promised 1.4 million acres of land in Manitoba in order to protect existing Métis residence patterns against the flood of incoming White settlers from Ontario. Delays, mismanagement, fraud, and corruption meant that most Métis never received any land, and that the land we were inhabiting was stolen from us and given to White settlers. For more on the Manitoba Act and scrip, see Canada, Manitoba Act; Fillmore, "Half-Breed Scrip"; Murray, "Métis Scrip Records"; O'Toole, "Métis Claims to 'Indian' Title in Manitoba"; Fiola, *Rekindling*; and Chapter 6.

16 *Miigwetch* to the anonymous peer reviewer who pointed this out to me.

17 Fiola, *Rekindling*.

18 Benton-Banai, *The Mishomis Book*; Fiola, *Rekindling*.

CHAPTER 1 – Searching for Our Stories in Oral History

1 See Introduction, n9.

2 Nicks and Morgan, "Grande Cache"; Gilbert, *Entitlement to Indian Status*; Lawrence, *"Real" Indians and Others*; Lawrence, "Identity, Non-Status Indians, and Federally Unrecognized Peoples"; and Fiola, *Rekindling*. Exceptions exist in the 1875 adhesion into Treaty 3 (*Adhesion by Halfbreeds of Rainy River and Lake*) and the Manitoba Act of 1870, referred to by some Métis, including Riel, as the "Manitoba Métis Treaty." Chartrand, "Métis Treaties in Canada," 29; Shore, "The Emergence of the Métis Nation." For more on treaties and the Métis, see Chartrand, "Métis Treaties in Canada."

3 Lawrence, *"Real" Indians and Others*; and Fiola, *Rekindling*.

4 Dickason, *Canada's First Nations*; Gilbert, *Entitlement to Indian Status*; and Fiola, *Rekindling*.

5 While both options extinguished Indian title to land (according to the government), most of the 1.4 million acres of land promised to the Métis in the Manitoba Act (1870) ended up in the hands of White bankers, land speculators, priests, and government officials due to delays, mismanagement, illegal amendments, fraud, and corruption. See Milne, "The Historiography of Métis Land Dispersal"; Augustus, "Métis Scrip"; Fillmore, "Half-Breed Scrip"; Sealey, "Statutory Land Rights"; Sprague, "Government Lawlessness"; Murray, "Métis Scrip Records"; Lawrence, *"Real" Indians and Others*.

6 Despite finally acknowledging Métis Indigeneity and rights in section 35 of the Constitution Act (1982), the federal government often continues to refuse to honour Métis rights unless forced to by the courts. Until *Daniels v. Canada* (2016), the government interpreted section 91(24) of the original British North America Act 1867, which states that the federal government has jurisdiction over "Indians and lands reserved for Indians," in a narrower fashion that only included status Indians on reserves. See RCAP, *Report on the Royal Commission*; Morse and Groves, "Métis and Non-Status Indians"; Fiola, *Rekindling*. An example of rights protected by section 91(24) (and upheld by section 35) are Non-Insured Health Benefits such as dental and vision care, medication, and medical transportation; to date, only Inuit who are recognized by an Inuit land claim organization and First Nations people with registered Indian status are eligible. Canada, Non-Insured Health Benefits for First Nations and Inuit.

7 Canada, *Alberta (Aboriginal Affairs and Northern Development) v. Cunningham*.

8 The Cunninghams, a Métis family registered to and living in the Peavine Metis Settlement in Alberta (one of eight constitutionally protected Métis settlements in Canada, all found in Alberta) obtained Indian status (thanks to newer amendments to the Indian Act) to access medical assistance for an ill family member. The Cunninghams were then removed from the settlement as per the Métis Settlements Act, which prohibits anyone with registered Indian status from living there. The Cunninghams sought a declaration from the courts that the Alberta Métis Settlements Act breached their section 15 equality Charter rights. The Supreme Court disagreed with the Cunninghams, upholding the Alberta Métis Settlements Act. For more on the settlements, see Métis Settlements of Alberta.

9 As of 1951, the "marrying out" clause in the Indian Act (section 12[1]b) stipulated that when a woman with registered Indian status married a man without status (even if he was Indigenous, including Métis), she would automatically lose her status and so would her children (i.e., forced enfranchisement). As of 1985 and 2011, Bills C-31 and C-3, respectively, allowed for the reinstatement of Indigenous women, children, and grandchildren who were stripped of status as a result of sexual discrimination in the Indian Act (Canada, Background on Indian Registration). However, discrimination has persisted. See Green, "Exploring Identity and Citizenship"; Coates, "Being Aboriginal"; Giokas and Groves, "Collective and Individual Recognition in Canada"; Lawrence, *"Real" Indians and Others*; Eberts, "McIvor: Justice Delayed"; and McIvor and Grismer, *Communication Submitted for Consideration*. In 2019, the courts demanded that the federal government remove all remaining sexual discrimination from the Indian Act's identity registration (Canada, Bill S-3).

10 Fiola, *Rekindling*.

11 Siggins, *Riel*.

12 Ibid., 3.

13 Families like the Riels and Lagimodières (Riel's maternal family) were members of the Métis elite and, according to scholar Lesley Erickson, they sought "distinction by fostering close ties with the Catholic clergy. . . . Consequently, they increasingly divorced themselves from the unlettered and unpropertied *engages*, tripmen, hunters, petty traders, and small farmers who made up the majority of the Métis communities at St. Francis-Xavier and Pembina. Métis hunters and their families were only nominally Catholic, they organized their lives around the seasons of the hunt, and they engaged freely in social activities like drinking and dancing, which the clergy deplored" ("Bury Our Sorrows in the Sacred Heart," 22). In 1871, *Le Metis*, a French newspaper in St. Boniface, identified Sara Riel (Louis's younger sister) as "the first missionary from the Métis Nation of Red River" (as quoted in Erickson, "Repositioning the Missionary," 115; "Bury Our Sorrows in the Sacred Heart," 19). She had become the first Métis Grey Nun in 1868 (a few Country-born mixed-race women preceded her, the first being Marguerite Connolly in 1845) (Erickson, "Bury Our Sorrows in the Sacred Heart," 19, 40 n10; "Repositioning the Missionary," 116, 123). Using her knowledge of French, English, Michif, and Cree, Sara taught at the mission in Ile-à-la-Cross beginning in 1871. Erickson notes that "mixed-race women could turn Christianity and missionization attempts to their advantage to pursue distinguished careers at a time when their pivotal fur trade role as women 'in between' was coming to an end" ("Repositioning the Missionary," 134). She elaborates, "A religious vocation, therefore, remained one of the few remaining avenues by which Métis and Mixed-Blood women could achieve social status

independent from a husband or father during the declining decades of the fur trade" ("Bury Our Sorrows in the Sacred Heart," 30). Sara internalized the "nineteenth-century devotional Catholicism, which sought to promote and preserve patriarchy and paternalism in French-Canadian society . . . [and Ultramontanism which] "declared patriarchal principles, medieval devotionalism, and rural living as necessary to the survival of the French-speaking Catholic family," as well as the hierarchical principles of authority: "pope over king, king over man, man over woman" (Erickson, "Bury Our Sorrows in the Sacred Heart," 24–27). "Riel distanced herself increasingly from the Red River Métis and dedicated herself to 'Christianizing' and 'civilizing' the Métis, Cree, and Dene of the North" (Ibid., 20). However, as Erickson notes, Riel also "suffered repeated crises of faith and, at one point, contemplated taking her own life" (Ibid., 20). During a near-death experience, she promised to "rededicate her life to God and to renounce the Riel name" if she recovered; upon recovery, she took the name Sister Marguerite-Marie (Ibid., 34). For more on Sara Riel and the way gender shaped Métis responses to Christianity and colonization, see Erickson, "Bury Our Sorrows in the Sacred Heart," and "Repositioning the Missionary."

14 Here Bawdwaywidun was referencing the fallout from the suppression of Indigenous ceremonies that were made illegal by the Canadian government from 1884 until 1951—though many Indigenous people continued to believe they were illegal for decades afterwards. Some brave individuals and families continued to participate in ceremonies in secret, but many did not teach these ways to the next generation for fear of repercussions against themselves and their loved ones. For more on government repression of Indigenous ceremonies, see Pettipas, *Severing the Ties That Bind.*

15 Eddie Benton-Banai, personal communication with author, 28 August 2018.

16 Ibid.

17 This would be the last time I saw Uncle; he was called home to the spirit world on 30 November 2020. He helped countless people on their spiritual journeys, including me, and he is greatly missed. His spiritual legacy resonates beyond time, including for Métis people, who he said also have a birthright to the Midewiwin. Fiola, *Rekindling.*

18 Interestingly, the family in question comes from Montana, where Riel spent considerable time after he was exiled from Canada. By the late 1870s, Montana was the last place bison herds could still be spotted, making the area attractive to Plains Indigenous peoples, including the Métis. Around this time, Riel intensified his efforts to encourage an Indigenous confederacy in the Plains and tried to persuade powerful chiefs, like Sitting Bull, to join (Siggins, *Riel,* 285–87). Bitter about the broken promises in Manitoba, Riel would gain U.S. citizenship and prepare a petition with 101 signatures, urging the U.S. government to create a "Half-breed reservation" in Flat Willow Creek, along the Musselshell River in Montana (Siggins, *Riel,* 298). The petition was unsuccessful, but Riel stayed in Montana, becoming a schoolteacher at St. Peter's Mission and marrying Marguerite Monet *dit* Bellehumeur. Monet's family was part of a band of Métis who wintered in Montana and had elected Louis Riel as their chief (ibid.); she and Riel had three children, —two did not survive into adulthood and the other died in his mid-twenties. It was from Montana that Gabriel Dumont would petition Riel to return to the region that would become Saskatchewan to resume leadership among the Métis and pressure the Canadian government once again to honour Métis rights. The Northwest Resistance (1885) followed, and as punishment for Riel's efforts to protect Métis sovereignty, Canada took his life.

19 Red Rising Collective, Métis issue (#9), *Red Rising Magazine.*

20 Maria adheres to moontime (menstruation) teachings and restrictions: I was not permitted to help prepare food for others, and she asked me not to go in the main cabin while food was being prepared. Moontime teachings are usually carried orally by aunties and grandmothers and centre on women's power during these cleansing ceremonies and the importance of resting and being served by others during this time. Some worry these teachings have been influenced by patriarchal and misogynistic Christianity and perpetuate (male) control over women's bodies, movements, and sovereignty. For critiques decolonizing menstruation taboos and advocating for body sovereignty, see Simpson, "Indigenous Queer Normativity," and A. Wilson, "Our Coming In Stories: Cree Identity, Body Sovereignty, and Gender Self-Determination," and "Skirting the Issues: Indigenous Myths, Misses, and Misogyny."

21 Maria Campbell, personal communication with author, 24 July 2018.

22 Ibid.

23 Ibid.

24 Ibid. Many Indigenous nations carry pipe teachings, including how the pipe came to the people, how to harvest and carve the stem and pipestone, how to care for it, which medicines to smoke, and for what purposes. Pipe ceremonies can stand on their own, be part of significant occasions (e.g., treaty negotiation), or can occur within more elaborate ceremonies.

25 During her keynote address at the "Rising Up" conference, Maria explained that she was raised in a matriarchal community and spoke of recently translated stories from her Aunt Lita, who lived to the age of ninety-six—one of these was the story of Thunderbird Pipe. Chief Ahtahkakoop (Maria's relative) is said to have carried that pipe; it is now carried by his descendants. This story is told often in Maria's home; she also shared that her family smokes the pipe in offering. Some Métis families, like Maria's, continue to participate in these ancestral ceremonies.

26 Maria Campbell, personal communication with author, 24 July 2018.

27 McCrady, "Louis Riel and Sitting Bull's Sioux," 205.

28 As quoted in ibid., 209. All quotes from historical sources in this book are reproduced as written, retaining original spellings and punctuation.

29 As quoted in ibid., 210. "Brulés," the name of a Sioux band, is not to be confused with the term "Bois-Brulées," which the French called the Michif and some Michif called themselves before the term "Métis" became popular.

30 Barkwell, Préfontaine, and Carrière-Acco, "Métis Spirituality," 185.

31 In Red River at the time Welsh was born, "Métis," or more precisely, "Bois-Brulées" or "Michif," were the terms used to describe Métis individuals with Indigenous and French ancestry who birthed the Métis Nation, and "Halfbreed" was a term for people with Indigenous and English (or Scottish or Icelandic) ancestry who came to be citizens of the Métis Nation. However, Welsh uses "Halfbreed" (never "Métis") for both and refers to people like Gabriel Dumont as his chief when the latter is elected Captain of the Hunt. The term "Halfbreed" did not fall out of favour until after the confederation of Manitoba in 1870. By the 1980s, the name "Métis" had become the most popular and was used to describe Michif and Halfbreeds alike in Western Canada. Today, some folks are returning to the name "Michif," as it more accurately describes our lineage (and distinguishes us from raceshifters who are co-opting the term "Métis"). Given that Weekes's book was first published in 1939, the language is, unsurprisingly, dated.

32 Weekes, *The Last Buffalo Hunter*, 51, 99.

33 As quoted in ibid., 47.

34 Ibid., 47–48.

35 Ibid., 49–50.

36 As quoted in ibid., 51.

37 Ibid., 52.

38 Ibid.

39 Pettipas, *Severing the Ties That Bind.*

40 As quoted in Weekes, *The Last Buffalo Hunter*, 132.

41 Ibid., 133, 134.

42 Barkwell, Préfontaine, and Carrière-Acco, "Metis Spirituality"; Vrooman, "The Metis Receive Sun Dance Song," 187–91.

43 Vrooman, "Many Eagle Set Thirsty Dance," 16; and Barkwell, Préfontaine, and Carrière-Acco, "Métis Spirituality."

44 Vrooman, "Many Eagle Set Thirsty Dance," 16; emphasis added.

45 Ibid., 16; and Barkwell, Préfontaine, and Carrière-Acco, "Métis Spirituality."

46 Vrooman, "Many Eagle Set Thirsty Dance," 16. According to Vrooman in "The Metis Receive Sun Dance Song," the Iron Confederacy was "one of the most significant alliances ever to occur at the centre of the continent ... [because] common interests and shared heritage create the strongest bonds. The Cree, Assiniboine, and Chippewa [Ojibwe] were intermarried. The Michifs shared the blood of each of them from their mother's side" (187). *Dibaajimowin*, a blog written by Kade Ferris (enrolled citizen of the Turtle Mountain Band of Chippewa, North Dakota), shared a post explaining that the confederacy was a military and political alliance of Plains Cree, Plains Ojibwe, Métis, and Assiniboine people and included the following bands: Pembina Band, Little Shell Band, Turtle Mountain Band, St. François Xavier Saulteaux/Metis, Nakawiniul (Wilkie's) Band, Big Bear's Band, Poundmaker's Band, Crazy Bear Band, Canoe Band of Nakota, Four Claws (Gordon) Band, Nekaneet Band, Carry the Kettle Band, Rocky Boy's Band, Montana Band, Muscowequan Band, Beardy's Band, One Arrow's Band, Carlton Stragglers Band, Petaquakey Band of Muskeg Lake, Dumont's Band, Big Bear's Band, Red Stone Band, Maski Pitonew Band, Piche (Bobtail) Band, Moose Mountain group of White Bear Band, Striped Blanket Band, Prison Drum Band, Crooked Lakes group of Cowessess Band, Ochapowace Band, Pasqua Band, Kahkewistahow Band, and Sakimay Band" (Ferris, "Nehiyaw-Pwat"). The blog post explains that the confederacy lost its power as a result of the decline of the fur trade and the collapse of the bison herds after the 1860s, but that members nonetheless "heeded Gabriel Dumont's call to participate in the 1885 rebellion and after the battle of Batoche, they scattered to various areas where they were placed on reserves or settled into other communities" (ibid.). Innes corroborates that the Iron Confederacy seems to have mostly dissolved around 1870; *Elder Brother and the Law of the People*, 61.

47 Spaulding, "Métis Receive Sundance Song," 1.

48 Barkwell, Préfontaine, and Carrière-Acco, "Métis Spirituality"; and T. Belcourt, "Many Eagles Set Song Ceremony."

49 Weekes, *The Last Buffalo Hunter.*

CHAPTER 2 – Combing the Written Record for Our Stories

1   Thompson's *Red Sun* came out after *Rekindling*; I am happy for its existence.

2   Thompson, *Red Sun*, 8.

3   Ibid., 3.

4   According to Woodcock, "Ai-caw-pow" translates to "The Stander." Woodcock, *Gabriel Dumont*, 5.

5   Thompson, *Red Sun*, 3 and 253n24.

6   Ibid., 192, 213.

7   Ibid., 44.

8   Woodcock, *Gabriel Dumont*, 19.

9   Thompson, *Red Sun*, ii.

10   Ibid., 16, 53.

11   Woodcock, *Gabriel Dumont*, 8.

12   Thompson, *Red Sun*, 6, 9. Note, the written historic record often contains a gender bias that excludes women's voices. Gabriel's spirituality was also likely influenced by the women in his life.

13   Ibid., 55–56.

14   Ibid., 56. The story of Gabriel's vision quest was relayed to Thompson via an interview with Élie Dumont, Gabriel's grandnephew, who himself carried two cures, "a compound to stop heavy bleeding and an elixir for heart trouble." Gabriel may have even possessed surgical abilities. Thompson, *Red Sun*, 261n249.

15   Ibid., 145.

16   Campbell, *Riel's People*.

17   Ibid., 22.

18   Thompson, *Red Sun*, 214.

19   Ibid., 240.

20   Ibid., 213.

21   Ibid., 237.

22   Ibid., 229.

23   Ibid., 118. Thompson was gifted a pipestem which he believes may be the original. Ibid, 278n794.

24   Préfontaine, *Gabriel Dumont*, 91. According to Préfontaine, a pipe attributed to Big Bear was bought by the Hobbema Cree at a Montreal auction house and repatriated to their community, where the elders confirmed it had belonged to Big Bear. They later believed the pipe had also belonged to Dumont and should be returned to the Métis; the Métis Nation-Saskatchewan has been trying to repatriate the pipe.

25   I photographed this plaque when I visited the Batoche museum during my stay with Maria Campbell in July 2018. Also of interest is an illustration by Peter Myo titled "Dumont, Gabriel, Smoking Peace Pipe" (2003), wherein Gabriel is participating in a pipe ceremony with five other Indigenous men; everyone is seated cross-legged, in a circle around a fire.

26   Thompson, *Red Sun*, 54.

27   Accounts of Métis using tobacco as an offering can also be found in Kermoal, "Métis Women's Environmental Knowledge," Adese, "Spirit Gifting," Dorion, *Relatives with Roots*, Ghostkeeper, *Spirit Gifting*," and Leclair, "Métis Environmental

Knowledge." In "Métis Women's Environmental Knowledge," Kermoal also discusses gendered intergenerational transmission of medicinal knowledge via Métis mothers and grandmothers. Hodgson-Smith and Kermoal, "Community-Based Research and Métis Women's Knowledge" add that Métis women's medicinal knowledge is often combined with ceremonies and prayer, as they are stewards of the land. Likewise, Dorion's bilingual (Michif/English) children's book focuses on Métis women's connection with land, use of traditional medicines, including tobacco and smudge, and pays homage to Michif spiritual knowledge learned from our Cree and Anishinaabe relatives; it is also a good example of syncretic blending of Indigenous and Christian traditions.

28   Sweat lodges are purification ceremonies where a lodge is built and covered in cloth tarps (formerly animal hides); "grandparents" (rocks) are heated in a fire and brought into a pit in the centre of the lodge. Participants "wash" themselves in the steam and pray. Sundance, perhaps the most demanding of all, is a four-day-and-night ceremony held in the summer (though preparations occur all year long) where dancers sacrifice water, food, and comfort to humble themselves before Creator, seeking blessings and healing for themselves and others.

29   Thompson, *Red Sun*, 50–51, 242.

30   Ibid., 32, 51, 243, 246.

31   Ibid., 135, 176.

32   Ibid., 242.

33   This became the site of the Battle of Batoche, and a cemetery was erected there. Ibid., 117, 140, 203, 248. In 1906, Dumont died of a heart attack; he is buried in the cemetery in the old Sundance grounds. Ibid., 248.

34   Ibid., 177.

35   Ibid., 267n452.

36   Ibid., 134.

37   Ibid., 258n178.

38   Ibid.

39   Ibid., 177.

40   Ibid., 183.

41   Ibid., 134.

42   Ibid., 87, 91, 93; Woodcock, *Gabriel Dumont*, 11, 22, 38.

43   Campbell, *Riel's People*, 19.

44   Ibid., 27.

45   McCarthy, *To Evangelize the Nations*.

46   Ibid., 6.

47   Ibid., 12.

48   Ibid., 12–14.

49   Huel, *Proclaiming the Gospel*, 1996; Payment, *The Free People*, 2009; and Fiola, *Rekindling*.

50   McCarthy, *To Evangelize the Nations*.

51   Ibid., 16.

52   Ibid., 17.

53   Ibid., 18.

54 Anglicans preferred sedentary missions, which they would establish, for example, in St. Peter's.

55 McCarthy, *To Evangelize the Nations*.

56 Ibid., 21–22.

57 Duval, "The Catholic Church," 67–68.

58 McCarthy, *To Evangelize the Nations*, 21.

59 Ibid., 234.

60 Ibid., 29–30.

61 McCarthy, *To Evangelize the Nations*, 30. St. François-Xavier, St. Laurent, Lorette, and Ste. Anne are among the Métis communities selected for this study. Mission schools at Lac Caribou, Duck Bay, and Fort Alexander (outside the "Postage Stamp Province") are not included in McCarthy's list.

62 Duval, "The Catholic Church," 75.

63 Ibid.

64 McCarthy, *To Evangelize the Nations*, 233–34.

65 Duval, "The Catholic Church."

66 Ibid., 76–77; and Fiola, *Rekindling*.

67 Angélique Nolin and Marguerite Nolin, born in Sault Ste. Marie and educated by nuns in Montreal, arrived with the first priests in Red River in 1818 and taught at the first formal Catholic school for Indigenous girls in Red River (St. Boniface) from 1829 to 1834.

68 St-Onge, *Saint-Laurent, Manitoba*.

69 The MMF only accepts genealogies prepared by Le Centre du patrimoine for Métis citizenship applications.

70 The binder contains letters dated to 1860 or later that are mostly political in nature. See Centre du patrimoine, Collection Louis Riel.

71 Duval, "The Catholic Church," 87.

72 Ibid., 70.

73 Ibid.

74 These terms were used by Father Belcourt; see Centre du patrimoine, Fonds Provencher, Cahier H, 31 mars 1818–10 juillet 1848, P-2882–P-3282, pp. 11–13 and 91–92. The terms were also used by other priests.

75 Centre du patrimoine, Fonds Provencher, Lettre à Mr. Bazeault (illegible), Secrétaire pour Msgr. L'Éveque de Quebec, de G.A. Belcourt, Saint Paul des Sauteuse, Août 1841 (94). Emphasis added. All translations of excerpts are mine; any errors are my own.

76 Ibid; emphasis added.

77 Centre du patrimoine, Lettre à La Grandeur Mr. L'Évêque de Québec Bas-Canada, de G.A. Belcourt, Rivière Rouge, 26 août 1836, Saint Paul des Sauteuse. Emphasis added.

78 Centre du patrimoine, Lettre à P.-F. Turgeon, Évêque of Sidyme à QC, Canada, de J.-N. Provencher, St-Boniface, Rivière Rouge, 14 juin 1847, Cahier G, 27 mars 1818–6 juillet 1852, P-2526–P-2881.

79 Paul L. Gareau (Métis) discusses the priests' disappointment in the Métis people's apparent ambivalence regarding Catholicism and the stereotype that "Métis are bad Catholics," explaining that Métis could only be considered "bad Catholics" if one

was using an Oblate definition of Roman Catholicism that upholds Whiteness and settler colonialism. When Métis people failed to uphold the standards of Whiteness via Catholicism, they were viewed as backsliding into racial savagery. Gareau discourages a racialized understanding and instead recognizes agency in Métis relationships with Catholicism in ways that suited them, resisted White settler colonialism, and promoted Métis sovereignty. See Gareau, "Mary and the Métis."

80 Centre du patrimoine, Lettre à Monseigneur Alexandre-Antonin Taché, de Charles Camper, Mission de St-Laurent, Lac Manitoba, 12 septembre 1868, *Les Cloches de St-Boniface*, vol. 25, avril 1936, 102–10. Emphasis added.

81 McCarthy, *To Evangelize the Nations*; Fiola, *Rekindling*; and this volume, Chapter 4.

82 Centre du patrimoine, Lettre à Monseigneur Alexandre-Antonin Taché, de Père Laurent Simonet, St-Laurent, Lac Manitoba, 2 avril 1866, 7. Emphasis added.

83 COVID-19 has meant modifications to ceremonies as a safety precaution; for example, only those who presented proof of double vaccination were permitted to enter the Sundance grounds. We also modified our postpartum ceremonies; normally, extended family and friends would be invited to bear witness.

84 See Fiola, "Prenatal/Postpartum Ceremonies and Parenting as Michif Self-Determination." Readers may also be interested in urban Cree-Métis scholar Kim Anderson's reflections upon her birthing experience, incorporation of medicines, and pondering the ways ceremonies attempt to simulate birth ("New-Life Stirring: Mothering, Transformation and Aboriginal Womanhood").

85 Barkwell, Préfontaine, and Carrière-Acco, "Métis Spirituality," 184.

86 Ibid., 185.

87 Vrooman, "The Metis Receive Sun Dance Song"; Vrooman, "Many Eagle Set Thirsty Dance (Sun Dance) Song." For more on the Iron Confederacy, see Introduction n9, and Chapter 1 n44.

88 Barkwell, Préfontaine, and Carrière-Acco, "Métis Spirituality," 196.

89 Ibid., 197.

90 Leclair, "Métis Environmental Knowledge," 3.

91 Barkwell, Préfontaine, and Carrière-Acco, "Métis Spirituality," 197.

92 Leclair does not adhere to the Métis National Council's definition of "Métis" or boundaries of the homeland in her dissertation.

93 Leclair, "Métis Environmental Knowledge," 98.

94 Ibid., 50.

95 Ibid., 104.

96 Ibid., 143.

97 Ibid., 141–44.

98 Ghostkeeper, *Spirit Gifting*. See Adese, "Spirit Gifting," for an in-depth discussion on Ghostkeeper's book.

99 Préfontaine, Paquin, and Young, "Métis Spiritualism," 1.

100 Ibid.

101 Kumar and Janz, "An Exploration of Cultural Activities," 64. The Métis population examined in the Aboriginal Peoples Survey includes "those who reported identifying as Métis (either as a single response or in combination with North American Indian and/or Inuit). . . . The Métis supplement was designed specifically for the Métis population . . . who identified themselves as Métis and/or who have Métis ancestry."

102 Ibid., 67.

103 Ibid.

104 Flaminio, Gaudet, and Dorion, "Métis Women Gathering," 57.

105 Ibid., 58.

106 Ibid., 63n1; emphasis added. Similarly, as noted earlier, Barkwell, Préfontaine, and Carrière-Acco refer to a "First Nations' post-partum practice" involving the placenta but describe this ceremony as a characteristic of Métis spirituality. "Métis Spirituality," 196.

107 For more on syncretism and Indigenous Christianity, see Treat, *Native and Christian*; Twiss, *Rescuing the Gospel from the Cowboys*; McDonald, *The Black Book*; and Shrubsole, *What Has No Place, Remains*. These sources favour Christianity and are First Nations–focused—they neglect Métis experiences. Particularly disappointing is Shrubsole's book, which reviews contemporary Indigenous religious freedom in Canada but completely ignores the Métis—an example of the ongoing erasure of Métis as Indigenous people.

108 This volume, Chapter 1; and Fiola, *Rekindling*. For more on Métis relationships with Catholicism, see Foran, *Defining Métis*; Freynet, *Red River Mission*; and Gareau, "Mary and the Métis." Gareau cautions against perpetuating a false dichotomy between Indigenous spirituality and Christianity—I comment on this in the final chapter of this book.

109 Barkwell, Préfontaine, and Carrière-Acco, "Métis Spirituality."

CHAPTER 3 – A Métis-Centred Study and Approach

1 Sturm, *Becoming Indian*; Leroux, *Distorted Descent*; Leroux, "'Eastern Métis' Studies"; and O'Toole, "Wiisaakodewininiwag ga-nanaakonaawaad."

2 Michell, "Pakitinâsowin"; Michell, "Offering Tobacco in Exchange for Stories"; Smith, *Decolonizing Methodologies*; S. Wilson, *Research Is Ceremony*; and Kovach, *Indigenous Methodologies*.

3 S. Wilson, *Research Is Ceremony*.

4 I situated myself at the beginning of this book, too. Carol Leclair identifies this as Métis protocol: "[A] standard practice within Metis oral tradition which requires that whoever speaks/writes 'as Metis' identifies themselves and their family, community and place, before continuing on to speak to issues of interest to contemporary Metis." "Métis Environmental Knowledge," 1. She begins her dissertation in this way: "I have decided to begin in a traditional way, as I would speak at a gathering or a ceremony, smudging with sage, and remembering to be grateful to my ancestors and teachers, visible and unseen, animate and inanimate." Ibid., 5. See also Adese, "Spirit Gifting."

5 The late Gerard Lavallée (Chubby) was working in the housing department at the MMF at the time.

6 Fiola, *Rekindling*.

7 Ibid., 12.

8 Fiola, *Rekindling*.

9 Benton-Banai, *The Mishomis Book*; Pitawanakwat, "Bimaadziwin Oodenaang"; Simpson, *Lighting the Eighth Fire*; Simpson, "Oshkimaadiziig, the New People"; and Fiola, *Rekindling*. As noted in the Introduction, the Seven Fires Prophecy predicted the advent of the Midewiwin, the arrival of Europeans, and the resulting devastating consequences for Indigenous peoples. It foretold that during the seventh fire, the Oshkibimaadiziig (New People) would emerge and restore our ancestral ways of life.

10 My adopted father, Mizhakwanagiizhik, a fluent Anishinaabewomin-speaker, explained to me that *mikwayndaasowin* refers to "recalling, or remembering, that which was there before," including "knowledge of our past, and our beginnings" (personal communication with author). The Nêhiyawawin equivalent, *miskâsowin*, means "finding one's sense of origin and belonging, finding 'one's self,' or finding 'one's centre'" (Cardinal and Hildebrandt, *Treaty Elders of Saskatchewan*, 21), or "going to the centre of yourself to find your own belonging" (Kovach, *Indigenous Methodologies*, 179). *Mino-bimaadiziwin* refers to a good, healthy life in balance with Creation (Fiola, *Rekindling*).

11 Dumont, "Journey to Daylight-Land"; Weber-Pillwax, "What Is Indigenous Research?" and Anderson, *Life Stages and Native Women*.

12 Michell, "Pakitinâsowin"; Michell, "Offering Tobacco in Exchange for Stories"; Smith, *Decolonizing Methodologies*; S. Wilson, *Research Is Ceremony*; Kovach, *Indigenous Methodologies*; and Anderson, *Life Stages and Native Women*. Nêhiyaw scholar Herman Michell explains that "when you take something from nature, balance is disrupted. And when balance is disrupted, there is a need for the restoration of harmony" ("Pakitinâsowin," 6). He goes on to say that "when you take a story from a person, you are taking something from that person. You are taking something from nature that leads to the disruption of balance" (9). This occurs when researchers listen to stories shared by participants—offering *asemaa* (tobacco), food, and/or a gift can help restore balance.

13 Dumont, "Journey to Daylight-Land"; Benton-Banai, *The Mishomis Book*; Ermine, "Aboriginal Epistemology"; and Gaywish, "Prophesy and Transformation." I mobilized this by fasting, offering participants *asemaa* and medicine bundles to say *miigwetch*, smudging before interviews and throughout the data analysis, and participating in ceremony often.

14 Fiola, *Rekindling*.

15 Bryman and Teevan, *Social Research Methods*. Quota sampling refers to non-probability sampling, where participants are selected by the researcher in the hopes of hearing from many segments of the population.

16 Ibid.

17 An equal number of participants were male, female, did or did not have Indian status, and ranged in age from twenty-five to seventy-six years.

18 Fiola, *Rekindling*.

19 I caution readers against reproducing biological determinism (defining Métis as simply mixed race) through concepts such as hybridity and métissage. See Dolmage, "Metis, Mêtis, Mestiza, Medusa"; Donald, "Forts, Curriculum, and Indigenous Métissage"; Chambers et al., "Métissage"; and Scott, "Reconciliation through Métissage." Métis are not "hybrids" or half of anything; we are whole and complete beings. Our culture, world view, and nationhood are not mixed or mixed up; we are not confused.

20 LaVallee, Troupe, and Turner, "Negotiating and Exploring Relationships"; Gaudet, "Keeoukaywin"; and Flaminio, Gaudet, and Dorion, "Métis Women Gathering."

21 LaVallee, Troupe, and Turner, "Negotiating and Exploring Relationships," 177. Elder Maria Campbell expressed the same thing to me (Chapter 1); Troupe was staying with Maria while our group visited her in July 2018.

22 Ibid.; emphasis added.

23 Gaudet, "Keeoukaywin," 47.

24 Ibid., 48.

25 Ibid., 50.

26 Ibid., 53.

27 Ibid.

28 Ibid., 54.

29 Ibid., 55.

30 Ibid., 59.

31 Gaudet maintains a gender dichotomy by not considering 2SLGBTQ and non-binary folks.

32 Flaminio, Gaudet, and Dorion, "Métis Women Gathering," 55.

33 Ibid., 57.

34 Ibid., 57–58.

35 Ibid., 58.

36 Ibid.

37 Gaudet, "Keeoukaywin."

38 Ibid., 4.

39 Leclair, "Métis Environmental Knowledge," 107.

40 Ibid., 137.

41 Ibid., 108.

42 Ibid., 13.

43 Ibid., 113.

44 Ibid., 143, 141–44.

45 Barron-McNab, "Métis-Specific Gender-Based Analysis Framework."

46 The principles concern reciprocal relationships, respect, safe and inclusive environments, recognition of diversity, 'research should' (objectives), and Métis context. NAHO, "Principles of Ethical Métis Research."

47 Bartlett, Carter, Sanguins, and Garner, "Case 8."

48 After the *Profile of Metis Health Status and Health Care Utilization in Manitoba: A Population-Based Study* (a.k.a. "the *Métis Atlas*") was published, it was interpreted via Knowledge Network discussion tables, the Knowledge Translation model, and the

"Life Promotion Framework" methodology, which is not culturally specific to the Métis but was adapted for use with the Métis population. Martens et al., *Profile of Metis Health Status.*

49 University of Manitoba, *Framework for Research Engagement.*

50 Bartlett, Carter, Sanguins, and Garner, "Case 8."

51 Flaminio, Gaudet, and Dorion, "Métis Women Gathering."

52 NAHO, "Principles of Ethical Métis Research."

53 One of the anonymous reviewers of this book wondered whether working with a "Métis organization" automatically equated to using a Métis methodology and said they did not think it did. I agree; however, the MMF is the Métis *government* (not an organization) for Manitoba Métis citizens. In this respect, MMCREP can be understood as part of a Métis-specific methodology.

54 The other researcher was a Métis graduate student doing research for her master's degree.

55 The MMF Caucus/Cabinet consists of the Chief Executive Officer (President), the Vice-Presidents and Executives of each Region, and the Spokeswoman of the Infinity Women Secretariat.

56 At this point, efforts were made to sign a MoC between myself, my institution (University of Winnipeg), and the MMF. This process proved to be complex, and legal advice was sought on both sides. Incremental progress was made, but unfortunately, the TSN Department dissolved (as I explain below) before the MoC could be signed. I maintain communication with the former director of MMCREP and continue to enjoy her support—she circulated my poster and invited the VPs to the presentation of findings I held in all six Métis communities, and she provided thoughtful feedback on sections of this book before its publication.

57 Director of the TSN, personal communication with author, 2019.

58 Leclair, "Métis Environmental Knowledge," 138.

59 Ibid., 140. For example, Gloria Campbell, the CR for Duck Bay (suggested to me by the MMF) and I have become friends, going for coffee, calling each other on the phone, and keeping each other in our prayers.

60 Charlie was Chief of the Western Doorway of the Three Fires Midewiwin Lodge but later raised the Minweyweywigaan Midewiwin Lodge, becoming its chief. Recently, the lodge grandmothers also lifted up his youngest son, my little brother, as a chief.

61 Fiola, *Rekindling.*

62 Peterson and Brown, *The New Peoples*; and Devine, "The Plains Metis."

63 Bakker, "'A Language of Our Own'"; Bakker, *A Language of Our Own*; Bakker, "Ethnogenesis, Language, and Identity"; and Crawford, "What Is Michif?" My sisters and I are the first generation within our family who cannot speak Michif, and the third generation who cannot speak Anishinaabemowin (Saulteaux/Ojibwe) and Nêhiyawawin (Cree). Fiola, *Rekindling.*

64 Andersen, *"Métis."*

65 Andersen, *"Métis"*; Gaudry and Leroux, "White Settler Revisionism"; Gaudry, "Communing with the Dead"; Leroux, "Self-Made Métis"; Leroux, *Distorted Descent*; Leroux, "'Eastern Métis' Studies"; Leroux and O'Toole, "An Analysis of the MNO's Recognition"; and O'Toole, "Wiisaakodewininiwag ga-nanaakonaawaad." Leroux, in *Distorted Descent*, identifies three such practices. In *lineal descent*, White settlers trace their genealogy and discover one Indigenous ancestor 200 to 400

years ago. *Aspirational descent* occurs when White settlers refashion a French female ancestor into an Indigenous one. In *lateral descent*, White settlers attach themselves to a historic Indigenous person who is not their own direct ancestor. Leroux's website (raceshifting.com), identifies raceshifters, their organizations (seventy-five plus), and their attempts to get federal recognition as Métis with Métis rights through the courts (over 120 failed cases to date).

66 Canada, *R. v. Powley*. The Powley decision resulted in the ten-part Powley Test.

67 O'Toole, "Wiisaakodewininiwag ga-nanaakonaawaad," 69.

68 Gaudry, "Communing with the Dead."

69 Gaudry and Leroux, "White Settler Revisionism." In an attempt to demonstrate that they are claimed by community, raceshifters create organizations of fake métis (referred to by some as *Fetis*) active on social media. Anyone who questions them gets vilified and accused of lateral violence and genocide against the Métis Nation; this twisted logic and bullying are examples of gaslighting and settler colonial violence.

70 In 2020, a prominent raceshifter was awarded a $200,000 research grant by a national funding agency.

71 Tuck and Yang, "Decolonization Is not a Metaphor."

72 Leroux, in "Self-Made Métis," unearthed court transcripts exposing raceshifting leaders as White supremacists fighting against Indigenous rights before newly identifying as "métis."

73 Leroux, *Distorted Descent*. At the 2019 MMF Annual General Assembly, the Métis Nation citizens in attendance (myself included) were told of the efforts under way (since 2013) to trademark the Métis infinity flag and the name "Métis Nation."

74 I also examined the complex relationship between Métis, registered Indian status, and some non-status Indians calling themselves Métis in *Rekindling*. I continue to have these concerns (Introduction n9) and explore these complex relationships (Chapter 6). However, in this book, when I discuss raceshifting, I do not include non-status Indians—I am referring strictly to White settlers who suddenly claim an Indigenous (especially Métis) identity.

75 Métis National Council, "Métis Nation Citizenship."

76 Barkwell, *The Métis Homeland*. See also Chapter 4, this volume.

77 Leclair, "Métis Environmental Knowledge," 148.

78 *Miigwetch* to the anonymous peer reviewer who helped me come to the following realizations.

79 Adese, "Spirit Gifting," 51.

80 Ibid., 63.

81 Ibid., 51.

82 Ibid., 63.

83 Ibid.

84 Leclair, "Métis Environmental Knowledge," iv.

85 Ibid., 60.

86 Ibid., 146–47.

87 After meeting for the first time and visiting over tea in Gripette's home in St. Laurent, I drove back to Winnipeg and shipped her a copy of my first book upon her request. One month later, she invited me back and accepted my tobacco to

participate. Her knowing my relatives helped build trust between us. Afterwards, when I treated her to a meal at the local restaurant, she proudly introduced me to everyone who walked in: "*C'est la pchit fiiy de Robert et Dorothée [née Guiboche] Normand*; she's writing a book!" (This is the granddaughter of Robert and Dorothée [née Guiboche] Normand!) A year later, I had the opportunity to reciprocate when she invited me to collaborate on a project; we maintain an ongoing friendship.

88 Leclair, "Métis Environmental Knowledge," 146–47.

89 Kovach, *Indigenous Methodologies*, 43.

90 Ibid.

91 Leclair as quoted in Adese, "Spirit Gifting," 53; and Leclair, "Métis Environmental Knowledge."

92 Similarly, I sent sections of my manuscript that were based on our conversation to Elder Maria Campbell and followed up with her colleague Cheryl Troupe. Unfortunately, I have not heard back from Maria. I tried to do the same with Elder Eddie Benton-Banai; however, the care home he lived in was in lockdown during COVID-19. He returned to the spirit world in November 2020. I say *miigwetch* to Midewiwin Rainey Gaywish for reviewing and approving the relevant sections, since she had accompanied me to visit Uncle Eddie and participated in our conversation.

93 Fiola, *Rekindling*.

94 There were two exceptions to the generally positive reception to these presentations: in one case, a man approached me afterwards (he was angry because he was raised Métis and wanted to be Métis but was informed as an adult that he is a non-status Indian) and told me women should not touch the drum—some adhere to this controversial belief, while others critique it as influenced by patriarchal and misogynistic Christianity. In the second case, one CR was unable to join me for the presentation, and six community members arrived to angrily voice their dissatisfaction with the MMF—they mistakenly believed my talk was an MMF event or a Liberal party event (elections were occurring).

95 Michell, "Pakitinâsowin"; Michell, "Offering Tobacco in Exchange for Stories"; Smith, *Decolonizing Methodologies*; S. Wilson, *Research Is Ceremony*; Kovach, *Indigenous Methodologies*; Barron-McNab, "Métis-Specific Gender-Based Analysis Framework"; Martens et al., *Profile of Metis Health Status;* NAHO, "Principles of Ethical Métis Research"; *University of Manitoba,* "Framework for Research Engagement"; FNIGC, "The First Nations Principles"; and *Tri-Council Policy Statement: Ethical Conduct for Research Involving Humans.*

96 LaVallee, Troupe, and Turner, "Negotiating and Exploring Relationships"; Gaudet, "Keeoukaywin"; and Flaminio, Gaudet, and Dorion, "Métis Women Gathering."

CHAPTER 4 – Six Red River Métis Communities

1 Barkwell, *The Metis Homeland.*

2 Several other Métis communities in Manitoba fit this description; however, because of time and financial constraints, I was limited to six.

3 Peterson and Brown, *The New Peoples*; and Howard, *Strange Empire.*

4 Howard, *Strange Empire*, 25–26; and Bell, "The Old Forts of Winnipeg."

5 Henderson, "The Lord Selkirk Settlement."

6 Howard, *Strange Empire*, 28. According to Howard, Pembina had been inhabited since 1780 and is considered "the oldest community in the American northwest";

the first White children in the American or Canadian northwest were born there. From the perspective of many White chroniclers, the arrival of White settlers marks the beginning of "history"; this erases and obscures long-standing Indigenous inhabitation and land rights while justifying White settler presence and reinforcing settler land claims (or theft of Indigenous lands).

7   Manitoba Government, "Postage Stamp Province."

8   Ferris, "The Postage Stamp Province."

9   I am indebted to the late Lawrence Barkwell's *The Metis Homeland* and Martha McCarthy's *To Evangelize the Nations* for much of the history on Métis communities that I share in this chapter. Also, special thanks to genealogist Gail Morin and historian Nicole St-Onge for helping me make sense of the historic census data herein. Census records are notoriously difficult to comprehend due to missing pages; crossed-out entries; faint, smudged, or obscured entries or sections; illegible handwriting; convoluted numbering and totals that do not always add up correctly; phonetic spellings of French and Indigenous names [mentioned below, n53]; and human error. Despite these challenges, it is possible to get a sense of population totals and breakdowns in terms of Métis identity, and often religion and country of origin. See map of communities, Figure 1.

10   Barkwell, *The Metis Homeland*.

11   McCarthy, *To Evangelize the Nations*.

12   Ibid., 52; and Barkwell, *The Metis Homeland*.

13   McCarthy, *To Evangelize the Nations*, 51.

14   Ibid., 55.

15   Ibid.

16   Ibid., 56.

17   Ibid., 61. McCarthy notes that while Darveau reportedly drowned on Lake Winnipegosis, it is more likely he was killed by a Saulteaux person he had angered. More on this at note 65, below.

18   Ibid., 59.

19   "St. François-Xavier, Roman Catholic Parish."

20   Ibid., 68.

21   Ibid., 70.

22   Ibid., 70–71.

23   Ibid., 71.

24   Ibid.

25   See Manitoba Archives, Census Returns for Red River Settlement and Grantown, 1827, Digital Image Number: HB13-002637.JPG, Location Code: E.5/1 (H2-136-1-2), Additional Image Information: Census returns 1827, E.5/1 fos. 9d-10.

26   This represents a seventy-three-person increase since 1844 as mentioned by McCarthy, above. The 1849 Red River Census also includes population information for the Saulteaux Village, the Swampy Village, and other areas. See Manitoba Archives, Council of Assiniboia Fonds, Red River Census 1849, Location P7537/5, Microfilm M160.

27   See Manitoba Archives, Council of Assiniboia Fonds, Red River Census 1870, Location P7537/7, Microfilm M160; see also Council of Assiniboia Fonds, Finding aid for Red River Settlement Census 1870, Location P7539/3.

28　Entries for St. François-Xavier appear in four sections of the census (with other communities' statistics appearing in between these); each named individual is given an entry number and these numbers climb sequentially across every community. The entries (i.e., named individuals with a number in the census) appear as numbers 1 through 744, then 751 through 1464, then 2273 through 2275, then 2284 through 2784 (with communities such as the parish of St. Charles enumerated between these ranges). When the enumerated individuals for St. François-Xavier are added, the total is 1,959; however, when individual entries are counted across all four sections manually, the total is closer to 1,850.

29　When discussing Statistics Canada data, I replicate their use of the term "Aboriginal."

30　Statistics Canada, *Aboriginal Population Profile, 2016 Census.*

31　In the 2016 Canadian Census, Aboriginal identity is based on self-identification as First Nation, Métis, and/or Inuit. Aboriginal identity is more affected than other categories by the incomplete enumeration of certain Indian reserves and Indian settlements in this census.

32　No communities are identified as "Métis communities" in the 2016 Census, even when the Métis population outnumbers all others. This erases Métis history (especially Métis relationships with territory) and ongoing Métis presence in the present.

33　Hourie, "St. Laurent History."

34　Lavallée, "The Métis of St. Laurent"; and St-Onge, *Saint-Laurent, Manitoba.* My ancestors are the Pangmans (and a few Chartrands and Lavallées) from St. Laurent.

35　Hourie, "St. Laurent History."

36　St. Laurent and District History Book Committee, *The Land between the Lakes.*

37　Lavallée, *The Métis of St. Laurent.*

38　McCarthy, *To Evangelize the Nations*, 120–21.

39　Hourie, "St. Laurent History."

40　McCarthy, *To Evangelize the Nations.*

41　As quoted in ibid., 124. Emphasis added.

42　In 1875, a standalone building would be constructed for a school; ever larger school buildings would replace the former in 1888, 1897, 1908, and so on until a collegiate was built in 1961, then a new elementary school in 1970. Pauline Mercier, Sœur, "Reinseignements sur Saint-Laurent, Manitoba," 24–25, 28, 31–33.

43　In 1870, the Manitoban government passed the Public School Act which was meant to safeguard the rights of the French-speaking Catholics of Manitoba, set up a dual school system with Roman Catholic and Protestant superintendents, and recognize both English and French as the official languages of Manitoba. However, when an influx of English-speaking Protestants from Ontario became the majority population, the Manitoba government passed the Manitoba School Act of 1890 which abolished French as an official language and meant that Catholic schools would no longer receive public funding. For years, Catholics took the fight all the way to the Supreme Court of Canada and the Privy Council in England to no avail. Then, in 1896 the Laurier-Greenway Compromise was reached and the following year the Manitoba Schools Act was amended to allow (Catholic) religious instruction between 3:30 pm and 4:30 pm, and to allow for instruction in both English and French when there were two or more French-speaking students. Robert Smith, "The Manitoba School Act of 1890: An Insult to the French Roman

Catholics." A French school was opened again in St. Laurent in 1990. St. Laurent and District History Book Committee, *The Land between the Lakes*, 10.

44 Personal communication, Dorothée Guiboche and Donna Fiola (née Normand), 1 May 2021.

45 McCarthy, *To Evangelize the Nations*, 128.

46 Lavallée, "The Métis of St. Laurent."

47 McCarthy, *To Evangelize the Nations*; and Hourie, "St. Laurent History."

48 Lavallée, "The Métis of St. Laurent."

49 As quoted in Barkwell, *The Metis Homeland*, 188.

50 Lavallée, "The Métis of St. Laurent." Recall that my sisters and I are the first generation in our family who cannot speak Michif, and the third generation who cannot speak Anishinaabemowin (Saulteaux/Ojibwe) and Nêhiyawawin (Cree)— we are the first generation who did not grown up in St. Laurent.

51 Ibid., 91–92.

52 Ibid.

53 Ibid., 93.

54 Hourie, "St. Laurent History."

55 McCarthy, *To Evangelize the Nations*.

56 See Manitoba Archives, Census of the Indian Population of Fond du Lac, 13 December 1857, Location B.72/z/1 fos. 2-3, Microfilm 1M876.

57 This number excludes heads of households themselves, since they are usually duplicated in either the column for husbands or wives (i.e., the head of household is also the husband). The 1857 Fond du Lac Census has nearly illegible handwriting, and names of individuals (heads of households) sometimes include only a first name or a nickname, and the names themselves seem to be in Indigenous and French languages with phonetic spelling and spaces added between syllables.

58 Statistics Canada, *Aboriginal Population Profile, 2016 Census*.

59 Barkwell, *The Métis Homeland*.

60 McCarthy, *To Evangelize the Nations*, 99.

61 Ibid.

62 Again, it is likely there were Métis families present as well, given the makeup of this and surrounding communities as is made clear below.

63 McCarthy, *To Evangelize the Nations*, 108–9.

64 Ibid.

65 Ibid., 117. McCarthy offers the following version of this story: In 1884, Darveau left Duck Bay with Jean Baptiste Boyer and Ignace Emmanuel Odjickajaban (a fourteen-year-old Swampy Cree boy hired by Darveau) and encountered Cetakkwen (a Cree guide previously hired by Darveau; their relationship had soured) and his friend Tcimékatis. Cetakkwen accused Darveau of being a *windigo* (cannibal) and causing an epidemic that hit The Pas; he then killed both Boyer and the boy and had Darveau killed and threw the bodies in the lake to make it look like they drowned. Palmer, in "Camperville and Duck Bay: Part 2," offers another version: Father Darveau's death was the result of Swampy Cree medicine men "who were afraid they'd lose their influence over their people as a result of the new religion of the White men."

66 McCarthy, *To Evangelize the Nations*, 112–13.

67 Ibid., 113; emphasis added.

68 Ibid.

69 Palmer, "Camperville and Duck Bay: Part 1"; and Barkwell, *The Metis Homeland*.

70 Barkwell, *The Metis Homeland*; Barkwell, "Surrender of Duck Bay Reserve." Those who left included Pierre Chartrand, William Chartrand, Joseph Chartrand, Joseph Genaille, Louis Guiboche, Patrice Ferland, François Chartrand, Antoine Bone, Baptiste Chartrand Sr., Baptist Chartrand Jr., Joseph Beauchamp, Edouard Guiboche, Alexis Ferland, and the widow Rosine Ferland.

71 Barkwell, *The Metis Homeland*, 43; Barkwell, "Surrender of Duck Bay Reserve."

72 Barkwell, *The Metis Homeland*; Barkwell, "Surrender of Duck Bay Reserve."

73 Palmer, "Camperville and Duck Bay: Part 1."

74 Eight boys ran away from the school at once, in 1928; children also tried to burn the school down at various times. For a list of children who died while attending the school, see National Centre for Truth and Reconciliation (NCTR), "Pine Creek Residential School." For photos of the school before it was demolished, the field where it once stood, and a commemorative monument, see Manitoba Historical Society, "Pine Creek Indian Residential School."

75 The day school was destroyed by arson in 1972 and rebuilt. Palmer, "Camperville and Duck Bay: Part 1."

76 McCarthy, *To Evangelize the Nations*, 114.

77 The St. Boniface Archives do not have historic population counts for Duck Bay, either.

78 Here, a cautionary note in the census warns readers about a discrepancy in Aboriginal identity population and overall population.

79 Palmer, "Camperville and Duck Bay: Part 1"; and Barkwell, *The Metis Homeland*.

80 Barkwell, *The Métis Homeland*.

81 Palmer, "Camperville and Duck Bay: Part 1"; and Barkwell, *The Metis Homeland*.

82 Barkwell, *The Metis Homeland*.

83 McCarthy, *To Evangelize the Nations*, 128.

84 Barkwell, *The Metis Homeland*.

85 Personal communication, Ron Richard, 1 May 2021.

86 Barkwell, *The Metis Homeland*.

87 The St. Boniface Archives do not have historic population counts for Camperville, either.

88 Statistics Canada, *Aboriginal Population Profile, 2016 Census*.

89 The Aboriginal population count appears higher than the overall population for Camperville. Here, the 2016 Census does not offer an explanation for the discrepancy but offers a caveat cautioning readers to also refer to the 2011 population count amendments. Statistics Canada, *2011 National Household Survey*.

90 Barkwell, *The Metis Homeland*.

91 McCarthy, *To Evangelize the Nations*; and Barkwell, *The Metis Homeland*.

92 McCarthy, *To Evangelize the Nations*, 198.

93 Barkwell, *The Metis Homeland*.

94 Except Père (Father) Morin, who likely moved there after the 1852 flood.

95 McCarthy, *To Evangelize the Nations*, 189–200.

96 Ibid., 202.

97 Ibid; and Barkwell, *The Metis Homeland.*

98 McCarthy, *To Evangelize the Nations.*

99 Ibid., 208.

100 McCarthy, *To Evangelize the Nations*, 208, 210.

101 McCarthy, *To Evangelize the Nations*; and Barkwell, *The Metis Homeland.*

102 Barkwell, *The Metis Homeland*, 183–84.

103 McCarthy, *To Evangelize the Nations*, 204.

104 Quoted in ibid., 205.

105 Ibid., 205–6.

106 Ibid.

107 This is another example where numbers do not properly add up. See Manitoba Archives, Council of Assiniboia Fonds, Red River Census 1870, Location P7537/7, Microfilm M160; see also Finding aid for Red River Settlement Census 1870, Location P7539/3.

108 Statistics Canada, *Aboriginal Population Profile, 2016 Census.*

109 Barkwell, *The Metis Homeland*, 150. According to Barkwell, Petite Pointe des Chênes had its name changed to Lorette by Bishop Taché to honour a priest in France who made a sizeable donation to the St. Boniface Cathedral.

110 Ibid., 150.

111 Lorette History Book Committee, *Paroisse Notre-Dame de Lorette*, 2.

112 Ibid., 2–3.

113 Ibid., 3.

114 Ibid., 3–4.

115 Ibid., 3.

116 Barkwell, *The Metis Homeland*, 150.

117 Lorette History Book Committee, *Paroisse Notre-Dame de Lorette*, 17.

118 Ibid., 5.

119 Ibid.

120 Lorette History Book Committee, *Paroisse Notre-Dame de Lorette*, 46; The Sisters of Saint Joseph of Saint-Hyacinthe, "Lorette."

121 Lorette History Book Committee, *Paroisse Notre-Dame de Lorette*, 17. Julie Reid, an archivist from the St. Boniface Archives, helped me locate a census taken in Lorette in 1910 by the parish priest (0075/L20412-L20448). According to Julie, "these were French-Canadian families only. They would all have been francophone and Catholic. He counted 92 families with a total population of 516. He does not mention if any of them were Métis. This document is in the Archdiocese of Saint-Boniface's archives and has not been digitized." Reid, personal communication with author, 15 October 2020. See Louis-Philippe-Adélard Langevin Series, Corporation Archiépiscopale Catholique Romaine de Saint-Boniface, Fonds # 0075, Centre de patrimoine. However, I find it difficult to believe that there were only French-Canadian families living in Lorette in 1910 (or that the priest would have only enumerated French-Canadian families and excluded Métis families) since the community was founded by Métis families, Father Fillion noted a dominant Métis population in 1874, and Métis families still live there today.

122 Recall that the 2016 Census cautions that statistics for Aboriginal identity can be unreliable and contain inconsistencies resulting from incomplete enumeration, among other issues.

123 Métis children were more likely to attend day schools than residential schools because of the government's differential treatment of Métis and First Nations children in their overall agenda of forced assimilation. Despite this, many Métis children did end up in residential schools. Those who attended day schools had the same clergy as teachers, were subjected to the same forms of abuse and assimilation, and experience the same struggles with intergenerational trauma as those who attended residential schools. However, day schools were excluded from the Truth and Reconciliation Commission, and the Indian Residential School Settlement Agreement of 2006; though class action lawsuits are underway. Truth and Reconciliation Commission (TRC), "Residential School Locations"; University of British Columbia, "Indian Day Schools." For a more detailed discussion on this matter, see Chapter 3 in Fiola, *Rekindling*; Chartrand, Logan, and Daniels, *Métis History*; TRC, *Canada's Residential Schools*; and, Chapters 7 and 9 below.

124 McCarthy, *To Evangelize the Nations*, 99.

125 Ibid., 104.

126 Ibid., 112–13. Manitoba House was an HBC trading post with an adjacent Métis community called Manitoba House Settlement until 1889 when it became known as Kinosota. Barkwell, "The Metis Homeland," 128.

127 McCarthy, *To Evangelize the Nations*, 124. Emphasis added.

128 Ibid., 113.

129 Centre du patrimoine, Lettre à Monseigneur Alexandre-Antonin Taché, de Charles Camper, Mission de St-Laurent, Lac Manitoba, 12 septembre 1868, *Les Cloches de St-Boniface*, vol. 25, avril 1936, 102–10. Emphasis added.

130 McCarthy, *To Evangelize the Nations*, 113–14.

131 Ibid., 114.

132 Lorette History Book Committee, *Paroisse Notre-Dame de Lorette*, 17.

133 Barkwell, *The Metis Homeland*.

CHAPTER 5 – Meeting the Participants

1 Twenty-seven people accepted a tobacco tie. On three occasions, when I was on my moontime, I did not offer it in case this would have been disrespectful toward their own teachings; on two other occasions, I was unable to offer tobacco because the interviews were done via Skype. Twenty-two people smudged; five individuals declined for their own reasons, three times I did not offer because I was on my moontime, another individual smudged before I arrived at his house (the beautiful smell still lingered), and in one instance, smudging was against the fire code in the participant's office. Some of these communities are illustrated on the map (see page xi).

2 One CR conducted four interviews in her community, and another CR conducted one interview. I conducted the remaining twenty-seven interviews.

3 More specifically, one participant was under twenty, one was in their twenties, seven were in their thirties, four were in their forties, seven were in their fifties, another seven were in their sixties, four were in their seventies, and one was over eighty.

4 However, Ron maintains a home in his Métis community of Camperville (he was the CR for that community) as well as one in Winnipeg.

5 The order in which I discuss the six communities in this chapter is from the farthest north to the closest in geographic proximity to Winnipeg.

6   Four of the six interviews for St. Laurent were conducted by Jacinthe Lambert, the CR for that community; I conducted the remaining two.

7   Fiola, *Rekindling*.

8   Ibid.; Statistics Canada, *2006 Aboriginal Population Profile*; and Statistics Canada, *2011 National Household Survey*.

9   Peters, Stock, and Werner, *Rooster Town*.

CHAPTER 6 – Métis Family Relationships with Land, Language, and Identity

1   Métis communities mentioned by the participants included: Ashern, *Boggy Creek, *Eddystone (formerly Cayer), Ile des Chênes, *+Kinosota, Prairie Grove, Richer (formerly Coteau-de-Chênes, then Thibaultville), *Roblin area, Ross, *San Clara (formerly Ste. Claire), *Ste. Agathe (formerly Petit Point au Roches, Pointe à Grouette, or Petite Pointe à Saline), *St. Ambroise, *St. Boniface, *+St. Eustache (formerly Baie St. Paul), St. Lazare, *+Ste. Madeleine, St. Malo, *+St. Norbert (formerly Rivière Sale), *+Ste. Rose du Lac, *St. Pierre(-Jolys), *St. Vital, and *+Turtle Mountain region. (Communities with "+" appear on map, page xi.) Most of these communities are corroborated as historic Métis Nation communities according to Barkwell, *The Metis Homeland* (denoted by * above) and remain identifiable as such today. A few communities also have a large French population and may be identified by some as "French communities," especially contemporarily; however, they were established on Métis land and Métis inhabitation preceded French settlement.

2   For more on the history and destruction of Ste. Madeleine from the perspective of Métis inhabitants, see Zeilig and Zeilig, *Ste. Madeleine*; and Herriot, *Toward a Prairie Atonement*.

3   The Municipality of Ellice-Archie's website indicates that St. Lazare began as a Catholic mission and that "in 1900, Father Favreau conducted a census of the mission, the census which included men, women and children was 89 families, 456 souls in all broken down as follows. Métis 342, French Canadians 34, French 15, Irish 30, Scotch 19 and Germans 18." See Rural Municipality of Ellice-Archie, "History of St. Lazare."

4   This was land occupied and travelled by Métis located on the historic Dawson Trail (just north of Lorette), where, according to the tourism website for Prairie Grove, settler families were given land to form a community "in the middle of the land set aside for Métis grants"; soldiers brought in to quash the Red River Resistance (1869–70) also took up land nearby. See Treasures of the Dawson Trail, "Prairie Grove."

5   I did not inquire beyond their grandparents' generation; however, it is likely that even earlier generations lived in the same communities—some possibly since the community's origins in the early 1800s (as is the case for my Métis family and the community of St. Laurent).

6   Recall that scrip was supposed to distribute the 1.4 million acres of land that had been promised to Métis in the Manitoba Act of 1870. It was a lottery system of land allotment whereby Métis would receive a coupon for land or money in their name; however, for many reasons (including delays and fraud), most Métis were swindled out of their land, with many feeling forced to sell their land for far less than its value. My family has two dozen scrip—explained to my ancestors in Saulteaux,

Cree, "Indian," and French; we do not know what became of them. For an example of Métis scrip explained to my ancestor Marie Desjarlais (from Oak Point, which neighbours St. Laurent) in the Saulteaux language, see Figure 24.

7   Remember that each community had six participants except Ste. Anne and Lorette, which had four each.

8   For more on the history of treaties and scrip, as well as similarities, differences, and overlap in experiences of Métis and status Indians, see Fiola, *Rekindling*.

9   Jules may be mistaken about the year being 1828, since the Manitoba Act was signed in 1870 and the first Métis scrip were issued in 1876.

10   *Miigwetch* to University of Manitoba Press acquisitions editor Jill McConkey for reminding me that Louis's comparison of Métis to dandelion seeds blown in the wind is reminiscent of how Métis Elder Maria Campbell's spiritual teacher compared Métis to scattered puzzle pieces, as a result of colonization. Maria explains:

> One day he was talking to me about *wahkootawin*, about our foundational philosophy, the foundation of our culture and our governance structure, and I was having a hard time wrapping my head around all this, and he said it's like this puzzle, this thing that you do with your kids. He said, "If I picked this up," and he picked it up—because we had it all finished and were ready to hang it on the wall—and he picked it up and he lifted it up, a way up, and then he tossed it in the air and it flew into one million pieces. I don't remember how many pieces were in that puzzle but it looked like one million, and pieces flew all over there, bouncing all over the place and bouncing off the wall and the ceiling. EVERYWHERE! My kids were all shocked. And he said, "That's what happened to us Metis, to our history, to our kin"— talk about understanding it. He said it was like somebody came and they just threw us all up in the air and all these pieces flew all over, and he said we had nothing left: they took our land, our livelihoods, put our kids in foster homes, residential schools, and everyone was all over. But he said people like you, you might have two or three pieces, and your friend over there might have one and that one over there has got six, and he said you come together and you start to rebuild the puzzle and pretty soon you have it all done and it'll be all there. And he said that's what happened with *wahkootawin*—it all broke up—but, he said, don't give up because we can put it all back together." As quoted in Thistle, "The Puzzle of the Morrissette-Arcand Clan," 2.

In "We Need to Return to the Principles of Wahkotowin," Campbell explains the concept of *wahkootawin* as follows:

> Today it is translated to mean kinship, relationship, and family as in human family. But at one time, from our place it meant the whole of creation. And our teachings taught us that all of creation is related and inter-connected to all things within it. Wahkotowin meant honouring and respecting those relationships. They are our stories, songs, ceremonies, and dances that taught us from birth to death our responsibilities and reciprocal obligations to each other. Human to human, human to plants, human to animals, to the water and especially to the earth. And in turn all of creation had responsibilities to us. (5)

11   See Chapter 1 n9.

12   Brenda later added the following details: "My mom's family originates from Key First Nation, Saskatchewan, Duck Bay and St. Laurent [Manitoba] and my father's

family from Duck Bay, Sandy Bay First Nation and St. Laurent [Manitoba]." Personal communication, 3 May 2021.

13 See Chapter 4, notes 69 to 72.

14 It can also be noted that Duck Bay is the home community of David Chartrand, who has been President of the MMF for twenty-four years; his family members also occupy leadership positions within the MMF governance structure.

15 See Introduction, n9.

16 Linguists recognize Michif as a distinct Indigenous language that emerged among Métis people in the early days of Métis ethnogenesis; it is a blend of mostly Cree verbs and French nouns (and sometimes Saulteaux words). There are different dialects of Michif, with some that rely more heavily on Cree or French. See works by Bakker in the bibliography.

17 Bakker, "Ethnogenesis, Language, and Identity"; Bakker, *A Language of Our Own*; Bakker, "A Language of Our Own"; and Crawford, "What Is Michif?"

18 George may be referring to Heather Souter (Michif), a well-regarded Michif language instructor who resides in Camperville with her husband and teaches Michif classes at the Universities of Manitoba and Winnipeg.

19 Chandler and Lalonde, "Cultural Continuity"; McIvor, Napoleon, and Dickie, "Language and Culture as Protective Factors"; and Whalen, Moss, and Baldwin, "Healing through Language."

20 Of these, seventeen said "Métis" only; one said "Michif" only; two said "Métis and Halfbreed" (one of these also said "Apitowgoshaanuk"); another two said "Michif and Métis"; and one said "Halfbreed" only.

21 One person's adopted family identified as English/White Anglo-Saxon Protestant (WASP); another's as White Catholic; and one person indicated that some family members self-identified as White and others as Métis.

22 There was overlap between the categories—some family members identified with more than one term, or different family members used different terms. Such overlap appears in some of the other findings as well. It is also the case that some responses are not reflected in the findings chapters of this book—there was simply too much data to discuss every response; therefore, only larger patterns (and occasionally, unique and telling deviations from these) are shared.

23 Six people indicated no change over time, and four mentioned having at least one family member who had obtained Indian status and currently identified as that instead of, or in addition to, being Métis. Several others also discussed family members obtaining status, but this did not alter their ongoing self-identification as Métis (or at least as Métis and Cree/Saulteaux/First Nation).

24 Barbara later added that they all knew they were Métis, so no one felt the need to voice it.

25 See Chapter 8, note 3, for a discussion of the term "Apitowgoshaanuk."

CHAPTER 7 – Métis Family Relationships with Culture and Religion

1 Smaller themes mentioned in connection with Métis culture included Catholicism; Métis culture as a lived reality; Métis culture existing underground, as private or hidden because of internalized racism and shame; involvement with Métis organizations and governance; poverty; Métis clothing; storytelling; medicines; and sports.

2 Thirty-five percent of those who identified subsistence activities as an important aspect of their family's relationship with Métis culture mentioned a decrease in this aspect of their relationship over time.

3 Smaller themes relating to family relationships with First Nations cultures included intermarriage, friends, sports, Catholicism, school, powwow , family stories, foster care (assimilation and strained relationships with First Nations), employment, subsistence activities, poverty, ceremonies and medicines, and embracing diversity.

4 Eight others indicated no change in their family's relationship with First Nations cultures.

5 "Racism" was the term used by participants. However, the definition of racism recognizes that it is about power and oppression, and is systemic and ubiquitous. As a collective, Indigenous people do not have access to the systems of power that maintain status quo; therefore, they cannot be racist toward other Indigenous people. More accurate terms are *discrimination* and *lateral violence*; the latter occurs when individuals in a minority group lack the power to lash out at their oppressors and so lash out within or across their own peer group when frustrations boil over. This behaviour is common in countries with a history of ongoing colonization, oppression, and intergenerational trauma. For more on these concepts, see Native Women's Association of Canada, "Aboriginal Lateral Violence"; and Bombay, Matheson, and Anisman, *Origins of Lateral Violence*.

6 Other smaller patterns or unique responses with respect to Euro-Canadian culture included family, employment, "White institutions," urbanity, adoption, foster care, and intermarriage.

7 For more on the shortcomings of Métis representation in mainstream curriculum, see Fiola, *Rekindling*, and Fiola, "Expanding Métis Curriculum."

8 For a documentary depicting the phenomenon of overcoming shame about one's Métis identity (and acknowledging one's Métis identity after identifying as French Canadian due to internalized racism for so long), see Wookey and Wookey, *Mémére Métisse*.

9 One person also identified grandparents who were Methodist, Baptist, Anglican, and "not Catholic." Not every participant discussed their grandparents.

10 By the time they were adults, the other three participants who grew up in the child welfare system had located their biological families, which were all Roman Catholic. Two people also mentioned their family's religious identification as Anglican, and one each mentioned Protestant, Lutheran, Mennonite, United Church, "anti-Catholic," and atheist. Sometimes one parent was Christian and the other was not, or each parent adhered to a different denomination of Christianity. For instance, George (Duck Bay) shared that his father was Protestant but had converted to Catholicism upon marrying George's mother. Family affiliations other than Catholicism were mentioned as follows: Duck Bay—Protestant and Lutheran; Lorette and Ste. Anne—Anglican; and St. François-Xavier—Mennonite, United Church, atheist, and anti-Catholic. No denominations other than Catholicism were identified by participants from Camperville and St. Laurent.

11 Of these, Louis's mother was the only one to attend a residential school as opposed to a day school. Later, we learn that Bobbie-Jo's (St. Laurent) father and George (Duck Bay) are also residential school survivors (Chapter 9).

12 While there was overlap between these two groups, not every individual who noted a decline in their family's relationship with the church mentioned their family's

participation in Indigenous spirituality. Eight people said their family's relationship with religion or spirituality had not changed over time.

13 *Ruugaruus, rugarus, roogaroos* are variations in spelling the Michif pronunciation; the term translates in French to *loup-garoux* and in English to "werewolves." *Maarsii* (thank you) to Michif language teacher Heather Souter for providing assistance with spelling.

14 See Chapter 4, note 123.

15 *Windigo* is understood (especially by Michif, Nêhiyawak, and Anishinaabeg) as an insatiable cannibal person or spirit. I've also heard Western or dominant culture described as *windigo* because of capitalism's insatiable greed, materialism, and consumption despite the social and environmental toll this is taking.

16 By community, the percentage of people who discussed a decrease or total cessation in their family's participation in the church was as follows: 83 percent in Duck Bay; 75 percent in Lorette; 50 percent in Camperville and in Ste. Anne; 33 percent in St. François-Xavier; and 17 percent in St. Laurent. Of those who indicated no change in their family's relationship with spirituality, 50 percent were in Camperville and St. François-Xavier and 17 percent in Duck Bay and Lorette.

17 By community, the percentage of people who indicated an increase in their family's relationship with Indigenous spirituality was 100 percent in St. Laurent; 75 percent in Lorette; 50 percent in St. François-Xavier and Ste. Anne; 33 percent in Duck Bay; and 17 percent in Camperville.

18 Fiola, *Rekindling*, Chapter 3.

CHAPTER 8 – Exploring Self-Identification

1 Ten people also used the term "Cree," five used "Anishinaabe," four used "Saulteaux," two used "Ojibwe"—there was overlap in use of these terms. In addition to Cree and Anishinaabe terms, four individuals also identified as (non)status/treaty, two as Canadian, and one each as the following: Sioux, Chipewyan, Indigenous, Aboriginal, First Nation, Traditionalist, mixed, two-spirit and transgender, Mennonite, and human. One person also shared their spirit name and clan at this point, and another described themselves as "person, Creator's child, and Mother Earth's child."

2 Below is a list of unique term combinations used by some of the Métis people in this study:
   • Métis-Cree and Ojibwe/Anishinaabe
   • Cree, Ojibwe, and Métis
   • Anishinaabe/Saulteaux, Nêhiyawak/Cree, Michif/Métis, and Sioux
   • Treaty, Saulteaux Métis, and Cree
   • Métis and treaty
   • Métis and non-status
   • Métis and Cree
   • Métis with Saulteaux and Cree ancestors
   • Métis, and sometimes adding details about ancestry: Cree, Saulteaux, Blackfoot
   • Métis, but also Aboriginal/Indigenous, depending on context
   • Métis with Cree and Anishinaabe ancestors; also "mixed"
   • Métis and Mennonite

- Métis, Canadian, Swedish, and Scottish
- Michif; tries not to say Métis; explains ancestry as Anishinaabe/Saulteaux/ Chippewa, Cree, Scottish, and French
- Cree, Saulteaux, Chipewyan, French and Scottish; of the Métis Nation
- Cree and Métis, and sometimes mentioning Euro-Canadian ancestry
- Métis, and lists Indigenous and Euro-Canadian heritages
- Métis but prefers avoiding proper nouns/labels entirely

3   "Apitowgoshaanuk" is a dialectical variation of the pronunciation of *Âpihtawikosisân*. Métis scholar Chelsea Vowel explains that this "is the name the Cree have given to the Métis, and literally translated it means 'half-son.'" See About page on Vowel, *Âpihtawikosisân* (blog). Though no participant used the name "Otipemisiwak" (The Ones Who Own Themselves) when asked pointedly, "How do you self-identify?" I know that at least one person (Barbara, St. Laurent) also uses this term to identify herself and Métis people in general. Interestingly, in response to a recent Facebook post where someone said "Otipemisiwak" is what Cree people called Métis people, well-known Indigenous rights advocate and Métis artist Christi Belcourt replied: "Otipemsiwak is what we [Michif/Métis] called ourselves. In our own Cree language. The root of the word means 'to own' but also 'freedom.' The 'wak' on the end is what makes it a plural 3rd person. It's a Cree word because that is the language we [Michif/Métis] spoke. My grandparents spoke Cree. Cree language isn't seoerate [separate] from us. It is us and we are it. As well as Michif in all of our dialects." Belcourt, "Just a quick clarification," Facebook comment, 10 March 2020.

I agree that Métis people are not separated from the Cree (or Saulteaux/ Anishinaabemowin) language(s), despite being forcibly disconnected via linguistic assimilation. As I mentioned earlier, the Métis were and are a multilingual people and Cree (and Saulteaux/Anishinaabemowin) was one of the languages we spoke and continue to speak (including in my own family). Christi's comment makes me wonder if something similar has occurred with the term "Âpihtawikosisân"—did our Cree relatives give us this name, or is it a name we gave ourselves? Either way, as George and Chelsea illustrate, it is a name that some Métis people have adopted for themselves.

4   Use of the term "Cree" appeared as follows across the communities: two each in Camperville, St. Laurent, Ste. Anne, and Duck Bay (one person in Duck Bay also used the term "Nêhiyawak"), and one each from St. François-Xavier and Lorette. Use of the terms "Anishinaabe/Saulteaux/Ojibwe" appeared as follows across each community: Camperville (one Anishinaabe, one Ojibwe, and one used both); Duck Bay (one Saulteaux, and one used both Saulteaux and Anishinaabe); Lorette (one each for Anishinaabe and Saulteaux); St. Laurent (Saulteaux); and St. François-Xavier (Anishinaabe). No one connected to Ste. Anne used the terms "Anishinaabe," "Saulteaux," "Ojibwe," or "Cree."

5   Upon review, Bethany wanted to add the following: "When I'm saying anti-White, I don't think I had the full vocabulary to explain myself properly. I believe I was saying how many Indigenous people are uncomfortable with their Whiteness given the history of our relationships with White settlers so that's one reason why I feel shame about recognizing my own Métis identity."

6   The following terms were mentioned once each—except when otherwise indicated in parentheses—across each community (sometimes the same participant mentioned more than one term):

- Duck Bay: treaty (2); non-status; Sioux; two-spirit transgender woman

- St. François-Xavier: Canadian (2); Mennonite; mixed
- Camperville: First Nation; status (upon marriage); spirit name and clan
- Ste. Anne: Indigenous; traditionalist; human
- Lorette: Chipewyan; person, Creator's child, Mother Earth's child
- St. Laurent: Indigenous/Aboriginal

7   Self-identification was context specific for two people each in Lorette, Ste. Anne, Camperville, and St. François-Xavier, and for one person each in Duck Bay and St. Laurent.

8   Elizabeth alludes here to the use of DNA testing as problematic. For an explanation of why this is so, see TallBear, "DNA, Blood, and Racializing the Tribe."

9   Ronnie is among the oldest participants in the study and the least connected to Métis culture and ceremonies.

10 Canada, *Daniels v. Canada.*

11 For more on *Daniels v. Canada*, see Andersen and Kermoal, *Daniels v. Canada.*

12 Three people discussed racism as intersectional and inseparable from other forms of discrimination, including transphobia, sexism, and misogyny. The following experiences related to racism were also mentioned by one or two individuals each: threats of violence (including against Indigenous women at sites of pipeline resistance); a hierarchy of Indigeneity; racism perpetrated by members of the RCMP and the army; intergenerational racism; linguistic discrimination; racism at the library; being forced to listen to racist "jokes" because of one's ambiguous appearance; being encouraged to deny one's own Indigeneity; and attempting suicide as a result of lived experiences with racism.

13 Brenda has dedicated her career to bettering ACCESS Programs in universities. Also recall that Ron Richard, mentioned here in Brenda's story, was the community researcher for Camperville; he was also a participant in Fiola, *Rekindling.*

14 The theme of racial hierarchy among Indigenous people also arose in *Rekindling* (84–85).

CHAPTER 9 – Spirituality, Types of Ceremonies, and Disconnection Factors

1   Other characteristics mentioned included powerful and strong; personal and individual; searching and finding; special and sacred; higher power and faith; collectivity; and spirituality as distinct from religion (with the latter being institutionalized). Other values mentioned included humility; acceptance, openness, and fluidity; safety; and sobriety. Some of these themes come up more centrally in later discussions on connection and disconnection factors. Some of the elements I have termed "characteristics" may also fit under "values" or vice versa; the way I have presented them here is just one way of understanding them.

2   The following challenges were also highlighted: internalization of the harmful stereotype that Métis people only go to church and First Nations only go to ceremonies; tensions and struggles around time and familial commitments and finding a balance; longing to be gently corrected after making a mistake in ceremony (instead of harshly, publicly); and colonial divisions between Indigenous and non-Indigenous people.

3   The highest number of distinct ceremonies participated in (one or more times) by a single person was sixteen, followed by twelve ceremonies practised by two people, then one person who practised eleven ceremonies. Only Debbie (St. Laurent) and

Ronnie (St. François-Xavier) had not participated in multiple types of ceremonies; they both continue to identify as Catholic. Recall that Vern (St. François-Xavier) and Jules (St. Laurent) also continue to identify with Christianity; however, they have both participated in more than one type of Indigenous ceremony (sweat lodge and smudging, and sharing circles and smudging, respectively).

4 In decreasing frequency, the following nations' ceremonies were identified: Cree, Ojibwe (Anishinaabe), Peruvian (a "Peruvian tobacco ceremony" and a "Mesa bundle carrier"), Dakota, Lakota, and Blackfoot ceremonies.

5 Interestingly, here Nicki (Lorette) spoke of being a firekeeper and helper at a fast for a two-spirit elder and a two-spirit knowledge holder as they were preparing for an upcoming Sundance. In her own words,

> I was a fire keeper at a fast for Barbara and [her friend] when they were preparing for their. . . . [Sundance]. I think that was four years ago or five maybe. It was the two of them and they were just fasting where Barbara's old sweat lodge was in Anola there on their friends' property, who happen to be two-spirit Métis wives. There were two sweat lodges on that ground, so they each set up their own little bedroll in each sweat lodge. I brought an actual tent and I just stayed in the tent and was fire keeping for them while they did that. I did two days of fire keeping and then [another friend/colleague] came in and did the last two days.

Women are not usually firekeepers as many people hold teachings that this is supposedly "men's work." Two-spirit people often recognize gender roles and norms in ceremony as unnecessarily dogmatic and influenced by patriarchal, heterosexist Christianity and therefore modify them in an effort to honour diverse gender and sexual expressions.

6 This list should not be considered definitive or exhaustive, as folks may have simply not recalled other types of ceremonies they are involved with in the moment they were discussing these. For instance, this is the case for participation in drum ceremonies because neither Charlotte (Ste. Anne) or Nicki (Lorette) mentioned being drum carriers; however, I know they both are. Charlotte (a two-spirit elder) helped us both make a drum. Later, she and Barbara (St. Laurent; another two-spirit elder, and another participant in this study) helped us follow protocol for readying our drums for ceremonial use, including "birthing" them in a sweat lodge and feasting them. We have since helped them build a two-spirit sweat lodge and we bring our drums inside.

7 Some readers may be interested in a more precise breakdown of participant involvement in these ceremonies: 81 percent participate in sweat lodge; 66 percent participate in Sundance; 56 percent participate in smudging; 50 percent use traditional medicines in ceremony; 47 percent participate in pipe ceremonies; 38 percent mentioned receiving their spirit name and spoke about their naming ceremony; another 12 percent explicitly named or identified a particular nation (or region) associated with one or more particular ceremonies; 34 percent participate in fasting and/or vision quest; 28 percent participate in drum ceremonies; 25 percent participate in singing ceremonies and in being on the land harvesting medicines for ceremonies; 22 percent participate in ceremonial feasts and powwows; and 16 percent participate in Midewiwin ceremonies, shake tent ceremonies, and sharing circles. The list of ceremonies that these Métis people participate in is thorough and warms my heart. In fact, additional ceremonies that were mentioned by a few people each included dreams or visions; clan belonging; *Jiibay* (Ghost dance); *Windigokaan*

(Contrary ceremony); syncretic activities (i.e., baptism, and the Native American Church); erecting a lodge on their property; *Yuwipi* (Tie Up ceremony. One person spoke of a "dark ceremony"—this could be a Yuwipi or a Jiibay, as both are sometimes referred to in this manner; however, using this terminology interchangeably should be avoided. *Miigwetch* to traditional knowledge holder Cecil Sveinson for talking with me about this); Indigenous funerals or wake ceremonies; and traditional camps (i.e., healing, spring, fall camps; excluding fasting camps). In addition, the following types of ceremonies were mentioned by one person each: New Moon ceremony; moontime (menstruation) ceremonies; round dances; bison ceremony; Native American Church; Indigenous ceremonial weddings; ayahuasca ceremonies; use of rattles in ceremonies; elders' gatherings; Four Worlds ceremonies; the White Bison Wellbriety Movement; cleansing with cedar and eagle fan; beading as ceremony; two-spirit ceremonies; chicken dance; horse dance; and water ceremonies.

8   For instance, recall that Gabriel Dumont carried the spirit names Red Sun and Buffalo Child and was recognized as belonging to the buffalo clan (Thompson, *Red Sun*, 192, 213, 44), and Louis Riel carried the name *Uneeyen* (Ibid., 267 n452). Moreover, Dumont was put out on a four-day vision quest ceremony before puberty by his father (Ibid., 55–56), used medicines and performed doctoring rites (Ibid., 56), was a pipe carrier and conducted pipe ceremonies (Ibid. 118, 213; Prefontaine, *Gabriel Dumont*, 91), was a firekeeper for sweat lodges, built sweat lodges, and participated in them (Thompson, *Red Sun*, 50–51, 242), and attended Sundances (Ibid., 32, 51, 243, 242, 246).

9   Folks from Camperville indicated they participated in five to eight types of ceremonies; from Duck Bay, between five and nine types; from St. Laurent, between two and twelve types; from St. François-Xavier, between two and sixteen types; from Lorette, between four and eleven types; and from Ste. Anne between nine and twelve types.

10   Linda shared stories about participating in the following ceremonies: sweat lodge, Sundance, smudging, using traditional medicines, naming ceremony, drumming, singing, powwow, sunrise ceremony, having a vision, fasting, full moon ceremony, pipe carrier, Jiibay ceremony, Windigokaan ceremony, and using a rattle as part of her bundle.

11   Other sources of fear, anxiety, and self-doubt included worrying that one did not "fit in" at ceremonies and wondering whether one was "supposed to be there"; not feeling "Native enough" in appearance to be accepted at ceremonies; generalized shyness and anxiety; fear of burning out and taking on too many responsibilities along with the time commitment that comes with ceremonies; difficulty facing one's true self in ceremonies; anxiety over mispronouncing one's own spirit name in an Indigenous language; fearing "bad medicine"; and residual fear and spiritual wounds from when the Canadian government made Indigenous ceremonies illegal, burned lodges and bundle items, and imposed imprisonment or fines. For more on the latter, see Pettipas, *Severing the Ties That Bind*.

12   Such divisions were identified as being fuelled by confusion over who can claim Métis identity and being discouraged from identifying as both Métis and First Nation; unfair criticism that many Métis cannot speak our Indigenous language (Michif) when the same is also true for many First Nations people; the challenge of untangling Métis practices from First Nations practices and being unsure why such practices cannot be recognized as belonging to both; the stereotype that Métis people only go to church despite rumours that even the highest levels of

the Metis governance structure utilize the services of medicine people; Métis people assimilating into a "White world view"; being made to feel there was no room for Métis people in ceremonies when these began returning in the 1970s and '80s; and being (Red River) Métis but living in Quebec and having to navigate misinformation about Métis people in eastern Canada.

13 Several other disconnection factors were mentioned by six or fewer people each (in decreasing order): lack of opportunity and connection to ceremonies; lack of family support; struggles with alcohol and drugs; poor health (e.g., cancer, chronic headaches); traumatic experiences (e.g., death, sexual abuse, rape and resulting abortion and divorce); seeing others fall off the Red Road (spiritual path); moving away (e.g., spiritual mentor or ceremonial friends moving away, or having to move away from one's spiritual community); the foster care system; being "White coded" (being mistaken for White, not accepted by First Nations people because of light skin colour or being Métis, or being silenced by a First Nations person with an implicit accusation of appropriation); racism; work responsibilities and burnout; financial challenges or poverty; homelessness; gang involvement; living in a White neighbourhood; not knowing one's Indigenous language; government; transportation challenges; difficulty with genealogy (specifically the fact that Indigenous women are often unnamed in the records); and the MMF inhibiting Métis people from finding their way back to ceremonies. The only person who said they have never experienced any factors that discouraged their participation in ceremonies was Jules (St. Laurent).

14 These folks were Anungoohns, Brenda, Louise, and Karen (Camperville); George, Ray, Lightning Rattle Woman, and Whistling Eagle Child (Duck Bay); Barbara, Debbie, and Gripette (St. Laurent); Linda and Nancy (St. François-Xavier); and Charlotte and Louis (Ste. Anne).

15 This was discussed by Maryanne, George, and Whistling Eagle Child (Duck Bay); Bobbie-Jo, Lucille, and Barbara (St. Laurent); Brenda and Karen (Camperville); and Louis and Charlotte (Ste. Anne).

16 The Pine Creek Residential School was located in Camperville from 1890 to 1969; the school and surrounding farmland covered 632 acres. Eight boys ran away from the school at once, in 1928; children also tried to burn the school down at various times. When the Roman Catholic mission could no longer finance the school, they turned it over to the government who continued its operation but as a day school. For a list of children who died while attending the school, see National Centre for Truth and Reconciliation (NCTR), "Pine Creek Residential School." For photos of the school before it was demolished, the field where it once stood, and a commemorative monument, see Manitoba Historical Society, "Pine Creek Indian Residential School."

17 More specifically, these were Elizabeth, Denise, and Linda (St. François-Xavier); Nicki, Andrea, and Bethany (Lorette); Justin and Amanda (Ste. Anne); Maryanne and Lightning Rattle Woman (Duck Bay); and Karen (Camperville).

18 This was the case for Brenda and Karen (Camperville); Maryanne and Whistling Eagle Child (Duck Bay); Denise and Elizabeth (St. François-Xavier); and Louis (Ste. Anne). This issue also arose in *Rekindling*.

19 Negative experiences at ceremonies were mentioned by Nicki, Andrea, and Bethany (Lorette); Barbara and Lucille (St. Laurent); Maryanne and George (Duck Bay); Louis (Ste. Anne); and Denise (St. François-Xavier).

CHAPTER 10 – Spiritual Connection Factors, Impacts upon Identity, and Others' Reactions

1   Specific family members identified included grandparents, mothers, wives, children, sisters, extended family relatives, and a relative through marriage; Jason spoke movingly about his Métis stepfather.

2   In addition, the following categories of people were each mentioned by three or fewer people: teachers and mentors (e.g., Métis professor, and a traditional knowledge holder who happens to also be a friend); Indigenous people (excluding the categories already mentioned, so non-biological grandmothers, Indigenous women, and Métis women specifically); and non-Indigenous allies.

3   Besides conferences, the following places were identified: reserves (Moose Factory Cree Nation, the Turtle Lodge in Sagkeeng First Nation, and Little Saskatchewan First Nation); Indian and Métis Friendship Centres; the city; Indigenous healing centres (especially those specializing in recovery from sexual abuse); The Forks (Winnipeg); Thunderbird House (in Winnipeg); land or property to conduct ceremonies on; and Indigenous organizations (in Winnipeg). Upon reviewing her transcript and quotes, Denise added the following: "While living in Tucson, I was fortunate to be invited to join a traditional drum group, all the members were ceremonial people, most were Sundancers. They invited me to *inipi* (sweat lodges) and it was there that I felt like I was home. They also invited me to support/sing at various Sundances, which were powerful, healing experiences for me."

4   Connection factors identified by six or fewer people included employment (especially in Indigenous-specific organizations and/or Indigenous-specific jobs); Indigenous resurgence and the Indigenous Sovereignty Movement (e.g., the American Indian Movement); dreams or visions; sobriety; a feeling of searching or longing; syncretism (blending Christianity and Indigenous spirituality); learning about one's Indigenous identity despite growing up in the child welfare system; spiritual awakening; society unlearning stereotypes regarding Indigenous people; and use of bundle items and traditional medicines.

5   This was the case for five people each in St. Laurent and St. François-Xavier, for four people in Camperville, everyone in Lorette, and for three people each in Ste. Anne and Duck Bay.

6   Mae Louise Campbell appears as a Métis participant in my first book, *Rekindling the Sacred Fire.*

7   This was the case for two people each from Ste. Anne, St. François-Xavier, and Duck Bay, and for one person each in Camperville, St. Laurent, and Lorette.

8   As we have seen a couple of times with other participants, Jules seems to have internalized the belief that ceremonies are specifically First Nation (not Métis).

9   Three people from Camperville, two each from St. Laurent and St. François-Xavier, and one from Lorette discussed this.

10 Lest raceshifters latch on to the "one drop of Indigenous blood" notion to fuel their co-optation of Indigenous identity, I remind readers that the participants in this study are all Métis today because they are descended from Métis ancestors and connected to legitimate (historic) Métis communities. Notions such as blood memory are sometimes useful to understand powerful connections to our Métis ancestors and Métis communities that persist despite the legacy of colonization. This is not to be confused with using "blood memory" as a justification for claiming an Indigenous identity, despite only having a single Indigenous ancestor in one's family lineage over a 200-year span.

11 Five people each from Camperville and Duck Bay, four people each from St. Laurent, St. François-Xavier, and Ste. Anne, and three people from Lorette replied in this way.

12 A few people also spoke of a heightened sense of purpose or path in life; confidence in knowing that Métis people also participate in ceremonies; thinking differently; Métis pride; a deeper understanding of self; humility; issues around safety; and ongoing internalized self-doubt regarding one's own Indigenous identity.

13 Other family reactions included no aversion/discouragement/neutral; curiosity; unsurprised/expected; respectful; proud; and one (non-Indigenous) husband felt left out but was supportive, nonetheless.

14 Other reactions participants reported from their Indigenous spiritual communities included divisiveness; no divisiveness (especially no divisions between First Nations and Métis people); mixed reactions; respect; feeling safe; and, empathy. A few people shared reactions by people other than family or spiritual community members; notably, several people indicated unsupportive reactions from the general public or specifically from Christians. A couple of others indicated members of the general public being curious about ceremonies and happy for them.

15 Charlotte is referring to a month-long confrontation over unceded Indigenous land in British Columbia between unarmed Sundancers who had gathered for Sundance, a White cattle farmer, and the heavily armed RCMP in 1995.

CHAPTER 11 – Métis Spirituality Today

1 Woodcock, *Gabriel Dumont*; Préfontaine, *Gabriel Dumont*; and Thompson, *Red Sun*.

2 Centre du patrimoine, Lettre à Monseigneur Alexandre-Antonin Taché, de Laurent Simonet, St-Laurent, Lac Manitoba, 2 avril 1866.

3 Métis National Council, "Métis Nation Citizenship."

4 Gaudry and Leroux, "White Settler Revisionism"; Gaudry, "Communing with the Dead"; Leroux, "Self-Made Métis"; Leroux, *Distorted Descent*; Leroux, "'Eastern Métis' Studies"; Leroux and O'Toole, "An Analysis of the MNO's Recognition."

5 In *Rekindling*, eighteen people aged twenty-five to seventy-six with Red River Métis ancestry (from Manitoba who participate in ceremony) were interviewed (with an equal number of females and males). In the present book, we heard from thirty-two Métis people who participate in ceremony, range in age from eighteen to eighty-three years (twenty-three females, including two transgender women, and nine males), and are connected to at least one of the six selected historic Métis communities.

6 One reason for the higher educational levels in the first study is that participants were drawn largely from my own and my dissertation committee member's/spiritual advisor's personal contacts (we both have a PhD and work in academia). In contrast, the six community researchers who assisted me with the current study have a broad range of educational attainment, as do their contacts.

7 An explanation for the higher percentage of Indian status among participants in the first study is the fact that they did not have to meet the criteria for Métis identity according to the MNC, nor did they have to be connected to a recognized historic Métis community (though most met those criteria nonetheless).

8 In decreasing order, the languages were Anishinaabemowin, Nêhiyawawin (Cree), and Michif in *Rekindling*, and Michif, Anishinaabemowin, and Nêhiyawawin in this book.

9   Recall that the remaining participants have a familial connection to one (or more) of these communities (through ancestral scrip, and/or through relatives who live there).

10   From the first study, only Ron (from Camperville) continues to live in his Métis community (though he also has a home in Winnipeg); in the current study this is the case for twelve people.

11   In one exception, Ron knew his ancestors had redeemed their scrip for land in Camperville and put it into a trust with the Catholic Church in the 1920s; the church later gave it to the federal government without his family's consent. Most Métis did not receive the land promised to them in the Manitoba Act (1870).

12   In this study, 72 percent; in *Rekindling*, 67 percent.

13   In *Rekindling* I noted family members who used multiple terms to self-identify but not in this study; however, this came up here in participants' personal self-identification.

14   Participants in *Rekindling* were not asked about changes in family self-identification over time; however, similarities to the ones just mentioned can nonetheless be gleaned across their stories.

15   Participants in *Rekindling* also discussed relating to Aboriginal cultures *kiimoochly* (secretively), with such relationships marked by denial, disconnection, shame, marginalization, distrust, silence, and internalized racism.

16   Participants in *Rekindling* were not asked to reflect upon family relationships with First Nations cultures.

17   For example, laws regarding hunting, fishing, midwifery, natural resources and child and family services.

18   Cree (Nêhiyaw) and Anishinaabe (Saulteaux, Ojibwe) were the most frequently mentioned identity terms, in addition to Métis or Michif.

19   While one person indicated this in the current study, this term was rarely identified as being used by families in the first place.

20   In the current study, 69 percent, and in *Rekindling*, 67 percent.

21   Participants in *Rekindling* described more physical violence, death threats, and being urinated on, as well as loss of friends, denial of services (by hotels, police, utilities providers), being refused romantic dates, and being paid less than White employees for the same job despite the same skill level and seniority.

22   See Pettipas, *Severing the Ties That Bind*.

23   *Maarsii* to my Métis colleague and friend Dr. Paul L. Gareau for reminding me to avoid binaries and dichotomies. Personal communication with author, 2 November 2020.

24   As quoted in Herriot, *Toward a Prairie Atonement*, 72–73.

25   *Miigwetch* to the anonymous peer reviewer who posed this question.

26   These reasons include the following: ceremonial and spiritual knowledge must be earned, not taken from books; people must "put their hands to the work and show their face"; obtaining knowledge before people are ready can mean it will not be understood in any depth or that it can be misused with harmful consequences; certain knowledge is shared only in certain contexts or at certain times of year, with certain people; the ongoing secrecy surrounding ceremonies that was internalized as a result of the persecution Indigenous people faced when Canada made ceremonies illegal between 1884 and 1951; and so on. See Fiola, *Rekindling*, 5–7; and Pettipas, *Severing the Ties That Bind*.

27 Flaminio, Gaudet, and Dorion, "Métis Women Gathering," 57.

28 Ibid., 58.

29 Barkwell, Préfontaine, and Carrière-Acco, "Métis Spirituality"; Spaulding, "Métis Receive Sundance Song"; Vrooman, "Many Eagle Set Thirsty Dance"; Vrooman, "The Metis Receive Sun Dance Song"; and Chapter 1 in this volume.

30 Examples of this include when Midewiwin Grand Chief Benton-Banai received instruction from Spirit to allow English translation in the Midewiwin lodge, and when Sundance Chief David Blacksmith allowed an Indigenous reporter and camera crew from the Aboriginal Peoples Television Network (APTN) to film parts of a Sundance ceremony after having a dream instructing him to do so and obtaining permission from his elder. Fiola, *Rekindling,* 5–6, 78–79.

31 I do believe it is possible for Indigenous people to appropriate things from other Indigenous people if they have indeed taken something without permission or acknowledgement. To avoid this, one can be transparent about one's lineage, as I describe below.

32 *Maarsii* to Michif Elders, Barbara and Charlotte, for reading this section of the book's manuscript, offering feedback, and helping me to remain accountable. In their wisdom, they reminded me to express gratitude to our First Nations relatives for originally (and, in some cases, currently) teaching us these ways. I was reminded that First Nations have been practising these ways since time immemorial, much longer than the Métis—but that some Métis have also been practising these ways as long as Métis people have existed. They acknowledged the Métis Nation citizens across our homeland (and who now live elsewhere) who are Sundancers, sweat lodge keepers, pipe carriers—especially those who carry two-spirit teachings. They encouraged me not to fixate on a comparison between First Nations ceremonial practices and Métis ceremonial practices, as such a comparison is unnecessary. Rather, I was to remember that the Métis uniquely adapted what has been taught to us in ways that resonate with us, that the gifts we carry come through a lineage of different ways that are each important. Indeed, this is what makes Métis people so rich: our distinct ways of being, our culture, our spirituality, our nationhood. Finally, they echoed the importance of Métis Nation leadership recognizing and supporting Métis citizens who participate in ceremonies.

33 Fiola, "Two-Spirit Identity and Faith"; Fiola, "We've Always Been Here"; Fiola and Ruprai, "The Findings of C2C"; Fiola and Ruprai, "Two-Spirit and Queer Trans People of Colour"; and Fiola and McLeod, "Two-Spirit and LGBTQ Resurgence in Winnipeg" (forthcoming).

34 Canada, "Coronavirus Disease (COVID-19)."

BIBLIOGRAPHY

Centre du patrimoine de la Société historique du Saint-Boniface (St. Boniface Archives)

Collection Les Cloches de Saint-Boniface

Lettre à Monseigneur Alexandre-Antonin Taché, de Charles Camper, Mission de St. Laurent, Lac Manitoba, 12 septembre 1868, vol. 35, avril 1936.

Lettre à Monseigneur Alexandre-Antonin Taché, de Laurent Simonet, St-Laurent, Lac Manitoba, 2 avril 1866.

Fonds Louis Riel, 0003, collection formerly known as MG3 D1

Fonds Corporation archiépiscopale catholique romaine de Saint-Boniface (CACRSB, fonds # 0075)

a) Série Louis-Philippe-Adélard Langevin
Recensement à Lorette, 1910. 0075/L20412-L20448.

b) Série Joseph-Norbert Provencher

Fonds CACRSB, Série Joseph-Norbert Provencher. 0075/4/P2526 à P3584.

Fonds CACRSB, Série Joseph-Norbert Provencher. Cahier H 31, mars 1818–juillet 1848, 0075/P2882 à P3282.

Fonds CACRSB, Série Joseph-Norbert Provencher. Lettres de M.G.A. Belcourt, Cahier I, 29 août 1835–15 avril 1857, 0075/P3283 à P3584.

Fonds CACRSB, Série Joseph-Norbert Provencher. Lettre à La Grandeur Mr. L'Évêque de Québec Bas-Canada, de G.A. Belcourt, Rivière Rouge, 8 juillet 1836.

Fonds CACRSB, Série Joseph-Norbert Provencher. Lettre à La Grandeur Mr. L'Évêque de Québec Bas-Canada, de G.A. Belcourt, Rivière Rouge, 26 août 1836, Saint-Paul des Sauteuses.

Fonds CACRSB, Série Joseph-Norbert Provencher. Lettre à Mr. Bazeault (illegible), Secrétaire pour Msgr. L'Éveque de Québec, de G.A. Belcourt, Saint-Paul des Sauteuses, août 1841.

Fonds CACRSB, Série Joseph-Norbert Provencher. Cahier G, 27 mars 1818–6 juillet 1852, P2526 à P2881

Lettre à P.-F. Turgeon, Évêque de Sidyme à QC, Canada, de Joseph-Norbert Provencher, St-Boniface, Rivière Rouge, 14 juin 1847.

Manitoba Archives

Census of the Indian Population of Fond du Lac, 13th December 1857, Location B.72/z/1 fos. 2-3, Microfilm 1M876.

Census Returns for Red River Settlement and Grantown, 1827, Digital Image Number: HB13-002637.JPG, Location Code: E.5/1 (H2-136-1-2), Additional Image Information: Census returns 1827, E.5/1 fos. 9d-10.

Council of Assiniboia Fonds, Finding aid for Red River Settlement Census 1870, Location P7539/3.

Council of Assiniboia Fonds, Red River Census 1849, Location P7537/5, Microfilm M160.

Council of Assiniboia Fonds, Red River Census 1870, Location P7537/7, Microfilm M160.

Legal Cases, Statutes, Treaties, and Government Sources

Adhesion by Halfbreeds of Rainy River and Lake. Confederation Debates 1865–1949, Treaty Document(s), 13 October 1873, Treaty No. 3. University of Victoria. https://hcmc.uvic.ca/confederation/en/treaty_03.html (accessed 6 April 2020).

Canada. *Alberta (Aboriginal Affairs and Northern Development) v. Cunningham.* Supreme Court of Canada. 2011. https://scc-csc.lexum.com/scc-csc/scc-csc/en/item/7952/index.do (accessed 6 April 2020).

———. Background on Indian Registration. 2018. (last modified 28 November 2018.) https://www.rcaanc-cirnac.gc.ca/eng/1540405608208/1568898474141 (accessed 6 April 2020).

———. Bill S-3: An Act to amend the Indian Act in response to the Superior Court of Quebec decision in *Descheneaux v. Canada.* 2019. https://openparliament.ca/bills/42-1/S-3/ (accessed 6 April 2020).

———. British North America Act. 1867. https://www.justice.gc.ca/eng/rp-pr/csj-sjc/constitution/lawreg-loireg/p1t11.html (accessed 6 April 2020).

———. Constitution Act. 1982. https://www.canlii.org/en/ca/laws/stat/schedule-b-to-the-canada-act-1982-uk-1982-c-11/latest/schedule-b-to-the-canada-act-1982-uk-1982-c-11.html (accessed 6 April 2020).

———. "Coronavirus Disease (COVID-19): Being Prepared." 4 April 2020. https://www.canada.ca/en/public-health/services/diseases/2019-novel-coronavirus-infection/being-prepared.html (accessed 6 April 2020).

———. *Daniels v. Canada (Indian Affairs and Northern Development).* 2016. Supreme Court of Canada. https://scc-csc.lexum.com/scc-csc/scc-csc/en/item/15858/index.do (accessed 6 April 2020).

———. Manitoba Act. 1870. https://www.solon.org/Constitutions/Canada/English/ma_1870.html (accessed 6 April 2020).

———. Métis Nation Protocol. 2013. https://www.canada.ca/en/news/archive/2013/04/metis-nation-protocol.html (accessed 6 April 2020).

———. Non-Insured Health Benefits for First Nations and Inuit. 2020. (last modified January 24) https://www.sac-isc.gc.ca/eng/1572537161086/1572537234517 (accessed 6 April 2020).

———. Reference as to whether "Indians" in s. 91(24) of the B.N.A. Act includes Eskimo in habitants of the Province of Quebec. Supreme Court of Canada, 1939.

https://www.canlii.org/en/ca/scc/doc/1939/1939canlii22/1939canlii22.html (accessed 6 April 2020).

———. *R. v. Powley.* Supreme Court of Canada. 2003. https://scc-csc.lexum.com/scc-csc/scc-csc/en/item/2076/index.do (accessed 6 April 2020).

Manitoba. *Final Report of the Aboriginal Justice Inquiry of Manitoba.* Aboriginal Justice Implementation Committee, 2001. http://www.ajic.mb.ca/reports/final_toc.html (accessed 6 April 2020).

———. *From the Past into the Future: Manitoba Métis Policy.* 2010. https://www.gov.mb.ca/inr/major-initiatives/pubs/metis_policy_en.pdf (accessed 6 April 2020).

———. "Postage Stamp Province." n.d. https://www.gov.mb.ca/chc/hrb/plaques/plaq0945.html (accessed 6 April 2020).

Statistics Canada. *2006 Aboriginal Population Profile.* Minister of Industry, 6 December 2010. http://www12.statcan.ca/census-recensement/2006/dp-pd/prof/92-594/Index.cfm?Lang=E (accessed 6 April 2020).

———. "2011 National Household Survey: Aboriginal Peoples in Canada: First Nations People, Métis and Inuit." *The Daily,* 8 May. Minister of Industry, Component of Statistics Canada catalogue no. 11-001-X, 2013. http://www.statcan.gc.ca/daily-quotidien/130508/dq130508a-eng.htm?HPA (accessed 6 April 2020).

———. *Aboriginal Population Profile, 2016 Census.* Minister of Industry, 21 June 2018. https://www12.statcan.gc.ca/census-recensement/2016/dp-pd/abpopprof/index.cfm?Lang=E (accessed 6 April 2020).

Scholarly and Other Sources

Adese, Jennifer. "Spirit Gifting: Ecological Knowing in Métis Life Narratives." *Decolonization: Indigeneity, Education and Society* 3, no. 3 (2014): 48–66.

Andersen, Chris. *"Métis": Race, Recognition, and the Struggle for Indigenous Peoplehood.* Vancouver: UBC Press, 2014.

Andersen, Chris, and Nathalie Kermoal, eds. *Daniels v. Canada: In and Beyond the Courts.* Winnipeg: University of Manitoba Press, 2021.

Andersen, Chris, and Tahu Kukutai. "Reclaiming the Statistical 'Native': Quantitative Historical Research beyond the Pale." In *Sources and Methods in Indigenous Studies,* edited by Chris Andersen and Jean O'Brien, 41–48. New York: Routledge, 2017.

Andersen, Chris, and Jean O'Brien, eds. *Sources and Methods in Indigenous Studies.* New York: Routledge, 2017.

Anderson, Kim. *Life Stages and Native Women: Memory, Teachings, and Story Medicine.* Winnipeg: University of Manitoba Press, 2011.

———. "New-Life Stirring: Mothering, Transformation and Aboriginal Womanhood." In *"Until Our Hearts Are on the Ground": Aboriginal Mothering, Oppression, Resistance and Rebirth,* edited by Memee Lavell-Harvard and Jeannette Corbiere Lavell, 13–24. Toronto: Demeter Press.

Augustus, Camie. "Métis Scrip." *Our Legacy.* University of Saskatchewan Archives, 2008. http://scaa.sk.ca/ourlegacy/exhibit_scrip (accessed 6 April 2020).

Bakker, Peter. "Ethnogenesis, Language, and Identity: The Genesis of Michif and Other Mixed Languages." In *Contours of a People: Metis Family, Mobility, and History,* edited by Nicole St-Onge, Carolyn Podruchny, and Brenda Macdougall, 169–93. Norman: University of Oklahoma Press, 2012.

————. "'A Language of Our Own': The Genesis of Michif, the Mixed Cree-French Language of the Canadian Métis." PhD diss., University of Amsterdam, 1992.

————. *A Language of Our Own: The Genesis of Michif, the Mixed Cree-French Language of the Canadian Métis.* New York: Oxford University Press, 1997.

Barkwell, Lawrence. *The Metis Homeland: Its Settlements and Communities.* Winnipeg: Louis Riel Institute, 2016. http://www.metismuseum.ca/resource.php/11956 (accessed 6 April 2020).

————. "Surrender of Duck Bay Reserve." Louis Riel Institute. https://www.scribd.com/document/90782311/Surrender-of-Duck-Bay-Reserve (accessed 2 May 2021).

Barkwell, Lawrence, Darren Préfontaine, and Anne Carrière-Acco. "Metis Spirituality." In *Metis Legacy II*, edited by Lawrence Barkwell, Leah Dorion, and Audreen Hourie, 183–99. Saskatoon: Gabriel Dumont Institute and Winnipeg: Pemmican Publications, 2006.

Barron-McNab, Deborah. "Métis-Specific Gender-Based Analysis Framework for Health." Prairie Women's Health Centre of Excellence (PWHCE), 2009. http://www.pwhce.ca/pdf/metisGBAFramework.pdf (accessed 6 April 2020).

Bartlett, Judith, Sheila Carter, Julianne Sanguins, and Brenda Garner. "Case 8: The Use of a Holistic Wellness Framework and Knowledge Networks in Métis Health Planning." In *Citizen Engagement in Health Casebook.* Ottawa: Canadian Institutes of Health Research (CIHR), 2013. https://cihr-irsc.gc.ca/e/47596.html (accessed 6 April 2020).

Belcourt, Christi. "Just a quick clarification, Otipemsiwak is what we called ourselves." Facebook comment, 10 March 2020. https://www.facebook.com/metis.women/posts/10158318718263856?comment_id=10158318808088856.

Belcourt, Tony. "Many Eagles Set Song Ceremony." YouTube video, 6 January 2018. https://www.youtube.com/watch?v=CVUWMJyGSaA (accessed 6 April 2020).

Bell, Charles. "The Old Forts of Winnipeg, 1738–1927." *Manitoba Historical Society Transactions*, series 2, no. 3. Manitoba Historical Society, 1927. http://www.mhs.mb.ca/docs/transactions/2/oldfortsofwinnipeg.shtml (accessed 6 April 2020).

Benton-Banai, Edward. *The Mishomis Book: The Voice of the Ojibway.* Hayward, WI: Indian Country Communications, 1988.

Bombay, Amy, with Kim Matheson and Hymie Anisman. *Origins of Lateral Violence in Aboriginal Communities: A Preliminary Study of Student-to-Student Abuse in Residential Schools.* Ottawa: Aboriginal Healing Foundation (AHF), 2014. http://www.ahf.ca/downloads/lateral-violence-english.pdf (accessed 6 April 2020).

Bryman, Alan, and James J. Teevan. *Social Research Methods.* Toronto: Oxford University Press, 2005.

Cameron, Michelle. "Two-Spirited Aboriginal People: Continuing Cultural Appropriation by Non-Aboriginal Society." *Canadian Woman Studies* 24 (2005): 123–27.

Campbell, Maria. *Riel's People: How the Métis Lived.* Toronto: Douglas and McIntyre, 1992.

————. "We Need to Return to the Principles of Wahkotowin." *Eagle Feather News* 10, no. 11 (November 2007): 5. https://www.eaglefeathernews.com/quadrant/media//pastIssues/November_2007.pdf.

Cardinal, Harold, and Walter Hildebrandt. *Treaty Elders of Saskatchewan: Our Dream Is That Our Peoples Will One Day Be Clearly Recognized as Nations*. Calgary: University of Calgary Press, 2000.

Chambers, Cynthia, Erika Hasebe-Ludt, Dwayne Donald, Wanda Hurren, Carl Leggo, and Antoinette Oberg. "Métissage: A Research Praxis." In *Handbook of the Arts in Qualitative Research: Perspectives, Methodologies, Examples, and Issues*, edited by J. Gary Knowles and Ardra Cole, 142–54. Thousand Oaks, CA: Sage, 2008.

Chandler, Michael, and Christopher Lalonde. "Cultural Continuity as a Hedge against Suicide in Canada's First Nations." *Transcultural Psychiatry* 35, no. 2 (1998): 191–219.

Chartier, Clément. "The Case against the Tri-Council": A Letter from the President of the Métis National Council to the Leaders of the Tri-Council. Métis Nation.ca, 3 December 2020. https://www2.metisnation.ca/news/the-case-against-the-tri-council/ (accessed 9 December 2020).

Chartrand, Larry. Métis Treaties in Canada: Past Realities and Present Promise. 2020. https://indigenouslaw.usask.ca/publications/metis-treaties-in-canada.php (accessed 19 April 2021).

Chartrand, Larry, Tricia Logan, and Harry Daniels, eds. *Métis History and Experience and Residential Schools in Canada*. Ottawa: Aboriginal Healing Foundation, 2006.

Coates, Ken. "Being Aboriginal: The Cultural Politics of Identity, Membership and Belonging among First Nations in Canada." In *Aboriginal Peoples in Canada: Futures and Identities*, edited by Michael Behiels, 23–41. Canadian Issues 21. Montreal: Association for Canadian Studies, 1999.

Crawford, John. "What Is Michif? Language in the Métis Tradition." In *The New Peoples: Being and Becoming Métis in North America*, edited by Jacqueline Peterson and Jennifer Brown, 231–41. Winnipeg: University of Manitoba Press, 1985.

Devine, Heather. "The Plains Metis." In *Native Peoples: The Canadian Experience*, edited by C. Roderick Wilson and Christopher Fletcher, 328–55. Don Mills, ON: Oxford University Press, 2014.

Dickason, Olive. *Canada's First Nations: A History of Founding Peoples from Earliest Times*. Toronto: Oxford University Press, 1992.

Dolmage Jay. "Metis, Mêtis, Mestiza, Medusa: Rhetorical Bodies across Rhetorical Traditions." *Rhetoric Review* 28, no. 1 (2009): 1–28.

Donald, Dwayne. "Forts, Curriculum, and Indigenous Métissage: Imagining Decolonization of Aboriginal-Canadian Relations in Educational Contexts." *First Nations Perspectives* 2, no. 1 (2010): 1–24.

Dorion, Leah Marie. *Relatives with Roots: A Story About Métis Women's Connection to the Land*. Saskatoon: Gabriel Dumont Institute, 2011.

Dumont, Jim. "Journey to Daylight-Land: Through Ojibwe Eyes." *Laurentian Review* 3, no. 2 (1979): 31–43.

Duval, Jacinthe. "The Catholic Church and the Formation of Métis Identity." *Past Imperfect* 9 (2001–3): 65–87.

Eberts, Mary. "McIvor: Justice Delayed—Again." *Indigenous Law Journal* 9, no. 1 (2010): 15–46.

Egale Canada. *The Just Society Report—Grossly Indecent: Confronting the Legacy of State Sponsored Discrimination against Canada's LGBTQ2S1 Communities.* Egale Human Rights Trust, 2016.

Erickson, Lesley. "'Bury Our Sorrows at the Sacred Heart': Gender and the Métis Response to Colonialism—the Case of Sara and Louis Riel, 1848–83." In *Unsettled Pasts: Reconceiving the West Through Women's History*, edited by Sarah Carter, Lesley Erickson, Patricia Roome, and Char Smith, 17–46. Calgary: University of Calgary Press, 2005.

———. "Repositioning the Missionary: Sara Riel, the Grey Nuns, and Aboriginal Women in Catholic Missions of the Northwest." In *Recollecting: Lives of Aboriginal Women of the Canadian Northwest and Borderlands*, edited by Sarah Carter and Patricia McCormack, 115–134. Edmonton: Athabasca University Press, 2011.

Ermine, Willie. "Aboriginal Epistemology." In *First Nations Education in Canada: The Circle Unfolds*, edited by Marie Battiste and Jean Barman, 101–12. Vancouver: UBC Press, 1995.

Ferris, Kade. "Blurred Lines and Kinship Tales: A Case against Colonial Separation of Indigenous People." *Dibaajimowin* (blog), 16 August 2018. http://www.dibaaji-mowin.com/tawnkiyash/blurred-lines-and-kinship-ties (accessed 6 April 2020).

———. "Nehiyaw-Pwat: The Iron Confederacy." *Dibaajimowin* (blog), 15 August 2018. https://www.dibaajimowin.com/tawnkiyash/nehiyaw-pwat-the-iron-confederacy (accessed 6 April 2020).

———. "The Postage Stamp Province." *Dibaajimowin* (blog), 29 December 2018. https://www.dibaajimowin.com/metis/the-postage-stamp-province (accessed 6 April 2020).

Fillmore, W.P. "Half-Breed Scrip." In *The Other Natives: The-Les Métis*, vol. 2, edited by Antoine Lussier and D. Bruce Sealey, 31–36. Winnipeg: Manitoba Métis Federation Press, 1978.

Fiola, Chantal. "Expanding Métis Curriculum." In *Research Journeys in/to Multiple Ways of Knowing*, edited by Jennifer Markides and Laura Forsythe, 185–95. New York: DIO Press, 2019.

———. "Naawenangweyaabeg Coming In: Intersections of Indigenous Sexuality and Spirituality." In *Good Relation: History, Gender, and Kinship in Indigenous Feminisms*, edited by Sarah Nickel and Amanda Fehr, 136–53. Winnipeg: University of Manitoba Press, 2020.

———. Prenatal/Postpartum Ceremonies and Parenting as Michif Self-Determination." In *Strong Métis Women Academics: Our Contributions*, edited by Laura Forsythe and Jennifer Markides. Forthcoming.

———. *Rekindling the Sacred Fire: Métis Ancestry and Anishinaabe Spirituality.* Winnipeg: University of Manitoba Press, 2015.

———. "Two-Spirit Identity and Faith": A Conversation with Chantal Fiola by Alana Trachenko. *Geez* 49 (Summer 2018). https://geezmagazine.org/magazine/article/two-spirit-identity-and-faith/ (accessed 6 April 2020).

———. "We've Always Been Here: Two-Spirit People in the Midewiwin Creation Story." Two-Spirit issue, *Red Rising Magazine* 7 (2018): 10–13.

Fiola, Chantal, and Shauna MacKinnon. "Urban and Inner-City Studies: Decolonizing Ourselves and the University of Winnipeg." In *Decolonizing and Indigenizing*

Education in Canada, edited by Sheila Cote-Meek and Taima Moeke-Pickering, 155–77. Toronto: Canadian Scholars Press, 2020.

Fiola, Chantal, and Albert McLeod. "Two-Spirit and LGBTQ Resurgence in Winnipeg." In *Indigenous Resurgence and Institutional Development in Winnipeg: 1950–2019*, edited by Lorena Fontaine, John Loxley, Shauna MacKinnon, and Kathy Mallett. Forthcoming.

Fiola, Chantal, and Sharanpal Ruprai. "The Findings of C2C: Two-Spirit and Queer Trans People of Colour—Calls to Action." University of Winnipeg, 2019. https://www.uwinnipeg.ca/c2c/docs/c2c_calls-to-action_final.pdf (accessed 6 April 2020).

———. "Two-Spirit and Queer Trans People of Colour: Reflecting on the Call to Conversation Conference (C2C)." *Canadian Journal of Native Studies* 39, no. 1 (2020): 45–64.

Flaminio, Anna, Janice Gaudet, and Leah Dorion. "Métis Women Gathering: Visiting Together and Voicing Wellness for Ourselves." *AlterNative* 16, no. 1 (2020): 55–63.

FNIGC. "The First Nations Principles of OCAP®." First Nations Information Governance Centre, 2015. https://fnigc.ca/ocap (accessed 6 April 2020).

Foran, Timothy. *Defining Métis: Catholic Missionaries and the Idea of Civilization in Northwestern Saskatchewan, 1845–1898*. Winnipeg: University of Manitoba Press, 2017.

Freynet, Robert. *Red River Mission: The Story of a People and Their Church*. Winnipeg: Vidacom, 2018.

Gareau, Paul L. "Mary and the Métis: Religion as a Site for New Insight in Métis Studies." In *A People and a Nation: New Directions in Contemporary Métis Studies*, edited by Jennifer Adese and Chris Andersen, 188–212. Vancouver: UBC Press, 2021.

Gaudet, Janice. "Keeoukaywin: The Visiting Way—Fostering an Indigenous Research Methodology." *Aboriginal Policy Studies* 7, no. 2 (2019): 47–64.

———. "Rethinking Participatory Research with Indigenous Peoples." *Native American and Indigenous Studies* 1, no. 2 (2014): 69–88.

Gaudry, Adam. "Communing with the Dead: The 'New Métis,' Métis Identity Appropriation, and the Displacement of Living Métis Culture." *American Indian Quarterly* 42, no. 2 (2018): 162–90.

Gaudry, Adam, and Darryl Leroux. "White Settler Revisionism and Making Métis Everywhere: The Evocation of Métissage in Quebec and Nova Scotia." *Critical Ethnic Studies* 3, no. 1 (2017): 116–42.

Gaywish, Rainey. "Prophesy and Transformation in Edward Benton-Banai's Revitalization of the Midewiwin Heart Way: 'Neegawn I-naw-buh-tay Aynnayn-duh-mawn.' My Thoughts Flow Forward to the Future." PhD diss., Trent University, 2008.

Ghostkeeper, Elmer. *Spirit Gifting: The Concept of Spiritual Exchange*. Raymond, AB: Writing on Stone Press, 2007.

Gilbert, Larry. *Entitlement to Indian Status and Membership Codes in Canada*. Scarborough, ON: Carswell/Thompson Professional Publishing, 1996.

Giokas, John, and Robert Groves. "Collective and Individual Recognition in Canada: The Indian Act Regime." In *Who Are Canada's Aboriginal Peoples? Recognition, Definition, and Jurisdiction*, edited by Paul Chartrand, 41–82. Saskatoon: Purich Publishing, 2002.

Green, Joyce. "Exploring Identity and Citizenship: Aboriginal Women, Bill C-31 and the 'Sawridge Case.'" PhD diss., University of Alberta, 1997.

Henderson, Anne. "The Lord Selkirk Settlement at Red River, Part 1." *Manitoba Pageant* 13, no. 1 (1967). Manitoba Historical Society. http://www.mhs.mb.ca/docs/pageant/13/selkirksettlement1.shtml (accessed 6 April 2020).

Herriot, Trevor. *Toward a Prairie Atonement.* Saskatchewan: University of Regina Press, 2016.

Hodgson-Smith, Kathy, and Nathalie Kermoal. "Community-Based Research and Métis Women's Knowledge in Northwestern Saskatchewan." In *Living on the Land: Indigenous Women's Understanding of Place*, edited by Nathalie Kermoal and Isabel Altamirano-Jiménez, 139–67. Edmonton: Athabasca University Press, 2016.

Hourie, Audreen. "St. Laurent History." In *The Metis Homeland: Its Settlements and Communities*, edited by Lawrence Barkwell, 55–56. Winnipeg: Louis Riel Institute, 2016. http://www.metismuseum.ca/resource.php/11956 (accessed 6 April 2020).

Howard, Joseph Kinsey. *Strange Empire: A Narrative of the Northwest.* St. Paul: Minnesota Historical Society Press, (1952) 1994.

Huel, Raymond. *Proclaiming the Gospel to the Indians and Métis.* Edmonton: University of Alberta Press, 1996.

Hunt, Sarah. "An Introduction to the Health of Two-Spirit People: Historical, Contemporary, and Emergent Issues." National Collaborating Centre for Aboriginal Health, 2016. https://www.ccnsa-nccah.ca/docs/emerging/RPT-HealthTwoSpirit-Hunt-EN.pdf (accessed 6 April 2020).

Innes, Robert. *Elder Brother and the Law of the People: Contemporary Kinship and Cowessess First Nation.* Winnipeg: University of Manitoba Press, 2013.

———. "Multicultural Bands on the Northern Plains and the Notion of 'Tribal' Histories." In *Finding a Way to the Heart: Feminist Writings on Aboriginal and Women's History in Canada*, edited by Jarvis Brownlie and Valerie Korinek, 122–45. Winnipeg: University of Manitoba Press, 2012.

———. "Challenging a Racist Fiction: A Closer Look at Métis–First Nations Relations." In *A People and a Nation: New Directions in Contemporary Métis Studies*, edited by Jennifer Adese and Chris Andersen, 92–114. Vancouver: UBC Press, 2021.

Kermoal, Nathalie. "Métis Women's Environmental Knowledge and the Recognition of Métis Rights." In *Living on the Land: Indigenous Women's Understanding of Place*, edited by Nathalie Kermoal and Isabel Altamirano-Jiménez, 107–37. Edmonton: Athabasca University Press, 2016.

Kovach, Maggie. *Indigenous Methodologies: Characteristics, Conversations, and Contexts.* Toronto: University of Toronto Press, 2009.

Kovach, Margaret. "Conversational Method in Indigenous Research." *First Peoples Child and Family Review* 5, no. 1 (2010): 40–48.

Kumar, Mohan, and Teresa Janz. "An Exploration of Cultural Activities of Métis in Canada." Statistics Canada Catalogue, no. 11-008-X, Canadian Social Trends, 2010.

Lamirande, Todd. "Three Metis Nations Sign Historic Self-Government Agreement in Ottawa." Aboriginal Peoples Television Network, 27 June 2019. https://aptn-news.ca/2019/06/27/three-metis-nations-sign-historic-self-government-agree-ments-in-ottawa/ (accessed 6 April 2020).

Lawrence, Bonita. "Identity, Non-Status Indians, and Federally Unrecognized Peoples." In *Aboriginal History: A Reader*, edited by Kristin Burnett and Geoff Read, 196–205. Don Mills, ON: Oxford University Press, 2012.

———. *"Real" Indians and Others: Mixed-Blood Urban Native Peoples and Indigenous Nationhood*. Vancouver: UBC Press, 2004.

LaVallee, Amanda, Troupe, Cheryl, and Turner, Tara. "Negotiating and Exploring Relationships in Métis Community-Based Research." *Engaged Scholar Journal: Community-Engaged Research, Teaching, and Learning* 2, no.1 (2016): 167–82.

Lavallée, Guy. "The Métis of St. Laurent, Manitoba: Their Life and Stories, 1920–1988." Published by author. Winnipeg, Manitoba, 2003.

Leclair, Carol. "Métis Environmental Knowledge: La Tayr Pi Tout Li Moond." PhD diss., York University, 2003.

Leroux, Darryl. *Distorted Descent: White Claims to Indigenous Identity*. Winnipeg: University of Manitoba Press, 2019.

———. "'Eastern Métis' Studies and White Settler Colonialism Today." *Aboriginal Policy Studies* 8, no. 1 (2019): 104–14.

———. Raceshifting. 2021. http://www.raceshifting.com/ (accessed 6 April 2020).

———. "Self-Made Métis." *Maisonneuve*, 1 November 2018. https://maisonneuve.org/article/2018/11/1/self-made-metis/ (accessed 6 April 2020).

Leroux, Darryl, and Darren O'Toole. "An Analysis of the MNO's Recognition of Six New Historic Métis Communities: A Final Report." Manitoba Metis Federation, 2020.

Levin, Clare. "The Unheard Majority: A History of Women Educators in Manitoba." Manitoba Women's Directorate, 2002.

Lorette History Book Committee. *Paroisse Notre-Dame de Lorette Parish: The History of Lorette, Manitoba, 1875–2000*. Lorette, MB, 2000.

Macdougall, Brenda, and Nicole St-Onge. "Metis in the Borderlands of the Northern Plains in the Nineteenth Century." In *Sources and Methods in Indigenous Studies*, edited by Chris Andersen and Jean O'Brien, 257–65. New York: Routledge, 2017.

Manitoba Historical Society. "Pine Creek Indian Residential School/Camperville Indian Residential School." Page revised 6 February 2021. http://www.mhs.mb.ca/docs/sites/pinecreekresidentialschool.shtml (accessed 1 May 2021).

Manitoba Metis Federation. "MMF Annual General Assembly with Standing Ovation Votes Unanimously to Pass Resolution #6—Authorization for Manitoba Metis Federation to Withdraw from the Métis National Council." News release, 22 September 2019. http://www.mmf.mb.ca/news_details.php?news_id=417 (accessed 6 April 2020).

———. "MMF and Canada Sign Historic Self-Government Recognition Agreement." News release, 6 July 2021. https://www.manitobametis.com/news/mmf-and-canada-sign-historic-self-government-recognition-agreement (accessed 7 July 2021).

———. "Protecting the Citizens of the Métis Nation." News release, 29 November 2019. http://www.mmf.mb.ca/news_details.php?news_id=338 (accessed 6 April 2020).

Martens, Patricia, Judith Bartlett, Elaine Burland, Heather Prior, Charles Burchill, Shamima Huq, Linda Romphf, Julianne Sanguins, Sheila Carter, and Angela Bailly. *Profile of Metis Health Status and Healthcare Utilization in Manitoba: A Population-Based Study. Winnipeg: Manitoba Centre for Health Policy, 2010.* http://www.mmf.mb.ca/docs/metis_health_status_report.pdf *(accessed 6 April 2020).*

McCarthy, Martha. *To Evangelize the Nations: Roman Catholic Missions in Manitoba, 1818–1870.* Winnipeg: Manitoba Culture Heritage and Recreation Historic Resources, 1990.

McCrady, David. "Louis Riel and Sitting Bull's Sioux: Three Lost Letters." In *The Western Métis: Profile of a People*, edited by Patrick Douaud, 203–12. Regina: Canadian Plains Research Centre, 2007.

McDonald, Thomas Michael. *The Black Book: Native Americans and the Christian Experience: Overcoming the Negative Impact of Nominal Christianity.* Norway House, MB: Goldrock Press, 2017.

McIvor, Onowa, Art Napoleon, and Kerissa Dickie. "Language and Culture as Protective Factors for At-Risk Communities." *Journal of Aboriginal Health* 5, no. 1 (November 2009): 6–25.

McIvor, Sharon, and Jacob Grismer. *Communication Submitted for Consideration under the First Optional Protocol to the International Covenant on Civil and Political Rights.* Submitted to United Nations Human Rights Committee, Office of the High Commissioner for Human Rights, Geneva, 24 November 2010. http://www.socialrightscura.ca/documents/legal/mcivor/McIvorPetition.pdf (accessed 6 April 2020).

Mercier, Pauline, Soeur. "Renseignements sur Saint-Laurent, Manitoba." Unpublished manuscript compiled for Division Scolaire de la Prairie du Cheval Blanc (White Horse Plain School Division). Elie, Manitoba, 1974.

Métis National Council. "Métis Nation Citizenship." n.d. https://www2.metisnation.ca/about/citizenship/ (accessed 19 April 2021).

———. "The Métis Nation Flag." n.d. https://www2.metisnation.ca/news/the-metis-nation-flag/ (accessed 19 April 2021).

Metis Settlements of Alberta. 2018. https://msgc.ca.

Michell, Herman. "Offering Tobacco in Exchange for Stories: The Ethic of Reciprocity in the First Nations Research." In *Kitaskino: Key Issues, Challenges and Visions for Northern Aboriginal Communities in Canada*, edited by Herman Michell and Cathy Wheaton, 196–216. Vernon, BC: J. Charlton Publishing, 2014.

———. "Pakitinâsowin: Tobacco Offerings in Exchange for Stories and the Ethic of Reciprocity in First Nations Research." *Journal of Indigenous Thought* 2, no. 2 (1999).

Milne, Brad. "The Historiography of Métis Land Dispersal, 1870–1890." *Manitoba History* 30 (1995): 30–41.

Morse, Bradford, and Robert Groves. "Métis and Non-Status Indians and Section 91(24) of the Constitution Act, 1876." In *Who Are Canada's Aboriginal Peoples? Recognition, Definition, and Jurisdiction*, edited by Paul Chartrand, 41–82. Saskatoon: Purich Publishing, 2002.

Murray, Jeffrey S. "Métis Scrip Records—Foundation for a New Beginning." *The Archivist* 20, no. 1 (1993): 12–14.

Myo, Peter. "Dumont, Gabriel, Smoking Peace Pipe" (illustration). Saskatoon: Gabriel Dumont Institute, 2003. http://www.metismuseum.ca/resource.php/02016 (accessed 6 April 2020).

NAHO (National Aboriginal Health Organization). "Principles of Ethical Métis Research." Ottawa, 2010. https://achh.ca/wp-content/uploads/2018/07/Guide_Ethics_NAHOMetisCentre.pdf (accessed 6 April 2020).

———. "Suicide Prevention and Two-Spirited People." Ottawa, 2012. https://ruor.uottawa.ca/bitstream/10393/30544/1/Suicide_Prevention_2 Spirited_People_Guide_2012.pdf (accessed 6 April 2020).

Narine, Shari. "Claims of 'new' Métis communities in Ontario rejected by MMF's research document." *Windspeaker*, 3 February 2021. https://windspeaker.com/news/windspeaker-news/claims-new-metis-communities-ontario-rejected-mmfs-research-document (accessed 21 April 2021).

National Centre for Truth and Reconciliation (NCTR). "Pine Creek Residential School." n.d. https://memorial.nctr.ca/?p=1432 (accessed 1 May 2021).

Native Women's Association of Canada. "Aboriginal Lateral Violence." Ottawa, 2011. http://www.cwhn.ca/en/node/43914 (accessed 6 April 2020).

Nicks, Trudy, and Kenneth Morgan. "Grande Cache: The Historic Development of an Indigenous Alberta Métis Population." In *The New Peoples: Being and Becoming Métis in North America*, edited by Jacqueline Peterson and Jennifer Brown, 163–84. Winnipeg: University of Manitoba Press, 1985.

O'Toole, Darren. "Métis Claims to 'Indian' Title in Manitoba, 1860–1870." *Canadian Journal of Native Studies* 28, no. 2 (2008): 241–71.

———. "Wiisaakodewininiwag ga-nanaakonaawaad: Jiibe-Giizhikwe, Racial Homeopathy, and 'Eastern Métis' Identity Claims." *Aboriginal Policy Studies* 8, no. 2 (2020): 68–95.

Palmer, Gwen. "Camperville and Duck Bay: Part 1—Camperville." *Manitoba Pageant* 18, no. 2 (1973). Manitoba Historical Society. http://www.mhs.mb.ca/docs/pageant/18/campervilleduckbay1.shtml (accessed 6 April 2020).

———. "Camperville and Duck Bay: Part 2—Duck Bay." *Manitoba Pageant* 18, no. 3 (1973). Manitoba Historical Society. http://www.mhs.mb.ca/docs/pageant/18/campervilleduckbay2.shtml (accessed 6 April 2020).

Passante, Lisa. "Aboriginal Two-Spirit and LGBTQ Mobility: Meanings of Home, Community and Belonging in a Secondary Analysis of Qualitative Interviews." MA thesis, University of Manitoba, 2012.

———. "Becoming Home: What Two-Spirit and LGBTQ People Say about Home, Community, and Belonging." Paper presented at the Canadian Alliance to End Homelessness Conference, Montreal, QC, 2–4 November 2015.

Payment, Diane. *The Free People—Li Gens Libres: A History of the Métis Community of Batoche, Saskatchewan.* Calgary: University of Calgary Press, 2009.

Peters, Evelyn, Matthew Stock, and Adrian Werner. *Rooster Town: The History of an Urban Métis Community, 1901–1961.* Winnipeg: University of Manitoba Press, 2018.

Peterson, Jacqueline, and Jennifer S.H. Brown, eds. *The New Peoples: Being and Becoming Métis in North America.* Winnipeg: University of Manitoba Press, 1985.

Pettipas, Katherine. *Severing the Ties That Bind: Government Repression of Indigenous Religious Ceremonies on the Prairies.* Winnipeg: University of Manitoba Press, 1994.

Pitawanakwat, Brock. "Bimaadziwin Oodenaang: A Pathway to Urban Nishnaabe Resurgence." In *Lighting the Eighth Fire: The Liberation, Resurgence, and Protection of Indigenous Nations,* edited by Leanne Simpson, 161–74. Winnipeg: Arbeiter Ring Publishing, 2008.

Préfontaine, Darren. *Gabriel Dumont: Li Chef Michif in Images and in Words.* Saskatoon: Gabriel Dumont Institute, 2011.

Préfontaine, Darren, Todd Paquin, and Patrick Young. "Métis Spiritualism." Saskatoon: Gabriel Dumont Institute, 2003. http://www.metismuseum.ca/resource. php/00727 (accessed 6 April 2020).

Racette, Sherry Farrell, Alan Corbiere, and Crystal Migwans. "Pieces Left along the Trail: Material Culture Histories and Indigenous Studies." In *Sources and Methods in Indigenous Studies,* edited by Chris Andersen and Jean O'Brien, 223–29. New York: Routledge, 2017.

RCAP (Royal Commission on Aboriginal Peoples). *Report on the Royal Commission on Aboriginal Peoples: Final Report.* 5 vols. Ottawa: Supply and Services Canada, 1996.

Red Rising Collective. Métis issue, *Red Rising Magazine* 9 (2019).

Ristock, Janice, Art Zoccole, and Lisa Passante. *Aboriginal Two-Spirit and LGBTQ Migration, Mobility, and Health Research Project: Winnipeg Final Report.* 2 Spirits, 2010. http://www.2spirits.com/PDFolder/MMHReport.pdf (accessed 6 April 2020).

Ristock, Janice, Art Zoccole, Lisa Passante, and Jonathon Potskin. "Impacts of Colonization on Indigenous Two-Spirit/LGBTQ Canadians' Experiences of Migration, Mobility, and Relationship Violence." *Sexualities* 22, nos. 5–6 (2019): 767–84.

Rural Municipality of Ellice-Archie. "History of St. Lazare." http://www.rmofellicear-chie.ca/p/history-of-st-lazare (accessed 19 March 2021).

Scott, Bryanna Rae. "Reconciliation through Métissage." In *Decolonizing and Indigenizing Education in Canada,* edited by Sheila Cote-Meek and Taima Moeke-Pickering, 31–49. Toronto: Canadian Scholars Press, 2020.

Sealey, D. Bruce. "Statutory Land Rights of the Manitoba Métis." In *The Other Natives: The-Les Métis,* vol. 2, edited by Antoine Lussier and D. Bruce Sealey, 1–36. Winnipeg: Manitoba Métis Federation Press, 1978.

Shore, Fred. "The Emergence of the Métis Nation in Manitoba." In *Métis Legacy: A Métis Historiography and Annotated Bibliography,* edited by Lawrence J. Barkwell, Leah Dorion, and Darren R. Prefontaine, 71–78. Winnipeg: Pemmican Publications, 1999.

Shrubsole, Nicholas. *What Has No Place, Remains: The Challenges for Indigenous Religious Freedom in Canada Today.* Toronto: University of Toronto Press, 2019.

Siggins, Maggie. *Riel: A Life of Revolution.* Toronto: Harper Perennial, 1995.

Simpson, Leanne, ed. "Indigenous Queer Normativity." In *As We Have Always Done: Indigenous Freedom through Radical Resistance.* Minneapolis: University of Minnesota Press, 2017.

———. *Lighting the Eighth Fire: The Liberation, Resurgence, and Protection of Indigenous Nations.* Winnipeg: Arbeiter Ring Publishing, 2008.

———. "Oshkimaadiziig, the New People." In *Lighting the Eighth Fire: The Liberation, Resurgence, and Protection of Indigenous Nations,* edited by Leanne Simpson, 13–22. Winnipeg: Arbeiter Ring Publishing, 2008.

Smith, Linda Tuhiwai. *Decolonizing Methodologies: Research and Indigenous Peoples.* New York: Zed Books, 2001.

Smith, Robert. "The Manitoba School Act of 1890: An Insult to the French Roman Catholics." Educational Resources Information Center (ERIC). April 1994. https://files.eric.ed.gov/fulltext/ED372017.pdf (accessed 2 May 2021).

Spaulding, Tom. "Métis Receive Sundance Song." *Métis Voyageur,* September–November 2004, 1, 16.

Sprague, Douglas N. "Government Lawlessness in the Administration of Manitoba Land Claims, 1870–1887." *Manitoba Law Journal* 10, no. 4 (1980): 415–41.

"St. François-Xavier, Roman Catholic Parish." Community website. https://www.sfx-rcparish.ca/history.html (accessed 2 May 2021).

St. Laurent and District History Book Committee. *The Land between the Lakes: R.M. of St. Laurent.* St. Laurent, MB: St. Laurent and District History Book Committee, 2010.

St-Onge, Nicole. *Saint-Laurent, Manitoba: Evolving Métis Identities, 1850–1914.* Regina: Canadian Plains Research Centre, 2004.

Stranger, Darrell. "Métis of Ontario Suspended by National Council." Aboriginal Peoples Television Network, 22 January 2020. https://aptnnews.ca/2020/01/22/metis-of-ontario-suspended-by-national-council/ (accessed 6 April 2020).

Sturm, Circe. *Becoming Indian: The Struggle over Cherokee Identity in the Twenty-First Century.* Santa Fe, NM: School for Advanced Research Press, 2011.

Surtees, Robert J. "The Robinson Treaties (1850)." Treaties and Historical Research Centre, Department of Indian and Northern Affairs Canada, 1986. https://www.rcaanc-cirnac.gc.ca/eng/1100100028974/1564412549270 (accessed 6 April 2020).

TallBear, Kimberly. "DNA, Blood, and Racializing the Tribe." *Wicazo Sa Review* 18, no. 1 (2003): 81–107.

Teillet, Jean. *The North-West Is Our Mother: The Story of Louis Riel's People, the Métis Nation.* Toronto: Patrick Crean, HarperCollins, 2019.

The Sisters of Saint Joseph of Saint-Hyacinthe. "Lorette." 2021. http://www.sjsh.org/92-field-lorette.html?t=1 (accessed 1 May 2021).

Thistle, Jesse. "The Puzzle of the Morrissette-Arcand Clan: A History of Metis Historic and Intergenerational Trauma." MA thesis, University of Waterloo, 2016.

Thompson, Charles Duncan. *Red Sun: Gabriel Dumont, The Folk Hero.* Saskatoon: Gabriel Dumont Institute Press, 2017.

Treasures of the Dawson Trail. "Prairie Grove." https://dawsontrailtreasures.ca/index. php?page=prairie-grove (accessed 19 March 2021).

Treat, James. *Native and Christian: Indigenous Voices on Religious Identity in the United States and Canada.* New York: Routledge, 1996.

Tri-Council Policy Statement: Ethical Conduct for Research Involving Humans. Canadian Institutes of Health Research, National Sciences and Engineering Research Council of Canada, Social Sciences and Humanities Council. Ottawa: Secretariat on Responsible Conduct of Research, 2018. https://ethics.gc.ca/eng/documents/tcps2-2018-en-interactive-final.pdf (accessed 6 April 2020).

TRC (Truth and Reconciliation Commission of Canada). *Canada's Residential Schools: The Métis Experience.* Vol. 3 of *The Final Report of the Truth and Reconciliation Commission of Canada.* Montreal: McGill-Queen's University Press, 2015. http://www.trc.ca/assets/pdf/Volume_3_Metis_English_Web.pdf (accessed 6 April 2020).

———. "Residential School Locations." http://www.trc.ca/about-us/residential-school. html (accessed 2 May 2021).

Tuck, Eve, and K. Wayne Yang. "Decolonization Is Not a Metaphor." *Decolonization: Indigeneity, Education, and Society* 1, no. 1 (2012.): 1–40.

Twiss, Richard. *Rescuing the Gospel from the Cowboys: A Native American Expression of the Jesus Way.* Downers Grove, IL: IVP Books, InterVarsity Press, 2015.

Two-Spirited People of Manitoba. Welcome page. 2019. https://twospiritmanitoba.ca/ (accessed 6 April 2020).

L'Union Nationale Métisse Saint-Joseph du Manitoba. Welcome page. 2020. http://www.unmsjm.ca/ (accessed 6 April 2020).

University of British Columbia. "Indian Day Schools." https://irshdc.ubc.ca/learn/indian-residential-schools/indian-day-schools/ (accessed 2 May 2021).

University of Manitoba. *Framework for Research Engagement with First Nation, Metis, and Inuit Peoples.* 2014. University of Manitoba, Faculty of Health Sciences, 2014. https://umanitoba.ca/faculties/health_sciences/medicine/media/UofM_Framework_Report_web.pdf (accessed 6 April 2020).

Vowel, Chelsea. About page. *Âpihtawikosisân* (blog). https://apihtawikosisan.com/about-2/ (accessed 19 March 2021).

Vrooman, Nicholas. "Many Eagle Set Thirsty Dance (Sun Dance) Song." *Métis Voyageur* September–November (2004): 1, 16.

———. "Many Eagle Set Thirsty Dance (Sun Dance) Song: The Metis Receive Sun Dance Song." In *Metis Legacy II*, edited by Lawrence Barkwell, Leah Dorion, and Audreen Hourie, 187–91. Winnipeg: Pemmican Publications, 2006.

Weber-Pillwax, Cora. "What Is Indigenous Research?" *Canadian Journal of Native Education* 25, no. 2 (2001): 166–76.

Weekes, Mary. *The Last Buffalo Hunter.* Markham, ON: Fifth House Publishers, (1939) 1994.

Whalen, D.H., Margaret Moss, and Daryl Baldwin. "Healing through Language: Positive Physical Health Effects of Indigenous Language Use." *F1000Research*, 9 May 2016. https://f1000research.com/articles/5-852 (accessed September 2020).

Widder, Keith. *Battle for the Soul: Métis Children Encounter Evangelical Protestants at Mackinaw Mission, 1823–1837*. East Lansing: Michigan State University Press, 1999.

Wilson, Alex. "How We Find Ourselves: Identity Development and Two-Spirit People." *Harvard Educational Review* 66, no. 2 (1996): 303–17.

———. "N'tacimowin inna nah': Our Coming In Stories." *Canadian Woman Studies* 26, no. 3–4 (2008): 193–99. http://cws.journals.yorku.ca/index.php/cws/article/viewFile/22131/20785 (accessed 6 April 2020).

———. "Our Coming In Stories: Cree Identity, Body Sovereignty, and Gender Self-Determination." *Journal of Global Indigeneity* 1, no. 1 (2015): 1–5.

———. "Skirting the Issues: Indigenous Myths, Misses, and Misogyny." In *Keetsahnak: Our Missing and Murdered Indigenous Sisters*, edited by Kim Anderson, Maria Campbell, and Christi Belcourt, 161–74. Edmonton: University of Alberta Press, 2019.

Wilson, Shawn. *Research Is Ceremony: Indigenous Research Methods*. Winnipeg: Fernwood Publishing, 2008.

Woodcock, George. *Gabriel Dumont*. Markham, ON: Fitzhenry and Whiteside, 2003.

Wookey, Janelle, and Jérémie Wookey, dirs. *Mémére Métisse*. Wookey Films, 2009.

Zeilig, Ken, and Victoria Zeilig. *Ste. Madeleine: Community without a Town—Métis Elders in Interview*. Winnipeg: Pemmican Publications, 1987.

INDEX